The aftermath of the Popish Plot and the subsequent succession crisis of the years 1678 to 1681 are the context of this new study. It asks two key questions: Was there an exclusion crisis? and, Did these years witness the birth of modern political parties? Through a detailed analysis of Parliament, the court and the country, the author argues that the unrest was not simply due to a centrally organised party machine based around the single issue of exclusion, but was a broad-based controversy about the succession, fears of popery and arbitrary government which produced ideological polarisation and political sophistication. Part I examines central politics to explore the succession crisis within the context of the court and an emergent fluid but partisan political structure. Part II explores public opinion in the country as a whole, and argues that propaganda, electioneering, religious conflict and petitions and addresses committed men to organised networks of belief, but also ensured a struggle about the representation of the will of the people.

Cambridge Studies in Early Modern British History

POLITICS AND OPINION IN CRISIS, 1678–81

Cambridge Studies in Early Modern British History

Series editors

ANTHONY FLETCHER
Professor of Modern History, University of Durham

JOHN GUY
Professor of Modern History, University of St Andrews
and JOHN MORRILL
*Reader in Early Modern History, University of Cambridge and
Fellow and Tutor of Selwyn College*

This is a series of monographs and studies covering many aspects of the history of the British Isles between the late fifteenth century and the early eighteenth century. It includes the work of established scholars and pioneering work by a new generation of scholars. It includes both reviews and revisions of major topics and books which open up new historical terrain or which reveal startling new perspectives on familiar subjects. All the volumes set detailed research into broader perspectives and the books are intended for the use of students as well as of their teacher.

For a list of titles in the series, see end of book.

POLITICS AND OPINION IN CRISIS, 1678–81

MARK KNIGHTS
Lecturer in History, Leicester University

CAMBRIDGE
UNIVERSITY PRESS

Published by the Press Syndicate of the University of Cambridge
The Pitt Building, Trumpington Street, Cambridge CB2 1RP
40 West 20th Street, New York, NY 10011–4211, USA
10 Stamford Road, Oakleigh, Melbourne 3166, Australia

First published 1994

Printed in Great Britain by Redwood Books, Trowbridge, Wiltshire

A catalogue record for this book is available from the British Library

Library of Congress cataloguing in publication data
Knights, Mark.
Politics and opinion in crisis, 1678–1681 / Mark Knights.
    p.   cm. – (Cambridge studies in early modern British history)
Based on the author's thesis.
Includes bibliographical references.
ISBN 0–521–41804–6
1. Great Britain–Politics and government–1660–1688.
2.   Great Britain–Kings and rulers–Succession–Public opinion.
3.   Public opinion–Great Britain–History–17th century.
I. Title.   II. Series.
DA448.K62   1994
941.06'6—dc20   93–42095   CIP

ISBN 0 521 41804 6

CONTENTS

LIST OF ILLUSTRATIONS

ACKNOWLEDGEMENTS

In the course of my research I have incurred a number of debts of thanks. The greatest is to my supervisor, Blair Worden, who guided me towards my subject, and who has always commented incisively and helpfully on the content and the presentation of my work. I am very grateful for the amount of time he has spent in reading drafts, and for his warm support. His seminars at Oxford, run in conjunction with Anne Whiteman, and those organised by Donald McKenzie on the seventeenth-century book trade, have also taught me a great deal and introduced me to a number of scholars whose comments have always been extremely useful. I have greatly benefited from discussions with Steve Pincus, John Spurr, Giles Mandlebrote, Alan Marshall, Jonathan Scott, Andrew Swatland and Peter Dickson, and I am particularly grateful to Colin Lee and Perry Gauci who read parts of this work. My work has undoubtedly benefited from the atmosphere of friendliness and scholarship created by my colleagues at the History of Parliament, Perry Gauci, Stuart Handley, Andrew Hanham and David Hayton, who have kindly checked a number of references for me in their travels through various record offices. I gladly acknowledge the profound influence of David's expertise, and can only hope for the reader's sake that some of his stylistic flair has rubbed off on me. The examiners of my thesis, Clive Holmes and Mark Goldie, as well as my editors, Anthony Fletcher and John Morrill, have also been extremely helpful in suggesting ways in which my thesis could be improved for publication, and John has steered me expertly through the process of revision. I should also like to thank Alasdair Hawkyard for his helpful advice on the structure of the index.

My research was made possible by the generous help of all the staff at the libraries and archive offices listed in the bibliography, but especially by the staff at the Bodleian and Dr J Hall of Cambridge University Library. I have been funded by the British Academy, not only as a graduate but also as a post-graduate by means of a Thank-Offering to Britain Fellowship and a small personal grant. I have also been aided by a Huntington Library Fellowship, and by miscellaneous grants from Oxford University's Arnold, Bryce and Reid Fund.

I would like to thank the following for permission to quote from manuscripts in their possession: the Marquess of Bath, the Duke of Devonshire, the Trustees of the will of Major Peter George Evelyn, Major Ralph Verney, the Huntington Library, the Harry Ransome Humanities Research Centre at the University of Texas at Austin, the Warden and Fellows of All Souls College Oxford, the Master and Fellows of Magdalene College Cambridge, the National Trust, Lord Kenyon, The Library of Congress, the Trustees of the National Library of Scotland, the Folger Shakespeare Library, Leicestershire County Council, and the Leeds Archive Office. I am also grateful to the Trustees of the History of Parliament for allowing me to take some unpaid leave to finish drafting my work.

Finally, I would like to thank my wife, Emma, whose support, financial as well as emotional, has been invaluable. She nursed me through glandular fever, which interrupted my writing for some while, and was subsequently prepared to uproot from York to enable me to join the History of Parliament. This book's appearance therefore owes much to her loving patience and sacrifices.

LIST OF ABBREVIATIONS

The place of publication is London, unless otherwise stated.

Ailesbury Memoirs	*The Memoirs of Thomas Bruce, Earl of Ailesbury*, ed. Buckley, W.E. (The Roxburghe Club, 1890)
AO	Archive Office
BIHR	*Bulletin of the Institute for Historical Research*
BL	British Library
Bod.	Bodleian Library
Bulstrode newsletter	Newsletters sent to Sir Richard Bulstrode, now in the Harry Ransome Humanities Research Center at the University of Texas at Austin
Burnet Letters	*Some Unpublished Letters of Gilbert Burnet*, ed. Foxcroft, H.C. (Camden Miscellany, third series, xi, 1907)
Cal. Treas. Bks.	*Calendar of Treasury Books*
Congress newsletter	London newsletters (MF.18,124), at the Library of Congress, Washington
CJ	*Journal of the House of Commons*
CHJ	*Cambridge Historical Journal*
CSPD	*Calendar of State Papers Domestic*
Dering Diaries	*The Diaries and Papers of Sir Edward Dering Second Bart 1644–84*, ed. Bond, M.F. (House of Lords Record Office Occasional Publications 1976)
Diary of Henry Sidney	*The Diary of the Times of Charles II by Henry Sidney*, ed. Blencowe, R.W. (1843)
Domestick Intelligence	The newspaper of this title, including those issues under the amended title of *The Protestant Domestick Intelligence*

EHD	*English Historical Documents 1660–1714*, ed. Browning, A. (1953)
EHR	*English Historical Review*
Grey, *Debates*	A. Grey *Debates of the House of Commons 1667–1694* (1769)
Halifax Letters	'Some Unpublished Letters of George Savile, Lord Halifax', ed. Poole, D.L, *EHR* xxvi (1911), 535–42.
Hatton Corresp.	*The Correspondence of the Hatton Family*, ed. Thompson, E.M. (Camden Society, new series, xxii, 1878)
History of Parliament	*The History of Parliament : The House of Commons 1660–1690*, ed. Henning, B.D. (1983)
HJ	*Historical Journal*
HLQ	*Huntington Library Quarterly*
HMC	Historical Manuscripts Commission
Hyde Corresp.	*The Correspondence of Henry Hyde, Earl of Clarendon and his brother Lawrence Hyde, Earl of Rochester*, ed. Singer, S.W. (1828)
JBS	*Journal of British Studies*
LJ	*Journal of the House of Lords*
Loyal Protestant	*The Loyal Protestant and Domestick Intelligence*
Luttrell, *Brief Relation*	*A Brief Historical Relation of State Affairs* (Oxford, 1857)
Newdigate newsletter	Newsletters addressed to Sir Richard Newdigate, now in the Folger Shakespeare Library
NLS	National Library of Scotland
NLW	National Library of Wales
Original Papers	*Original Papers; containing the Secret History of Great Britain*, ed. MacPherson, J. (1776)
P&P	*Past and Present*
POAS	*Poems on Affairs of State*, ed. Mengel, E.F. (New Haven 1965–6), vol. ii
Popish Plot Catalogues	*Narcissus Luttrell's Popish Plot Catalogues*, ed. Francis, F.C. (1961)
Prideaux Corresp.	*The Letters of Humphrey Prideaux to John Ellis*, ed. Thompson, E.H. (Camden Society, new series, xv, 1875)
PRO	Public Record Office

Reresby, *Memoirs*	*The Memoirs of Sir John Reresby*, ed. Browning, A. (1936)
RO	Record Office
Russell Letters	*The Letters of Rachel Lady Russell*, ed. Russell, R. (1853)
Savile Corresp.	*The Savile Correspondence: Letters to and From Henry Savile*, ed. Cooper, W.D. (Camden Society, lxix, 1858)
Sidney Letters	*Discourses Concerning Government by Algernon Sidney with his letters, trial, apology and some memoirs of his life*, ed. Hollis, T. (1763), letters appended in final section of volume
Somers Tracts	*A Collection of Scarce and Valuable Tracts [belonging to Lord Somers]*, ed. Scott, W. (1809–15)
State Trials	*A Complete Collection of State Trials*, ed. Howell, T.B. (1816)
TRHS	*Transactions of the Royal Historical Society*
UCNW	University College of North Wales, Bangor
Van Prinsterer, *Archives*	*Archives ou Correspondance inédite de la Maison d'Orange-Nassau*, ed. Van Prinsterer, G. Groen (Utrecht 1861), v (1650–88)
Williamson Letters	*Letters … to Sir Joseph Williamson* (Camden Society, new series, viii and ix, 1874)
Wing	*Short Title Catalogue 1641–1700* (second edition, 1972–88), ed. Wing, D.
Wing Index	*An Index to Wing's Short Title Catalogue*, compiled by Morrison, P. G. (Virginia, 1955)

NOTES ON DATES AND STYLE

Dates are given according to the old style calendar, but the beginning of the year is considered to have been 1 January rather than 25 March. Letters and dispatches written abroad, or sent abroad, have the new style date given after that of the old style.

Contractions have usually been extended, superscriptions ignored, and 'ye' and 'yt' transcribed as 'the' and 'that', but spelling has otherwise only been altered where the original version would have impeded understanding.

Part I

'A GREAT CRISIS IN POLITICS'

We now come to a great crisis in politics, the discovery of the popish plot...

W. Kennett, *A Complete History of England* (1706), iii. 364.

I may aforehand prophesy, that, unless th[e historian's] Pen had Eyes and Ears at work in the very time when the Plot was fragrant, it is impossible, out of the Rubbish in Print, to shew the character of the Age, and what witchcraft prevailed over the understandings of the many.

R. North, *Examen* (1740), p. 187.

He that would give a Punctual and Particular Account of all the Narratives, Discourses, Tryals, Executions, Speeches, Votes, Accusations, Examinations, Commitments, Tumultuous Elections, Petitions, Ryots, Libels, and Seditious Attempts of all Sorts, during the said time, must write a History more Voluminous than Fox or Hollinshead.

A Compendious View of the late Tumults and Troubles (1685), preface.

1

Introduction

AN EXCLUSION CRISIS?

In October 1678 the Cavalier Parliament began investigating revelations made by Titus Oates of a Popish Plot to assassinate the King. The Plot inflamed long-standing fears of popery and had ominous implications for the duke of York, whose conversion to catholicism had been widely suspected since his refusal to comply with the Test Act of 1673. Oates did not directly implicate James in the Plot itself, but he did accuse Edward Coleman, the duke's former secretary, whose papers proved to contain treasonable letters to Louis XIV's confessor about catholic designs in England. The vulnerability of James's position was clear. Charles dissolved the Cavalier Parliament on 24 January 1679 and called a new one, but before Parliament sat on 6 March, the duke had been forced into temporary exile. A bill to exclude James from the succession to the throne was introduced in the Commons on 15 May and passed a second reading six days later, though the session was prorogued before it could proceed any further. When Parliament met again on 21 October 1680 a similar bill reached the Lords where, on 15 November, it was decisively rejected; and a third exclusion bill was read in the short-lived Parliament held in Oxford in March 1681. Exclusion bills thus linked all three new Parliaments of the period.

The years 1678–81 were also seen by contemporaries as a time of crisis,[1] when the nation drifted slowly towards violent unrest. Throughout the period disorder appeared to be imminent. In January 1679 a rabble gathered daily outside Newgate to inquire about the fate of three convicted priests, 'to the putting some in fear of an outrage'.[2] The following month Sir James Hayes reported that he was 'very much afray'd of great troubles at hand'.[3] In May 1679 one observer reported that England was 'on the very brink of

---

[1] For use of the term see *The Countries Vindication* (1679), p. 4; *HMC Ormonde*, iv. 244; Bod., MS Rawl. C.727, f. 56, Sir Leoline Jenkins to Gabriel Sylvius, 20 July 1680; BL, Add. 32,681, f. 12, Jenkins to Henry Sidney, 20 July 1680.
[2] *CSPD 1679–80*, p. 21.
[3] NLS, MS 7008, f. 189, Hayes to earl of Tweeddale, 17 February 1678/9.

confusion',[4] and when a rebellion actually erupted in Scotland the following month, the knock-on effect south of the border was dreaded.[5] At the end of the summer disorder was again expected after the King fell seriously ill.[6] 'Never was a civil war feared more than now', wrote one anxious observer.[7] In December 1679 it was feared that the people would 'not be quiet long'.[8] In March 1680 rumours circulated that London's apprentices intended to rise in arms, whilst in July renewed political agitation prompted a parliamentary clerk to predict that trouble might soon break out.[9] By November Sir William Temple could see nothing to prevent the nation 'falling into violent and popular tumults' if Parliament ended without an agreement with the King.[10] In February 1681 Algernon Sidney, who had surely witnessed much unrest in his lifetime, remarked that he had never seen 'men's minds more heated than at present', and a few months later Sir William Coventry remarked that 'all things worked for bringing ruin'.[11] Looking back over the period, Roger North could 'not remember at any time, a more hared and giddy temper of the people'.[12] Prognostications of chaos and civil war had been voiced throughout the 1660s and 1670s; but never so continuously, nor from so many different quarters, nor perhaps so desperately, as between 1678 and 1681. Even if fears of disorder were greatly exaggerated, the years 1678–81 witnessed an unrest that made the likelihood of civil war at least seem possible. In the words of one contemporary historian, the period was 'the most deplorable time that was ever seen in England'.[13]

The extraordinary political events that took place between the Popish Plot and the dissolution of the 1681 Oxford Parliament have consequently been described by modern historians as the 'Exclusion Crisis'.[14] I have generally avoided that term, not on grounds of dogma or a belief that it should never be used, but because I want in the following pages to shift the emphasis away from an interpretation of the controversy as one generated by, and revolving around, the single issue of exclusion, and because the label incorrectly implies that the crisis was merely a parliamentary one, centering on one piece of legislation. The 'exclusion crisis' is a well-known short-hand title, but, for

[4] HMC Ormonde, v. 104.
[5] Bod., MS Carte 232, f.44, earl of Longford to earl of Arran, 5 July 1679.
[6] Sidney Letters, p. 97.
[7] Bucks. RO, Verney mss, M11/33, Cary Gardiner to Sir Ralph Verney, 15 September 1679.
[8] BL, Trumbull mss, 60, R. Trumbull to W.Trumbull, 1 December 1679.
[9] HMC Lords 1678–88, p. 156.
[10] Van Prinsterer, Archives, v. 447.
[11] Sidney Letters, p. 60 (Hollis dates the letter 3 February 1678/9, but it refers to 1681); BL, Longleat mss, M/904, reel ix, vol. xvi, f. 328, Coventry to Sir Thomas Thynne, 24 May 1681.
[12] North, Examen, p. 504.
[13] R. Halstead, Succinct Genealogies (1685), p.433.
[14] The nearest contemporary use of the phrase is Anthony Hammond's retrospective entry in his diary for 1679, which reads 'Bill of Exclusion, the great & epidemical Controversy then depending' (Bod., MS Rawl.A.245, f. 44).

reasons that will become apparent, it is best reserved for the brief period between the rejection of the bill in the House of Lords in November 1680 and the dissolution of the Oxford Parliament in March 1681. When the slogan is used, it should be remembered that it does not do justice to the depth and complexity of what was the critical period in Charles II's reign, when politics and opinion were in crisis.

For a long time the 'attempted revolution', as the crisis has also been called,[15] has been overshadowed by the successful revolutions of 1640–60 and 1688–9, and received relatively little attention from historians. Only recently has the period come under greater and more penetrating study as historians have questioned whether or not the exclusion bill was the central or most important feature of these years, and even whether contemporaries were justified in regarding it as a crisis. In order to ask the question 'was there an exclusion crisis?' we therefore need to review the historical debate which has forced this question on to the agenda.

INTERPRETING THE PERIOD

Recent interest in the period has centred on the development of political parties, and of the Whig party in particular. Such an approach is not new. As early as 1740, in what became the classic delineation of the Tory perspective of the crisis, Roger North in his *Examen* argued that by 1673 there existed a Country party of well-meaning but politically naive men, and a group of 'desperadoes' of old republicans and 'malcontents'. They were led, he suggested, by the earl of Shaftesbury, whose motives ranged from a desire for a commonwealth, an ambition to manage affairs himself, and a sheer wish for 'experiment'. To achieve his aims, North claimed, Shaftesbury developed a powerful propaganda machine and party organisation, which worked hand in hand with dissenters from the Church of England. 'So united and so uniformly did they move and act, as if one single soul animated the whole', that the party temporarily dominated politics; but, North gleefully pointed out, after a period of irresolution, the Court outwitted its opponents, with the result that far from destroying the monarchy, the crisis encouraged 'a second Restauration' of royal power. Although North admitted that he wrote from a partisan point of view, modern historians have, with some refinements and modifications, largely followed the outline he gave of a tightly organised and thrusting opposition to the King.

Acceptance of North's interpretation has been made easier because the alternative Whig analysis shares his stress on the crisis as a turning point in the formation of parties. Thus William Cowper, son of the earl of Shaftesbury's political associate Sir William Cowper and himself a Whig, argued (even

---

[15] F.S. Ronalds, *The Attempted Whig Revolution of 1678–81* (Urbana, 1974).

before North published) that parties had their origin 'about the time the Bill of Exclusion was set on foot in the reign of King Charles II', and came into being for two reasons: the Court's persecution of protestant dissenters, and the exclusion bill.[16] Cowper's account differs from North's mainly in the priority he assigned to the role of principle as the cohesive force behind opposition to the Court. Concern for religion and a sincere belief that Parliament had the power to alter the succession were thus far more important than factious ambition, hatred of the church, or a desire to see the restoration of a commonwealth.

Given the agreement about the rise of parties, the modern historical debate has, until recently, focused on the novelty of 1679–81 as the turning point in their emergence, and on the date at which parties became recognisable. To understand this debate, however, it is necessary to examine interpretations of the 1660s and 1670s in order to assess earlier political developments.

One strongly argued body of opinion suggests that parties emerged in stages during the whole Restoration period. This view was most eloquently stated by Andrew Browning, who argued that the rise of parties in the reign of Charles II was an inevitable consequence of the increase in the power and prestige of Parliament during the civil wars and Commonwealth. He identified three Court parties under the administrations of Clarendon, Arlington–Clifford–Williamson, and Danby, seeing in Shaftesbury the leader of a fourth, opposition, party.[17] The most serious challenge to this view has come from historians of the Cavalier Parliament. Dennis Witcombe's study of the Parliament up to the rise of Danby, 'demolished the idea, so attractive and convenient, of a neat two-party system. In place of disciplined "Court" and "Country" parties logically and inevitably opposed to one another, he presents a picture of complicated groupings, shifting allegiances and confused motives.'[18] The most recent historian of the early years of the Restoration, Paul Seaward, has likewise warned against seeing anything very new in the parliamentary management of these years, regarding the organisation of Bennet (later earl of Arlington) and Clifford as essentially faction driven.[19]

Browning's model has therefore been modified by a number of historians who have sought to push forward the date for the emergence of parties. In his thesis of 1923, Esmond De Beer advanced the idea that it was only during

---

[16] J. Lord Campbell, *Lives of the Lord Chancellors* (1846), iv. 421–2.

[17] A. Browning, 'Parties and Party Organisation in the Reign of Charles II', *TRHS*, xxx (1948), 21–36.

[18] D.T. Witcombe, *Charles II and the Cavalier House of Commons 1663–1674* (Manchester, 1966), foreword by B.D. Henning, who nevertheless employed a Court–Opposition dichotomy when analysing the behaviour of MPs in the *History of Parliament* volumes covering the Cavalier Parliament.

[19] P. Seaward, *The Cavalier Parliament and the Reconstruction of the Old Regime 1661-7* (Cambridge, 1989), pp. 79, 99.

Danby's administration that parties first became organised and established on a permanent basis. In response to this Court initiative, De Beer argued, Shaftesbury tried to consolidate the opposition to Danby's management into a power strong enough to force Parliamentary control on the King, though the disparate nature of his support made this possible only for so long as the Court was aimless.[20] Until 1677, de Beer suggested, this struggle took place within the two Houses of Parliament; thereafter, however, there was a profound change to the type of conflict between Parliament and the King that had characterised the earlier part of the century. After the Popish Plot all semblance of a party conflict disappeared, and the exclusionist Whigs appeared as a faction.[21]

An alternative to De Beer's thesis argues the almost opposite point of view mainly because it examines the Court's critics rather than its supporters. This rival analysis, which has been the most widely accepted, suggests that, although there was increasing opposition to the Court in the 1670s, it was still largely factional, and personal in character; parties had not yet formed, and needed the impetus provided by the Popish Plot to develop around the issue of exclusion. David Ogg therefore concludes that the exclusion crisis witnessed the birth of the modern party system.[22] Although stressing that provincialism still counted for much in political life, he saw 1678–81 as a period in which national politics predominated, and observed that 'it was the simple choice of exclusion or a popish successor that crystallised amorphous masses of prejudice, instinct, and misgiving into the clear-cut forms of political party'.[23]

In *The First Whigs* James Jones gives the clearest and fullest expression of this line of thought. His work, which remains the standard text for the study of the period, seeks to deny that Walcott's analysis of early eighteenth-century politics, which had focused on family connections and interest groups, had relevance for the period 1678–81, and argues that the upheaval after 1678 cannot be explained in terms of mere personalities or factions; instead, opponents of the Court became 'a coherent and highly organised body which can properly be described as a party'.[24] Regarding it as a political rather than a religious crisis, Jones argues that the party formed itself round the single issue of exclusion, and placed itself under the leadership of the earl of Shaftesbury, who used an unprecedented degree of party management and organisation. Jones admits, however, that this effort was entirely geared to

---

[20] E.S. de Beer, 'The Development of Parties during the Ministry of Danby' (London MA thesis, 1923), chapter 1. K. Feiling, *History of the Tory Party* (Oxford, 1924), p. 165 argues along a similar line.

[21] de Beer, 'Development of Parties', pp. 151, 167–74.

[22] D. Ogg, *England in the Reign of Charles II* (Oxford, 1984 re-issue of 1956 2nd edition), p. 606.

[23] Ibid., p. 612.

[24] Jones, *The First Whigs* (Oxford, 1961), p. 9.

pushing through exclusion, and did not permanently affect the nature of the political system. He also believes that the first Whigs had not developed an ideological programme. In a subsequent work Jones enlarges his views about the rise of parties. 'There can be no doubt that the first Whigs were a party', he argues, because they possessed 'a clearly defined and accepted group of leaders, headed by Shaftesbury, who made the decisions, pre-arranged the tactics that were to be followed in Parliament and elections, and issued orders and instructions which individual MPs and leaders in the localities accepted.'[25] Much of Jones's analysis has been recently taken up by Richard Ashcraft in his study of Locke and revolutionary politics. Like Jones, Ashcraft sees the first Whigs as 'much more organised and disciplined than a mere alliance established among a few aristocratic leaders and their immediate followers would suggest';[26] unlike Jones, however, he dates the first formal political organisation to the year 1675. In a sense, North's view of a highly organised revolutionary party under the direction of Shaftesbury has come full circle.

A number of difficulties are apparent in Jones's argument. At times he seems to argue that the period witnessed the birth of a two-party system, whilst on other occasions he suggests that it was only the Whigs who developed into a party between 1679 and 1681, an inconsistency which raises questions about the extent to which a party can exist on its own. He also argues for the emergence of parties, even though he admits that there was no stable structure of politics. The cautions made at the start of the book about the fluidity of politics and the fragmentary nature of the opposition are soon forgotten, and he regards the political struggle as mainly confined to Parliament and Whitehall, making it unclear how far the divisions permeated the country as a whole. He argues that issues were what mattered, but believes the ideology of the Whigs to have been largely unformed and incoherent; and he concentrates instead on the pivotal role of exclusion, a measure to deal with a religious as much as a political problem, in a purely secular way. Moreover, his insistence on the crisis revolving around the single concern of exclusion rests on a case that fails to consider some of the other issues at stake.

Uneasiness has been voiced on a number of these scores. John Miller regards the politics of the Restoration as having been shaped by men who were ambitious for office, and by differences of principle, with no clear-cut party divisions; challenges to the King's power were thus *ad hoc* responses to particular events and problems, rather than a systematic campaign.[27]

---

[25] Jones, *The Revolution of 1688 in England* (1972), p. 39; Jones, 'Parties and Parliament', in *The Restored Monarchy*, ed. Jones (1979), pp. 48–70.

[26] R. Ashcraft, *Revolutionary Politics and Locke's Two Treatises of Government* (Princeton, 1986), pp. 141, 175.

[27] J. Miller, 'Charles II and his Parliaments', *TRHS*, xxxii (1982), 1–24.

Similarly, Kenneth Haley's excellent biography of Shaftesbury, which has provided so much of the detail for students of the period, does not present a straightforward portrait of a party leader: 'Even in the Whig heyday of the Exclusion crisis,' he says, 'it is foolish to talk as though all the Whigs were Shaftesbury's obedient "henchmen".'[28] Sir John Plumb also warns that Shaftesbury and his followers 'never possessed half the coherence of purpose that is often attributed to them'.[29]

A comprehensive revision of the accepted structure of Restoration politics is, however, only now emerging. It is taking place on two main fronts, the religious and the organisational, and has sprung from the idea that 1679–81, or even 1660, was less of a watershed than has previously been thought. In his study of seventeenth-century puritanism, Michael Finlayson has argued that the political and religious outlook that was prevalent in the pre-civil war period persisted after the Restoration. Anti-popery and fear of arbitrary government were the same issues that dominated men's minds before and after the civil war, so that 'what shaped the political consciousness of many who supported the policy of Exclusion was a sense of continuity with generations of post-Reformation protestants'.[30] The idea that the Restoration did not resolve the abiding problems of the seventeenth century is not new; but historians have often not followed through the implications of their own observations. Mark Goldie and others, most notably Tim Harris, have therefore pursued the religious context of Restoration politics, and see it shaping both attitudes and organisation.[31] They have succeeded in placing a new emphasis on the importance of the struggle between dissent and the established church. Indeed, Harris's study of politics under the later Stuarts literally aims to put dissent back into discussions of the period, by suggesting that political divisions were at root religious ones, born out of the failure of the Restoration religious settlement.[32] Whilst admitting that the conflict between episcopacy and dissent must be linked to constitutional issues in order to explain how religious factors generated party politics, he accords religious factors 'primacy of place' in establishing party identity. Yet he does

---

[28] K.H.D. Haley, *The First Earl of Shaftesbury* (Oxford, 1968), p. 349.

[29] J. Plumb, *The Growth of Political Stability 1675–1725* (1967), p. 51.

[30] M. Finlayson, *Historians, Puritanism and the English Revolution* (1983), p. 152. This argument has been challenged by S. Zwicker, who argues that the exclusion crisis was not 'an example of godly politics after the manner of the 1640s' but 'the conduct of political battle under the open aegis of party' (S. Zwicker, 'Lines of Authority: Politics and Literary Culture in the Restoration', in *The Politics of Discourse*, ed. S. Zwicker and K. Sharpe [California, 1987], pp. 234–5).

[31] *The Politics of Religion in Restoration England*, ed. T. Harris, P. Seaward and M. Goldie (Oxford, 1990); T. Harris, *London Crowds in the Reign of Charles II* (Cambridge, 1987). See also R.L. Greaves, *Radicals and Nonconformists in Britain 1664–1677* (California, 1990), which concludes (p. 244) that 'virtually all dissidents were Protestant nonconformists but the majority of the latter had no real ties to the radicals'.

[32] Harris, *Politics under the Later Stuarts* (1993), pp. 8–9, chapter 4.

not explain why and how the character of the religious dispute was different to the divisions of the earlier seventeenth century, about which historians have been reluctant to talk in terms of parties. If the post-Restoration period mirrored tensions which existed before 1660 and which were unresolved at the King's return, why should we call the divisions of the later period 'parties', but not those of the earlier seventeenth century?

This is exactly the question posed, and answered, by Jonathan Scott. He has argued that the crisis of 1679–81 had more in common with the 1620s, 1630s and 1640s than historians have previously recognised, and that the Restoration was more of a reaction than a settlement, creating a fragile and unstable situation in which the problems of politics and religion that had bedeviled the country between 1625 and 1660 could erupt.[33] He accordingly sees the crisis of 1679–81 partly as a response to the Counter-Reformation, and identifies three underlying causes: fear of popery, fear of arbitrary government and the disruption in England's client relationship with France. Perhaps what is most important about Scott's claims is that, just as the issues were the same for the early and later Stuarts, so the structure of politics remained the same: 'the whole idea of the "exclusion crisis" giving rise to the "whig" and "tory" parties (and so to the political structures of the eighteenth century) is', he suggests, 'another case of the "long eighteenth century" giving premature birth to itself from the depths of a different period'.[34] As an alternative framework, Scott suggests that there were competing factions, and that any cohesion that existed among the 'sides' was ideological rather than organisational.

Scott's views are put forward with flair and enthusiasm, and a number of his lines of enquiry are extremely valuable. Indeed, I shall be endeavouring to enlarge on a number of themes which he highlights. His review of the importance of the exclusion bill and the leadership offered by Shaftesbury, and his emphasis on the importance of ideology, faction and the fears of popery and arbitrary government, including the survival of Parliament, are all extremely important arguments which rightly challenge some of the imbalances of other accounts of the period. His recognition of the rupture of Anglo-French relations as an essential component of the crisis also adds a useful dimension omitted by many other commentators, and his lively and provocative style has reinjected a welcome vigour and vitality into the debates about the period.

[33] J. Scott, 'Radicalism and Restoration', *HJ*, xxxi (1988), p. 458; *Algernon Sidney and the Restoration Crisis 1677–1683* (Cambridge, 1991), passim, but especially pp. 1–49. Ironically, Scott builds on Jones's argument that the Restoration settlement left many problems of the 1640s and 1650s unresolved, and that the balance of power between King, Parliament and the church had still to be worked out after the Restoration (Jones, *The Revolution of 1688*, pp. x, 3).

[34] Scott, 'Radicalism and Restoration', pp. 458, 464; Scott, *Restoration Crisis*, pp. 11–14.

A number of reservations nevertheless need to be made about the stress he puts on some points because he pushes valuable insights too far, and similarities (which will become clearer) in some of our arguments make it necessary to state at the outset where we differ.

The fact that there was continuity between the late and early seventeenth century does not mean, as Scott insists, that 1679–81 'was a repeat screening of the crisis of the reign of Charles I'.[35] Of course, there were many parallels between the periods and a good deal of propaganda was produced to highlight them; but the cry that '1641 had come again' was made by the Court and its supporters, in whose interest it was to emphasise the similarities and even to claim that history was repeating itself.[36] Scott admits, and emphasises, that contemporaries were 'the prisoners of memory';[37] but at times he seems unaware of the motives of those who sought to stir it. As we shall see, the memory of the civil wars was to play an important factor in shaping the attitudes of the Tory reaction after 1681, for the past was not just determining the structure of the debate, but was also being deliberately manipulated for partisan reasons, and we must be careful not to accept the assertions of a prejudiced contemporary press at face value. Scott's reluctance to recognise that propaganda was part of the political process means that he sees the 'Whigs' of 1678 simply becoming the 'Tories' of 1681.[38] Whilst some shift of opinion did occur, the apparent Toryism had as much to do with a struggle to represent the will of the nation as it had with the change of will, and, when Scott says that his formula works for all except some hardliners, he seems to forget that elsewhere he argues that it was those hardliners who really made up the Whigs and Tories (such as they were) in the first place.

Moreover, although the crisis of 1678–81 needs to be viewed from the perspective of the past, the perspective of the future is also important. Whilst it is true that historians have concentrated too much on the fears for the future under a popish successor at the expense of studying the crisis of government under Charles II, it is impossible to ignore the fact that there were grave anxieties about the imminent impact of popery under James that gave a new dimension to the political and religious problems. As I shall discuss later, it is unnecessary to see a crisis of popery and arbitrary government and a crisis about the succession as mutually exclusive themes. Fear of what James would do when he became King triggered alarms about popery and arbitrary government; but similarly, Charles's handling of the succession crisis seemed to place the future of Parliament at risk and open the way to the destruction

---

35 Scott, *Restoration Crisis*, p. 7.
36 For a survey of some of the material relating to the civil wars reprinted 1679–81, see chapter 6.
37 Scott, *Restoration Crisis*, p. 3.
38 Scott, *Restoration Crisis*, p. 45.

of protestantism. Scott is right to see 'consecutive phases' in the nation's thinking, with fear of popery giving way to fear of fanaticism, and fear of royal tyranny giving way to fear of parliamentary tyranny; but this merely explains how, by 1681, a loyalist reaction could take place, and it does not follow that shifts in emphasis of expression corresponded to an absence of fundamentally held views, or that divisions did not continue beyond 1681 into the first age of party. The years 1679–81 therefore did have, and were seen to have, significance retrospectively after 1688. A collection of the debates of the 1680 and 1681 Parliaments were printed in 1689, and appended to them was the text of *A Just and Modest Vindication*, which Scott's hero Algernon Sidney had probably helped pen in 1681.[39] If 1679–81 had such little significance for post-Revolution political alignments, it is hard to see why contemporaries living in the first age of party looked back to the crisis as a crucial stage in the process of division;[40] and at least some degree of continuity was ensured by the fact that many of the MPs elected in 1681 were called to sit in the assembly summoned in December 1688, and sat in Parliament thereafter.[41]

Although he sees the crisis as one about popery, Scott considers religious divisions chiefly in terms of a European catholic conspiracy, to the neglect of paying detailed attention to the role of the heated domestic debate about, and within, the Church of England concerning an accommodation with protestant dissenters.[42] After the Restoration, many dissenters or zealous protestants saw the high-churchmen's insistence on ceremonies as indicative of popish inclinations, and condemned them as papists in masquerade. The controversy by 1681 was thus also about whether those antipathetic to nonconformity or the dissenters themselves were doing the work of the Pope. Some anglicans saw dissenters as misguided protestants who ought not to be persecuted because they helped reinforce the bulwark against the catholic threat, whilst others saw them as working to divide the protestant community, thereby weakening it and rendering it vulnerable to papist attack.

[39] *An Exact Collection of the Debates of the House of Commons* (1689). The work was also reprinted separately as *The Design of Enslaving England Discovered* (1689).

[40] See Lord Cowper (son of Sir William Cowper, MP 1679–81), *An Impartial History of Parties*, printed as appendix to life of Cowper in Campbell, *Lives of the Lord Chancellors*, iv. 421–2; H. St John, Lord Bolingbroke, dated the birth of parties to 1679 but added that they 'did not grow up into full maturity or receive their names till about two years afterwards' (cited in C.B. Kent, *The Early History of the Tories 1660–1702* [1908], p. 11). The period was also formative for several members of the future Whig Junto, Charles Montagu, John Somers and Thomas Wharton. Edward Russell, future earl of Orford, also distanced himself from the Court in 1683 after the execution of his cousin Lord William Russell. John Smith, the future Whig chancellor of the exchequer, entered Parliament in 1679.

[41] R. Beddard, 'The Revolution of 1688', in *The Unexpected Whig Revolution*, ed. Beddard (Oxford, 1991), pp. 31–41.

[42] The best account of anglicanism's identity is J. Spurr, *The Restoration Church 1646–1689* (1991).

Both dissenters and high anglicans, therefore, saw each other as part of the problem of popery.

However, the most serious weakness of Scott's work is his handling of Parliament, especially in terms of the networks of influence that he identifies. He makes very strong assertions about the absence of party, for which he offers relatively little analysis, and his focus on Sidney distorts and exaggerates the importance of a 'republican interest' that he never adequately defines. Nor does he explain why ideological unity failed to crystallise into some form of organisational cohesion, especially in Parliament, or in London where he admits opposition to the Court was strongest. It is of course true that for the debate about the degree of organisation and co-ordination that existed to be a fruitful one the discussion must avoid becoming bogged down in an exchange of definitions of what constituted a 'party'; clearly we need to relate in some detail what the term meant to contemporaries with the structure of politics around them, and what it means to historians.

Whilst Scott at least admits that there was considerable unrest between 1679 and 1681, Ronald Hutton has recently doubted whether contemporaries were right to think that there was any crisis at all.[43] For Hutton the real troubles which Charles faced were not the failures of the political or religious settlements negotiated at the Restoration, so much as the difficulties the King created for himself by 'committing a string of mistakes amounting in some cases to real idiocy', a character flaw more usually attributed to his brother James. Hutton is right about the errors made by the King, but this does not mean that contemporaries were wrong to think there was no crisis that underlay or even contributed to them. His work is, however, particularly valuable in restoring a Scottish and Irish dimension to the conventional picture, and he rightly seizes on the King's quest for men and measures as one of the central features of the period.

Recent research has explored other aspects of the crisis besides those of party organisation. In particular, interesting questions have been asked about the relationship between politics, opinion and propaganda during the period. Richard Ashcraft's work on John Locke and revolutionary politics,[44] Tim Harris's on London crowds,[45] and James Sutherland's analysis of Restoration newspapers,[46] have all explored the organisation and impact of propaganda on politics, political thought and public opinion. Ashcraft has mined

---

[43] R. Hutton, *Charles II* (Oxford, 1989), p. 357.

[44] R. Ashcraft, 'Revolutionary Politics and Locke's *Two Treatises of Government*: Radicalism and Lockean Political Theory', *Political Theory*, viii (1980), 429–86; R. Ashcraft, 'The *Two Treatises* and the Exclusion Crisis: The Problem of Lockean Political Theory as Bourgeois Ideology', *Papers Read at the Clark Library Seminar, 10 December 1977* (Los Angeles, 1980); Ashcraft, *Revolutionary Politics*.

[45] Harris, *London Crowds*, pp. 133–44.

[46] J. Sutherland, *The Restoration Newspaper and its Development* (Cambridge, 1986).

the pamphlet literature of the period in order to reconstruct the intellectual milieu in which Locke wrote, and found that Jones's dismissal of the Whig propaganda as superficial misrepresents the nature of a rich vein of political thought. Harris has similarly charted the Whig creed, but has then looked at how the Tory response to it was based on a number of shared slogans, such as popery and tyranny. Harris is very much concerned with the propaganda message that reached the London crowds, and Sutherland's survey of newspapers in the period probes one format that perhaps reached the highest number of readers.

A number of regional studies have also examined how news and opinion about events at Whitehall and in Parliament were transmitted into the localities, and what attitudes formed there. Some historians have taken the county as the basis for analysis of opinion,[47] others the town or groups of opinion within the corporation, town or city.[48] Although studies of localities have not been nearly so plentiful as those undertaken for the earlier half of the century, those that have been made have generally made up for the lack of quantity by their high degree of quality. In particular, they have deepened our understanding of political and religious groupings. James Rosenheim has argued that outside Westminster elections occasioned party disputes, and highlights the difficulty of distinguishing between party and groupings of faction or local ties. This emphasis on local influences is also apparent in two excellent studies of East Anglian towns, Norwich and Great Yarmouth,

---

[47] P.J. Challinor, 'Restoration and Exclusion in the County of Cheshire', *Bulletin of the John Rylands University Library of Manchester*, lxiv (1981–2), 360–85; A.M. Coleby, *Central Government in the Localities: Hampshire 1649–89* (Cambridge, 1987); C. Holmes, *Seventeenth Century Lincolnshire* (Lincoln, 1980); J. Hurwich, 'Dissent and Catholicism in English Society: A Study of Warwickshire 1660–1720', *JBS*, xvi no. 1 (1976), 24–59; P. Jenkins, *The Making of a Ruling Class : The Glamorgan Gentry 1640–1790* (Cambridge, 1983); L.M. Munby, 'Politics and Religion in Hertfordshire 1660–1740', *East Anglian Studies* (1968); P.J. Norrey, 'The Restoration Regime in Action', *HJ*, xxxi (1988), 789–813; M.S. Child, 'Prelude to Revolution: The Structure of Politics in County Durham 1678–1688' (Maryland Ph.D., 1972); P.E. Murrell, 'Suffolk: The Political Behaviour of the County and its Parliamentary Boroughs from the Exclusion Crisis to the Accession of the House of Hanover' (Newcastle Ph.D., 1982); N. Key, 'Comprehension and the Breakdown of Consensus in Restoration Herefordshire', in *Politics of Religion*, ed. Harris *et al.*, pp.191–215.

[48] J.T. Evans, *Seventeenth Century Norwich : Politics, Religion and Government 1620–1690* (Oxford, 1979); G. De Krey, *A Fractured Society : The Politics of London in the First Age of Party 1688–1715* (Oxford, 1985); J. Hurwich, 'A Fanatick Town: The Political Influence of Dissenters in Coventry 1660–1720', *Midland History*, iv (1977), 15–48; J.W. Kirby, 'Restoration Leeds and the Aldermen of the Corporation', *Northern History*, xxii (1986), 123–75; M. Mullett, 'The Politics of Liverpool 1660–1688', *Transactions of the Historical Society of Lancashire and Cheshire*, cxxiv (1972), 31–56 ; M. Mullett, 'Conflict, Politics and Elections in Lancaster 1660–1688', *Northern History*, xix (1983), 61–87; M. Mullett, '"Deprived of our former place"' – The Internal Politics of Bedford 1660–1688', *Bedfordshire Historical Record Society*, lix (1980), 1–42; P. Gauci, 'The Corporation and the Country: Great Yarmouth 1660–1720' (Oxford D.Phil., 1991); C. Lee, '"Fanatic Magistrates": Religious and Political Conflict in Three Kent Boroughs, 1680–4', *HJ*, xxxv, no. 1 (1991), 43–61.

which point to the importance of strong local patrons, as well as to the impact of religious disputes. Attacks on the Restoration church settlement have been examined by most historians of the provinces, stressing the need to re-examine the role of religion in politics. But a great deal about the crisis in the country as a whole is still unknown. The *History of Parliament* volumes covering the Restoration period tell us much about the conduct of elections in terms of local interests, but are often significantly silent about what the contests at the polls were about in terms of issues, suggesting that Jones's view that the 1679 and 1681 elections were fought on exclusion needs re-assessment; and, although Lionel Glassey and Andrew Colbey have success-fully examined the impact of national politics on the localities in terms of officeholdings, we also need to know more about how the boroughs and counties reacted to events at the centre.

THE FRAMEWORK OF DISCUSSION

As this brief survey of recent research shows, the period has become the centre of an exciting controversy, with many questions left to be explored. Is the concept of exclusion as the central, almost sole, demand which dominated the political scene any longer tenable, and if not, where does this leave the party organisation that allegedly formed around this one issue? Was there in fact a first Whig party based on a much broader agenda, or must we abandon the idea of the birth of modern party politics entirely? If there were no parties, who made up the factions that shaped politics? If factions are the key to understanding the period, is the whole crisis explicable in terms of person-alities rather than issues such as popery and arbitrary government? Or if the factions had an ideological slant, what distinguished them from what have been called parties? If the factions shared ideological convictions, to what extent did the co-ordination between them become structured? If there was some such structure, when did it emerge, and was it new? If there was no development of party organisation, how are we to explain the new labels of Whig and Tory that seem to denote a polarised society neatly divided into two sides? How was public opinion manipulated, and why did it shift? Was there any difference between the character of politics at Westminster and politics in the provinces? Were the divisions purely religious, or were there other factors complicating the picture? What were elections fought over, and what were the issues agitating the localities?

This book attempts to tackle at least some of these questions. It will divide into two basic themes: politics and opinion. The first section of the book will examine the issues at the heart of the loudest current controversy about the period, namely the debate about the problem of the succession and the structure of politics in which that debate took place. It will focus almost entirely on high politics, that is to say on Parliament and the Court, though I do not wish to suggest that this was the only issue at stake in either arena. The attempts to settle the succession problem will be examined in order to understand how and why exclusion emerged as the demand of the House of Commons. Since it will be argued that distrust of the Court and the King's own problems in finding a coherent ministry created the framework within which the succession problem must be viewed, the nature of Charles's administrations will also be explored. The first part will conclude with an overview of the structure of politics. The second part of the book will turn to public opinion in the country as a whole. Another chronological analysis will still consider the role of exclusion, but from the perspective of opinion outside Westminster and Whitehall; it will still attempt to question the extent of party organisation, but will examine how this affected London and the rest of the country. In an attempt to widen the debate, I shall also look at how opinion was expressed, by the press, by the petitions and addresses that were promoted during the period, and at elections. I shall tell the story of a struggle to represent the will of the nation, and consider how far religious concerns influenced political divides. The narrative will reveal what issues were considered important outside Parliament, and show how attitudes shifted or appeared to shift over the period.

The chronological parameters for the following discussion will be from the Popish Plot and the final session of the Cavalier Parliament in the autumn of 1678, until the dissolution of the Oxford Parliament in 1681 and its immediate aftermath. Some histories of the period continue the crisis until 1683, when Charles finally regained control of appointment to London's key offices of power, but most commentators, both modern and contemporary, agree that the spring and summer of 1681 marked a turning point in the course of events. Most of the characteristics of the next two years were already apparent by then, and can therefore be included in assessments of the main body of the crisis. Similarly, for the beginning of the crisis, no attempt will be made to re-examine the intricacies of the Popish Plot, which has been fully described elsewhere,[49] though it will now be necessary to sketch the state of the nation at that time.

POLITICS AND RELIGION AT THE TIME OF THE POPISH PLOT

The crisis of 1678–81 cannot be seen simply in terms of the events of those years, extraordinary though they were. Many of the disputes in 1678–81 were over issues that had been unresolved by the Restoration settlements, and

[49] For accounts of the plot see J.P. Kenyon, *The Popish Plot* (1974); Sir John Pollock, *The Popish Plot* (1903); and J. Miller, *Popery and Politics in England 1660–1688* (Cambridge, 1973).

had been debated, with increasing vigour, ever since 1660.[50] So deep-rooted were the problems that one pamphleteer thought that 'the Popish Plot, the uncertainty of his R[oyal] H[ighness] His religion, the want of Lawful Issue to inherit after his Majesty, and the like … [were] things that occasion rather than cause our sickness'.[51] This is not the place for a detailed study of the 1670s, though such a work is urgently required; but it is important to recognise that the succession crisis of 1678–81 brought into sharp focus a debate about the relationship between King and Parliament, and between anglican and dissenter, that had been rumbling, and at times raging, since 1660, and that the storm had been gathering head especially since the early 1670s.[52]

The grievances that underpinned the crisis can be summed up by the deceptively simple slogan of 'popery and arbitrary government'. 'Some think that plot called the Popish Plot', the Rye House Plotter James Holloway planned to tell Charles in 1684, 'was a twofold plot, one for settling arbitrary government as in France … the other for settling popery, when the first was obtained.'[53] Such a view was best expressed by Andrew Marvell's *Account of the Growth of Popery and Arbitrary Government in England*, published in 1677 (and republished soon after Marvell's death in August 1678[54]), which opened with the claim that 'there has now for divers years a design been carried on to change the lawful government of England into an absolute tyranny; and to convert the established protestant religion into downright popery'.[55] Marvell began his narrative in 1665 and charted attempts by the Court since then, and since 1670 in particular, to 'introduce French slavery and Roman idolatry' into England.

Charting the growth of popery, Marvell noted how the 1672 Declaration of Indulgence had been aimed at tolerating catholics, and that the other side of this coin was the attack on dissent. Marvell therefore commented on how the ministers at Court had appealed to the old cavalier spirit of intolerance

---

[50] R. Hutton, *The Restoration* (Oxford, 1985), p. 290; Norrey, 'The Restoration Regime in Action', p. 812; Scott, 'Radicalism and Restoration', pp. 453–67; Scott, *Restoration Crisis*, pp. 6–9. William Sacheverell claimed that 'All our misfortune arises from the late times. When the King came home, his ministers knew nothing of the Laws of England, but foreign Government, things managed by a premier minister of State' (Grey, *Debates*, vii. 35).

[51] E. Bohun, *An Address to the Freemen* (1682), p. 5; cf. Nevile's statement that 'the evil counsellors, the pensioner-parliament, the thorough-paced judges, the flattering divines, the busy and designing papists, the French counsels, are not the causes of our misfortunes; they are but the effects' of a general decay of government (*Plato Redivivus*, printed in C. Robbins, *Two English Republican Tracts* [Cambridge, 1969], p. 81).

[52] Sir Edward Dering dated 1672/3 as a turning point (*Dering Diaries*, pp. 125–6).

[53] *CSPD 1683–4*, p. 366.

[54] It was answered by L'Estrange in *The Parallel or An Account of the Growth of Knavery*, which was reprinted in 1679 with a preface complaining about the posthumous re-appearance of Marvell's tract.

[55] Printed in *The Complete Works of Andrew Marvell*, ed. A. Grossart (1875), iv. 248–414.

against dissent in order to attract a body of supporters. Whilst this observation was undoubtedly true at an ideological level, it was paradoxically the
case that, even after the cancellation of the 1672 Declaration of Indulgence
(which had eased restrictions on both catholic and protestant dissenters),
the enforcement of the laws against protestant nonconformists was patchy
in the 1670s, and very lax by the end of the decade.[56] Nevertheless, nonconformists bitterly resented being prosecuted under legislation aimed
primarily at catholic recusancy, and wished to redirect the Court's energies
against popery.[57] They, and a number of churchmen, sought a new 'reformation' within the church itself, the result of which, it was hoped, would be a
broader, more comprehensive church or a general toleration of protestant
dissent.[58]

Marvell argued that arbitrary power was concomitant with popery. He
observed that the catholic party looked to Louis XIV, 'the Master of Absolute
Dominion ... the declared Champion of Popery', for support, but that,
although France was regarded as the nation's enemy, war with Louis was
resisted. Swimming against the tide of public opinion meant side-lining or
corrupting the nation's mouthpiece, Parliament. The Court, Marvell claimed,
used insidious arts of bribery and management of MPs, so that the prize of a
seat at Westminster encouraged vice at the polls in by-elections, from which
divisions in the provinces spread. Inside the Commons the Court party sold
their consciences in return for pensions; Members either opposed the Court in
order to attract attention and force the Court to buy them off, or, once they
had office or rewards, formed such a strong crew that there was 'no place for
deliberation, no perswading by reason'. Ministers whipped the Court party
into line by 'frighting them with dissolutions, comforting them with long,
frequent and seasonable adjournments, now by suspending, or diminishing
their pensions, then again by increasing them; sometimes by scorn, and
othertimes by a favour'.

Marvell's concern about the direction of English foreign policy is particularly striking. He saw the inclination of the Court to ally with France as one of
the most important causes of the nation's domestic problems, and given this
close relationship between the foreign and internal situation it is worth
fleshing out some of his analysis. By the end of the Dutch war in 1674,

[56] A. Fletcher, 'The Enforcement of the Conventicle Acts 1664–1679', in *Persecution and Toleration* (*Studies in Church History*, xxi, 1984), ed. W.J. Sheils, p. 245.

[57] Prosecution under Elizabethan anti-catholic legislation accelerated under Danby (R. Clark, 'Anglicanism, Recusancy and Dissent in Derbyshire 1603–1703' [Oxford D. Phil., 1979], p. 248), though it was said to have begun earlier (Grey, *Debates*, vii. 422).

[58] For the use of the term 'reformation' see *HMC Ormonde*, iv. xviii; R. L'Estrange, *A Seasonable Memorial* (1680), pp. 11–12; *A Letter to a Friend in the Country touching the Present Fears* [1680], p. 1; *Observator*, no. 11, 7 May 1681; *Declaratory Considerations upon the Present State of Affairs* (1679), p. 101; *A Perswasive to Reformation and Union* (1680).

antipathy to France, encouraged by William of Orange who had risen to power after the murder of the De Witts, had reached a new height; but instead of following this mood Charles had secretly renewed his alliance with Louis XIV in 1676 by a treaty which provided payments if Charles avoided meeting Parliament. France had pursued an aggressive policy towards the Dutch which had been militarily successful in the spring of 1677, prompting the House of Commons to pass a series of motions requesting active measures to halt French expansionism. Charles ostensibly responded by moving closer towards an alliance with the Dutch, but nevertheless continued to negotiate simultaneously with the French. In February 1678 the Commons voted money for war against France, and an army was raised, but Charles failed to use it. By not declaring war or disbanding the army Charles therefore alienated both the French and Parliament. The earl of Danby, the King's main adviser, now feared for his own as well as for his master's position and a new Anglo-French treaty was agreed in May 1678 which granted Charles more money. Yet, despite the negotiation of a general peace, the King still did not disband the army, perhaps because he or Danby intended to use it to coerce internal dissent or perhaps because he believed it increased his value in Louis' eyes. In either case, the policy backfired, for in late 1678 Charles found himself diplomatically isolated abroad and hence forced to rely on Parliament and with an unpopular standing army at home which had no enemy to fight. In this situation, the parliamentary session in the autumn of 1678 was always likely to have been a stormy one, even without the Popish Plot, as the repercussions of the disastrous foreign policy were all too obvious. On 19 December 1678 the former ambassador in Paris, Ralph Montagu, revealed the double-dealing of the King and Danby, thereby exposing the deviousness of policy at the centre of government. The succession was thus at first just one more layer of the problem of popery and arbitrary government, especially since James was both a catholic and one of the allies of France.[59]

Charles's foreign policy had important consequences for the domestic situation. The standing army increased fears about the King's desire to introduce arbitrary government. MPs thus at first thought that the Popish Plot was a device to justify the maintenance of the troops, and on 1 April 1679 the Commons passed a vote on the illegality of a standing army.[60] Even after the soldiers had been disbanded, suspicions of Charles's military intentions persisted in hostility to the King's guards and to the personnel in charge of the armed forces.[61] The cost of paying the army had also wrecked the Crown's

---

[59] *Popery and Tyranny* (1679), p. 18; *Europe a Slave* (1681), p. 55.
[60] Bucks. RO, M11/32, Edmund Verney to Sir Ralph Verney, 7 October 1678; K.H.D. Haley, *The First Earl of Shaftesbury* (Oxford, 1968), p. 457; Burnet, *History*, ii. 156; Grey, *Debates*, vi. 218; vii. 73.
[61] *A Seasonable Warning to the Commons of England* (1679), p. 2; *CSPD 1679–80*, pp. 177, 201; *HMC Verney*, p. 474; *The Observator*, 16 April 1681.

solvency. One of the most important weaknesses of the Crown during the crisis was a financial one.[62] The roots of the problem lay, courtiers claimed, in the Restoration settlement that had failed to grant adequate revenue to the Crown, but the burden of preparations for war had overstretched the Exchequer in 1672, and increases in the customs and excise revenue after 1674 failed to cover expenditure.[63] Danby presided over a huge floating debt by 1678 – larger than that which led in 1672 to the Stop of the Exchequer – and the situation deteriorated as a result of a three-year ban on imported French goods, from which the King had derived lucrative taxes. The decision to dissolve the Cavalier Parliament before it had granted money for the disbandment of the army therefore threatened to plunge the exchequer into crisis.[64]

The extremely delicate financial state of the Crown had political implications for the Court's position. Lord treasurer Danby was replaced in 1679 by a Treasury Commission that instituted a severe retrenchment programme on the King's household, wardrobe, chamber and privy purse expenditure.[65] Salaries went unpaid, with the result that service of the Court was not a financially attractive proposition at a time when it needed to attract support.[66] Moreover, Charles was forced throughout the period to place money high on his agenda, and to let his need for it influence his policy. According to one of its architects, the remodelling of the privy council in April 1679 was based partly on the concept of giving the nation's wealthiest men a say in government, since the councillors 'might out of their own Stocks, and upon a Pinch, furnish the King so far, as to relieve some great Necessity of the Crown'.[67] Financial considerations were quite nakedly prominent in royal

---

[62] For a good summary of the forms of royal revenue see Ogg, *England in the Reign of Charles II*, chapter xii.

[63] Clarke, *James II*, i. 593. Exchequer receipts did not cover expenditure until 1681 (W.R. Scott, *The Constitution and Finance of English, Scottish and Irish Joint-Stock Companies to 1720* [Cambridge 1910–11], iii. 534–5, 540–1).

[64] Modern scholarship has estimated the total debt in 1679 at £2,720,194 (*Cal. Treas. Bks*, vii. pt. 1 [1681–5], introduction by W. Shaw, p. xxviii), a figure remarkably close to the £2,740,879 calculated at the time by Sir Robert Howard (*An Account of the State of His Majesties Revenue* [1681], p. 20), although a lower figure of £1,457,834 has also been suggested (Scott, *Joint Stock Companies*, iii. 544). Newdigate newsletter Lc.735, 23 January 1679, reported that Parliament might have to be recalled specifically in order to grant money for disbanding, though according to BL, Add. 10,118, f. 40, the duke of York supplied the money.

[65] C.D. Chandaman, *The English Public Revenue 1660–1688* (Oxford, 1975), p. 250; HMC *Ormonde*, v. 151; Newdigate Newsletter Lc.974, 21 August 1680; Huntington Lib., Stowe MS STT 2451, Sir Ralph Verney to Sir Richard Temple, 9 February 1681; All Souls, MS 171, f. 133, newsletter, 14 February 1681; N. Luttrell, *Brief Relation*, i. 68.

[66] The King's household expenditure fell from £111,000 in 1679 to £57,000 by 1682, and pensions of grace were slashed from £120,000 to £50,000 in 1679 (BL, Add. 10,119, ff. 52, 55).

[67] Temple, *Memoirs*, p. 333.

policy in early 1681. On 17 January 1681 the privy council discussed whether or not the ban on French goods expired in March, and it did not escape the King's notice that the prohibition lapsed after 20 March if MPs failed to renew it.[68] Parliament sat on 21 March and was dissolved a week later, before any legislation could be passed.

The Court's supporters were acutely aware of the obstacle the shortage of money placed in the way of resolute action, and sought means to rescue the King. In March 1680 it was reported that Edward Seymour had a plan to raise money in Ireland that could be used in England, though Shaftesbury dismissed this as another attempt 'to make the king independent of his people'.[69] Seymour was by no means alone in his inventiveness. Soon after the failure of the petitioning campaign requesting Charles to let Parliament sit in January 1680, Sir Richard Grahme appears to have drawn up a proposal for a 'free loan' from the counties to raise £300,000, with the names of subscribers to be entered into an Exchequer Roll; unlike the signatures on the mass petitions presented to the King, this subscription would 'bee a kind of Numbering of the K[in]g's friends'.[70] Although the scheme was not apparently pressed any further, Grahme was working in the autumn of 1680 on another project to raise £485,000 through the sale of honours and titles.[71] Charles wisely left both these early Stuart expedients alone, as well as plans to raise revenue by a strict prosecution of papists, and by collecting first fruit and tenths from the clergy,[72] though in the wake of the dissolution of the Oxford Parliament some voluntary contributions to the royal coffers were reported.[73]

In January 1680, when it was thought 'miraculous [that] the government does yet subsist', Sir Robert Southwell remarked that some of the Court's critics had a 'shrewd calculation of our wants'.[74] The poor state of the Exchequer increased the number of opportunities to exploit the Court's financial weakness. Sometime after the elections in the autumn of 1679 a paper was drawn up by an opposition hand to map out future action in Parliament, and concluded that if Charles dissolved it he should be deprived of revenues by a campaign to stop up hearths and drink as little liquor as possible.[75] In May 1680 it was said that Shaftesbury believed that the expiry

[68] PRO Baschet Transcripts, 31/3/148, f. 27, Barrillon dispatch, 17/27 January 1681.
[69] *CSPD 1679–80*, p. 416; *HMC Ormonde*, v. 351.
[70] BL, Add. 63,773, ff. 4–5, 'A free loan', n.d.
[71] BL, Add. 63,773, f. 9, 'A project to raise money', 2 November 1680.
[72] *CSPD 1679–80*, p. 535; All Souls, MS 239, f. 267, Stephen Allen to [Jenkins], 7 February 1681.
[73] *Loyal Protestant*, no. 14, 22 May 1681.
[74] *Hatton Correspondence*, i. 214; *HMC Ormonde*, iv. 576.
[75] BL, Longleat mss, M/863, Coventry papers, vi. ff. 248–51, 'Several Usefull and Indispensably Necessary Cautions', n.d.

of the 1677 Excise Act and Law Duty would make the King's 'wants more pressing' so that he could the more easily be 'constrained', and in August 1680 the French ambassador Barrillon reported that the malcontents wanted Charles to have to maintain the costly defence of Tangier because it drained his coffers.[76] It was also later claimed that some MPs persuaded the East India Company to deliberately enter into bonds rather than pay Charles ready money for custom dues.[77] When Parliament met again, the Commons resolved to bring in a bill against the illegal exaction of money, effectively forbidding loans to the King and making Parliament the sole means by which money could be raised.[78] As we shall see, MPs were increasingly inclined to view supply as a carrot to dangle before the King as an incentive to grant their demands. According to one tract, Shaftesbury often asked Oates 'are they not all starved yet at Whitehall?', and on 23 December 1680, in a speech that was published, he warned that 'the Nation is betrayed, if upon any Terms we part with our Money till we are sure the King is ours'.[79] Perhaps following this lead, the Commons voted on 7 January 1681 that all anticipation on any branch of revenue was illegal, and that anyone who lent money was a public enemy.[80] As Burnet remarked, it was thought that this 'must certainly bring the king to their terms', though MPs were, of course, mistaken.[81]

One of the arguments Marvell used to justify a war against France was that a trade deficit of almost £1,000,000 meant that 'the treasure and money of the nation was yearly exhausted and carried into France, and all this by unnecessary wines, silks, ribbons, feathers etc.'.[82] Though perhaps exaggerated, the effects of this imbalance had prompted a group of merchants to complain about the situation as early as November 1674. Alarms about France causing a decay of England's trade, particularly its cloth trade which was hard hit by

[76] Bod., MS Carte 243, f. 473, newsletter 11 May 1680; PRO, 31/3/146, f. 47, 2/12 August 1680. Tangier cost £1,600,000 to maintain (*Cal. Treas. Bks*, vii. pt 1 [1681–5], p. xxvii). Chandaman, *English Public Revenue*, p. 249, notes that the Crown's net income fell to £1,281,000 1680–1.

[77] All Souls, MS 239, f. 260, memorandum about East India Company. Barrillon reported that due to the influence of Thomas Papillon (MP and deputy governor) it refused to loan Charles money in October 1680 (PRO, 31/3/146, f. 107, Barrillon dispatch, 7/17 October 1680). In October 1681 the Company nevertheless loaned the King 10,000 guineas (Scott, *Joint-Stock Companies*, ii. 143).

[78] *CJ*, ix. 682–3; PRO, 31/3/147, f. 82, Barrillon dispatch, 20/30 December 1680.

[79] *The Intrigues of the Popish Plot Laid Open* (1685), p. 30; *A Speech lately made by a Noble Peer* (1681).

[80] *CJ*, ix. 702.

[81] Burnet, *History*, ii. 264.

[82] Marvell, *Complete Works*, p. 360. S. Bethel, *An Account of the French Usurpation upon the Trade of England* (1679), p. 6, put the imbalance at £1,600,000. The 1670s are 'statistically blank' for trade figures (R. Davis, 'English Foreign Trade 1660–1700', *Ec. Hist. Rev.* 2nd series, vii (1954), 155).

Colbert's tariffs, were voiced increasingly noisily as the 1670s progressed.[83] *The Art of Good Husbandry* (1675) complained of 'the great decay of trade and want of money, which is now the general cry of all people both in city and country';[84] in January 1676 Thomas Overbury thought that English money was 'carried into foreign parts for toys and trifles we had better be without, which has already reduced us to so great want and beggary, that were not God merciful in affording us yet plenty of corn, our poor would starve and the rich be hardly enough put to it to live'.[85] In 1677 a crop of tracts railed against the French monopoly of trade, and such attacks did not cease when the war did.[86] Thus in 1680 *Britannia Languens* insisted that even in peace time 'our land-rents are generally much fallen, and our home-commodities sunk from their late value and price; our poor are vastly increased, and the rest of our people generally more and more feel the want of money';[87] and another tract argued that 'at present we have so little work that many thousands of families of salt-workers, rope-makers, weavers, dyers, potters, tanners &c have no employment'.[88] The Levant Company, which exported far more cloth than its rival, was also going through hard times as a result of East India Company imports, and one writer thought there were as many as 200,000 idle poor in England in 1679.[89] This economic discontent could be channelled into political unrest: the petitions of 1679 and 1680 owed some of their support to economic grievances and James Holloway, the Bristol linen draper whom we have already met as a Rye House Plotter, was sucked into national politics

[83] M. Priestley, 'Anglo-French Trade and the "Unfavourable Balance" Controversy 1660–1685', *Ec. Hist. Rev.* 2nd series, iv (1951–2), 37–52. See also S. Pincus, 'From Butterboxes to Wooden Shoes: the Shift in English Popular Sentiment from hatred of Holland to hatred of France in the 1670s', *HJ*, forthcoming 1994; D. Hall, 'Anglo-French Trade Relations Under Charles II', *History* n.s. vii (1923), 17–30.

[84] *Seventeenth Century Economic Documents*, ed. J. Thirsk and J. Cooper (Oxford, 1972), p. 97. cf. *A Discourse of Trade* (1675).

[85] *CSPD 1675–6*, p. 499.

[86] *A Short Discourse upon the Designs, Practices and Counsels of France* (1677); *The Present State of Christendom* (1677); *A Commentary upon the Present Condition of the Kingdom* (1677); *Europe a Slave, Unless England Break Her Chains* (1681, but first printed in French 1677).

[87] *Britannia Languens*, introduction. cf. *Discourses Upon the Modern Affairs of Europe* (1680). Sir Edward Dering thought that a decline in the value of the gentry's rents since the Dutch war had put 'very many men out of humour' (*Dering Diaries*, p. 126).

[88] J. Collins, *A Plea for the Bringing in of Irish Cattel* (1680), p. 10.

[89] A.C. Wood, *A History of the Levant Company* (Oxford, 1935), p. 102; Scott, *Joint-Stock Companies*, ii. 136; *The Proposals for Promoting the Woollen Manufactory Promoted* (1679), p. 3. North, *Examen*, p. 463 claimed the leaders of the Turkey Company were also 'the demagogues or heads of the faction in the city'. In April 1680 Lord Chandos was elected as the company's ambassador to Constantinople having received support from 'all those who any way dissent from the government' (BL, Althorp MS C5, Thomas Thynne to Halifax, 26 April 1680). In February 1681 an attempt to remove Lord Berkeley as the Company's head was seen as 'a tryall of skill amongst the chiefest merchants of London' (Bulstrode newsletter, 10 February 1681).

after attending Parliament in 1679 to promote a bill for the encouragement of linen manufacture.[90]

Not only did these conditions create unrest among the artisans in London and the provinces, but they also alienated a number of influential merchants, many of whom became prominent opponents of the Court, such as Patience Ward, Thomas Papillon, Michael Godfrey (the brother of Sir Edmund Berry Godfrey, the murdered JP to whom Oates gave his evidence) and John Dubois. Furthermore, as the puritanical tone of many of the pamphlet quotations suggest, the interest of trade was seen as linked to religious freedom, and hence the economic grievances increased pressure for toleration or comprehension of dissenters, and for a protestant foreign policy.[91] Henry Nevile's *Plato Redivivus* also argued along Harringtonian lines that a large part of the nation's problem was that the balance of political power no longer followed the balance of economic power.[92] On the other hand, economic considerations ultimately worked in favour of the Court, once the political and religious crisis of 1678–81 itself caused 'a sensible decay and poverty, a wasting of the very spirit and life of the city and Nation'.[93] Thus an address from Bristol in April 1681 lamented that the city's inhabitants talked politics to the 'great detriment of our trade', and Barrillon reported that the rich London merchants had no wish to see serious unrest.[94] One tract advising

[90]   T. Sprat, *A True Account and Declaration of the Horrid Conspiracy* (1685), p. 75; J. Latimer, *The Annals of Bristol in the Seventeenth Century* (1900), p. 394; M. Knights, 'London Petitions and Parliamentary Politics in 1679', *Parliamentary History*, xii (1993), 41–2. The *Loyal Intelligence*, no. 1, 16 March 1679/80 nevertheless claimed that for all the reports of bad economic conditions in London, 'there was never more trade here in the memory of man'.

[91]   *Early English Tracts on Commerce*, ed. J. McCulloch (Cambridge 1952), p. 360, citing *Britannia Languens* (1680); *A Commentary upon the Present Condition of the Kingdom* (1677), pp. 9–27; *A Discourse of Trade* (1675), pp. 9–40; E. Ellis, 'The Whig Junto' (Oxford D.Phil., 1961), pp. 65–8, discussion of a 'Remonstrance' written by John Somers in 1681; *The Emperour and Empire Betray'd* (1681), pp. 113–18; S. Bethel, *The Interest of Princes* (1680). It has been suggested that Penn obtained the charter for Pennsylvania because Charles wished to syphon off discontented merchants and dissenters from England (F. Mood, 'William Penn and English Politics 1680–1), *Journal of Friends' Historical Society*, xxxii (1935), 3–21.

[92]   Robbins, *Two English Republican Tracts*, pp. 61–200. The socio-economic dimensions of the crisis have only recently been studied after a period of long neglect. Ashcraft has argued that the Whigs wanted to form an alliance between the industrious merchants, tradesmen, artisans and the gentry (*Revolutionary Politics*, chapter 6). His use of the term 'class' is, however, unfortunate, and there are a number of problems with his argument. If, as he suggests, there was an element of 'class conflict', why were so many of the leading critics of the Court aristocrats? How could there have been 'a greater polarisation of the nation along class-divided lines' than at any time since the Restoration when criticism of the aristocracy was 'muted' and 'indirect' ? Why were some merchants more active than others in opposing the Court?

[93]   *A Seasonable Address to the Right Honourable Lord Mayor* (1680), p. 2.

[94]   Bristol address cited by J. Barry, 'The Press and the Politics of Culture in Bristol 1660–1775', in *Culture, Politics and Society*, ed. J. Black and J. Gregory (Manchester, 1991), p. 53; PRO, 31/3/146, f. 32, Barrillon dispatch, 12/22 July 1680; 31/3/147, f. 21, Barrillon dispatch, 8/18 November 1680, f. 41, 18/28 November 1680; Bohun, *An Address to the Freemen and Freeholders of the Nation* (2nd part) (1682), pp. i–xxv.

corporations how to vote in 1681 even claimed that the decay in trade was due to the dissenters, a complete reversal of the argument that persecution of nonconformists damaged the economy.[95]

Finally, Marvell's tract revealed his loathing of Charles's advisers, the most prominent being the earl of Danby, who had dominated politics since 1674. In 1675 an attempt to impeach him had failed, but the perception that he presided over the growth of popery and arbitrary government, together with the personal resentments aroused by his creation of a Court interest composed of officeholders, pensioners and his own relatives, ensured that hostility towards him crescendoed in the autumn of 1678, almost to the exclusion of all else. Thus Sir Francis Rolle asked Daniel Finch why he was so zealous in promoting bills against popery when evil ministers were still advising the King, and argued that 'till they were removed all was in vaine'.[96] It was not the Plot alone that brought Danby's administration down – ironically he actually sought to use it to his own advantage – but a mixture of the same blend of 'country' opposition and faction that had marked the first attempt to impeach him in 1675. Indeed, the role played by faction is worth reconstructing to show an element in the structure of politics at the beginning of the crisis that is often overshadowed by the issue of popery. The study of Danby's downfall reveals the fluid and cabal-ridden nature of Court groups and alignments, as well as the personal nature of politics. It also contributes to our understanding of the political legacy which the impeachment bequeathed: one of six months of strife about Danby's fate, dissatisfaction about the pardon he was granted and the role of bishops as judges at trials of peers, but above all, the power vacuum that it created at the centre of affairs.

Danby's initial attempt in the autumn of 1678 to harness the wave of anti-catholic feeling inevitably placed a strain on his relationship with the duke of York, who correctly suspected that Danby advised the King to abandon his brother. This division was exploited by opponents of Danby who sought to drive a wedge between the Court factions.[97] Rivalry between York and the duke of Monmouth, Charles's illegitimate son, between Danby and Charles's mistress, the duchess of Portsmouth, and between Danby's formidable wife and lord chancellor Finch fractured the Court further.[98] In the Commons, the Court's majority dissolved and its supporters were increasingly disorganised. For example, on 2 December a vote against Charles's

---

[95] *Considerations Offered to all the Corporations of England* (1681), p. 1.

[96] Leics. RO, Finch mss, DG7/4957/57 (diary), f. 1, 31 October 1678.

[97] PRO 31/3/141, f. 47, Barrillon dispatch, 4/14 November; f. 51, Barrillon dispatch, 7/17 November; f. 57, Barrillon dispatch, 14/24 November 1678; Reresby, *Memoirs*, pp. 157–8.

[98] Clarke, *James II*, i. 525–6; PRO, 31/3/141, f. 72, Barrillon dispatch, 21 November/1 December 1678; Bucks RO, Verney mss, M11/32, John Verney to Sir Ralph Verney, 11 November 1678.

decision to veto the militia bill was carried because 'many of those whom they call the Court Party were absent, being gone to dinner'.[99] The disarray had also been clear enough the day before, when some of the duke's supporters voted in favour of a resolution about the ill state of the nation that struck directly at the lord treasurer;[100] privately the duke's supporters Lords Clarendon and Feversham pressed Charles to abandon his minister.[101]

Danby also faced opposition from other factions at Court. Information to be found in his personal papers about the co-ordination of the groups sheds interesting light on the confused state of political alliances. The duke of Ormonde was said to have fallen in with an 'Irish interest' of the earl of Essex and Lord Longford, who opposed Danby's alliance with the earl of Ranelagh, and who worked through Sir Henry Capel, William Harbord and Sir Cyril Wyche in the Commons. A group of Exchequer officials, including Sir Robert Howard, Sir Robert Carr, Sir Stephen Fox and Sir John Duncombe, were reported to have been alienated by Danby's alleged financial malpractice. Other courtiers such as Sir Allen Apsley, Sir Robert Holmes, Sir Thomas Chicheley, Secretary Coventry, Solicitor General Sir Francis Winnington and Edward Seymour, Speaker of the Commons, motivated either by loyalty to the duke or dislike of Danby, joined the Court malcontents.[102]

Another dangerous figure at Court for Danby was Arlington, who had supported the impeachment of 1675, and was again prominent in 1678.[103] He and Prince Rupert encouraged the group of 'Country' MPs who had served in the earlier assault, amongst whom a degree of faction is noticeable. Thomas Littleton, Henry Powle, Lord Cavendish, Colonel Birch and Silius Titus all had a strong hatred of popery and arbitrary government, and wished to see a rapid disbandment of the army; but they were also motivated by personal considerations in their attack on Danby. Powle had ambitions to be a commissioner of the Treasury, Littleton had lost his office as commissioner of the Navy as a result of Danby's rise to power, Cavendish believed that his alienation from Court stemmed from Danby's influence, and Titus admitted that nonpayment of £4,000 owed to him for his offices on the council of plantations and groom of the bedchamber sharpened his appetite for the lord treasurer's fall.[104] The personal nature of many of the grievances against Danby is evident in an impeachment article drawn up, though eventually dropped, which accused him of having made Sir Robert Atkyns, Lord

[99] Huntington Lib., MS HM 30315 no. 195, newsletter, 3 December 1678.
[100] Reresby, Memoirs, p. 161.
[101] BL, Add. 28,049, f. 34, J. Netterville to Knox, 24 December 1678.
[102] BL, Add. 28,049, f. 34, Netterville to Knox, 24 December 1678; f. 36, same to same, n.d.; Huntington Lib., MS HM 30315, newsletter no. 202, 20 December 1678.
[103] A. Browning, Thomas Osborne, Earl of Danby (Glasgow, 1944–51), iii. 1–2.
[104] BL, Add. 28,043, f. 1, 'Mr Crosse', 20 November 1678; Add. 28,049, f. 36, Netterville to Knox, n.d.; Grey, Debates, vi. 362.

Halifax, Lord Holles, Lord Dorset, Sir Robert Carr, Sir John Duncombe, Sir Robert Howard and secretary Coventry 'a sacrifice to his ambition pride and avarice'.[105] Even the earl of Strafford, whom the King thought should have been influenced by the fate of his famous father, was 'violent' against Danby 'from a personal peake he had to him for obstructing a pension'.[106] The articles of impeachment eventually levelled against the treasurer were, significantly, focused on the general charge of fiscal misconduct, and sympathy to popery and arbitrary government, allegations which were broad enough to unite all factions.

The most dangerous figure for Danby was the ex-courtier Ralph Montagu, another of Arlington's protégés and the former ambassador to France. Montagu resented Danby's refusal to appoint him as Secretary of State on his return in 1678, and possessed letters from Danby that were incriminating enough to deal the final blow to the Treasurer. Montagu's designs had been encouraged by Barrillon, the French ambassador, in order to secure the disbandment of Charles's army, and in order to create enough unrest in England to diminish England's capacity to act in Europe. Barrillon therefore exploited the grievances of Montagu, Littleton, Powle and Harbord, thereby encouraging and assisting, rather than instigating, the impeachment.[107] The ambassador was also in contact with the duke of Buckingham,[108] though Buckingham mistrusted another enemy of Danby, the earl of Shaftesbury, and was in turn mistrusted by the other opposition groups.[109]

The attack on Danby thus reveals a very confused and loose state of politics, driven by faction rather than by party organisation, with many of those allying against him motivated by different and sometimes diverging reasons. It was no wonder that Secretary Coventry thought 'all things both in Court, Parliament, Town and Country full of confusion',[110] or that he found 'so many subdivisions in our divisions, both in Court and Parliament that I think ere long we shall divide so nicely as to have no factions, which is the best I can hope of it'.[111] Indeed, the co-ordination of opposition, if not the unity shown by many of the members of the Cabal administration which Danby had supplanted, offers an intriguing insight into the extent to which the government's problems were at this stage caused by an alliance of Court and

---

[105] BL, Add. 28,049, f. 38, draft articles of impeachment.

[106] Reresby, *Memoirs*, p. 167.

[107] PRO, 31/3/141, f. 25, Barrillon dispatch, 14/24 October; f. 28, Barrillon dispatch, 17/27 October; f. 96, Barrillon dispatch, 12/22 December 1678. These dealings were nearly exposed in the House (Leics. RO, DG7/4957/57, f. 22, 7 November 1678).

[108] PRO, 31/3/141, f. 52, Barrillon dispatch, 7/17 November 1678.

[109] PRO, 31/3/141, f. 63, Barrillon dispatch, 14/24 November. 1678.

[110] BL, Longleat mss M/874, reel ii, f. 128, Coventry to Ormonde, 26 November 1678.

[111] *HMC Ormonde*, iv. 269.

Country. The impeachment also highlights the danger of taking the grievance of 'popery and arbitrary government' simply at face value. The rallying cry hid factional motives as well as tying together a raft of festering grievances. The involvement of a number of York's followers further indicates the impossibility of describing the main supporters of Danby's impeachment as a proto-exclusionist party. Yet distrust of Danby did have important consequences for the succession problem, which had not yet come to a head. Firstly, it pushed the ever-restless Montagu into a dangerous alliance with Monmouth that was to last throughout the crisis. Secondly, the issue of Danby's impeachment was to continue to deflect attention away from the duke of York. Thirdly, in order to bolster his own position, Danby had planned to sacrifice the duke of York, and had thereby linked the survival of his administration to James's position. Ironically, the Court's disintegration ensured that the succession issue became part of the struggle for power, and it is on that intertwined problem that we must now focus.

2

Politics and the succession, 1678–9

The last section outlined some of the problems facing the Court in 1678 at the time of the Popish Plot. The growth of suspicions in the 1670s that Charles or Danby intended to introduce popery and arbitrary government focused attention on the perceived misrule of the King, fears that were heightened, though not primarily caused, by increasing alarm about the possible tyranny of his catholic brother James. Mistrust of the Court was increased by the ambiguities of Charles's foreign policy and by his maintenance of a standing army, the cost of which placed enormous burdens on the royal coffers. The principal target for many MPs in the autumn of 1678 was thus the King's chief adviser, Danby, not the duke of York. Factions at Court, centring on the lord treasurer's old rival Arlington but including a large number of the government's own officials, allied with the leaders of the Country party to bring down the lord treasurer.

Yet although most hostility, even by James himself, was directed towards Danby, the rifts at Court had also exacerbated and exploited uneasiness about the duke of York's claim to the throne, and we need now to explore how the succession problem was viewed at Whitehall, Westminster and among the opposition cabals. This chapter will focus on the early stages of the crisis, because by concentrating on the months between November 1678 and May 1679 it is possible to examine how and why exclusion emerged as the means chosen by the House to meet the succession problem. This, and following sections, will examine the politics of the succession issue rather than its ideology, and will reconstruct debates in Parliament and at Whitehall. It will be argued that in order to tackle the subject properly, we need to look not just at the progress of the exclusion bill, but also at the possible alternatives to it, which have generally been neglected by historians. A wide variety of ideas to safeguard the future were discussed and promoted, and exclusion was a measure somewhat reluctantly adopted by MPs. In other words, the period witnessed a succession crisis, not just an exclusion crisis. Having accepted that broader framework we can then ask why the House resolved on the bill, and suggest that its acceptance was the result as much of a failure of the alternatives, of Court management, and of faction, as of the positive pressure of parliamentary opinion. The succession must thus be seen against the backdrop of Court politics, and such an approach will require a study of the Court's internal difficulties, which will in turn force us to re-examine the parameters within which politics was being conducted.

James had virtually admitted his conversion to catholicism by refusing to comply with the Test Act in 1673, yet exclusion had by no means been the tactic immediately embraced by MPs to deal with the situation. The idea of exclusion had, it is true, been raised in 1674, but only in the House of Lords.[1] The Cavalier House of Commons had shown considerable moderation in approaching the problem of the succession. Although in 1673 Charles had feared that bills might be introduced in Parliament to exile James and exclude catholics from the throne, no such legislation appeared,[2] and MPs continued to be cautious even after the revelations of the Popish Plot in the autumn of 1678 had increased the urgency of ensuring adequate safeguards for the King's life and increased the need to protect the religion and property of the subject. According to a number of sources, a bill excluding papists from the succession 'had bin whispered' after Parliament resumed sitting on 21 October 1678;[3] but it was not until 4 November that William Sacheverell asked the House of Commons whether King and Parliament were able to dispose of the succession,[4] and even then, MPs were markedly reluctant to pursue the idea. On 21 November Sir George Hungerford moved for the exclusion of papists from the succession, but Finch recorded that 'no man seconded this motion'.[5] This hesitancy did not mean that there was not considerable anxiety about the prospect of a catholic King. Next day MPs expressed more fears about a popish successor, but 'whether they intended a particular Bill by itselfe for it or whether they intended there should be no Popish King' Finch was unable to tell.[6] Yet whatever their motives, MPs had debated James's position 'with all [the] respect & tendernesse possible',[7] and did not, so far as

---

[1] The Lauderdale Papers, ed. O. Airy (Camden Society, n.s. xxxviii, 1885), iii. 33; HMC Kenyon, p. 100; Diary of Ralph Josselin, ed. A. Macfarlane (Oxford, 1976), p. 573. cf. CSPD 1673–5, pp. 131–2.

[2] Haley, Shaftesbury, p. 331; Witcombe, Cavalier Parliament, chapter 11.

[3] Clarke, James II, i. 525; Luttrell, Brief Relation, i. 3; Leics. RO, Finch mss, DG7/4957/57, f. 23, 9 November 1678.

[4] Grey, Debates, vi. 132; PRO, 31/3/141, f. 51, Barrillon dispatch, 7/17 November 1678; Leics. RO, Finch mss, DG7/4957/57, ff.16–21, 4 November 1678.

[5] Leics. RO, Finch mss, DG7/4957/57, f. 34, 21 November 1678. Grey did not record Hungerford's speech but does give earlier speeches that may have encouraged Hungerford: Sir Philip Warwick had said he 'would rather consider that a Popish Successor may not be, but a Protestant of our Religion', and Sir Robert Howard asked 'what will hold all you have done, if the Crown come to [the duke of York?]' (Grey, Debates, vi. 248–9).

[6] Leics. RO, Finch mss, DG7/4957/57, f. 36, 22 November 1678.

[7] Huntington Lib., MS HM 30315/180, newsletter, 5 November 1678.

we know, mention exclusion again before the Cavalier Parliament was dissolved on 24 January 1679.

The reticence shown by Members of the Cavalier Parliament to bar James from the throne is perhaps not surprising, though we should expect the new Parliament that met on 6 March 1679, which is known as the first Exclusion Parliament, to have been more enthusiastic about the measure. Nevertheless, most MPs in the new assembly were slow to embrace exclusion.[8] It was not until 27 April that speeches were made in favour of a protestant successor,[9] and even then the debates about the succession do not seem to have been conscientiously attended, for on 11 May Sir Francis Winnington complained that it was left 'for a few Gentlemen to debate and argue, and the rest to slip away'.[10] Four days later, when the exclusion bill received its first reading, it was noticed that attendance at the Commons was thin, many MPs being lured away by a dog match at Hampton Court and a horse race at Banstead.[11] When the House finally voted on the bill, on 21 May, only 335 MPs voted, twenty-five less than had voted on 8 April for a committee of the whole house to discuss the Irish Cattle Bill.[12] The bill had thus not drawn the largest turnout of the session, and MPs from certain counties appear to have been particularly reluctant to commit themselves: only two of Nottinghamshire's eight MPs voted, as did only two of Oxfordshire's nine, and only one of Shropshire's twelve.[13] Most of the House of Commons had moved cautiously, hesitantly even, towards exclusion which even the bill's supporter Sir John Hobart referred to as 'soe sharpe & hazardous a remedie'.[14] Once the exclusion bill's long gestation period is recognised, it can be set in context as part of a much broader attempt to find answers to the succession problem. Exclusion had not been the only solution that had been proposed between November 1678 and May 1679. Yet many of the alternatives have been virtually ignored by historians, and must now be examined.

The most important of the alternatives was the project for limitations on the powers of the monarchy. After 1673 this scheme had been advanced in a variety of ways. The Cavalier Parliament had drawn up a new Test Act, and introduced bills to secure the education of the duke of York's children as protestants, to expand provisions for habeas corpus, to ensure that judges

---

[8] Harris, *Politics under the Later Stuarts*, p. 83, suggests that the opposition did not dare bring in the bill immediately in the face of explicit royal hostility. Yet hostility was far from explicit, and royal antipathy did not prevent the promotion of the bill in later stages of the dispute.

[9] Grey, *Debates*, vii. 140.

[10] Grey, *Debates*, vii. 251.

[11] *HMC Ormonde*, v. 102.

[12] 'An Exclusion Bill Division List', ed. A. Browning and D.J. Milne, *BIHR*, xxiii (1950), 207: 'the total vote of 335 ... must be regarded as a small one'.

[13] Ibid., p. 217. Haley, *Shaftesbury*, p. 522, suggests that an informal system of pairing may have been operating.

[14] Norfolk RO, WKc/7/6/39, Sir John Hobart to William Wyndham, 13 May 1679.

held office during good behaviour rather than at the King's pleasure, to prosecute catholic recusants, to prevent the illegal exaction of money, and to disband the army.[15] 'Fear of the Duke ma[de] them every day fetter the Crown', remarked the earl of Conway.[16] Although all these bills had been lost as a result of prorogations, the earl of Danby had not been insensitive to MPs' alarm, and had responded to the pressure by espousing a cautious policy of limitations restricted to the eventuality of a popish successor rather than limiting the Crown's powers *per se*. In 1677 he had introduced a bill in the Lords which would have imposed an oath on every King concerning transubstantiation; those who failed to take it were to have their children educated by the episcopacy as protestants, and the catholic King would no longer have an unrestricted right to appoint bishops. But the bill had been buried in committee, possibly because it proposed to turn the ecclesiastical hierarchy into a self-appointing oligarchy above the power of the Crown.[17]

Danby nevertheless returned to the idea of limiting a popish successor in the aftermath of the Popish Plot. Perhaps prompted by a speech made on 4 November by Col. Birch, who declared in the Commons that until laws were made 'to begin in the next king's time, that, whoever he is, he may not be able to destroy the Protestant Religion, nor our Property, we can never be safe',[18] Danby actively considered a bill of limitations 'to pare the nailes ... of a popish successor', a proposal to which Charles agreed.[19] The suggestion for such a bill was made formally in the King's speech on 9 November, with the provisos that the true line of the succession was not to be altered and that limitations should not restrict the rights of a protestant successor.[20] The lord chancellor added that Parliament would sit continuously for a year if a papist succeeded to the throne.[21] These speeches were reported to have been met 'with very great satisfaction'.[22] On 22 November Secretary Coventry restarted the initiative by proposing that a popish successor be deprived of the right to dispense with penal laws against papists, and, with an unknown degree of official support, Speaker Seymour continued by suggesting that

---

[15] Haley, *Shaftesbury*, p. 359; de Beer, 'Development of Parties', pp. 55–61; Witcombe, *Cavalier Parliament*, pp. 156–7, 159–61.

[16] Quoted by Haley, *Shaftesbury*, p. 359.

[17] Feiling, *Tory Party*, pp. 166–7; *HMC Lords 1671–1678*, pp. 81–2; BL, Add. 28,091, ff. 59–60, notes on debate 20 March 1677; BL, Longleat mss, M/863, reel v, vol. viii, ff. 244–5, 'Abstract of the Bill Concerning the Succession', n.d.; BL, Add. 35,865 (Hardwicke Papers), ff. 205–8, 'Breveat of Proposals to be made in Parl[iamen]t for the preservac[i]on of [sic] Popery In Case the Crown should descend to a Prince of the Romish perswasion'.

[18] Grey, *Debates*, vi. 137.

[19] Reresby, *Memoirs*, p. 157.

[20] Grey, *Debates*, vi. 172.

[21] PRO, 31/3/141, f. 57, Barrillon dispatch, 14/24 November 1678.

[22] Leics. RO, Finch mss, DG7/4957/57, f. 25, 9 November 1678; Newdigate newsletter Lc.705, 12 November 1678; *HMC Ormonde*, iv. 470. The proposals were, however, attacked by Sacheverell as 'a rattle, to keep us quiet' (Grey, *Debates*, vi. 172).

'dependencies in Church or State, and power to dispose of the Public Revenue, or the Militia' be taken from a popish successor.[23] MPs warmly embraced these suggestions and ordered articles to be drawn up;[24] but the attack on Danby displaced other business for the rest of the session, and the progress of the scheme was halted.

Despite Danby's impeachment, which resulted in his fall from power and a new privy council, limitations on a popish successor remained government policy in the new Parliament. On 30 April 1679 the lord chancellor declared that Charles was prepared to pass a test to distinguish a papist from a protestant successor, to provide for the automatic sitting of Parliament after his death, to agree to the transfer of the power of appointment of judges, privy councillors, JPs, lord lieutenants and navy officers to Parliament in the time of a popish successor, and to recognise Parliament's sole right to raise money, as well as the provisions outlined in November 1678.[25] In other words Seymour's suggestions had been incorporated more formally into the government's proposals. According to Richard Baxter 'this offer took much with many, but most said that it signifyed nothing',[26] and, for reasons that will be discussed later, the limitations proposal failed to make any further headway. It is ironic to note, however, that it was the government which had acknowledged these matters as suitable for legitimate political discussion, for much of the struggle in the future was to centre on whether or not these provisions for a protestant and parliamentary government could be linked to exclusion or come into effect during, rather than after, Charles's reign.

'Limitations' were not the only measure designed to safeguard religion and liberties in case a popish successor ruled England. One expedient was that the subjects' right to resist such a king, if he should invade religion or property, should be acknowledged, in the form of an 'association of protestants', based on Elizabethan precedent. Right from the start, the crisis thus incorporated a debate about the right to resist a popish king, and by extension questioned the nature of monarchical authority and the extent to which allegiance was owed to it, a controversy that was to preoccupy much of the rest of the decade. In late October and November 1678 the idea of an association was being discussed at Westminster,[27] and on 7 December there was a long debate in the House of Commons about provisions to enable protestants 'to withstand and defend themselves against any Papists whatsoever that should come with commission and bear arms in any military employment, and to dispense with those laws that at present made it rebellion so to do'; at the end, the

[23] Grey, *Debates*, vi. 264–6; *HMC Ormonde*, iv. 478–9.
[24] *HMC Ormonde*, iv. 479.
[25] Grey, *Debates*, vii. 158; J. Oldmixon, *The History Of England* (1730), p. 631.
[26] R. Baxter, *Reliquiae Baxterianae* (1696), pt iii, p. 185.
[27] Haley, *Shaftesbury*, p. 471; *HMC Ormonde*, iv. 465.

Elizabethan Act of Association was read out.[28] Its reading was again demanded on 27 April 1679,[29] and an 'association' was expected to be moved during the debate on 30 April on measures to secure the King and religion,[30] though formal proposals failed to materialise.

A second expedient was that the duke of York should rule in name, but as if he were a minor or lunatic, a proposal put forward in private conversations in the House of Commons on 22 November 1678, when MPs were considering Seymour's suggestions to limit a popish successor,[31] and repeated on 27 April 1679.[32] William of Orange, the duke's son-in-law and heir apparent, was the natural candidate to act as Regent in such a situation, and as early as 6 November 1678 there were rumours that he would come to England.[33]

A third expedient was to secure protestantism whilst Charles was still alive. One way to do this was by passing anti-catholic legislation, for example by making convictions of popish recusants more easy and more frequent.[34] Anthony Gylby, MP for Hull, duly reported that the House of Commons was 'prepairing Bills against the Papists, soe severe, that ... if they be put in Execution, noe Papist can live in England'.[35] One close follower of parliamentary debates, who disliked both exclusion and limitation proposals, went so far as to suggest that the best security for protestantism was to legalise the murder of catholics who attended mass and offered any resistance to protestant vigilantes.[36] But the threat from catholic plotters also made the idea of a union of protestants more attractive. As Sir Robert Southwell observed, there were demands for 'a greater circle to the Church of England'.[37] Attempts to promote the comprehension of dissenters within the Church should therefore be regarded as part of a wider attempt to safeguard religion and property.[38]

Limitations and expedients were measures protecting subjects once a popish successor was on the throne; but there were also proposals to circumvent the duke of York's claims altogether. One alternative was that Charles

[28] Grey, *Debates*, vi. 328–34; *HMC Ormonde*, iv. 489. William Sacheverell was instrumental in urging this measure, as he had been on 22 November 1678.

[29] Grey, *Debates*, vii. 142. Bennett had desired 'that by some law we may have power to arm ourselves against [the duke of York] if he would bring in Popery amongst us' (Ibid., p. 138).

[30] *Sidney Letters*, p. 76.

[31] *HMC Ormonde*, iv. 479.

[32] Grey, *Debates*, vii. 140.

[33] PRO, 31/3/141, f. 67, Barrillon dispatch, 18/28 November 1678.

[34] J. Miller, *Popery and Politics*, pp. 163–5.

[35] Hull RO, Corporation MS L.911, Gylby to the Mayor, 10 December 1678. Daniel Finch also thought that the bills 'would have extirpated' popery in England (Leics. RO, Finch mss, DG7/4957/57, f. 70, 28 December 1678).

[36] Hereford and Worcester RO (Hereford), W15/1, 'Sir Harry Coningsby's Expedient', n.d.

[37] *HMC Ormonde*, iv. xix.

[38] For an excellent discussion of these, throughout the period, see H. Horwitz, 'Protestant Reconciliation in the Exclusion Crisis', *Journal of Ecclesiastical History*, xv (1964), 201–17.

should divorce his wife and remarry a protestant. This idea had been raised as early as 1667/8, pursued in 1670, resurrected by Shaftesbury in 1673, and revived once again in the aftermath of the Popish Plot.[39] On 7 October 1678 Barrillon, the French ambassador, reported a rumour that Charles would divorce, and observed that the idea was being discussed throughout October and November.[40] Oates decided to add weight to the scheme by accusing the Queen of engaging her physician Sir George Wakeman to poison the King. On 28 November the House of Commons therefore resolved on an address to the King that the Queen and other catholics should be removed from Court; but when the matter was debated in the House of Lords the next day, only a handful of peers supported the address, and the matter fell.[41] Danby was himself toying with the idea of a royal divorce, and urged the King to take a new wife. Charles replied that he 'should rather fear his forwardnesse to imbrace the expedient than any way obstruct itt if any of the Bishops could but satisfy him of the lawfulness of doing itt', so Danby sent archbishop Sancroft, who was 'very well disposed in the matter'; but the lord treasurer later claimed he was 'prevented by the troubles' surrounding his impeachment from furthering the project.[42] In fact, MPs had noticed that no courtiers opposed the motion against the Queen in the Commons, and suspected a Court trick to hasten a dissolution.[43] It was not until after Danby had lost office that talk of a divorce resurfaced, and even then it remained private discourse. On 12 April Sir Robert Southwell reported that, although the idea was not yet under open discussion, it was expected to 'fill the minds of all';[44] but it was only 'glanced at' in the debate on 11 May,[45] and failed to be formulated as a serious proposal.

If no way could be found by which Charles could remarry and thereby have a legitimate son, another alternative to exclusion was to legitimise his natural son, the duke of Monmouth. Rumours that the King would acknowledge his marriage to Monmouth's mother had been circulating for many years,[46] but it was not until after the popish plot that Monmouth himself seems to have taken his claim to the throne seriously. This development arose largely

---

[39] Haley, *Shaftesbury*, pp. 199, 276, 330, 337, 344; Miller, *Popery and Politics*, pp. 128–9.

[40] PRO, 31/3/141, f. 16, Barrillon dispatch, 7/17 October; f. 28, Barrillon dispatch, 17/27 October; f. 35, Barrillon dispatch, 24 October/3 November; f. 59, Barrillon dispatch, 14/24 November 1678.

[41] Haley, *Shaftesbury*, p. 485; Chatsworth, Devonshire Collection, Group 1A, Roger Jackson to the earl of Devonshire, 30 November 1678; Huntington Lib., MS HM 30315 no. 194, newsletter, 29 November 1678.

[42] Reresby, *Memoirs*, p. 161; BL, Add. 28,043, f. 67, 'Queries about the Queen'.

[43] Leics. RO, DG7/4957/57, f. 47, 28 November 1678; Chatsworth, Devonshire Collection, Group ID, 28 November 1678.

[44] *HMC Ormonde*, iv. 503. On 4 April 1679 Downing opened a debate about provisions against a future royal marriage with a catholic (All Souls, MS 242, f. 471, newsletter).

[45] *HMC Ormonde*, iv. 512.

[46] Haley, *Shaftesbury*, pp. 199, 277, 327.

because of his association with opponents of Danby, who flattered his hopes in order to secure his co-operation in bringing about the fall of the lord treasurer.[47] Monmouth was also encouraged by popular support for him as the 'protestant duke'. Whether spread by the opposition cabals, or as a result of a genuine misunderstanding, a rumour swept through London on 9 November that Charles had told the House of Commons of his resolution to choose a protestant successor, and that Monmouth was to succeed.[48] The suggestion that the King could nominate his successor even seems to have formed the basis for dealings between Danby and Shaftesbury that took place before the 1679 Parliament sat;[49] but Monmouth's hopes at this stage relied principally on pressure on the King to declare him legitimate.[50]

The last, but least hopeful, alternative to exclusion was to persuade the duke of York to return to the protestant fold. Following the visit of an episcopal delegation, which had been sent with Charles's backing in February 1679 to try to persuade James to convert,[51] there were reports that the duke intended to go to church again,[52] though these proved unfounded. There were renewed rumours that he had returned to the reformed religion on the eve of the first reading of the exclusion bill,[53] although the reports were probably encouraged at this time by the duke's friends in an effort to sap support for the measure.

This brief analysis of the alternatives to exclusion has attempted to show how many ideas were considered during the period. Exclusion was just one of many projects, and MPs were divided in their choice. A number of contemporary reports clearly reveal the wide spectrum of opinion that existed on the eve of the 1679 Parliament as to what policies should be pursued. The first is a report from one of Danby's intelligence gatherers, James Netterville.[54] Although Netterville observed that 'the hearts and minds of the people will

[47] Haley, *Shaftesbury*, p. 485; Clarke, *James II*, i. 526, 530; BL, Add. 28,043, f. 1, 'Mr Crosse 20 November [16]78'; PRO, 31/3/141, f. 98, Barrillon dispatch, 12/22 December 1678.

[48] *HMC Ormonde*, iv. 470. There were many bonfires lit that night (Newdigate newsletter Lc.705, 12 December 1678; Chatsworth, Devonshire Collection, Group 1H, newsletter, 12 November 1678).

[49] BL, Add. 28,053, f. 133, Robert Brent to Danby, 21 January 1679; *The Collection of Autograph Letters and Historical Documents Collected by Alfred Morrison*, ed. A.W. Thibaudeau (1883–92 privately printed), i. 181–2.

[50] Clarke, *James II*, i. 530; *HMC Verney*, p. 472.

[51] Clarke, *James II*, i. 537–8; All Souls, MS 242, f. 464, newsletter, 25 February 1679; Bod., MS Tanner 39, f. 184, memorandum of the episcopal visit to James; Bod., MS Carte 228, f. 147, newsletter, 25 February 1679; Chatsworth, Devonshire Collection, Group 1F, newsletter, 25 February 1679.

[52] Norfolk RO, Bradfer-Lawrence MS 551c, earl of Yarmouth to his wife, 26 February 1678/9; Eustace Burneby to Lady Yarmouth, 16 February 1678/9.

[53] All Souls, MS 171, f. 30, newsletter, 9 May 1679; BL, Add. 70,013, f. 10, letter of news, 10 May 1679. Such rumours circulated again before the Lords' vote on the second exclusion bill in 1680 (Bulstrode newsletter, 15 November 1680).

[54] BL, Add. 28,049, f. 32, [?Netterville] to [?Knox], n.d.

not be at rest till the succession be confirmed in a protestant', he pointed out that opinions about how to proceed varied, for some wanted 'several bills for the entyre suppression of Popery', whilst others were for 'bills for the preservation of libertie and propertie'.[55] A letter from John Evelyn to Sidney Godolphin, reporting his conversations with several MPs and others who came to London in March 1679, found other views prevalent.[56] Evelyn had been told by all of them that only a settlement of religion could secure the nation and that popery had to be rooted out, a policy which, Evelyn remarked, 'they think cannot effectually be done, without qualifying the successor ... and passing a Bill for a kind of Comprehension', the latter a measure which was to include presbyterians and independents, and which Evelyn himself appears to have supported. Netterville's report and Evelyn's letter suggest that opinions were not yet fixed on the single issue of exclusion, and this impression is reinforced by other comments. On 17 February Secretary Coventry told Sir Richard Bulstrode that it was not easy to predict how the new Parliament would act because 'men differ[ed] in their guesses as in theire wishes',[57] and as late as 5 May, barely a week before the House of Commons resolved to bring in an exclusion bill, Algernon Sidney reported that he did 'not know three men of a mind'.[58]

Exclusion did not stand out as superior to other schemes. Yet historians, in so far as they have considered them, have been quick to point out the disadvantages of limitations and expedients, presumably because with the benefit of hindsight they know they did not succeed. To some extent it *is* justified to point out the weaknesses of the alternatives to exclusion, for the inherent problems in several of the proposals were indeed part of the reason for their failure. The divorce project relied on there being enough time for Charles to remarry and produce a child, yet the revelations of catholic attempts on the King's life suggested that an immediate solution to the succession crisis was necessary. Moreover a divorce jeopardised the aspirations of James, Monmouth and William of Orange, who found common ground in resenting limitations, though for very different reasons.[59] Indeed there was an uneasy rivalry between the main contenders for the throne. The King must have been aware that his brother, and perhaps his nephew, would never submit to Monmouth's claims to the Crown, even if Charles officially recognised them, and that legitimising his son might therefore bequeath civil war to the nation on his death. Moreover, the idea of an 'Association'

---

[55] The 'presbyterians', led by Lord Holles, drew up a programme of legislation to preserve liberty and property (BL, Add. 28,047, f. 47, Knox to Danby, 23 January 1679).

[56] Christ Church, Oxford, John Evelyn's Letter Book, Letter no. cccc, 6 March 1679.

[57] BL, Add. 62,585, f. 74, Bulstrode Letter Book, 17/27 February 1679.

[58] *Sidney Letters*, p. 77.

[59] For James's opposition see Bod., MS Clarendon 87, f. 334, James to Hyde, 7 December 1680. For William's opposition see Dalrymple, *Memoirs*, ii. 307.

threatened the King's own power over the militia and raised the possibility of armed conflict; the idea of William as Regent was not acceptable to some of the opposition who saw him as merely another Stuart with the family's inclinations for arbitrary power;[60] and the idea of broadening the Church was a highly contentious one. Expedients were thus fraught with difficulty.

But one might as easily point out that many of the contemporary objections to the expedients were fallacious. For example, William Sacheverell complained on 30 April 1679 that a catholic king could survive financially without Parliament;[61] yet the scheme of limitations which he had just heard included provisions that when Charles died, Parliament was to be the sole source of revenue, and that 'the Parliament then in being may continue indissolvable for a competent time; or if there be no Parliament in being, then the last Parliament which was in being before that time, may re-assemble, and sit a competent time, without any new summons or Elections'.[62] Had this been accepted, James II might well have faced the hostile 1681 Parliament, rather than the tame one elected in 1685. On the same day as Sacheverell voiced his doubts, Sir Thomas Littleton, who was to show that he was unconvinced by his own arguments against limitations when he spoke in their favour eleven days later, complained that it would be illegal to say the King was a papist, and that therefore provisions against a catholic king could not be enforced;[63] yet he had just heard an offer for a test to distinguish between a catholic and a protestant successor which could easily be worded to overcome his reservation. On 11 May Sir Nicholas Carew said that the duke of York would break the bonds and fetters of an act of Parliament imposed on the Crown when he inherited, so that the limitations offered no security.[64] This was one of the most common arguments against the scheme;[65] but what security was there that the duke of York would pay any more regard to an act which excluded him?[66] If security was the issue, what would happen if the duke of York had children,[67] or if Scotland upheld his claims?[68] Moreover, some of the exclusionists' arguments could equally apply to limitations. The right of Parliament to limit the descent of the succession was equally the right of Parliament to limit the powers of the successor; and, if the exclusionists

---

[60] *A Vindication of His Royal Highness The Duke of York* (1683), p. 8, claimed that Oates had declared against William, saying he 'was a Canary Bird'. cf. PRO, 31/3/148, f. 55, Barrillon dispatch, 14/24 February 1681. William's protestantism was also questioned by some (K.H.D. Haley, 'No Popery in the Reign of Charles II', *Britain and the Netherlands*, v [1975], 103).

[61] Grey, *Debates*, vii. 160.   [62] Grey, *Debates*, vii. 158–9.

[63] Grey, *Debates*, vii. 162, 253–4.

[64] Grey, *Debates*, vii. 238.   [65] Grey, *Debates*, vii. 243–4.

[66] Secretary Coventry argued that the duke of York might recourse to force if the bill passed (Grey, *Debates*, vii. 242).

[67] Grey, *Debates*, vii. 242.   [68] Grey, *Debates*, vii. 256–7.

claimed that limitations altered the constitution by establishing a common-wealth,[69] the limitationists could turn this argument round and claim that exclusion threatened to introduce an elective monarchy.[70] Indeed exclusion itself was riddled with difficulties. The duke of York had not been convicted as a catholic,[71] and the doctrine of deposing a king was itself considered to be popish.[72] Exclusion was by no means the overwhelmingly logical solution.

COURT POLITICS

If exclusion was not necessarily the obvious policy for MPs to follow, and if MPs were seriously willing to consider alternatives, the question must be asked why the bill emerged in May 1679 as the solution embraced by the House of Commons. The answer lies not so much in the merits of exclusion, which have been exaggerated, as in the way they were propounded and in the political climate in which they would have to operate. Only by studying why the alternatives failed can we understand why exclusion was adopted.

Two reasons for the failure of limitations or expedients are immediately apparent. The key to the political crisis throughout the period was to win over the King himself; yet Charles remained ambiguous towards, or unconvinced by, any of the alternatives to exclusion. He appeared to back the limitations proposals, but was observed to be 'cheerful' when the exclusion bill was being read in the House,[73] and therefore failed to send a clear message to Court supporters.[74] He was also uncompromising about the alternative schemes. He scotched the idea of a divorce, or prosecution, of the Queen by remaining loyal to his wife,[75] and he claimed that his conscience refused to allow him to legitimise his son.[76] The attitude of the King therefore remained crucial. The success of limitations or expedients relied on the goodwill of the King not only

---

[69] Grey, *Debates*, vii. 251.   [70] Grey, *Debates*, vii. 257.

[71] Indictments against James for recusancy were attempted on 26 June 1680, 30 June 1680, 29 November 1680, and 8 February 1681.

[72] Grey, *Debates*, vii. 254–5; *Heraclitus Ridens*, no. 14, 3 May 1681; All Souls, MS 229, f. 278, draft speech by Sir Leoline Jenkins; *Religion and Loyalty* (1681), p. 55.

[73] Reresby, *Memoirs*, p. 182.

[74] Lord chancellor Finch thought that Shaftesbury had made MPs believe that Charles would agree to exclusion and that only by removing Shaftesbury from office would the King show his opposition to the measure (*Diary of Henry Sidney*, i. 2).

[75] Clarke, *James II*, i. 528–9. Burnet wrote in 1683 that 'tho' it may easily enough be believed that the King would not have been sorry to have been rid of her in a fair way, yet he could not endure to see her ruin'd for such odious crimes, of which he perswaded himself she was innocent' (BL, Add. 63,057B, Burnet's ms history, f. 44).

[76] On 3 March 1679 Charles declared that he had never been married to anyone except his present Queen (Burnet, *History*, ii. 203).

to back them, but also to pass the necessary legislation; and, even if MPs persuaded Charles, could they trust James to observe the bills his brother passed? Yet the attitude of the King, and shortcomings in the practicability of these alternative schemes, were problems which also applied to exclusion; the reasons for the failure of limitations must, therefore, mainly lie elsewhere. They are to be found in the mistrust MPs had of the Court, and the weakness of Court management. Detailed schemes of limitations were put forward by the Court in November 1678 and in April 1679; yet at both times mistrust of the Court could not have been greater.

We must therefore make an apparent digression in order to assess the state of the Court and attitudes of MPs towards it. Only by plumbing the depths of the internal problems faced by the Court, and the consequent difficulties these entailed in terms of the management of the House, can we set the succession question in its true and wider context. Studying the succession from the perspective of the Court shows clearly how the struggle for power affected government policy and influence inside Parliament, and how distrust of the Court wrecked any policy it put forward. On no other issue were these pressures more obvious than in the Court's attempts to promote limitations on a popish successor.

As we have seen, in order to bolster his own position, Danby had planned to sacrifice the duke of York, and therefore offered limitations to Parliament on 9 November.[77] MPs had to decide whether they were being offered a tactical manoeuvre by the lord treasurer, or a sincere measure to safeguard their future. Therefore, although the scheme was immediately the object of suspicion for parliamentary leaders such as Sacheverell, most MPs awaited the outcome of the second Test Act, which was considered 'the great touchstone for success, and remedy to several evils impending'.[78] The proviso exempting the duke of York from the act's provisions against catholics sitting in Parliament was a test in itself of Danby's sincerity, a test which he failed. On 21 November the bill exempting James passed the House of Commons, 'contrary to the expectation of all'.[79] Its passage had largely been due to a rare display of skilful Court management,[80] which signalled the temporary reconciliation of Danby and James,[81] and to the opposition's disorganisation.[82]

---

[77] Browning, *Danby*, i. 297–8.   [78] *HMC Ormonde*, iv. 472.

[79] Huntington Lib., MS HM 30315/190, newsletter, 21 November 1678; Burnet, *History*, ii. 176.

[80] A barrage of Court speakers performed well (Grey, *Debates*, vi. 240–53), and a large amount of money was said to have been distributed to Court pensioners the night before (PRO, 31/3/141, f. 74, Barrillon dispatch, 25 November/5 December 1678).

[81] PRO, 31/3/141, f. 71, Barrillon dispatch, 21 November/1 December 1678.

[82] Finch noted that many MPs who opposed the proviso 'were out of the House and did not think it would have come to so near a division, nay they thought it would have bin carried to disagree with the L[or]ds by a great plurality of voices or Else they had not been absent from the House' (Leics. RO, Finch mss, DG7/4957/57, f. 34, 21 November 1678).

The next day Seymour detailed his ideas for limitations to MPs 'with that vigour as drew many of them to attention and concurrence to the work',[83] but the type of Court organisation displayed the day before was no longer apparent, and distrust of Danby buried the scheme.[84] In other words, antipathy to Danby, compounded by mistrust of the Court's intentions and exacerbated by rivalries and divisions within the Court, prejudiced the scheme of limitations at precisely the time when attitudes towards the duke of York were still flexible and hence when there was a chance that the plan might have found acceptance.

If antipathy to Danby destroyed the limitations he offered, the question arises why the scheme continued to come under suspicion, and to answer that we must again return to the legacy of a divided Court bequeathed by the treasurer. The prorogation of the Cavalier Parliament on 30 December 1678 allowed a reorganisation of the King's administration. This failed to provide unity, and a brief sketch of the political situation will reveal the extreme confusion of affairs which prevented the formation of a coherent succession policy.

Danby sacked officeholders who had voted against him, but seemed to have no clear idea of which faction he should cling to. Thus both the earl of Salisbury, one of the Lords sent to the Tower in 1677 for asserting that the Cavalier Parliament was dissolved because of its long prorogation, and York's brother-in-law, the earl of Clarendon, were added to the privy council. At the same time, Danby began negotiations with the 'presbyterian' group of Holles, Littleton, Boscawen and Hampden, either to divide his opponents or really to attempt to have his impeachment reduced to a 'mild censure' in return for money, disbandment and a new Parliament.[85] Charles also seems to have been uncertain about how to proceed, and was reported to have told one peer that 'he had so much troubles on him that he could not tell which way to turn', though characteristically he looked to foreign aid.[86] He abjectly told the French ambassador that he would not refuse any condition which France asked in return for its support, claiming that he would rather depend on Louis XIV than on his own people.[87] Barrillon, however, had no intention of solving the difficulties which he had helped to stir by his liaisons with Montagu and others, calculating that England was still far from a civil war

---

[83] It is possible that Seymour's ideas were not backed by Danby.

[84] D.T. Witcombe, 'The Parliamentary Careers of Sir William and Mr Henry Coventry' (Oxford B.Litt., 1954), p. 196, argues that it is possible that 'a large group of moderates' might have been persuaded to oppose exclusion in return for the dismissal of Danby and the disbandment of the army.

[85] Burnet, *History*, ii. 187–8; PRO, 31/3/142, f. 17, Barrillon dispatch, 2/12 January; f. 25, Barrillon dispatch, 16/26 January; f. 35, 20/30 January; f. 40, Barrillon dispatch, 31 January/9 February 1679.

[86] *CSPD 1679–80*, p. 22.

[87] Dalrymple, *Memoirs*, ii. 209–10.

that might produce a francophobic commonwealth.[88] Charles was therefore left on his own, and dithered. He had resolved by 21 January 1679 to prorogue for a further week, and declared as much at privy council; but no proclamation was issued, and within days the decision had been reversed.[89] 'Good God, how uncertaine we are in our Resolutions', one Court watcher observed.[90] Political alignments were shifting daily. Confusion at Court was increased both by Shaftesbury's approaches to York, and the involvement of Arlington's secretary, Richard Cooling, in co-ordinating the factions.[91] Eventually, Charles was forced to take personal control of the situation, announcing on 24 January his decision to dissolve. He had made up his mind without the advice of privy councillors, telling them that 'the factions amongst themselves ha[d] rendered it uselesse and dangerous' to consult them.[92] When the earl of Devonshire's agent in London heard the news, he observed how 'such curious and suddaine counsells have of late been, that many neare the helme have not known or foreseen w[ha]t the next houre would produce.'[93]

The period between the prorogation and dissolution of Parliament high-lighted the collapse of ministerial administration. There was now a vacuum at Court, which Danby enlarged by continuing to purge officeholders whom he considered disloyal to himself. In a separate development, Secretary William-son, who had been sent to the Tower by the Commons and was now so afraid of the House that he refused to dispatch governmental orders, handed the seals to the earl of Sunderland.[94] These changes at Court set tongues wagging about who might be promoted. There was talk of removing Arlington as lord chamberlain, replacing him either by Danby's son, Lord Latimer, or the earl of Sunderland, whose secretaryship could be offered to Sir William Temple; there were also rumours about appointing the earl of Plymouth as Lord Steward and the earl of Ranelagh as Keeper of the Privy Purse.[95] Sunderland, demonstrating his prodigious powers of 'undertaking', began to prepare for Danby's departure, and tried to persuade Sidney Godolphin to accept office in the treasury, though the go-between in the matter, John Evelyn, found Godolphin 'so jealous and diffident of the complexion and stabilitie of

[88] PRO, 31/3/142, ff. 14–17, Barrillon dispatch, 2/12 January 1679.
[89] Huntington Lib., MS HM 30315/212, newsletter, 21 January 1679; Newdigate newsletter Lc.735, 23 January 1679.
[90] Bucks. RO, Verney mss, M11/32, Edmund Verney to Sir Ralph Verney, 20 January 1679.
[91] BL, Add. 28,053, f. 133, Brent to Danby, 21 January 1679; BL, Add. 28,047, f. 48, Knox to Danby, 23 January 1679.
[92] BL, Stowe 746, f. 7, H. Goodricke to Fairfax, 25 January 1679.
[93] Chatsworth, Devonshire collection, Group 1A, R. Jackson to Devonshire, 25 January 1679.
[94] PRO, 31/3/142, f. 46, Barrillon dispatch 10/20 February 1679.
[95] All Souls, MS 171, f. 23, newsletter, 24 February 1679; Bucks. RO, Verney mss, M11/32, Sir Ralph Verney to Edmund Verney, 27 February 1679; All Souls 242, f. 464, newsletter, 25 February 1679; Congress newsletter 6/184, 20 February 1679.

publique affaires' that he declined until matters were no longer 'in this tremulous posture'.[96] At about the same time, Shaftesbury was putting suggestions to Danby, via Lord Chandos, Thomas Stringer and Sir Josiah Child, about a reconciliation. Shaftesbury wanted Danby to agree to 'securing the Crown to a protestant successor, whom the King thought most fitt, soe he were a protestant according to the Church of England', the removal of the King's catholic mistress the duchess of Portsmouth and 'securing the government from the French and theyr mode of government'.[97] Danby's reply is unknown, but presumably was unfavourable.

All this jockeying for position did nothing to resolve the Court's weaknesses, and only contributed further to them, for Charles faced the new Parliament without a co-ordinated administration. He himself seemed prepared to make concessions, since he asked his brother to leave England, let it be known that 'he meant to cast himselfe into the armes of his Parliament',[98] and in his speech to MPs on 6 March, which was received 'with great hums of applause', said he wished for a 'healing Parliament'.[99] Charles pointed out that he had sent his brother away, had partially disbanded the army, and had pushed on with dealing with alleged catholic plotters. But his plea to moderate opinion, which was in the long run to win the struggle for the nation, nevertheless fell on deaf ears at this time. The King's strategy did not take account of the fact that his actions were not regarded as concessions but as necessities, that moderates and radicals in the House were not yet divided, and that Danby himself was part of the King's troubles.

Danby's disruptive influence became fully apparent in a spectacular fashion when the lord treasurer tried to save himself by sabotaging the session, right at its start, thereby destroying at a stroke any possibility of regrouping Court strength. The issue at stake was the election of the Speaker of the Commons. Danby pursued a personal rivalry with his former ally Edward Seymour, with each 'contending who should be uppermost'.[100] Danby's lack of management over the large gathering of over 400 MPs – it was said to be 'the fullest House that had been knowne at the first meeting' – was immediately apparent on the opening day. One observer thought there was no privy councillor present, 'soe that it seems at this tyme eyther to be

---

96 Christ Church, Oxford, Evelyn Letter Book, cccxciii, Evelyn to Sunderland, 'February [16]79'.

97 *Collection of Autograph Letters*, ed. Thibaudeau, i. 181–2. As early as December 1678 York's friends feared such a union (PRO, 31/3/142, f. 9, Barrillon dispatch, 25 December 1678/5 January 1679).

98 Chatsworth, Devonshire collection, Group IG, [-] to Devonshire, 6 March 1679. Charles is reported to have summoned a 'William Bloud', possibly a mistake for Col. Thomas Blood. For the latter's career see A. Marshall, 'Colonel Thomas Blood and the Restoration Political Scene', *HJ*, xxxii [1989], 561–82).

99 *LJ*, xiii. 449–50; *HMC Ormonde*, iv. 345.

100 *Second Part of the Growth of Popery* (1682), p. 232.

avoided to have the Speaker soe at first recommended or els noe diligence used to have it soe'.[101] This comment was not entirely accurate, since Sir John Ernley, who was present and 'who was to have recommended Sir Thomas Meres as a person that should be acceptable to the King', was given no time to speak.[102] Seymour was instead nominated, and dragged to the chair by Lee and Hampden, 'Country party' men who if the agreement between Danby and the presbyterians meant anything, should have been working to manage the House for the Court.[103] Seymour was not acceptable to Danby,[104] who persuaded the King that the former Speaker was 'the promoter of the most desperate addresses and proceedings of the House of Commons last sessions' and Charles refused the choice.[105] When the Commons returned to their seats, the Court's only manager, Ernley, bungled the renomination of Meres by calling him Sir Robert instead of Sir Thomas,[106] and Powle complained that 'of late, those things of the greatest moment are done without any council at all; done in a corner'.[107] On 8 March Lee tried to get the Commons to consider what it would do, though MPs were uncertain how to proceed and no guidance was offered from the Court. Serjeant-at-law Thomas Street tried to nominate Powle, 'but he was not suffered'.[108] On 11 March Birch, Powle, Maynard and others 'of the leading men' such as Sacheverell, Williams, Clarges, Garraway and Lee, spoke in favour of choosing a compromise candidate, but the House resolved, with only four or five negatives, to make a second representation to the King about their first choice, thereby deepening the deadlock between the Court and Parliament.[109] A prorogation was thought necessary to calm tempers and resolve on a candidate suitable to all parties. The dispute had sharpened animosities against Danby, ensuring that his impeachment would dominate much of the second session's debates. Moreover, it had also shown the incapacity of Court management, as well as the rejection of Meres or Powle, both prominent Country Members, as Speaker and hence signalled the impracticality of Danby's attempts to deal with leading MPs.

[101] Newdigate newsletter Lc.756, 8 March 1679; Bod., MS Tanner 39*, f. 213, [-] to John Hobart, 15 March 1679.

[102] All Souls, MS 242, f. 466, newsletter, 7 March 1679.

[103] Grey, *Debates*, vi. 402; Bod., MS Firth C2, f. 14, newsletter, 7 March 1679. According to All Souls, MS 242, f. 175, undated newsletter, it was Sir Thomas Whitmore, a gentleman of the privy chamber, who joined Lee.

[104] *HMC Finch*, ii. 47; BL, Add. 63,057B, Burnet's ms history, f. 47.

[105] Browning, *Danby*, ii. 71.

[106] BL, Add. 29,556, f. 431, Lord Grey to Lord Hatton, n.d (c. March 1679); Grey, *Debates*, vi. 405.

[107] Grey, *Debates* vi. 408.

[108] Grey, *Debates*, vi. 414. The duke of York favoured him 'for I hope he will be my friend, and further my return' (*HMC Dartmouth*, i. 30).

[109] All Souls, MS 242, f. 468, newsletter 14 March 1679; Newdigate newsletter Lc.758, 13 March 1679; newsletter Lc. 759, 15 March 1679.

The short prorogation allowed leading Members of the Commons to present a proposal to the King, via Monmouth, offering money and an end to the Speakership controversy in return for Danby's removal.[110] But whereas in 1680 the House would offer money in return for exclusion, the principle grievance at this stage was Danby, who had 'now become the subject of all discourse and is made the only obstacle that stands between the King and his people'.[111] Court management was in a state of collapse. 'All things pass on with a powerful stream, so that opposition is so far from being useful, that it is become dangerous', remarked one MP.[112] The government was nearing a state of paralysis. At the beginning of the session Lord Grey reported that 'the Court party [was] in some distress, since S[i]r John Earnley [was] their only speaker',[113] and even he was unseated on 5 April after a successful petition against his election.[114]

Not surprisingly, negotiations began for a new administration. The remodelled privy council announced on 20 April replaced Danby and some of his supporters with a number of his fiercest critics, including the earl of Shaftesbury, Lord Halifax, the earl of Essex and Lord Cavendish, and was preceded by the establishment of a treasury commission.[115] Yet suspicion of the Court was at such a height that MPs mistrusted anything it did, and even before the changes were announced the House of Commons indicated its intractability to Court management no matter who undertook it. One pamphleteer reviewing a century of conflict believed that religious distinctions 'by degrees began to wear away ... and now its Country man and Courtier' that really mattered.[116] Jealousies of Court management seemed almost as rife as fear of popery, and the independence of mind of the 'Country' party was certainly valued as piously as protestantism. Former members of the Country party who now looked for office were regarded as renegades. Thus on 29 March Lord Cavendish moved to consider disbanding the army, 'a thing very acceptable to the Court',[117] since the Treasury needed money; but William Garraway and Sir Thomas Meres continued to insist that no money should be given until the army had first been disbanded, and Sir Thomas Lee and Sacheverell were able to persuade the House to vote the existence of the army illegal.[118]

---

[110] Browning, *Danby*, ii. 112–13; PRO, 31/3/142, f. 71, Barrillon dispatch, 17/27 March 1679.
[111] All Souls, MS 242, f. 468, newsletter, 14 March 1679.
[112] Grey, *Debates*, vii. 24; *HMC Ormonde*, iv. 500.
[113] BL, Add. 29,556, f. 431, Grey to Hatton, n.d. (c. March 1679).
[114] *History of Parliament*, ii. 273.
[115] E.R. Turner, 'The Privy Council of 1679', *EHR*, xxx (1915), 251–70; Temple, *Memoirs*, pp. 333–6 (pp. 363–4 prints a list of the names of the Privy Councillors and new officeholders. For the new treasury team see *Dering Diaries*, p. 115).
[116] *Advice to the Nobility, Gentry and Commonalty of this Nation* (1679), p. 1.
[117] Huntington Lib., MS HM 30315/220, newsletter, 1 April 1679; Grey, *Debates*, vii. 64.
[118] Grey, *Debates*, vii. 67–73. Garraway, Lee and Meres possibly had their eyes on office and wanted to show their importance.

Shaftesbury and Halifax met with equal failure. They were unable to persuade the House of Commons to erase the word 'attainder' from the bill against Danby, a moderation which they had proposed 'in compliance with the King's desires'.[119] Moreover, although part of the reshuffle of offices was to have brought Seymour back as Speaker,[120] the latter found 'so much aversion' from the same men who had supported his candidature at the beginning of the session 'that all his industries [could] not prevail'.[121] On 12 April the House resolved 'that upon any vacancy of the chair, no motion be made for chusing a new speaker, till after eleven o' clock', a move clearly designed to prevent a surprise Court nomination.[122] On 14 April other Court recruits experienced a similar foretaste of the House's antipathy to management. Powle moved to consider the navy and Sir Gilbert Gerard to consider the militia, but Sacheverell immediately insinuated that they were Court mouthpieces who sought money, and the debate was diverted by Boscawen into an investigation into naval corruption.[123] Four days later Meres, Lee and Birch advertised their interest in office by praising the idea of a Treasury commission and supporting the transfer of money for disbanding to the Exchequer now that Danby was no longer in power there, only to be opposed by Cavendish and Russell, who had already been reconciled to the Court and were perhaps trying to show that they maintained their independence.[124] Anyone who sought preferment was 'immediately looked upon as a man infected', or, as Sir Robert Southwell put it, 'whoever comes voluntarily in to offer his service, or is called out of the crowd to assist, that man seems immediately to lose all the power and virtue that was in him by coming to Whitehall'.[125] Even before the new ministry was officially recognised there had been signs that its influence over Parliament would be uncertain and limited.[126] Having berated Court corruption for so long, the leaders of the Country party of the 1670s found they had contributed to an ideology of critical opposition which now restricted their freedom of action.

It is not surprising, therefore, that when Charles announced his new privy

---

[119] *Sidney Letters*, p. 62; All Souls, MS 242, f. 474, newsletter, 11 April 1679; A. Browning, *Danby*, i. 328.

[120] BL, Longleat mss, M/904, reel x, vol. xx, f. 372, Sjt. Gregory to Henry Thynne, 30 March 1679. All Souls, MS 171, f. 28, newsletter, 2 April 1679 mentioned Sir John Trevor as a possible Speaker.

[121] *HMC Ormonde*, iv. 502; All Souls, MS 242, f. 476, newsletter, 18 April 1679.

[122] Grey, *Debates*, vii. 106.

[123] Grey, *Debates*, vii. 107–14.

[124] Grey, *Debates*, vii. 118–21; All Souls, MS 242, f. 476, newsletter, 18 April 1679.

[125] *HMC Ormonde*, iv. pp. xviii, 502.

[126] *HMC Ormonde*, iv. p. xviii.

council to the Commons the news was received 'with most coldness',[127] and the House did not even move a vote of thanks.[128] Burnet remarked that many MPs 'finding themselves forgot, while others were preferred to them, resolved to make themselves considerable, and they infused in a great many a mistrust of all that was doing'.[129] The earl of Conway came to a similar conclusion: 'no sooner doth any man get the least employment, but an hundred others are immediately contriving to turn him out'.[130] Edmund Verney feared that his Buckinghamshire neighbour Sir Thomas Lee's recent patriotic performances had been only to gain office, and that now he and others were 'bought off and Advanc'd, they'r zeal for their countrys good ... [would] coole'.[131] As Secretary Coventry remarked, 'the bare being preferred maketh some of them suspected',[132] and the newswriter Francis Benson observed, perhaps with Montagu and Sacheverell in mind, that there were 'those in the House of Commons that are not pleased to see others advanced and themselves left behind'.[133] But the idea that Charles foresaw the reorganisation's divisive qualities, and used it in a machiavellian ploy to destroy the credit of his former opponents, is to endow the King with long-term planning that was largely absent from his calculations, and it was probably mere necessity and the lure of money that had most persuaded him into agreement.[134]

The result of the reorganisation of offices was to diminish, not increase, Court influence, which was further undermined by internal rivalries in the new privy council. The remodelling of the council had removed some of Danby's supporters, but a group had remained, including the lord chancellor, the earl of Bath, the duke of Lauderdale and Sir John Ernley, and these men were 'not very agreeable to the rest' because of their association with the previous ministry.[135] More importantly, the new intake of privy councillors

---

127 Temple, *Memoirs*, p. 335. There are, however, contradictory reports about the reaction in the Commons, some suggesting that MPs favoured the changes: All Souls, MS 171, f. 29, newsletter, 21 April 1679. William Ramsden reported that 'soe farr as [he] could apprehend [the news of the new council] was pleasing in the Countenance of all sorts of quallityes in the houses both of L[or]ds & Commons' (Hull RO, MS L.934, William Ramsden to the Corporation of Hull, 22 April 1679).

128 All Souls, MS 242, f. 480, newsletter, 22 April 1679.

129 Burnet, *History*, ii. 210. Those 'forgot' included Sacheverell, Garraway and Montagu.

130 *HMC R.R. Hastings*, ii. 387.

131 Bucks. RO, Verney mss, M11/32, Edmund Verney to Sir Ralph Verney, 28 April 1679. Reresby remarked: 'so true it is that the court and country liverey can never be worn together' (Reresby, *Memoirs*, p. 178).

132 *HMC Ormonde*, v. 57.

133 All Souls, MS 242, f. 480, newsletter, 22 April 1679. The writer, Benson, also observed that 'most people are of [the] opinion that this will be to the advantage of the earl of Danby'.

134 Dalrymple, *Memoirs*, ii. 211.

135 All Souls, MS 242, f. 478, newsletter, 25 April 1679. Bennett remarked that though the council had been 'in some degree ... reformed, no good could reasonably be expected' so long as Lauderdale and Anglesey remained on it (*Sidney Letters*, p. 76).

were themselves divided, largely because the changes in personnel had been brought about by two different interests. Sir William Temple, one of the chief promoters of the remodelling, shared with the earls of Sunderland, Essex and Halifax a sympathy towards Holland and William of Orange, and a moderate attitude towards James. However, in order to settle the nation internally, it had also been thought necessary to include Shaftesbury, Russell and Monmouth, who put domestic issues above foreign ones and who were hostile to the duke of York. The split was exacerbated by a personal rivalry of some long-standing between Shaftesbury, a vain and proud old man,[136] who was 'ambitious beyond what ever enter'd into the designs of any man',[137] and his nephew Halifax, 'one that could draw with no Body',[138] and who, as one lampoon put it,

> for empire has as great an itch
> as ever dog had for his salt-swollen bitch.[139]

The rivalry between Shaftesbury and Halifax developed into a struggle for domination of the council, in which Halifax was initially at a disadvantage because of the King's dislike of him.[140] Charles at least knew Shaftesbury's skills in office, whereas Halifax was a dark horse.

THE POLITICS OF EXCLUSION

The details of Court politics during and after Danby's fall from power allow us to explain why the succession became caught up in the factional intrigues at Whitehall. Danby had left a regime in tatters and a legacy of distrust that was hard to dispel, for even when Charles gave offices to some of Danby's critics, neither they nor the Court as a whole enjoyed renewed popularity. Thus, in the context of the succession, any solution proffered by the Court would be suspected by many MPs. To make matters worse, the new privy council was not even a united body, for Halifax not only pursued his rivalry with Shaftesbury, but did so by using the succession as one of his weapons.

The effect of the clash between the two ministers should not be underestimated if we are to believe the account of Gilbert Burnet. 'The personal animositys between Shaftesbury and Halifax', Burnet remarked in the first

---

[136] Haley, *Shaftesbury*, pp. 370–1; Burnet, *History*, ii. 109–10. cf. *Ailesbury Memoirs*, i. 25.

[137] Halstead, *Succinct Genealogies*, p. 432. He probably wanted to be lord chancellor (*HMC Ormonde*, iv. 508). Burnet described Shaftesbury as 'intolerably vain' in his desire to govern the council (*History*, ii. 213). In November 1680 Shaftesbury told Sir John Davys that he believed a fortune teller's prediction that he 'should live to bee the second man in England' (Bod., MS Carte 219, f. 285, Davys to Ormonde). cf. *Supplement to Burnet's History of My Own Time*, ed. H.C. Foxcroft (1897), p. 58.

[138] Temple, *Memoirs*, p. 336 (Temple reports a comment made by the earl of Sunderland).

[139] *POAS*, ii. 334. Halifax wanted to become lord lieutenant of Ireland (*HMC R.R. Hastings*, ii. 387).

[140] Burnet, *History*, ii. 208–9. For the quarrel see also Haley, *Shaftesbury*, pp. 530–1.

version of his history, 'was so great an Ingredient [in the nation's fate] that when I think of it, I often call that sentence of St James to mind, Behold how great a Pire, a little fire hath kindled.'[141] The personal conflict was to have important consequences for the political situation: 'since the Exclusion was considered as a project of Shaftesbury's, [Halifax] saw that if it were carryed, the honour of it would fall chiefly on him, and [Halifax] was not of a temper to bear that easily'.[142] Hitherto Halifax had not shown a reluctance to pursue exclusion. Indeed, in 1674 he had supported the imposition of the penalty as a means of preventing members of the royal family from marrying a catholic,[143] and had made derogatory remarks about the wisdom of primogeniture.[144] Yet, Burnet implies, because of a factional dispute with a rival,[145] he now championed the rival policy of limitations. Burnet was in a good position to know because in July he 'went between them twice or thrice', but found that the quarrel 'could not be made up'.[146] It continued to smoulder throughout the crisis, occasionally flaring up in public, such as in December 1679, May 1680 and November–December 1680.[147] Burnet was so shocked 'how violently resentments wrought upon' Halifax, that he altered his hitherto favourable opinion of that politician. Nor is Burnet's testimony the only indication of the severity of the dispute. The earl of Ossory astutely remarked on 6 May that 'a rupture may happen amongst the new men now in affairs', and in 1682 a pamphleteer referred to Halifax's position being motivated by 'the peak between him and Shaftesbury'.[148]

Burnet had remarked that exclusion was 'considered as a project of Shaftesbury's'. Yet how far was Shaftesbury responsible for the adoption of the bill? On 11 May Thomas Bennett, one of Shaftesbury's mouthpieces in the Commons, was the first to be named to the committee to draw up the bill,[149] suggesting that the earl's influence was the prime factor in its emergence. The bill's gestation, however, proves to have been more complex, and linked to the factional politics of the Court. Rather than aiming to reject limitations from the start, Shaftesbury may have been concerned primarily to disrupt

141 BL, Add. 63,057B, Burnet's ms history, f. 55.
142 BL, Add. 63,057B, Burnet's ms history, f. 54.
143 Haley, *Shaftesbury*, p. 360.
144 Burnet, *History*, ii. 212.
145 Burnet, *History*, ii. 256. Halifax may not have been as averse to exclusion as he appeared to be: Burnet records in his 1683 History that Halifax believed that 'if the king were once prevail'd on to pass a Bill of Expedients, by which the duke would be highly disobliged, and all parties disheartened, a Bill of Exclusion would be so much the nearer for that' (BL, Add. 63,057B, Burnet's ms history, f. 58).
146 BL, Add. 63,057B, Burnet's ms history, f. 52.
147 HMC Ormonde, iv. 566–7; BL, Longleat mss, M/904, reel viii, vol. xv, Thynne papers, f. 9, Halifax to Thynne, 6 May 1680; M/904, f. 323, Sir William Coventry to Sir Thomas Thynne, 19 January 1681. See chapters 3 and 4 for further details of the rivalry.
148 HMC Ormonde, v. 87; *Second Part of the Growth of Popery* (1682), pp. 277–8.
149 CJ, ix. 620.

their smooth passage in order to force his inclusion into the select inner group of advisers, consisting of Halifax, Essex, Sunderland and Temple, from which he had initially been excluded.[150] Evidence for his opposition to limitations at this time comes mainly from the memoirs of Sir William Temple, yet the latter had always opposed Shaftesbury's inclusion in the new privy council, and was to blame him for its failures.[151] Temple's impartiality is, therefore, suspect. Indeed there is evidence that Shaftesbury's hostility to limitations may not have been implacable.[152] According to the duke of Buckingham, Shaftesbury had reputedly written that part of a pamphlet published in 1677 called *Some Considerations Upon the Question whether the Parliament is Dissolved* which had claimed that Parliament had the power to 'bind, limit, restrain, and govern the descent and inheritance of the Crown itself, *and all the rights and titles thereto*' [my emphasis], a phrase suggesting that he believed both exclusion and limitations were theoretically possible.[153] In other words, Shaftesbury had been more concerned to champion the cause of parliamentary sovereignty than any particular solution to the succession problem.

The speeches made in the Commons by Thomas Bennett, whom Barrillon described as a 'grand parleur', are also illuminating.[154] Daniel Finch observed that 'Mr Bennett is so intirely my L[or]d Shaftesbury's Creature that we call him his Bennett for distinction [from his namesake MP for Marlborough] and therefore w[ha]t he says is the more regarded.'[155] On 27 April Bennett talked about trying to secure a son for the King and measures for protection against a catholic king, not specifically about exclusion.[156] Moreover, after the lord chancellor had outlined the King's offer of limitations on 30 April, Bennett opened the debate by moving a vote of thanks, and was seconded by Sir Francis Russell, the ally of the limitationist Sir Henry Capel, as well as by Meres, Maynard and Williams.[157] In other words it is possible that Bennett and Russell were signalling that both factions in privy council were in agreement with the proposals. Those who opposed the motion, Sacheverell

---

[150] Temple, *Memoirs*, pp. 336–7.

[151] Temple, *Memoirs*, p. 337, says that only himself and Shaftesbury opposed limitations in council, yet it must remain very doubtful whether Russell and Monmouth were not also opponents of the scheme. Temple was writing his account in retrospect, when it was commonplace to blame Shaftesbury for the unrest of these years.

[152] J.P. Kenyon, *Robert Spencer, Earl of Sunderland 1641–1702* (1958), p. 26, remarks that in 1679 Shaftesbury's aim was probably to prune the King's prerogative and then run the administration. Acceptance of limitations and office would have achieved this.

[153] Haley, *Shaftesbury*, p. 414. The tract is attributed by Wing to Lord Holles (Wing H2467).

[154] PRO, 31/3/146, f. 27, Barrillon dispatch, 12/22 July 1680.

[155] Leics. RO, Finch mss, DG7/4957/57, f. 17, 4 November 1678.

[156] Grey, *Debates*, vii. 138–9. Shaftesbury appears to have been in contact with York to secure a reconciliation at this time through Lord Townshend or George Pitt (*HMC Dartmouth*, i. 32).

[157] Grey, *Debates*, vii. 159–62. Haley, *Shaftesbury*, p. 518 ascribes Bennett's speech to 'impetuosity'.

and Littleton, and Titus, who urged caution on the House, were all MPs who had not been taken into office.[158] Even after the debate on 30 April the House of Commons had still not resolved on exclusion, and there is evidence that Shaftesbury was still not yet the champion of the measure. According to Temple's memoirs, Sunderland, Halifax and Essex took Shaftesbury and Monmouth into 'the first digestion of affairs' at about this time 'to agree with them in the Banishment of the Duke, either for a certain term, or during the King's life'.[159] During the period of such negotiations consideration of the succession was deliberately kept out of the House, despite the restlessness of some MPs to tackle the matter.[160] Originally put off to 5 May, the issue was not debated until 11 May, when Bennett once more opened the proceedings by moving that the duke of York should not return without leave of King and Parliament, and that MPs would stand by the King in case of any popish attack. Bennett was thus proposing the banishment of the duke and provisions if James broke this measure; 'expedients', as contemporaries called them, rather than exclusion.[161] But Bennett was outmanoeuvred in the debate by a group of radical MPs who had a strong dissent-sympathising, neo-republican, London-interest bias, such as Pilkington, Dubois and Player, aided by Hampden and Foley.[162] These Members pushed for exclusion.[163] It is, of course, possible that in these debates Bennett was acting independently of his patron, or that Shaftesbury, whilst appearing to give some support to his colleagues on privy council, was privately encouraging such exclusionists,

---

158 Grey, *Debates*, vii. 159–64. Titus was later backward in supporting exclusion (*History of Parliament*, iii. 573) and he may have been trying to show how necessary it was for the government to buy him off with office. Vaughan supported an adjournment. He had been given office and may have been seeking to limit the damage done to government proposals, or to maintain his credit in the House.

159 Temple, *Memoirs*, p. 337. Temple's account is slightly ambiguous since he says that Halifax, Essex and Sunderland negotiated with Shaftesbury and Monmouth, but that 'within a Fortnight or a little more' they began to find them unreasonable and decided on a prorogation; Temple claimed that he went into the country for two days and came back to London to find the Parliament was to be prorogued that morning. Since Parliament was prorogued on 27 May, this implies that the negotiations began after the Commons resolved on 11 May to bring in an exclusion bill, but it is possible that negotiations began on 30 April, as a result of the defeat of limitations. This timing would also fit with Temple's explanation that the three Lords wanted Shaftesbury's and Monmouth's support for a bill of banishment (see below), and with the fact that between 30 April and 7 May the succession was not discussed in Parliament, until Leveson Gower forced a debate for 11 May.

160 PRO, 31/3/142, f. 108, Barrillon dispatch, 8/18 May 1679; *HMC Ormonde*, v. 89.

161 In November 1680 Shaftesbury and his allies ridiculed Halifax in the Lords when he suggested the banishment of James (*Original Papers*, p. 108); but the political situation was very different by then, and the personal rivalry between them very bitter.

162 For the meetings of Pilkington, Player, Ward and City radicals see *CSPD January–June 1683*, p. 356. Both Papillon and Dubois attended the French Church in Threadneedle Street.

163 According to Grey's *Debates*, Bennett made fewer and fewer speeches as the crisis progressed.

many of whom he knew;[164] but, given this piecing together of rather fragmentary evidence, it seems more likely that Shaftesbury did not lead, so much as side with, the exclusionists once it was clear that limitations had failed.[165] At the very least, his position was ambiguous, and there may well have been more underhand dealings that explain the delay of the bill's second reading from the 19th to the 21st.[166] It would appear that Shaftesbury took advantage of the mistrust of the privy council of which he was nominally the head. The astute politician appreciated the fact that limitations were suspected because they were proposed by the Court, that they encouraged the radical elements in the Commons to push further, and that only by appearing to head the opposition could he exert influence over the King and be 'absolutely at the Head of all Affairs'.[167] The prize was that a further reorganisation of officeholders in England, and even in Scotland and Ireland, was clearly envisaged once one faction had triumphed.[168] The succession was thus part of a power struggle.

On 21 May the exclusion bill received its second reading, but the Halifax–Essex–Sunderland faction, which still supported limitations, was able to prevent its further passage by persuading Charles to prorogue the session on the 27th. The limitationist faction seemed to have triumphed, fuelling the antipathy between Halifax and Shaftesbury, the latter swearing he 'would have the Heads of those who were the Advisers of this prorogation'.[169] In the privy council there was 'perpetuall appearance of ill Humour ... which broke into spighted Repartees often betwixt [Shaftesbury] and Lord Halifax', and between Monmouth and Essex, which 'grew into a spirited quarrell'.[170] Lord chancellor Finch believed that Shaftesbury and Monmouth would 'obstruct all till they are at the top of all affairs'.[171] It was no wonder, then, that Charles was observed to be 'sullen and thoughtful'.[172]

Personal and factional, as much as ideological, factors thus explain the emergence of exclusion as the solution adopted by the House of Commons to solve the crisis.[173] It is clear that the collapse of the Court's control over Parliament, mistrust of courtiers and disputes between groups at Court

---

[164] Haley, *Shaftesbury*, pp. 234, 499, 500, 520.

[165] cf. Haley, *Shaftesbury*, p. 745.

[166] On 15 May the House ordered the bill to be read again on the 19th, *CJ*, ix. 623.

[167] Temple, *Memoirs*, p. 338.

[168] Huntington Lib., Hastings MS 5962, Huntingdon to John Guy, 6 May 1679; All Souls, MS 242, f. 485, newsletter, 8 May; PRO, 31/3/142, f. 109, Barrillon dispatch, 8/18 May 1679.

[169] Temple, *Memoirs*, p. 338.

[170] Temple, *Memoirs*, p. 339.

[171] *Diary of Henry Sidney*, i. 2.

[172] Burnet, *History*, ii. 225.

[173] Although J.R. Jones recognises (*First Whigs*, p. 67), that the arguments for exclusion were based on necessity, 'on the immediate political situation', he puts forward the arguments in favour of exclusion rather than discussing why the alternatives to it failed.

played a major role in the failure of the House of Commons to adopt limitations. But even at this stage, exclusion was not the overriding concern of the House. The breadth of Members' demands was evident in the debate on 14 May 1679, when Powle and Cavendish had pushed for supply. The mood of MPs was summed up by Garraway, who proposed that no money be given until grievances had been redressed. These included Lauderdale's rule in Scotland, the army, militia and the navy, the failure to execute popish priests, the prosecution of the catholic lords in the Tower, a demand for commitment to the all-encompassing phrase 'the security of protestant subjects', and foreign alliances.[174] A printed *Narrative and Reasons* of the Commons' conduct was published in order to explain to the public not why the exclusion bill had been promoted, but why there had been a delay in trying the lords, including Danby, being held in the Tower. Fittingly, in the light of the problems which he had left in his wake, Danby was blamed for the dispute between the Houses that was the pretext for the end of the session just as he was blamed for the 'stumbling at the threshold' in March.

CONCLUSION

The parliamentary attack on Danby, together with the wave of anti-popery which the treasurer had initially tried to ride, had undermined the duke of York's position and heightened long-standing concern about the succession. Nevertheless, Members of the Cavalier House of Commons treated James's position with delicacy and sensitivity, and were reticent about openly attacking his claim to the throne. This caution continued to be apparent in the new Parliament which met in March 1679, when MPs showed a reluctance to commit themselves in important debates about the succession. Thus, rather than single-mindedly pursuing exclusion, the House accepted the bill only slowly, even somewhat reluctantly. The reasons for this lie in the broader context of the succession crisis. First, the idea of excluding James was considered alongside plans to limit the powers of a catholic king, to form an association of protestants based on Elizabethan precedent, to legislate for the King's divorce from his barren Queen, to legitimate Monmouth, to allow James to rule in name only, with a regent exercising power, and to strengthen protestantism by passing severe anti-catholic laws and by promoting measures to broaden the state church by comprehending dissenters or to tolerate conventiclers. Second, the broader context of the succession also includes the state of the Court. Exclusion was adopted for largely political reasons, which can only be explained by examining the Court's internal difficulties. Limitations were put forward by Danby, immediately suspected

---

[174] Grey, *Debates*, vii. 266–78; *HMC Ormonde*, iv. 514–15; Newdigate newsletter Lc.785, 17 May 1679.

as a trick to keep him in power at the expense of the duke, and when put forward by the new privy council of April 1679 they suffered from the mistrust of the Court that Danby had done so much to create. Moreover, the policy of limitations was championed by the dominant faction of the council. Their power, and Halifax's in particular, was resented by Shaftesbury, the council's new president, and this personal and factional conflict helped shape the divisions within Parliament. The succession issue thus became part of the struggle for power, a struggle that was to continue for the next two years as Charles searched for a coherent ministry. The King himself dithered about the right course of action to take, and thus failed to offer any clear guidance to the country. This, and a divided Court, spelt disaster for the Court's management of Parliament, and Shaftesbury took advantage of this situation to side with the exclusionists who opposed the proposals of the Halifax faction. The 1679 Parliament was thus characterised by mistrust of the Court, distrust within the Court, and a struggle for power in which the succession became embroiled.

3

'A King at chess'[1]: politics and the succession between Parliaments, May 1679–October 1680

The last chapter argued that Court weakness and faction, as well as MPs' mistrust of the Court, prejudiced the chances of alternatives to exclusion. In other words, the structure of politics affected the development of policy. The following sections will explore this theme further, and, in addition, try to redress the imbalance evident in many commentaries on the succession question. Historians have paid most attention to charting the actions of those who supported exclusion, without a full examination of the Court or of the cohesion of loyalists, even though neither the succession problem nor the apparent strength of the Court's opponents can be fairly assessed without a detailed study of the weaknesses of Charles's administrations throughout the period. Only once we have taken stock of the failings of the Court can a discussion about the character of opposition be undertaken, for otherwise there is a strong risk that the strength and organisation of voices critical of the government will appear exaggerated. The next two chapters therefore offer a chronological survey of the period 1679–81, closely interweaving the two strands of politics and the succession in order to show how attitudes towards the latter continued to be shaped by distrust of the Court and by Charles's failure to find a long-lasting ministry. This approach seeks to deepen our understanding of the structure of politics, and to correct the view that it is possible to examine the succession debate in isolation.

One of the major threads running through the period is, as we have seen, the weakness of the Court.[2] The fall of Danby wrecked unity amongst Charles's advisers, and the following years were marked by the King's search for a suitable set of ministers. Charles's own policy of playing the factions against each other, though ultimately successful, created uncertainty and irresoluteness in the short term. Only in 1681 was some order restored to royal management, and even then it largely followed, rather than led, loyalist opinion outside Whitehall. But we also need to introduce another part of the political equation which Charles found so difficult to solve. In part, the King's difficulty in finding a ministry of substance was due to his own ambiguous

[1] *Burnet Letters*, p. 27.
[2] Hutton, *Charles II*, chapter 14, comes to a similar conclusion.

foreign policy, the main plank of which mirrored the domestic policy of divide and rule by seeking to play the Dutch off against the French, and vice versa. Just as the attempt to steer between the factions and interest groups ended in failure at home, so too did Charles's ambition to play off Louis XIV and William of Orange. By 1681 he had been forced to develop a more coherent foreign policy in the form of England's adherence to France. Thus both at home and abroad the King sacrificed what he loved most, the flexibility to choose between a number of options, in order to achieve a restoration of stability and his own survival. It is the process by which the King was forced to abandon his independence from France, and the political effects this process had, which provides one of the threads running through the next two chapters.

THE COURT IN CHAOS, JUNE 1679–JANUARY 1680

Although the prorogation of Parliament had seemed to augur the triumph of the Halifax–Essex–Sunderland faction at Court, events, as was so often to happen over the next two years, intervened to destroy any embryonic stability. The Scottish rebellion in June 1679 'altered the whole face of affairs'[3] because Monmouth's success in quelling it, and his subsequent restraint against the rebels, made him a popular hero in whose reflected glory Shaftesbury could bask. The prospect of the Shaftesbury–Monmouth alliance grasping power pushed the triumvirate of Halifax, Essex and Sunderland into persuading Charles to dissolve Parliament on 10 July.[4] The internal Court debates that led to the decision were nevertheless grossly mismanaged, with the result that councillors who had not been briefed spoke almost unanimously with Shaftesbury against a dissolution, and Anglesey and Finch even dined with the earl afterwards;[5] but, to the evident discontent of the majority, the King insisted on breaking up Parliament.[6] Despite a reminder from Shaftesbury that the King had promised to govern with the advice of the privy council, that faction-riven body was not, as many had expected, dissolved along with Parliament.[7] Its retention meant that throughout the ensuing election period the situation at Court was very unclear, with the privy council rent by division and anomalies: Shaftesbury was anti-France, but his ally Monmouth flirted with French support for his pretensions to the throne; Charles's toleration of Monmouth's role in politics seemed at odds with his professions to his brother James; Lord Holles, the leader of the presbyterians,

[3] *Diary of Henry Sidney*, i. 5.
[4] Bod., MS Carte 232, f. 47, earl of Longford to earl of Arran, 8 July 1679.
[5] Bod., MS Carte 233, f. 233, newsletter, 6 July; BL, Add. 18,730, unfol. Anglesey's diary, 6 July 1679; Temple, *Memoirs*, p. 341.
[6] All Souls, MS 242, f. 504, newsletter, 11 July 1679.
[7] HMC *Ormonde*, iv. 530; Bod., MS Carte 243, f. 369, newsletter, 16 July 1679.

was more favourable to France, and feared domination by William of Orange; Temple, on the other hand, wanted to establish William; and Shaftesbury and Halifax continued to rail at one another in public.[8] There was thus nothing coherent enough, except the very concept of the corrupt Court, against which an opposition could throw itself, certainly not in the area of the succession where virtually all shades of opinion were represented amongst the King's advisers. The result was a fragmentation of authority, illustrated by Henry Coventry grumbling in August that the 'the truth is, all of us councillors are so scattered that we meet not but by accident'.[9]

Throughout the summer of 1679 the state of the Court continued to be very confused. Lord Robartes found the King 'too artificiall' to be able to guess at any of his intentions, and others found him 'careless of matters'.[10] It was very difficult to tell who, including even which royal mistress, was in favour.[11] Although Charles seemed resolved to uphold Danby's pardon, he took advice from Danby's enemies, Halifax and Essex, but also dined with their rivals, Shaftesbury and Lord Wharton.[12] Shaftesbury, although still president of the council, nevertheless found himself increasingly isolated and ignored, and increasingly did not even 'come near to Court'.[13] The King, however, hinted to some privy councillors that he had resolved to reconcile himself with Parliament, a policy that would surely have meant the earl's triumph.[14] Moreover, Charles was caught in a vicious circle where the uncertainty about his plans fuelled speculation about a further re-organisation of offices, rumours which only served to increase the uncertainty.[15]

Behind this smoke-screen of conflicting signals, Charles was pursuing a double-edged foreign policy that did nothing to resolve his domestic difficulties. A treaty between England and Holland, promoted by the Halifax–Sunderland–Temple faction but apparently also supported by Shaftesbury, was read at the committee of intelligence on 17 June, and approved by the King the next day.[16] Sunderland and Henry Sidney worked to strengthen

---

8 For the influence of the ministers see *HMC R.R. Hastings*, ii. 388; Bod., MS Carte 39, f. 64, Sir Nicholas Armorer to Arran, 9 August 1679; f. 68, Mr Cholmley to Arran, 24 September 1679; PRO, 31/3/143, ff. 33–6, Barrillon dispatch, 3/13 July 1679; *Diary of Henry Sidney*, i. 25, 28.

9 *HMC Ormonde*, v. 185

10 BL, Add. 28,049, f. 62, Danby to Bath, 5 August 1679; *HMC R.R. Hastings*, ii. 388.

11 *Diary of Henry Sidney*, i. 86; Bucks. RO, Verney mss, M11/33, Cary Gardiner to Sir Ralph Verney, 20 August 1679.

12 BL, Add. 28,049, f. 62, Danby to Bath, 5 August 1679; Newdigate newsletter Lc.815, 26 July 1679.

13 All Souls, MS 171, f. 50, newsletter, 9 August 1679; Congress newsletter 6/257, 10 August 1679; *HMC R.R. Hastings*, ii. 388.

14 PRO (Kew), FO.95/565, d'Avaux dispatch, 21/31 August 1679.

15 Bod., MS Carte 39, f. 64, newsletter, 9 August 1679.

16 BL, Add. 15,643, ff. 13–14, register of committee of intelligence, 17 and 18 June 1679.

relations between the two countries by secretly inviting William to England.[17] But the Dutch States General faced a dilemma. If they ratified the treaty, there was a possibility that William would become too powerful; yet if they did not make the alliance, France might become too strong. In August, one newswriter noticed, the Dutch were still at 'a greate stand [about the alliance], fearing that if they joyne with us it may Advance the P[rince] of Orange to a Kingly Power, and to Joyne with the French ag[ain]st us may prove fatall and is contrary to their Conscience to assist a Popish Prince'.[18] Charles, meanwhile, approached Barrillon in July in hopes of procuring French aid.[19] The King was juggling ministers and policies, keeping as many balls in the air as possible in order to allow him to pursue a number of options, with the one aim of biding time in order to secure his own survival.[20] As he told Barrillon at this time, his 'one and only interest was to subsist'.[21]

Events, rather than any resolution on the King's part, dispelled the fog of uncertainty and ambiguity that had descended over Whitehall. In late August 1679 Charles fell seriously ill, and James rushed back from exile to be at his bed-side. The triumvirate of Halifax, Essex and Sunderland, who were said to 'engross all',[22] combined with James to strip Monmouth of his offices, though they wanted York to return to Brussels if Monmouth also left the Kingdom.[23] On the advice of Montagu and 'all the Presbyterians and Dissenting people' who flocked to him,[24] Monmouth contemplated refusing Charles's wishes, but a number of amicable meetings in September between father and son seem to have convinced Monmouth of the necessity of his departure.[25] The ministers' motives in securing his leaving had been partly factional, hoping that 'thereby [Shaftesbury] would be quite deprived of his instrument and the divisions in [Court] cease, which had hitherto distracted all the' privy council. Shaftesbury was 'to be shaken off and left to do his worst'.[26] The remodelled privy council was finally breaking up, and its factions jockeyed for position. One observer remarked that they were 'like the Children of some[e] old father,

---

[17] Diary of Henry Sidney, i. 3–35.

[18] Newdigate newsletter Lc.823, 24 August 1679.

[19] PRO, 31/3/143, f. 25, Barrillon dispatch, 26 June/6 July; ff. 29–32, Barrillon dispatch, 3/13 July 1679.

[20] Sunderland was doing the same thing, ostensibly supporting Henry Sidney's efforts in Holland and courting the presbyterians at home, whilst informing James of the King's French policy (BL, Add. 28,049, f. 68, Latimer to Danby, 21 August 1679; Clarke, James II, i. 564).

[21] PRO, 31/3/143, f. 53, Barrillon dispatch, 21/31 August 1679.

[22] HMC Ormonde, iv. 536. In September Halifax was said to be always at the King's elbow (Hatton Corresp. i. 193)

[23] Clarke, James II, i. 568.

[24] Dalrymple, Memoirs, ii. 249.

[25] All Souls, MS 171, f. 62, newsletter 23 September 1679.

[26] HMC Ormonde, iv. 536; Hatton Corresp. i. 195; Clarke, James II, i. 568–9; Temple, Memoirs, p. 344.

every one seek[ing] to gett what he cann for himselfe'.[27] Towards the end of September there were therefore strong rumours of changes at Court, and even of the arrest of Shaftesbury and Buckingham.[28]

Charles was attempting to restore a unified Court by allowing one faction to dominate, but Halifax and Essex soon found that they 'were but other Men's Dupes and did other Men's work',[29] as York's influence grew and displaced their own. The ministers had been preparing for the new Parliament's sitting, planning to consolidate their power by concluding investigations into the Plot, and offering Danby as a sop to public opinion and to boost their own popularity, though once again Halifax may have been driven by his personal grudge against Shaftesbury, since Danby had sent his ally the earl of Bath to join Shaftesbury's cabals with Monmouth.[30] But James threw his weight against MPs sitting,[31] a policy which also flew in the face of Shaftesbury's hopes for a Parliament, where he apparently hoped to press for a royal divorce and for a war against the French.[32] There were thus three main factions, two in support of Parliament's sitting, though at odds with each other, and one against its assembly. It is not surprising that Algernon Sidney remarked that there was 'the strangest confusion that I ever remember to have seen in English business. There never was more intrigues.'[33]

The King did nothing to resolve this highly complex and fluid situation, hoping to play a waiting game. Ironically, however, by doing nothing Charles ensured the victory of York and Sunderland, since Essex and Halifax sought assurances of 'surer terms' of office and felt aggrieved when these were not forthcoming.[34] Halifax fell ill and was 'dejected in his ambition', and both he and Essex feared the accusation that they had failed to secure a meeting of Parliament.[35] Although James left for Brussels on 25 September, it was apparent by early October that his influence was so much in the ascendant in England that Parliament would not sit, and on the 7th he was told by Charles

27 Longleat, Coventry mss, vol. vi, ff. 127–8, anon. letter to Coventry, 5 September 1679.
28 Bucks RO, Verney mss, M11/33, Cary Gardiner to Sir Ralph Verney, 22 September 1679. Buckingham's electioneering was rumoured to have been outrageous enough to merit prosecution, and he had also publicly accused Lord Chief Justice Scroggs of having secret orders to favour papists (PRO, 31/3/143, f. 75, Barrillon dispatch, 22 September/2 October 1679; Bod., MS Don. C38, f. 265, newsletter, 23 September 1679).
29 Temple, *Memoirs*, p. 344.
30 BL, Add. 28,049, f. 72, Danby to Latimer, 2 September 1679; *HMC Ormonde*, iv. 536; Bod., MS Carte 39, f. 68, Cholmley to Arran, 24 September 1679. Temple nevertheless broke with his former allies at this time (Temple, *Memoirs* pp. 344–5).
31 PRO, 31/3/143, f. 67, Barrillon dispatch, 11/21 September 1679.
32 *HMC Ormonde*, iv. 538.
33 *Original Letters of John Locke, Algernon Sidney and Anthony Lord Shaftesbury*, ed. T. Foster (1830), p. 97.
34 *HMC Ormonde*, iv. 538.
35 *HMC Ormonde*, iv. 539; Burnet, *History*, ii. 246.

that he could retire via England to Scotland.[36] This gave James a refuge in a power-base where any bill passed in the English Parliament against him would not apply without separate ratification north of the border. The privy council had not been consulted, and a furious Shaftesbury used the matter to force his own dismissal from office on 14 October, after insisting that his opposition to York's return be recorded and allegedly suggesting that the duke might be seized and kept prisoner until Parliament sat.[37] Three days later, about 150 Commoners and twenty-six Lords met on 17 October to hear that Parliament was prorogued until 26 January 1680.[38] The King had forbidden the council to debate the decision, and had twice told Sir Henry Capel to sit down when he had tried to complain.[39] Halifax and Essex had sought to use James's return to exclude Shaftesbury from power; the latter had indeed been dismissed, but only at the expense of the ministers' own standing and their domestic and foreign policies. Only their colleague, the supple and subtle Sunderland, gained from the intrigues because he had the confidence of both the King and the duke, and had successfully negotiated a treaty with Barrillon, which when ratified would have given Charles money and Louis an assurance of English subordination to French aspirations.[40]

The combination of Monmouth's exile, Shaftesbury's dismissal, York's second return to England en route for Scotland, and the prorogation of Parliament seemed to augur a new strength of Court action. 'Some think that resolute counsels are now taken up', wrote Sir Robert Southwell.[41] Yet the struggle at Court left the King with a narrowing field of advisers. Sir William Jones, who may have co-ordinated with Shaftesbury about the planned arrest of the duke of York, resigned as attorney general,[42] and rumours circulated that lord chancellor Finch would also ask leave to quit.[43] In the end Charles had no choice but to insist that his brother leave, though in turn the duke's departure for Scotland on 27 October removed the head of the one faction that seemed capable of restoring order to the Court, even if it caused disorder outside it.

Moreover, swift-moving events brought about another complete revo-

---

[36] *Diary of Henry Sidney*, i. 161.
[37] *The Second Part of the Growth of Popery* (1682), p. 261; All Souls, MS 171, f. 72, newsletter, 14 October 1679; Newdigate newsletter Lc.850, 16 October 1679.
[38] *Domestick Intelligence*, no. 31, 21 October 1679.
[39] HMC *Verney*, p. 476; HMC *Ormonde*, iv. 545.
[40] PRO, 31/3/143, f. 45, Barrillon dispatch, 24 July/3 August; ff. 50–2, Barrillon dispatch, 21/31 August; ff. 63–8, Barrillon dispatch, 11/21 September; ff. 73–5, Barrillon dispatch, 22 September/2 October; f. 78, Barrillon dispatch, 25 September/5 October; ff. 83–8, Barrillon dispatch, 29 September/9 October 1679.
[41] HMC *Ormonde*, iv. 546.
[42] PRO (Kew), FO.95/565, d'Avaux dispatch, 23 October/2 November 1679. Others thought that Jones 'lost his place in tro[u]ble for to see how the [duke of York] governs all' (Bucks. RO, Verney mss, M11/33, Cary Gardiner to Sir Ralph Verney, 30 October 1679).
[43] Newdigate newsletter Lc.851, 18 October 1679.

lution in the political scene within days. Any prospect of the Court regaining the political initiative was destroyed by the discovery at the beginning of November of the Meal Tub Plot, an ill-conceived attempt by a group of catholics, orchestrated by Lady Powis and a midwife named Mrs Cellier, to persuade a Popish Plot witness, Stephen Dugdale, to change his evidence, and to manufacture evidence of a presbyterian plot. The exposure of these activities, when implicating papers were found concealed at the bottom of Mrs Cellier's meal tub, revived the fears of popery that Oates had aroused only a year earlier. Shaftesbury was in a particularly good position to benefit from this renewal of anti-catholic feeling since Thomas Dangerfield, the main witness of the Plot, claimed that there had been several attempts to assassinate the earl.[44] Rumours consequently began to circulate that Shaftesbury would be restored to office as a result of overtures made to him by the earl of Sunderland.[45] Halifax was deeply worried that his rival might return to favour, and remarked that London buzzed with so much politicking that 'a wasp's nest is a quieter place to sleep in than this town is to live in'.[46]

Shaftesbury realised, however, that if he took office he would be an isolated figure with only Sunderland as an ally. His public response was therefore that he would not come to Whitehall until he saw he could 'doe some good'.[47] The Court was once again in disarray, and the King indecisive. Conflicting rumours of an impending dissolution, and of a proclamation declaring that Parliament would sit, created great uncertainty. This reached a peak on 9 November when Charles refused to allow any discussion in the privy council about the timing of the next session, even after Essex and several others had proposed that Parliament should meet.[48] Russell had also raised Shaftesbury's idea that Parliament should sit 'not as a valid house, but as a Great Councill', but this provoked Charles's anger, and the council broke up with the lord chancellor reprimanding Russell for being 'too quick' with the King.[49] The result of, and in part because of, the renewed paralysis at the

---

[44] *Mr Thomas Dangerfield's Particular Narrative* (1679), pp. 22–3, 37–9.
[45] UCNW, Mostyn MS 9089, f. 187, newsletter, 4 November 1679; All Souls, MS 171, f. 85, newsletter, 5 November 1679; Newdigate newsletter Lc.859, 6 November 1679; 'The Journal of Edmund Warcup', ed. K. Feiling and F. Needham, *EHR*, xl (1925), 245–7; *HMC Ormonde*, iv. 557–8.
[46] *Diary of Henry Sidney*, i. 181; *Savile Corresp.* 134.
[47] Newdigate newsletter Lc.860, 8 November 1679.
[48] All Souls, MS 171, f. 83, newsletter, 7 November 1679; Newdigate newsletter Lc.860, 8 November; Lc.861, 11 November 1679; *Diary of Henry Sidney*, i. 182–3. It is likely that Capel supported his brother (*Diary of Henry Sidney*, i. 179, 182). Anglesey also 'dealt very freely w[i]th King & Councell' (BL, Add. 18,730, 9 November 1679). Other speakers were Russell and Cavendish (*HMC Ormonde*, v. 238), and possibly even the moderate Lord Robartes (BL, Longleat mss M/863, reel vii, vol. xi, f. 433, newsletter endorsed 'Fox A Bookseller in Westminster', 15 November 1679).
[49] Bucks. RO, Verney mss, M11/33, John Verney to Sir Ralph Verney, 10 November; Cary Gardiner to Sir Ralph Verney, 13 November 1679; *HMC Ormonde*, iv. 558.

heart of government was a political scene 'very different to what was four months ago'.[50] Halifax and Sir William Temple were discontented,[51] attendance at Court slumped,[52] and the moderate Sir Robert Southwell decided to retire as clerk of the council.[53] Essex resigned as first lord of the Treasury, though he retained his seat on privy council,[54] and was replaced by York's brother-in-law, Laurence Hyde, who had participated in the negotiations with Barrillon about the French treaty.[55] Seven privy councillors were thought to be on the verge of retiring.[56] With little sign that the King was receiving advice from anyone around him except Sunderland and Hyde, it is not surprising that petitions were launched to remind the King that he should have over five hundred counsellors if he let Parliament sit.[57]

Reports that Charles had made an agreement with France in return for a promise not to summon MPs not only encouraged the petitions, but also damaged the King's credibility, since the rumours suggested to some observers 'that the French ambassador [wa]s our chief statesman'.[58] The European situation continued to affect, and restrict the King's domestic policies. Like Charles himself, Louis XIV had pursued a double-handled foreign policy by sanctioning Barrillon's talks with the English Court at the same time as trying to secure a Franco-Dutch alliance. The latter, which by late 1679 was looking increasingly possible, threatened Charles with diplomatic isolation and reliance on Parliament. In order to support Henry Sidney's ultimately successful efforts at the Hague to prevent the States General agreeing to the French offers, and to promote an Anglo-Dutch accord instead, Charles had at the very least to play down his differences with MPs, and even prepare to work with them. This strait-jacket of circumstances explains why the King renewed negotiations with Shaftesbury and others, and why he was so annoyed by the presentation of the petitions, which highlighted his internal difficulties at a time when he needed to present to European powers a

---

[50] Diary of Henry Sidney, i. 183.
[51] BL, Add. 32,680, ff. 155–8, Henry Sidney to William of Orange, 11 November [1679]; Diary of Henry Sidney, i. 183–4.
[52] Bucks. RO, Verney mss, M11/33, Cary Gardiner to Sir Ralph Verney, 11 November 1679.
[53] HMC Ormonde, v. 248.
[54] HMC Ormonde, iv. 558–9; Original Papers, p. 98; CSPD 1679–80, p. 283; BL, Longleat mss, M/904, reel xvii, Thynne Papers, f. 47, Thomas Thynne to Henry Frederick Thynne, 20 November 1679; Bucks. RO, Verney mss, M11/33, Cary Gardiner to Sir Ralph Verney, 17 November 1679.
[55] Hyde was appointed to the council on 19 November 1679.
[56] Bucks. RO, Verney mss, M11/33, William Denton to Sir Ralph Verney, 17 November 1679.
[57] See chapter 8.
[58] Bucks. RO, Verney mss, M11/33, Cary Gardiner to Sir Ralph Verney, 20 November 1679.

picture of a united nation. Domestic and foreign policy were thus inseparable.[59]

They were knit together to an even greater extent by William of Orange's increasingly strong conviction that James would never succeed to the throne, and by William's own desire to be 'put in a way of having it himself'. Unwilling to become a pawn in the manoeuvrings of the English Court, where James desired William's presence to bolster his own position against that of Monmouth, William decided not to visit England, as he had been urged to do by Charles's envoy, Henry Sidney.[60] In part, William was cautious because he suspected that Sidney was part of Monmouth's faction, but also because the Prince thought that Charles might be forced to abdicate, pushing Parliament into calling Orange over.[61] William may also have been alarmed by the conclusions of an agent named Freeman, who had been in England to discuss the European situation with leading parliamentarians and who found that mistrust of Charles would jeopardise any attempt to secure funding for an Anglo-Dutch league, which was feared by sections of both English and Dutch opinion.[62] William perhaps hoped that the perceived danger of French designs to become Europe's 'universal monarchy' would, given time, outweigh suspicions about his own motives; but, in the more immediate objective of securing English support against France, William wished to see Charles agree with his Parliament by passing an act excluding all catholic successors.[63] Ironically, it was at precisely this time that the idea of excluding the

---

[59] *Archives ou Correspondance inédite de la Maison d'Orange Nassau*, ed. G. Groen Van Prinsterer (Utrecht 1861), v. 377–9; PRO, 31/3/143, ff. 97–138, Barrillon dispatch, 18/28 December 1679; 31/3/144, ff. 1–25, Barrillon dispatches, 22 December 1679/1 January 1680, 25 December 1679/4 January 1680, 29 December 1679/8 January 1680, 1/11 January, Barrillon dispatch, 5/15 January 1680.

[60] *Diary of Henry Sidney*, i. 130, 142, 143–4.

[61] PRO (Kew), FO. 95/565, d'Avaux dispatch, 28 August/7 September, 25 September/5 October 1679.

[62] PRO (Kew), FO. 95/565, d'Avaux dispatch, 28 August/7 September, 4/14 September, 11/21 September, 26 September/ 6 October 1679; PRO, 31/3/143, f. 68, 11/21 September; f. 81, 25 September/5 October 1679; *Sidney Letters*, pp. 98–9; Scott, *Restoration Crisis*, pp. 116–20. The Dutch republican in correspondence with Algernon Sidney was identified by d'Avaux as a Monsr. Pacts (FO.95/565, d'Avaux dispatch, 20/30 November 1679), and this may have been the Mr Potts of the Hague with whom Col. John Scott was involved in espionage (J.A. Marshall, 'Sir Joseph Williamson and the Development of the Government Intelligence System in Restoration England 1660–1680' [Lancaster Ph.D., 1991], p. 411). Shaftesbury, as much as Sidney, feared the domestic implications of an Anglo-Dutch alliance (PRO, 31/3/144, ff. 72, 9/19 February 1680). 'Freeman' may have been the nephew of John Trenchard, who had acted under this name as one of du Moulin's agents during the third Dutch war. A 'memorial' dated May 1680 written by Freeman, outlining the need for a grand alliance against France, is printed in *Diary of Henry Sidney*, ii. 326–370. Its conclusions and wording were used in *Discourses Upon the Modern Affairs of Europe* (1680) – compare *Diary of Henry Sidney*, ii. 366 and *Discourses*, p. 20, for suggestions about how to promote the alliance in Parliament by means of the leaders of the Commons and Shaftesbury's 'party' in the Lords.

[63] *Diary of Henry Sidney*, i. 143.

duke of York was being put on one side, and other expedients were being embraced.

This detailed study of the complex factional manoeuvrings at Court has been necessary to show how the Court continued to be fragmented, and how the situation abroad influenced domestic considerations. Instead of charting the rise of the opposition, it has been possible to show that a power vacuum had been created which would be filled by the Court's critics. The perspective of the Court thus sheds light on both its own organisation and on the reasons why critics were so easily able to take advantage of a situation that inevitably made them appear stronger than they were. Moreover, instead of a conflict between Shaftesbury and the King, the emphasis has been on the internal shifts within the Court of which Shaftesbury was himself part; only once he had lost power at the centre did he turn to using public opinion in his fight for control.

EXPEDIENTS TO SETTLE THE SUCCESSION, JUNE 1679–JANUARY 1680

Having outlined the political background for the second half of 1679, it is now possible to examine attempts to settle the succession during that time in their proper context. The period of weakness and uncertainty forced Charles to keep an open ear to any proposals made to him; and these proposals could now be whispered in secret meetings and followed up in private, in a very different atmosphere to the public platform of Parliament. As a result, the period between October 1679 and January 1680 saw a concerted effort, even on the part of Shaftesbury, to settle the succession problem by means other than exclusion, an effort that was nearly successful. This argument may appear surprising since it is sometimes assumed or implied that once the Commons had resolved on the bill, there were no more discussions about alternative solutions, and that nothing very important happened after May 1679 until Parliament met again in October 1680. Too often it is accepted that exclusion was the single cry of the opposition, maintained loudly and consistently throughout the period. In fact the clamour for the bill receded in the autumn of 1679, despite, or perhaps because, of the duke's return from exile. The secret nature of the talks makes them difficult to reconstruct fully, but there is enough evidence to show that discussion of expedients predominated over exclusion.

Soon after the dissolution of Parliament in July 1679 Thomas Thynne wrote that he thought MPs had 'spent their powder' in relation to the duke, and, presumably referring to limitations, 'would have accepted of what was offered'.[64] Although in late August one of York's friends heard that James's

---

[64] H. Foxcroft, *Life and Works of Sir George Savile ... Earl of Halifax* (1898), i. 174.

exclusion would again be proposed in the new Parliament, or, if that failed, that a bill should be introduced declaring that a catholic could never be King, the focus of attention swung towards the alternative solutions to the succession problem.[65] For a number of months expedients were under active consideration by all the interested parties, and agreement was almost reached. A solution to the succession crisis seemed to be in sight. A week after Parliament was dissolved Lord Massereene predicted that

a pleasing antidote ag[ain]st a popish successor ... shallbee reddy cut and Dryed before the parliam[en]t open, & then [they] will all strive who shall open his country-man's purse widest for the supply of a necessitous and meriting court if this expedient ag[ain]st popery be found out, w[hi]ch as it is as rare, so will be valued equall w[i]th the philosopher's stone.[66]

In mid October the earl of Huntingdon believed there would be endeavours for expedients 'to secure religion even from the Court partie'.[67] Presumably as part of this initiative Southwell promised to send the duke of Ormonde a copy of a limitations bill 'making everything as strict as can be devised'.[68] The Meal Tub Plot then altered the state of politics and nothing further is known of the project until in early December Southwell dispatched the bill which had been 'handed amongst the great men of all sides some months ago', and in which Holles and Littleton had 'laboured'.[69] Both drafters were at this time in contact with Barrillon, via the intermediary Sir John Baber, and the ambassador noted that Holles opposed exclusion and favoured limitations.[70] Barrillon also recorded that the King was being pressured to declare safe-guards for protestantism in the case of a popish successor, in addition to the prosecution of Danby and the popish lords in the Tower, and meetings of Parliament every two years; in return, the attack on the Queen would be dropped.[71] The blue-print under discussion also included a proposal to restrict the revenue of a catholic king in order to force him to rely on Parlia-ment.[72] Barrillon thought the negotiations were not without hopes of success, but although it was said that York had agreed to the provisions of the draft bill, Southwell believed that James's failure to take the oaths when he became

65 PRO (Kew), FO.95/565, d'Avaux dispatch, 21/31 August 1679. The informant was Col. Fitzpatrick.
66 BL, Add. 29,910, f. 114, Lord Massereene to John Swinfen, 17 July 1679. A month later he reported that 'one expedient now in discourse for securing the p[ro]test[ant] Religion, is that none shall bear any office but such as are conformable' (Add. 29,910, f. 123, Massereene to Swinfen, 19 August 1679).
67 Huntington Lib., Hastings MSS 5965, Huntingdon to John Guy, 14 October 1679. He added that it was feared that the expedients would be impracticable.
68 *HMC Ormonde*, iv. 547–8.
69 *HMC Ormonde*, iv. 567.
70 PRO, 31/3/143, f. 113, Barrillon dispatch, 4/14 December 1679. James believed Holles to be 'very much his friend' (Bod., MS Clarendon 87, f. 321, James to Hyde, 29 January 1680)
71 PRO, 31/3/143, f. 127, Barrillon dispatch 11/21 December 1679.
72 PRO, 31/3/144, ff. 2–3, Barrillon dispatch, 22 December 1679/1 January 1680.

a privy councillor in Scotland caused the limitationists to 'abandon any further thoughts of what they were about'.[73]

Yet this was not the whole story. On 29 December Barrillon, who thought the talks more than an attempt to buy time, reported that both limitations and exclusion were under discussion with the Court;[74] and at the same time a number of rumours circulated suggesting that several 'eminent' men would 'get preferm[en]t by undue practices'.[75] It appeared that Charles was smoothing away differences with some of his critics, and using the lure of office. Monmouth duly wrote to William that 'in a little while he would be restored to favour with the King', and was noted to have had frequent meetings with Charles.[76] Hyde was sufficiently worried about York's position to write him a tetchy letter, warning him that if he continued to be awkward about the repression of catholics Hyde could no longer serve him. Even Louis XIV was concerned about the possibility of a reconciliation between the Court and the factions, ordering Barrillon to restart the stalled negotiations with Charles about an Anglo-French alliance.[77]

Sometime between late December 1679 and early January 1680 Charles had made an important decision not to buckle to domestic pressures, whilst pursuing measures abroad to maintain the balance between English, Dutch and French power. In part this was a tactical manoeuvre to buy time, but the King may also have hoped that by siding with the country's antipathy to France he could regain popularity, defuse the charge of popery and arbitrary government that was being levelled against him, and hence split his critics. It was certainly a painful policy for him, since it meant refusing a treaty with the French, and turning down Louis' money,[78] and preparations for agreement with Parliament also meant continuing to negotiate with opposition cabals. It also meant that the succession question remained on the political agenda.

The basis for the ensuing back-stair dealing was a royal divorce, a policy that had long been dear to Shaftesbury. Early in November he had insisted as a condition of his possible return to Court that Charles 'part with the Queen and Duke', and for a while it had seemed as though the King might agree.[79] There had been a report that the Queen was to be confined to her chamber,

[73] HMC Ormonde, iv. 569.
[74] PRO, 331/3/144, f. 17, Barrillon dispatch, 29 December 1679/8 January 1680.
[75] Newdigate newsletter Lc.889, 29 December 1679; Longleat, Muddiman newsbook, unfol. 1 January 1680.
[76] PRO (Kew), FO.95/566, 1/11 January 1680; Congress newsletter 6/311, 20 December 1679.
[77] Clarke, James II, i. 583–4; PRO, 31/3/144, f. 19, Barrillon dispatch, 1/11 January 1680.
[78] PRO, 31/3/144, f. 25, Barrillon dispatch, 5/15 January; ff. 47–8, Barrillon dispatch, 19/29 January; f. 51, Barrillon dispatch, 22 January/1 February 1680.
[79] Diary of Henry Sidney, i. 181; HMC Ormonde, iv. 557–8. Another demand may have been the return of Monmouth (Newdigate newsletter Lc.860, 8 November 1679.

and that the King had told her something which had made her cry all night.[80] But although the idea was shelved at that time, interest in a royal divorce was re-awakened early in the new year, coinciding with renewed hostility to Charles's French mistress, the duchess of Portsmouth.[81] By 8 January 1680 Barrillon had learned that Charles had been promised money for life, and an end to calls for exclusion or limitations, in return for his divorce from the barren Queen Catherine, and subsequent remarriage to a protestant. Shaftesbury went secretly each night to Whitehall, while by day he maintained pressure on the King by encouraging the petitioning campaign for a new Parliament.[82] The difficulties about the scheme were nevertheless significant ones: Charles's sincerity in listening to the proposal was questionable; the duchess of Portsmouth, James, William and Monmouth could all be expected to oppose it, though some of the duke's friends favoured it, and William's hostility was softened with promises of being made Protector over an heir who was a minor; Holles knew of the divorce proposal, but was lukewarm in his support, especially when he learnt that Lauderdale backed it, and he even revealed the talks to Barrillon; and there was always the possibility that Parliament would not be satisfied with the solution.[83] Ironically, before any of these factors came into play, the petitions which Shaftesbury had helped to promote, and which now had a momentum of their own that he was powerless to stop, destroyed hopes of his scheme's success. On 13 January, when negotiations on an agreement were at their most delicate, the first roll of signatures was presented to the King, forcing Charles to recognise that opposition was now a country-wide phenomenon that threatened his own prerogatives as well as those of his successor. Furthermore, Holles's illness, followed by his death in February, were a serious blow to the men searching for an expedient to the succession problem; whilst the receding threat of a Franco-Dutch alliance further stalled the negotiations, which ground to a halt after the prorogation of Parliament on 26 January 1680.

It might be objected that although these discussions came near to success, Charles would have had no intention of standing by what he negotiated. There is no doubt some truth to this argument, if one assumes that the King had a free hand; but it is also true that Charles may have had no option but to yield and stand by his concessions. If France had secured an alliance with the States General, Charles would have been isolated and forced to rely on Parliament; MPs would have demanded safeguards for protestantism, and

80 All Souls, MS 171, f. 83, newsletter 7 November 1679. This rumour was later denied (Newdigate newsletter Lc.861, 11 November 1679).
81 Twenty-two articles of impeachment were drawn up against her (Newdigate newsletter Lc.883, 5 January 1680; Bod., MS Carte 72, f. 520, 'articles of high treason', n.d.).
82 PRO, 31/3/144, f. 31, Barrillon dispatch, 8/18 January 1680.
83 PRO, 31/3/144, ff. 32–45, Barrillon dispatches, 8/18 January, 12/12 January, 15/25 January 1680.

would have been in a good position to ensure that they extracted them. The negotiations were a safety belt as far as the King was concerned, but it was one he might well have needed.

TOWARDS A NEW MINISTRY, JANUARY–AUGUST 1680

After Charles's refusal to concede to the petitioners' demands a more cohesive Court appeared to emerge. In part this was due to the disintegration of opposition after its peak of organisation during the petitioning campaign. At the end of January 1680 Shaftesbury advised his allies on the privy council to seize a propaganda victory by resigning 'in a body together', on the highly improbable grounds that within a few weeks the papists, led by James, would try to alter church and state with the assistance of France.[84] However, only Russell, Cavendish, Powle and Capel retired from the privy council, and Lee and Vaughan from the admiralty;[85] whilst Essex, Halifax, Winchester and Fauconberg, who, it had been said, would also resign, remained in office.[86] Elsewhere Shaftesbury's support began to evaporate without Parliament to give it a voice, and as the splits amongst opposition groups widened.[87] Some were alienated by the earl's continued reliance on exerting the 'weight of the nation'[88] on the King; the presbyterians lacked direction after the death of Lord Holles; whilst others were pacified into quietness by the Court's new ministry and the prospect of a general pardon.[89] In the City Shaftesbury's credit was noticed to have 'mitily fallen',[90] and it was not only in London that Shaftesbury's empire seemed to be collapsing. The Court's new mixture of firmness and prudence was said in Lancashire to have had such good effect that the petitioners were 'reduced to private murmurings'.[91] Indeed, by the spring of 1680 Shaftesbury's 'mutineers', as the Court now called his

---

[84] W.D. Christie, *Life of Anthony Ashley Cooper, First Earl of Shaftesbury* (1871), ii. 357.

[85] When they asked leave to withdraw Charles replied 'with all my heart' (Luttrell, *Brief Relation*, i. 33). For Capel's reasons for resigning see *Diary of Henry Sidney*, i. 270–1.

[86] HMC *Ormonde*, iv. 578; Newdigate newsletter Lc.897, 5 February 1680; Congress newsletter 6/15, 5 February 1680; BL, Althorp MS C2, Sir William Hickman to Halifax, 15 Feb. 1680. The earl of Radnor had been instrumental in persuading them to stay, though one newswriter listed him as one of those who might have resigned (Congress newsletter 6/14, 3 February 1680).

[87] The duke of York remarked on his return to England in February that Shaftesbury's support was waning (Clarke, *James II*, i. 588).

[88] Christie, *Shaftesbury*, ii. 357.

[89] Newdigate newsletter Lc.897, 5 February 1680. John Locke was told on 5 February 1680 that the rumour of a pardon was being hushed (*Correspondence of John Locke*, ed. E.S. de Beer [Oxford. 1976], ii. 155), but it was still being repeated in early March (*CSPD 1679–80*, p.409).

[90] *Hatton Corresp.* i. 224.

[91] Lancs.R.O., Kenyon MS DDKe/6/21, letter dated 25 February [1680]. In Somerset the proceedings against the petitioner Thomas Dare 'very much humbled the party' (*CSPD 1679–80*, p.428).

followers,[92] faced collapse. Although a group of peers which met at Wharton's house resolved in March to meet weekly,[93] Shaftesbury could only muster Monmouth, Huntingdon, Grey, Howard and Paget to a meeting at the end of that month.[94] It was even reported that 'the Green Riband Confederacy [the notorious Green Ribbon Club] is almost as good as broke'.[95] Sir William Coventry informed Halifax in April that Shaftesbury's influence grew 'every day lesse, even amongst those from whence he hopes his greatnesse should spring'.[96]

But in part, the decline of opposition was also due to a growing sense of purpose at Court. Charles took advantage of the opposition's difficulties to purge dissent among his judges,[97] and to remodel his Court, though as much with an eye to diplomacy as internal strength. In February 1680 Sir Leoline Jenkins, experienced in foreign negotiations, became Secretary of State and a privy councillor; Daniel Finch and Sidney Godolphin were also recruited to the new administration, the latter on account of his financial acumen, which Hyde had probably noticed at the treasury.[98] The trio of young statesmen Godolphin, Hyde and Sunderland formed what was known as the 'Chits' ministry.[99] All were on good terms with the duke of York, but committed to working with William of Orange to construct a network of alliances that would restrain the aggrandisement of France in order to preserve the balance of power in Europe. Charles lost nothing by pursuing such a policy. If successful, it would not only provide security but would also appease discontent at home; if unsuccessful it would at least have bought the King time, and convince France of the need to buy his friendship at a higher price as a result of the demonstration of his ability and readiness to pursue an independent policy. Crucially, the duke of York, who returned from Scotland on 24 February, appeared willing to support the ministry's efforts. 'The duke falls into our measures so much beyond what we could expect, both at home and

[92] *Diary of Henry Sidney*, ii. 24–6, 41.

[93] *Hatton Corresp.* i. 224.

[94] *Currant Intelligence*, no.15, 31 March 1680; *Domestick Intelligence*, no. 78, 1 April 1680. According to Reresby, Russell and Cavendish also attended meetings in April 'which changed from hous to hous for more privatie every night' (Reresby, *Memoirs*, p. 193). Sir John Coventry was possibly another participant of these cabals (BL, Longleat mss M/904, reel ix, vol. xvi, ff. 290–1, Sir William Coventry to Sir Thomas Thynne, 3 April 1680).

[95] *CSPD 1679–80*, p. 432. Pepys's transcript of Green Ribbon Club meetings shows a gap between May and November 1680 (Pepys Library, Magdalene College, Cambridge, Pepys MS 2875, f. 484).

[96] BL, Althorp MS C4, Coventry to Halifax, 20 April 1680.

[97] All Souls, MS 171, f. 114, newsletter, 6 February 1680.

[98] It was also rumoured that Hyde, or even the old survivor Arlington, would become lord treasurer (All Souls MS 171, f. 114, newsletter, 4 February 1680; UCNW, Mostyn MS 9089, f. 227, newsletter, 17 January 1680). Arlington replaced the earl of Suffolk as lord lieutenant of Suffolk (All Souls, MS 241, f. 206, newsletter, 17 February 1680).

[99] The name was mentioned in the verse 'On the Young Statesmen', *POAS*, ii. 340–1; Burnet, *History*, ii. 250.

abroad, that I will venture to say the King's affairs are in a better condition than they have been these seven years', Sunderland told Henry Sidney.[100] In May 1680 the Chits made great efforts to win over parliamentary leaders in preparation for a Parliament,[101] and by the middle of the month Lord Townshend, assuming the role of leader of the presbyterians, was offering to 'undertake for a good session', even without Shaftesbury's help.[102] For a while, as we shall see in more detail later, peace and tranquillity appeared to have returned.

But the calm could always be ruffled by events, such as Charles's illness in May, which temporarily rallied opposition forces at a meeting at the end of the month at the Sun tavern, attended by between forty and sixty MPs.[103] Moreover, although it was the most successful ministry of the period, the strength of the Chits was always illusory.[104] They shared a belief that their anti-French foreign policy would settle the nation;[105] but by the end of the summer the only result of the diplomatic initiatives was a defensive treaty with Spain, signed on 10 June. Other states were reluctant to commit themselves until England and Holland had concluded an alliance; but the Dutch wished first to see whether Parliament and Charles could work together. Charles in turn refused to call a Parliament until he had an agreement to present to them. Moreover, the prospect of Parliament's sitting widened the differences between Hyde and Sunderland over the position of the duke of York,[106] exposing the ministry's failure to recruit the support of Temple, Halifax and Essex. James himself had quite quickly reverted to his francophile inclinations,[107] and a strained politeness was the best of his relationship with William. Since much of the Chits' domestic policy rested on their foreign diplomacy, their failure abroad spelt disaster at home and fragmentation of the Court into its different interest groups. As early as 21 March, Sir William Hickman reported to Halifax that whilst 'things above board appear yet very calme ... it's said there has been some disquiet amongst the great ones',[108] and on 10 April the earl of Conway wrote that 'our present cabal of

100 *Diary of Henry Sidney*. i. 292.
101 PRO, 31/3/145, f. 43, Barrillon dispatch, 10/20 May 1680.
102 Bod., MS Carte 243, f. 473, newsletter, 11 May 1680; PRO, 31/3/145, f. 57, Barrillon dispatch, 28 May/8 June 1680.
103 *Burnet Letters*, p. 31; Newdigate newsletter, 27 May 1680.
104 Sir William Hickman observed that 'things above board appear yet very calme though its sayd there has been some disquiet amongst the great ones' (BL, Althorp MS C2, Hickman to Halifax, 21 March 1680).
105 *Diary of Henry Sidney*, ii. 6–8.
106 Sunderland believed the sacrifice of the duke of York to be inevitable (*HMC Ormonde*, v. 454; *Diary of Henry Sidney*, ii. 99; Bod., MS Carte 243, f. 506, Longford to Arran, 24 August 1680). Hyde, however, remained committed to upholding the York interest (PRO, 31/3/146, f. 40, Barrillon dispatch, 24 July/3 August 1680).
107 PRO, 31/3/145, f. 21, Barrillon dispatch, 15/25 April 1680.
108 BL, Althorp MS C2, Hickman to Halifax, 21 March 1680.

governors are all to pieces among themselves, and they cannot agree either who is wisest or most in favour'.[109] The administration desperately needed a wider bottom. In mid June a meeting at Sunderland's seat at Althorp marked an attempt to draw Halifax into the ministry,[110] and Sir William Jones was offered the lord chancellorship in an unsuccessful 'endeavour to gaine men of credit to their party'.[111] By the end of the summer the Court was once more divided,[112] a state of fragmentation to which Charles's mistress, the duchess of Portsmouth, was contributing. Fearing for her own position, she looked to York's enemies as a means of self-preservation, and allied with Sunderland and Godolphin, who supported William of Orange's interests, against Hyde, who supported James and who planned to replace Portsmouth's charms with those of her former rival, the duchess of Mazarin.[113]

Although an open rupture at Whitehall was not apparent for some time, there were strong rumours in August of a new round of changes at Court, including the return of Shaftesbury.[114] As usual, such reports echoed private dealing with opposition leaders. The negotiations that took place in September and October 1680 for a reconciliation between the Court and its critics once again turned to a large extent on the issue of the succession, since that problem had become inextricably linked to a struggle for power. Indeed, the period immediately before Parliament's sitting on 21 October witnessed intense factional intrigues, with a host of secret meetings 'held at untimely hours'.[115]

INTRIGUE AND THE SUCCESSION, AUGUST–OCTOBER 1680

The background to the negotiations that took place prior to Parliament's assembly lay in projects, which had been put forward during the spring and summer whenever a meeting of MPs seemed likely, to limit the duke's powers as King or in attempts to find other expedients that stopped short of exclusion but which would settle the nation. In March 1680 Charles had listened to proposals from leaders of the parliamentary cabals, apparently supported by the Chits, to abandon exclusion if the King allied against France and dropped both Portsmouth and Lauderdale from favour, but the King had walked away

---

[109] *HMC Portland*, iii. 365.
[110] *Diary of Henry Sidney*, ii. 75.
[111] *Diary of Henry Sidney*, ii. 71–2; *Russell Letters*, p. 114; Foxcroft, *Halifax*, i. 222–3. Jones met with James at the end of June (*Russell Letters*, p. 122).
[112] *Locke Corresp.* ii. 226.
[113] PRO, 31/3/146, f. 40, Barrillon dispatch, 24 July/3 August 1680.
[114] *CSPD 1679–80*, p. 597; UCNW, Mostyn MS 9090, f. 62, newsletter, 10 August 1680; Bod., MS Carte 243, f. 506, newsletter, 24 August 1680.
[115] Foxcroft, *Halifax*, i. 242, quoting Dutch dispatch dated 12/22 October 1680.

when he heard his mistress being attacked.[116] Early in June, Barrillon had reported rumours that James would agree to limitations on his power as King if exclusion was abandoned; and there had been a number of well-informed reports that York had received positive assurances from the principal Members of the Commons that in the next session they would not talk about either the duke in particular or the succession in general.[117] Admiring Charles's apparent open-mindedness, Arlington admitted that he had not believed the King 'would ever be brought to what he now does', and, in order to complete preparations for a meeting of Parliament, Sunderland had hoped William could be persuaded to come to England.[118] With a successful session imminent, and in danger of isolation if Halifax and Jones had succumbed to the enticements of the Court, Shaftesbury had been observed to be 'pettish and out of humour extremely'.[119] The earl had desperately sought a way to force his way back into consideration, even if this meant wrecking the delicate compromise being worked out with the 'presbyterian' moderates over the succession. He and a number of MPs had found a sensational way to do so on 26 June, when they indicted the duke of York as a popish recusant.[120] Charles had been forced to further prorogue the opening of Parliament, thereby reopening the opportunity for Shaftesbury to regain influence.

Faction dominated the complex secret dealing that occurred in September and October 1680, with each cabal attempting to dominate at the expense of the other and using the succession issue for positional advantage.[121] This is not to suggest that there was no ideological element involved, but that the cabals aimed at the same goal of the security of protestantism, and sought it by different routes. Some wanted to pursue limitations, others to enforce measures against catholics in general; exclusionists, such as Russell, sought to impeach the duke, whilst 'some honest gentlemen' sought to delay the consideration of exclusion on the grounds 'that if the House did immediately fall upon the laying aside the Duke of York, it was more than ten to one they

---

[116] PRO, 31/3/144, ff. 99–100, Barrillon dispatch, 4/14 March 1680; 31/3/145, f. 19, Barrillon dispatch, 12/22 April 1680; *Burnet Letters*, p. 12; *Diary of Henry Sidney*, i. 298. The talks appear to have been conducted by Sir John Baber, a presbyterian doctor at Court.

[117] PRO, 31/3/145, ff. 70–1, Barrillon dispatch, 3/13 June 1680; PRO (Kew), FO.95/566, d'Avaux dispatch, 24 June/4 July 1680. The sources for the latter were John Churchill, and the Spanish Ambassador in London.

[118] *Diary of Henry Sidney*, ii. 74–5.

[119] *Russell Letters*, p. 117.

[120] The presenters were Lords Shaftesbury, Grey, Huntingdon, North, Howard of Escrick, Russell, Cavendish, Brandon, Thomas Wharton, Thomas Thynne, Sir Scrope Howe, Sir Edward Hungerford, Sir Gilbert Gerard, Sir Henry Calverly, Sir William Cowper, John Trenchard and William Forester (*HMC Verney*, p. 479; BL, Althorp MS C5, Thynne to Halifax, 26 June 1680; *Reasons for the Indictment of the Duke of York* [1680]). According to Newdigate newsletter Lc.955, 29 June 1680, nearly 200 MPs had followed behind.

[121] PRO, 31/3/146, f. 87, Barrillon dispatch, 20/30 September 1680.

had nothing at all'.[122] The centrifugal force of the impending Parliament began to separate both the Court and its critics into their different components, a division from which Charles may have hoped to profit, since he began negotiations with the leaders of the City of London with the purpose of moderating their position on the succession and splitting them from other interest groups.[123]

The most important figure at Court at this stage was Sunderland, whom Godolphin largely followed. Relentless in the belief that foreign affairs provided the key to domestic tranquillity, the two ministers needed agreement between King and Parliament, which they thought in turn necessitated the sacrifice of James. They now threw their weight behind William, whom they once again tried to persuade to visit England, especially since the idea of the Prince acting as regent was again being floated.[124] At Sunderland's suggestion, the Dutch envoy Van Lewen was also dispatched to England to foster unity between Charles and MPs, and, as d'Avaux suspected, to maintain a Williamite party that could declare the prince the successor the moment things became heated.[125]

But, unable to rely on a single power-base in the Commons, Sunderland was also forced to try to mediate between the factions in order to pave the way for a smooth meeting of Parliament. His support was probably behind Henry Capel's running between Sir William Temple and Russell in mid September, when it was proposed that James retire from Court and agree to limitations in return for an undertaking not to alter the succession and for money to be administered by parliamentary nominees. Part of the deal may have included a plan for York to renounce his own claim to the throne in favour of those of his children, and for Monmouth to leave England too in return for restoration to his offices.[126] These proposals came to nothing because few were prepared to commit themselves to any line of action before it was clear what the mood of MPs would be. Support for the scheme was in any case thin and undisciplined. Temple was by now an isolated figure; Halifax's aloofness kept him

---

122 Clarke, *James II*, i. 594; Van Prinsterer, *Archives*, v. 417; *Second Part of the Growth of Popery*, pp. 281–3. Newdigate newsletter Lc.974, 21 August 1680, referred to '24 articles ready to be presented to the p[ar]l[ia]m[en]t ag[ains]t the D[uke] of Y[ork]'.

123 Kent AO, U1015/043/5, notes of a meeting between Secretary Jenkins and Thomas Papillon, 27 August 1680; PRO, 31/3/146, f. 74, Barrillon dispatch, 6/16 September 1680.

124 *Hatton Corresp.* i. 237; PRO, 31/3/146, f. 106, Barrillon dispatch, 7/17 October 1680; PRO (Kew), FO.95/566, d'Avaux dispatch 12/22 October, 15/25 October, 21/31 October 1680; J.P. Kenyon, 'Charles II and William of Orange in 1680', *BIHR*, xxx (1957), 95–101.

125 Van Prinsterer, *Archives*, v. 415–16; *Diary of Henry Sidney*, ii. 104–5; PRO (Kew), FO.95/566, d'Avaux dispatch, 23 September/3 October 1680, summarised in *Négociations de Monsieur le Comte d'Avaux* (1754), i. 104–6.

126 *Diary of Henry Sidney*, ii. 107; PRO, 31/3/146, f. 87, Barrillon dispatch, 20/30 September; ff. 99–100, Barrillon dispatch, 27 September/7 October 1680; PRO (Kew), FO.95/566, d'Avaux dispatch, 12/22 October 1680; Bod. MS Carte 104, f. 38, Jenkins to Middleton, 1 October 1680.

away from London until a fortnight before MPs met, by which time the chance for promoting limitations had passed; and Essex had thoughts of retiring from Court.[127] Henry Sidney worked hard, but unsuccessfully, to bring other players, such as Montagu and Sir William Jones, into partnership,[128] and, with few voices pleading its cause, the scheme was left to break up under the pressure of James's refusal to voluntarily retire.[129]

Sunderland was therefore increasingly forced to look for support elsewhere, which meant dealing with Shaftesbury. A correspondence between the two had already been established in September, even though Shaftesbury was opposed to William's designs which Sunderland supported.[130] In the first week of October Sunderland suggested to Shaftesbury the exile of James, followed by his exclusion, in return for supply.[131] In effect Sunderland was proposing to rely on Shaftesbury, Russell and others to 'undertake' for a peaceful session, a high-risk strategy given the divergence of their long-term objectives.[132] Shaftesbury himself recognised that any agreement had to be reached before Parliament sat, otherwise he risked losing his credit, and that even he had to follow, rather than dictate to, the wishes of Members.[133] Sunderland was now trying to rally all anti-York groups into one alliance, which was to be tied to the Court. He was aided by the Spanish and Dutch ambassadors, together with Henry Sidney, who hoped to unite all parties behind exclusion,[134] and by the duchess of Portsmouth who still saw her own salvation in James's demise. Having been legally presented as a common nuisance only a few months earlier, she now went to London several times 'to make up matters with Shaftesbury and his party, by the canal of Lord Howard of Escrick, and having done it, promoted their measures'; she even met with Monmouth.[135]

The consequence of this re-alignment was to fracture the Court on the eve of Parliament's meeting. The latent divisions amongst the Chits surfaced, as the factions struggled over the issue of James being sent back once more into exile. Although the duke had alienated many at Court, Hyde and Clarendon

[127] Foxcroft, *Halifax*, i. 241; *HMC Fitzherbert*, p. 23.

[128] *Diary of Henry Sidney*, ii. 108, 111–2. In early September there had been more talk of Jones becoming lord chancellor (Newdigate newsletter Lc.980, 9 September 1680).

[129] PRO, 31/3/146, f. 78, Barrillon dispatch, 6/16 September; f. 81, Barrillon dispatch, 13/23 September 1680.

[130] PRO, 31/3/146, f. 77, Barrillon dispatch, 9/19 September; f. 101, Barrillon dispatch, 27 September/7 October 1680.

[131] PRO, 31/3/146, f. 107, Barrillon dispatch, 7/17 October 1680.

[132] Van Prinsterer, *Archives*, v. 423.

[133] PRO, 31/3/146, f. 107, Barrillon dispatch, 7/17 October 1680. Shaftesbury 'professe[d] himself to be amazed why the parliament should be called to sit at this time, there being not, as he says, the least probability of their doing good to the King' (*CSPD 1680–1*, p. 45).

[134] PRO, 31/3/145, f. 110, Barrillon dispatch, 11/21 October; f. 119, Barrillon dispatch, 18/28 October 1680.

[135] *Original Papers*, p. 105; *HMC Ormonde*, v. 445.

remained firm in their support and pressed Charles to dissolve Parliament in order to save his brother;[136] yet if the King stuck to James he risked provoking a revolt, thereby endangering his own position. For some time Charles's own attitude was inscrutable, with some saying that he would abandon his brother, and others declaring the contrary.[137] Perhaps to keep the factions guessing, he did not return to London until early in October, even though his presence in the capital was thought by Jenkins to be the only way 'to give heart to his friends and check the cabals that are formed against him'.[138] Some decision was necessary, however, about whether or not James would be allowed to remain in England, and hence whether or not Parliament would sit. Sunderland, Essex, Halifax and Godolphin all argued for sending the duke away, supported behind scenes by the duchess of Portsmouth.[139] But the privy council was split down the middle over the issue, and, after the failure of a last-ditch attempt to persuade James to embrace protestantism, Charles ordered him to return to Scotland.[140] The only consolation for Charles was that just as his own advisers were divided, so were the opposition, with Russell temporarily falling out with Shaftesbury over whether or not the duke ought to go.[141]

At the beginning of the second new Parliament of the crisis an unconfirmed alliance between Sunderland, Portsmouth, Monmouth and Shaftesbury had thus been negotiated to favour the passage of exclusion; but this group was far from securing dominance at Court. It was still unknown how the King would act, though Henry Sidney correctly predicted that Charles would not consent to exclusion.[142] Yet the period between the Parliaments, from July 1679 and October 1680, had witnessed the failure of repeated attempts to find alternatives solutions to the succession problem which were both practicable and acceptable to all the parties involved. Expedients and limitations continued to be advocated after October 1680, as we shall see, but, as Halifax

---

136 Foxcroft, *Halifax*, i. 241; Van Prinsterer, *Archives*, v. 423.
137 Foxcroft, *Halifax*, i. 241.
138 *CSPD 1680–1*, p. 42.
139 All Souls MS 171, f. 128, newsletter, 13 October 1680; *Original Papers*, p. 104.
140 *Diary of Henry Sidney*, ii. 109–10; Clarke, *James II*, i. 596; All Souls MS 171, f. 128, newsletter, 13 October 1680; *HMC Ormonde*, v. 459. Barrillon reported that the lord chancellor, the earls of Clarendon and Anglesey, the marquis of Worcester, Hyde, Seymour, Jenkins, the Archbishop of Canterbury and the bishops of Durham and London all opposed the idea of the King ordering James away, though according to one newsletter Chancellor Finch told the King that 'it was very requisite the D[uke] of Y[ork] should dep[ar]t' (PRO, 31/3/146, f. 117, Barrillon dispatch, 18/28 October 1680; Newdigate newsletter, Lc.996, 19 October 1680). Those in favour of James's departure included Essex, Prince Rupert, Halifax, Sunderland, Godolphin, Radnor and Fauconberg (Bod., MS Carte 233, f. 295, newsletter, 19 October 1680).
141 PRO, 31/3/146, f. 117, Barrillon dispatch, 18/28 October 1680. Russell, who wanted James to stay to face trial for treason, told Shaftesbury that the duke would not return in Shaftesbury's lifetime, but that York would revenge himself on his younger opponents.
142 Van Prinsterer, *Archives*, v. 430–1.

recognised, 'the waves beat so high against [James] that [a] great part of the world will not hear of anything lesse than exclusion'.[143] Halifax himself must bear some responsibility for this situation. Had he thrown his weight whole-heartedly behind the Chits, they might have been successful in the Spring of 1680, when opposition forces lay in disarray. But, in a sense, Halifax's unwillingness to engage himself on behalf of the Court was part of a wider malaise of distrust of the King, created by suspicions about Charles's real opinions and intentions. Only somebody as intelligently devious as Sunder-land could sympathise with the windings of the royal mind, and even he misunderstood it. Charles's love of keeping all his options open was ironically beginning to restrict them, for his reticence to take any positive action about the position of his brother increasingly tied him to upholding James's suc-cession. Perhaps this was machiavellian genius; but it also magnified much of the unrest that he now had to face.

CONCLUSION

The virtual collapse of the Court, characterised by the internal rivalry be-tween ministers, shaped the development of the succession crisis, and it is only after we have recognised the weakness of the government that we can properly assess the strength of opposition forces. By turning the spotlight on to the Court, the factors of faction and foreign policy assume a new import-ance. James himself headed one of these factions, whilst his son-in-law William of Orange, who wished Charles and Parliament to agree so that they could unite against French power, sought James's exclusion as the most likely way to achieve reconciliation between King and MPs. This dynastic struggle overlay disagreements in 1679 between Shaftesbury and Monmouth, on the one hand, and an alliance of Halifax–Sunderland–Essex, on the other. Yet even this latter faction disintegrated under the pressure first of James's return in September from exile, and then the resurgence of Shaftesbury's power in the winter of 1679–80. This turbulence at Whitehall ensured that a variety of ways to settle the succession were discussed. Indeed, consideration of limi-tations and expedients predominated over talk of exclusion; a limitations bill was produced in the autumn of 1679, and a royal divorce formed the basis for negotiations between Shaftesbury and Charles in January 1680. But the earl's decision to look outside the Court to popular support in his struggle for power undermined the King's readiness to work with him, and frightened Charles that his own power was at stake.

The winter of 1679–80 therefore appeared to mark a turning point in the state of Court politics. As a result of the failure of the petitioning campaign to try to awe Charles into summoning Parliament, opposition groups continued

[143] Foxcroft, *Halifax*, i. 241.

to be deprived of a national platform and had become associated with rebellious designs and tumultuous popular pressure. Their disintegration seemed further ensured by the death in February 1680 of Lord Holles, one of the champions of limitations and an important co-ordinator of opposition cabals; and by a new cohesion at Court in the spring and early summer of 1680 with the Chits' administration, headed by Sunderland, Hyde and Godolphin, which aimed to achieve domestic tranquillity partly by negotiating an anti-French European alliance and by trying to put the succession issue to one side. Yet York's reluctance to see Parliament re-assemble widened cracks that began to appear in the narrow-based ministry once it was apparent that the Dutch would only ally with England when King and Parliament were united. These rifts were exploited by those discontented with the state of the nation and with their own circumscribed political role. A series of complex, intense, factional intrigues therefore took place in the autumn of 1680, with the different cabals jockeying for position and using the succession as one of the decisive issues. After initial exploration of the limitations scheme, Sunderland decided that the pressure for exclusion was overwhelming. This assessment fractured his partnership with Hyde, who supported James's interest, and pushed Sunderland into an uneasy alliance with Shaftesbury. Once more the King faced Parliament with a divided and weak Court.

The period of almost a year and a half between Parliaments makes an understanding of Court politics essential. So long as MPs were not sitting, attention turned towards Whitehall. Charles faced a number of important decisions: on whom should or could he rely for advice? what should he do to try to settle the succession problem? and what foreign policy should he adopt? His shifting responses to these three inter-related questions had helped determine the nature of politics during this period, and it is difficult to discern in the King's actions any long-term policy. Essentially he seems to have been willing to react to events as they happened, as though he hoped the problems might simply go away. But in October 1680 the problems were still there, and now the focus of politics turned back to Parliament.

4

Politics and the succession, 1680–1

The previous two chapters have argued that for 1679 and most of 1680 exclusion was part of a much wider succession crisis, intertwined with the European situation and the factional struggles that followed from the collapse of Court power. Whilst these factors continued to affect and determine the succession debate, the character of politics did change in the autumn of 1680, since the meeting of Parliament not only restored a legitimate platform for opposition, but also witnessed a hardening of attitudes in the House of Commons over the need to bar James from the throne. On 21 October Charles opened the session with a speech that promised concurrence 'in any remedies which shall be proposed that may consist with the preserving of the Crown in its due and legal course of descent', and five days later Russell moved to consider ways of securing the government and religion against a popish successor; but instead of heeding the King, the Commons resolved *nemine contradicente* to suppress popery and prevent a popish successor, and on 2 November Harbord successfully moved for another exclusion bill.[1] Russell presented the bill two days later, and on 6 November it had a second reading. Two days after that, the bill was debated in a committee of the whole House, and passed on 11 November.[2] On the 15th the bill was carried up to the Lords, where it was nevertheless defeated, thirty votes to sixty-three.[3] Unlike the 1679 Parliament, therefore, MPs had immediately resolved on the bill, and now faced new problems of how to achieve their aim. The rejection of the bill thus marks the beginning of the exclusion crisis proper.

Detailed examination of high politics in the period between November 1680 and April 1681 is necessary for a number of reasons. Scott has recently warned against viewing the exclusion bill in isolation and out of context.[4] He quite rightly points out that the bill must be placed in its wider setting, for a bald outline of its fate sheds no light on the attitudes of MPs; and he correctly

---

[1] Grey, *Debates*, vii. 347, 357–65.
[2] Jenkins told William that 'the number ag[ains]t the bill was considerable', but they had refrained from forcing a division (PRO, SP.104, For. Entry Bk. 67, f. 17, 12 November 1680).
[3] *CJ*, ix. 647, 651; *LJ*, xiii. 666; *HMC Ormonde*, v. 488.
[4] Scott, *Restoration Crisis*, p. 79.

emphasises that the bill was becoming caught up in the call for the redress of other grievances, most notably the abuse of the King's power to summon MPs. Yet his assertion that the second Westminster Parliament exactly mirrored the first is overdrawn, not least because his analysis stops in November, and his consideration of the role of Algernon Sidney leaves little room for the continuing debate about limitations, which was now conducted in the Upper House rather than amongst sections of the Lower. Indeed, Scott does not attempt to treat the parliamentary politics of the period in any depth, and therefore a more detailed, and differently angled, revision of the 'exclusionist' account is necessary. Moreover, our analysis of the period can be widened in other ways. It will be argued here that the period between the second Westminster Parliament and the short Parliament held in Oxford in March 1681 was as much a period of crisis for the exclusionists, as an exclusion crisis. The bill's supporters faced a variety of options. They could either force or persuade the Lords and the King to pass the measure; if so, they needed to find a way in 1680 of reintroducing exclusion, or something like it, since the same piece of legislation could not legally be read twice in one session; alternatively, or perhaps additionally, they could look outside Parliament for support in the face of an increasingly fierce battle for public opinion. Choosing which course of action to pursue put increasing strain on the unity of opposition groups, and caused disputes about tactics and strategy, revealing splits within the parliamentary leadership. This chapter aims to explore these themes by taking the narrative of politics and the succession up to the dissolution of the Oxford Parliament at the end of March 1681, and, like earlier sections, will also try to assess the impact of foreign affairs on domestic politics, as well as seeking to approach the succession debate from the perspective of the Court.

There was certainly still much to play for in 1680 in terms of the struggle for control of the King's ear. Shortly before MPs sat, Barrillon believed that Sunderland and Portsmouth had promised Shaftesbury, Monmouth and Russell that Charles would appoint them to high office, and agree to all Parliament's demands in return for supply and Charles's freedom to name his successor.[5] Events showed that this initiative failed, opening the possibility of power for a rival Court cabal. But success in the power struggle meant that politicians had first to weigh up Charles's opaque intentions. Charles at first seemed about to cave in to opposition demands. At the beginning of November Barrillon thought the King had slid into a lethargy, an indication that he might submit to Parliament; Sunderland, Portsmouth and Godolphin were similarly convinced that the bill would pass the Upper House

---

[5] PRO, 31/3/147, ff. 1–3, Barrillon dispatch, 25 October/4 November 1680. Barrillon mentioned Seymour, Arlington and St Albans as one such cabal.

because the King had been 'contrived into a passive neutrality'.[6] Yet, as the debate on the bill in the Lords grew nearer, Charles's resolution against it also seemed to grow. On 13 November he received a long address from the Commons 'without one word in answer', displayed impatience when the 'part w[hi]ch mentioned the ill councells w[hi]ch had been given for dissolving & proroguing of Parl[iamen]ts' was read,[7] and 'went about himself to sollicite against' the bill in the Lords.[8] Politicians had to weigh up whether Charles's new-found resolution was permanent, or whether he had opposed exclusion so that he could later claim that he had been forced into making concessions. The crisis of authority at Court was thus an integral part of the nation's problems.

THE SUCCESSION AND THE WESTMINSTER PARLIAMENT OF 1680–1

A number of features of the political debate after the loss of the exclusion bill in the Lords were apparent even before it left the Commons. Large numbers of MPs seem to have deliberately absented themselves from the succession debates in 1680, just as they had done the previous year. On 2 November 'a great many left the House before the vote passed and so it went nemine contradicente',[9] and on the 8th, the same day as the bill's reading, a division on the controverted Montgomery election mustered only 207 votes. Indeed, when Pulteney took the chair that day for the committee of the whole on the exclusion bill he moved that the serjeants-at-arms should call in MPs.[10] Once again, Members seem to have been reluctant to commit themselves at a personal level. One explanation is that the debates showed an early tendency towards division, and rule by a faction. On 2 November Garraway declared that he wanted a committee established to consider the alternatives to exclusion, such as a bill to convict all popish recusants prior to their banishment, and provisions for frequent Parliaments; but Winnington tried to smooth things over by claiming that differences between the supporters of expedients and the exclusionists were only 'to the manner and not the thing', and the House accordingly rejected any attempt to consider expedients separately.[11] Nevertheless, although uncertainty about the wisdom of

---

[6] PRO, 31/3/147, f. 12, Barrillon dispatch, 1/11 November 1680; *HMC Ormonde*, v. 496. Charles had been pressed to accept a first reading of the bill, which could then be amended (*Original Papers*, p. 107; Clarke, *James II*, i. 615).

[7] *HMC Ormonde*, v. 488; John Rylands Lib., Legh mss, Richard Sterne to Richard Legh, 13 November 1680. Courtiers had never seen the King so angry (BL, Add. 28,930, f. 201, Samuel Ellis to John Ellis, 13 November 1680).

[8] Clarke, *James II*, i. 615.

[9] BL, Add. 28,875, f. 146, newsletter by John Ellis, 2 November 1680.

[10] *CJ*, ix. 648.

[11] Grey, *Debates*, vii. 398–40; BL, Add. 32,681, f. 67, Jenkins to Sidney, 2 November 1680.

pursuing alternatives to exclusion was thus suppressed, at least in the short term, the process of division amongst the bill's supporters, which its defeat accelerated and exposed, can be detected in the evolution of the bill's wording. The nomination of Charles's successor was a particularly sensitive issue, since it forced a contest between the different wings of the exclusionist ranks as interest groups formed round each of the rival claimants to the throne.[12] Sunderland and Henry Sidney tried to persuade William to come to England,[13] Monmouth abandoned the bar of illegitimacy on his coach's coat of arms,[14] whilst a third group wanted the open declaration of neither duke nor Prince. Algernon Sidney and several leading Members thus wrote to a Dutch republican that they feared an alliance with Holland because it would increase the authority of both Charles and William; but also that Monmouth 'n'est pas si bien qu'il pense dans la chambre basse [et] qu'on y a trop de défiance de lui'.[15] These rifts soon became apparent. On 5 November Secretary Jenkins observed that unlike the first exclusion bill of 1679, which had stipulated that the Crown was to pass to the next in line of succession as if the duke of York were dead (and hence to the Princess of Orange), the new one left the nomination 'in suspense'.[16] In the debate the next day, Sir Richard Temple pointed out that the draft bill could be interpreted as disabling the duke of York's relatives, including his children. Halifax's ally Sir William Hickman therefore urged that the Crown should descend to the next lawful heir, and Harbord went further in support of the Orangist line by suggesting that he would oppose a bill that excluded James's protestant children. Birch, Sir John Knight and Titus, however, all successfully resisted the attempt to name a successor, despite the fact that this blank laid the bill open to the charge that it would 'cause an interregnum'.[17] The House resolved that the bill was to apply to the duke only, leaving the question of the heir undecided, but the Williamites were stronger behind the scenes for when the House resumed the debate on 8 November, Russell added a proviso that the Crown was to descend as if the duke were dead, a confirmation of the Orangist claims, even if the Princess's rights were not specifically declared.[18]

Besides MPs' reticence and shaky long-term unity, the early debates of the session showed that the Court's critics wanted more than exclusion. Even

---

12 PRO, 31/3/147, f. 6, Barrillon dispatch, 25 October/4 November 1680.
13 *Diary of Henry Sidney*, ii. 117, 119; Van Prinsterer, *Archives*, v. 435, 448.
14 *Sidney Letters*, pp. 101.
15 PRO (Kew), FO.95/566, d'Avaux dispatches, 28 October/7 November, 4/14 November 1680. Buckingham was similarly on bad terms with both the Williamites and Monmouthites, and was even thought to have been reconciled with James (PRO, 31/3/146, ff. 125–6, 21/31 October 1680).
16 PRO, SP.104/67, f. 17, Jenkins to William, 5 November 1680.
17 Grey, *Debates*, vii. 425–30; *An Exact Collection of the Most Considerable Debates* (1681), pp. 56–9.
18 Grey, *Debates*, vii. 431–2.

before Parliament sat, Barrillon had thought they aimed to control the government by extending Parliament's power over officeholding, the armed forces and Ireland and Scotland.[19] His observation was confirmed by a long, wide-ranging and influential speech made on 26 October by the former opponent of exclusion, Sir Henry Capel, who gave an account of the growth of popery since the Restoration, attacked the influence of France and questioned the government of all three British kingdoms, thereby dispelling any doubts that this was a one-issue crisis.[20] The actions of the House after the exclusion bill's defeat merely emphasised that many of the limitations or expedients which had previously been voiced in the Commons as alternatives to exclusion were now demanded alongside it as additional safeguards, a phenomenon which helps explain why former opponents of the bill, such as the Capels, now supported it. Exclusion thus became one, albeit very important, part of a much larger programme of demands once it had become fused with the measures originally designed to make it unnecessary.

The debates also reveal that MPs were prepared to offer supply in order to entice the King to pass the bill. On 27 October Sacheverell condemned Sir William Temple's attempt to direct debate towards the European situation as a ploy to obtain money, and suggested that the House give no money before domestic grievances had been redressed;[21] but although a resolution to support the King at home and abroad was opposed 'because such addresses in [the] past had always drawn Parliaments in to grant money', the motion was nevertheless passed, even if it did not have the clause some wanted to support the government 'as established by law'.[22] MPs were very aware of the power of the purse over the King, and would use it in the coming months of struggle. As early as 2 November Treby was advised that 'a very simple and easy' way of achieving security for the nation was by 'tacking the revenue of the Crown to the Laws established for Religion'.[23]

Suspicions between and amongst MPs, the merger of expedients with demands for exclusion, the importance of supply, and distrust of the King's uncertain policy were all manifest in the proceedings of the Lower House after the decisive vote in the Lords on 15 November. On 17 November Hampden proposed 'a plain bargain' with the King in an address informing the King of the state of the nation, in which Charles was to be offered supply

[19] PRO, 31/3/146, ff. 109–10, Barrillon dispatch, 11/21 October 1680.

[20] Grey, *Debates*, vii. 360–2. *An Exact Collection*, pp. 2–12, gives a much longer version of the speech recorded by Grey. Newdigate newsletter Lc.999 described it as 'an excellent speech opening the state of the nation'.

[21] Grey, *Debates*, vii. 375.

[22] *An Exact Collection*, p. 19; Leics. RO, Finch mss, DG7/4957/61/1, notes on debate 27 October 1680.

[23] HMC Fitzherbert, p. 23.

in return for the security of protestantism.[24] The House duly agreed to make a representation about the dangerous condition of the kingdom, though Grey records the inclusion of the phrase 'by reason of the fears and apprehensions of popery and a popish successor', omitted from the resolution in the *Journals*.[25] When the address was reported on the 27th it revealed some of the differences between the leaders of the House. Sacheverell found the address's attack on popery as the cause of all the nation's problems to be too simplistic, preferring a wider attack on present ministers and the arbitrary policies of the 1670s, though he was causticly reminded by Hampden that in 1678 he had thought catholicism the root of all evils, and the bickering continued when Booth and Cavendish expressed reservations about the wording of the address.[26] Despite the open differences of approach and analysis of the nation's problems, the House approved the text unamended in what was regarded as a victory for 'the moderate party'.[27]

After the trial of the earl of Stafford early in December, the House was again unsure about how to proceed. As Sir Edward Dering rather poetically put it, MPs 'seemed to ly at hull, & let the wind drive, neither spreading their sailes nor drawing their anchors to make any way'.[28] By mid December Members realised that they were 'not one bit safer' than at the beginning of the session, and 'had better have half a loaf, than no bread'.[29] On 15 December the King made a speech in which he repeated his promise to agree to any remedy consistent with the legal succession,[30] but this failed to appease the House. In a committee of the whole, Cavendish remarked on 'a silence in the House', and therefore began a debate about forming an association of protestants. Those who refused to join were, he suggested, 'to be declared incapable to bear any office', a proposal that sparked tangential speeches about judges holding their places for life, abuses of the Corporation Act, the role of the clergy, the fleet, militia and guard, and a call for Parliament to sit after the King's death to determine whether the successor was a papist. Despite opposition from Birch, the House resolved on an association bill which named the duke of York, thereby effectively reintroducing exclusion by another means.

24 Grey, *Debates*, viii. 8. *A Collection of the Substance of Several Speeches and Debates* (1681), p. 4, prints a speech by Sir Nicholas Carew, not recorded by Grey, which made a similar proposal.
25 Grey, *Debates*, viii. 21. Nearly every significant leader of the House was named to the committee to draw up the address (*CJ*, ix. 655). One of them, Capel, repeated the need for the address on 19 November (Grey, *Debates*, viii. 36).
26 Grey, *Debates*, viii. 99–106.
27 *HMC Ormonde*, v. 511.
28 Kent AO, U1713 C2, f. 9, Dering to Southwell, 14 December 1680.
29 Grey, *Debates*, viii. 129, 135. The debate showed that Jones felt under attack by Capel and Birch.
30 For accounts of this day's proceedings see Grey, *Debates*, viii. 147–71; Leics. RO, Finch mss, DG7/4957/61/11, notes; *The History of the Association* (1682), pp. 1–5; *HMC Le Fleming*, p. 177.

Far from narrowing the scope of debate back down to the succession alone, the adoption of the association opened it wider. On 18 December Hampden moved for a resolution that without exclusion there could be no safety, and in favour of an association, but also urged that the House 'must go yet farther' by pressing for protestant judges, justices of the peace, lord lieutenants, deputy lieutenants and naval officers of integrity, in return for which the House would offer supply. Exclusion had thus become joined to a wholesale reform of current officeholding. The reaction to Hampden's speech revealed a split between those who were prepared to grant supply first, and those who insisted on the prior passage of exclusion. Sir William Jones, one of the most influential of the new Members, indicated in a carefully worded speech that money would be given in return for the redress of grievances, whilst Winnington and Birch duly suggested that the demands be set out in an address. Cavendish, whom Barrillon believed to be working on behalf of the Court and who had the support of moderates, nevertheless pressed for money first, and suggested that a committee composed of 'men of all opinions' be appointed to draw it up. This was agreed to 'by a very great majoritie', and Dering thought the debate had shown that 'the major part of the House are inclin'd to an accomodacon'.[31] But when the address was reported on the 20th it was evidently a victory for the hardliners. It highlighted the evils of a popish successor sitting on the throne, and warned that opposition to a catholic king would 'not only endanger the farther descent of the Royall line, but even Monarchy itself'; it called for royal assent to the exclusion and association bills, argued that judges should sit only as long as they behaved well, and requested a remodelling of the commission of the peace and the lieutenancies; but it did promise supply if the House's demands were met.[32]

The address articulated in public a deal that was already being offered in private, for we know that some of the leaders of the House were involved in negotiations with the Court. They offered to allow the King power to nominate his successor, and to grant supply of £600,000 in return for both Charles's assent to the bill and their own inclusion in a new administration. Probably encouraged by Sunderland and the duchess of Portsmouth, both of

---

[31] Grey, *Debates*, viii. 186–98; *History of the Association* (1682), pp. 8–9; Corpus Christi, Oxford, MS E298, f. 118, Sir William Jones's speech; NLW, Trevor-Owen mss, notes by Speaker William Williams; Kent AO, U1713 C2, Dering to Southwell, 18 December 1680; PRO, 31/3/147, ff. 85–6, Barrillon dispatch, 20/30 December 1680. According to Barrillon, the active members of the address committee were Russell, Hampden, Jones, Cavendish, Montagu and Harbord.

[32] *CJ*, ix. 684–5. Sir Michael Warton told his constituents at Hull that these were 'our desires for the pres[en]t ... but severall other things we should demand' (Hull RO, L985, Warton to Hull, 21 December 1680). For lord chancellor's Finch's notes on the address see Leics. RO, DG7/4958/73 [iii], possibly designed as an outline of how the King should reply.

whom had backed exclusion only to find themselves on the wrong side of the Lords' vote, a cabal known as the Southamptons, consisting of Montagu, Russell, Jones, Winnington, Hampden, Capel and Titus, offered the bargain in return for office.[33] The chances of success seemed to have increased when a rumour circulated that James had written to Charles offering to submit to the proposal.[34] Yet the scheme foundered because of mutual mistrust between the Court and cabals. Burnet, who was informed of the project by Montagu, thought that 'the jealousies upon the king himself were such, that the managers in the House of Commons durst not move for giving money till the bill of exclusion should pass, lest they should have lost their credit by such a motion; and the King would not trust them. So near was this point brought to an agreement, if Montagu told me true.'[35] It is difficult to know exactly when these negotiations had begun, though as early as 19 November the earl of Salisbury had unsuccessfully moved in the Lords for a prorogation in order to allow the bill to be reintroduced in a new session;[36] but it is clear that the negotiations intensified towards the end of December. When reports leaked out, or were deliberately leaked, during the Christmas recess that some of the leaders, including Montagu and Harbord, had been seen at Court, there was an unseemly haste on the part of the intriguers to disassociate themselves from the charge of self seeking.[37] On 30 December Winnington moved that no one was 'to have a place whilst he is a Member of Parliament, without acquainting the House before of it', which Harbord duly seconded; Titus refuted the truth of rumours about his attendance on the duchess of Portsmouth, though Jones, perhaps with one eye still on a legal post, thought the self denial should only apply to offices at Court. The Southamptons were nevertheless attacked by Lee, who paraded his 'country habitation' and wanted to remove the clause that allowed the House to approve the taking of places. Perhaps as Charles had hoped, the leaders of the House were dividing

---

[33] The scheme is mentioned by Barrillon (PRO, 31/3/148, ff. 11–12, Barrillon dispatch, 3/13 January 1681) and is detailed in *HMC Ormonde*, v. 562; *HMC Finch*, ii. 99; Burnet, *History*, ii. 267–8; *England's Concern in the Case of his R[oyal] H[ighness]* (1680), postscript. The earl of Bedford was to be made a duke, 'another earl to be Treasurer' (possibly Salisbury), Sir William Jones was to become Lord Chief Justice, and Col. Titus to be appointed Secretary of State. The plan was a revamping of the negotiations that had taken place with Shaftesbury at the beginning of the session, but this time the earl was omitted (Haley, *Shaftesbury*, pp. 615–16). For the friendship between Jones and Montagu see *Diary of Robert Hooke*. Montagu, Russell, Hampden, Winnington and Jones acted together in early December (PRO, 31/3/147, f. 74, Barrillon dispatch 9/19 December 1680).

[34] *England's Concern* (1680), postscript; Clarke, *James II*, i. 652.

[35] Burnet, *History*, ii. 268. Henry Sidney received information from the Dutch ambassador that Charles was willing to pass exclusion once Parliament resumed sitting after the Christmas adjournment (*Diary of Henry Sidney*, ii. 147).

[36] Newdigate newsletter Lc.1010, 20 November 1680. Harbord had hinted of the scheme in his speech on 15 December (Grey, *Debates*, viii. 155).

[37] *HMC Ormonde*, v. 541; *HMC Finch*, ii. 99.

over suspicions about the integrity of their allies. Never was an exclusionists' crisis more obvious.[38]

The success or failure of the scheme depended on the King's reply to the Commons' address. This was delivered on 4 January 1681, when instead of conceding to the demands, Charles surprised many by recommending MPs to reconsider ways other than exclusion, and by his cheek in requesting supply without redress of grievances[39]. But the old problem of MPs absenting themselves whenever the succession was discussed, a problem made worse by the Christmas recess, forced a deferral of the debate until the House could be 'called over', for the truth was that the leaders of the House headed a very thin crew. Winnington and Titus condemned the absentees as 'not true to their country'; Capel thought it strange to have witnessed the 'industry, pains and charge' Members had expended at elections 'and yet to see them not sit'; and Boscawen suggested physically shutting Parliament's doors as the best way of preventing his colleagues from slipping away.[40] The list of those ordered to be taken into custody for nonattendance included a number of MPs who had supported exclusion in the past, suggesting that even those who had previously committed themselves may now have sought to distance themselves from events at Westminster.[41]

A slightly fuller House sat on the 7th to consider the King's message, but backbench MPs were still in no mood to participate in debate. Perhaps because Members had been stunned by Booth's opening attack on the growth of arbitrary power and threats against anyone who lent money to the King, Capel saw 'no body offering to stand up' to speak, and launched into an invective against Charles's advisers and the King's own sincerity of ruling with Parliament. During the ensuing debate a suggestion that William act as regent 'as an ornament' to James was laughed at, and Cavendish threw caution to the wind by arguing that the duke's religion made him incapable of succeeding to the throne, moving that it should be legal to forcibly resist his accession. Tempers calmed slightly after more moderate interventions by Jones, Foley and Finch, but were recharged by a highly provocative speech from Secretary Jenkins about relying on God's providence rather than legal provisions for the nation's security. The House resolved that only exclusion would suffice, that no money would be granted until it had been passed, and

[38] PRO, 31/3/148, f. 6, Barrillon dispatch, 30 December 1680/9 January 1681; Grey, *Debates*, viii. pp. 222–5; Newdigate newsletter Lc.1025, 28 December 1680.
[39] *HMC Finch*, ii. 100. Charles had still been negotiating with the leaders of the House at this time (PRO, 31/3/148, ff. 11–12, Barrillon dispatch, 3/13 January 1681).
[40] Grey, *Debates*, viii. 235–7.
[41] *CJ*, ix. 699. Nineteen MPs were named, nine of whom had previously shown anti-Court sentiments (Samuel Starkey, Edward Nosworthy, Samuel Rolle, Sir Nathanial Napier, William Glyde, Sir Rice Rudd, Sir Robert Henley, Sir Philip Skippon and Alan Bellingham).

that the King's advisers ought to be removed.[42] The debate is important because it highlights the increasing radicalism of the crisis, moving from provisions against James to include direct action against Charles and his ministers. In part, this extremism may have been deliberate, aimed to provoke a prorogation so that exclusion could be reintroduced. An end to the session did follow only three days later, though not before the House had passed a series of votes, one of which condemned any prorogation that was not intended as a means of allowing the bill's passage.[43] Eight days later Parliament was nevertheless dissolved.

This account of the attempts to obtain exclusion has emphasised the degree to which the measure had become entangled with other expedients, many of which were to come into effect during Charles II's reign, and stressed the uncertainties amongst MPs. But the account of proceedings in the Commons is only part of the whole picture, for measures to safeguard the future were also actively considered in the Lords. Indeed, the fact that lists of the bill's opponents in the Lords were circulated and pinned up in coffee houses demonstrates that contemporaries temporarily turned their attention to the Upper House to see if it could produce a solution to the problems.[44]

After the rejection of the exclusion bill the House of Lords immediately agreed to consider other measures to secure religion and government if a catholic succeeded to the throne. On 16 November Halifax proposed a five year banishment for the duke of York, but this idea was ridiculed by Shaftesbury, who in turn suggested his old project of a royal divorce, and was opposed by Halifax again, as well as by the King.[45] A third measure, for an association of protestants, was far better received, partly because it was not as yet identified with any one faction, and a sub-committee was set up in order to frame such a bill,[46] whilst a fourth bill was also suggested 'for limitations on a popish successor, thereby making him incapable of doing prejudice either to religion or property'.[47] Efforts were therefore directed towards the refinement of these last two measures, though the first two continued to play a part in deliberations.

On 17 November the Lords considered the heads for the limitations bill. It

---

[42] Grey, *Debates*, viii. 260–85; *An Exact Collection*, pp. 243–67; *A Collection of the Substance of Several Speeches*, pp. 11–14.

[43] Grey, *Debates*, viii. 289–90.

[44] NLS, MS 14407, f. 72, Lord Fauconberg to earl of Tweeddale, 16 November 1680.

[45] *Original Papers*, p. 108; Clarke, *James II*, i. 619.

[46] For the text of the 'instrument of Association', dated as having been received from Sir Robert Southwell on 25 January 1679/80, see National Library of Ireland, MS 2395, ff. 239–40. I am very grateful to David Hayton for copying this document for me. For the wording of the association bill found in 1681 in Shaftesbury's possession see BL, Eg. 2979, f. 189. According to Burnet Shaftesbury 'did not like it and never made use of it' (BL, Add. 63057B, Burnet's ms history, f. 60). I hope to work further on the associations promoted in the 1680s and 1690s.

[47] *HMC Ormonde*, v. 488.

was proposed that all ecclesiastical and spiritual benefices in the gift of the Crown be conferred only on pious and learned protestants, that James be stripped of his power of legislative veto should he become King, that if he did succeed to the throne he should be treated as a minor, and that any bill concerning the protestant religion should pass automatically.[48] Further heads were added two days later, but progress was temporarily halted by a resolution to discuss Shaftesbury's proposal for a royal divorce, despite Halifax's denunciation of the latter's motives.[49] According to one newsletter, an extraordinary meeting of the privy council was called on 22 November to discuss the matter, and the following day the divorce was 'with modesty laid by', partly because Shaftesbury was absent, ill with gout, and partly because the King gave 'no encouragement to it, but much the contrary'.[50] Discussion in the Upper House therefore reverted to the limitations bill, or bill for the security of the protestant religion as it was called. In addition to the heads already discussed, the draft provisions included clauses that no forces were to be raised without consent of Parliament; that the Parliament in being at the time of the King's death should sit for six months into the new reign; that if there was no Parliament at the time then the last one should reassemble; and that in the absence of a Parliament a committee would dispose of all offices, subject to the ratification by MPs when they next met. The final bill also included a clause removing the duke's exemption from the 1678 Test Act, disabling him from any office without parliamentary approval. These measures would have imposed a very strict limitation of James's powers as King, with no power to appoint to any office without consent of Parliament.[51] Parliament was effectively to act as regent. On 25 November the Lords ordered the bill to be drawn up 'with all convenient speed', and two days later the bill was ordered to be presented on the 29th, when it duly received its first reading.[52] The second reading occurred on 10 December and the bill was committed to the consideration of the whole House. A number of additional clauses were consequently prepared, and agreed to on 8 January 1681. These included extending the power of a council of forty-one members over foreign policy, the government of Ireland, and banishing James during Charles's life to at least 500 miles from England on pain of treason for himself or his followers.[53] The bill was lost on the prorogation on 10 January, but, had it

[48] LJ, xiii. 674; HMC Lords 1678–1688, p. 209.

[49] LJ, xiii. 678; HMC Lords 1678–1688, p. 209; PRO, 31/3/147, ff. 43–4, Barrillon dispatch, 22 November/2 December 1680.

[50] Newdigate newsletter Lc.1011, 23 November 1680; HMC Ormonde, v. 502. cf. Reresby Memoirs, p. 204.

[51] LJ, xiii. 684; Bod., MS Carte 228, f. 208, 'heads of a bill'; HMC Ormonde, v. 502. A proposal that the next protestant should inherit if the heir marry a catholic was 'laid aside'.

[52] LJ, xiii. 688, 692, 694.

[53] Bod., MS Rawl. A162, ff. 39–40, copy of bill; LJ, xiii. 711, 740; HMC Lords 1678–1688, pp. 222.

passed, would have conferred on Parliament and council powers not achieved even after the Glorious Revolution.

The drafting of the association bill paralleled the progress of the limitations bill. The heads drawn up by Essex, presented to the peers on 23 November, determined that all bishops, peers, voters, MPs, judges, lawyers, local office holders and clergy, including those in Ireland, had to subscribe to the association; that on the King's death all the associators were to take up arms until Parliament sat; that even in Charles's reign the command of the garrisons and ports was to be given to men nominated by the King but approved by Parliament; that the Act was to be read twice a year in church; and was to be compulsory for all over eighteen years.[54] The bill therefore deferred the succession crisis until after Charles's death, but until then militarised the political conflict and specifically justified the use of arms on behalf of Parliament, a direct refutation of the loyalists' fundamental tenets of passive obedience and nonresistance.

It will have become clear that limitations remained on the political agenda long after the defeat of the exclusion bill, though the arena for discussion of them had shifted from the Lower to the Upper House.[55] But it is legitimate to ask why the Lords' bills failed to proceed further, and why they were never sent to the Commons, even though the Lower House clearly needed some kind of direction or initiative. In part, the bills were delayed by Stafford's trial and the Lords' long Christmas break, impediments to rapid progress that contributed to the loss of the bills at the prorogation; but there were also other factors at work. One was the Commons' decision to address the King for the removal of Halifax, an indication of how little support the earl could muster there, and thus how hostile the Lower House would have been to measures of his promoting. Another consideration was the growing extremism of antipathy towards James. On 29 November, the day of the limitations bill's first reading, a Middlesex grand jury indicted the duke of York for popery in an attempt to force the pace in favour of exclusion,[56] and in late December Shaftesbury, Essex and Salisbury launched a bitter attack on the duke of York.[57] Sunderland also saw that the expedients fell between two stools: 'they will generally be thought either ineffectuall, or such as may endanger the monarchy', he told William.[58] Moreover, William himself protested against the limitations, and was now prepared to travel to England to protect his

---

[54] *HMC Lords 1678–1688*, pp. 210–11.
[55] Finch's concessions on 7 January 1681, proposing that Parliament appoint privy councillors, that severe laws be passed against catholics and that the throne pass to the next protestant heir, may nevertheless be seen as part of the limitations package.
[56] Longleat, Thynne mss, vol. xvi, Sir William Coventry to Thomas Thynne, 4 December 1680.
[57] Haley, *Shaftesbury*, p. 612.
[58] Van Prinsterer, *Archives*, v. 443.

interest by promoting exclusion.[59] 'It must not be imagined', he remarked with one eye on the possibility that he would himself succeed to the throne, 'that if they had once taken away from the Crown such considerable prerogatives as are talked of, that they would ever return again.'[60] In this, if not on other matters, James agreed, and castigated the limitations as worse than exclusion because they destroyed the monarchy.[61]

William's campaign to have exclusion pass in order to unite Charles and Parliament against the French was a reminder that once again the European situation was influencing British domestic policy against limitations. Both the Dutch ambassador in London, and his Spanish counterpart Ronquillo, with whom Montagu believed Shaftesbury had secret dealings, worked to obtain the approval of anti-French alliances and supply to enforce them, which they believed could only be achieved once King and MPs agreed on exclusion.[62] The debate on Europe on 27 October, in which Sacheverell and Garraway slighted the treaty with Spain as being no support to the Protestant religion, and which highlighted MPs' suspicions about William, showed the uphill task the envoys faced.[63] Sir William Temple wrote in his memoirs that MPs had laughed at talk of foreign alliances as nothing more than 'Court tricks'.[64] Yet, although the conclusion of treaties was unsuccessful, the arguments used in their favour supported exclusion because the bill was regarded as the best route to domestic unity. In mid December Henry Sidney translated and distributed copies of a memoir written by the Dutch States General which urged an accommodation with Parliament, and another from Spain followed shortly after.[65] Yet, although Sunderland continued to try to convince Charles of the necessity of the policy of exclusion and the Dutch treaty, rumours that an Anglo-Dutch alliance had been concluded actually damaged William's standing in the Commons by increasing fears of the resulting powers of both King and his nephew.[66] The French ambassador did all he could to foster these suspicions of William, and used his contacts amongst

---

[59] BL, Add. 32,681, f. 92, Sidney to Sunderland, n.d.

[60] Dalrymple, *Memoirs*, ii. 307. Halifax reassured the Dutch envoy that the measures only applied to James (Van Prinsterer, *Archives*, v. 454–5).

[61] Bod., MS Clarendon 87, f. 334, James to Hyde, 7 December 1680.

[62] PRO, 31/3/146, f. 119, Barrillon dispatch, 18/28 October; 31/3/147, f. 9, Barrillon dispatch, 28 October/7 November; f. 14, Barrillon dispatch, 1/11 November; f. 69, 6/16 December 1680. The duke of York thought Spain 'would be glad to see a republic settled in England' and that the Dutch 'do not care how little authority there is left to a king' (*Hyde Correspondence*, i. 50)

[63] Grey, *Debates*, vii. 375–6; PRO, 31/3/147, ff. 36–7, Barrillon dispatch, 18/28 November; f. 51, 22 November/2 December 1680.

[64] Temple, *Memoirs*, p. 351.

[65] *Diary of Henry Sidney*, ii. 146; Clarke, *James II*, i. 641–3; *Négociations d'Avaux*, i. 116; *An Intimation of the Deputies of the States General* [1680]; *The Last Memorial of the Spanish Ambassador* (1680).

[66] PRO, 31/3/147, f. 56, Barrillon dispatch, 25 November/5 December 1680.

opposition MPs to hinder promises of supply in relation to the alliances.[67] The diplomatic situation, together with observations that England was sliding towards a republic which was not in France's interest, and the calculation that exclusion might pass, with the consequent success of William's aims, forced France to offer a treaty with Charles. Talks resumed with vigour at the beginning of January, at exactly the time when Charles was dealing with the leaders of the Commons and having to decide whether or not to agree to their demands.[68] The French offer of money thus played an important part in the King's decision not to concede to Parliament, and hence in the rejection of exclusion. In a sense, this was more important than the conclusion of the negotiations with France a few months later, which are usually regarded as the reason why Charles finally broke with Parliament.

COURT CABALS, OCTOBER 1680–FEBRUARY 1681

Charles's dilemma about how to act had been reflected by a paralysed and factional Court, with the old Halifax–Shaftesbury antipathy still very much apparent at the centre of a power struggle in which the succession continued to play an important part. The debate on 15 November inevitably became an oratorical contest between Halifax, who spoke 'incomparably' sixteen times, and Shaftesbury, who was supported by Halifax's former ally, Essex.[69] Attempts by two clergymen, John Tillotson and Gilbert Burnet, to dissuade Halifax from speaking against the exclusion bill had therefore failed because it had 'become a point of honour, and he resolved to value himself upon his managing that matter'.[70] Halifax's zeal against Shaftesbury had also been motivated by envy of Sunderland. According to Temple, Halifax 'saw himself topp'd by Lord Sunderland's credit and station at Court' and consequently resolved to oppose exclusion 'so that falling into confidence with the King upon such a turn, he should be alone chief in the ministry without competitor'. These tactics produced 'an outrageous quarrel' between the two, spiced by Halifax's knowledge of Sunderland's secret meetings with his old rival, Shaftesbury.[71]

Sunderland's position as chief minister during the period of the second Westminster Parliament, on a platform of opposition to France and support for exclusion and William of Orange, was naturally under threat after the defeat of the bill on 15 November. But although his credit plummeted he was not dismissed. Charles simply extended his circle of inner advisers by taking

[67] PRO, 31/3/147, f. 86, Barrillon dispatch, 20/30 December 1680.
[68] PRO, 31/3/148, ff. 8–9, Barrillon dispatch, 3/13 January 1681.
[69] *Original Papers*, p. 108.
[70] T. Birch, *Life of Tillotson* (1752), p. 82; BL, Add. 63,057B, Burnet's ms history, f. 54. Others had also tried to divert Halifax (*Diary of Henry Sidney*, ii. 127).
[71] Temple, *Memoirs*, p. 354.

Halifax, the 'riseing man and first favourit', into his confidence, and also conferring with Hyde, Seymour, Jenkins and the ever-present Arlington.[72] The influence of Halifax and Seymour was recognised by the attack MPs made on them. Even so, their weights did not pull in the same direction. Seymour was impeached for trying to prorogue or dissolve Parliament, but Halifax's advice had been to let it sit in the hopes of raising supply and passing limitations.[73] Charles meanwhile asked his treasury officials whether he could survive financially without Parliament, a question that further divided Hyde and Godolphin.[74] Indeed, there was very little cohesion at Court. Sunderland, Halifax, Hyde and Seymour all held different views about how to deal with Parliament and the succession, forming a smokescreen of opinion behind which Charles could sit and await events.[75] Although James urged his brother to purge Sunderland, Essex, Sidney and Godolphin from government, Charles refused to rush into a reorganisation,[76] with the result that on 18 December Henry Coventry observed the government to be 'in a kind of derout', and he saw little hope of rallying its forces.[77] The attack in the Lords on 21 December on Hyde, Feversham and Legge for 'their too great addiction to the duke' was a further blow,[78] and confusion about the Court's direction only increased as news spread of Sunderland's dealings with the prominent MPs. The King, though outwardly cheerful, kept 'his thoughts very secret', and chatted to his thin and melancholy Court about piety rather than politics.[79] Thus although Charles's decision not to end the session after the vote in the Lords has been seen as part of a shrewd policy to give his critics 'rope enough ... [to] hang themselves', there was little design to the King's action.[80] Sir William Temple privately observed that 'the Lords throwing out the bill have left so many in both Houses desperate, that they are like to runn in with any thing that they can hope will support them against the Duke', a situation

[72] Reresby, *Memoirs*, pp. 203, 205; PRO, 31/3/147, f. 38, Barrillon dispatch, 18/28 November; ff. 49–50, Barrillon dispatch, 22 November/2 December 1680. Charles continued to meet Sunderland daily in late November, but spoke angrily of him to others (PRO, 31/3/147, f. 63, Barrillon dispatch, 29 November/9 December 1680).

[73] PRO, 31/3/147, f. 68, Barrillon dispatch, 6/16 December 1680. For articles of impeachment against Seymour see Grey, *Debates*, viii. 39–40. The House resolved on an address against Halifax on 17 November 1680.

[74] PRO, 31/3/147, f. 69, Barrillon dispatch, 6/16 December 1680.

[75] PRO, 31/3/147, f. 74, Barrillon dispatch, 9/19 December 1680.

[76] James wanted to replace them by lords Chesterfield, Ailesbury, Peterborough and Craven, with Hyde or Clarendon as Secretary, Finch in the Treasury, and to find places for Sir John Chicheley in the Admiralty, George Legge and Sir Christopher Musgrave in the Ordinance, with John Churchill as ambassador to France (*Hyde Corresp.*, ed. Singer, i. 48–51).

[77] HMC *Ormonde*, iv. 528.

[78] PRO, SP104/67, f. 23, Jenkins to William, 21 December 1680. The Commons followed on 7 January 1681 with a similar attack on Feversham, the marquess of Worcester, Clarendon, Hyde, Seymour and Halifax.

[79] HMC *Hastings*, ii. 391; *Ailesbury Memoirs*, i. 37–8; Reresby, *Memoirs*, p. 208.

[80] *Ailesbury Memoirs*, i. 40.

of recourse to extremities that would play into Charles's hands.[81] But it was luck rather than judgment that produced this situation. The King was content to play his usual waiting game (only this time it proved the right thing to do), and the fact that he did not immediately dismiss Sunderland from office suggests that he was content for a while to have a Court looking in two different directions.

Danby believed that the King could only rescue his position if he gave up 'mixt councills w[hi]ch hitherto have alwaies undone his businesse'. But although it was evident that Sunderland would eventually be replaced and that without his support the duchess of Portsmouth would withdraw from meddling in politics, it was not clear which group would emerge as the dominant faction.[82] Charles was forced to take a more active role, and personally made the decision to dissolve Parliament, though such a breach was opposed in council by Sunderland, Godolphin, Salisbury, Essex, Fauconberg and Carr, who were refused permission to speak. In fact, the credit for the dissolution probably belonged to Seymour, who had joined with Danby and Charles's go-between with the French ambassador, the earl of St Albans.[83] Halifax, resenting the Commons' address against him on 7 January, which labelled him as the promoter of popery and the betrayer of the nation, 'had thoughts to retire from Court', but he too had probably finally supported the decision.[84] It was thought that Seymour and Halifax, 'the great and ... only councillors' now planned to 'clear the Court of all factions'.[85] There was immediate talk of 'great alterations att Court, and of the retiring of great men into the country', including the lord chancellor,[86] though in reality only Sunderland was replaced as Secretary by Seymour's candidate, the earl of Conway.[87]

Although apparently poised in a position of strength with the King, Halifax and Seymour nevertheless found it difficult to work together. The former sought limitations as a means of reconciling King and Parliament, and

[81] BL, Add. 32,681, f. 100, to Henry Sidney, 30 November 1680. cf. Temple's letter to William, printed in Van Prinsterer, *Archives*, v. 445–9.

[82] *HMC Ormonde*, v. 551; PRO, 31/3/148, f. 26, Barrillon dispatch, 17/27 January 1681; BL, Add. 28,053, f. 222, Danby to Conway, 12 January 1681. cf. *HMC Ormonde*, v. 46 for James talking of 'half councells'. There was even talk of Portsmouth going abroad to live 'as a recluse' (All Souls, MS 171, f. 132, newsletter, 24 January 1681).

[83] BL, Add. 18,730, entry in Anglesey's diary for 18 January 1681; *Original Papers*, p. 115; All Souls, MS 171, f. 131, newsletter, 18 January 1681; *HMC Ormonde*, v. 563; PRO, 31/3/148, f. 33, Barrillon dispatch 24 January/3 February 1681.

[84] Reresby, *Memoirs*, p. 210.

[85] *Diary of Henry Sidney*, ii. 159.

[86] Hull RO, L994, Warton to Hull, 18 January 1681; Newdigate newsletter, Lc.1231, 18 January 1681; Congress newsletter 7/150, 20 January 1681; All Souls, MS 171, f. 132, newsletter 25 January 1681.

[87] Clarke, *James II*, i. 659. Daniel Finch had been offered the post, but turned it down.

possibly to that end began meetings with the duke of Buckingham;[88] whilst Seymour, although a supporter of limitations, seems to have been much more sympathetic to the rising power of the duke of York, and allied himself with the Hyde faction.[89] Seymour's triumph seemed possible when Temple and Essex, with whom Halifax could possibly have worked, were dismissed from council,[90] and Halifax retired to the country;[91] but Seymour's dominance was curtailed ironically by the growing influence of York, and his champion, Hyde.[92] Thus when Seymour also left London briefly at the beginning of February, Hyde was left in control, aided by new appointments of Yorkists to the council,[93] and Arlington, whose ascendancy Halifax suspected, joined with him.[94] On his return to London, Seymour went to lodge with the earl of St Albans,[95] with whom Hyde was working on the secret negotiations with the French; and James naturally threw his weight behind the Anglo-French alliance.[96] Not surprisingly in this confused and complex situation, jealousies continued to distract courtiers throughout March 1681,[97] and Jenkins wished that the Court's preparations for the new Parliament 'did bear proportion with the diligence of the adverse party'.[98]

THE PUSH FOR EXPEDIENTS, FEBRUARY–MARCH 1681

The political manoeuvrings at Court after the dissolution had important consequences for the succession debate. Although Sir Edward Dering thought there was still some chance that the exclusion bill might pass, its supporters and the Williamites at Court had been purged, leaving the limitationists and Yorkists in an uneasy alliance.[99] Charles let it be known that he would offer the new Parliament some 'proposition', though he would not clarify what he meant by that, leaving observers at a loss as to how he

---

[88] PRO, 31/3/148, f. 30, Barrillon dispatch, 20/30 January 1681. James expected Halifax to promote a bill that limited him as a minor when King (*HMC Dartmouth*, p. 47).

[89] *HMC Dartmouth*, p. 46.

[90] *Sidney Letters*, p. 60, (misdated as 1678/9); PRO, PC.2/69, f. 192, privy council register, 24 January 1681.

[91] *Savile Corresp.* pp. 177–8.

[92] PRO, 31/3/148, f. 74, Barrillon dispatch, 7/17 March 1681.

[93] PRO, 31/3/148, f. 41, Barrillon dispatch, 1/10 February 1681. The earls of Chesterfield, Oxford and Ailesbury had been made privy councillors on 26 January and the earl of Craven on 9 March 1681.

[94] PRO, 31/3/148, f. 64, Barrillon dispatch, 21 February/3 March 1681; BL, Longleat mss, M/904, reel viii, vol. xv, f. 23, Halifax to Thynne, 2 February 1681.

[95] PRO, 31/3/148, f. 68, Barrillon dispatch, 1/10 March 1681.

[96] Dalrymple, *Memoirs*, ii. 295.

[97] Reresby, *Memoirs*, p. 217; PRO, 31/3/148, f. 74, Barrillon dispatch, 7/17 March 1681.

[98] *HMC Ormonde*, v. 599.

[99] Kent AO, U1713 C2, f. 35, Dering to Southwell, 19 January 1681. Godolphin, always Sunderland's junior partner, nevertheless retained his seat in council.

intended to act.[100] Even James did not know Charles's mind, though he suspected that Halifax's bill of banishment would be promoted.[101] Yet Halifax had few allies. Sunderland shrewdly observed that although the King may have been sincere in espousing expedients, 'I do not thinke so of any man about him. It is an extraordinary method to remove all that would be for any fair propositions, and then make them. The distrust is so great that the difficultyes will be almost insuperable.'[102] Similarly Temple thought the project would be 'but the rest of an expedient that was thought of before that Parliament broke, and which, for ought I know, might have done then, but I doubt not now'.[103] Only gradually did details of Charles's plan emerge, and even those seemed half-formed. On 23 February he informed the council about the speech he would give in Oxford, in which he proposed James's banishment until his own death, though a variety of other measures were also being actively discussed at Court, including an exclusion bill against all catholics, a bill declaring the duke's children to be his heirs, and a royal divorce. The scheme most talked of, however, was a regency.[104] According to Barrillon, it was Halifax and the ever-resourceful Arlington who had made the regency proposal, but Halifax may have been inspired by Burnet and Littleton, who are known to have 'dressed up a scheme of this' and showed it to him and Seymour, who both liked it.[105] Most importantly, so did the King. Discussions were nevertheless interrupted when Charles listened to approaches from Monmouth and malcontent MPs. On 8 March it was reported that Charles was 'off' expedients 'to the great dissatisfaction of the ministers', and that he would restore Monmouth to favour 'to oblige his Parliam[en]t'.[106] James thought Charles was also again offered money in return for exclusion.[107] William added his weight behind exclusion, though Hyde told him that the Prince was not asking for 'an accommodation but a submission',

---

100 PRO, SP104/67, f. 28, Jenkins to William, 18 January 1681; Bod., MS Carte 222, f. 236, newsletter, 22 January 1681; Congress newsletter, 7/151, 22 January 1681; Van Prinsterer, *Archives*, v. 478.
101 *HMC Dartmouth*, p. 56.
102 BL, Add. 32,681, f. 157, Sunderland to Sidney, 4 February 1681. This distrust was evident in another attempt to indict James for recusancy (see All Souls, MS 243, f. 172, 'The case of vindicating his R.H.').
103 *Diary of Henry Sidney*, ii. 177, referring to the idea of 'the kingdom to be governed by a protector and Council and the Prince of Orange to be the protector'.
104 *CSPD 1680–1*, p. 184; PRO, 31/3/148, f. 68, Barrillon dispatch, 1/10 March; f. 70, Barrillon dispatch, 3/13 March 1681; PRO (Kew), FO.95/567, 3/13 March 1681; *Négociations d'Avaux*, i. 149–50, which claims that William wanted to rule as joint regent with the duke of Hanover. Barrillon believed that Seymour masterminded the plans.
105 Dalrymple, *Memoirs*, ii. 311; Burnet, *History*, ii. 281.
106 *HMC Le Fleming*, p. 180; Nottingham University Library, DDSR 219/14, L. Champion to Halifax, 8 March 1681.
107 Clarke, *James II*, i. 670.

and advised him to use his influence to persuade the opposition to back the expedients.[108] William was at a complete loss as to how to proceed.[109]

Despite his wobbling resolve, Charles opened Parliament on 21 March by proposing that 'the administration ... be putt in protestant hands in relation to a successor'.[110] Once again we have to question the King's sincerity. Was this speech a mere propaganda exercise, as he later seemed to imply, or was Charles genuinely seeking a solution?[111] The answer is that it was both. The King was always reluctant to follow a single clear-cut policy, and his offer brought the best of both worlds: he offered a last chance for a settlement, but if it failed he could only gain advantage from the obstinacy of the Commons, whose leaders he hoped to divide.[112]

On 24 March, as the House was on the point of rising, Carew moved for the exclusion bill, but Birch and Ernley (who had regained his seat) countered that expedients ought to be considered first, and the debate was adjourned.[113] Barrillon reported that the parliamentary leaders were divided between those who wanted to continue the policies of the last session and those who wanted to offer Charles money to persuade him to pass exclusion,[114] but others thought the deferral to consider expedients an 'artifice to make a shew to the world that they have tryed all methods and finde ... onely [exclusion] effectuall'.[115] Attention now turned to events in the Lords, where Shaftesbury proposed that Charles settle the Crown on the duke of Monmouth, the first public declaration of the alliance between the duke and the earl. Charles replied that he would be happy if he had a legitimate child who could reign, but that he would sooner lose his life 'than ever part with any of [his] Prerogative, or betray his Place, the Laws, or the Religion, or alter the true succession of the Crown, it being repugnant both to conscience and Law'. Shaftesbury suggested making a law legitimising Monmouth but Charles replied it could not be done 'without overthrowing all Religion, and all Law'.[116] The next day the King asked Shaftesbury if no other expedient but exclusion could be found, and although the earl replied that there was none, the King suggested that Shaftesbury and two others should meet him and two of his advisers, and 'he doubted not but he should find out a better expedient'. Shaftesbury wittily retorted that the meeting should take place

---

108 Van Prinsterer, *Archives*, v. 484.
109 *Diary of Henry Sidney*, ii. 182.
110 Hull RO, L1000, Warton to Hull, 21 March 1681; Grey, *Debates*, viii. 291–2.
111 Clarke, *James II*, i. 673.
112 Henry Sidney thought it would have had more chance of success if the King had outlined his scheme himself (PRO [Kew], FO.95/567, 21 April/1 May 1681).
113 Grey, *Debates*, viii. 295–6.
114 PRO, 31/3/148, ff. 91–2, Barrillon dispatch, 24 March/3 April 1681.
115 *HMC Finch*, ii. 106; Clarke, *James II*, i. 671–2.
116 *The Earl of Shaftesbury's Expedient* (1681); Loyal Protestant no. 10, 24 March 1681; PRO, 31/3/148, f. 94, Barrillon dispatch, 28 March/7 April 1681.

in Arlington's chambers because the latter had good wine, which he thought
would be the best thing to come out of the meeting.[117]

Encouraged by these exchanges, the exclusionists in the Lower House met
the limitationists head on. On 26 March Clayton moved for exclusion, but
Ernley promoted the regency as well as provisions for a Parliament to sit at
Charles's death.[118] Littleton added that James could be banished 500 miles
on pain of forfeiting his estates, and that commissioners should be sent
immediately to the Prince and Princess of Orange to obtain their oaths that
they would enforce such a regency. These proposals were later published as
The Heads of the Expedient Proposed in the Parliament at Oxford. They
suggested that if the duke of York had a son he was to be educated as a
protestant; that the regent was to nominate the privy council, possibly subject
to parliamentary approval; that it would be treason to take up arms on
James's behalf or to say that possession of the title of King purged him of the
disabilities of the act; that an oath was to be tendered to civil and military
officers to abide by the act; that a Parliament in Scotland should pass the same
act;[119] that if the duke returned from exile he was to be excluded and
sovereignty would be entirely invested in the Regent; that papists should be
banished; and that their children would be educated as protestants. The
document concluded that this would lay a sure foundation for a league with
Holland against France. These tactics and bill heads were drawn up before the
debate, probably given to Court speakers,[120] and may also have been shown
to opposition MPs in order to persuade them to support it.[121]

Yet 'exclusion was the word' and the House resolved, with only about
twenty dissenting voices, to bring in the bill.[122] There were a number of

---

[117] Haley, *Shaftesbury*, p. 635.

[118] Grey, *Debates*, viii. 309–10, 315; Leeds AO, Mexborough (Reresby) mss 17/27a, 'Abstract
of Saterdays debate March 26'; *Dering Diaries*, pp. 122–4.

[119] Later in the year when a Parliament did sit in Scotland Lord Belhaven was sent to the Castle
for proposing limitations on the Crown which, James wrote in a letter to William, 'is a thing
not suffred here' (Van Prinsterer, *Archives*, v. 514).

[120] Hyde claimed that Charles had 'commanded all his servants in the House of Commons, to
promote [expedients] the most that was in their power' (Van Prinsterer, *Archives*, v. 490).
Draft 'Heads of Expedient touching the Succession' are among Jenkins's papers (All Souls,
MS 242, f. 114), and list the points made in the printed sheet, together with a note 'to try if the
House will turn itself into a Committee of the whole House'. The House refused to do so
(Van Prinsterer, *Archives*, v. 488) The document in Jenkins's papers also added that on the
King's death 'the last Parli[a]m[en]t that sate, doe of course, convene; and do continue
sitting, for a time limited, even after that the Regent is enter'd upon the Governm[en]t'.

[121] Bod., MS Jones 17, ff. 212–32, ms tract, suggests that an eminent Member 'was consulted
about the expedient then proposed, & did not only seem to approve it, but promised his
assistance for carrying it in the House, & yet after consulting with his pillow, opposed it with
the greatest violence imaginable the next day'.

[122] Reresby, *Memoirs*, p. 221; *Dering Diaries*, p. 122. Parliamentary control of the militia, fleet,
garrisons, an association of protestants had again been mooted as demands to be made
alongside the bill (Reresby, *Memoirs*, pp. 223–4; Van Prinsterer, *Archives*, v. 489).

reasons for the rejection of the regency proposal. First, it was put forward by recent and not very effective recruits to a weak Court which was mistrusted. The 'men of expedients' never operated as a coherent pressure group. Although Powle and Birch had pressed on 24 March for the consideration of expedients other than exclusion, and Meres and Littleton supported the regency proposal on the 26th, the latter was thought 'too high spirited' to work with Halifax; Birch and Vaughan actually spoke against it; Meres and Lee were named to the committee to draw up the exclusion bill; neither Powle nor Garraway are known to have spoken in the crucial debate; Finch was absent; and the King had even dissuaded Sir William Temple from being elected to the Parliament.[123] The Court had tried to rely on the leaders of the 1670s Country party, but with as little success as Danby had found when he had tried a similar tactic in 1679.[124] Their failure to carry the House is a neat illustration of how politics had changed from the 1670s.

Secondly, the rejection of the scheme showed the strength of MPs' suspicions of William. Hampden put this bluntly when he said that Parliament might not intend the Princess of Orange to be the beneficiary of her father's misfortune.[125] William, the nation's saviour only seven years later, was·in 1681 considered to be part of England's problems. Monmouth, on the other hand, was more popular and Secretary Conway believed that had the duke been nominated as the regent 'there were very probable grounds to beleeve they would have accepted it'.[126] Thirdly, Hyde reported that in private the leaders of the House acknowledged that the proposal 'might goe a great way to quiett men's minds, but, as they were of the Parliament, they had engaged themselves so farr in the Exclusion, they could not recede; they should be ruined in their reputations and interests, if they should be guilty of such a change in their resolutions'.[127] Exclusion had developed a self-propelling logic, based on informal pressures such as reputation and interest, and had become part of the structure of political groupings in the House; to that extent, there was a party dependent on exclusion. Moreover, Birch claimed that 'where ten were of the mind for this bill a twelve-month ago, there are an hundred now that will bleed for it'.[128]

Two more general factors were also important in the rejection of the regency. The first was that the nature of the expedients in case James

---

[123] HMC Ormonde, vi. 5.
[124] Browning, Danby, i. 312, 321.
[125] Leeds AO, Mexborough (Reresby) MS 17/27a. In June 1680 Hampden had said that a league with the Dutch meant that 'we shall have the Prince of Orange here with an army' (Russell Letters, p. 117).
[126] Van Prinsterer, Archives, v. 492. cf. Foxcroft, Halifax, i. 290 n.2; PRO (Kew), FO.95/565, d'Avaux dispatch, 10/20 July 1679.
[127] Van Prinsterer, Archives, v. 491.
[128] Grey, Debates, viii. 330.

succeeded to the throne had changed. Until 1681 limitations had been proposed in order to appeal to moderates, but they had also found favour with some of those with commonwealth principles,[129] such as John Wildman,[130] Algernon Sidney,[131] the duke of Buckingham[132] and Henry Nevile, whose *Plato Redivivus*, a tract arguing for limitations on royal power, was printed prior to the Oxford Parliament and was 'much read by the discontented partie'.[133] According to Burnet, in 1679 Halifax had therefore sought to bolster his limitations proposals by encouraging their radical, as well as their moderate, supporters. He had 'studied to infuse in some a zeal for a commonwealth', saying that limitations would bring one in,[134] and at least one MP shared his opinion. Littleton declared that the commonwealth party was mad to oppose limitations which

seem'd so advantageous to public liberty that a man that was fond of it would have wished for a Popish King for the sake of the limitations, and it was very indecent for many of them to pretend a zeal against them because they would bring on a change of Governm[en]t when it was visible that there was nothing which they desired more earnestly.[135]

---

[129] J. Walker, 'The Republican Party in England from the Restoration to the Revolution 1660–1688' (Manchester Ph.D. 1930), chapter 8, 'The Republicans and the Exclusion Bill'; Z. Fink, *The Classical Republicans* (Northwestern University Studies, no. 9, 1945), pp. 136–9.

[130] M. Ashley, *John Wildman, Plotter and Postmaster* (1947), p. 223.

[131] James recorded that 'Algernon Sidney and the ablest of the republican party said, that if a bill of limitations was once got, they should, from that moment, think themselves sure of a republic' (*Original Papers*, p. 111; Clarke, *James II*, i. 635). Sidney's *Discourses Concerning Government* argued for a limited monarchy. For William Penn's belief in a contract form of government and his links with Sidney see M.M. Dunn, *William Penn: Politics and Conscience* (Princeton, 1967), pp. 32–41, 56. Scott argues that 'it would be missing the point to say that he supported limitations over exclusion, or vice versa' (*Restoration Crisis*, p. 147).

[132] W. Gardner, Lady Burghclere, *George Villiers, Second Duke of Buckingham* (1903), p. 379. On 23 November 1680 Buckingham called for a joint committee of both Houses to find the best methods of securing the protestant religion, a proposal in favour of limitations on James (*LJ*, xiii. 683; PRO, 31/3/147, f. 60, Barrillon dispatch, 25 November/5 December 1680).

[133] Bod., MS Film Dep.936 (Petty Papers), no. 84, Robert Wood to Petty, 1 March 1681. Wood summarised the tract's most important arguments as arguing for annual Parliaments, summoned without royal writs; regulated elections; government by four parliamentary committees (to control foreign affairs, militia, treasury and principal offices of state); rotation of office. For comment on Nevile's work see Robbins, *Two English Republican Tracts*, pp. 67–200; J. Pocock, *The Machiavellian Moment* (Princeton, 1975), pp. 417–420; Z. Fink, *Classical Republicans*, pp. 129–35; C.C. Weston and J.R. Greenberg, *Subjects and Sovereigns* (Cambridge, 1981), pp. 198–9.

[134] Burnet, *History*, ii. 212. Burnet believed that Halifax was more set on the idea of limitations 'because it would bring the prerogative so low that it would be little more than a name' (BL, Add. 63,057B, Burnet's history, f. 49). For common ground between Halifax and Sidney see J. Scott, *Algernon Sidney and the English Republic 1623–1677* (Cambridge, 1988), p. 217; *Restoration Crisis*, pp. 140–4.

[135] BL, Add. 63,057B, Burnet's ms history, f. 49. cf. Vaughan's comment that limitations took 'away all Royal Power and ma[d]e the Government a Commonwealth' (Grey, *Debates*, vii. 251).

Yet instead of an alliance of radicals and moderates in support of limitations, a natural reconciliation of radical ideas had occurred as limitations had become joined with exclusion. By December 1680 the association of protestants, the replacement of royal appointments by parliamentary ones, a fixed session of Parliament and parliamentary control over the guards and revenue, had become demands additional to, rather than alternatives to, exclusion.[136] This development had important consequences. Limitations had encouraged some MPs to consider circumscribing the powers of the monarchy under Charles rather than under a popish successor, a move which understandably frightened the King, who regarded the association as 'a deposing of himself'.[137] Daniel Finch had noted in 1679 that Shaftesbury had argued that limitations would introduce a republic,[138] and as the crisis wore on, Charles was to see the truth in this objection. Limitations had thus at once been a measure sponsored by the Court and a measure supported by some of those who wished to see the power of the Court restricted, a paradox that weakened the proposals' chances of acceptance both by the Court and by Parliament, and which forced Charles to shift the terms of the discussion from constitutional change to a regency under which the powers of the monarchy would be left largely intact.[139] Once this shift had occurred it was natural that radical support for expedients should have withered away.

The anomaly that limitations restricted a King's power and yet were sponsored by the Court may also explain why so few tracts had been produced supporting the proposals, or even discussing them.[140] The Court's proposals found few champions amongst those who supported arguments about the King's power. Limitations implied that a king's powers were bound by law and by Parliament, and that there would be penalties for a monarch's breach of the subjects' rights, ideas that sat ill at ease with claims that the King was appointed by God, to whom alone he was responsible.[141] At least one

---

[136] Grey, *Debates*, viii. 186–98 (in the Commons Hampden seems to have been the main voice for the neo-republicans in favour of adding limitations to the demand for exclusion); *CSPD 1680–1*, p. 105; PRO, 31/3/147, f. 82, Barrillon dispatch, 20/30 November 1680. J. Walker, 'Republican Party', p. 231, argues that if the proposals had been accepted the constitution would have been similar to that of 1649 except that there would be a bicameral Parliament and a nominal king.

[137] Burnet, *History*, ii. 266.

[138] *HMC Finch*, ii. 52; Burnet, *History*, ii. 212. James also opposed the limitations on the grounds that they would destroy the monarchy (Bod., MS Clarendon 87, f. 334, letter from the duke of York, 7 December 1680; Van Prinsterer, *Archives*, v. 481).

[139] Littleton explicitly stated that the regency altered the constitution 'the least imaginable' (Grey, *Debates*, viii. 317).

[140] M. Goldie, 'The Roots of True Whiggism', *History of Political Thought*, i (1980), p. 206.

[141] John Mathew, the loyalist author of *Certain Material and Useful Considerations* (1680), p. 7, rejected limitations outright. He argued that 'where Power is invested in any, and by custom and free consent is made Hereditary, I conceive it cannot afterwards be *limited* with other conditions that at first was agreed on, without the consent of him that hath it'.

pamphlet, *Advice to the Men of Shaftesbury* (1681), mentioned limitations more out of a desire to show the illogicality of the exclusionists' arguments than seriously to champion the proposals. On the other side, the majority of opposition writers preferred to glory in the loyalists' discomfort about the proposed limitations on royal powers. *A Just and Modest Vindication* (1681) pointed out that courtiers sometimes claimed the monarchy to be by divine right and at other times allowed that the King could be limited by law, concluding that the Court's proposals must have been drawn up only to delude Parliament and the people.[142] Similarly *The Character of a Popish Successor Compleat* (1681) argued that if limitations were possible 'then there's Jure divinum quite laid aside: for Divine Right of Birth entitles a Prince to the Power as well as the name of a King, and if that Right be sacred and inviolable, no one part of it more than another ought or can lawfully be alienated'.[143] The author of *A Dialogue at Oxford* (1681) also showed that 'giving a solitary and empty Name of King to one Man, and placing the Execution of the Kingly Power in the hands of another, does not only divide the office from the person ... but strikes at the very Being of Monarchy itself'.[144] Other opposition pamphlets simply highlighted the insincerity, or the impracticality, of the Court's proposals.[145] It was left to a few individuals, most notably Henry Nevile, to argue out the idea in print.[146] *A Letter from a Student* (1681), *The Protestants' Remonstrance* (1681), *The State and Interest of the Nation* (1680), *Religion and Loyalty* (1681), *An Answer to a Late Pamphlet entitled A Character of a Popish Successor* (1681), *The True Englishman* (1681) and a manuscript tract entitled 'An Answer to the Vindication of the Last Two Parliaments' did all advocate limitations to some degree,[147] even if only in passing; but most of them did so only in 1681, after the debate in favour of them had been lost and, significantly, when limitations had evolved into proposals for a regency.

The second general point about the failure of the regency related to the prospect of civil war, which many felt was brought nearer by the prospect of a clash between James and his regent William. As Jones remarked, 'if there must be an army to maintain the bill of exclusion, there must be four armies to

---

[142] *A Just and Modest Vindication*, pp. 32–3. For the question of authorship of this tract, and further discussion of it, see chapter 10.

[143] *The Character of a Popish Successor Compleat*, p. 28.

[144] *A Dialogue at Oxford* (1681), p. 19.

[145] *The Character of a Popish Successor* (1681), p. 21; *The Case of Protestants in England Under a Popish Prince* (1681), p. 31; *Reasons for His Majesties Passing the Bill of Exclusion* (1681), p. 5; *Pereat Papa* (1681), p. 4; *Mr Hunt's Postscript* (1682), preface.

[146] In the first version of his history Burnet also claimed to have written a treatise in 1679 supporting limitations (BL, Add. 63,057B, ff. 49–50). The tract may be *A Few Words among Many* first published in 1679 and reprinted in 1681 as *The Moderate Decision*.

[147] Bod., MS Smith 17, 'An Answer to a Vindication', ff. 212–32.

maintain the expedient'.[148] The measures to settle the succession had often been debated less on ideological grounds than in terms of whether they would cause or avoid war. The crux of the matter was, as Secretary Coventry asked, 'How will that word "secure" be interpreted?' Thus in May 1679 exclusion had been condemned as likely to 'entail a war for ever upon England' and Capel had argued that 'the safest way to preserve us, is not to take away the duke's right to the Crown'. 'How little security have we,' asked Powle, 'that this exclusion of the duke ... shall not end in a civil war?' The supporters of exclusion did not at first deny the possibility that the bill would lead to war, but still thought it the safest option available: 'Do what you can, all may come to blood; but you will secure the Protestant Religion by making the Duke incapable of the Succession, by Act of Parliament', Foley told the House.[149] By 1680 the supporters of the bill admitted that it needed to be backed up by an armed association of protestants; but they were increasingly sure that the alternatives were by then more dangerous. When, on 2 November, Hyde asserted that exclusion would lead to war and questioned 'whether a civil war is more dangerous than a Popish successor?', Birch replied that the nation should not fear such a war if the alternative was 'idolatry'. 'We are now come to that pass', agreed Boscawen, 'that we must be either papists or protestants, one or other, and I see no expedient in that case'.[150] Both sides had tried to use the spectre of war to win their point, and both had used the slogan of 'security'; but the longer the matter went unresolved the less expedients seemed to offer safeguards against war. Capel, a convert to exclusion, argued against the position he had taken in 1679 and claimed that if the bill did not pass 'all the nation will be in blood'.[151] Denial of the bill was itself regarded as increasingly dangerous. By 1681 such attitudes had hardened. Swinfen declared that 'all the Expedients have been to increase the fears of the kingdom, and to hasten our undoing', and Vaughan thought 'the Regency must be supported by war as well as the Bill of Exclusion'.[152] Regency and limitations schemes were thus opposed because of their risk of increasing, not decreasing, the chances of conflict by allowing James the legal title of King.

The rejection of the regency expedient spelt the end for the Oxford Parliament. On 28 March the Commons only had time to read the exclusion bill for the first time before black rod knocked on the door to summon MPs to hear the King's speech of dismissal. Sir John Reresby recorded in his diary that 'it was plane by this dissolution ... that the King would not relinquish his brother, and did not thinke of calling another Parlament of a long time'.[153]

---

[148] Grey, *Debates*, viii. 322.   [149] Grey, *Debates*, vii. 242–56.
[150] Grey, *Debates*, viii. 402–5.   [151] Grey, *Debates*, viii. 457.
[152] Grey, *Debates*, viii. 312, 327. [153] Reresby, *Memoirs*, p. 223.

'Now is the grand crisis, of all this political ferment, over', remarked North, and Burnet observed that 'the Court took a new ply, and things went in another channel'.[154] Part of the new resolution had come from the more coherent group of advisers with which Charles now surrounded himself. The most flamboyant of these was Seymour, who had helped advise the timing of the dissolution, and in whose coach Charles had left Oxford.[155] In mid April Seymour resigned his lucrative post of treasurer of the navy, obviously in hopes of higher office, and Charles was observed to be forever in his company and that of his cronies, Conway and Ranelagh.[156] But the hoped-for preferment never came and Seymour's imperiousness eventually proved his undoing.[157] He lost influence to Halifax, who was described in July as 'the entire favourite', an adviser always hovering to give advice but shrinking from embracing power too tightly.[158] He shared power with Hyde, the negotiator of the French alliance, who was raised to the peerage at the end of April as a sign of his growing favour.[159] Charles had finally found a Court in which internal jealousies certainly still existed but which were not sufficiently serious to impair smooth administration, partly because the tensions were not exploited or deepened by the pressure of a parliamentary session. With a more united council, and the indefatigable Jenkins as secretary of state, central government was relatively strong. But perhaps more importantly, it was by 1681 buttressed by a tide of loyalty in the country which had not been there to shore up earlier administrations. In 1688 the dependence of the state on the church and anglican gentry would be one of the Crown's weaknesses; but in 1681 it was its major strength.

CONCLUSION

The rejection of the exclusion bill by the House of Lords on 15 November 1680 marks the beginning of the exclusion crisis proper, or, more accurately, a crisis for the exclusionists, who began to differ over how to proceed to achieve their aim. No sooner had exclusion become the most important item on the political agenda than the latent tensions within the exclusionist camp became apparent. The jealousies among the parliamentary leaders came to a head around Christmas 1680, when a cabal known as the Southamptons offered Charles money in return for office and his assent to the bill. In the event, Charles turned the proposal down, partly because, with crucial timing, France decided that it was not in its interests to allow Charles's power to

---

154 North, *Examen*, p. 106; Burnet, *History*, ii. 286.
155 Luttrell, *Brief Relation*, i. 72; *Ailesbury Memoirs*, i. 57.
156 Luttrell, *Brief Relation*, i. 76–7; HMC *Ormonde*, vi. 59.
157 *History of Parliament*, iii. 418.
158 Reresby, *Memoirs*, p.227.   159 HMC *Ormonde*, vi. 48.

crumble. Rather than having to concede to parliamentary demands, Charles could therefore look forward to restored relations with Louis XIV. This undercut the Commons' most useful tool, the lure of supply, and the King's resolve against exclusion prompted howls of anger in charged and impassioned debates and resolutions.

Yet the desire to pass exclusion should not obscure the renewed interest in other expedients to settle the succession problem, particularly those promoted in the Upper House. The heads of the limitations bill offered the most stringent curtailment of royal authority so far envisaged, whilst the association bill, promoted by Essex, would have militarised the conflict and ensured that Parliament, backed by arms, would decide the succession issue on Charles's death. Yet William of Orange, with a shrewd eye to the future, threw his weight against any restriction of royal power. Moreover, the type of restrictions proposed in the Lords as an alternative to exclusion were increasingly being voiced in the Commons as a means of buttressing exclusion.

The Court had been paralysed for much of the 1680–1 session by divisions between Essex, Sunderland and the duchess of Portsmouth, who supported exclusion, and Halifax, Hyde and Seymour who opposed it; by personal rivalries between Halifax and Sunderland; by differences between Halifax and Seymour over Parliament's sitting; and between Hyde and Godolphin over the state of the King's finances. Charles did nothing to resolve the chaos, using the confusion as a cover for his own manoeuvres and freedom of action, and although the dissolution of Parliament in January 1681 ushered in a minor purge of Sunderland, Essex and Temple, the Court continued to be riven by jealousies. Although Charles decided to offer an 'expedient', in the form of William's regency if James succeeded to the throne, Halifax and Seymour were unable to work together on the project. The latter sided with the York faction, leaving Halifax isolated. The regency proposal was also doomed to failure because Charles had purged the Williamites from Court, and the 'men of expedients' recruited from the old country party of the 1670s were no longer able, and in some cases did not even try, to sway the House. Moreover, William was not popular amongst MPs, who in any case felt they had engaged themselves too far to retreat from exclusion. The fact that, unlike the limitations previously on offer from the Court, the regency did nothing to curtail the powers of the Crown, further ensured that the scheme did not satisfy MPs, and, with impasse reached in only a week, Charles dissolved Parliament.

It has been argued over the last three chapters that weakness at Court between 1678 and 1681 created a power vacuum. The collapse of Danby's administration had left the King without any one group at Court on which he could rely for advice. Forced to adopt an experiment in council, the mixture of factions had proved disastrous and had brought Charles to an almost desperate plight by the winter of 1679–80. In the spring of 1680, however, the triumvirate of the 'Chits' did offer some stability and coherent policy, but this ministry too dissolved under latent and external pressures. The autumn and winter of 1680 witnessed a struggle at Court amongst the different interest groups, and it was only early in 1681 that a more unified Court, purged of its exclusionist element, emerged. During this process the succession had played an important part in the struggle for power. Accepting that the succession problem was intertwined with the political manoeuvrings at Court has thrown up a greater degree of factionalism than is usually admitted for the period, with rivalries at Court and in Parliament helping to shape the course of the crisis, which passed through different levels of intensity. The narrative has also placed the push for the exclusion bill in a wider context, within a succession crisis, rather than a simple exclusion crisis. Once the bill against James was adopted by the Commons in May 1679 discussion about other means to settle the nation did not cease, even when Parliament was not sitting. The King was forced by necessity to listen to proposals made to him, and, by examining the discussions at Westminster and Whitehall about the limitations and expedients, it has been possible to show how political considerations as much as ideological ones determined the lines of confrontation. Part of those considerations included the state of Europe, and it was no coincidence that Charles should resolve both his diplomatic and domestic dilemmas at the same time.

Yet the struggle at Court for the King's ear had not been resolved by any decisiveness on Charles's part. In a sense, he did not so much find a ministry, as find one foisted on him by the logic of his reluctance to pass exclusion; in return he gained some of his new-found resolution after 1681 from those around him. For most of the period the King's short-term and confusing policies had exacerbated many of the problems he faced. By trying to keep all his options open, and listening to more than one adviser, he had encouraged and maintained divisions within the Court. For Charles the idea of a balanced policy meant pursuing mutually contradictory policies simultaneously, and the crisis was thus in part one about his own style of government. It is possible, of course, that he had deliberately pursued ambiguous policies in order to exploit the differences amongst opposition groups, especially when Parliament was not sitting, and in order to gain valuable time for a reaction of public opinion to occur.[160] But the price of ambiguity had been increased suspicions about the Court's sincerity in seeking a solution, and a belief that

---

[160] North, *Examen*, pp. 98–9, 119. Barrillon commented that negotiations with the opposition always occurred when there was no prospect of Parliament sitting (PRO, 31/3/144, f. 105, Barrillon dispatch, 11/21 March 1680).

the King might concede to exclusion.[161] Both factors worked against a quick settlement of the succession problem. With hindsight Charles's policy was successful; but it is very difficult to find in his clever tactical responses to events any long-term strategy which might justify the idea that he had planned to defeat the bill in the way he did. Indeed it was in part frustration with the King's irresolution, rather than his leadership, that provoked the loyalist reaction in the country. Yet it was also this irresolution that made the polarisation of the country into two parties a much slower and more uncertain development than many have recognised. Without a firm Court party, the opposition to it was inevitably diffuse and loose, made to appear more coherent by the weakness of central control. With this in mind, we are now in a position to review the structure of politics, and to re-examine the state of an opposition party.

[161] 'In the course of these troublesome times the loyalists were never secure in their own minds that the King would stand the siege which had environed him' (R. North, *Lives of the Norths* [1826 edition], i. 379). cf. Temple's claim that exclusion was supported in 1680 partly because MPs believed Charles had secretly resolved to pass it 'upon the observation of such lords of the Court engaged so far in sending away the duke' (*Memoirs*, p. 350).

5

The structure of politics

The previous sections have sought to revise our interpretation of the succession problem, suggesting that concentration on the exclusion bill has oversimplified the complex issue of the succession crisis, that an important aspect of the crisis was the collapse of strong central government, and that factionalism did at least bear some part in fuelling the divisions. These conclusions raise questions about our understanding of the workings of politics at this time: if the Court's weakness contributed to the degree of the crisis, how does this affect our view of a thrusting opposition party? If we question the nature of the debate about the succession, and the place of exclusion on the political agenda, we must necessarily question the structure of politics that has been constructed by earlier analyses of the period, which have argued that the succession controversy cannot be described in terms of faction, and that the crisis therefore heralds the emergence of modern parties, based on the struggle between exclusionists and anti-exclusionists.

J.R. Jones's attack on Robert Walcott's ideas about the importance of familial and factional groupings in late seventeenth- and early eighteenth-century politics in turn laid undue stress on the sophistication of party organisation around one leader, Shaftesbury, and on the importance of the single issue of exclusion. It is no longer necessary to swallow this thesis whole. But equally it is unnecessary to counter it with its mirror image, which denies any existence of party groupings, and reduces the succession debate to a near irrelevance, since that analysis would miss the subtleties and complexities of the situation as much as the first. This chapter attempts to refine rather than to entirely reject the concept of parties.

I hope, therefore, to build on the discussion of political alignments and rivalries already undertaken in the preceding sections, and to explore the caveats about the looseness and fluidity of party politics that are often made by commentators in passing, but all too often ignored in detail. Of course, a complete picture can only be fully achieved by looking at the rest of the country as well as at Parliament, and this will be attempted in the second half of the book; but I wish here to focus mainly on the structure of politics at its

107

most rarefied level, in Parliament, where it has been claimed we should find the development of techniques associated with a modern political party. Although the focus of the following discussion will therefore be on the supporters of exclusion, their activity will be related to that of courtiers. Of course, a juxtaposition of exclusionist or opposition and courtier must also be questioned. The fact that prominent members of the Country party of the late 1670s spoke (however ineffectively) on behalf of the Court in 1681, as we saw in the last chapter, immediately raises questions about how we should, and how contemporaries did, label their positions in the political spectrum.

CONTEMPORARY VIEWS ON A DIVIDED SOCIETY: TERMS AND TERMINOLOGY

One historian's 'faction' can easily be another's 'party' or another's 'interest group', and the existence of 'party' would seem to be very much in the eye of the beholder, now as much as in the seventeenth century. A great deal depends on the explanation of men's motives, a complex and controversial question, and on what we choose to call men who shared similar motives. In the following discussion I shall be examining a number of features which a modern party might reasonably be expected to display, such as leadership, membership, cohesion, discipline and organisation, a long-term ideology and a short-term agenda of means to achieve it. Such criteria may themselves be debatable, though such an argument would quickly become a sterile one if unaccompanied by a review of our knowledge of contemporary attitudes and allegiances. A controversy over political models is only useful if it stimulates new research into the ways politics actually worked.

A good starting point for any discussion of the political framework is to look at contemporary attitudes, in order to assess how those living through the crisis regarded the structure of politics around them. Did they talk in terms of parties, and if so, what did they mean by them? We can begin to answer these questions by looking at contemporaries' revealing use of language. Although there is no need to see every term of abuse as a true reflection of an opponents' character, a brief glance at the terminology used in correspondence and pamphlets can serve as a useful guide to how those rivals were perceived.

Contemporaries did identify 'parties',[1] although one of the striking

---

[1] For a discussion of the evolution of the term party see M. Kishlansky, 'The Emergence of Adversarial Politics in the Long Parliament', *JMH*, xlix (1977), 624–6.

features about the nomenclature of the period is its sheer diversity. Men close to the seat of government often referred to the 'Loyall Party', meaning men loyal to the church and state as they were then established by law;[2] in other words, supporters of the church settlement and the monarchy.[3] But by their opponents such men were given the names of 'Yorkists', 'Tantivies', 'Sham Plotters', 'Masqueraders', 'Church Papists', 'Pensioners', 'God-damnees' and finally Tories.[4] One satire rolled a number of these sobriquets together to form the remarkable compilation 'Toryrory damnee plotshamee Younkercraper'.[5] The critics of the Court, on the other hand, were castigated as the 'adverse party', the 'malignant party', the 'discontented' or the 'restless party', with Ralph Montagu even identifying his own allies as 'mutineers'.[6] Such men were 'patriots', 'True Blues', a reference to the distinguishing ribbons they wore, 'Birmingham Protestants', an allusion to the false groats coined there, 'Whirligigs', and finally Whigs.[7] In 1681 L'Estrange even published his paper, *The Observator*, in the form of a dialogue between Whig and Tory. As he remarked elsewhere, 'calling of names is speaking to the people in a language that they do both understand and believe', a view

2 Sir John Kaye set out 'loyalty to our sovereign and the Protestant religion as wee have it now by law happyly established' as the basic tenets for 'true-hearted and honest-principled men' (Leeds AO, Mexborough mss, Reresby 15/69, Kaye to Reresby, 20 November 1680).
3 For use of the term see UCNW, Mostyn MS 9090, f. 119, newsletter, 30 April 1681; Bucks. RO, Verney mss, M11/33, Cary Gardiner to Sir Ralph Verney, 15 September 1679; *Heraclitus Ridens* no. 20, 14 June 1681; Van Prinsterer, *Archives*, v. 410.
4 For Yorkist see: *The Diaries and Letters of Philip Henry* ed. M.H. Lee (1882), p. 284; *London's Choice of Citizens* (1679), p. 3; *CSPD 1679–80*, p. 429. The term was apparently the invention of Shaftesbury (*Original Papers*, p. 109). For Tantivy ('riding to Rome') see *The Oxford Health* (1681), *A Prospect of a Popish Successor* and *The Time Servers* (1681), all printed in F.G. Stephens, *Catalogue of Political and Personal Satires* (1870), vol. i (1320–1689). For Masqueraders, Church Papists and Pensioners see *The True Protestants' Appeal* (1681), p. 2. For God-damnees and Sham-plotters see *The Character of a Modern Sham Plotter* (1681), pp. 1–2; *The Tryal of Slingsby Bethel* (1681), p. 11; *A New Satirical Ballad* (1679), printed in *Political Ballads of the Seventeenth and Eighteenth Centuries*, ed. W. Wilkins (1860), i. 221. For Tory see p. 150, *A New Ballad with the Definition of the Word Tory* (1682); North, *Examen*, p. 321.
5 *A Sermon prepared to be preached … by the Reverend Toryrory* (1682).
6 *HMC Ormonde*, v. 599; UCNW, Mostyn MS 9090, f. 119, newsletter, 30 April 1681; *Certain Material and Useful Considerations* (1680), p. 9; *HMC Ormonde*, iv. 567; *CSPD 1679–80*, p. 558. For Mutineers see: *Russell Letters*, p. 120; *The Glory of the English Nation* (1681) refers to Londoners as 'mutineers'. Sir John Reresby referred to the 'mutineers' of York (Reresby, *Memoirs*, p. 581).
7 BL, Longleat mss, M/863 reel v, Coventry papers vol. vii, ff. 148–9, Bishop of Bath and Wells to Coventry, 22 February 1679; Bod., MS Jones 17, 'an Answer to a Vindication', f. 212; *The Manner of the Election of the Honourable Approved Patriots* (1681); North, *Examen*, p. 321; *A Letter from Mr Edward Whitaker* (1681), p. 2; *The Character of a Fanatick* (1681), p. 1; *The Character of the True Blue Protestant Poet* (1682); *Essexian Triumviri* (1684), p. 1. Longleat, Muddiman newsbook, 5 March 1681 refers to Birmingham protestants 'who with a counterfeit stamp and a disguised face pass currant among the greater number of people, though upon Examination they prove counterfeit and of the basest of metalls'.

confirmed by the cleric Edmund Hickeringill's reference to 'these dayes of Part-taking and distinguishing who men are for'.[8]

Not only did contemporaries identify parties, but they also saw them in opposition to one another. Division seemed to permeate all aspects of life. The earl of Ailesbury later remembered his shock when, at the time of the Oxford Parliament, the 'rancour' went so far that even in church some MPs 'would not sit promiscuously but separated from us'.[9] By 1681 Norwich was noted as being 'divided into two factions, Whig and Torys ... and both contend for their way with the utmost violence'.[10] Luttrell thought that by 1682

all things are come to that passe ... that if any thing of Whig or Tory comes into question, it is ruled according to the interest of the party; if in the citty of London, against the Tories; if in any of the counties, against the whiggs; so that neither side will believe either of the contrary parties.[11]

Indeed, in late 1681 a London rabble 'went to blows among themselves by the distinction of Whig and Tory';[12] and one defender of the Court thought that 'things are brought to that height of both sides that good bills are often flung out onely because they are brought in by the contrary faction'.[13] Although contemporaries did see parties in conflict with each other, we must nevertheless beware of taking their comments at face value. We must guard against applying the divisions apparent in 1681 to earlier stages of the crisis. Harris, who otherwise draws an excellent account of the propaganda of the period and skilfully points out the overlap in the rhetoric between the two sides, sees a clash of rival Whig and Tory mobs in London before 1681, even though, apart from a few isolated incidents, the phenomenon of two antagonistic groups *active at the same time* in London does not really occur until 1681–2, as he himself at one point seems to admit.[14] The 'fundamental divide along whig–tory lines at the level of the crowd' thus occurred as a consequence of the parliamentary crisis, not during it.[15]

It is therefore worth emphasising that a Whig–Tory party analysis does not

---

[8] *Citt and Bumpkin, the second part* (1680), p. 26; Hickeringill, *The Naked Truth, the Second Part* (1681), p. 52.

[9] *Ailesbury Memoirs*, i. 54–5.

[10] *Prideaux Corresp.* (Cam. Soc. n.s. xv), p. 90.

[11] Luttrell, *Brief Relation*, i. 198.

[12] *CSPD 1680–1*, p. 588.

[13] Bod., MS Jones 17, 'An Answer to a Vindication', ff. 212–32.

[14] Harris, *London Crowds*, chapter 7, especially pp. 157, 172– 80, 188.

[15] This disagreement partly arises because of a difference over dates. Harris considers 1681–3 and 1678–81 as part of one crisis, and to some extent the crisis in London up until the surrender of its charter did grow out of earlier unrest; but I believe that nationally there had been a fundamental sea-change in politics by 1681 which justifies using that date as a termination point. The point may seem pedantic, but is important because, as Jones points out (*First Whigs*, chapter 7), the Whigs were in decline after 1681 and heading for collapse.

explain the cause, or even the course, of the unrest during 1679–81, so much as the results of it, and even then such an approach is only really useful in examining the actions of the extremes of each side. Before 1681, contemporaries used the term party to describe the political situation rather than to explain it, and the labels of Whig and Tory only became common usage in 1681, after the dissolution of the Oxford Parliament.[16] In other words, a Whig–Tory structure imposed on the years before 1681 is not only premature in its chronology, but oversimplifies the situation by blinding us to important shifts in opinion, and in the expression of opinion, that occurred during the period. Some fluidity must be reinjected into the discussion. Even if Robert Webb, who 'among Tories ... was a Whig and when with Whigs a Tory',[17] was an idiosyncratic devil's advocate, we must allow room for the fickle who swam with the tide,[18] and, more importantly, for the body of moderate opinion, or the 'party volant' that Lord Keeper North believed to be crucial in determining the strength of the Court.[19] A number of publications indicate the dislike of divisions, and of being categorised by labels. The title of *The Character of a Good Man, neither Whig nor Tory*, published in 1681, speaks for itself and a broadside entitled *The Condemnation of Whig and Tory*, published in January 1682, proclaimed that its author was 'neither Whig nor Tory, but a Subject truly loyal'.[20] Such men, soon to be identified as 'trimmers', included those who moved away from supporting exclusion when it became politically expedient to do so, as well as those who had never embraced any one measure irrevocably.[21] Their creed was eloquently stated by Halifax in a letter written on 5 March 1681 to Gilbert Burnet: men should go to Parliament

16 Burnet, *History*, ii. 286; R. Willman, 'The Origins of Whig and Tory in English Political Language', *HJ*, xvii (1974), 247–64. A newsletter nevertheless states that two MPs, Sir Richard Newdigate and Thomas Mariet, were dismissed from the Warwickshire commission of the peace 'for being whiggs' (Congress newsletter 6/313, 25 December 1679).

17 *CSPD 1680–1*, p. 646. cf. Lord keeper North's comment that 'some are always of two partys, the country party outwardly, of the court party privately, so are safe whoever thrives' (BL, Add. 32,518, f. 10).

18 A loyalist writer believed that the 'unthinking crowd ... are certainly of his minde that speakes last' (Bod., MS Jones 17, 'An Answer to a Vindication', ff. 212–32).

19 Dalrymple, *Memoirs*, ii. 322. See J.P. Montano, 'Courting the Moderates: Ideology, Propaganda and Parties in the 1670s', (Harvard Ph.D., 1987), for a discussion of the middle ground.

20 BL, C.20 f. 4 (46), endorsement of date by Luttrell. cf. *A Brief Discourse between a Sober Tory and a Moderate Whig* [1682].

21 For a discussion of trimming see D.R. Benson, 'Halifax and the Trimmers', *HLQ*, xxvii (1963–4), 115–34; R. Beddard, 'The Retreat on Toryism: Lionel Ducket, MP for Calne, and the Politics of Conservatism', *Wiltshire Archaeological Magazine* lxxii–iii (1977–8, published 1980), 75–106; S. Pincus, 'Shadwell's Dramatic Trimming', forthcoming. Lord Chief Justice Scroggs identified 'many worthy & sober persons in both Houses, whos minds are sett upon the reall good of the Nation, not hunting after faults only, but rather sorry when they find 'em' (BL, MS Add. 28,091, f. 79).

with no schemes ready drawn, nor resolutions taken beforehand, let there bee no Lords of the Articles to exclude the consideration of anything they do not propose, and then let all men bee tryed and judged whether they do not in their severall stations promote everything that may tend to healing and reconcilement.[22]

Moreover, the 'Whigs' were themselves composed of shades of opinion and different interest groups.[23] Subordinating these groups to fit one umbrella term forces a unity and cohesion which did not always exist.

For these reasons I have not used the terms Whig and Tory until 1681, preferring instead to refer to 'loyalist' and 'opposition' groups. The word 'loyal' was itself a label that was fought over, as will become apparent, and it does not fully distinguish between loyalty to the Court, constitution or the church; but, perhaps because of that ambiguity, it is at least a consistent label used by contemporaries throughout the period 1679–81. The term 'opposition' is a modernisation of the 'adverse party' seen by observers, though the label 'the faction', or Halifax's description of them as 'confederates' might just as easily have been used.[24]

FACTION IN PARLIAMENT?

The obvious question with which to start, given the arguments put forward so far and the fact that Courtiers used the term 'the faction' to describe their opponents, is whether what have been called parties were merely factions. The role accorded to faction in political groupings depended ultimately, as it does for modern commentators, on interpretation of the motives behind men's actions. Loyalists saw little principle guiding their opponents. One satirist depicting the reasons for the political unrest saw a confusing tangle of factors with only self-interest as predominant:

> Paint here Ambition making humble Court,
> To Popular Ears, and shewing Scripture for't.
> There, draw me Envy, and here, private Pique,
> Looking Demure while Deep Revenge they seek.
> Here one who lost his Crown and Bishop Lands,
> Clapping for joy his sacrilegious hands.
> Draw busie jealousie among the Crowd,
> And whispering Fear, and Calumny still Loud.
> Paint Armed Zeal in fighting Gospel Buff;
> Paint what thou wilt, for't to be confused enough.[25]

---

[22] Halifax Letters, p. 540.
[23] Jones, First Whigs, pp. 9–19; J. Ferguson, Robert Ferguson 'The Plotter' (Edinburgh, 1887), pp. 409–10; Observator no. 8, 30 April 1681; J. Childs, '1688', History lxxiii (1988), 407.
[24] Longleat, Thynne mss, vol. xv, ff. 23, 27, Halifax to Thynne, 27 February, 16 April 1681.
[25] New Advice to a Painter (1679), p. 2. cf. Seasonable Advice to all Protestant People of England (1681), p. 37.

Such cynicism was repeated elsewhere. Another writer, possibly even Halifax, identified the restless spirits as 'men turn'd out, or that would get into Court-Imployments, that account themselves slighted or disoblig'd; men of great Ambition, or of Desperate Fortune', and listed ex-courtiers Sir William Jones and Sir Francis Winnington as men who, if taken back into favour, 'wou'd stand up for the Court, as much as now they do against it'.[26] The earl of Essex was cited as another lost sheep that could be enticed back into the fold. As one poet put it, for such men

> Preferment is their End, their only Aim,
> Stop but their mouths with this, they'l soon grow tame'.[27]

It was believed by one pamphleteer that the ambitious man sought election 'to make himself popular, so as to be taken off by the Court party, as now term'd, to have his end that way; or if not, to render things so uneasie to the Publick, as that unless his Ends be answered, we must have things run upon his private ends in to confusion'.[28] Indeed, blaming the crisis on ambitious men was official policy: Charles Bertie was sent as envoy to the German states with an instruction to explain that the unrest in England was due to a 'disaffected party ... because they have not such authority and sway in the government as their ambitions and restless spririts aym at'.[29]

Although such views were usually expressed by loyalists, the author of one pro-exclusion tract also bemoaned 'a sort of men that pass with the Vulgar for very publick Spirits, yet no otherwise for the Publick Good, than as they think it may conduce to their own private Designs'.[30] Sir William Temple complained in 1679 'how ill Lord Chumleigh, Mr Montague and Sir William Carr behave themselves, what mischief they do, because they are not uppermost', whilst the following year Dorothy Sidney observed that the malcontents' aim was 'still themselves, which keeps them from agreeing'.[31] Even Robert Ferguson, Shaftesbury's friend, believed that the earl's main objective had been 'obtaining upon the principal conduct of affairs'.[32] Somewhat hypocritically, William Harbord, who accepted money from the French ambassador and who was not himself above suspicions of place hunting, wished that 'every man in his station would prefer the cause of the public before his own advantage',[33] and it was in part to try to ensure such restraint that the

---

26 *A Seasonable Address to both Houses of Parliament* (1681), p. 11. Sir Roger North ascribed Jones's dissatisfaction to his failure to be appointed lord chief justice (*Examen*, pp. 515–16). For placing the blame for the political turmoil on men 'in hopes to make or retrieve crack'd fortunes', see *Three Great Questions Concerning the Succession* (1680), p. 18.
27 *The Good Old Cause Reviv'd* (n.d.), p. 1.
28 *Observations on the Single Query* (n.d.), p. 2, cf. *Mischief of Cabals* (1685).
29 All Souls, MS 241, f. 344.
30 *Reasons for his Majesties Passing the Bill of Exclusion* (1681), p. 1.
31 *Diary of Henry Sidney*, i. 30; *Russell Letters*, p. 133.
32 Ferguson, *Ferguson the Plotter*, pp. 410–11.   33 *Diary of Henry Sidney*, i. 243.

Country wing of the opposition introduced a place bill in May 1679 forcing any Member who accepted office to seek re-election.[34]

At its most cynical, the suggestion was that the succession crisis had only been an opportunity for 'a pack of beggarly miscreants ... to enrich themselves upon the spoyls of three kingdoms'.[35] 'No sooner doth any man get the least employment but a hundred others are immediately contriving to turn him out, so that there will be nothing but tumbling down one another till they come all to the bottom of the hill', remarked Conway.[36] In a sense there was a struggle between rival administrations, with exclusion as one of the keys which could unlock the door to preferment. The degree to which ambition fuelled grievances about popery and arbitrary government was reflected in the number and bitterness of attacks on the King's advisers, and the increasing importance of parliamentary regulation of officeholding. Even those observers who took a less jaundiced view of individual honesty and motive could still see faction powering the crisis by talking in terms of

> Mistaken Men, and Patriots in their Hearts,
> Not Wicked, but seduc'd by Impious Arts.[37]

This analysis focused on a faction perverting honest men, who were 'sound at bottom' and seemed 'wors than they are'.[38] One author thus warned Monmouth that he had been 'drawn in by designing Politicians for ends of their own', a view of the duke adopted in Dryden's *Absalom and Achitophel*.[39] The strength of the belief in an evil faction deliberately seducing men from affection to the Court to further their own ends can be seen in the attention paid to Shaftesbury, whose apparently vacillating loyalties over the course of his career made him the obvious candidate for the part of unprincipled puppeteer.

It was, of course, in the loyalists' interest to describe their opponents as factious men, and to exaggerate their organisation so that it appeared a greater threat to stability. In an age when opposition to the Crown was still seen as disloyal it was to some extent inevitable that critics should be seen as a group of conspirators leading the rest of the country astray. Part of the reason for the emphasis on faction was thus the pejorative sense of the word party. Both its individualistic and collective senses were perfectly compatible with a factional view of politics if the individual pursued private interest and the collective division was not regarded as being caused by genuine grievances. As

---

[34] The bill received its first reading on 5 May, and may have been introduced by Hampden (Bod., MS Locke e. 5, f. 147).

[35] *The Impostor Expos'd* (1681), pp. 22–3.

[36] *HMC R.R. Hastings*, ii. 387.

[37] J.Dryden, *Absalom and Achitophel*, lines 497–8.

[38] BL, MS Add. 28,091, f. 79, draft speech.

[39] *A Seasonable Address to Both Houses* (1681), p. 14.

Sir Roger L'Estrange remarked in *The Observator*, a party was 'a Confederacy ... a Combination against the Law'.[40] For L'Estrange and others the only 'loyal party' was one that supported the Crown. At the beginning of the crisis, however, the Court's critics could themselves claim loyalty to the King and church by arguing that their aim was to put the nation on a sound footing that would rescue it from danger. Supporters of exclusion thus presented themselves as defenders of the constitution, claiming to be 'patriots' whose loyalty to their country was their overriding concern. Only when a clear Court policy emerged that claimed to champion protestantism and liberty could any opposition to it be seriously and effectively charged with having a hidden, disloyal agenda. When such a Court policy was formulated in 1681, as subsequent chapters will show, it was natural that all protest and unrest should be regarded as factious.

Castigation of the idea of a loyal opposition does not mean that party lines could not have existed, as historians of the early eighteenth century have sought to show.[41] The claim that the first Whigs were more than a collection of individuals, groups or interests, and that they followed the direction of an effectively organised leadership which perfected new techniques in parliamentary tactics and management must therefore now be tested. What were the characteristics of this management, how new were its techniques, and how successful was it? Was it *party* management, and did division among MPs occur along party lines? To answer these questions, records about Parliament must be scrutinised for evidence about the nature of the political leadership, the existence of party programmes, the degree of co-ordination between MPs, and whether there were influential groups of speakers that might have led or dominated proceedings.

The focus of the commentary will be on the House of Commons, largely because this is where previous historians have seen the new developments as having taken place. This is not to say that organisation in London and the provinces is unimportant, for this will be considered in the second half of the book; nor that the House of Lords can be neglected, although one tract written in 1679 claimed that 'the people rarely or seldom' spoke of the Upper House, or did so 'with so much slight and indifferency as if they thought the Lords rather spoil'd than further'd the affairs and good of the nation'.[42] One of the most illuminating recent pieces of research on the Restoration period has nevertheless studied the politics in the Upper House with fruitful results, concluding that co-operation between members of the two Houses was an

---

[40] *Observator*, no. 1, 13 April 1681. The idea of such a combination may have contributed to an analysis of all opposition as tightly organised, and hence to a confusion between *an* opposition and *the* opposition.

[41] G. Holmes, *British Politics in the Age of Anne* (1987 revised edition), pp. 46–50.

[42] *Truth and Honesty in Plain English* (1679), chapter 2, p. 4.

important factor in the emergence of parties. Bi-cameral conflicts after 1675 were, Andrew Swatland argues, the consequence of the emergence of political parties in both Houses rather than the result of faction-fighting at Court; the Whig and Tory parties in the Lords had thus been in existence since the mid 1670s rather than developing in response to the exclusion crisis. He has concluded that the Whigs in the Lords consisted of between thirty and forty peers who voted fairly consistently together, and on matters of principle rather than out of personal ambition. Swatland shows that their agenda stretched far beyond the single issue of exclusion, and in this way challenges the idea of a Whig party based solely on one objective; but he suggests that this means that we should look to an earlier date for the development of parties than that of 1679–81, rather than abandon the idea of new forms of organisation entirely.[43]

There are also good grounds for looking at the Commons before 1678. If the claim was true that politics after 1679 showed a marked contrast to what went before, we can expect to find novel features of organisation. Yet precedents for the type of management that characterised the crisis can be found much earlier. The petitions of 1640–2, the alliance with the City of London, and a degree of parliamentary co-ordination had all been features of Pym's leadership before the civil war. During the 1640s and 1650s, some historians have argued, there was a polarisation of politics into 'adversarial' or 'party' politics,[44] and the development of parties has been charted for the 1660s by Professor Browning.[45] However, as both Swatland's comments and the survey of historiography in the introduction suggest, it was the 1670s that witnessed many of the developments normally attributed to 1679–81. By 1673 or 1674 many of the features of the crisis had already emerged. Dissatisfaction with foreign policy, the war with the Dutch, the perceived growth of popery, the duke of York's marriage, and concern over the constitutional position of Parliament had combined to bring forth many of the organisational features that have been claimed as innovations in or soon after 1679. A pope-burning procession, one of the most famous forms of mass propaganda associated with the era of the Popish Plot, was organised as early as November 1673, a time when London was in turmoil: the coffee houses buzzed with talk, clubs appeared, and pamphlets were published which carried details of Parliament's proceedings.[46] MPs met together to thrash out policy outside Parliament, and huddled together within it.[47] Observers saw

---

[43] A. Swatland, 'The House of Lords in the Reign of Charles II, 1660–1681' (Birmingham Ph.D., 1985), pp. 5, 251, 331, 346.

[44] D. Underdown, 'Party Management in the Recruiter Elections', *EHR*, lxxxiii (1968), 235–64; Kishlansky, 'The Emergence of Adversarial Politics', 624–30.

[45] *EHD*, viii. 229–69.

[46] *Williamson Letters* ii. 67–8, 82, 157.

[47] Ibid., pp. 51, 55–6, 59, 94, 105, 115, 127, 129, 157.

two sides and referred to a 'malitious party', co-ordinated from the Lords, and an 'old honest party', with a 'moderate party' in between.[48] In terms of ideology, too, the early 1670s prefigured later events. Much of the agenda for 1678–81 had already been set: bills for regulating elections, for extending Habeas Corpus, for a test between protestant and papist, against the growth of popery and for security in case of a popish successor, were all promoted during the decade.[49]

Although J.R. Jones is convinced that there was something new after 1679 in terms of party management, and discusses extra-parliamentary activity such as electioneering and petitioning, he offers little guidance as to what the new methods were *inside* Parliament, apart from pointing to the subordination of MPs to an exclusionist line. We must therefore turn to an examination of the workings of politics at Westminster in more detail in an attempt to find the novelty of party.

A number of factors after the dissolution of the Cavalier Parliament, far from making the Commons an easier arena for party management, in fact made it more complicated. Unlike the fairly consistent composition of the House between 1661 and 1678, the membership thereafter was altered by three general elections between 1679 and 1681. Forty-five per cent of MPs in 1679 were new. Admittedly, the re-election of many of the same MPs caused this figure to fall to 22 per cent for the second Westminster Parliament, and only 12 per cent for the Oxford Parliament; but a Member who had been newly elected in 1679, and sat in all three parliaments of the period, had only 170 days of parliamentary experience behind him by the time of the 1681 dissolution. This inexperience caused problems: the 1679 Parliament was said to be full of 'raw young men ... apt to run riot before they will understand the game',[50] men who were unused to 'party' discipline no matter who tried to enforce it. One writer referred to MPs 'of green Years, slender Parts, and small Experience',[51] and at the beginning of the second Westminster Parliament the earl of Longford noted that 'all the new members herded together', so that few of the old members were listened to.[52] Another pamphleteer remarked that the electorate was 'sending Boyes that have not yet worn the School-brand out of their Buttocks, to sit and consult upon the good of the nation'.[53] The average age of MPs did indeed fall from forty-eight at the end of the Cavalier Parliament to forty-two in 1679, and although the

---

48 Ibid., pp. 94, 126, 157; J.R. Jacob, *Henry Stubbe, Radical Protestantism and the early Enlightenment* (Cambridge, 1983), p. 112.
49 *Williamson Letters*, ii. 130, 136, 147–8, 156.
50 D'Oyley to Henry Coventry, 12 February 1679, quoted by Witcombe, 'The Parliamentary Careers of Sir William and Mr Henry Coventry', p. 209.
51 *Certain Material and Useful Considerations* (1680), p. 1.
52 *HMC Ormonde*, v. 647.
53 *A Vindication of his Royal Highness the Duke of York* (1683), p. 21.

History of Parliament could find no correlation between age and political opinion, the youth of some of the new recruits must have added to the problems of inexperience. Moreover, the number of what Prof. Henning describes as 'plain country gentlemen without other occupation' rose from 66 per cent in the Cavalier Parliament to 73 per cent in 1681, and these independent country gentry were unused to, and resentful of, discipline.[54] According to Barrillon, at the start of the first Westminster Parliament even those who had previously held most sway in the Commons did not know where they stood because of the large numbers of new, inexperienced country gentlemen, whom nobody dared to oppose, however irregular their proceedings.[55]

The effect of the changes in the personnel of the chamber was to exacerbate the already existing problems of poor attendance, infrequent activity and reticence to make speeches. Out of a total of 513 Members, the 'average attendance', determined from division figures, fell from 293 in the first Westminster Parliament to 230 in the second, the lowest figure since the February–May 1677 session of the Cavalier Parliament, though significantly higher than the 1660s and many of the meetings held after the Revolution.[56] Obviously non-attendance was not a new problem, nor one that was resolved at this time, but it did seem to be becoming more serious, and noticeable, during 1678–81, perhaps because full participation was expected in moments of crisis. On 23 November 1678 the House summoned all MPs, and on 11 December ordered several to take their seats, including such prominent Members as Sir William Coventry, whom Finch described as 'the most considerable and remarkable man in the House', and Sir Eliab Harvey, who had apparently abandoned parliamentary business in order to collect his rents.[57] Although these two MPs subsequently re-appeared, Finch believed that Coventry's absence had been 'on purpose that he might be turn'd out of the Hou[se], being weary of the attendance', and other Members may also have been slipping away, for on 14 December it was reported that the House would again be 'called over', and that those who failed to turn up would be taken into custody.[58]

Members also seem to have begun to slip away once conflict seemed likely in the 1679 Parliament. Despite a large showing of Members at the beginning of the session, an order was made on 25 April that absent MPs should be

---

[54] J. Miller, 'The Later Stuart Monarchy', in *Restored Monarchy*, ed. Jones, p. 42. The *History of Parliament*, i. 65 suggests that twice as many county MPs opposed the Court as supported it 1679–81.

[55] PRO, 31/3/142, f. 77, Barrillon dispatch, 27 March/ 6 April 1679.

[56] *EHD*, viii. app. iii.

[57] *CJ*, ix. 546; Leics. RO, Finch mss, DG7/4957/57, f. 38; *History of Parliament*, ii. 508.

[58] Leics. RO, Finch mss, DG7.4957/57, f. 38; Longleat, Muddiman newsbook, 14 December 1678. On 18 December forty-six MPs were ordered to be sent for (*CJ*, ix. 558).

taken into custody if they were not present in the Commons between 10 a.m. and noon,[59] and the situation apparently deteriorated so far that a bill for the better attendance of members was read on 5 May 1679.[60] Such legislation was not new,[61] but just as Danby had believed that if MPs could be brought to exert themselves the loyalism of the silent or absent majority would ensure victory, so the critics of the Court believed that greater control over members would work to their advantage. After Parliament's dissolution an unknown, anti-Court hand accordingly drew up a set of guidelines that would have ensured the attendance of all representatives, and stipulated that all matters of importance should be debated in the morning.[62] So concerned were opposition groups to enforce attendance that Lord Chief Justice North believed that a number of people from outside the House had taken on the task of reminding MPs to take their seats before a vote.[63] Even so, the number present towards the end of the following Parliament was dramatically low. On 9 December 1680 only 143 MPs voted in division, and only 129 could be mustered to vote on 7 January 1681. This was at the end of a session, when the House was habitually thinner, but, unlike in many other meetings, important business remained in agitation right up to the prorogation. Moreover, even when MPs did attend they often kept quiet. Silence did not, of course, necessarily mean indifference. Sir Joseph Ashe was not appointed to any committees and is not recorded as having made a speech in the 1679 or 1680 Parliaments, but in 1681 assured his constituents that he had 'been present when all our great businesses have been debated'.[64] Yet hesitancy to speak does suggest a reluctance to participate in the often heated debates. Fortunately the speeches are well reported, allowing us to make some, albeit rough, analysis of the debates. In 1679 about three quarters of MPs never made a recorded speech, and half of those that debated did so only five times or less. Moreover, a third of Members were never appointed to a committee, whilst in the very short-lived meeting at Oxford in 1681 just over a half of MPs failed to be appointed to any committee, and obviously even fewer spoke than in the previous sessions.

This level of inactivity makes the categorisation of Members into neat party groupings a hazardous exercise, which can often only be based on tenuous evidence. The views of even prominent politicians are often hard to identify even on important issues such as the succession. Sir Charles Sedley, for

[59] *CJ*, ix. 602; Chatsworth, Devonshire collection, Group 1B, newsletter, 26 April 1679.
[60] *CJ*, ix. 612.
[61] Witcombe, *Cavalier Parliament*, p. 157.
[62] BL, Longleat mss, M/863. reel v, Coventry mss, vol. vi. ff. 248–51, 'Severall Usefull and Indispensibly necessary Cautions and Instructions'.
[63] Dalrymple, *Memoirs*, ii. 323. cf. *The True Englishman* (1680), p. 9, which rebuked 'a new sect called undertakers' who tried to manage the London shrieval election.
[64] *History of Parliament*, i. 81–2. cf. Ibid., iii. 240.

example, is noted by the *History of Parliament*, still an underused work of reference, as an avowed opponent of the Court, and as having been marked 'worthy' by Shaftesbury.[65] He was nevertheless absent from the division on the exclusion bill, and only in the unpublished account of an obscure early eighteenth-century vicar do we have the chance recollection that, immediately before the Oxford Parliament, Sedley entered a coffee house, sat down at table where the author of the memoir was sitting, and declared

> how destructive such a method would be to the public affairs, and ... that for his part, tho' his aversion to popery was as great as any man's could be, and the Duke [of York] had been more injurious to him than to any private man in the Kingdom (for he had robbed him of his only child and daughter, whom he delighted in above all worldly comforts, deflowered her virgin innocence, and made her a whore of quality to himself), yet he would never give his vote to a bill against the succession of the Crown in the right line.[66]

The views of many less colourful MPs prove far more elusive, and discussions about the extent of party at this time deal with the visible tip of a largely unfathomable iceberg. The research of the *History of Parliament* for this period reveals how little as well as how much we know about the views of Members. Even those who sat in the House at the time were not quite sure where all their fellows stood. For example, in 1681 William Love wanted MPs to declare their position on exclusion 'because several Members who voted for it in the last Parliament had, after the Parliament was ended, disowned their having been for it', though Cavendish was quick to object to such a 'new way of declaring minds'.[67] Indeed, the fact that we do not know the sympathies of MPs on the issue may indicate that many were deliberately refraining from declaring one way or the other.

The fall in the number of Members who attended, spoke, or were appointed to committees, should urge caution about making sweeping assertions about allegiances. Yet the problems of management do not mean that some form of leadership was impossible, since they enabled a small group of MPs to dominate proceedings. To some extent a group of leading Members had always existed in Parliament, but there are indications that contemporaries were more awake to the rule of such a group during the parliaments of the crisis. One loyalist pamphleteer complained that the youth and inexperience of many new Members made them 'easy prey' to more experienced men, 'so that twenty, perhaps twelve men, represent the whole House of Commons, in such affairs as those touching the state of the nation in

[65] *History of Parliament*, iii. 409.
[66] BL, Add. 27,440, Charles Allestree, 'The Second Part of the Appendix to the Votes', f. 170.
[67] *HMC Ormonde*, vi. 8.

general, and what is concluded there, is their sense indeed, and not the free sense of the House of Commons'.[68] The point was echoed elsewhere. Votes in the Commons, another propagandist argued, were made 'Nemine contradicente, when there was not above a 7th or an 8th part of the whole House that did actually give their consent to it; and yet their being part of the ruling party, are to be received by us poor country folks as the unanimous determination of an undivided and infallible Parliament.'[69] The ability of 'a few private persons to govern the House of Commons', the author continued, was as bad as the King listening to a few favourites. Another writer attacked MPs for being cowed by 'leading men ... whereas every one should have wisdom and reason enough of his own to guide his opinion by, and not run and baa like a silly sheep after the law-bell of another's cant'.[70] It was said in November 1680 that the House lost credit with the public because votes had been carried by 'a small number of the major party', and Reresby believed the Commons to be 'managed by seven or eight angry and able lawyers and some few more disobliged persons'.[71] Thus the very unmanageability of the House contributed to the domination by what might be termed a steering group, though their control was far from total and should not be exaggerated: for example, on 7 January 1681 the leaders 'had purpose to vote the Chancellor, Privy Seal, Radnor, Halifax and Hyde evil counsellors, and to be removed from the King's presence. They began with Halifax and Hyde, but others were by accidental motions introduced against the sense of the managers', and one hostile observer delighted to 'see how the faction writhed' to defend the duchess of Portsmouth, who had become a temporary ally.[72]

The composition of the House's leaders is crucial to any understanding of how the Commons functioned during the period 1678–81. The problems of identifying the most influential members are, of course, numerous. Most obviously, the parliamentary records of the day are not exhaustive, though the Journals can offer important clues about activity in committee and in tellerships. Grey's version of the Commons' debates also makes it possible to point to key orators who were able to sway the House, or direct the course of discussions, and other versions of debates were produced, which help corroborate or fill gaps.[73] However, it is difficult to say how many speeches went unrecorded and a basic number count of contributions takes no account of

---

[68] All Souls, MS 240, f. 43, tract dated June 1679.
[69] Bod., MS Jones 17, ff. 212–32, 'An Answer to a Vindication'.
[70] *A Vindication of His Royal Highness the Duke of York* (1683), p. 21. L'Estrange also referred to 'leading Members' (*The Lawyer Outlaw'd* [1683], p. 28).
[71] *CSPD 1680–1*, p. 93; M. Geiter and W. Speck, 'The Reliability of Sir John Reresby's Memoirs and his Account of the Oxford Parliament of 1681', *BIHR*, lxii (1989), 110.
[72] *HMC Ormonde*, v. 563.
[73] The additional sources are discussed in the next chapter.

garrulity or conscientiousness as opposed to credit.[74] Although we have to rely on them, the Journals and debates can pose a false sense of certainty about who was important. For example, Barrillon ranked Richard Ingoldsby and Sir Thomas Byde as leading Members, though in the 1679 Parliament the former was not named to a committee, nor made any recorded speech, and the latter was only appointed to two relatively unimportant committees.[75] The earl of Lindsey thought that Secretary Jenkins must 'often' have heard Sir Richard Cust speaking in the House, though only three speeches of his are recorded by Grey.[76]

Nevertheless, the pattern suggested in the previous sections of declining Court influence on the floor of the House, and a corresponding rise in that of its critics, can be charted in terms of the activity of individual Members. By analysing Grey's debates, the most frequent speakers in the last session of the Cavalier Parliament in order of importance were William Sacheverell, Sir Thomas Lee, Henry Powle, Secretary Coventry, William Williams, Col. Birch, Silius Titus and Sir Thomas Meres, who all addressed the House over forty times, and were frequently named to committees.[77] Sir William Temple believed Sir William Coventry, who was active both as a speaker and in committee, 'had the most credit of any man in the House'.[78] The main pursuers of the Popish Plot's implications were thus members of the Country opposition who had distinguished themselves in earlier sessions, and who may now have been sitting together in the House.[79] Apart from Sir Henry Coventry, there were few able Court speakers to give direction, although Sir Joseph Williamson and Sir John Ernley did provide some support. The Court's vocal critics, on the other hand, were backed up by a barrage from colleagues such as Sir Nicholas Carew, William Cavendish, Sir Thomas Littleton and Thomas Bennett, each of whom delivered over twenty recorded speeches.

Although in 1679 there was some shift in the Court's position, it was only a turn for the worse. Of the new privy councillors only Powle and Lee were amongst the top ten speakers, though Capel and Cavendish took the floor on over fifteen occasions; but Secretary Coventry halved the number of

---

[74] The 'exclusionist' Arthur Onslow, for example, was said by one biographer to have 'had his credit too, though not engaging ... in the business' of the Commons in the sense of 'a leader or manager in a party' (*HMC Onslow*, p. 484).

[75] PRO, 31/3/146, ff. 24–9, Barrillon dispatch, 12/22 July 1680.

[76] *CSPD July–September 1683*, p. 180; *History of Parliament*, ii. 183.

[77] All spoke more than forty times, with Sacheverell leading on 59 contributions. Sacheverell was also nominated to the most committees (twenty-eight out of a possible thirty-nine).

[78] *History of Parliament*, ii. 162.

[79] Meres referred to 'this side of the House ... and that side of the House' (Grey, *Debates*, vi. 247), though it is quite possible that he was speaking metaphorically. Thomas De Laune, *Present State of England* (1681), p. 149 asserted that MPs sat 'promiscuously'.

contributions he made, whilst Ernley lost his seat. Seymour's quarrel with Danby and his failure to regain the Speakership had deprived the Court of one its best tools, whilst his replacement in the chair, Serjeant Gregory, was inept in controlling the House. Fears that Gregory's 'partes and experience would hardly carry him through his great charge' proved well-founded when on 10 May he 'whipped out of the chair' to carry up money bills to the Lords, despite 'the many calls on him to return', a disregard for the House's sensibilities that Sacheverell thought merited a spell in the Tower.[80] Winnington's dismissal from his post as solicitor general because of his support for Danby's impeachment had also lost the Court another able spokesman, and his disaffection, which nevertheless did not yet include supporting exclusion, prompted him to make the second highest number of speeches.[81] The leading contributor, as in the last session, was Sacheverell, whose spirit seemed all-pervasive,[82] with Sir Thomas Clarges, Garraway and Titus helping to dominate debates, aided by William Williams, Edward Vaughan, John Birch, Sir Robert Howard, Thomas Bennett and Sir Thomas Meres. But members of the old Country party, such as Lee, Meres and Littleton, were unable to keep up with the changed tempo,[83] and new Members such as Sir Thomas Player and Paul Foley were also able to emerge as leaders of the House.[84] In a similar process the Court was losing control of the committees, membership of which was always a minority pastime, where the exclusionists, such as Richard Hampden, Thomas Papillon, John Dubois, Sir John Hewley, Sir Francis Drake and Sir Robert Peyton were apparently indefatigable.[85] But an assumption that certain MPs dominated the House *because* they supported the exclusion bill is too simplistic, if only because the speeches ranged over the whole gamut of parliamentary issues. Active speakers such as Sir John Trevor, William Harbord, Sir William Coventry and Sir Thomas Clarges opposed exclusion, whilst Garraway and Sir John Knight (who was named

---

[80] Bod., MS Tanner 39*, f. 213, [-] to John Hobart, 15 March 1679; *HMC Ormonde*, v. 90.

[81] For his resentment against Danby see BL, Add. 63,057B, Burnet's ms history, f. 47. Burnet thought Winnington 'a man of much heat and a warm phancy, that was a fluent though good speaker' (ibid., f. 45).

[82] Though see *HMC Finch*, ii. 47 for even his difficulties in winning over the House.

[83] *HMC Ormonde*, v. 98.

[84] Williams spoke six times before 21 April and twenty times thereafter; Swinfen spoke twice before and eleven times after the Court reorganisation. Foley was described as 'one newly started up into great vogue in that House' (*History of Parliament*, ii. 336), and Barrillon believed that he drafted the exclusion bill (PRO, 31/3/146, f. 27, Barrillon dispatch, 12/22 July 1680).

[85] They were appointed to 38, 33, 34, 34, 35 and 41 committees respectively, though we do not know how many they actually attended. Those who reported from committees included Meres (privileges and elections), Winnington (Danby), Clarges (security against popery; habeas corpus), Hampden (regulating elections), Trevor (Irish cattle; trials of peers), and Sir Richard Cust (disbanding army). Hampden reported on seven occasions during the session; Trevor on six; Clarges on five; and Sacheverell and Winnington on four.

to thirty-nine of the sixty-six committees of the session) abstained from the division on the bill, though they worked with the other leaders on many different matters.

By the time Parliament sat again the 'league table' of MPs had again changed slightly. In July 1680 Barrillon listed the most considerable Members, and, although he admitted that they were not a firmly united party, all except Trevor and Clarges seem to have supported exclusion,[86] Harbord, Cavendish and Powle having become converted to the measure by this time. The differences between the leaders lay in who should succeed after Charles, with some supporting the pretensions of the duke of Monmouth, whilst others, like Sir John Coventry who blamed him for the slit nose he had received in 1670, were his enemies. Judging by the performances at Westminster in 1680–1, as recorded by Grey and the Journals, the Court still lacked strength. Its management had been weakened by the replacement of Henry Coventry as Secretary of State by Sir Leoline Jenkins, whose administrative skills vastly outweighed his oratorical talents,[87] and by the defection to the exclusionist cause of Sir Henry Capel, Lord Cavendish, William Harbord, Sir Edward Dering and Sir Francis Russell;[88] the most important Court voice was now Sir Christopher Musgrave. Halifax, the main patron of limitations, had only a limited number of supporters in the Commons,[89] and although Jenkins reported that the 'number ag[ains]t the [exclusion bill] was considerable',[90]

---

[86] PRO, 31/3/146, ff. 24–9, Barrillon dispatch, 12/22 July 1680. Apart from Ingoldsby and Byde who have already been noted, they were: William (possibly a mistake for Scorey) Barker, John and Richard Hampden, Sir Thomas Lee, Sir Roger Hill, William Williams, William (possibly a mistake for Edward or Hugh) Boscawen, Edward Nosworthy, William Cavendish, William Sacheverell, George Treby, John Trenchard, Sir John Coventry, Thomas Bennett, Henry Mildmay, Sir Harbottle Grimston, Henry Powle, Sir Edward Harley, Paul Foley, John Birch, Sir John Hobart, William Harbord, Sir Samuel Barnardiston, William Lord Russell, Sir Thomas Clarges, Sir John Hotham, Sir Gilbert Gerard, Sir Patience Ward, Thomas Papillon, Edward Vaughan, Sir Thomas Player, Robert Thomas, 'Varnond' [?George Vernon], Sir Francis Winnington, Sir John Trevor, Silius Titus and Algernon Sidney. The inclusion of the latter, who had yet to step foot in a Parliament held by Charles II, suggests that the French ambassador was taking reputation into consideration as much as proven parliamentary ability, and that Sidney may have been one of the ambassador's main sources of information. Barrillon also listed one Monsecours, possibly meaning Sir Christopher Musgrave.

[87] Jenkins made only sixteen speeches in the 1680 Parliament. He was not a spontaneous speaker, and made copious notes for set speeches (All Souls, MS 242, ff. 115–21; MS 229, f. 270, f. 273; MS 251, f. 169, ff. 256–61). Ailesbury thought him 'heavy in his way of discourse' (*Ailesbury Memoirs*, i. 42) and Burnet thought 'all his speeches and arguments against exclusion were heard with indignation' (*History*, ii. 257).

[88] *History of Parliament*, ii. 9, 38, 212, 486; iii. 362.

[89] These included Thomas Thynne, Sir William Hickman, Sir William Coventry (who did not sit after 1679), Sir Thomas Clarges and Daniel Finch (Witcombe, 'Parliamentary Careers of Sir William and Mr Henry Coventry', pp. 228–9; BL, Althorp MS C5, Thynne to Halifax, 26 July 1679; H. Horwitz, *Revolution Politics: The Career of Daniel Finch, Second Earl of Nottingham 1647–1730* [Cambridge, 1968], pp. 22–3).

[90] PRO, SP.104/67, f. 17, Jenkins to William of Orange, 12 November 1680.

the Court was unable to galvanize them to impede its passage. So fearful of Parliament had the Court's managers become that Sir Robert Carr, Jenkins and Godolphin all refused to deliver Charles's rejection of exclusion to the House on 4 January 1681, and the impeachment of Seymour silenced yet another able tongue.[91] Control of the House thus passed almost completely to the supporters of exclusion. William Williams was elected Speaker, a man of 'a fiery and vicious temper' who was nevertheless 'subservient' to the opposition leaders and 'pliant to them as a spaniel dog';[92] and Sir Francis Winnington (a convert to exclusion), Sir William Jones, Hampden, Harbord, Birch, Russell and Titus were able to dominate debates.[93] They were aided by Sir Gilbert Gerard, Dubois, Trenchard, Boscawen, Lee, Hotham, Foley and Sir Trevor Williams in committee,[94] and were able to use their influence to push bills through the lower House.[95] On the other hand, the more moderate Garraway and Lee still argued their views eloquently and frequently, and as the session progressed there may have been a growing sympathy for less strident voices. Indeed, there was enough of a split amongst the leaders that in 1681 the government attempted to recruit eloquent MPs to boost its speaking power. Powle, Littleton, Lee, Birch, Vaughan, Meres and Garraway formed a group of speakers labelled 'the Men of Expedients'.[96] But the impression given by the few debates of the Oxford Parliament is that Jones, Winnington, Hampden, Harbord and Boscawen continued to dominate, though Jenkins

[91] Temple, *Memoirs*, p. 352; *HMC Ormonde*, v. 530; *HMC Le Fleming*, p. 174.

[92] *Ailesbury Memoirs*, i. 45. Others talked of for the post were Sir John Trevor (PRO, 31/3/146, f. 28, Barrillon dispatch, 12/22 July 1680), Boscawen, Paul Foley and Evan Seys (Newdigate newsletter Lc.996, 19 October 1680). In June 1679 George Treby's name had been mooted, but he was handicapped by 'being so very short-sight'd he cannot see to distinguish Members in the House' (Bucks. RO, Verney mss, M11/32, John Verney to Sir Ralph Verney, 30 June 1679). Perhaps as compensation, Treby was made chair of the elections committee in 1680.

[93] Jones was a new recruit, and a 'courteous and fine speaker' who 'grew to be the chief man in the House', although L'Estrange referred to him as 'an imperious dictator' (*Ailesbury Memoirs*, i. 36; BL, Add. 63,057B, Burnet's ms history, f. 54; *The Lawyer Outlaw'd* [1683], p. 30). In 1680 Winnington's speeches made up 8.6 per cent of the total number recorded by Grey; Jones's made up almost 6 per cent, and Harbord and Hampden about 5 per cent. Interestingly Sacheverell's frequency of speeches dropped markedly after 1679. The earl of Longford claimed that of the old MPs only Russell, Titus, Winnington, Bennett, Harbord and Colt would be listened to (*HMC Ormonde*, v. 467).

[94] Hampden, Foley, Winnington, Williams, Dubois, Jones, Gerard, Boscawen, Lee and Trenchard were all appointed to more than thirty committees. Reporters from important committees included Trenchard (petitioning, removal of Halifax), Trevor (Irish cattle), Winnington and Birch (Popish Plot), Clayton (removal of Jeffreys), Sacheverell (protestant dissenters), Powle (security against popery), Hampden (address on state of kingdom 27 November; address on King's Speech 20 December), Pulteney (impeachment of Seymour), and Sir Richard Corbet (proceedings of judges, Scroggs impeachment).

[95] Others considered influential included Montagu, Maynard, Sir Nicholas Carew, Vernon and Hotham (*HMC Ormonde*, v. 561).

[96] *HMC Ormonde*, vi. 5. Littleton was the 'ablest and vehementest arguer of them all'; although unsuccessful at the second election of 1679 he secured a government seat in 1681 (*History of Parliament*, ii. 748–51).

and Ernley were more strenuous in pleading for the alternatives to the bill than in previous sessions.[97] MPs may nevertheless have been slipping out of control: William Leveson Gower was becoming an increasingly important voice on the exclusion issue, and had to be stopped from finishing an intemperate speech, as did Sir William Cowper, whilst North claimed that Jones's pre-eminence had been short-lived, for 'his authority sunk and little of his proposing would succeed'.[98] Unfortunately, the extremely curtailed length of the session makes it difficult to gauge the status of MPs in the House accurately.

Three features of the steering group of MPs need further comment. The first is the rather obvious point that it was relatively small in number, making it difficult to term the group a 'party' in the modern sense of the word. In 1680 only eleven MPs made more than twenty recorded contributions from the floor. Secondly, the group's composition was not static. The leaders of 1681 were no longer those who had managed the investigations into the plot and who had led the impeachment of Danby. Sacheverell, in particular, had become almost mute by December 1680, whilst new men, such as Jones, had risen to the top. Powle, Meres, Littleton, Bennett and Cavendish were all waning stars by 1681, giving way to Winnington, Harbord, Hampden and Boscawen. The third point is that although the group of Members spoke or acted together over a whole range of issues that came before the Commons, they did not necessarily do so in organised unison, or to effect, especially when interest cut across their cohesiveness. In 1679, for example, divisions over the renewal of the Irish cattle bill, largely determined by MPs' local concerns, cut across exclusionist lines.[99] The limits to party loyalty were in fact clearly spelt out by one supporter of exclusion, who can probably be identified as Lord Cavendish.[100] He wanted the bill passed 'because I think it is just and necessary, not because it is contended for by a party; for I hold myself as free to differ with that party, when I think them in the wrong, as to agree with them when they have reason on their side'.[101] Nor did John Dutton Colt feel himself constrained by party loyalty when in 1680 he defended Sir John Davys against attacks by Sir Robert Clayton and others, even though he was 'otherwise a hot, disobliged and fierce speaking man against the

---

[97] Jenkins in fact made the largest number of speeches (nine). 'A Dialogue Between the Ghosts of the Two Last Parliaments' (*POAS*, ii. 406) referred to Maynard, Jones and Winnington as the rulers of the Commons at Oxford.

[98] Leeds AO, Reresby mss 17/27a, abstract of debate, 26 March 1681; North, *Examen*, p. 568. According to Burnet, Jones helped Littleton to manage the debate on the regency proposals (BL, Add. 63,057B, f. 58, ms history).

[99] C. Edie, 'The Irish Cattle bills: A Study in Restoration Politics', *Transactions of the American Philosophical Society*, vi (2), (1970), 47–8, 54.

[100] Dalrymple, *Memoirs*, ii. 285; HMC *Ormonde*, v. 561.

[101] *Reasons for His Majesties Passing the Bill* (1681), p. 4.

Court'.[102] On 8 November 1680 George Vernon, who moved the second reading of the exclusion bill and was one of the 'hot and violent conductors' of the session, defended Lord Ferrer's chaplain against an accusation, driven on by Harbord and Birch, that he had annotated a copy of the votes of the House with scandalous words.[103]

Indeed, a number of jealousies amongst the leaders of the House rose to the surface, especially after the rejection of the exclusion bill by the Lords in November 1680, when, as we have seen, some of the leaders appeared to be involved in negotiations with the Court to grant the King supply in return for his assent to the bill and their inclusion in a new administration. Opposition was most cohesive when it was most in opposition, so that the nearer it seemed, or even came, to success the more differences within its composition began to become apparent. The attacks in late 1680 on Charles's advisers signalled tensions among the steering group, and suspicions of the leaders by the rest of the House. Jones, Winnington and Montagu had apparently been the chief promoters of the factious attack on Halifax in revenge for his eloquent opposition to the bill, even though other leaders, such as Cavendish and Russell, opposed or disowned the assault.[104] 'Four score' Members were reported to have left the chamber in disgust at the display of malice.[105] Jones's position seems particularly factious since he had recently been on good terms with Halifax.[106] As Winnington observed, 'when against Popery and Arbitrary Government we are all of a mind; but when we come upon particular persons, then we differ'.[107] Other personal attacks also highlighted rifts between the leaders. Birch was a strenuous opponent of the impeachment of Seymour, for which Winnington and Titus made insinuations about his motives, though Titus himself seems to have been unpopular with some sections of the exclusionists.[108] Harbord was suspected of attacking Seymour for personal gain, and was forced to deny that he coveted the old Speaker's

---

[102] *HMC Ormonde*, v. 547. Colt had been softened on this point by his brother, who knew Davys.

[103] Grey, *Debates*, vii. 430.

[104] *Diary of Henry Sidney*, ii. 135. Cavendish, Booth and Garraway were also said to have become moderate in late November 1680 (*HMC Le Fleming*, p. 174).

[105] *Diary of Henry Sidney*, ii. 128.

[106] Jones was a slippery character who, North claimed, 'despised' his fellow lawyer and parliamentary ally, Sir Francis Winnington (*Examen*, p. 568), even though he seems to have sat next to him in the House (Grey, *Debates*, viii. 270). The earl of Ailesbury asserted that Jones was intimate with Sir Allen Apsley, the duke of York's treasurer, whom he may have used to draw up the exclusion bill 'in so violent a strait that he was well assured that the House of Peers would never pass it' (*Ailesbury Memoirs*, i. 36–7), and North reported that at that time Jones and Charles 'would stand together [in Parliament] and sometimes lean on the hanging, in conversation for a considerable while' (*Examen*, p. 538). Even when he had resigned from office he was careful not to burn all bridges with the Court, and in June 1680 talked with James (*Russell Letters*, p. 122).

[107] Grey, *Debates*, viii. 145.

[108] *History of Parliament*, i. 659; *HMC Legh*, p. 269.

office of treasurer of the navy, though he may have been trying to curry favour at Court on 9 December by defending Secretary Jenkins against accusations of having tried to stifle the investigation into the plot.[109] Bickering between the leaders of the House was quite open by December. On 13 December Jones thought himself slighted by Birch and Capel, and the next day Titus voiced his wonder at Birch's moderation in favour of Sir Robert Peyton, sarcastically commenting that the colonel was usually 'always against great men accused', and Titus again reflected on Birch's opinions on the 31st.[110] On 20 December angry words passed between Jones and Vaughan, the latter criticising Jones's negotiations with the Court for a prorogation.[111] The leadership of the House in 1679–81 was thus in an uncertain and insecure position, constrained by the prejudices and suspicions of the other Members and other leaders.

Having outlined the limits to the cohesion and influence of the steering group of MPs on the floor and in committees, we now need to consider what means were at their disposal to manage their colleagues, besides the power of their voices. The most obvious way of co-ordinating their strength was to meet with other Members outside the House. One observer complained in June 1679 about what 'Caballing there is in Parliament time, how the leading men do busy themselves in making their Court to such as they would bring over to their Party', and thought that as a consequence there was 'but little freedom in the Votes of the House of Commons, men bringing their opinions along with them stiff and unalterable by debate and reason'.[112] The earl of Ailesbury thought that John Arnold and John Dutton Colt 'had their parts given them', and a tract, possibly written by the earl of Halifax, claimed that 'all transactions of Parliament are first design'd and hammer'd, collections made, [and] a Common Purse manag'd'.[113] The propagandist exaggeration of such allegations should not be discounted, but they did contain some factual basis. Extra-parliamentary debate was, for example, openly called for on 16 November, the day after the Lords' rejection of the exclusion bill, when, on Sir John Hotham's motion, the Commons adjourned for a day 'to the end the Members may consult together and consider what is most fitting to be done'.[114] Consequently five or six 'great clubbes' were held that evening, including one at the Sun tavern, a favourite haunt of the discontented where over 100 MPs had met before the start of the session (in what one

[109] Grey, *Debates*, viii. 87–93, 115.
[110] Grey, *Debates*, viii. 135–6, 144, 231.
[111] Grey, *Debates*, viii. 198–201.
[112] All Souls, MS 240, ff. 43–4, ms tract.
[113] *Ailesbury Memoirs*, i. 45; *A Seasonable Address to both Houses* (1681), p. 19.
[114] Bod., MS Eng. Poet. C25, f. 52. 'private debates in the House of Commons'; NLW, Wynnstay mss, L491, ms version of the resolutions of the House, 16 November 1680, omitted from the Journal.

pamphleteer described as 'a rehearsal' of speeches and proceedings to be made in the House), and where another meeting was to take place after the session's prorogation.[115]

The most famous forum for such discussions is the Green Ribbon Club, which the Tory historian Roger North described as 'a sort of executive power' for the Court's opponents.[116] Thirty-seven MPs were almost certainly members, and another four may have been,[117] but, apart from a handful, they were not leaders of the House, and at least two of them defected from opposition ranks.[118] The Club was important in terms of its ability to organise propaganda or petitioning, and as a link with City radicals, not, as has recently been re-asserted, as 'a kind of party headquarters for the Whigs and as the locus of its party activists', if this means a machine to co-ordinate parliamentary procedure.[119] Even North admitted that the Club's strength lay in creating and spreading news quickly in London and in the country,[120] and the minutes of the Club, as transcribed by Pepys, suggest that it may not have formally sat between March and September 1679, May and November 1680, and February and June 1681. It was thus probably inactive for long periods when Parliament was in session, and could not have influenced the course of debates.[121]

---

[115] BL, Add. 28,930, f. 203, Samuel Ellis to John Ellis, 16 November 1680; *CSPD 1680–1*, p. 86; *A Dialogue betwixt Sam the Ferriman* (1681), p. 6; *The Speech and Carriage of Stephen College* (1681), p. 3; *HMC Kenyon*, p. 124. About sixty peers and commoners had met with Shaftesbury at the Sun at the end of June 1680 (Newdigate newsletter Lc.956, 1 July 1680), and the tavern was later the scene of alleged discussions about the Rye House Plot (*State Trials*, ix. 366, 490).

[116] North, *Examen*, p. 572.

[117] Using the membership list transcribed by Pepys (Pepys Library ms 2875, ff. 489–91) the following can be identified as having joined: Col. Robert Austen, William Ashe, Robert Apreece, Edward Ashe, John Ashe [possible], Sir Hugh Bethell, Henry Booth, Maurice Bockland [possible], Thomas Pope Blount, Sir William Courtenay, Sir William Cowper, Sir Francis Drake, Sir William Ellis, Thomas Freke junior and senior, Sir Richard Grahme, Sir George Hungerford, John Hall, Arthur Harris, Thomas Horde, Sir John Holman, John Leigh [possible], Sir John Mallet, Henry Mildmay, Edward Nosworthy, Edward Norton, Sir Robert Peyton, Gerard Russell, Paulet St John, Francis Stonehouse, John Smith, Richard Southby, George and John Speke, George Treby, three Trenchards (William, John and Henry), Henry Whithed [possible], Sir William Waller and Sir Walter Yonge.

[118] Sir Robert Peyton was expelled from the Commons for trying to bargain with the duke of York (*History of Parliament*, iii. 234), and Sir Richard Grahme, whose brother James held a place in the duke's household, went over to the Court in 1679 (ibid., ii. 430).

[119] Ashcraft, *Revolutionary Politics*, pp. 143–5. For the club's role in petitioning see Knights, 'London's "Monster" Petition', pp. 53–5. For its propagandist role see chapter 6; Harris, *London Crowds*, pp. 92–3, 100–1; J.R. Jones, 'The Green Ribbon Club', *Durham University Journal* xlix (1956), 17–20.

[120] North, *Examen*, pp. 572–3. He may have based his comments on notes made by his brother, Lord Keeper Francis North (Dalrymple, *Memoirs*, ii. 322–3).

[121] Magdalene College, Cambridge, Pepys Library MSS, 2875, ff. 465–88. Since it was noted in April 1680 (*CSPD 1679–80*, p. 432) that the club had virtually collapsed, the gaps do not seem to be mere breaks in Pepys's note-taking though see p. 203 for activity in May 1679.

Almost as legendary as the influence of the Green Ribbon Club is the political sway of the earl of Shaftesbury. Attempts have already been made to point to the limits on Shaftesbury's power as the head of a party in the Commons, particularly during late 1680 when a group of MPs decided to negotiate with the Court without him. The earl said he did 'no more understand the House of Commons than he does the Court', and his biographer notes that at this time 'the House was slipping out of control'.[122] He had not been the scheme's promoter, and it is suggested that it collapsed as a result of the icy blast of his anger.[123] Whatever the cause of the failure of the negotiations, they reveal Shaftesbury, who is all too often put forward unreservedly as the head of the opposition to the Court, struggling to control members of his own faction. His role outside Parliament will emerge in later chapters; but his control of Parliament, and in particular the Commons, is worth questioning here in order to emphasise and expand some of the reservations that Haley's invaluable biography made about the earl's powers. The issue of his leadership is important because historians have seen his hand behind the creation of the first modern political party and the promotion of exclusion. Once both aspects are put in context, so evidence for Shaftesbury's control of MPs diminishes.

Contemporary comments go some way to suggesting that MPs were 'influenced very much by the Lord Shaftesbury', who was thought to have had 'a great influence on the House of Commons, who were ruled much by his persuasions'.[124] Dorothy Sidney noted that 'all the several parties' of the opposition were called 'my Lord Shaftesbury's followers', and another writer of news referred to the 'Sha[ftesbury] men'.[125] Yet it is significant that many of the comments which magnify his power were made after the earl's trial in 1681, by which time the government itself had focused attention on him as the ring-leader of disaffection. It is extremely difficult to extricate the reality of Shaftesbury's power in 1679–81 from the propaganda version pedalled by the Tories. For example, *A Modest Vindication of the Earl of Shaftesbury* (1681) was not what its title suggested, but a satire including an imagined ministry that the earl might form. Among those listed was John Dryden, who

---

[122] *Diary of Henry Sidney*, ii. 135.
[123] Haley, *Shaftesbury*, pp. 615–16. Shaftesbury's opposition might, in any case, have been thought hypocritical since he and Sunderland had been involved in similar discussions before the start of the session, promising to 'do great matters for the King, if he will part with the duke' (ibid., p. 590). It is also likely that support for the proposal disintegrated because the King would not agree to it until he saw that its supporters could manage Parliament, and this they were unable to do.
[124] *The Second Part of the Growth of Popery* (1682), p. 283; *CSPD 1680–1*, p. 653.
[125] *Russell Letters*, p. 121; *HMC Le Fleming*, p. 168. Sir John Davys claimed he was attacked in the second Westminster Parliament by Clayton 'and some other vassals of my Lord S[haftesbury]' (*HMC Ormonde*, v. 546).

seems to have been included simply because he had once written a panegyric to Oliver Cromwell, and therefore fitted the image of Shaftesbury as a republican, even though the poet was now one of the Court's chief writers, and was to pen the most stylish attack on the earl in *Absalom and Achitophel*. Slingsby Bethel's inclusion on the list as chief headsman was a reference to the London sheriff's alleged involvement in the execution of Charles I, another jibe about the earl's radical civil war connections. The roll-call of names was thus clearly not a serious study of the extent of Shaftesbury's support. Moreover, attitudes towards the extent of Shaftesbury's influence were always as flexible as his own alleged political waverings. The French ambassador, for example, remarked in a memorandum to Louis XIV in July 1680 that the earl directed all the opposition, yet in his dispatch dated the same day noted that many of the Court's opponents acted on their own; and a few months later reported that Shaftesbury wanted a speedy resolution of negotiations that he was currently pursuing with the Court because it was necessary to follow the Commons.[126] As Temple remarked about him, 'boldness looked like strength'.[127]

The number of Shaftesbury's followers is problematic, and, apart from Walcott, who thought that sixty commoners and peers might be counted in the group, which had an inner 'core' of only a dozen, historians have been reluctant to list them.[128] J.R. Jones, the most zealous asserter of the earl's powers, only mentions Russell, Sacheverell, Swinfen, Cavendish and the Hampdens as his lieutenants in the Commons.[129] Of these Russell was by far the most important, and Thomas Bennett, the earl's secretary, should be added; but Shaftesbury's reliance on the others who are named is more questionable. Russell had influence over Cavendish, but the latter voted against exclusion in 1679, and though he changed his mind on the issue, he kissed the King's hand in 1681 as reconciliation to the Court. Sacheverell dined with Shaftesbury in 1679, but it is difficult to find any other evidence that they were acting in concert; and there is even less evidence linking the earl and Swinfen, whose patron was Lord Paget. Similarly, the Hampdens owed more to Lord Wharton than to Shaftesbury, though the latter did support Richard Hampden's candidature for Parliament. This is not to say that these men did not act on the earl's orders; merely, that there is only sketchy

---

126 PRO, 31/3/146, ff. 24, 30, Barrillon dispatch, 12/22 July 1680; 31/3/146, f. 107, Barrillon dispatch, 7/17 October 1680.

127 Temple, *Memoirs*, p. 349.

128 R. Walcott, *English Politics in the early Eighteenth Century* (Oxford, 1956), pp. 78–9. Shaftesbury's most recent and best biographer is cautious about the extent of the earl's power (Haley, *Shaftesbury*, pp. 523, 606, 611, 744–5). V.H. Simms, 'Organisation of the Whig party during the Exclusion Crisis' (London MA, 1934), appendix ii (pp. 401–6), lists fifty-eight 'leaders of the Whig party' in the Commons, and appendix i (pp. 395–400), forty-two peers who supported Shaftesbury.

129 Jones, *First Whigs*, p. 18.

surviving evidence with which to back such a claim. We must rely on contemporary assessments, which vary in the quantity and quality of observed support. Burnet thought Shaftesbury had 'a great dexterity in engaging plain and well-meaning men that had no depth of understanding to admire him and depend on him, but even these were often disgusted with his vanity and indiscretion'; and Colonel Scott, a spy with an extensive knowledge of London's low-life, dismissed them as a motley crew of 'enemies to the government and discontented and disappointed persons and such as hoped for preferment, with fools and others deluded'. The most upbeat remark about Shaftesbury's followers was made by Daniel Finch, who reckoned in June 1679 that the earl was 'intimate with 75' MPs.[130]

Shaftesbury's power over MPs was limited by a number of factors. The first was that he did not personally have a strong regional power base from which to control election returns, and could not rely on a large clientele of compliant Members in the lower House. He therefore had to join with a number of other nobles and gentlemen who had far greater electoral strength than he did. Secondly, though the point is an obvious one, the fact that he was a peer, and not present during the Commons debates, necessarily restricted his ability to direct proceedings, again forcing him to rely on other men. Although the power of the peerage has perhaps been underestimated, the Commons after the Restoration was not an assembly where the wishes of a patron could simply be implemented on the floor of the House. Only a very few MPs could be considered to be the earl's mouthpieces in the Lower House. This is not to say that Shaftesbury did not help to formulate overall strategy, and co-ordinate it with a number of leading MPs. For example, before the opening of the session in October 1680 he met with Lord Herbert, Sir Thomas Armstrong, Lord Macclesfield, Lord Brandon, Colonel Whitley, Sir John Bowyer and Sir Richard Corbet in order 'to consult of matters in relation to that Parliament'; their discussion probably included consideration of who should be elected Speaker, since the earl's friend Francis Charlton offered the job to William Williams two days before Parliament's opening.[131] After the dissolution of the Oxford Parliament he similarly met a number of Herefordshire's MPs, such as Birch, Coningsby, Foley and John Dutton Colt.[132] But there is an important difference between influence and control. We know from the

---

[130] Foxcroft, *Supplement to Burnet*, p. 58; *CSPD July–Sept. 1683*, p. 390; *HMC Finch*, ii. 52. Perhaps the MPs who subscribed money for a contribution to Oates's maintenance made up some of this number, since the initiative appears to have come from the earl (*CSPD July–Sept. 1683*, p. 256). See also chapter 3 for those who followed the earl's lead in June 1680 in presenting the duke of York for popery.

[131] *CSPD July–Sept. 1683*, p. 175; *State Trials*, xiii. 1439. Armstrong was described in September 1679 as 'a Shaftesbury intriguer' (Bod., MS Carte 243, f. 390, Longford to Arran, 13 September 1680).

[132] *CSPD 1682*, p. 291.

lists that he compiled of MPs allegiances how he viewed them,[133] but we know little of what even sympathetically minded Members thought about him, though it is clear that Sir William Jones, for one, had no love for him.[134] Thirdly, Shaftesbury's status, credit, power and influence all fluctuated during the period, particularly as he passed in and out of office. By 1680–1 he was increasingly seen by the Court as the source of discontent ironically at a time when his power was on the decline, and when illness increasingly drained his energies. Frustration with him was summed up by Ferguson's punning rebuke that the diminutive earl was 'so little a statesman' that he rejected all expedients except exclusion even though its passage 'was next to an impossibility'.[135] Shaftesbury's single-minded pursuit of the bill against James was seen by one loyalist as proof that all the 'noise and clamour' of the period arose 'from a personal quarrel between' him and York.[136] Yet Shaftesbury was a master of propaganda. Many of his actions were designed as much for effect as to effect change. At face value he seemed to have been behind much of the unrest, but once we delve a little deeper the image has less substance. It was entirely fitting that the Court focused on his prosecution in 1681 as part of its own propaganda drive, though in the process it buttressed Shaftesbury's own self projection as the single head of opposition.

The attention paid to Shaftesbury's organisational skills as leader of the Whigs, and the single issue of exclusion, has overshadowed the broader ideology that helped bind MPs together. A party must have a set of ideals and a working list of priorities in order to achieve them. Apart from the so-called 'instructions' to MPs, which will be considered later, Shaftesbury's role in formulating the 1679 agenda for the opposition to the Court was subordinate to that of another peer who commanded a great deal of respect in the Lower House, Lord Holles. It is significant that the document that Shaftesbury probably drew up prior to the 1679 Parliament described the state of the nation, rather than what ought to be done to remedy it.[137] If the reports

---

133 J.R. Jones, 'Shaftesbury's "Worthy Men"', *BIHR*, xxx (1957), 232–41. Even if Shaftesbury was totally accurate in his categorisations, it would not prove that he was their leader but that he was a shrewd political observer. *History of Parliament*, ii. 123 uses the list to suggest that only twenty-eight on the 'worlay' list voted against exclusion, and eighteen who voted for the bill had been marked 'base' or 'vile', 'an error of some 8 per cent'. In fact, this percentage does not include the abstainers, who increase the error rate to 14 per cent, and it is also worth asking why ninety-five 'worthy' men failed to vote, compared to only thirty 'vile' or 'base' men, a fact that tends to count against Haley's idea that an informal system of pairing may have operated (Haley, *Shaftesbury*, p. 522). If we add the abstainers to the other voters who surprised Shaftesbury's calculation, we find just over 27 per cent of MPs failing to live up to expectations, besides the thirty-six Members whom the earl marked as 'doubtful'.

134 Scott, *Restoration Crisis*, 61.

135 *The Second Part of the Growth of Popery* (1682), pp. 259–60.

136 All Souls, MS 240, f. 63, manuscript tract, June 1679. cf. *Plain Dealing* (1681), p. 14.

137 The tract is discussed by Haley, *Shaftesbury*, pp. 502–3.

compiled by Barrillon and others are an accurate reflection of the state of politics in 1678–9, it was Lord Holles, rather than Shaftesbury, who seems to have been instrumental in drawing up programmes of action.[138] As we have seen, negotiations took place before the dissolution of the Cavalier Parliament, between Danby and a group of 'presbyterians' led by Holles, for the disbandment of the army, for a new Parliament that was to sit for a minimum of six months and a maximum of three years, and for a thorough investigation of the Popish Plot before the new assembly met.[139] When the Cavalier Parliament was dissolved, Holles had another opportunity to draw up a plan of how to proceed when the new Parliament met. The agenda for the meeting in March 1679 is thus of particular interest in assessing the state of party planning early in the crisis, and indicates what issues were considered to be important.[140] According to one report sent to Danby, Holles's first priority was 'the enacting of some laws whereby the liberty and property of the subject might be preserved'.[141] This meant a series of measures designed to ensure that the legal system was used for corrective purposes 'and not destruction': a Habeas Corpus Act, the appointment of judges for life rather than at the pleasure of the King, and a law regulating the trial of peers. Holles also aimed at a militia bill and bills 'for the entire suppression of popery'.[142] Another report suggests that the leader of the 'presbyterians' was preparing a bill to remedy some of the abuses which had been apparent during the recent parliamentary elections.[143] All these measures were duly introduced in the new Parliament. Conspicuous by its absence was any demand for exclusion.

A rudimentary form of a modern political party's programme of action was therefore available at the start of the first Westminster Parliament, and another detailed set of objectives was drawn up, apparently soon after its dissolution, entitled 'Severall Usefull and Indispensibly necessary Cautions and Instructions to the Members of Parliament'.[144] In order to avoid being caught out by a sudden end to the next session, as had happened in May, it urged MPs to consider 'what bills are fittest to be first entered upon and dispatched ... to be ready for the Royal assent in case of a dissolution or

---

[138] In December 1679 Barrillon described him as 'the man of all England for whom the different cabals have the most consideration' (Dalrymple, Memoirs, ii. 260).

[139] These negotiations are further considered by D. Lacey, Dissent and Parliamentary Politics 1661–89 (New Jersey, 1969), p. 95.

[140] The Plowman's Complaint [1679] set out a programme in print. It called on MPs to put out papists from the fleet and militia, bring the plotters to justice, repeal the laws against protestant dissenters, and attack those who had purloined taxes, concluding that 'if these things be Deny'd, Delay'd, or You sent Home, then English-Free-Men, Sound your Trumpet, Beat your Drum'.

[141] BL, Add. 28,047, f. 47, Thomas Knox to Danby, 23 January 1679.

[142] BL, Add. 28,049, f. 32, J. Netterville to ?Knox, 11 January [1679].

[143] All Souls, MS 171, f. 27, newsletter, 27 February 1679.

[144] BL, Longleat mss, M/863, reel v, Coventry mss, vol. vi, ff. 248–51.

prorogation'. It gave detailed guidance about what resolutions should be followed, including votes about the plot, the trials of the catholic lords who stood impeached, a denial of the King's right to pardon anyone who was impeached or of the right of bishops to vote on such matters, about the King's guard being a grievance, about the navy, and about the King's revenue. One tract printed in 1685 may have been referring to such a document when it complained that the votes and addresses of the 1679–81 Parliaments had been 'contrived and hammer'd by Factious Clubs and Cabals, several months before the Parliament sat, and divers copies distributed among the leading men'.[145]

The opposition to the Court had plenty of time to draw up plans in the autumn of 1680 although, as Secretary Jenkins observed, the various factions had 'so many hares on foot' that they found it difficult to agree on a concerted line of action for the new Parliament.[146] Apart from measures to settle the succession, there were plans to 'justify petitioning [and] make a remonstrance, to get a certain time to sit', to extend parliamentary control of the navy, the garrisons, the Exchequer, Ireland and Scotland.[147] The French ambassador reported that nobody now thought that exclusion alone would satisfy MPs.[148] Shortly after the session had opened, Algernon Sidney believed that the Members would never agree with the King until he had renounced his right to prorogue or dissolve Parliament, and surrendered the power to choose the commanders of the armed forces and finance commissioners.[149] It is clear that there was a considerable amount of informal discussion amongst MPs before Parliament sat, but that the agenda they were setting was becoming increasingly unwieldy and wide ranging. The programme for the Oxford Parliament was set out in a number of addresses, or 'instructions' which will be discussed later, since they show how the localities were beginning to have a say in the formulation of the parliamentary agenda.

Having established the existence of objectives for MPs to follow, albeit worked out in an increasingly *ad hoc* fashion after Holles's death, it is necessary to stress that they were aims rather than day-to-day directions on how to proceed. Unlike the Court party under Danby, the opposition did not possess rewards to hand out to loyal followers, and there was no 'whipping' system of threats or enticements that could be applied to independently minded Members. As a result objectives were often not achieved. For example, Lord Holles had negotiated with Danby for the dissolution of the Cavalier Parliament and the exile of the duke of York, in return for reducing

145 *The Mischief of Cabals* (1685), p. 8.
146 PRO, SP.104/67, Jenkins to William of Orange, 24 August 1680, 28 September 1680; Bod., MS Carte 104, f. 38, Jenkins to Middleton, 1 October 1680.
147 *CSPD 1680–1*, pp. 25, 44; PRO, 31/3/146, ff. 109–10, Barrillon dispatch, 11/21 October 1680.
148 PRO, 31/3/146, f. 118, Barrillon dispatch, 18/28 October 1680.
149 PRO, Kew FO.95/566, d'Avaux dispatch, 4/14 November 1680.

Danby's punishment to a mild censure if he withdrew from affairs and agreed to disband the army; but unless he had all along intended to trick the Court, Holles was unable to deliver what he promised, a failure that Barrillon had shrewdly predicted.[150]

The reports of the French ambassador, who paid MPs for services and news, indicate that outside influences were also at work in influencing the House of Commons, even if they did not alter the structure of politics.[151] In the autumn of 1678 Barrilon worked closely with Country MPs in the downfall of Danby. Of particular use were Montagu, Harbord, Sacheverell, Littleton, Powle and Hampden, many of whom were connected to Lord Holles, though the latter refused a preferred gift of a jewelled box. But it is important to remember that Barrillon was only making use of discontented MPs, not creating an opposition party, and certainly not a party that directly promoted French interests. In order to frustrate English alliances with Spain and the Dutch, he was increasingly thrown back on to two main pressure groups of MPs who could influence the House. The first was a group of the duke of Monmouth's friends, although they were really only a subset of the exclusionist camp, who were useful because they kept the English Court concerned with domestic rather than European concerns, and because they could help to frustrate attempts to name William of Orange, or his wife Mary, as the beneficiaries of a successful exclusion or regency bill. Barrillon included Montagu, Cavendish, Lee, Trenchard, Russell, Vaughan and Winnington among the Monmouthites.[152] Counting those who entertained the duke on his progresses through England in 1680, together with other evidence about whose company he kept, a group of over twenty more Members of the Commons, as well as a handful of peers, can be identified as Monmouth's associates.[153] However, the extent to which this pressure-group co-ordinated their activity must remain doubtful, for amity could not necessarily be translated into political cohesion: Cavendish, for one, was on good personal

---

[150] PRO, 31/3/142, f. 25, Barrillon dispatch, 16/26 January; f. 35, 20/30 January; f. 40, 30 January/9 February 1679; Reresby, *Memoirs*, p. 168.

[151] For the influence of Spanish envoys see PRO, 31/3/146, f. 58, Barrillon dispatch, 16/26 August; f. 64, Barrillon dispatch, 23 August/2 September; f. 119, Barrillon dispatch, 18/28 October 1680.

[152] PRO, 31/3/146, ff. 24–9, Barrillon dispatch, 12/22 July 1680.

[153] They are: Sir Thomas Armstrong, Thomas Thynne, George Speke, Sir John Sydenham, William Strode, Edmund Prideaux, Sir Walter Yonge, Richard Duke, Sir William Courtenay, Michael Harvey, Thomas Horde, William Wright, Brome Whorwood, Sir William Portman, Sir William Waller, Major John Braman and Sir Ralph Dutton. In addition, Sir Scrope Howe, Thomas Wharton, Sir John Stonhouse and Nicholas Bayntun were created freemen of Oxford at the same time as Monmouth in September 1680. Less firm friends include Sir William Jones and Viscount Colchester. Noble friends included Shaftesbury, Huntingdon, Stamford, Lovelace and Grey. For Monmouth's supporters in Cheshire in 1682 see Cheshire RO, DDX/7, deposition by Peter Shakerley, 19 September 1682.

terms with the duke, but not in favour of his succession to the throne. Indeed, according to Godolphin in December 1680, there were only ten MPs 'attached' to Monmouth at the beginning of the second Westminster Parliament, although he believed their number to be growing.[154]

Algernon Sidney had no great liking for the King's illegitimate son,[155] but was an important member of a second, closely connected neo-republican group through which Barrillon and D'Avaux worked to wreck Court policy directed against France. It has recently been claimed that there was a revival of republicanism in Parliament during the crisis, and that it helped provide both leadership and the repetition of the agenda of the 'good old cause'.[156] Such a view exaggerates the influence of the republicans, just as propagandists did at the time. The labels 'republican' or 'commonwealthsman' were freely banded about, especially after the discovery of the Rye House Plot to kill the King in 1683, and modern historians have been equally imprecise about the criteria employed in identifying them.[157] The number of men actively seeking the overthrow of the monarchy was very small, though those seeking to learn from classical antiquity, who emphasised ideas of contract and natural rights and who spoke a rhetoric of civic virtue were undoubtedly more numerous.[158] The number of 'good old cause' republicans in Parliament was tiny. Barrillon listed only the two Hampdens, Ingoldsby, Hill, Foley, Hobart and Hotham, though he might have added Mildmay and Braman.[159] For all his efforts, Sidney never made it into the House, and in any case was always something of a loner; as the French Ambassador put it, 'il ... prétend faire figure par lui même'.[160] Important as he was in the role of political observer, intriguer and theorist, he did not occupy a pivotal role in

---

154 Van Prinsterer, *Archives*, v. 455–6.

155 PRO, 31/3/146, f. 28, Barrillon dispatch, 12/22 July 1680.

156 Scott, *Restoration Crisis*, pp. 60–4.

157 For a clear study of the nature of republicanism see B. Worden, 'English Republicanism' in *The Cambridge History of Political Thought 1450–1700*, ed. J. Burns and M. Goldie (Cambridge, 1991), pp. 443–75. Scott (*Restoration Crisis*, p. 70) claims that Jones, Titus, Maynard, Sir Henry Capel and William Harbord were 'veterans of the first long parliament'; in fact, Jones did not enter the House until 3 November 1680, and whilst all the others sat in the Cavalier Parliament, only Maynard had sat in the 1640 Long Parliament.

158 J. Duke-Evans, 'The Political Theory and Practice of the English Commonwealthsmen 1695–1725' (Oxford, D.Phil. 1980) has argued that the ideas promoted by the commonwealthsmen were part of main-stream thought and assumptions.

159 PRO, 31/3/146, ff. 24–9, Barrillon dispatch, 12/22 July 1680; M. Houlbrooke, 'Paul Barrillon's Embassy in England 1677–1688' (Oxford, B.Litt. 1971), p. 145. Foley's inclusion is curious, and Richard Ingoldsby's brother Henry, who did not sit in Parliament, was a far more active associate of Sidney. Dorothy Sidney also regarded Lord Russell as a commonwealthsman (*Russell Letters*, p. 132).

160 PRO, 31/3/146, f. 28, Barrillon dispatch, 12/22 July 1680. Barrillon noted that Sidney's contacts were with 'obscure and concealed persons' (Dalrymple, *Memoirs*, ii. 287), and Sidney had signed the 1680 London mass petition on a sheet subscribed by exactly such men, indicating his relative isolation from other groups of radicals (see Knights, 'Petitioning and the Political Theorists', p. 106).

either parliamentary or, before 1680, in City politics, though his past and his persuasive tongue may have convinced Barrillon that he did.[161] Slingsby Bethel similarly failed to obtain a seat, and John Wildman only secured one for the short-lived Oxford Parliament, where he made no known contribution.[162] The republicans' most obvious leader was the duke of Buckingham, who had nurtured links with radicals in the City of London,[163] but because he was a curious and unreliable figurehead, many were forced to turn to Shaftesbury instead.[164] Problems of leadership may partly explain why those republicans who were in the House were not very good at working together: although Braman and Mildmay acted as tellers on 11 December 1680 on behalf of Sidney's election return, the tellers on the other side were William Harbord, who like Sidney had been in the pay of the French Ambassador, and John Arnold, a member of the Green Ribbon Club, who was accused in 1681 of saying that he would 'bring the King's head to the block'.[165] Moreover, the Sidney–Jones–Titus–Maynard connection, which Scott identifies and emphasises, was considerably less important in forging links with the radicals of London than the City's own MPs and merchants.[166] Sir Thomas Player (City chamberlain 1672–83, MP for London), Thomas Pilkington (City bridgemaster 1680–1, MP for London), Thomas Papillon (City auditor 1680–2, MP for Dover), Sir Robert Clayton (London's lord mayor 1679–80 and MP), John Dubois (City auditor 1679–80, MP for Liverpool) and Sir Patience Ward (lord mayor 1680–1, MP for Pontefract)

[161] Although Barrillon ascribed Bethel's election as sheriff in 1680 to the intrigues of Sidney (Dalrymple, *Memoirs*, ii. 287), his information probably came from Sidney himself, and one newsletter ascribed Bethel and Cornish's election to the MPs Player, Pilkington and Dubois (Leeds AO, Mexborough mss, Reresby 15/73, 15 July 1680). For the significance of this group of London officials see below.

[162] On 31 October 1678 Daniel Finch noted that Wildman was 'very active and busy' (Leics. RO, DG7/4957/57, f. 7), but his role as secretary to the Lords' committee investigating the plot was handed over to Shaftesbury's steward, Thomas Stringer (Haley, *Shaftesbury*, pp. 473–4).

[163] Buckingham may have sought to patronise the Green Ribbon Club (*The Litany of the D. of B.*, endorsed as 1679 on BL C. 20. f. 4 (252).

[164] In March 1679 Buckingham negotiated for a pardon and promised to discover designs against the government, promises which he may have repeated the following year (*HMC Lindsey*, p. 403; BL, Add. 28,053, f. 135, 'Mr Hebdon 16 March ab[ou]t the D[uke] of Bucks pardon'; Congress newsletter 7/50, 13 May; 7/54, 25 May; 7/63, 17 June 1680; Bucks. RO, Verney mss M11/34, Cary Gardiner to Sir Ralph Verney, 31 May 1680; UNCW, Mostyn MS 9090, f. 29, newsletter, 5 June 1680). In January 1680 Barrillon remarked that Shaftesbury managed the republicans (PRO, 31/3/144, f. 29, Barrillon dispatch, 5/15 January 1680), and it is significant that the following month Buckingham's barge greeted the duke of York on his return (*Mercurius Anglicus*, no. 28, p. 84, 24 February 1680).

[165] *CJ*, ix. 677. Tellerships are not, of course, proof of allegiance, but are often a useful indicator. Further evidence that the 'republicans' were not primarily a parliamentary force is provided by the fact that in November 1680 John Hampden left England for a European tour (*History of Parliament*, i. 546).

[166] Jones's credentials as a 'good old cause' republican are highly suspect. See Burnet, *History*, ii. 282.

were all more influential in terms of City and parliamentary politics, and were on good terms with Shaftesbury and Buckingham, who lived in the City and became members of City livery companies.[167] Indeed, Scott's argument that in the summer of 1680 Shaftesbury was at odds with a radical, republican faction in the City is based on a misreading of evidence.[168] It is precisely *because* of Shaftesbury's contacts there that the earl was an important figure.

Although the revival of republicanism in Parliament may have been exaggerated, Scott is right to suggest that there is value in viewing the crisis from the perspective of the past as well as the future. Sir Roger L'Estrange and other pamphleteers claimed that the design of the exclusionists was exactly the same as that of the rebels of the 1640s and 1650s, and that if men examined the present disturbers of the state they would 'find the old Republicans to be the Ring-leaders', that there were 'the same faces now at work again' and that the disaffected were 'all descended from the right forty one breed'.[169] Even Oliver Heywood, a puritan minister, believed that Whig and Tory had simply replaced roundhead and cavalier.[170] In other words, the past dictated the structure of politics. One way of testing this claim is to correlate the opinions of MPs in 1679–81 with their, or their families' allegiances, between 1640 and 1660. Of course, such a correlation could lay no claims to great accuracy, since the categorisation of Members into neat groups is impossible, especially when the definition of those groups helps to determine the outcome of the enquiry; when many MPs had no personal experience of the earlier period; and when evidence about allegiances on either personal or present issues is often vague or nonexistent. Even so, the task is worth attempting, so long as these caveats are remembered. Using the labels given by

---

167 *History of Parliament*, ii. 84–7, 237–8; iii. 202–5, 245–7, 250–2, 667–70; Luttrell, *Brief Relation*, i. 69; Haley, *Shaftesbury*, pp. 640–1; *Original Papers*, p. 112. Shaftesbury referred to a 'City party' in May 1681 (*Loyal Protestant*, 20 May 1681). After the Oxford Parliament, it was alleged that Pilkington, Player and Clayton, William Strode, Sir Richard Cust and George Treby (MP for Plympton Erle and Recorder of London 1680–3) were said to have held frequent meetings with Shaftesbury, Grey, Howard and Chandos, and wanted a 'free state' (*CSPD 1680–1*, p. 232).

168 Scott uses the evidence of the 1680 shrieval election to support his claim that J.R. Jones made factually incorrect assertions about Shaftesbury that flew in the face of contrary evidence. He also uses it as as evidence of 'the public boiling over' of the acrimony between Shaftesbury and Sidney. (*Restoration Crisis*, pp. 59, 164–5). In fact, the letter Scott quotes on p. 165 refers to 1679, not 1680, and to a general election, not a City election; he offers no evidence that Sir William Russell, a juror for the 1683 treason trials, was a 'client' of Shaftesbury's or that the earl campaigned on his behalf; moreover, Sidney tried to patch up the quarrel with Shaftesbury (which was over the earl's allegation that Sidney was a pensioner of France), at least so far as to undertake to 'know his mind' (*Russell Letters*, p. 136).

169 *A Dialogue between the Pope and a Phanatick* (1680), p. 18; *Citt and Bumpkin* (1680), p. 28; *A Word Concerning Libels* (1681), p. 11; *The Protestants' Remonstrance* (1681), p. 24; *A Letter to the Earl of Shaftesbury* (1680), p. 2.

170 Cited by Willman, 'Origins of Whig and Tory', p. 263.

the Henning volumes of the *History of Parliament*, an interesting pattern emerges. Analysis of the MPs who voted in the division for the exclusion bill on 21 May 1679, for which a list is extant, shows that, of those whose background could be identified with some degree of certainty, ninety-three came from Parliamentarian and 122 from Royalist camps. Only one seventh of these Parliamentarians voted against the bill, compared to a third of Royalists who supported the measure. Those from Parliamentarian backgrounds were thus far more likely to support the bill than oppose it, whilst a significant minority of Royalists also backed it. This basic result is repeated if the total number of MPs sitting in the period are categorised in terms of past and present attitudes.[171] Two features about these findings are striking. Firstly, many pre-Restoration groupings survived the Restoration, especially among Parliamentarian families; secondly, and paradoxically, a significant number of MPs with a 'Royalist' background opposed the Court and/or voted for exclusion.[172] The caricatures and oversimplifications of the pamphleteers thus contained some true-to-life strokes, though the past did not so much cause certain behaviour as add another layer of political consciousness that helps explain it.

Like the past, another plane of influence on the behaviour of MPs was religion. The labels of Whig and Tory had religious connotations, derived from names given to Scottish covenanting (presbyterian) rebels, and Irish (catholic) thieves. A polarity had emerged between protestants of all hues and so-called 'papists in masquerade', men whose devotion to the reformed religion was thought to be lukewarm or a cloak for for catholicism: 'Whoever have been Neutrals in this last Grand Contest between Religion and Popery, ought to be more than suspected for your Enemies', exclaimed one pamphleteer.[173] To what extent, then, were the political divisions in Parliament merely a reflection of religious ones? And what in particular was the relation-

---

[171] Of MPs with readily identifiable backgrounds, 268 came from the Royalist camp and 214 from the Parliamentarian. Only one seventh of the latter supported the Court, compared to about a half of the former.

[172] Eighty-two fought personally for the King, twenty-four of whom voted for exclusion. cf. P.J. Challinor, 'Restoration and Exclusion in the County of Cheshire', *Bulletin of the John Rylands University Library of Manchester*, vol. 64 (1981–2), 360–85. Anthony Wood remarked that 'those that before were thought to be royallists shew themselves to be whiggs' (note on MS Tanner 102, f. 120, cited in Wood, *Life and Times*, ii. 431). William Cowper later claimed that the supporters of exclusion were 'those, generally speaking, who by themselves or their ancestry had been royalists and had taken part with King Charles I' (Campbell, *Lives of Lord Chancellors*, iv. 422). The earl of Ailesbury suggested that Royalist dissatisfaction with the Restoration land settlement contributed to the formation of the Whigs (*Ailesbury Memoirs*, i. 6).

[173] *A Seasonable Warning to the Commons of England* (1679), p. 3. cf. 'The quarrel is now purely betwixt Protestant and Papist' (*The Countries Vindication* [1679], p. 3).

ship between political and religious dissent? One pamphleteer thought that 'the present jealousies which do possess the minds of the people, especially the vulgar sort, may solely be attributed to the great increase of sects and factions amongst us, who though they differ on some points of Religion, yet the aversion of them all is the same to the Church of England'.[174] Protestant nonconformists or occasional conformists did tend to support the exclusion bill – Sir Thomas Clarges said all the supporters of the bill were 'either Presbyterians or their sons' – whilst only a few of them opposed it; but they do not account for all the bill's supporters.[175] William Cowper later claimed that the bill was 'promoted by members of the Church of England (there being but two or three dissenters or thereabouts in any of those Parliaments)'.[176] He perhaps overstated his case, but, even so, in 1679 a quarter of 'anglicans', and almost half of 'probable anglicans', in the House voted for the bill.[177] Furthermore, when looking at a broader range of MPs' attitudes, the *History of Parliament* tentatively suggests a 'movement of anglicans and probable anglicans towards opposition' as the crisis developed.[178] In a sense, these figures really only show how the term 'anglican' can be misleading, since attitudes towards dissent were, as Cowper himself recognised, the important factor in polarising the nation, rather than membership of the church itself. Those who conformed to the church settlement themselves, but who saw no need to enforce the penal laws, either in theory or simply at a time of heightened fears about the threat from popery, seem to have comprised the bulk of 'anglican' supporters of the bill, though a minority of such men, such as Halifax, Anglesey and Buckingham in the Lords, or Sir Richard Temple and Finch in the Commons, opposed it or were unenthusiastic about its passage. Although not vociferous in 1678–9, when anti-popery temporarily papered over divisions within the protestant community, anglicans who could not understand the objections of the dissenters, and even those who sympathised with their reservations about conformity but increasingly found them frivolous or mistimed, had by 1681 come to see conventiclers as an example of opposition for the sake of opposition, a view which in its most extreme expression pictured dissent as a cover for a desire to overthrow the existing political as well as religious system. The factional view of religion thus merged with the factional view of politics to give it even greater potency. This union was expressed by the term 'faction', which we have seen used against men in a secular way, and which also had a religious meaning, being one of the terms applied to nonconformists.

As Robert Ferguson's comments about the frustration felt by some

[174] *A Letter to a Friend in the Country Touching the Present Fears* (1680), p. 1.
[175] Dalrymple, *Memoirs*, ii. 219–20; *History of Parliament*, i. 52–3.
[176] Campbell, *Lives of the Lord Chancellors*, iv. 422.
[177] *History of Parliament*, i. 13, 52.
[178] *History of Parliament*, i. 51.

Members about the lack of progress on measures to safeguard protestantism show, religion was certainly on the agenda of MPs;[179] but the agenda itself was not purely religious. For example, at the end of October 1678, when fears of popery were at their height in the immediate wake of the Popish Plot revelations, Sir Francis Rolle approached Daniel Finch 'and tould me he wonderd I was so zealous in Promoting those Bills [against popery], & used many Argum[en]ts to dissuade me from desiring any bills for the security of the Protestant Religion as long as there were such Ministers [as Danby] about the King, for till they were removed all was in vaine'.[180] Not all parliamentary politics was the politics of religion. Algernon Sidney assured a republican friend in Holland that it was wrong to believe that religion motivated the principal men in England, claiming that it was only a pretext for the recovery of their liberty and ancient privileges.[181] From the other side, the thrust of loyalist pamphleteering on the succession was that James's religion was being used as a mask to hide the malcontents' more sinister aims against the state.[182] Thus whilst religious sympathies helped fire the clamour for the subject's legal rights, which were necessary for the security of protestantism, a significant part of the constitutional debate took place on a purely secular level about the rights and powers of Parliament and the King. Religion was part of a citizen's liberty and property, which was why those words became such important slogans.

Religion, therefore, was one bond of cohesion, but it was part of a broader shared ideology. Whig tenets were defined by opponents as support for liberty of conscience and an association of protestants, insistence on exclusion, the replacement of the King's advisers, and a reformation of all judges and other officers appointed by the Crown.[183] The 'modern Whig' or 'à la mode true loyal protestant' was 'bred in the corruption of the late rebellion', took his religion from Geneva, shouted rallying cries of the Plot, popery and arbitrary government, subscribed petitions, and had 'blasphemed his R[oyal] H[igh-ness the duke of York] beyond all hopes of pardon, that therefore his all is at stake';[184] he believed no form of government to be *jure divino*, and that fundamental laws limited the powers of Kings.[185] The Whig drawn by the pen of his opponents was, of course, a stereotype, and in reality his commitment to this whole programme may have varied; yet the features identified show that the critics of the Court were more than just exclusionists. True Whigs believed in natural, fundamental rights and the idea of the sovereignty of the

---

[179] *The Second Part of the Growth of Popery* (1682), p. 260.
[180] Leics. RO, Finch mss, DG7/4957/57, f. 7, 31 October 1678.
[181] PRO (Kew), FO.95/566, d'Avaux dispatch, 4/14 November 1680.
[182] See, for example, *Fiat Justicia* (1679), p. 1, and *Observator*, no. 1, 13 April 1681.
[183] *Observator*, no. 29, 2 July 1681.
[184] *The Character of a Modern Whig* (1681), pp. 1–2.
[185] *The History of Whiggism* (1682), p. 5.

people, leading to a view of the constitution which stressed the rights of the subject rather than the prerogative of the King, as well as the right to self defence against a tyrant, and greater freedom of worship than the Restoration settlement allowed. This complex web of ideology deserves greater investigation than this chapter will permit, and is so important to our understanding of the crisis that the second half of the book seeks in part to relate the ideas which separated men to the context of events.

Turning to less formally organised influences on MPs, such as those of the past and of religion, allows a greater understanding of their behaviour. We should look for the community of sentiment rather than the structure of party. Such an approach, if taken at a psychological level, also helps explain why most MPs remained committed to the exclusion bill.[186] Having voted on, or supported, exclusion, many felt they had engaged themselves too far against James, who was not known for his forgiving nature,[187] to back a milder measure. Burnet remarked that some MPs 'thought in point of honour they must go on as they had done hitherto'.[188] It was personal obligation that was binding the exclusionists together as much as any party discipline. Fear, too, played its part. Daniel Finch observed that, although support for exclusion was partly motivated by concern for the perceived interests of the nation and security, it was also 'partly as a security to those who had most signally opposed the Duke, and so were afraid to trust him'.[189] Henry Savile likewise told Sir Richard Bulstrode that MPs were

too far engag'd to thinke themselves safe without finishing what they have begun; every perticuler man apprehending a personall revenge from the animosity of the duke if it ever bee in his power to shew his resentment against men who have so publickly undertooke his destruction that he must turne saint to forgive them.[190]

Mrs Cellier, the popish midwife, allegedly found 'divers' of the opposition ready to be 'taken off' but they feared York's 'revenging the injuries they might formerly have done him'.[191] On occasions these powerful emotions resembled a loyalty to party, and the attacks on the turn-coats Sir Robert Peyton, Justice Warcup and Judge Sir Francis Pemberton suggest that many of

---

[186] About thirty-five MPs nevertheless shifted their stance over the bill, mainly from opposition to consent.

[187] Russell had told the Commons that James was 'a Prince implacable and that never forgot injuries' (*Ailesbury Memoirs*, i. 27). Shaftesbury described James as 'heady, violent and bloody' (Christie, *Shaftesbury*, ii. 314).

[188] Burnet, *History*, ii. 282.

[189] *HMC Finch*, ii. 98.

[190] BL, Eg.3678, Henry Savile to Sir Richard Bulstrode, 14/24 January 1681. cf. Temple, *Memoirs*, p. 350; Reresby, *Memoirs*, p. 221.

[191] Halstead, *Succinct Geneaologies* (1685), p. 435. Ironically, James's employment of dissenters and Whigs after 1687 suggests that he could forget former opposition to him when necessary.

their colleagues felt betrayed when they 'joined with the King'.[192] In the first version of his *History*, in a passage that was subsequently dropped from the final text, Burnet wrote that the 'hot men' among what people called the Whig party were a 'violent and unjust sort of people, and if a man does not in all points come up to their humours, they will defame him with more virulence and spight that in if he were in all points of the opposite party'.[193] But the tie of personal loyalty could work both ways. For example, Sir William Jones, on account of his 'old friendship' with Laurence Hyde, 'got the words relating to popery to be struck out of the address against him', and the 'exclusionist' Sir William Portman gave security for the courtier, but fellow west-countryman, Seymour.[194]

CONCLUSION

The distorting influence of simple but powerful emotions such as friendship and fear remind us of the personal and individual side of politics at Westminster, and force us to question the extent to which modern party management came into being. We must be careful not to equate all division with party, and organisation with an organisation. The crisis was an important stage in the seventeenth-century evolution of faction towards party, but the feats of political organisation in Parliament that have been claimed for the first Whigs have been exaggerated. The large roles accorded to the exclusion bill and to Shaftesbury's parliamentary control need to be slimmed down, to make way for greater emphasis on the domination of the Commons by a steering group of important MPs who worked with, but not always under, the earl, and on a loose, often informally organised, structure of politics that owed more to the bonds of ideology than to party-enforced cohesion. The term Whig – at least before the remodelling of the borough charters and the Tory reaction which again, and permanently broadened its applicability – is best reserved for the ideological remnant of the opposition to the Court in 1681 once it had been stripped of its adventurers, trimmers and those country gentry who were either won over or neutralised by the rhetoric used by the Court, or whose fear of civil war outweighed their fear of royal misgovernment. Whig and Tory in 1681–3 thus represent the extremes of ideological, political and religious polarities, and it would be futile to try to pigeon-hole all contemporaries into these categories.

Perhaps the best way to convey the complexity of allegiances and groupings is to employ a term used frequently by the Court to describe its critics, the

192 *CSPD 1680–1*, p. 365.
193 BL, Add. 63,057B, Burnet's ms history, f. 44.
194 Burnet, *History*, ii. 262; Grey, *Debates*, viii. 181.

'factious party'. The two elements of this label were, for contemporaries, interchangeable in a way no longer acceptable to modern definitions of the words. For example, in the 1683 version of his history, Burnet referred to men 'forming themselves out of Parliament into a faction against the Court'; but in the later published text substituted the word 'party' for 'faction'.[195] In part, Burnet's revision reflects the political developments between the early 1680s and the early eighteenth century when the work was published, but it also shows a greater flexibility of language than we now employ. The term 'factious party' neatly captures the many nuances behind the motivation, composition and organisation of the Court's opponents. It rightly depicts the movement, which had not yet been completed, towards party from faction. Of course, the phrase is loaded with value judgments, and does not sufficiently cater for the input of ideology, but it does imply a group of men, held together by some degree of common bond, who could nevertheless on occasion display characteristics associated with a faction. Politics was a constantly spinning double-sided coin, with faction on one surface, and party on the other.

[195] BL, Add. 63,057B, Burnet's ms history, f. 54.

A Prospect of a Popish Successor (1681)

Sir Roger L'Estrange

THE TIME-SERVERS: Or, A TOUCH OF THE TIMES.

Being a DIALOGUE between

Tory, Towzer, and Tantivee,

At the News of the Diffolution of the

Late **Worthy Parliament at Orford,**

The Time Servers (1681)

The effigy of an 'abhorrer' of petitions in a pope-burning procession

1 d.

A New BALLAD,

With the Definition of the Word

TORY.

7. June 1682.

THE Word *Tory's* of *Irish* Extraction,
   'Tis a Legacy they have left here,
They came here in their Brogues,
And have acted like Rogues,
In endeavouring to learn us to Swear.
Those Papists, I may rather say Atheists,
Was sent with a Sham to the Town,
To Swear one Plot up and another Plot down.

With a thick *Irish* Air, like the same that they
                    (Swear,
Contradiction in every Line ;
But this I conclude, their understanding's not
                    (good,
Their Reason's left in *Ireland* behind.

Towzer.
I will Write on
and Sham as I
have begun.

Thomson.
And I will Lie in
Print as you have
done.

Church of ENGLAND.   **PRESBYTER.**
There's nothing essential that divides us two. | Let us combine against the common Foe.

A New Ballad (1682)

Part II

PUBLIC OPINION, 1679–81: THE SUCCESSION, POPERY AND ARBITRARY GOVERNMENT

'I would fain understand what is meant by the People? for now every man calls himself the People; and when one man calls for one Thing and another for Something directly opposite, both cry out, that if this or that be done the People is betray'd.'

A Letter from Scotland (1681), p. 1

'It is not the sense and interest of a few that can long sway a nation; for if the public spirit be averse, at the long run it will prevail.'

Roger L'Estrange, *The State and Interest of the Nation* (1680), p. 9

❖ *6* ❖

'This outrageous liberty of the press'[1]

INTRODUCTION

The analysis so far has been very much concerned with high politics, examining the succession problem and party organisation almost exclusively from a parliamentary perspective. Yet, although one pamphleteer claimed that 'the language of the House of Commons is the unanimous voice of all the people of England' and Sir William Waller claimed that a vote of its Members was 'not ours only but everybody's opinion', Parliament was not the only political arena, nor was the succession the only problem contemporaries considered.[2] The second half of this book therefore turns to the nature of the crisis outside Westminster and Whitehall. In part it will explore earlier themes from a new angle, assessing the relevance of exclusion to the wider public and examining the structure of politics in the country as a whole; but it will also seek to broaden the discussion by considering questions about public opinion: how did the crisis at the centre affect London and the localities? Were the same issues considered to be important in Parliament and in the provinces? How much influence did local politics have on national politics? How was the national will voiced, and did its message shift, or appear to shift, during the period?

In answering these questions, and by setting the political and religious unrest in its local as well as in its national context, the thrust of the argument will be that there was both a succession crisis *and* a crisis about popery and arbitrary government in England between 1679–81. I shall argue that the succession, on the one hand, and crises about the relationship between the established church and dissent, as well as about the constitutional role of Parliament and the people, on the other, are not mutually exclusive themes. There is no need to argue that the discontent of 1679–81 was concerned

---

[1] *L'Estrange's Case* (1680), p. 16.
[2] *A Letter from a Gentleman in the City to one in the Country Concerning the Bill* (1680), p. 15; Grey, *Debates*, vi. 129.

153

wholly with one single issue. To focus entirely on exclusion or entirely on religion or the constitution is to miss the point that these themes were interrelated: the depth of the crisis about popery had much to do with fears about James's succession and the arbitrariness of Stuart government; whilst fears for the survival of Parliament were related to MPs' frustrated attempts to secure the succession and religion. As one pamphleteer put it, those who favoured a popish successor were '1) against the interest of the Church of England and the Protestant Religion 2) against the interest of England your native Country 3) against the interest of all Parliaments, and so against your own freedomes and Liberties ... Remember Popery and Slavery are linked together.'[3] The following pages seek to explore both the context of the succession crisis and the context of popery and arbitrary government. They will slim down, without dismissing, the role of exclusion, because it has often been overstressed; and give greater prominence to the controversy surrounding Parliament's place in government, the attempt to reform the church to comprehend dissenters, and the struggle to represent the will of the people, topics which have often been sidelined by accounts of the period. But it was the joint force of these issues, rather than any single strand, that gave the crisis its potency.

A study of the interplay between central politics and public opinion is also both necessary and productive because of the extent to which the political debate extended outside Parliament during the crisis. Pamphleteers commented on the vigour and frankness of political discussions in coffee houses and in taverns.[4] They observed it to be a time 'when every private and ordinary person turns statesman, and with a judicious gravity canvasses, and determines the particular interests and designs of Kings and princes';[5] a time when, as another pamphleteer put it, 'little citizens become (in their own opinion) states-men, and instead of minding their Shops and Business, are hearded into little Parties, to consider what are the fit Instruments to be set up to carry on their little Policies against the Establish'd Government and Laws';[6] a time when 'the Bounds of Sovereign Power [are] debated by Potters and Carmen over Pots of Ale',[7] and when 'the meanest Coblers dare censure the greatest States-men'.[8] Dryden complained that the theatre-going public cared for nothing but news, the exchange of which had become the theatre of

---

[3] *A Most Serious Expostulation* (1679), pp. 2, 4.
[4] *A Word without Doors* (1680), p. 1, claimed that discussions in taverns were more private.
[5] *The Mischiefs and Unreasonableness* (1681), p. 40.
[6] *A Seasonable Address to the Right Honourable the Lord Mayor* (1680), p. 2.
[7] *The Free-Born Subject* (1679), p. 12.
[8] *The Power of Parliaments in Case of Succession* (1680), p. 2.

'vast resort'.[9] Although the political crisis was most severe in London, and Sir William Hickman observed that news 'allay[ed] much in its passage' into the country,[10] the nation as a whole was affected by three general elections, as well as petitioning and addressing campaigns, making a survey of opinion in the localities as important as the study of London.

Defining public opinion is, however, problematic in a number of ways. The most obvious difficulty is the conflicting claims of groups, each claiming to speak for the 'people'. As one pamphleteer remarked, 'I would fain understand what is meant by the People? For now every man calls himself the People.'[11] The problem of 'what was really the sense of the Nation' was also one to which Roger North was sensitive.[12] He pointed out that the opinion of a few could appear as that of many, 'and on the other side, the true many, that are dispersed and unactive ... shall seem but a few'. As these comments indicate, much of the bitterness of the crisis was the result of debate over what institution or group represented the will of the nation. Was it the monarchy, Parliament, the grand juries who sent addresses to the King, or the groups of individuals who signed mass petitions? The question of determining the true sense and representation of the country was central to the political crisis, and will form one of the main concerns of the following chapters.

A second problem lies in the sources, which are themselves a form of opinion. Sir Leoline Jenkins recognised that if anyone was to 'measure the temper of the nation by the humour of our coffee houses, and by the venomous bitternesse of a few writers of Libells' the reader would find the prevalence of a different set of opinions to those really espoused by the bulk of the nation, which Jenkins believed was generally 'not so unjust, nor so ill-natured'.[13] Even an opposition tract recognised that 'we must not judge of the Temper of the People from Loud Clamour'.[14] Yet all too often it is only through sometimes inaccurate or biased printed newspapers and manuscript newsletters that an 'opinion' about events can be determined, while the views of the illiterate, inactive or unvocal majority are difficult to establish. Before turning to the debate over the will of the nation, we therefore need to examine the methods used to convey opinion and news to people outside Parliament.

[9] Prologue to Lee's *Caesar Borgia*, quoted by G.W. Whiting, 'The Condition of the London Theatres 1679–83: A Reflection of the Political Situation', *Modern Philology*, xxv (1927), 197–8.

[10] BL, Althorp MS C2, Hickman to Halifax, 27 March 1680.

[11] *A Letter from Scotland* (1681), p. 1.

[12] North, *Examen*, p. 491.

[13] PRO, SP.104/3, f. 16, Sir Leoline Jenkins to Lord Bodmyn, 13 August 1680.

[14] *London's Choice of Citizens* (1679), p. 3.

THE ORGANISATION OF THE PRESS

Politics and propaganda were inextricably linked during the period after the expiry of the Licensing Act in May 1679.[15] Their symbiotic relationship was noted by Sir Roger L'Estrange who believed that the press must bear responsibility for the political unrest. 'Tis the press that has made 'um Mad, and the Press must Set 'um Right again', he wrote.[16] Similarly, a writer in 1681 blamed the liberty of the press as the chief factor in 'spreading contagions of our divisions, both in Church and State' and that 'a few tuggs at the press shall immediately produce that which shall with ease speak to the whole nation at once',[17] whilst according to intelligence that William of Orange later received, it was precisely because the exclusionists lost control of the press that they were defeated.[18] An understanding of both the organisation of the printing world and the content of the propaganda it produced is therefore germane to later discussions about politics, propaganda and opinion.

This first part of this chapter will deal with the organisation of the press, and will concentrate on some bibliographical aspects of the subject to which relatively little attention has been paid by political historians, but which have important implications for our study of the period. The second section will examine the distribution of printed and manuscript material, and will ask what impact such literature, and in particular the part of it relating to parliamentary proceedings, may have had on the literate public. A final section will indicate the main themes of the literature, and hence suggest the direction of the ensuing discussion.

Some impressions about the organisation of the press can be gained by looking at a sample of the tracts printed during the period. About 600 titles of pamphlets produced between 1679 and 1681 have been selected in order to investigate the role and the messages of propaganda during the crisis.[19] This number represents a fairly small proportion of the total output

---

[15] The exact date of the expiry has been variously described as 13 March 1679 (R. Astbury, 'The renewal of the Licensing Act in 1693 and its lapse in 1695', *The Library*, xxxiii [1978], p. 296) and 10 June (T. Crist, 'Government Control of the Press after the Expiration of the Licensing Act in 1679', *Publishing History*, v [1979], p. 50, and M. Treadwell, 'London Trade Publishers 1675–1750', *The Library* [1982], p. 129.) Algernon Sidney wrote at the end of March as though the Act had already expired (T. Foster, *Original Letters of John Locke, Algernon Sidney and Anthony Lord Shaftesbury* [1830], p. 94, Sidney to Benjamin Furley, 23 March 1679). The confusion arises because the statute of 1662 was renewed in 1665 until the end of the session of the next Parliament. The first session of the 1679 Parliament was adjourned on 13 March, but without having transacted any business as a result of the dispute over who should be Speaker; the session proper was prorogued on 27 May, when privy council noted that the Act had expired (PRO, PC.2/68, f. 221, privy council minutes).

[16] *The Observator*, no. 1, 13 April 1681.

[17] *Some Reflections upon a late Pamphlet* (1681), p. 1

[18] Quoted by J.R. Jones, *The Revolution of 1688 in England* (1972), p. 227 (citing Nottingham University Portland MSS, MS PWA.2159, Intelligence from England).

[19] See bibliography.

of the press during these years. W.G. Mason's count of Wing-listed titles shows that in 1678 over 900 titles were published, compared to 800 in 1677; in 1679 this figure rose to over 1,300 and peaked in 1680 at almost 1,800 titles, before falling back in 1681 to just under 1,600.[20] My own sample was chosen purely on the basis of relevance to the controversial political and religious problems discussed in later chapters, and is thus not an average cross-section of the output of the press during these years; nor can it claim to be totally comprehensive even of those issues. Nevertheless, when backed up with information from other sources, especially P.G. Morrison's *Index to the Wing Catalogue*, it does provide a basis for discussion about the practices of printers, publishers and authors.

Only seventeen tracts in the sample carried the full names of their authors, seven of which were by L'Estrange, though a further thirty-one printed their initials. To avoid revealing their identities a number of authors preferred to use cryptic names, such as Theophilus Rationalis, Philanax Verax, Democritus, Philanax Misopappas and Pantophilus.[21] Deliberately designed to conceal the author from contemporaries they can also cause confusion for a modern reader: one pseudonym, Philanglus, was used by William Penn for *One Project for the Good of England* (1679), and also by the unknown author of *The Protestants' Remonstrance* (1681), which attacked Penn's friends, the dissenters, although both tracts are ascribed to Penn in the Wing Catalogue.[22] L'Estrange accused opposition libellers of being ashamed to put their names to their work,[23] but the same accusation might have been made with equal validity against loyalist authors. The significance of the fictitious names or the absence of names altogether is that the vast bulk of the pamphlet material was penned anonymously, often making it impossible to identify the source of the propaganda's inspiration. Thus whilst it offers insights into public opinion it must also be treated with caution since it was a 'public' that is often unknown.

Just under one fifth of the pamphlets in the sample were also issued without a date; and even those with one could be misleading. *The History of Self Defence* has its date printed as 1680, but refers to a tract not printed until 1689; and *A Letter to a Person of Honour Concerning the King's disavowing his having been married to the Duke of Monmouth's Mother* has the year

20 W.G. Mason, 'The Annual Output of Wing-Listed Titles 1649–1684', *The Library*, xxxix (1974), pp. 219–20. These yearly figures are probably underestimates since they include only pamphlets of which there are surviving copies.
21 These are the names used by the authors of *Multum in Parvo* (1681), *A Letter to his Royal Highness* (1681), *The Petitioning Comet* (1681), *A Tory Plot* (1682) and *The Plain Truth* (1681).
22 M.M. Dunn, *William Penn: Politics and Conscience* (Princeton 1967), p. 75 n. 4, recognises that the latter tract was unlikely to be Penn's work. *England's Alarm* (1679) also claimed to have been written by 'Johannes Philanglus'.
23 *Discovery upon Discovery* (1680), p. 28.

1610 instead of 1680, suggesting a rushed production. *An Excellent New Ballad*, a dialogue between two prisoners called 'Tom the Tory' and 'Tony the Whig', has the year 1678 on the imprint, suggesting that the political labels were in use at the beginning of the crisis; but since 'Tom' is a thinly disguised Thomas Osborne, earl of Danby, and 'Tony' is Anthony Ashley-Cooper, earl of Shaftesbury, and the two men were not in prison at the same time until July 1681, the printed date seems incorrect. Fortunately, this can be confirmed, for the book collector Narcissus Luttrell owned a copy, dated it as 'August 18', and placed it chronologically amongst other pamphlets published in 1681.[24] Similarly the Bodleian's copy of *A Praefatory Discourse* has a printed date of 1681, altered in a manuscript hand to '1680.3.Nov', suggesting that the publisher had tried artificially to extend the life of the tract by postdating it.[25]

Some tracts were published under more than one title. Thus *A Few Words Among Many* (1679) was republished in 1681 as *A Moderate Decision on the Point of the Succession*. *A Plea for Limited Monarchy* was first published in 1660, reprinted in 1680 with some topical additions as *The State and Interest of the Nation*, and again as *The Interest of the Three Kingdoms*. Two tracts in the sample did not change the title itself, but the imprint on the title page. The Huntington Library's copy of *A Brief Survey (Historical and Political) of the Life and Reign of Henry III* (1680), which at first was printed and published anonymously, has the label 'Printed for James Vade' glued to it.[26] More puzzling is the Huntington's copy of *The Grand Question Resolved* (1681), which shows that it had originally been printed for Richard Baldwin, and that a piece of paper stuck over it renamed the publisher as 'B. Pratt'.[27] There is no entry in the *Index to Wing* under this name, and the tract was very loyalist in tone, suggesting that the renaming may have been intended to ridicule Baldwin.

The imprints also show that, although the vast majority of pamphlets were printed in London, a few claimed to have been printed abroad, such as *Two Speeches made in the House of Peers* (1680) which declared its origin as Holland. The need to print abroad seems surprising after the expiry of the Licensing Act. Yet it is known that in August 1679 a nonconformist made a journey to Holland especially 'to print a book',[28] and in October 1680 the privy council was informed that 3,000 copies of *Discourses upon the Modern Affairs of Europe* had been printed there, at the instigation of one Robert Archer of London, and were shipped to London.[29] William Carr reported from Amsterdam that books printed by a Brownist named Smart or

---

[24] Huntington 135844.   [25] Bod., G.Pamph 1125 (29).
[26] Huntington 235926.   [27] Huntington 84491.
[28] *Diary of Henry Sidney*, i. 61.
[29] PRO, PC.2/69, f. 132, privy council minutes, 27 October 1680.

Swartz[30] were being shipped to London by a constant relay of small vessels.[31] Material about English affairs was not only sent from Holland to England, but from Holland to the rest of Europe,[32] a distribution network that worried Charles's government and his ambassadors and envoys abroad. Sir Robert Southwell had to complain three times in the summer of 1680 to the Elector of Brandenburg about the false claim made by his host's gazette that the English Parliament had been dissolved before it had even sat.[33] The appointment of Robert Plott and William Carr as special envoys in Holland facilitated control over the foreign press.[34] In November 1680 Plott gave 'a very sharp reprimande' to the *Rotterdam Gazette* for reporting that the affairs of England were 'in such confusion that a revolt was dayly expected',[35] and Carr adopted similar tactics to curb *The Haarlem Courant*.[36]

Approximately 40 per cent of the pamphlets in the sample have no record of either the printer or publisher on the imprint. At first this figure seems surprisingly high. Given the expiry of the Licensing Act in May 1679, and the simultaneous passage of the Habeas Corpus Act, which lord chancellor Finch noted as giving greater press freedom,[37] it might be expected that printers and publishers had less to fear from putting their names to their work. In fact, even before the expiry of the Act about half the publications appeared without a printer's name,[38] indicating that censorship was not the main factor behind the blank imprints. The sample therefore suggests that the lapse of restraints on the press affected printers' and publishers' anonymity very little.[39] But it did create an opportunity for some enterprising and courageous

---

30 PRO, SP.84/216, f. 154, Carr to Jenkins, 25 March 1681. Secretary Jenkins referred to 'one Swartz the phanatick printer' in Amsterdam who infringed Richard Royston's copyright of Dr Hammond's works (PRO, SP.104/68, f. 15, Jenkins to Henry Sidney, 31 August 1680). 'Mr Stephen Swartz Bookseller' was also reported to have copies of a treasonable reply to the King's *Declaration* of April 1681 (BL, Add. 37,981, f. 32, Carr to Conway, 19/29 April 1681).

31 PRO, SP.84/216, f. 154, Carr to Jenkins, 25 March 1681.

32 Ibid.

33 Kent AO, U350/C4, f. 140, Charles Dering to Sir Edward Dering, 8/18 September 1680. Henry Savile in Paris requested the publication of a pamphlet to put forward the Court's case for distribution in France (*Savile Correspondence*, pp. 112, 117).

34 Carr had been instrumental in suppressing Lord Howard's and Du Moulin's propaganda in the early 1670s (PRO, SP.84/216, f. 159, Carr to Jenkins, 2 May 1681).

35 PRO, SP.84/216, ff. 52–3, Plott to Jenkins, 1 November 1680.

36 PRO, SP.84/216, f. 150, Carr to Jenkins, 5 March 1681.

37 'He that publishes false and seditious news is by law to ly in prison til he can find his author; now his own recognisance frees him' (*Morrison Collection*, ed. Thibaudeau, ii. 37–8). I am very grateful to Lois Schwoerer for suggesting to me the importance of this aspect of the Habeas Corpus Act.

38 D.F. McKenzie, 'The London Book Trade in 1668', *Words*, iv (1974), 81.

39 In an attempt to remedy the situation an order was issued in March 1681 to the Stationer's Company to ensure that all publications by its members should contain the name of the printer (*CSPD 1680–1*, p. 208).

men to take risks on behalf of others. Michael Treadwell has shown that a number of publishers handled many small, low-profit items, often of a topical, controversial nature, in return for a small fee, and concludes that '1680 is obviously the crucial year for the emergence of the trade publisher', citing Langley Curtis, Randall Taylor, Richard Janeway and Richard Baldwin as examples.[40] The most prolific publisher in my sample is Richard Janeway, who was responsible for thirty tracts. Altogether, Janeway, whose name appeared on only one pamphlet before 1679, put his name to 106 pamphlets between 1678 and 1681.[41] Richard Baldwin's name appears on nine of the tracts in my sample,[42] and Langley Curtis's on five.[43] Prepared to act as a buffer between those really responsible for the publications and the authorities, the trade publishers such as Janeway, Curtis and Baldwin, dealt fairly consistently with works opposing government policy,[44] as did another publisher, Benjamin Harris, whose name appears on seven of the sample.[45] Henry Brome, on the other hand, generally published works that were loyalist or anglican in content, and his name appears on twenty-four of the tracts in the sample, including those by the Court's principal defender, L'Estrange. Brome's efforts on behalf of the loyalists or anglicans were seconded by publishers like Walter Kettilby and Benjamin Tooke, who were respectively responsible for seven and six of the sample publications, and by Randal Taylor, who published nine more of them.[46]

The question of whether such men were the tools of a party propaganda machine, or independent operators with strong personal convictions, is a complex one. John Hetet has shown that a number of publishers such as Benjamin Harris and Thomas Parkhurst,[47] and printers such as Francis Smith,[48] were heavily committed to a political, or religious, cause, but also

[40] Treadwell, 'Trade publishers', pp. 99–135. See also L. Rostenberg, 'Richard and Anne Baldwin, Whig Patriot Publishers', *Papers of the Bibliographical Society of America*, 47 (1953), 1–42.

[41] These figures exclude newspaper publications. Thomas Benskin, who had published only one tract before the crisis, published thirteen tracts in the period 1680–1.

[42] Twenty-nine in the period as a whole according to the *Wing Index*.

[43] Seventy-six overall in the period according to the *Wing Index*.

[44] They were attacked by L'Estrange in *A Word Concerning Libels* (1681), pp. 5–7.

[45] Thirty-six in the period as a whole according to the *Wing Index*. For Harris's career see Sutherland, *Restoration Newspaper*, pp. 186–93.

[46] Tooke was described in Randall Taylor's will as a 'good Friend' (W.H. Phelps, 'The will of Randall Taylor, a Restoration Bookseller', *Papers of the Bibliographical Society of America* [1978], p. 337).

[47] Parkhurst published tracts advocating a broadening of the ecclesiastical settlement such as *The Plain Truth* (1681), *Liberty of Conscience* (1680), *An Endeavour for Peace among Protestants* (1680), and *Certain Considerations Tending to Promote Peace* (1679).

[48] For Smith's career see T. Crist, 'Francis Smith and the Opposition Press in England 1660–1688' (Cambridge, Ph.D. 1977); J. Hetet, 'A Literary Underground in Restoration England 1660–89' (Cambridge Ph.D. 1987), pp. 113–14.

that principle was not the only motive of publishers.[49] That this was a lucrative time for the book trade is indicated bny Ezerel Tonge's statement in November 1680 that some printers said 'they ha[d] got money enough & can beare Imprisonm[en]t for a 12 moneth',[50] and by the fact that the number of printers increased greatly in the period.[51] The profit motive could, and did, cut across 'party' lines. Thus in 1680 Thomas Benskin published *A Just and Modest Vindication of His Royal Highness the Duke of York* and in the following year *The Vindication of His Grace James Duke of Monmouth*.

The printer and publisher Nathanial Thompson is another good example of the dangers in analysing the press unreservedly in terms of 'Whig' and 'Tory'.[52] In 1676–7 Thompson had printed libels against the government,[53] and in November 1679, by 8 a.m. of the day of Monmouth's return from his brief exile in Europe, had published celebratory verses, arousing suspicion that he had received prior warning from the duke's friends.[54] It also seems likely that he was the first printer of *An Appeal from the Country*, a tract which was sympathetic to Monmouth;[55] and that in the autumn of 1679 he printed *The Sale of Esau's Birthright*, which ridiculed Sir Richard Temple, a Court supporter who stood as a candidate at Buckingham.[56] Yet in the same year he also began printing *The True Domestick Intelligence* to rival Harris's *The Protestant Domestick Intelligence*. Reported to have been arrested in January 1680 'for printing the King's speech false',[57] Thompson appears to have altered his political stance in that year. In March 1681 he began printing *The Loyal Protestant*, 'publisht for no other end but to undeceive his Majesties Loyal Subjects', and became a self-appointed spokesman for the government.[58] Thompson's shifting and ambiguous political position highlights the danger of talking in terms of fixed political allegiances.[59]

[49] Hetet, 'Literary Underground', pp. 78–84; J. Walker, 'Censorship of the Press under Charles II', *History*, xxxv (1950), 236–7.

[50] BL, Stowe MS 746, f. 38, Tonge to Capt. J. Tonge, 17 November 1680.

[51] Hetet, 'Literary underground', p. 105.

[52] For Thompson's career see Sutherland, *Restoration Newspaper*, pp. 193–7; L. Rostenberg, *Literary, Political, Scientific, Religious and Legal Publishing, Printing and Bookselling in England 1551–1700* (New York 1965), ii. 315–43.

[53] *HMC Lords 1671–8*, pp. 69–79.

[54] *A Congratulatory Poem* (1679); *HMC Ormonde*, v. 244.

[55] Sutherland, *Restoration Newspaper*, pp. 188–9.

[56] BL, Add. 52,475A, unfoliated, deposition of 21 July 1679 by Richard Griffin.

[57] All Souls, MS 171, f. 113, newsletter, 19 January 1680.

[58] L'Estrange allegedly employed him to print *A Letter to a Noble Peer of the Realm about His Late Speech and Petition* (1681) (*Domestick Intelligence*, no. 93, 1 February 1681).

[59] He was described as 'a mercenary fellow for any side that pays him well' (*CSPD May 1684–February 1685*, p. 187).

Shaftesbury has often been seen as the guiding spirit behind much of the output of the opposition press.[60] Evidence about his relationship with the press is, however, patchy.[61] His contacts included some who had an acquaintance with the publishing world, such as Murray and Wrey, who were described as 'Emissaries of my Lord Shaftesbury's and most zealous dispersers of the damned libels now in Print ag[ains]t the Gov[ernmen]t', and who were arrested in 1679.[62] The lawyer Thomas Percivall, who according to Thomas Watson was 'as great ... with Lord Shaftesbury as anybody', used to send for Benjamin Harris to engage him 'in printing severall papers'.[63] Such arrangements would have been unnecessary if, as Danby was informed, Shaftesbury had a printing press in his house and 'could have what he pleas'd printed, and that in a night's time'.[64] The most direct piece of evidence of Shaftesbury's involvement is a letter in the earl's papers from William Lawrence, who presented him with two previous publications and hinted that with support he could publish a third proving that 'the King's Eldest son is the next not only Lineal but Lawfull Heir both by the Law of God and of the Land'.[65] Shaftesbury's reply, if he made one, is unknown; but in 1681 *The Right of Primogeniture* appeared, written by Lawrence. Yet, although Shaftesbury encouraged the printing of some literature, there is less evidence that he wrote any of it. Although it was rumoured that *The Narrative of Mr*

[60] *Honesty's Best Policy* (1677), p. 1, observed that there were 'a sort of people that not long ago were as busy as bees to publish and disperse at large whatever they thought might be for the Honour and Advantage of his Lordship'. *Memoires of the Life of Anthony late Earl of Shaftesbury* (1683), p. 6, claimed that the booksellers Smith, Harris and Starkey, and the writers Care and Ferguson were entertained at Thanet House and that 'whole shoals of lewd and seditious pamphlets – "Letters to Friends", "Appeals to the City", "Dialogues between Tutor and Pupils", were written, printed and dispersed by his direction and approbation'. North, *Examen*, p. 88, claimed that Shaftesbury had 'a great Judgement and dexterity in Managing and Putting forth Libels'.

[61] O.W. Furley, 'Pamphlet Literature in the Exclusion Crisis 1679–81', *CHJ*, xiii (1957), 20; Hetet, 'Literary underground', p. 114; Haley, *Shaftesbury*, pp. 553–4.

[62] Bod., MS Carte 243, f. 398, Longford to Arran, 18 October 1679. Wrey, or Rea, turned government informer (*CSPD 1680–1*, pp. 259–60, 317). A Mr Murray acted as intermediary between Shaftesbury and Lord Wharton in 1676 and was arrested for having distributed *An Appeal from the Country to the City* (1679), see Haley, *Shaftesbury*, pp. 413, 424–6, 553 n. 3.

[63] *CSPD 1680–1*, p. 489.

[64] BL, Add. 28,047, f. 47, Thomas Knox to Danby, 23 January 1678/9. *The Intrigues of the Popish Plot Laid Open* (1685), p. 31, claimed that there was a secret printing press in the Temple, operated by Shaftesbury's friend John Harrington.

[65] PRO, 30/24/6A, pt 1, f. 179, 25 October 1680. *CSPD 1680–1*, p. 440, prints a letter from William Helyar to John Brydall in September 1681 remarking that Shaftesbury had been sent a copy of Lawrence's *Marriage by the Moral Law Vindicated*, suggesting that the letter among the Shaftesbury papers became common knowledge after the earl's arrest.

John Smith (1679) was 'written or at least reviewed' by him,[66] and he made a few corrections to Settle's *Character of a Popish Successor* (1681),[67] it is significant that the only tract which can be ascribed to him with any degree of certainty was never published.[68] A speech supposedly delivered by him in the Lords was printed and thought seditious enough to merit being burnt by the Common Hangman; but, though Shaftesbury said 'he believed he might say some such thing', it may well have been edited and spiced up by its printer Francis Smith.[69]

Probably more important than the earl in the organisation and distribution of opposition literature was the Green Ribbon Club. The publisher Benjamin Harris was said 'to be frequent' with one of the Club's most important members, Slingsby Bethel.[71] Indeed Harris was reported to be present at the Southwark election when Bethel stood as a candidate,[72] and was visited by him after his commitment to Newgate in 1681.[73] Bethel's other friends included the baptist printer Francis Smith,[74] and Henry Care. Smith dedicated his *Account of the Injurious Proceedings of Sir George Jeffreys* (1680) to Shaftesbury;[75] whilst Care was the author of *The Weekly Pacquet of Advice from Rome*, and a subscription was raised by the Club to support him

---

[66] *HMC Ormonde*, iv. 560. Ferguson later claimed to have been its author (Bod., MS Smith 31, f. 30).

[67] *A Narrative written by Elkanah Settle* (1683), Epistle Dedicatory.

[68] Parts of it are printed in Christie, *Shaftesbury*, ii. 281–3, and 309–14. Haley, *Shaftesbury*, p. 502, speculates that it was not published because James's departure in March 1679 made it 'no longer applicable'.

[69] Newdigate newsletter Lc.1028, 4 January 1681; Luttrell, *Brief Relation*, i. 62. Barrillon claimed that Shaftesbury himself distributed copies of the printed speech (PRO, 31/3/148, f. 13, Barrillon dispatch, 3/13 January 1681). Verney nevertheless endorsed his copy with a note that Shaftesbury 'disowned to have said all of it in the House' (CUL, Sel.2. 118 [178])

[70] Ashcraft, *Revolutionary Politics*, p. 144; Harris, *London Crowds*, pp. 92–4, 100–1; Jones, 'The Green Ribbon Club', 17–20; North, *Examen*, pp. 572–4. For membership of the Club see *Mr Thomas Dangerfield's Particular Narrative* (1679). His list compares well with that drawn up by Pepys from the Green Ribbon Club minutes Pepys Lib. mss, 2875, ff. 489–91. For comments on the lists of names see G. Sitwell, *The First Whig* (Scarborough 1894), appendix, pp. 197–203, and J. Potenger's *Private Memoirs*, ed. C.W. Bingham (1841), p. 34.

[71] *Mercurius Bifrons*, no. 2, 24 February 1681.

[72] Ibid.

[73] *Heraclitus Ridens*, no. 17, 24 May 1681.

[74] *Loyal Protestant*, no. 13, 19 April 1681.

[75] As lord chancellor, Shaftesbury had ordered the return of Smith's books (*The Case of Francis Smith*, appended to *A Speech lately made by a Noble Peer* [1681]). In 1681 Smith revealed that Shaftesbury's 'attorney' gave him 'Lying Stories out of Scotland' which he had printed (Bulstrode newsletter, 16 April 1681).

during imprisonment.[76] The bookseller John Starkey's shop was one of the places where the members gathered,[77] and in December 1680 was the mailing address for the MP and recorder of London, George Treby.[78] Other members of the club included the propagandists John Ayloffe and Charles Blount, as well as Dr Harrington, who had connections with Shaftesbury and the booksellers of the Temple.

Historians have paid most attention to the organisation of printers and publishers who clashed with the government, partly because they seem to be in the vanguard of press, religious and political freedom, but also perhaps because information about the loyalist press is harder to find. There is only sparse evidence that literature was promoted by the Court, yet what does survive points to Danby's awareness of the value of propaganda. He sponsored a controversial tract by John Nalson called *A Letter from a Jesuit at Paris*, which was published a week before the 1679 Parliament sat, and drew up a memorandum 'about directing some body to write both about the present state of things to give the world a better impression of them then they are now possesst w[i]th & to give constant weekly acc[oun]ts of what is done att any time w[hi]ch may bee for the satisfaction on men's minds'.[79] This may have inspired Francis North to draw up the heads of a pamphlet 'for un-deceiving the people about the late popish plott', and North, who believed that the Court should set up 'counter-writers that as every libel came out, should take it to task and answer it', was also influential in promoting the pro-Court newspapers in 1681.[80] Secretary of State Sir Leoline Jenkins may also have had an interest in helping Court propagandists, for the heads of a pamphlet, to be called *An Address to all the Freeborn Subjects of England in Vindication of Liberty and Property*, are to be found amongst his papers.[81]

---

[76] Pepys Lib. mss, 2875, minutes of the Green Ribbon Club, f. 474. *The Trial of Henry Care* (1681), p. 20, reveals that by July 1680, much to the enjoyment of Scroggs, Care had been abandoned by his party, who failed to pay his fines. Care was nevertheless later at All Souls, Barking, when Bethel and two churchwardens conspired to have George Hickes presented for idolatry (Bod., MS Misc.e.4, 'Life of Hickes', f. 14; see chapter 9). Care was described as 'a Common Instrument to the Faction' (*L'Estrange His Appeal* [1681], p. 22).

[77] *CSPD 1679–80*, p. 21.

[78] *HMC Fitzherbert*, p. 24. Treby had defended Starkey in Court in 1677, and they had remained friends (L. Schwoerer, *The Declaration of Rights* (1981), pp. 43–5). For Starkey's importance as an organiser of opposition tracts see Hetet, 'Literary underground', p. 114, n. 68.

[79] Wood, *Life and Times*, ii. 444; Grey, *Debates*, vii. 32–3; BL, Add. 28,042, f. 19, memorandum, n.d.

[80] BL, Add. 32,518, f. 144, notes by North; R. North, *Lives of the Norths* (1826), i. 320–4; *State Trials*, vi. 1497–502.

[81] All Souls, MS 240, f. 363, 'the Scheme of a Paper to be offered to publique consideration', n.d. Jenkins, as Secretary of State seems to have been seen as a co-ordinator or protector of Court propagandists *CSPD 1679–80*, p. 425; *CSPD 1680–1*, pp. 52–3, 375). The duchess of Portsmouth also employed a servant, Mrs Dawson, who passed on tracts to the King (PRO, SP.77/52, f. 276, 7/17 August 1680).

Sir Roger L'Estrange, described by Burnet as 'the chief manager' of the Court's publications,[82] was rumoured to be financed partly by a pension from the King,[83] and partly by voluntary contributions from loyalist bodies such as the Bristol Artillery, Cambridge University and the clergy of Worcester.[84] Generally, however, ministers were cautious about employing authors to defend the government, and the Court seems to have been more concerned about keeping an eye on pamphlets printed by the opposition than on promoting its own. This policy may have reflected the opinion of Halifax, who seems to have held a strong view that the government ought not to 'employ small authors ... whose officiousness or want of money may encourage them to write', though he possibly took up his own pen on the government's behalf.[85]

L'Estrange and the other loyalist pamphleteers had a bleak view of their situation, and emphasised the literary caution shown by supporters of the Court. He complained that he was 'charg'd for writing more than [his] share; when the true Reason of it was that others wrote less ... and finding other people more cautious than [he] thought was either Needful or Expedient, in so Publick a Case, [he] engag'd himself fur[t]her then [his] neighbours'.[86] He even believed that his opponents were 'Supported and Abetted, by men of no small Trust in the Government'.[87] In 1681 another supporter of the Court, John Nalson, complained that he had

waited with some impatience, to see some bold and generous Pen endeavour to arrest the Torrent, and stem the Tide [of opposition publications], but have still been defeated in my expectation; deterred, I suppose, by a prevailing Timorousness, lest they should be branded with the infamous Names of Jesuit, Papist or Popishly affected.[88]

---

82 Burnet, *History*, ii. 221.
83 Newdigate newsletter Lc.921, 3 April 1680; Wood, *Life and Times*, ii. 484.
84 *Protestant Mercury*, no. 15, 12–16 February 1681; Luttrell, *Brief Relation*, i. 93; *Impartial Protestant Mercury*, no. 11, 31 May 1681. The claims were refuted by L'Estrange in *The Observator*, no. 21, 8 June 1681, and he claimed that he received no compensation from the Court except 'fair words' (*The Freeborn Subject* [1679], p. 14). For connections between the clergy and propagandists see Bod., MS Tanner 38, f. 45, Bishop of Exeter to Archbishop Sancroft, 14 June 1679; Bod., MS Tanner 37, f. 21, Bishop Barlow to Sancroft, 11 May 1681; Bod., MS Tanner 37, f. 228, Sir William Crooke to Sancroft, 5 January 1681.
85 Foxcroft, *Halifax*, ii. 292. *Observations upon a Late Libel* (1681) has been ascribed to him.
86 *L'Estrange His Appeal* (1681), p. 27.
87 *Observator*, no. 17, 26 May 1681, a reference perhaps to the earl of Anglesey who had been a 'friend' to Francis Smith (*CSPD 1661–2*, p. 109).
88 *The True Protestant's Appeal to the City and Country* (1681), p. 1.

Nalson's contention that loyalists wrote and published less was supported by other writers. When no reply to *A Just and Modest Vindication of the last Two Parliaments* (1681) was immediately forthcoming, the opposition tract was said by its eventual critic to be 'look't upon as unanswerable'.[89] The author of *Heraclitus Ridens* agreed that 'the Loyall Party have been very apt to be less active than the other, whose Mercury makes them Restless and indefatigable'.[90] The loyalists themselves therefore believed that they produced insufficient numbers of pamphlets. The claim that loyalists were cautious in publishing their work does appear to have some foundation. Even after the expiry of the licensing laws a number of tracts circulated in manuscript form,[91] and five tracts of loyalist sentiment have been found which seem never to have been printed.[92] It is not clear whether any of these works ever reached an audience, but their common feature of loyalty to the established succession, church and state suggests that, despite a period of relative press freedom, loyalists were reluctant, especially in 1679, to go into print, presumably because of fears of parliamentary punishment should the authors be discovered.

Loyalists also believed that their publications were either not bought or not read in the quantities achieved by their rivals. Part of the problem, thought the future licenser of the press Edmund Bohun, was that loyalist pamphlets remained on gentlemen's bookshelves whereas 'base' pamphlets were quickly bought up.[93] Yet his conviction that loyalist tracts went unread may not have

---

[89] Bod., MS Jones 17, ff. 212–32. cf. BL, Stowe MS 425, ff. 106–9, 'Sober Reflections and Inquiries upon the Proceedings of the three last Parliaments'. Burnet, however, claimed that *A Just and Modest Vindication* 'had no great effect' (Burnet, *History*, ii. 289), a comment corroborated by the fact that Edmund Bohun complained that he did not hear about the pamphlet for six months after its printing, and could not obtain a copy of it for a further six months (*Reflections on a Pamphlet stiled A Just and Modest Vindication* [1683], 'Author to the Reader'). On the other hand a Capt. Nicholls, in September 1681, repeated several of the pamphlet's charges about the King's *Declaration* of April 1681 (*CSPD 1680–1*, p. 492), a good example of how propaganda helped form political opinion. For further discussion of the tract and its context see chapter 10.

[90] *Heraclitus Ridens*, no. 20, 14 June 1681. cf. *Grimalkin* (1681), p. 10.

[91] *A Word concerning Libels* (1681), p. 12 referred to pamphlets 'both written and printed'; and *Citt and Bumpkin, the Second Part* (1680), 'To the Reader', referred to an answer 'in Manuscript'.

[92] Bod., MS Rawl. D. 1064, ff. 19–72, 74–9; All Souls, MS 240, ff. 314–51; BL, Add. 32,518, ff. 75–81; Bod., MS Jones 17, ff. 212–32. A sixth, 'Animadversions upon a Pamphlet, Entitled A Brief History of the Succession' (BL, Add. 22,589, ff. 98–105) is dated as c. 1682. For another manuscript reply to the *Brief History* see BL, Add. 27,402, f. 169.

[93] Bohun, *The Third and Last Part of the Address to the Freemen* (1683), 'Epistle Dedicatory', p. vii. Francis North observed that reports that 'were Scandalous were Greedily received ... and libellous books were applauded & to be had everywhere' (BL, Add. 32,520, f. 185). cf. *Honest Hodge and Ralph* (1680), p. 2.

reflected the true picture. In the absence of evidence about how political sympathies affected reading habits it is difficult to determine if there was a party readership,[94] but one, albeit very rough, guide to the popularity of individual titles is the number of reprints made of them.[95] Only seventy-three (15 per cent) of the sample were reprinted at some time before the end of the century, including eighteen which had editions printed only after 1681, leaving fifty-five tracts first printed and then reprinted during the years 1679–81. Of this fifty-five a surprising number, thirty-two, were loyalist tracts, a figure which suggests that a much larger demand for loyalist propaganda existed, especially in 1680 and 1681, than has been thought. The single most reprinted writer was that champion of the loyalists, Sir Roger L'Estrange, who was not only prolific,[96] but highly popular in some quarters. For example, his *Further Discovery of the Plot* (1680), went through six impressions in this period.[97]

The statement that loyalists produced fewer publications than their protagonists also requires qualification since there were significant fluctuations in output on both sides during the period. Unfortunately an analysis of output has often to rely on piecemeal contemporary comments, and on the pattern of government repression,[98] both of which reveal more about the quantity of tracts considered to be seditious than they do about loyalist works. More accurate guides to the output on a monthly basis are the manuscript annotations, relating to the precise date of printing or publication, which were made by a number of bibliophiles in the period. Narcissus Luttrell, who may have derived the idea from Thomason's collection of Revolution tracts, marked his copy of Clavell's printed *Popish Plot Catalogues*, and the Verney tracts in the Cambridge University Library, as well as a number of collections in the

---

[94] Both Anthony Wood, who was a loyalist, and Sir Richard Newdigate, who sympathised with the opposition, must have read newsletters by John Gay [Corpus Christi College, Oxford, MS 310, Wood to Fullman, 13 March 1680, and Newdigate newsletter Lc.911, 9 March 1680 contain strikingly similar phrases, suggesting that Wood was repeating to Fullman the contents of the newsletters.] Sutherland, *Restoration Newspaper*, p. 146, asserts that in 1679 'Englishmen became accustomed to choosing which paper they would read', but the evidence for this remark is unclear.

[95] Using the number of reprints to determine popularity can be misleading since the size of the original print run is usually unknown. On the other hand, reprints were made because the first impression had already sold. This suggests either that demand was high or that the size of sales was originally underestimated.

[96] Wing ascribes him thirty-three titles 1678–81. Burnet referred to his 'unexhausted copiousness in writing' (Burnet, *History*, ii. 221).

[97] V. Jordan has estimated that 64,000 copies of L'Estrange's tracts circulated 1679–81 (*Selections from the Observator* [Augustan Reprint Society, no. 141 1970], introduction, p. 1).

[98] Crist, 'Government Control of the Press', 49–77.

Bodleian Library, also have notes about the date of issue.[99] Using such information, the fluctuations in the output, type and content of publications, will be examined in the following chapters, where it will be shown that by late 1680 the loyalists were mounting a strong and increasingly effective challenge to what they saw as the sedition of the press.

THE IMPACT OF THE PRESS AND NEWSLETTERS

> Their libels fly to every shire
> As thick as Atoms in the air.
> *A Panegyrick Upon the Ensuing Spring* (1681).

If an assessment of the variations in the output of the press must be impressionistic, an appraisal of the impact of the press must be even more so. Yet although it is not possible to state exactly how many tracts were produced, since the number of pamphlets printed at each impression varied, a rough estimate can be calculated by multiplying the total number of titles by an average print run.[100] Evidence survives about eight impressions of different tracts printed during the years under consideration, and gives an average print run of 2,300.[101] Other pamphlets printed since the Restoration, however, ran to only about 1,000 copies.[102] These figures put the number of pamphlets in circulation in 1679–81 at between five and ten million, a huge volume by any reckoning. Indeed L'Estrange, commenting on the tracts published against church and state, claimed in 1681 that it was the 'opinion of Men well versed in the Trade of Book-Selling that there has not been so little as 30,000 Reams of Paper spent upon this Seditious Subject, in this Late

---

99 See bibliography. In 1678 Luttrell owned Thomason's annotated copy of *Some Sober Inspections* (1655) [Wing Films 1151/208]. I am very grateful to Blair Worden for this reference, and to Arnold Hunt for drawing the Verney collection to my attention. The latter is described in P. Hopkins, 'The Verney Collection', *Bulletin of the Friends of Cambridge University Library*, no. 9 (1988). There is also an index of Luttrell pamphlets at the Beinecke Library, which I have as yet been unable to consult.

100 A figure of 4,700 for the number of titles is derived from the totals given by Mason, 'Annual output', p. 220.

101 Four thousand of Stillingfleet's sermon 27 November 1678, and 3,000 for the second impression (*HMC Verney*, p. 471); 2,000 of a pamphlet sponsored by Sir R. Walsh in 1679 (*CSPD 1680–1*, p. 25,); 1,400 of *Vox Populi* (*CSPD 1680–1*, p. 237); 1,500 for the first impression of *A Letter*, and 1,500 for its second edition, 3,000 of an answer to the King's *Declaration*, 2,500 copies of the *Two Conferences* and 1,000 of *Reasons for the Indictment of the Duke of York* (Ferguson, *Ferguson the Plotter*), p. 55; and 3,000 copies of *Discourses upon the Modern Affairs of Europe* (PRO, PC.2/69, f. 132, privy council minutes, 27 October 1681).

102 *CSPD 1661–2*, p. 287 (500); *CSPD 1663–4*, p. 595 (1,500); ibid., p. 603 (1,000); *CSPD 1668–9*, p. 110 (200); *CSPD 1675–6*, p. 36 (2,000); and *CSPD 1677–8*, p. 406 (750). I am grateful to Donald McKenzie for these references. He uses 1,000 as a rough average for a print run ('London Book Trade in 1668', p. 79). It is possible that print runs were higher during the crisis because of the extent of public interest.

liberty of the Press'.[103] With so much printed paper available, it would be surprising if it did not have an important effect in shaping and reflecting public opinion.

Yet large volume does not *necessarily* imply a large readership. Indeed Tim Harris has recently concentrated on newspapers, ballads, broadsides and short pamphlets in the belief that their pithy statements were more likely to appeal to and reach a mass audience than longer and less succinct works.[104] There is undoubtedly good reasoning behind this approach: 'two Sheets is enough in all Reason for a Dose for the Strongest Constitution, and one for the Weaker', observed a pamphleteer,[105] and Henry Care openly admitted that his periodical diatribe against popery was printed as a single sheet in order to reach the hands of the 'vulgar'.[106] The author of *The Englishman's Happiness under a Protestant Prince* complained that many useful (in other words loyalist) pamphlets were not read 'because they were not crowded into the narrow compass of a Penny Sheet',[107] and London's common council Address of May 1681 was ordered to 'bee printed in one sheet of paper close written for every man's buying'.[108] Roger North also thought that different styles were designed to win different audiences. He commented that some pamphlets were 'adapted to deceive Men of Fortune and Education, well penned, and, perhaps, in Heroic Verse; others for the Rabble, and drunken, sottish Clubs, in Ballad Doggerel, with witty Picture affixed'.[109] But there is nevertheless a danger of drawing too close a distinction between an élite and popular readership, particularly in London, where literacy rates were higher than elsewhere.[110] Newspapers may have appealed to the 'vulgar', but they were also read by people higher in the social scale,[111] and James Sutherland has recently gone so far as to conclude that they were written 'for the middle-class reader' interested in the Court and City dealings.[112]

One of the main factors affecting readership would have been the cost of buying the prints; yet by spending £5.17.5 and £3.9.9 Narcissus Luttrell was

---

103 *A Word Concerning Libels* (1681), pp. 1, 10. This would have made a total of about 15 million sheets.
104 Harris, *London Crowds*, p. 100.
105 *Clod-pate's Ghost* (1679), p. 12.
106 *The Weekly Pacquet of Advice from Rome*, 3 December 1678. Even L'Estrange's *Observator* (no. 1, 13 April 1681) was published 'for the Enformation of the Multitude'.
107 *The Englishman's Happiness under a Protestant Prince* (1681), p. 1.
108 BL, Add. 29,558, f. 272, William Longueville to Lord Hatton, 14 May 1681. cf. Grey, *Debates*, viii. 211, speech by Hotham.
109 North, *Examen*, p. 101.
110 It has been estimated that by 1675 artisans and tradesmen had a 75–85 per cent literacy rate (L. Stone, 'Literacy and Education in England 1640–1900', *P&P*, xlii (1969), 109–12; D. Cressy, *Literacy and the Social Order* [Cambridge, 1980], pp. 134–7).
111 Bucks. RO, Verney mss, M11/34, Edmund Verney to John Verney, 15 January 1680.
112 Sutherland, *Restoration Newspaper*, p. 232.

able to collect 409 and 208 items respectively.[113] Many had cost him only 1d.[114] Similarly the Verney family collected 251 pamphlets for only £1.15.1.[115] For the gentry such sums were trifles, but they were also not beyond the reach of artisans and labourers who, according to Lord Chief Justice Scroggs, were ready to make great sacrifices to satisfy their lust for the printed word: they would 'deny their children a penny for bread, they will lay it out for a pamphlet ... the temptations were so great, that no man could keep two pence in his pocket because of the news'.[116] This may have been an exaggeration, but it was also a claim made by a pamphleteer who believed that 'every body was so desirous to hear News, that they would buy it, if they left not another Penny in their Pockets'.[117]

Moreover, items did not necessarily have to be bought to be read, for some tracts were simply given away. At the indictment of a hawker of books at Ely, for example, it emerged that 'what he could not dispose of for money, he scatter'd up and down Gratis'.[118] In 1679 *The Sale of Esau's Birthright* was distributed free in Buckingham, and one of its promoters was reprimanded by a colleague who told him that he would 'give soe many away that [he would] spoile the trade or market at the next towne'.[119] The free distribution of propaganda may have ensured a readership for pamphlets that did not sell well, but the tactic seems to have been used chiefly to achieve maximum impact for highly controversial material. The tract *A Vindication of the English Catholics*, for example, was 'scatter'd about', presumably in order to reach an audience that would never buy catholic propaganda.[120] But the technique was also used by the quakers and the more radical protestant pamphleteers in an attempt to by-pass Government censorship.[121] Thus before the lapse of the Licensing Act *A Remonstrance to Both Houses of*

[113] *Popish Plot Catalogues*, pp. 6–7. Luttrell may have been inspired to record the price by a catalogue which he owned of books published in the sixteenth and early seventeenth century with the price of each piece written in the margin by Humphrey Dyson (All Souls, MS 117).

[114] There were nevertheless complaints about artificially inflated prices. See advertisement in *Horae Mathematicae* (1680), the latter cited in S. Morrison, *Ichabod Dawks and his Newsletter* (1931), p. 13.

[115] P. Hopkins, 'Verney collection', p. 7. The account books of Verney's Buckinghamshire neighbour, Sir Richard Temple, also show his expenditure on pamphlets (Huntington, MSS ST 175 and ST 152).

[116] *The Trial of Henry Care* (1681), p. 23.

[117] *A Pleasant Discourse between Two Sea Men* (1681), p. 1.

[118] *Observator*, no. 7, April 27 1681. The hawker may have been Lawrence Morris who was imprisoned at Ely for dispersing *Vox Populi* (*CSPD 1680–1*, p. 237).

[119] BL, Add. 52,475A, information brought to the King's Bench.

[120] UCNW, Mostyn MS 9090, f. 31, newsletter 8 June 1680. *Domestick Intelligence*, no. 97, 15 February 1681 said the catholics distributed their pamphlets gratis and sent them into the country. cf. *Mercurius Anglicus*, 10 October 1681.

[121] For William Penn's activities in distributing literature see M.M. Dunn, *William Penn*, p. 25; Hetet, 'Literary underground', p. 151.

Parliament was 'scattered about Towne';[122] and in 1680, when the liberty of the press had been to some extent controlled by the 'Chits' Ministry of Hyde, Sunderland and Godolphin, 'many pap[er]s were dropt ab[ou]t the town questioning the D[uke] of York's being heire to the Crown'.[123] Lord keeper North remarked that libellous books were 'sometimes sent about the post for nothing'.[124] Tracts which supported Monmouth's claims to the throne were 'scattered and taken up on the Exchange',[125] and 'throwne into coaches'.[126] This method of scattered distribution was apparently so successful that a rival pamphleteer complained that one tract dispersed in this way had become 'almost as publick as a News-Book'.[127]

Such tracts could also be distributed through an underground network. Sir Ralph Verney was informed of 'the most abominable libels that walk in the dark, but no getting sight of them', and was told that a pamphlet about the succession, 'not fit for publik sight', was 'red about privetly'.[128] *A Speech lately made by a Noble Peer* was similarly 'secretly circulated among the Faction'.[129] Luttrell referred to two works, *Articles of High Treason and Misdemeanours against the Duchess of Portsmouth* and *A Satyr on D,[sic] Judge and a Whore*, as 'private things'.[130] The duke of Chandos received two copies of the *Appeal*, another pro-Monmouth pamphlet, from an agent of the Green Ribbon Club,[131] and the loyalist newswriter Henry Muddiman complained in March 1681 that 'the ranker sort [of libels] c[a]me generally from under a sister's apron or a brother's pocket'.[132] For a while there was no comparable distribution system amongst the loyalists. Lord keeper North complained that in contrast to the spread of opposition libels 'ingenious books wrote for the Governm[en]t were not disperst'.[133] This situation was nevertheless partly remedied with the loyalist reaction of spring 1681. In March 1681 one loyalist informed Sir John Reresby that he had sent copies of the King's Speech to his neighbours and had recommended his cousin to do

---

122 Bucks. RO, Verney mss, M11/32, John Verney to Sir Ralph Verney, 7 November 1678. Ironically, however, Verney had difficulties in obtaining a copy.
123 Newdigate newsletter Lc.972, 12 August 1680. A copy was also sent to the duke of York.
124 BL, Add. 32,520, f. 185, notes by North.
125 *CSPD 1679–80*, p. 487.
126 Bucks. RO, Verney mss, M11/34, John Verney to Sir Ralph Verney, 5 July 1680 (printed *HMC Verney*, p. 479).
127 *The Impostor Expos'd* (1681), p. 154. The same phrase is used to describe the successful distribution of *An Appeal from the Country to the City* (1679) (*An Answer to the Appeal* [1680], p. 35).
128 *HMC Verney*, p. 496; Bucks. RO, Verney mss, M11/34, Cary Gardiner to Sir Ralph Verney, 7 June 1680.
129 *A Letter from Scotland* (1681), p. 1.
130 *Popish Plot Catalogues*, pp. 8, 17.
131 *CSPD 1680–1*, p. 259.
132 Longleat, Muddiman newsbook, 5 March 1681.
133 BL, Add. 32,520, f. 185, notes by North.

likewise;[134] and in the previous month copies of a tract highlighting Monmouth's suspected love-affair with Lady Grey had been handed about 'privately' by Sir George Jeffreys and others.[135]

There were other ways in which propaganda could be absorbed without being paid for. In August 1679 Henry Robinson sang an election libel, directed against Sir Richard Temple at the George Inn at Buckingham, making fiddlers accompany him;[136] and in 1680 Stephen College read a pamphlet, 'in Quarto of two sheets, about the Duke of York', to a group of people invited to a treat in the Crown Tavern.[137] Contemporaries also begged, borrowed or stole pamphlets. Sir Ralph Verney lent tracts to his nephew;[138] Lord Hatton was sent one on the understanding that he pass it on to two further readers;[139] and a woman selling copies of Staley's *Trial* was kicked by a soldier because he wanted to read it without paying for it.[140]

The most common place of access to printed material for those who did not wish to buy it was 'the Great Pond or Puddle of News, the Coffee House'.[141] The connection between the latter and seditious propaganda was not new. The earl of Clarendon had complained in 1666 that the coffee houses were 'the places where the boldest calumnies and Scandals were raised'.[142] In the winter of 1675/6 Danby had sought, unsuccessfully, to have the coffee houses suppressed, but despite such official disapproval they had continued to act as a focal point for the exchange of news and gossip.[143] The latest prints, it was observed, were 'the Cumber and Pest of every Coffee House',[144] and without them, one pamphleteer remarked, the coffee houses 'would have no Trade'.[145] As the petitioning campaign gathered momentum a 'complaint was made to the council against coffee houses, it being urged that they are the places where scandalous and seditious discourses are most frequently promulgated', but on the plea of the coffee merchants, which had also been

---

[134] Leeds AO, Mexborough mss, Reresby 18/119, J. Wentworth to Reresby, 30 March 1681.

[135] *CSPD 1680–1*, p. 159.

[136] BL, Add. 52,475A, unfoliated, 30 August 1679. Temple found that his election rival Sir Peter Tyrrell was responsible for promoting the ballad.

[137] *The Intrigues of the Popish Plot Laid Open* (1685), p. 27.

[138] Bucks. RO, Verney mss, M11/32, 20 January 1679. The earl of Anglesey kept a library of 'all the remarkable [tracts] relating to Government', which he allowed others to consult (Sale Catalogue, Bod., Ashm.1059).

[139] BL, Add. 29,557, f. 79, Manley to Lord Hatton, 30 November 1678.

[140] Leics. RO, Finch mss, DG7/4957/57, f. 39, 23 November 1678. One George Adams was prosecuted in March 1681 for stealing books and pamphlets (*Middlesex County Records* [Middlesex County Record Society 1892], ed. J.C. Jeaffreson, iv. 152).

[141] *The Snotty Nose Gazette*, no. 1, 24 November 1679. B. Lillywhite, *London Coffee Houses* (1963), p. 218, refers to a pamphlet which claimed that all the coffee houses round the Royal Exchange, except Garraway's, were 'whiggified'.

[142] Quoted by Seaward, *Cavalier Parliament*, p. 73.

[143] Browning, *Danby*, i. 194–5.

[144] *News From Colchester* (1681), p. 2.

[145] *A Pleasant Discourse between Two Sea Men* (1681), p. 1.

successful in 1675/6, the houses were allowed to remain open.[146] In the absence of central control it was left to local initiative to prosecute coffee house owners for sedition. Thus in Norwich in 1681 a coffeeman named Howman was presented for dispersing the *Address of the Corporation of London*, in retaliation for the indictment of the *Norwich Address* by the Middlesex Grand Jury.[147] In April 1681 the Bristol Grand Jury recommended that no news, printed or unprinted, and no pamphlet, should be suffered to be read in any coffee house without prior sanction by the mayor or aldermen.[148]

In London the coffee houses also served another important function in the dissemination of propaganda. The Penny Post, introduced in March 1680 by William Dockwra, used them as collection points.[149] The system ensured the quick and easy distribution of material within London. Although it was at first castigated by Oates as 'a farther branch of the Popish plot',[150] the new postal system was partly the result of demand for a swift and cheap means to distribute propaganda,[151] and was quickly exploited by opposition publishers.[152] For example, a dozen copies of a libel written by Edward Fitzharris, and a dozen *Answers to His Majesties Declaration*, were sent in 1681 anonymously through the penny post to a newswriter, who then distributed them at the Amsterdam coffee house.[153] 'There was never any thing so favourable to the carrying on and managing Intrigue', complained the author of *Heraclitus Ridens* about the new post.[154]

Publishers were often very aware of a country as well as a metropolitan market, and made use of the national postal network for distribution purposes. The periodical *A Weekly Advertisement of Books* declared that it

---

[146] *The True Domestick Intelligence*, no. 48, 17 December 1679; *Haarlem Courant*, no. 4, 6 January 1680; Newdigate newsletter Lc.876, 18 December 1679.

[147] *CSPD 1680–1*, p. 371; *Currant Intelligence*, no. 26, 20 July 1681. The Norwich Grand Jury also heard a presentment against Thomas Firman of London for exposing seditious pamphlets in a coffee house in Norwich.

[148] Latimer, *Annals of Bristol*, p. 403. Sir Robert Cann complained that 'some insulting Nonconformists' met at 'John Kymbar's coffee house ... where they frequently spread their false scandalous newes: if this coffee house were suddainly suppressed it may be a means to prevent some evill' (BL, Longleat mss, M/863, reel iv, Coventry papers vol. vi, f. 210, Cann to Henry Coventry, 10 January 1679/80). This letter is further evidence of pressure to suppress the coffee houses during the petitioning campaign.

[149] Lillywhite, *Coffee Houses*, p. 19; T. Todd, *William Dockwra and the Rest of the Undertakers: The Story of the London Penny Post 1680–1682* (1952), p. 34.

[150] *Currant Intelligence* no. 13, 23–27 March 1680 and no. 15, 30 March–3 April 1680. One of the undertakers of the new system was Henry Nevil Payne, a reputed sympathiser of the catholics (Todd, *Dockwra*, p. 16).

[151] *Will With a Whisp* (1680), p. 1.

[152] Todd, *Dockwra*, p. 10, claims the system had Shaftesbury's backing. One of the scheme's undertakers was Shaftesbury's agent Robert Murray.

[153] *CSPD 1683–4*, p. 52. A copy of Fitzharris's libel was also sent to James Douche, a clergyman (R. Clifton, *The Last Popular Rebellion* [1984], p. 68).

[154] *Heraclitus Ridens*, no. 5, 1 March 1681.

would use the penny post to distribute its issues in the City, but that it also intended 'to dispose of some hundreds weekly by the [general] Post, to the principal if not to all the Booksellers in England'.[155] On 27 May 1680, copies of *A Letter from a Person of Quality concerning the Black Box*, a pamphlet about Monmouth's claim to the throne, were sent under blank covers to Edward Neale, an inn-holder, and to a stationer in Chelmsford.[156] *The Worcestershire Ballad*, a poem satirising loyalist electoral efforts, was avowedly 'Printed to be sent by the Post', and a loyalist pamphlet later claimed that *A Letter Concerning His Majesties Declaration* had been sent 'in Post Letters to infect the Populace of every County'.[157] There were complaints that some postmasters turned a blind eye to such practices,[158] but with or without such help, penetration of the country became an important objective of the propagandists. One Lawrence White rode about to fairs and markets to disperse his stock;[159] and Mrs Cellier planned a double impression of her pamphlet *Malice Defeated* 'to furnish the Country as well as the Citty'.[160] In some cases a libel seems to have been distributed in the country before the city, presumably to delay the time of suppression and hence maximise impact.[161]

Dissemination of propaganda into the countryside was dependent on the post in two further ways. First, correspondents were able to include copies of newspapers and pamphlets to save them the task of transcription;[162] and, second, manuscript newsletters could be distributed to every part of the country.[163] The attention paid by historians to printed newspapers has unduly overshadowed the importance of manuscript newsletters in disseminating reports of events in Parliament and London. The first newspaper did not appear until after the dissolution of the 1679 Parliament and after their

---

[155] *Weekly Advertisement*, no. 1, 1 October 1680.
[156] *CSPD 1679–80*, p. 504. cf. *CSPD 1683*, p. 439; Longleat, Muddiman newsbook, 5 March 1681. See Ashcraft, *Revolutionary Politics*, pp. 172–3, for a discussion of the network of 'Whig' correspondents.
[157] *His Majesties Declaration Defended* (1681), p. 5. In Taunton letters were received from London members of the Green Ribbon Club and the local opposition then arranged for the distribution of broadsheets and flysheets (Clifton, *Last Popular Rebellion*, pp. 62–3).
[158] For the complicity of Mr Santell and Mr Leeson, officers of the Post Office, in sending newsletters see *CSPD 1683–4*, pp. 53–4; T. Gardiner, *A General Survey of the Post Office 1677–82*, ed. F.W. Bond (Postal History Society Special Series, no. 3 1958), p. 27.
[159] *CSPD 1680–1*, p. 237.
[160] UCNW, Mostyn MS 9090, f. 70, newsletter, 4 September 1680.
[161] BL, Longleat mss, M/863, reel iv, Coventry papers vol. vi, f. 71: L'Estrange to Coventry, 12 June 1679; *CSPD 1682*, p. 563.
[162] Bucks. RO, Verney mss, M11/34, John Verney to Sir Ralph Verney, 14 October 1680; Hull RO, MS L.993, M. Warton to the Mayor, 15 January 1681; Gardiner, *Post Office*, p. 27.
[163] For discussions of newsletters see J.B. Williams, 'The Newsbooks and Letters of News of the Restoration', *EHR*, xxiii (1908), 252–76; P. Fraser, *The Intelligences of the Secretaries of State* (Cambridge, 1956), pp. 2, 29, 116, 119–21, 126–30; J.G. Muddiman, *The King's Journalist 1659–1689* (1923), passim.

ban in May 1680 no newspaper was printed until December 1680, only a few weeks before the Parliament was dissolved.[164] Manuscript newsletters, therefore, provided a continuity of information unmatched by their printed counterparts. It was also of a high quality. The newswriters' coverage of parliamentary sessions during the crisis was so extensive that two writers transcribed the whole of the exclusion bill, and a draft religious bill was sent in a newsletter to Oxford in 1681.[165]

This manuscript information, however, may have been less generally available than its printed counterpart. Although newswriters such as Blackhall, Robinson, Pike and Bill supplied the coffee houses in London with their information, which was then sent to provincial coffee houses, some newswriters, such as John Gay and his son, wrote exclusively for country consumption,[166] and it is probable that in the country only the gentry and nobility could afford the letters. Indeed one newswriter, Richard Alsopp, boasted that he specialised in writing for these higher social groups.[167] Unless available in coffee houses, the cost of newsletters put them beyond the reach of many. The price varied from between 10 guineas to £5 *per annum*, though the former was said not to leave any margin of profit once the cost of paper and postage had been considered.[168] Nevertheless, the trade was lucrative enough, for Giles Hancocke, who charged £4, £5 or £6 *per annum*, made £100–150 a year; and Gay boasted 'he had £16 or £20 a year out of one county'.[169]

One of the most important newswriters was Henry Muddiman, whose papers survive at Longleat.[170] Muddiman kept a journal in which he recorded all the information he received. He then placed crosses by the side of paragraphs that were to be omitted from the finished letters, leaving the rest as the basis from which copies could be made. The journal gave Muddiman flexibility, since he could begin a newsletter at the date when he last wrote to any

---

[164] Sutherland, *Restoration Newspaper*, p. 16.
[165] Congress newsletter 6/163, n.d.; Newdigate newsletter Le.789, 26 May 1679; Bod., MS Ballard 70, ff. 48–51. See Bucks. RO, Verney mss M11/32, John Verney to Sir Ralph Verney, 2 June 1679 about the circulation of the exclusion bill.
[166] *CSPD 1680–1*, p. 535; *CSPD 1683–4*, pp. 53–4. Gay's newsletters were described as 'fanatical' by Thomas Hyde (*CSPD 1680–1*, p. 422). *L'Estrange's Case* (1680), p. 8 describes Gay's newsletter as 'intended for country consumption, not town'. Gay published the zealously anti-catholic *Account of Queen Mary's Methods* (1680), which was dedicated to Shaftesbury.
[167] Chatsworth, Devonshire Collection, Group II, Richard Alsopp to the earl of Devonshire, 26 November 1678.
[168] Bod., MS Carte 222, f. 233, 'advertisement from Whitehall', 15 January 1680; Williams, 'Newsbooks', p. 252. *HMC Leeds*, p. 20 gives the price as £10 *per annum* c. June 1678.
[169] *CSPD 1683–4*, p. 53.
[170] I hope to publish parts of the Journal, together with extracts from the Bulstrode and other newsletters, in order to provide a 'Restoration newsbook'. For Muddiman's career see Muddiman, *The King's Journalist*.

of his recipients, a practice which does not seem to have been unique.[171] Muddiman seems not to have had to pay postage at all on his newsletters, which achieved a wide circulation.[172] Although not alone in reporting news in a way sympathetic to the Court, since writers such as Francis Benson[173] and Robert Yard[174] wrote from within Whitehall,[175] Muddiman's importance in conveying loyalist sentiments to the gentry and nobility was possibly second only to that of L'Estrange.

In the 1660s Muddiman had published his news in a printed form as *The Kingdom's Intelligencer*, thereby underlining the close relationship between newspapers and newsletters. Benjamin Claypool wrote for both media,[176] and the publisher Benjamin Harris also seems to have sent newsletters, as did Francis Smith.[177] There was often a remarkable similarity of wording between newsletters and papers,[178] and sometimes even between newsletters by different authors.[179] Moreover, as in the newspapers, accounts in newsletters of the same incident could be completely contradictory or contain false information.[180]

The government was as sensitive about the potentially seditious nature of manuscript news as it was about printed material. On 28 February 1679

---

[171] Congress newsletters 7/204 and 7/205, for 14 and 16 June 1681, overlap in content.

[172] Longleat, Thynne mss, vol. 41, f. 18, Muddiman newsletter, 3 January 1680, endorsed 'M.H. Free'.

[173] Benson's newsletters to Sir Leoline Jenkins are at Huntington, HM 30314–15, and All Souls, MS 242.

[174] Copies of Yard's newsletters to Sir Richard Bulstrode are at the Harry Ransome Research Centre, University of Texas at Austin. Yard promised to send Sir John Reresby 'the news constantly' (Leeds AO, Mexborough mss, Reresby 12/81, letter dated 20 August 1678).

[175] The duke of Ormonde received a frequent flow of intelligence from within Court circles (Bod., MS Carte 222, 228, 72).

[176] Luttrell thought Claypool wrote Thompson's *True Domestick Intelligence* (*Popish Plot Catalogues*, p. 20, n. 2). Claypool, or Cleypoole, was arrested in December 1679 (*London Gazette* no. 1467, 8–11 December 1679) and was prosecuted in September 1680 for writing scandalous newspapers (Congress newsletter 6/246, 27 September 1680). He was said to 'word things well if not in drink' (*CSPD 1683–4*, p. 54). He received his intelligence from Mr Netterville, who also supplied William Cotton (*CSPD 1683–4*, p. 51; *CSPD 1680–1*, p. 482). This is probably the Netterville who sent reports to Danby (see chapter 2).

[177] BL, Longleat mss, M/904, reel xxi, vol. xli, f. 179, newsletter, 11 December 1679, endorsed 'upon enquiry we finde that this letter comes from one Benjamin Harris'; *CSPD 1680–1*, p. 422. Smith in turn passed news to another newswriter, William Raddon, who wrote for baptists and other dissenters (*CSPD 1682*, pp. 435, 476).

[178] Sutherland, *Restoration Newspaper*, p. 101. See also the *Protestant Mercury*, no. 30 and Congress newsletter 7/175 for 7 April 1681; and compare the *Loyal Protestant*, no. 10, 8 April 1681 and Newdigate newsletter Lc.1062, 7 April 1681. Giles Hancocke was both a newswriter and publisher of printed material, and supplied the domestic information for the *Impartial Protestant Mercury* (*CSPD 1682*, p. 200). For Gay see n. 166.

[179] Compare Longleat, Muddiman newsbook, 12 November 1678 with Newdigate newsletter Lc.705, 12 November 1678. cf. *CSPD 1683–4*, pp. 53–4.

[180] Compare Bod., MS Carte 232, f. 82, anon. to [?Arran], 16 September 1680, and Congress newsletter 7/101, 16 September 1680. Chatsworth, Devonshire Collection, Group IB, newsletter, 26 April 1679, complained about incorrect information in other letters.

Samuel Amey was sent to Newgate for writing and dispersing seditious libels and letters;[181] in August 1679 a newsletter writer called Sindge wrote an account of Wakeman's trial that was sent to the Lord Chief Justice for action;[182] and in September 1679 the marquess·of Worcester and the earl of Anglesey complained about a newsletter which was 'publickly read att a coffee house in Bristol', and which they thought libellous.[183] In December 1679, during the petitioning campaign, several authors of newsletters were examined by privy council, among them Smallbridge, Hancocke, Combes, Biggs and Ford.[184]

Fortunately information, supplied after the Rye House Plot in 1683 by their colleague William Cotton, survives about some of these writers.[185] Combes had been involved in the 'Coffee trade', and 'must have some considerable information from Court, for he has not gone abroad himself for some time'; his letters were 'in great request in the country'. Hancocke seems to have been responsible for many of the most provocative letters, partly because he had 'great intelligence both from Court and Council', and partly because he was closely allied with the opposition to the Court: in April 1680, when several newswriters were seized, Hancocke was summoned before the privy council, and in June 1681 he was one of the clerks who took the poll in the shrieval election.[186] In September 1680 a complaint was also made against Claypool, whose newsletters, together with those by Gravely and Wood, were observed to arrive at the posthouse in Lombard Street 'at very late howers of the night the better to obscure ... their Evill practices'.[187] Hancocke, Cotton and Claypool were, not surprisingly, among the tribe of newsletter writers who descended on Oxford to report the session of March 1681.[188]

Newsletters and newspapers provided details of parliamentary proceedings, but they were not the only source for such important information. Sheila

---

181 PRO, PC2/67, f. 115, privy council minutes 28 February 1679. He was probably the 'S. Amy', author of *A Memento for English Protestants* (1680) and *A Praefatory Discourse* (1681).

182 Newdigate newsletter Lc.839, 12 August 1679.

183 Congress newsletter 6/250, 26 July 1769.

184 *London Gazette*, no. 1469, 15–18 December 1679; UCNW, Mostyn MS 9089, f. 203, newsletter, 16 December 1679; Newdigate newsletter Lc.875, 16 December 1679.

185 *CSPD 1683–4*, pp. 53–4. Cotton certainly knew about the trade. He had been summoned before privy council in April 1680, and had a further complaint made against him, in September 1680, for writing scandalous newsletters (Congress newsletter 6/267, 6 September 1680).

186 *Currant Intelligence*, no. 21, 23 April 1680; *CSPD 1680–1*, p. 334. cf. *CSPD 1682*, p. 280. Some of Hancocke's letters are in All Souls, MS 171 (see note by T. Crist in the college's catalogue).

187 *CSPD 1680–1*, p. 466; All Souls, MS 264, f. 98, 24 September 1681. William Smallbridge gave evidence that Claypool employed Henry Paris, Thomas Collyns and Christopher Fleet to write his newsletters (Bod., MS Eng.Hist.B.204, f. 76).

188 *Iter Oxoniense* (1681).

Lambert has already listed the extent of printed material officially sponsored by Parliament,[189] but it is worth examining the impact of this material, as well as that of the unofficial publications that related events at Westminster.

The 'votes', which were a condensed version of the *Commons Journal*, were the most important source of information about proceedings in Parliament. Before 1680 these were available in manuscript form, but had the disadvantage of being of limited distribution as well as sometimes containing inaccuracies.[190] Although in April 1679 Sir Francis Russell claimed that it was 'the right of every commoner of England to have [the House of Commons'] votes communicated to him',[191] the printing of the votes which Russell went on to propose was not embraced by the House until the following year. On 30 October 1680 the Commons, apparently on the motion of Sir William Cowper, a kinsman of Shaftesbury, decided to print their votes daily.[192] The decision was taken 'partly for the advantage of the Speaker, who had £6 a day from the printer', but partly for less ulterior motives, 'to render them publick to the people'.[193] The House resolved that the votes should be 'first perused and signed' by Speaker William Williams, presumably to eradicate the possibility of mistakes. Amongst Williams's papers drafts of the votes survive, and reveal that the wording was revised often as many as three times before being initialled, usually by William Goldesbrough, the parliamentary clerk of the House.[194] The revisions seldom changed anything material, though occasionally information was deleted.[195]

[189] S. Lambert, *Printing for Parliament 1641–1700* (List and Index Society, xx, 1984).

[190] Grey, *Debates*, vi. 118–19. A newsletter to Sir Francis Parry, dated 12 November 1678, complained that the Votes were 'written so very ill, that [one could] hardly make sense of them'. (BL, Add. 41,568, f. 45).

[191] Grey, *Debates*, vii. 74.

[192] *CJ*, ix. 643. The decision to print was partly the result of pressure from booksellers (D. Knott, 'The Booksellers and the Plot', *The Book Collector*, xxiii [1974], 205–6). Barrillon remarked that the printing of votes had been one of the first things done before the outbreak of the Civil War (PRO, 31/3/147, f. 14, Barrillon dispatch, 1/11 November 1680).

[193] *HMC Finch*, ii. 95; Bucks. RO, Verney mss, M11/34, John Verney to Sir Ralph Verney, 3 November 1680. Ironically the Speaker, William Williams, opposed the printing of votes in 1689 (Grey, *Debates*, ix. 145–6). Colin Lee has suggested to me that the votes were printed partly as an attempt to influence the conduct of proceedings in the House by enhancing awareness of future business. I am grateful to him for allowing me to read a version of his unpublished paper 'Whose business is it anyway?: the Initiation and Control of Proceedings in the Restoration House of Commons', delivered at Cambridge, 2 November 1992.

[194] NLW, Wynnstay MS L.465–517.

[195] For example, the order made on 1 November 1680 that the report on the Popish Plot should be finished 'with all possible speed' was watered down to read 'be perfected by the said committee' (NLW, Wynnstay mss, L470); the manuscript vote for 22 November records that the name of Oliver St John as well as that of William Strode should be struck out of the Stockbridge election return (ibid., L501); the list of the names given in the manuscript vote for 27 November as nominees to the committee to confer with the Lords about Stafford's trial differs from that given in *CJ* (ibid., L501). For other differences see also ibid., L483 and L516.

Once printed, the votes could be distributed around the London coffee houses where they provoked discussion and sometimes abuse;[196] or they could be sent into the provinces to inform the localities about events at the centre. Sir Ralph Verney, living in Buckinghamshire, wrote to his son in London requesting the printed votes, for although he thought 'there is nothing of moment in them [he] desired to have them all'.[197] One pamphleteer even advised the country that if it would 'but lay out a little money, you may have the Proceedings in Print; and I would advise you in your several Neighbourhoods to joyn together, and then you may have them for a very small matter; besides the great benefit you will find in conferring with each other, at the reading of them'.[198]

The printed votes were especially useful for MPs, or aspiring MPs, who wished to report to their constituencies. Sir Peter Tyrrell, it was said, 'obligeth his Electors very much, by sending Them Downe all sorts of Intelligences every Weeke',[199] and Thomas Coningsby was encouraged to send 'all the proceedings of Parliament ... to encourage the people to choose him again'.[200] Sir Matthew Andrews, MP for Shaftesbury, sent the votes every week to the mayor,[201] and it was claimed that there was 'scarce a parish but one or more bought them and lent them to their neighbours, by which most of them knew what was done'.[202] A memorandum drafted by an opponent of the Court even proposed to legislate for MPs to inform their electors about proceedings in Parliament, 'not onely the bare naked votes and resolutions of the House and the Bills, but the reasons, motives and Inducements which moved the House to such resolutions'.[203] Besides the votes, MPs sent personal accounts of parliamentary proceedings, such as those written to the Corporation of Hull,[204] or were implored to report on events by their constituents. For example, Samuel Key wrote from Ilminster to Hugh Speke, that 'the rest of our town request you would afford us the news ... every one's ears itching to hear the proceedings in Parliament'.[205] This thirst for information about Parliament's activities found expression in the demands of some of the 'instructions' given to MPs at the elections for the Oxford Parliament. The Essex and Shropshire 'instructions' expressed satisfaction

---

196 Lord Ferrer's chaplain had written 'foolish words (being in drink)' on the printed votes (John Rylands Library, Legh mss, Richard Sterne to Legh, 9 November 1680).
197 Bucks. RO, Verney mss, M11/35, letter to John Verney, 6 December 1680.
198 *Vox Regni* (n.d. 1680?), p. 3.
199 Bucks. RO, Verney mss, M11/32, Edmund Verney to Sir Ralph Verney, 17 April 1679.
200 *History of Parliament*, ii. 116.
201 Ibid., i. 535.
202 *CSPD 1683–4*, p. 368.
203 The suggestion is made in 'Several Usefull and Indispensibly Necessary Cautions' (BL, Longleat mss M/863, reel v, vol. vi, ff. 248–52).
204 Hull RO, Corporation Correspondence.
205 *CSPD 1680–1*, p. 60.

that the votes were being printed for all to read,[206] and the Cheshire address asked that the practice be continued.[207] The House of Commons duly obliged on the 24 March 1681 when the votes were once again ordered to be printed.[208] 'I think it not natural, nor rational', argued Winnington, 'that the People who sent us hither, should not be informed of our actions.'[209] Although their printing was opposed by the government, the very success of the distribution of the votes was ironically thought to help the loyalist cause 'by exposing to publick view the Irregularity of their owne proceedings'.[210] In a sense the Crown's opponents in the Commons were hoist with their own petard.

There was also a good deal of information about parliamentary transactions that was unofficially sponsored by the Commons. Speaker Williams appointed John Wright and Richard Chiswell to print the Commons' Address on the state of the kingdom in November 1680, though he sent a note to the printers asking them not to print his authorisation.[211] In November 1678 Sacheverell moved that two of Coleman's letters be printed, and though the Lords never agreed because of James's opposition, the incriminating correspondence did appear 'with a title particularly reflecting on the Duke'.[212] A number of pamphlets such as *England's Safety* (1679), *An Exact Collection of all Orders, Votes, Debates* (1679), *The Narrative and Reasons of Proceedings betwixt the two Houses* (1679), *An Impartial Account of Divers Remarkable Proceedings* (1679) and *A True and Perfect Collection of all Messages, Addresses* (1680), all of which contained information about proceedings hitherto regarded as unsuitable for the public domain, were left unmolested by Parliament. With the expiry of the Licensing Act in May 1679 it was observed that 'many of the late passages in Parliament c[a]me forth in print',[213] and Roger North later claimed that anything 'with the Word

206 *Vox Patriae* (1681), pp. 2, 12.
207 Ibid., p. 17. The author of *The Loyalty of the Last Long Parliament* (1681), p. 20, believed that if men could 'but hear the Debates in Parliament, [they] would give their Suffrage to the same things they now condemn'.
208 Grey, *Debates*, viii. 292–4.
209 Ibid., viii. 294.
210 BL, Add. 28,091, f. 97, Danby's draft declaration 1681.
211 NLW, Wynnstay MS L.519, 29 November 1680. Williams later begged James II's pardon for having appointed Newcombe and Hills to print Dangerfield's 'information' in November 1680, claiming he did it 'by inadvertancy in obedience to an order of the late House of Commons' when he was 'a minister only to their Exorbitant commands' (NLW, Wynnstay MS C34).
212 Leics. RO, Finch mss, DG7/4957/57, f. 21, 6 November 1678. The tract was called *Mr Coleman's two letters to Monsieur L'Chaise ... together with the D[uke] of Y[ork's] letter to the said Monsieur L'Chaise* (1678). A reward of £100 was offered for the discovery of its printer (*London Gazette*, no. 1368, 26–30 December 1678).
213 *HMC Ormonde*, iv. 524.

Parliament in the Front; such as Votes, Speeches, Protests, Conferences with Reasons, and the like' was dispersed with energy and profit.[214]

The world 'without doors' could even listen to some of the parliamentary debates. A number of speeches, such as those supposedly delivered by Powle, Winnington, Clarges and Williams, circulated in manuscript form,[215] though not without complaint in the first two instances that they were inaccurate versions.[216] Complete debates were available in manuscript form,[217] or in printed versions such as those of the 1680 Parliament in *An Exact Collection of the Most Considerable Debates*, which claimed to print speeches 'as they were *pro re nata* spoken'.[218] *A Collection of the Substance of Several Speeches and Debates in the Honourable House of Commons*, appeared in print in February or March 1681,[219] most of it having first circulated in manuscript form under the title *Fragmenta Parliamentaria*.[220] The Oxford Parliament was similarly well reported. *The Debates in the House of Commons Assembled in Oxford* appeared at the end of April 1681, a contemporary printing of part of what is now known as *Grey's Debates*, the collection compiled by the MP Anchitell Grey.[221] The Oxford debates were printed a second time in 1681 for a different publisher who appended to them the *Proceedings of the Honourable House of Commons* (1681), material which had previously been printed separately. *Historical Collections or a Brief Account of the Most Remarkable Transactions of the last two Parliaments* was also published to inform the public about the proceedings of the 1680 and 1681 Parliaments.

Many loyalists had severe misgivings about making parliamentary information so readily available. The author of *Heraclitus Ridens* argued that if the people were going to be informed 'it must either be for something or for

---

214 North, *Examen*, p. 88. On 23 December 1680 the House ordered the printing of a committee report about the 'arbitrary' actions of judges (*CJ*, ix. 692). I am grateful to Lois Schwoerer for pointing out the rarity of this action.

215 Copies of a speech by Winnington are at Bod., MS Firth C.13, f. 29; BL, Add. 61,903, f. 94; Huntington, EL.8925; Huntington, STT Parliament, Box 3, folder 13; Bod., MS Carte 72, f. 456; Newdigate newsletter Lc.766. Copies of a speech by Powle are at BL, Add. 28,046, f. 47; BL, Add. 61,903, f. 84; Bod., MS Rawl.A.137, f. 4; Newdigate newsletter Lc.764. A copy of a speech by Williams is at NLW, Coedyman Papers, Group I/50–1. For speeches made by other MPs see BL, Add. 61,093, ff. 152–4, 159; Bod., MS Carte 72, ff. 466, 467; Dr Williams's Library, MS 31.P, ff. 192–4.

216 Newdigate newsletter Lc.767, 3 April 1679.

217 Bulstrode newsletter, 12 March 1679; Newdigate newsletter Lc.1058, 24 March 1681.

218 *An Exact Collection of the Most Considerable Debates* (1681), 'To the Reader'.

219 It was advertised in *Smith's Protestant Intelligence*, no. 12, 7–10 March 1681.

220 Queen's College, Oxford, MS 33, endorsed 15 January 1680[1].

221 Richard Sterne, MP, thought 'that though it be lame & imperfect the substance is impartially related, though there are some circumstanciall errors, & some omissions. But by that [publication] you may be able to guess what passed among us at our last meeting'. (John Rylands Library, Legh mss, Sterne to Legh, 30 April 1681).

nothing; if for nothing, they may as well continue ignorant; if for something, that something supposes that they are to Judge' Parliament's actions, a capacity which was claimed to be beyond them.[222] The government's official attitude was expressed by Secretary Jenkins when he called the publication of the votes 'an Appeal to the People',[223] and by the Solicitor General, who stated during the trial of Fitzharris that parliamentary debates could not be used as evidence because 'they ought not to be divulged and because they are uncertaine'.[224] Parliamentary debates were too important and serious to be made public, one loyalist argued.[225]

It was this attitude that prevented publication of the proceedings of the Upper House. In 1679 a loyalist pamphlet suggested that 'the people not knowing what the Lords do in a session of Parliament makes them think they do nothing at all', and recommended that the proceedings of the peers be made public.[226] But, although the votes of the Commons were printed in 1680 and 1681, those of the Lords remained unpublished. When in April 1680 one enterprising printer, Ralph Holt, tried to capitalise on, or stimulate, the public's interest by putting the *Lords Journal* to the press the privy council ordered it to be seized.[227] Although Samuel Mearne, Master of the Stationer's Company, was granted access to the *Lords Journals* for research on an intended publication of state papers,[228] the clerk of Parliament, John Browne, wrote that Mearne 'meddle[d] with those matters he understands not', and Browne intended, when the Lords met again, to propose to them 'that some course may be taken that the Journals may not be exposed or prostituted to the designs of such inferior sort of people.'[229]

Despite attempts to hinder its distribution, information about parliamentary proceedings was circulated widely. From his desk in London William Longueville could 'heare the streete ring w[i]th the newly printed votes',[230] and after the Oxford Parliament Sir John Reresby was told about the 'extraordinarie diligence used to disperse papers of the last session'.[231] Although two impressions of *The Narrative and Reasons of the House of Commons* (1679) were seized, it was observed that the publication could 'not

---

222 *Heraclitus Ridens*, no. 16, 17 May 1681.
223 Grey, *Debates*, viii. 293.
224 NLW, Wynnstay MS L.702, proceedings against Fitzharris, 7 May 1681.
225 *The Freeborn Subject* (1679), p. 33.
226 *Truth and Honesty in Plain English* (1679), chapter 2, p. 4.
227 PRO, PC.2/68, f. 626, privy council minutes 2 April 1680; *Domestick Intelligence*, no. 80, 9 April 1680.
228 *CSPD 1679–80*, p. 529.
229 *HMC Lords 1678–88*, p. 156.
230 BL, Add. 29,558, f. 211, William Longueville to Lord Hatton, 28 March 1681. *A Pleasant Discourse between Two Sea Men* (1681), p. 1, complained that the newsmongers made such a noise 'that a body could not Discourse in the streets with ones Friends for the Clamour they made'.
231 Leeds AO, Mexborough mss, Reresby 18/119, J. Wentworth to Reresby, 30 March 1681.

be prevented, they are so thick bought up', and a third impression escaped the messengers of the press.[232] Copies of the tract were 'in every man's hands, & such as did never read them do mightily magnify them'.[233] Just how quickly Londoners learnt about events at Westminster is revealed by Lord Fauconberg's complaint that the day after the Lords rejected the exclusion bill the names of its opponents were posted up in the coffee houses, and that he expected to see their names in ballads and libels.[234]

The effectiveness of the dissemination of manuscript and printed propaganda is difficult to measure, largely because few records remain about reading habits, and those that do relate chiefly to the educated gentry. The picture must remain necessarily impressionistic. Nevertheless the evidence suggests that tracts penetrated all sections of society, especially in London. Even the royal family was a target for distributors. A copy of one pamphlet was dropped at the King's feet at Windsor as he was walking in a courtyard overlooked by Prince Rupert's tower,[235] and hawkers had to be restrained from selling papers at the Court's gates.[236] MPs were likewise the targets for propagandists.[237] Further down the social scale printed propaganda seems to have reached a wide audience. One loyalist pamphleteer complained that 'you shall sometimes find a seditious libel to have passed through so many hands that it is at last scarce legible for durt and sweat'.[238] Another author complained that pamphlets had become so intermingled with daily life that contemporaries were in danger of eating them at the bottom of their pies or used them to light tobacco.[239] Certain pamphlets were particularly eagerly bought up. The whole impression of Stillingfleet's sermon on 27 November 1678 was sold before nightfall of the very first day of its publication;[240] 1,500 copies of George Hickes's *The Spirit of Popery Speaking out of the Mouths of Fanatical Protestants* sold in one morning;[241] and Roger Morrice recorded that a ballad 'telling the world the Papists have now no interest in' Parliament

---

232 *HMC Ormonde*, v. 119.
233 Bod., MS Tanner 38, f. 45, Bishop of Exeter to Sancroft, 14 June 1679.
234 NLS, MS 14407, f. 72, Fauconberg to the earl of Tweeddale, 16 November 1680 (cf. North, *Examen*, p. 357). Fauconberg's prediction proved accurate (see *Poems on Affairs of State*, ii. 374–9, 'A Ballad November 1680 Made Upon Casting the Bill of the Duke of York out of the House of Lords'). George Powell wrote to Hugh Speke, 15 November 1680, requesting the names of the opponents of the bill in the House of Lords 'that the country might know their betrayers' (*CSPD 1680–1*, pp. 85).
235 *HMC Verney*, p. 479.
236 PRO, PC.2/68, f. 475, privy council minutes 12 December 1679.
237 BL, Add. 28,047, ff. 287–8, 'a paper disperst in the towne'; Bod., MS Tanner 38, Womock to Sancroft, 16 April 1679; *HMC Ormonde*, iv. 365; Muddiman, *King's Journalist*, p. 237.
238 Bohun, *The Third and Last Part of the Address to the Freemen* (1683), 'Epistle Dedicatory', p. vii.
239 *Tears of the Press* (1681), p. 4.
240 *HMC Verney*, p. 471.
241 Bod., MS Eng. Misc. E. 14, f. 14.

could 'scarcely be printed so fast as it was sold'.[242] Some tracts were so popular that obtaining a copy became difficult. Ralph Sheldon had to write to Anthony Wood in Oxford to ask him to buy a copy of *The Seasonable Address* since he found it 'very scarce to be had' in London.[243] The overall impression is of a trade that was successfully selling its product to a wide number of people, particularly in London and other major urban areas. As one pamphleteer asked in 1681, 'what Age ever brought forth more, or bought more Printed Waste Paper?'[244]

THE THEMES OF PROPAGANDA

Besides helping to explain how the controversies at the centre were disseminated to a wider public, propaganda also had an important role in shaping opinion. A study of the content of the voluminous pamphlet literature can therefore suggest some of the issues which contemporaries considered important. The material relevant to politics and opinion can be divided into six main topics: the succession, the parallels between the crisis and the civil wars, the constitution, elections, religion and miscellaneous tracts dealing with topical events. These distinctions are artificial, for a pamphlet could deal with any combination of the six concerns, but a brief consideration of them will help survey the issues considered in the rest of this book.

One pamphleteer observed that 'the Subject of His Royal Highness's Succession to the Crown is made the Common theme of the Press'.[245] Contemporaries were certainly aware of the seriousness of the succession problem. The succession issue was 'agitated in every Man's mouth'.[246] The period was a time 'when every Cobler is deciding who shall Reign',[247] and 'the matter indeed is what everybody thinks themselves engaged in, and everybody speak their minds of. There is no coffee house, and few private houses, but their Table talk is of these Things.'[248] The author of one pamphlet thought that the controversy over the terms heir apparent and heir presumptive 'hath gone so far, that the Plow-Man in the Country ... Argue, and Distinguish by it'.[249] Yet to focus entirely on the debate about the bill can

---

[242] Dr Williams's Library, Roger Morrice Ent'ring Book, MS 31.P, f. 130.
[243] Bod., MS Wood F.44, f. 178, Sheldon to Wood, 19 April 1681. According to the *English Gazette*, no. 5, 3 January 1681, the government had difficulties in obtaining two copies of *A Speech lately made by a Noble Peer* (1681).
[244] *Tears of the Press* (1681), p. 7.
[245] *The Free-Born Subject* (1679), p. 34.
[246] *A Letter from a Gentleman of Quality in the Country to his Friend Upon His being Chosen a Member* (1679), p. 8.
[247] *A Letter to a Friend Reflecting upon the Present Condition of this Nation* [1680], p. 8.
[248] *A Moderate Decision on the Point of Succession* (1681), p. 1.
[249] *Unio Dissidentium* (1680), p. 1.

distort our reading of the crisis. I have tried to find as many as possible of the pamphlets dealing *directly* with the succession, and have marked them with an asterisk in the bibliography. No doubt I have missed some, but for the years 1679–81 they total ninety.[250] To place this in context, the figure for the *three* years is only slightly higher than the number of pamphlets published in the *single* year of 1689 dealing with the 'allegiance controversy'.[251] I do not wish to argue that the succession debate was unimportant, or that, because it produced fewer tracts than some may have supposed, those that it did produce are uninteresting. On the contrary, they contain a rich source of political ideology, partly because they touched on so many other controversies. Far from subjugating discussion of other related issues, the succession debate reinjected vigour into the long-standing disputes about toleration or comprehension of dissenters, about the right of resistance and about the fundamental relationship between King, Parliament and the people. A solution to the succession problem was thus not the only topic debated in print, but the issue helped fuel discussion of other matters.

The controversy about the exclusion bill centred on how to interpret the constitution.[252] The succession crisis gave new life to a debate about the rights of the subjects and the origin and extent of royal prerogative, a debate which rapidly assumed a life and significance of its own. The attempt by Parliament to alter the royal line of inheritance created a dispute between those who asserted that 'the laws and statutes of the realm, with the Royal consent, have power to bind the right of the Crown, and to limit and govern the descent and succession', and those who argued that 'the descent of the Crown in the right line cannot (de jure) be impeached by any act or deed whatsoever', and that therefore 'if an act of Parliament were obtained to exclude his R[oyal] H[ighness it] would be unjust, unlawful, and ipso facto void, as contrary to the law of God and Nature, and the known Fundamental laws of the land'.[253] Besides generating an historical debate about whether

---

250 Nineteen in 1679, twenty-nine in 1680 and forty-two in 1681, figures which show the growing importance of the issue in 1681. Twenty-four of the total number had two or more impressions made of them during the period. A number of pamphlets dealing with the succession were, of course, published after 1681 which I have not counted, partly because they become increasingly interwoven with a debate on the right of resistance.

251 M. Goldie, 'The Revolution of 1689 and the Structure of Political Argument', *Bulletin of Research in the Humanities*, lxxxiii no. 4 (1980), 479, 521–2. Goldie gives the figures of eighty tracts in 1689, forty-eight in 1690, twenty-nine in 1691 and seventeen in 1692, giving an overall total of 192. He compares this with the 215 anti-papal tracts published in the reign of James II. On the other hand, the succession tracts were more numerous than those dealing with the 'engagement' controversy of 1649–52 (J. Wallace, 'The Engagement Controversy 1649–52: An Annotated List of Pamphlets', *Bulletin of New York Public Library*, lxviii (1964), 384–405) and the standing army debate of 1697–9.

252 *A Praefatory Discourse* (1681), p. 9.

253 *The Character of a Popish Successor... Part Two* (1681), p. 15; *The White Rose* (1680), p. 2; *The Great Point of Succession Discussed* (1681), p. 25.

Parliaments had altered the succession in the past, and about the biblical commands and precedents relating to human government, the exchange of views also centred on what constituted fundamental rights and laws. The rights of the monarchy, on one side, and those of Parliament and the people on the other, were vigorously contested, though even L'Estrange remarked 'it is a ticklish point to say what a King of Great Britain with his two Houses of Parliament either can or cannot do, when perhaps it would puzzle the three inns of Court to state and determine the very privileges of the single House of Commons'. The dispute, he added, split the people 'directly into two parties'.[254]

The outline of 'Whig' and 'Tory' positions on the succession and the constitution is now well known. Building on the work of earlier historians, Ashcraft and Harris have recently provided excellent, detailed reconstructions of the ideology of the period.[255] It would be quite unfair to suggest that neither Harris nor Ashcraft place the political thought in context – indeed, the latter's main concern is to place Locke's work in context – but their approach can be followed and extended with profit by further exploring the relationship between political theory and practice, and placing the ideological debate they have delineated more firmly in the events of the period. After all, events could themselves act as propaganda, for propaganda and politics were inextricably linked during this period. Furthermore, whilst there is agreement that by 1681 a 'Tory' interpretation had replaced a 'Whig' version of popery and arbitrary government, we need to know more about what prompted shifts of opinion during the crisis. In short, ideology and opinion needs to be set within a detailed political framework to give an account not only of what contemporaries thought, but why they chose to express such thoughts when they did. The second half of this book attempts to provide such an account.

One of the most important themes which will recur throughout the following chapters, and which Jonathan Scott has rightly emphasised,[256] was the King's perceived abuse of his powers to determine when Parliament met. One pamphleteer stated the fear of arbitrary power quite simply in his observation that 'one great design is to render Parliaments odious and thereby useless'.[257] The issue of securing Parliament was not, however, a new one in 1678. Shaftesbury had made frequent attempts after 1675 to secure the dissolution

---

[254] *The Case Put Concerning the Succession* (1679), pp. 6–7.
[255] For discussions of this topic see O.W. Furley, 'Pamphlet Literature in the Exclusion Crisis 1679–81', *CHJ*, xiii (1957), 19–36; B. Behrens, 'The Whig Theory of the Constitution in the Reign of Charles II', *CHJ*, vii (1941), 42–71; J.G. Pocock, *The Ancient Constitution and the Feudal Law* (Cambridge, 1957); Harris, *London Crowds*, chapters 5 and 6; Harris, *Politics Under the Later Stuarts*, chapter 4; Ashcraft, *Revolutionary Politics*, chapter 5; C. Edie, 'Succession and Monarchy: The Controversy of 1679–81', *American Historical Review*, lxx (1965), 350–70.
[256] Scott, *Restoration Crisis*, pp. 19–20, 33–8.
[257] *A Seasonable Warning to the Commons of England* (1679), p. 3.

of the Cavalier Parliament,[258] and in October 1676 it was reported that those who wore green ribbons in their hats, presumably members of the Green Ribbon Club, had done so to show that they were 'for a new Parlement'.[259] After Shaftesbury's imprisonment for suggesting that Parliament was dissolved because of the long prorogation, Members of the Lower House had vented their frustration at the adjournments of Parliament, a tactic which Charles employed instead of the more controversial prorogations. On 16 July 1677 a number of MPs had been outraged by Speaker Seymour's attempts to adjourn the House merely on the King's order: 'they say adiourning is an act of the house, and the speaker but their officer, and ought not therefore to doe everything as the act of the house w[i]thout first receyving the order and sense of the house'. Cavendish and William Williams had moved for the journals to be examined for precedents, but Seymour had refused to grant permission and had pronounced the House adjourned until 3 December 1677. On that day Sacheverell had 'offered to speak ... but the Speaker prevented him'.[260] The House was further adjourned until 15 February, when another adjournment was announced; this had occasioned 'some sport' when MPs moved to consider the adjournment, 'upon which some little heat arose' until Seymour rose from the chair, ending further debate.[261] Thus even before the Popish Plot, the issue of the King's power to summon, prorogue, adjourn and dissolve Parliaments had been questioned.

Yet it was as a result of the King's behaviour after 1678 that concern about Parliament's sitting became much more widespread. The response to Charles's repeated, and effective, use of his powers to prorogue and dissolve came in the form of petitions calling for Parliament's assembly. Mass petitioning of the King was not a new tactic. Pym had used it in 1640–2,[262] and though Parliament had passed an Act in 1661 forbidding petitions presented by more than ten people, the tactic had been suggested thereafter on several occasions to put pressure on the King to summon Parliament. In June 1667 there had been rumours about a petition from the City of London requesting that the Parliament be allowed to sit,[263] and in July 1676 a radical linen draper named Francis Jenkes had tried to move for the summoning of the

---

[258] Haley, *Shaftesbury*, pp. 371, 390, 401, 409.

[259] Bulstrode newsletter, 6 October 1676.

[260] Bulstrode newsletter, 16 July, 3 December 1677; BL, Add., 32,095, f. 52, newsletter, 4 December 1677. For notes by Williams of what he 'intended to say' on 3 December see NLW, Wynnstay mss, L422.

[261] Bulstrode newsletter, 15 January 1678.

[262] A. Fletcher, *The Outbreak of the English Civil War* (1981), chapter 6, 'Petitions'. L.F. Brown, *The First Earl of Shaftesbury* (1933), pp. 34, 36–7, argued that Shaftesbury learnt lessons from Pym that he never forgot.

[263] Seaward, *Cavalier Parliament*, p. 307.

London common council in order to petition for Parliament's assembly.[264] Jenkes may have seen himself as the link with the petitioning of the past, for he was the son-in-law of William Walwyn, the Leveller who had been highly active in framing and managing petitions in the 1640s.[265] Shortly after Jenkes's arrest, the MP Sir Philip Monckton was also taken into custody for agitating in the north for a petition 'ag[ain]st Popery, and to call the present Parliament againe very suddenly'.[266] It was therefore no surprise that it was to a petitioning campaign that the critics of the Court turned in 1679. The use of the tactic nevertheless sparked a struggle to represent the will of the nation, so that petitions and counter-petitions became sophisticated forms of propaganda as well as reflectors of opinion. A campaign of petitions in the winter of 1679–80 requested the King to let Parliament sit on 26 January 1680, and later in the year addresses 'abhorring' the earlier petitions were presented to the King. When Parliament met in the autumn these 'abhorrences' were investigated and condemned, and when Parliament was dissolved in January 1681 more addresses were presented, though this time to MPs, rather than to the King. When the Oxford Parliament was dissolved at the end of March 1681 a flood of addresses was presented to the King thanking him for the *Declaration* in which he had explained why the dissolutions had been necessary.

Yet this bald analysis, whilst showing how the petitions and addresses were linked responses to each other and to events, does little to convey the way in which the campaigns moulded and reflected opinion, and there is a considerable amount of information about them which has been largely unused, but which nevertheless illuminates the study of the interplay between central and local politics. The campaigns of petitions and addresses will therefore be examined in the following pages to ascertain the strength and organisation of the Court and of its opponents in London and in the country, to investigate the role of propaganda in politics, and to try to gauge shifts in public opinion. The petitions and addresses also offer insights into why, by 1681, moderates had been won over or neutralised by the Court, and why the opposition was stripped to a faction. It will be suggested that part of the answer lies in a struggle to control the ways of representing opinion, and that it was the campaign of addresses in 1681 that ensured and marked victory for the loyalists. Moreover, some observers remarked that 'petitioners' and 'addressers' were names prefiguring 'Whig' and 'Tory', an indication that we can also approach the emergence of party politics through

[264] Haley, *Shaftesbury*, p. 409.
[265] *The Writings of William Walwyn* ed. J. and B. Taft (1989), pp. 275–6, 283, 537.
[266] Bulstrode newsletter, 7 July 1676.

the campaigns.[267] Moreover, although it was not a new weapon, petitioning or addressing was a tactic that continued in use long after the political events which prompted its revival in 1679–81 had passed. Nationwide addresses were a propaganda weapon employed in the remaining years of Charles II's reign, during that of his brother, James II, and under William III. The petitioning and addressing campaigns of the crisis therefore have both short- and long-term consequence.

The general elections of 1679–80 also spawned propaganda that yields insights into public opinion. Southwell noted that at election time in 1679 the country swarmed with pamphlets,[268] and lord keeper North recognised the effect of such literature: the opposition, he thought, had 'a great advantage when it can dispers News so that it shall be thought the sense of the people. For by that means it will really become the sense of the people. By this means Elections will be Governed. For every idle Burger will beleev a ly in print rather than an honest neighbour.'[269] The general election campaigns them-selves are also revealing about opinion,[270] and it is mainly from the evidence they provide that J.R. Jones has concluded that Whig and Tory divisions emerged in 1679.[271] A re-assessment of the campaigns, therefore, offers the opportunity to test this claim. I have argued in the first half of this book that although exclusion was a significant political issue at Westminster it was by no means the only one polarising the nation, that its importance has been exaggerated, and that party groupings were rudimentary and fluctuating in their strength. A study of the electoral campaigns can help show whether these observations are valid for the country as a whole.

Alarmed by the hostility to the Court which the polls confirmed, few loyalist pamphleteers missed an opportunity to claim that 'the poysonous dregs and lees of the late horrid and unnatural rebellion begin again to rise'.[272] As proof, the author of *The Protestants' Remonstrance* accused the King's critics of using 'nothing but the fragments out of old Parliament

---

[267] Burnet remarked that the terms were introduced after the dissolution of the Oxford Parlia-ment, during the addressing campaign (Burnet, *History*, ii. 287). See also D. Neal, *The History of the Puritans* (1837), iii. 219; L. Echard, *The History of England* (1720), p. 988 (quoted by Willman, 'Origins of Whig and Tory', p. 247). UCNW, Mostyn MS 9090, f. 119, newsletter 30 April 1681, refers to 'the Petition by the Loyall Party by some called Tories'.

[268] *HMC Ormonde*, iv. 536.

[269] BL, Add. 32,518, ff. 35–6, notes by North.

[270] For discussions of the elections see E. Lipson, 'The Elections to the Exclusion Parliaments 1679–81', *EHR*, xviii (1913), 59–85; M.D. George, 'Elections and Electioneering 1679–81', *EHR*, xlv (1930), 552–78; W.A. Speck, 'The Electorate in the First Age of Party', in *Britain in the First Age of Party*, ed. C. Jones (1987), 45–62; Jones, *First Whigs*, pp. 34–48, 92–106, 159–73; Ashcraft, *Revolutionary Politics*, pp. 166–72, 228–44; M. Kishlansky, *Parlia-mentary Selection. Social and Political Choice in Early Modern England* (Cambridge, 1986).

[271] Jones, *First Whigs*, p. 92.

[272] *Vox Populi, Fax Populi* (1681), p. 1.

Pamphlets', and cited Thomas Fuller's *Ephemeris Parliamentaria* (1654) as a source.[273] The charge that old material was being reprinted because of its relevance to the present crisis was not without foundation. A sermon preached on 1 January 1651, described by Narcissus Luttrell as 'a prohibited thing; being first printed in the late times, ab[ou]t the Kings taking the Covenant', was reprinted in 1679.[274] *Jus Caesaris* (1681) and Charles Blount's *A Just Vindication of Learning* (1679) borrowed heavily from Milton's *Areopagitica* (1644);[275] and John Sadler's *The Rights of the Kingdom*, originally printed in 1649, was reprinted in 1682 with what L'Estrange called 'severall sly Variations, and Additions, and Many Things Omitted in the Latter Copy'.[276] But it was not only the opposition which made use of old tracts to justify their cause. A string of royalist pamphlets were reprinted during the crisis. The publication of the works of Sir Robert Filmer, including *Patriarcha*, was thus part of a more general reliance by the loyalists on texts written between 1640 and 1660 to counter opposition propaganda. L'Estrange republished *Presbytery Display'd* in 1681, a tract originally written in 1644 and published first in 1663, and is also likely to have been behind the printing of *Mr John Milton's Character of the Long Parliament*, a critical passage omitted from Milton's final version of his *History of Great Britain*.[277] *England's Black Tribunal*, a pamphlet first printed in 1659 which related Charles I's trial and 'the sufferings, and Death of divers of the Nobility and Gentry, who were Inhumanly Murthered for their Constant Loyalty to their Sovereign Lord the King', was reprinted in 1680 because it was 'much enquired after'.[278] *The Jesuits Letter of Thanks to the Covenanters in Scotland*, written in 1640, was reprinted in 1679 to highlight the parallels between the two times, and *The Late Keepers of the English Liberties* was a reprint of a satire of 1659 on members qualified to sit in the restored Rump. Works by the royalist Sir John Monson were published, one of them on the grounds that events were 'relapsing into the like Dangers'.[279] Given this awareness of the parallels with the civil wars, the following pages will chart how near to armed conflict men believed they were drifting, and how memories of earlier strife affected opinion between 1679 and 1681.

Persecutio Undecima, a tract first printed in 1648 to attack 'the Fanatick Persecution of the Protestant Clergy of the Church of England' was again

273 *The Protestants' Remonstrance* (1681), p. 27.
274 *Popish Plot Catalogues*, p. 4, (*A Sermon at the Coronation of King Charles the Second*).
275 G.F. Sensabaugh, *That Grand Whig Milton* (Stanford, 1952), pp. 54–65.
276 *A Word Concerning Libels* (1681), p. 2; CSPD 1682, pp. 31–2.
277 N. Von Maltzahn, *Milton's History of Britain* (Oxford, 1991), pp. 5–12. Sensabaugh, *Grand Whig*, p. 108, also discusses the tract by Milton.
278 *England's Black Tribunal* (1680), 'To the Reader'.
279 *Discourse Concerning Supreme Power* (1680), 'To the Reader'. cf. *Certain Material and Useful Considerations* (1680), written 1643/4 by John Mathew.

published in 1681, and illustrates the type of propaganda used against dissenters. The theme of much of the anti-nonconformist rhetoric can be summed up in L'Estrange's dictum that 'you cannot be a friend to the state without being one to the church too', and throughout his writings he pursued the idea of a conspiracy against both the established constitution and religion.[280] His approach was shared by many other writers, not least by John Nalson, whose *Character of a Rebellion* was subtitled 'the designs of the dissenters'. The author of *The Plain Truth* (1681) consequently lamented the 'fatal ferment' in religious tracts printed since the lapse of the licensing law, 'each book and pamphlet being pregnant with preternatural heat against the opposite party; each company and discourse imploy'd in unkind reflections upon others ... and, which is worst of all, the pulpit is abus'd by some on all sides to cast oyl into this woful flame'.[281] The explosive possibilities of provocative sermons in the heightened atmosphere of the popish plot was evident as much in the provinces as in London.[282] One minister at Gloucester, who had opposed the corporation in the two elections of 1679, upbraided the mayor and aldermen before the cathedral's congregation, calling them 'magistrates for the devill'; a complaint was duly dispatched to secretary Coventry, who was told that the offending preacher was a person of 'great parts and learning and his principles did not lead him to this, but his interest and ambition to be the leader of a faction'.[283] As the impeachment in Parliament of Richard Thompson of Bristol for a sermon delivered at Oxford illustrates, religious conflict was another factor in the interplay between local and national politics. Thompson was accused of slighting the plot, of attacking Parliaments for being 'seditious, rebellious and dangerous to the monarchs of this kingdom', and of 'aspersing his native good subjects, who were humble petitioners for the meeting and sitting of this Parliament, to be schismaticall'.[284] The dividing line between religious and political opinion was thus sometimes a faint one.

The themes of the succession, the sitting of Parliament, petitioning and addressing, elections, attitudes towards dissent, and fear of civil war will now be examined in a survey of public opinion from the dissolution of the Cavalier Parliament until the dissolution of the Oxford Parliament. The approach will be roughly chronological in order to show how opinion shifted over time, or at least how some opinions dominated over others at different times, and to

280 *A Further Discovery of the Plot* (1680), p. 18.
281 *Plain Truth* (1681), p. 1.
282 For an excellent study of a sermon and its context see D. Beaver, 'Conscience and Context: The Popish Plot and the Politics of Ritual 1678–82', *HJ*, xxxiv (1991), 297–327.
283 BL, Longleat mss, M/863, reel iv, Coventry papers vol. vi, f. 189, mayor and corporation to Coventry, 15 December 1679; ibid., ff. 193–4, Robert Frampton to Coventry, 20 December 1679; ibid., f. 195, mayor and corporation to Coventry, 27 December 1679.
284 NLW, Trevor-Owen MS 148, draft articles of impeachment for a sermon preached 30 January 1680.

stress that the crisis was not a uniform state of public alarm, but was punctuated by periods of relative calm, intervals which themselves affected how contemporaries viewed renewed unrest.

$$\text{---}\!\!\ll\!\!\text{---} 7 \text{---}\!\!\gg\!\!\text{---}$$

Public opinion in 1679

Who knows what Danger you are in of losing Parliaments? These frequent Dissolutions with some prognosticate an Anihilation; and then the Nation, whose Eyes are scarce dry from their Lamentations for their short-liv'd Parliaments must weep, as if it were but one great Eye for the Funeral of our Ancient Constitution.

A Seasonable Warning (1679), p.4.

This chapter examines public opinion in 1679. It places the themes of the succession, Parliament's sitting, attitudes towards dissent and fear of civil war in the context of the two general election campaigns of 1679 and the propaganda they spawned. It will argue that for much of 1679 exclusion was not *the* issue agitating the country. Instead, both the first and second general elections reveal a prevailing Court–Country conflict exacerbated by local factors and fears of popery and arbitrary government, with an undercurrent of division over the question of the unity of protestants. By the autumn of 1679 there was still no split of the nation into two different parties identifiable by their position on exclusion, although some degree of polarisation was beginning to occur, particularly in and around London. Thus by late 1679 many of the preconditions for division were in place, but they remained latent rather than fully or properly expressed.

THE FIRST GENERAL ELECTION OF 1679

Reaction to Charles's decision on 30 December 1678 to prorogue the Cavalier Parliament, which he is alleged to have made when 'pretty warm with liquor', provoked an almost universally hostile response.[1] Ironically the dissolution of the Cavalier Parliament had been eagerly sought by critics of the Court, but now its continuation was generally thought necessary to investigate the allegations of a Popish Plot,[2] and the moderate Edmund

[1] *Second Part of the Growth of Popery* (1682), pp. 223–4.
[2] *Diary of Ralph Josselin*, p. 619.

193

Verney thought the King 'strangely Infatuated at such a Nick to prorogue his Parliament . . . for instead of Disbanding his Army Hee in a manner Disbands his Parliament, w[hi]ch will Breed very ill blood among his people, & I am sorry for it'.[3] The prorogation was immediately blamed on the influence of papists at Court, and MPs went back home 'dissatisfyed and the more because they are afraid there will be a further prorogation on purpose to smother this damnable plot'.[4] A paper 'taken up on the Exchange', which may well have emanated from the Green Ribbon Club since its content echoed what we know many of its members were saying, accused Charles of meeting with some of the French and catholic contrivers of the Plot, accepting money from the French immediately prior to the prorogation, 'and all this is to make our King absolute by bringing in Popery and arbitrary Government'.[5] Furthermore, the document declared that Charles's word was worthless, and warned Londoners that the prorogation 'clearly tends to your ruine and advantage to the Papists'. In the light of such claims, Parliament's re-assembly became an immediate priority and headed a list sent to Secretary Williamson of ways to appease public opinion, a programme which also included executing the catholics convicted of participation in the Plot, bringing others to trial, replacing Danby, and disbanding the army.[6] Right from the start of the political crisis, therefore, the issue of Parliament's sitting was central to the crisis of faith in the Court, and was to remain one of the principal issues of the political unrest. The King's control over the times at which MPs could meet seemed to allow popery to go unchecked and threatened to introduce arbitrary government.

The desire to see MPs meeting at Westminster prompted the deployment of petitions requesting the King to allow Parliament's sitting, a tactic that was to shape much of the future conflict. By 13 January 1679, barely a fortnight after the prorogation had been announced, a petition was being organised in the City of London which requested that MPs should be allowed to sit at the time appointed, and called for the speedy execution of convicted plotters and the disbandment of the army. Although some were said to 'scruple' signing it for the moment, there was thought to be widespread agreement that Parliament ought to be reconvened, and as many as 20,000 Londoners were said to have subscribed. It was thought to be the 'opinion of most that the parl[ia]m[en]t must meet'; if not, even loyalists believed the result would be 'dreadfull'.[7] The

[3] Bucks. RO, M11/32, Edmund Verney to Sir Ralph Verney, 2 January 1679.

[4] *CSPD 1679–80*, p. 15; *HMC Le Fleming*, p. 153; *Diary of Philip Henry*, p. 278; All Souls, MS 169, f. 311, newsletter, 15 January 1679.

[5] All Souls, MS 169, f. 311–15, endorsed by Luttrell 'a base scandalous & malitious thing'; *CSPD 1679–80*, p. 21.

[6] *CSPD 1679–80*, pp. 15–16.

[7] Chatsworth, Devonshire collection, group 1A, R. Jackson to earl of Devonshire, 14 January 1679; *The Flemings in Oxford*, ed. J.R. Magrath (Oxford Hist. Soc. xliv, 1904), i. 273.

petition's promoters in London hoped to procure similar requests from 'all the considerable corporations in England'.[8] But before they could do so, the King dissolved the Cavalier Parliament.[9]

Historians seem to be agreed that the first general election of 1679 was influenced by local interests and a 'Court–Country' conflict, rather than by national political issues.[10] Organisation and groupings of candidates were fluid and unsystematic. With the Court's suspect zeal against popish plotters, and Danby's lame-duck administration, it was immediately apparent to contemporaries that men would be chosen 'everywhere that are averse to the Court'.[11] Even the King admitted that 'the country would choose a dog if he stood against a Courtier',[12] and no doubt aware that Court attempts at manipulation might only have been counterproductive, he largely refrained from intervention.[13] Although the nature of the elections is uncontroversial, two features nevertheless require comment. The first was the role of religion. The general election was the first in which the clergy could vote, enfranchisement being the reward given in 1664–5 for agreement to clerical taxation,[14] and some of the ecclesiastical hierarchy made use of this new sphere of influence to assume a high political profile. The Bishop of Norwich's letter recommending men of known loyalty to the church and King achieved notoriety, and the Bishop of Durham was reported to have recommended his elder brother to the electorate 'with some earnestness and a kind of little threatening'.[15] Loyalists, on the other hand, thought the nonconformists to be more active. One partisan, and retrospective, account claimed that the dissenters 'flew from their sullen retirements, and riding night and day about the villages, and trudging about the corporations, incited those they found willing, and persuaded, intreated and sometimes hired those they found less disposed to joyn with them'.[16] The earl of Lindsey believed that such zeal was effective partly because even the Court's supporters allied with the dissenters.

---

8 Knights, 'London Petitions and Parliamentary Politics in 1679', *Parliamentary History*, xii pt. 1 (1993), p. 31.
9 Parliament was dissolved by proclamation so that MPs need not meet, a sign of the government's nervousness (*CSPD 1679–80*, p. 50). No wonder that Charles was biting his nails so closely he could not sleep properly at night (*HMC Ormonde*, iv. 312).
10 The *History of Parliament* volumes nevertheless sometimes refer to candidates as 'exclusionists', presumably more as a label than a reflection of current political issues; and Simms, 'The organisation of the Whig party', p. 96, claims that the elections were 'really the first of the modern type, as fought by organised parties upon national issues.'
11 *Original Letters*, ed. Foster, p. 90.
12 *Diary of Ralph Josselin*, p. 619.
13 *Hatton Corresp.* i. 170–2.
14 I am grateful to Mark Goldie for drawing this point to my attention.
15· Bod., MS Tanner 39, f. 200, Thomas Long to Sancroft, 14 March 1679; *HMC Frankland*, p. 38. cf. Jones, *First Whigs*, p. 40; BL, Longleat mss, M/863 reel v, Coventry papers vol. vii, Bishop of Bath and Wells to Secretary Coventry, 11 February 1679.
16 Bohun, *The Second Part of the Address to the Freemen and Freeholders* (1682), p. 2.

He witnessed how some of the King's own servants 'made it their businesse industriously to discountenance the Loyall partys standing & so set up a Phanaticke interest', and reported the 'strange influence the nonconformists have over the corporations in w[hi]ch they live, & infallibly all Parliament men will bee of their choosing'.[17] The prominent role adopted by some nonconformists is undeniable. The quaker William Penn acted as election agent for Algernon Sidney at Guildford, and Sir John Hartopp was noted to have had 'fanatic' support in Leicestershire.[18] Yet the divide between opponents of dissent and those sympathetic to them was still embryonic. Lords Shaftesbury and Winchester pleased the King by writing letters 'in all which they gave their friends great caution not to choose fanatics', and the duke of Buckingham, for all his contacts with radical dissenters, originally supported Thomas Hackett, a churchman and a loyalist, at Buckingham against his former protégé Sir Richard Temple, who had espoused the Court interest.[19] Anti-popery or anti-Court sentiment was what mattered.

A second feature was the excessive cost of, and corruption at, elections, a problem which, in Restoration politics, had only previously been apparent in by-elections because there had been no general election since 1661.[20] The earl of Longford's entertainments in Surrey had cost £1,500–£2,000,[21] and the Buckinghamshire electorate had managed to consume 860 dinners and 800 bottles of sack, resulting in a bill for an estimated £1,600–1,700.[22] The effect was, Sir Robert Southwell suggested, that moderates and Court supporters would 'not be at the expense to stand'.[23] Corruption had not simply been limited to the vast expenses incurred at these elections, for intimidation of voters was also a cause for concern. For example Algernon Sidney claimed that several who would have polled for him at Guildford were threatened that, if they did not vote for his rival, 'they should not receive the Benefitt that others did of a considerable revenue that belongs to the Towne'.[24] Even worse, electoral officials had committed abuses to manipulate results. At the Westminster election a poll book containing 700 votes for Sir William Waller

[17] BL, Eg. 3331, f. 101, Lindsey to Danby, 15 February 1679.
[18] *History of Parliament*, i. 410–11, 295.
[19] *History of Parliament*, i. 244, 140.
[20] Ralph Montagu's by-election at Northampton in November 1678 cost him £1,000 in ale (*HMC Egmont*, ii. 77), prompting Edmund Verney to remark that 'if Things Goe on at this Rate, in a short Time longer, a Parliament will Be more Intolerable than a Standing Army' (Bucks. RO, Verney mss, M11/32, to Sir Ralph Verney, 20 February 1679). As early as 1674 an MP had complained that the cost of an election had 'grown so vast that it goes beyond all bounds' (cited by J. Cannon, *Parliamentary Reform 1640–1832* [Cambridge, 1973], p. 35).
[21] *HMC Ormonde*, iv. 341.
[22] Bucks. RO, Verney mss, M11/32, Edmund Verney to Sir Ralph Verney, 20 February 1679. The average cost of a seat a century later has been estimated at only £3,000 (Cannon, *Parliamentary Reform*, p. 35).
[23] Bod., MS Carte 39, f. 13, Southwell to Ormonde, 4 February 1679.
[24] A. Collins, *Letters and Memorials of State* (1746), i. 154.

had been 'artificially mislayed & lost by the officers',[25] whilst the proclamation of the Montgomeryshire election had been made so quietly that 'those in the next House to the market house where the fopp ceremonie passed, nay & some in the streete, heard it not'.[26] One tract claimed that fraudulent conveyances of land had been made in order to qualify what the author termed 'mushroom voters', a practice for which there does seem to be some evidence.[27]

The abuses at the elections were important because they strengthened Country sensibilities against corruption, and prompted consideration when Parliament met of how to reform polling procedures. On 4 April 1679 an elections bill was put before the House of Commons and received a second reading the next day, when it was recommitted. Although it never re-emerged for debate, the bill's provisions can be found in a printed version which circulated during the elections in the autumn of 1679 and thus ironically itself became a piece of electoral propaganda.[28] Primarily the bill dealt with the definition and punishment of all forms of electoral corruption, but also added a property qualification of £200 in fee for county voters, and allowed disenfranchisement as a penalty for infringement of the bill. The proposed measures also provided against a long continuance of the same Parliament by stipulating its automatic dissolution after two years.[29] Once again, the issue

---

25 BL, Add. 29,557, f. 114, William Longueville to Lord Hatton, 25 February 1679.

26 NLW, Wynnstay mss, Box 5/5, Edward Lloyd to Evan Vaughan, 13 May 1679.

27 Bohun, *Second Part of the Address* (1682), p. 8; Collins, *Letters and Memorials*, i. 153–4. *The Memorable Case of Denzil Onslow* (1681), pp. 2–5 protested that loyalists created shorthold leases purely to convey voting rights to his opponents. cf. *Impartial Protestant Mercury*, no. 27, 22–6 July 1681 (which reports the evidence offered by Onslow, including the accusation that one man 'convey'd to his sons Two Rods of his Cabbage Garden' to qualify them as voters); *A Dialogue between the Pope and a Phanatick* (1680), p. 13.

28 *The Bill for Regulating Abuses in Elections* (1679). *Heraclitus Ridens*, no. 15, 19 May 1681 claimed that this pamphlet 'was printed and dispersed after the dissolution of the Parliament of 1679'.

29 It may well have been based on Holles's bill regulating elections (see chapter 5). See also draft bills in Bod., MS Carte 80, ff. 827–8, 'breviat of a Bill for Regulating Election of Members of Parl[iamen]t Ap[ril] 1679'; BL, Add. 70,098, unfoliated, bill to prevent offences of bribery and debauchery at elections, with lists of amendments; and one in the Coventry papers probably dating from this time (BL, Longleat, M/863, reel v, vol. viii, f. 217). Another draft bill, endorsed 'Draught of a bill against long Parl[iament]s & for better attendance of members', and clauses for a bill are also amongst these papers (ff. 168–9, ff. 170–1). It is possible that these drafts are the result of the Commons' decision on 5 April to split the original bill (*CJ*, ix. 585). *The Nations Aggrievance* (1679), p. 4, suggested that election returns should be signed by the voters to prevent abuses by returning officials. cf. *The Benefit of the Ballot* (1679), and *A Safe and Easy Way to obtain Free and Peaceable Elections* (1680), which also advocated ballots. Biannual Parliaments seem to have been fixed on as a compromise between those who wanted triennial meetings (Grey, *Debates*, vii. 253; *HMC Ormonde*, v. 96) and those who favoured annual meetings: *English Liberties* (1681), p. 76; *An Impartial Account of the Nature* (1681), p. 19; *A Dialogue at Oxford* (1681), pp. 7–9. Their views were attacked by *Protestant Loyalty Fairly Drawn* (1681), p. 68; *Antidotum Britannicum* (1681), p. 72; *A Petition to the Petitioners* (1680), p. 1.

of control over the length and times of parliamentary sessions was under consideration, although now it was not in the form of petitions exerting pressure on the King's decision when or whether to dissolve, but as a bill which would, after two years, have removed his freedom to make the decision at all.

The issue of ensuring that Parliament met, and met often, remained prominent throughout the period. An undated manuscript, clearly written in the immediate aftermath of the Popish Plot, titled 'In Favour of frequent Parliaments', outlined the 'Advantages accrewing to the Publick by owneing the Act of the 16 of Cha[rles] the 1st for frequent Parliaments'.[30] Every future Parliament was to sit for an uninterrupted fifty days, long enough to enable members of the next Parliament 'to contract all necessary acts into one bill, as it were a Magna Carta against Popery &c as the first was ag[ains]t Tyranny'.[31] The Act enforcing frequent Parliaments would be, the document claimed, 'a strong bank to Religion and Liberty ag[ains]t Popish succeeding & usurping Kings, if they be not excluded by an act of settling the succession in the protestant heires'. Among Shaftesbury's papers is a draft act with very similar provisions 'for the prevent[ing I]nconveniencies happening by the long intermission of Parl[iament]s', which contained clauses requiring Parliament to sit for a minimum of fifty days, annual Parliaments and the automatic re-assembly of a Parliament prorogued for longer than three years.[32]

Such ideas continued to be aired throughout the period. In July 1679 Sir Robert Howard warned that the effect of frequent dissolutions was to foster 'a demand of a prefixed time of sitting', and the author of a paper written shortly after the end of the 1679 Parliament and in preparation for the next, had thought it 'necessary that the king be addressed to and the Lords concurrence desired, which they will hardly refuse, that the Parliament may sitt some competent time to dispatch the weighty affairs of the kingdom'.[33] Barrillon predicted that when MPs did meet, securing the length of the session would be one of their principal demands, and immediately before Parliament sat in October he noted that the demands discussed in the cabals included

---

[30] BL, Stowe 354, ff. 142–3. It refers to Oates's accusations, the danger of a popish successor, and the need for an Act of Association. Since it refers to Wakeman's trial it must be dated post July 1679. Another paper (ff. 144–5), written in the same hand, contains extracts of, and observations on, Thomas Phillip's *The Long Parliament Revived* (1661), which suggest that the unknown author envisaged a perpetual Parliament which would sit beyond Charles's death, dissolvable only by the unanimous consent of King, Lords and Commons.

[31] Barrillon refers to the Commons' resolution to have a Parliament assemble for fifty days (PRO, 31/3/147, f. 82, Barrillon dispatch, 20/30 December 1680). This specific length is not recorded in the Journals (*CJ*, ix. 682), but was the period stipulated by the 1641 Triennial Act.

[32] PRO, 30/24/30/44.

[33] *HMC Ormonde*, v. 156; BL, Longleat mss, M/863, reel v, Coventry papers vol. vi, ff. 248–51, 'Severall Usefull and Indispensibly Necessary Cautions'.

annual Parliaments.[34] The elections bill was accordingly reintroduced,[35] and on 15 December 1680 Ralph Montagu moved that a bill securing frequent Parliaments be taken into consideration.[36] Yet none of these proposals reached the statute book, and ideas about limiting the King's control over the timing of sessions remained the preserve of ideologues. Most contemporaries were interested in the practicalities of assembling MPs when they were needed, rather than the theoretical or legal regulation of the King's prerogative powers to summon and dissolve. This was an ambiguity not yet apparent in 1679, but it was to become more obvious as the crisis progressed.

THE UNITY OF PROTESTANTS

John Evelyn, who canvassed opinion at the beginning of the new Parliament, was struck by how people 'of such different interests, years & distant aboades should so universally be tainted, or inspir'd with the same zeale ... against the Court, poperie & plots, designes of Introducing Arbitrarie Governm[en]t &c'. When he remarked to those with whom he spoke that they had forgotten the civil wars, they replied that they abominated 'the sound of a Comonwealth', but that the desire to safeguard protestantism was so strong that the Court, which had 'alienated the hearts of loyal & honest people', would have to make concessions. Evelyn himself agreed that 'unless we alter the intire scheme of our late politics, and go upon another hypothesis, we shall run into suddain and inevitable confusion'.[37] His analysis of opinion on the eve of Parliament's opening is highly revealing. He depicted a unity of all sorts of men, forced together by their fear of popery and arbitrary government, their alienation from the Court and the conviction that the King's policies were leading to chaos. Two opposing political sides had clearly not yet emerged, and indeed Evelyn recorded that if it came to civil war Charles would stand alone. Evelyn's report echoes the anti-popery, anti-arbitrary government and anti-Court sentiment that had been revealed to be so widespread by the

---

34 PRO, 31/3/146, f. 6, Barrillon dispatch, 24 June/4 July 1680; ibid. f. 124, 21/31 October 1680
35 *CJ*, ix. 639; BL, Add. 70,098, unfoliated, notes made by Sir Edward Harley at elections committee 27 November 1680.
36 *The History of the Association* (1682), p. 3. Notes made that day by Daniel Finch record Hungerford as having moved for annual Parliaments (Leics. RO, Finch mss, DG7/4957/61/11). Grey did not record these motions but see Barrillon's comment that MPs aimed at frequent and annual Parliament (PRO, 31/3/147, f. 69, Barrillon dispatch, 6/16 December 1680), and *CJ*, ix. 682 for the resolution on 17 December 1680 for frequent Parliaments as security against arbitrary power. For discussions of attitudes to frequent Parliaments see Haley, *Shaftesbury*, pp. 370–1, 399–401, 412–13, 417–18; O.W. Furley, 'The Origins and Early Development of the Whig Party with special reference to Shaftesbury and Locke 1675–92' (Oxford, B.Litt. 1952), pp. 39–55; P. Croft, 'Annual Parliaments and the Long Parliament', *BIHR*, lix (1986), 155–71.
37 Christ Church, Oxford, Evelyn Letter book, letter no. cccc Evelyn to Godolphin, 6 March 1679.

elections. We must therefore turn to look for the reasons why this harmony began to dissolve.

Ironically, one divisive factor was the call for protestant unity. Evelyn had been told of the need for a comprehension of presbyterians and independents, and himself believed that the division of Christians over 'meere circumstantials' was wrong because it gave advantage to the nation's enemies. If it was so important that dissenters conformed, he asked, 'why was not Discipline vigorously exercised according to Law, when time was proper for it? Who are we to blame for this? Does the Credit, or activity of the Bishopps, the Zeale & Humility of the Cleargy, the Morals and Virtue of Court give us any hope of proselytyzing a Party who are every day more & more scandaliz'd? ... the Nation, the Church and (for ought [I] see) the intire protestant Interest of Christendome is at stake.'[38] Capitalising on such sentiments, and in an attempt to influence the proceedings inside the House of Commons in 1679, the growing debate outside Parliament about the relief of protestant dissenters found expression in the press. Thus *A Proposal of Union among Protestants*, 'humbly presented to the Parliament', and William Penn's *One Project for the good of England*, also 'humbly dedicated to the Great Council, the Parliament', were published during the main parliamentary session of 1679. The former parodied the chancellor's opening speech, and copies of the tract were 'privately conveighed into the hands of such members as are most likely to carry on' the dissenters' design.[39] Praising John Tillotson – who on 3 December had delivered a sermon in which he argued that in order to achieve a union of protestants the church hierarchy would 'not insist upon little things but ... yield them up ... to the plausible exceptions of those who differ from us' – the author remarked that 'a divine told us of late that the church of England is ready to open arms to embrace those that do dissent'.[40] The tract also suggested that to achieve protestant unity nothing should be imposed on ministers 'but what hath footing and warrant in the holy scriptures', necessitating concessions from the established church on ceremonies, which the author colourfully referred to as 'but chips in porridg'.[41] Penn argued equally eloquently for the unity of protestants, though from grounds of civil interest. Suggesting that men would no longer strive to maintain a government that failed to protect them from violence and injury, he concluded that since dissenters and conformists agreed on allegiance to England's

[38] Ibid.
[39] Bod., MS Tanner 38, f. 14, Bishop Womock to [Dr George Thorp], 16 April 1679.
[40] In 1667–8 Tillotson had been involved in comprehension plans; he favoured exclusion (T. Birch, *Life of Tillotson* (1752), pp. 42–4, 81. George Hickes, former chaplain to the duke of Lauderdale, claimed that in 1680 Tillotson frequently met with Shaftesbury and Secretary Sunderland, and that when Charles was informed of this he turned Sunderland out of office (Bod., MS Eng. Misc. e.4, f. 34).
[41] *A Proposal of Union among Protestants* (1679), p. 3.

civil government and resistance of papal domination, both their civil and religious interests coincided; such unity should not therefore be artificially broken, and protestant dissenters should be tolerated. Moreover, he argued, since only the papists gained from furthering divisions within the protestant community, obstruction to unity must come from those who were popishly inclined.

Both pamphlets show how the fear of popery fostered the belief that protestants needed to unite in order to face a common enemy, that such unity was to be achieved either through comprehension or toleration, and that whilst there were differences of opinion about which was the right way to proceed, the goal of union was paramount. These themes were repeated in other publications that year. Another tract, *To the Right Honourable the Lords and Commons*, stressed that 'every Protestant, dissenter or not, has the same thing to say against Popery. Agree then so far, and let a general negative creed be concluded upon, and from thence let some general positive truths considered of.' The author even suggested that 'a select assembly of some of all perswasions' should meet to draw it up.[42] The writer of *The Grounds of Unity in Religion* also advocated comprehension, since he believed this would give firmer unity than toleration: 'nothing conduceth more to unity and peace than by taking off things that are cavild at, provided only they are circumstantials'. In order to comprehend the presbyterians 'a few things will be sufficient, as dispensing with the surplice, and part of the oath in the Act of Uniformity, also the crossing in baptism, and kneeling at the sacrament left indifferent, and pluralities taken away'. Other sects were to have 'some connivance, but no legal liberty'.[43] *Certain Considerations Tending to promote Peace and Goodwill among Protestants*, whose author claimed to be 'a moderate conformist', similarly argued that once the established church had changed some of its ceremonies 'many thousand who now stand aloof off would joyn with our Church Assemblies'.[44] The advocates for the nonconformists assumed that all the concessions would have to come from the church, in order to make it less infected by popish influences, and in some way seem to have believed that the establishment of the church on new lines was possible. In short, they sought a second Reformation.[45]

Hostile replies to the advocates of unity and reform were nevertheless soon forthcoming, and both *A Proposal of Union* and *One Project* were answered.

---

[42] *To the Right Honourable the Lords and Commons* (1679), p. 12. The copy at Bod., G. Pamph. 1125 (14) has a manuscript endorsement of '1679'.

[43] *The Grounds of Unity in Religion* (1679), pp. 5–6.

[44] *Certain Considerations Tending to Promote Peace* (1679), contents page.

[45] See introduction for use of the term. Richard Baxter wrote copiously about the terms for 'unity' and 'concord' in order to promote reform: *A Moral Prognostication* (1680), pp. 41–56; *The True and Only Way of Concord* (1680), chapter xvii; *The Second Part of the Nonconformists' Plea for Peace* (1680).

Lawrence Womock undertook to refute the first in *The Late Proposal of Union ... Reviewed* (1679), having first obtained approval from the Archbishop of Canterbury. 'We readily grant', Womock wrote, 'that violent storms should drive the sheep together; but in such a season, all sober men will think that the straggling sheep should run into the common fold, and not quarrel with their faithful shepherd; nor labour to pluck down that fold which is their best shelter.' He therefore conceded nothing over ceremonies, for 'by offering these dissenters to yield them they know not what, upon the solicitation of we know not whom, we shall expose ourselves and our religion to no purpose'.[46] *The Reasons for Non-conformity Examined* (1679) similarly defended the church's stance on the disputed ceremonies. The answer to Penn's arguments was a little longer in appearing, but *A Seasonable Corrective* turned his arguments on their head.[47] Firstly, Penn's assertions about the conditional allegiance owed by subjects played into his opponent's hands, since it could be claimed that the dissenters aimed to 'unhinge the state and to undermine the government'. Secondly, the tract argued that the established church was the best bulwark against popery, and that the papists tried to attack the church by using the nonconformists to divide it. The arguments for unity that the dissenters had pressed on the church to change were therefore to be turned back on the dissenters, who were themselves exhorted to foster unity by conforming.[48] The message that it was time for the dissenters to conform was also that of *A Friendly Call* (1679), which neatly asked why, if they regarded disputed ceremonies as trifles for the church to concede, the nonconformists stood so stiffly for their abolition.[49]

The appeal for unity thus divided those who sought to achieve a union of protestants through concessions to the dissenters, from those who sought unity through a stronger national church that re-affirmed its unaltered beliefs and dogma, and to which the dissenters ought to rally if they were not the tools of the Pope. Since both sides believed themselves to be right, the rallying cry of a union of protestants thus had diverging and opposite meanings to different camps within and outside the church, and led ultimately to division.

Debates within the 1679 Parliament about the plight of dissenters help explain the presentation in May of a petition addressed to the City of London's court of aldermen acknowledging Parliament's proceedings 'in the pursuance of divers Methods, Means and Ways, In Order to the preserving of his Ma[jes]ties sacred Person, and the Protestant Religion'. Before the petition

---

[46] *The Late Proposal of Union amongst Protestants Reviewed* (1679), pp. 2, 6–7, 11.

[47] The tract had the same printers and publishers as Womock's reply to *A Proposal of Union among Protestants* (1678), and was written in a similar style, which may suggest Womock's authorship.

[48] *A Seasonable Corrective to the One Project* (1680), p. 4.

[49] The tract was reworked as *A Seasonable Advice to all True Protestants* (1679), and then reprinted in 1680 as *Friendly Advice to Protestants*.

was accepted, the court of aldermen added to this statement the clause 'according to the doctrine of the Church of England as it is now established by law', a matter of 'great disappointment' to the many dissenters who can be identified amongst the 1,536 subscribers. The petition was also designed to influence Parliament in another way. Originally intended to have been presented on 15 May, it would have coincided with the first reading of the exclusion bill, and was partly designed to show public support for the measure in order to increase its chances of adoption, though too much weight should not be attached to this motive, since an attempt by some of its promoters to add a clause specifically about the proceedings against the duke of York met with failure. The petition may also have sought to use the apparent weight of public opinion to deter the King from cutting the session short, before it had completed the redress of the nation's grievances. The petition which had circulated in January 1679, before the final dissolution of the Cavalier Parliament, had attempted to do just that, and the May petitioners promised to stand by Parliament (though with no mention of the King) 'with their lives and estates'. Yet Charles, perhaps in part reacting to the implied threat of the alliance of Parliament and the City, prorogued the session only a week after the petition had been presented. Clearly parliamentary politics had begun to move the City, and rumours that London's precedent would be followed in the provinces may have contributed to Charles's decision to nip the pressure of public opinion in the bud; but whilst trying to do so he inevitably sparked anger about the dismissal of MPs, which in the longer run created controversy about his powers to end sessions at his own whim.[50]

The prorogation on 27 May caused bewilderment and unrest. When 'a whisper went among [MPs] that they were to be prorogued or dissolved no body would believe it, but every body concluded it impossible', observed one newswriter.[51] The Green Ribbon Club exploited this dissatisfaction, congregating at Parliament's doors to blame the end of the session on James, and MPs once more returned to their constituencies 'full of anger and resentment at the prorogation'.[52] . The news had so disturbed even 'sober' men that Sir John Hobart thought 'all things as it were returned to October last ... I had almost said to a chaos'.[53] The feeling of outrage was particularly strong in London where the prorogation had 'wrought as great a consternation ... as hath been knowne of a long time',[54] and, as happened at the time of all

[50] This paragraph is a summary of my article 'London Petitions and Parliamentary Politics in 1679'. For the names of those appointed to draw up the revised petition see CLRO, common council papers 1679, minutes of the meeting of 23 May 1679.

[51] All Souls, MS 242, f. 489, newsletter, 27 May 1679.

[52] All Souls, MS 242, f. 489A, newsletter, 30 May 1679; Bulstrode newsletter, 29 May 1679.

[53] Bod., MS Tanner 38, f. 35, Sir John Hobart to John Hobart, 30 May 1679.

[54] Newdigate newsletter Lc.791, 31, 30 May 1679; Corpus Christi, Oxford, MS 310, Wood to Fullman, 30 May 1679.

prorogations or dissolutions, mercantile confidence plummeted to such a degree that one newswriter believed the prorogation to have caused 'the stopp of all trade'.[55] 'Never', wrote Daniel Finch to his uncle, 'were men's fears from abroad and from within greater than at this present.'[56] Once again, Charles's use of his prerogative powers to end a session had caused uproar and almost universal condemnation. Ominously, men began 'to look more than formerly into the means of preserving themselves', and the duke of York feared 'very great disorders'.[57]

By 8 June 6,000 rebels were indeed up in arms, though the uprising occurred north of the border, in Scotland.[58] The revolt of the covenanters had important effects on English public opinion, since it revived fears of what Charles or his brother would do with the army that had to be raised to quell it, and gave new weight to calls that Parliament be recalled. One newswriter viewed the Scottish rebellion as 'onely a trick to raise the army again', and the provisions of the 1640 Treaty of Pacification, which forbade armies the right to enter either country without the consent of Parliament, was 'insisted on in the common discourse to enforce thereby the necessity of calling presently our Parliament'.[59] The fact that the rebellion generated such fears forced James to conclude that the rising had not been accidental. Indeed, he told Charles that 'the rebellion in Scotland was contrived to make the king stand in greater need of his Parliament and to deliver him bound hand and foot into' the power of the malcontents.[60] Whatever its causes, the revolt did increase the pressure for Parliament to be held, and the newly free press exploited, or reflected, the mood. Thus on 17 June *An Impartial Account of Divers Remarkable Proceedings of the last Sessions of Parliament* was published, printing selected proceedings of the Commons, including Danby's impeachment and the exclusion bill, as well as a list of all the laws which had expired, amongst which

---

[55] Bulstrode newsletter, n.d. but written end of May/early June 1679. The uncertainty created by prorogations and dissolutions was bad for business. On 23 December 1678 John Verney had written that men's minds were 'soe disturbed for feare the Parl[iament] should be dissolved or prorogued for impeaching my Lord Tresurer that it brings a damp on all men's spirits, and the Traders utter little, for noe body will buy more than necessity requires' (Bucks. RO, Verney mss, M11/32, Verney to Edmund Verney). It was shortly afterwards observed that men grew 'so jealous of what may happen that no one will part with a farthing of money' (Bod., MS Carte 243, f. 428, Ellis newsletter, 18 January 1679). A similar crisis of confidence in the trading community occurred when Charles dissolved Parliament in January 1681, and Henry Ashurst advised his brother to wait for better markets before selling his silk (Bod., MS Don. C.169, f. 7, Ashurst letterbook, 24 January 1681. I am grateful to Perry Gauci for this last reference).

[56] *HMC Finch*, ii. 53–4.

[57] *Sidney Letters*, p. 83; Dalrymple, *Memoirs*, ii. 220.

[58] All Souls, MS 171, f. 33, 12 June 1679.

[59] All Souls, MS 171, f. 33, 12 June 1679 (passage crossed out); cf. *HMC Ormonde*, iv. 523; *HMC Verney*, p. 472.

[60] Clarke, *James II*, i. 563.

was the act restraining the press.[61] A speech which the Green Ribbon Club radical Francis Jenkes had made on 24 June 1676, calling for a new Parliament, was reprinted with the date 1679, possibly so as make it appear that he had repeated the demand.[62] In the privy council Shaftesbury also pressed for Parliament to be allowed to sit, and was presumably one of the 'noblemen and others Inhabitants in & about London' who signed a petition for 'calling the Parliament, [and] stopping the forces against the rebells in Scotland'.[63] Algernon Sidney observed that, if successful, the petition would be 'sent to the grand juries in the several counties and come up signed by so many as shall approve it'.[64] The campaign also attracted support from moderates such as Edmund Verney, who regarded the prorogation as 'a thing lamentable & intolerable, & of exceeding ill consequence', and 'many hands' were said to have signed it in London until, as one newswriter reported, the defeat of the Scots 'broke the neck of their designe'.[65]

Although shortlived, the petitioning had agitated the capital at a time when it was already disturbed by fears and suspicions about the Court's intentions. As one observer wrote, those who 'endeavour all they can to blow up sedi[ti]on' were helped by the fact that 'too many are troubled & discon[ten]ted'. The possibility of a rising was taken seriously, 'to prevent w[hi]ch the guards & watch of the citty are doubled, & the constables goe about to the shopkeepers that [th]ey keep [th]eir [ap]prentices within'.[66] Inflammatory papers were actually scattered in the streets to move people to take up arms, and Charles was so afraid of an insurrection that he refused to send his lifeguard to Scotland.[67] If the Scottish rebellion had not been suppressed at the battle of Bothwell Bridge, one newswriter claimed, it 'would in all appearances [have] been fatall to the king and the peace of the nation', and the duke of Ormonde believed the Scots in Ireland would have risen in sympathy.[68] Peace seemed highly fragile in the summer of 1679, and even the

---

61 Manuscript endorsement of the date on Bod. Nichols Newspaper collection; Longleat, Coventry mss, vol. vi, ff. 127–8, anon. letter, 5 September 1679; Bod., MS Carte 232, f. 52, Longford to Arran, 6 September 1679. Wood noted that it was 'onlie a collection made from coffey letters' (Wood, *Life and Times*, ii. 475).

62 *Mr Francis Jenk's Speech. Spoken in a Common Hall, the 24th of June 1679*. Compare with *CSPD 1676–7*, pp. 253–4. For further information about Jenkes see Knights, 'London Petitions and Parliamentary Politics', p. 41.

63 *HMC Drummond-Moray*, p. 131; BL, Add. 15,643, f. 17, minutes of the committee of intelligence, 21 June 1679.

64 *Sidney Letters*, p. 91.

65 Bucks. RO, Verney mss, M11/32, Verney to Sir Ralph Verney, 2 June 1679; UCNW, Mostyn MS 9089, f. 149, newsletter, 28 June 1679; *Sidney Letters*, p. 92.

66 Chatsworth, Devonshire Collection, Group 1A, R. Jackson to earl of Devonshire, 10 June ·1679; All Souls, MS 171, f. 33, newsletter, 10 June 1679.

67 PRO, 31/3/143, ff. 14–15, Barrillon dispatch, 12/22 June 1679.

68 All Souls, MS 242, f. 498, newsletter, 27 June; Bod., MS Carte 232, f. 44, earl of Longford to earl of Arran, 5 July; MS Carte 146, f. 192, letter from duke of Ormonde, 21 June 1679.

defeat of the covenanters had important consequences in England. In the short term, the rout of the rebels strengthened the prestige and popularity of Monmouth, who had led the English forces, and helped establish him as a popular Protestant hero in opposition to James. As Monmouth returned south he was 'treated in many places with the title of Highness which was no ways ill taken by him'.[69] But in the longer term the rebellion revived, or confirmed, fears of the insurrectionary nature of religious dissent. The author of the printed reply to Penn's tract advocating toleration wanted to 'send him into Scotland to take Recognizance of those Brethren ... and bring us in good bail to secure us the good behaviour of that party'.[70] The action of the Scots was also used to emphasise the alleged links between presbyterianism and popery. One of the original claims made by Oates had been that the catholics disguised themselves as dissenters in Scotland to foment rebellion, and a manuscript note on a copy of *The Jesuits Letter of Thanks to the Covenanters in Scotland: For their Compliance in divers Material Points of Roman Catholick Doctrine and Practice* (1679) makes it clear that the tract's purpose was to 'shew the agreement betweene the Jesuites doctrine and the Scotch presbyterians'.[71]

'OUT OF THE FRYING PAN INTO THE FIRE':[72] THE SECOND GENERAL ELECTION OF 1679

The decision in July 1679 to dissolve Parliament, the result chiefly of factional pressures at Court, threw the country into renewed turmoil, and was thought to be 'very unwelcome Newse to the Country, for it was a Parliament according to the People's mind'.[73] Many believed that it could only have been dismissed 'in hopes of having one that would be less careful of the public interest', so that the dissolution only heightened suspicions about the King's designs.[74] Yet the Court seems to have, rather naively, believed that the elections would witness a reaction against what it saw as the excesses of the last session, entertaining hopes that there were 'many who wish the proceedings of this [new Parliament] may be more moderate than those of the last were', and who would consequently choose moderate men.[75] Henry Sidney was to inform William of Orange that Charles had 'great hopes of this Parliament';[76] and one prospective candidate observed how the bishops

---

[69] Clarke, *James II*, i. 559.
[70] *A Seasonable Corrective to the One Project* (1680), p. 5.
[71] Kenyon, *Popish Plot*, p. 66; *The Jesuits Letter of Thanks to the Covenanters*, shelfmark Bod., C. 12. 14 (10).
[72] *HMC Ormonde*, v. 152.
[73] Bucks. RO, Verney mss, M11/33, Edmund Verney to John Verney, 14 July 1679.
[74] *Sidney Letters*, p. 95.
[75] All Souls, MS 242, f. 504, newsletter, 11 July 1679.
[76] *Diary of Henry Sidney*, i. 26.

boasted 'very much what they will doe in the election and also all the Court party I find hope great matters'.[77] Such optimism, if sincere, was thoroughly misplaced. Although Halifax's friend Thomas Thynne remarked that he thought 'this will be the last Par[liamen]t if it bee not a good one, and therefore wish all good men in it', the tide of opinion was flowing against, not with, the Court.[78] But did this mean, as J.R. Jones has argued, that the general election, the second in six months, was fought on national issues, with exclusion as '*the* issue'?[79] He analyses the election in terms of Whig and Tory, and suggests that the nation had divided on party lines as a result of the debates of the 1679 session and because of the efficient organisation of the opposition. It will be suggested here, however, that exclusion was not the overriding issue at stake, that a 'Court–Country' division often better explains attitudes than a 'Whig–Tory' one, and that the opposition was less well co-ordinated on a national scale than has been claimed.

One way of gauging opinion is to look at the political literature spawned by the election. The propaganda represents the first major debate on national politics after the expiry of the Licensing Act.[80] Even before the lapse of the act the output of the press had risen to disturbing levels, whilst the propaganda produced had been strongly anti-popish and also increasingly anti-Court in content.[81] In February or March 1679 Danby had drawn up a memorandum asking 'what can be done for the suppressing of seditious prints and papers?'[82] But after his fall from power no action was taken, and the number of anti-Court tracts increased: 'Never was there a[s] great [a] licence taken in dispersing such scandalous libels and Pamphletts as now', reported one loyalist newswriter at the beginning of April 1679.[83] With the end of the session the trickle from the presses became a flood. By the end of June it was observed that 'papers of all sorts fly about';[84] and in July a newsletter reported that 'the Streets doe every day Ring with Books and Pamphletts', with new tracts appearing each day.[85] In the same month another newswriter reported that the London printing presses began 'exposing to publique view

---

[77] Bod., MS Carte 103, f. 221, William Jephson to Thomas Wharton, 14 July 1679.

[78] Foxcroft, *Halifax*, i. 175.

[79] Jones, 'Parties and Parliament', p. 57.

[80] Lord Huntingtower complained that in Norfolk 'severall hundred of papers called the Norf[olk] Case' had been printed and dispersed earlier that year (Norfolk RO, KC/7/6/48, Sir John Hobart to William Wyndham, 24 May 1679).

[81] Wood, *Life and Times*, ii. 429.

[82] BL, Add. 28,042, f. 19, memorandum, n.d.

[83] Huntington, MS HM 30315, newsletter 220, Benson to Jenkins, 1 April 1679. Privy council noted that William Prynne's *The Soveraigne Power of Parliament* (1643) and other of his works had been on sale (PRO, PC.2/67, f. 155, privy council minutes 9 April 1679).

[84] *HMC Ormonde*, iv. 528.

[85] Newdigate newsletters Lc.808, 10 July 1679, and Lc.811, 15 July 1679.

all things [that] come to hand',[86] and Evelyn recorded in his diary that there was 'too shamefull a liberty' of the press.[87] Initially the 'paper war' seems to have affected London most, because that was where most presses and a large literate population were located. By August the capital was said to swarm with papers,[88] and the lord mayor issued an order suppressing hawkers of books and pamphlets, a measure which had some effect, 'the publisher perhaps not seeing his advantage to hazard such stuffe in the hands of booksellers who being of more substance would be more careful of what they should vend';[89] but the measure seems to have been more effective against the newspapers than against pamphlets,[90] which were observed to issue forth as before.[91]

In a sense, as Ashcraft has argued, all pamphlet literature was aimed at the electorate; and the 'swarms of pamphlets' on a variety of subjects added 'new flame' to opinion in the country.[92] But at least twenty-five pamphlets were published at this time which relate directly to the election.[93] Half of these reported polls that had already taken place, but about a dozen were printed with the sole purpose of influencing the electors' choice. The newswriter Henry Muddiman reported that 'No sooner were the writts sealed for the calling of a new Parl[iamen]t than the busy Fanatick had put forth in Print his Directory of what manner of men they ought to be who are sent forth on that great worke ... & these they disperse[d] abroad with the usuall industry of that tribe.'[94] Those pamphlets directing the electorate how to vote offer an

---

86 UCNW, Mostyn MS 9089, f. 155, newsletter, 8 July 1679. A poem written earlier by Andrew Marvell or by Henry Sidney, entitled *Advice to a Painter* was 'by the liberty of the press made publick' by early July (*Savile Corresp.*, p. 107. Hobbes's *Behemoth* (1679) was also in print by August (PRO, PC.2/68, f. 364, privy council minutes 5 September 1679).

87 *The Diary of John Evelyn*, ed. E.S. de Beer (Oxford 1955), iv. 172. cf. Wood, *Life and Times*, ii. 457.

88 Leeds AO, Mexborough mss, Reresby 14/63, E. Reresby to Sir John Reresby, 9 August 1679.

89 Longleat, Muddiman newsbook, 16 August 1679.

90 *HMC Verney*, p. 474; Bucks. RO, Verney mss M11/33, Cary Gardiner to Sir Ralph Verney, 15 September 1679.

91 *HMC Fitzherbert*, p. 21.

92 Ashcraft, *Revolutionary Politics*, p. 228; *HMC Ormonde*, iv. 536.

93 They are marked with an E in my bibliography. Twenty-three are listed in *A Compleat Catalogue of all the Stitch'd Books and Single Sheets* (1680), omitting *The Character of Popery and Arbitrary Government* (1679), *An Answer to a False and Scandalous Pamphlet, Entitled The Case of the Burrough of New Windsor* (1679), *The Nations Aggrievance* (1679) and *Tell Truth's Answer* (1679). Ogg, *Charles II*, p. 586, and *The Papers of William Penn*, ed. E.B. Bronner and D. Fraser (1986), v. 247, suggest that *England's Great Interest in the Choice of the New Parliament* (1679) was probably published for the first election of 1679, but the tract refers on its opening page to the King having restored the right of frequent Parliaments, a comment that would seem more applicable to the second election of 1679.

94 Longleat, Muddiman newsbook, 6 July 1679. cf. 'many papers have been lately published for the direction of the people in their next choice' (*The Domestick Intelligence*, no. 9, 5 August 1679).

insight into what issues were considered important by contemporaries, and can be used to test the claim that the opposition produced 'party' directives which the country was expected to follow.[95]

The content of the electoral propaganda suggests that the importance of the exclusion issue in elections has been exaggerated, though it would be foolish to deny that it had some bearing on voters. Two manuscript lists, written in the same hand, of opponents of the bill were drawn up apparently with the aim of advising the electorate, but they were not printed so far as we know and it is difficult to know how widely they circulated, if they were distributed at all.[96] Both *Sober and Seasonable Queries* and *A Seasonable Warning* also asked the electorate to consider whether they feared the papists murdering the King and bringing in a popish successor,[97] and *The Moderate Parliament* referred approvingly to Charles's offer of limitations.[98] Yet the bulk of the propaganda, both that designed for the specific market of freeholders and that for a more general market, did not focus on the succession issue, and analysis of the election literature suggests that it cannot be used as evidence of an organised exclusionist party. The dominant issue was not exclusion, but the undesirability of choosing Courtiers and 'pensioners' of the Court. The choice of rhetoric is important because it determines whether we see the division as being between Court and Country, or between Whig and Tory. *A List of One Unanimous Club of Voters* named MPs who had accepted pensions under Danby, and the attack on any candidate with Court ties was the keynote of many of the tracts. *England's Great Interest* and *The Character of Popery* warned against choosing pensioners or those who had

---

[95] Haley, *Shaftesbury*, p. 552, has argued that 'it is not misleading to describe these as party political literature'.

[96] One is calendared in *CSPD 1680-1*, pp. 675-8, without the names, and is dated there as relating to January 1681. However, the list of names attached is clearly of those who voted against the first exclusion bill, and is printed as such in Feiling, *Tory Party*, pp. 494-5. Internal evidence in the accompanying text suggests that it was written between the prorogation of 27 May and the dissolution of 12 July 1679, probably before the Scottish rebellion in June. A second version is at PRO, SP.29/444/51, endorsed 'animadvertissm[en]ts to freeholders'. There are discrepancies between the lists, though the names are arranged in a similar order. The second list is endorsed as having been 'fastened to Dugdale's letter of 9 August', presumably a reference to the letter (printed *CSPD 1679-80*, p. 214) which was sent in 1679 to the Green Ribbon Club member Hugh Speke. One tract published the following year (*The Power of Parliaments in Case of Succession* (1680), p. 7) did protest that after the exclusion bill had been published 'all that dissented to [it] were mark'd out and stigmatiz'd by the pamphleteers as the betrayers of their trust and deceivers of their country', but it is difficult to know whether or not this is a direct reference to the manuscript lists. It is interesting that Penn advised voters to review MPs' 'inclinations and votes as near as you can learn them' (*England's Great Interest in the Choice of the New Parliament* (1678), p. 3), though he offered no suggestion as to how they should go about doing this.

[97] *Sober and Seasonable Queries* (1679), pp. 1-2; *A Seasonable Warning to the Commons of England* (1679), p. 3.

[98] *The Moderate Parliament Considered* (1679), p. 4.

'any dependency on the Court';[99] *The Nation's Aggrievance* argued 'that all Court-officers, militia officers, Pensioners, and other Indigent officers, of what degree or Quality soever, are not in the apprehension of the Common People ... accounted competent in their judgement for your Majesties Great Counsel and Advisers'.[100] The author of *The Countries Vindication* drew a distinction between an honest, careful countryman and a Courtier, 'a pernicious piece of luxury, a Drone, a two faced Janus', whilst another pamphleteer claimed that the distinction among men was one between 'Country Man and Courtier.'[101] So virulent were the attacks that loyalist propagandists complained that the effect of the 'Country' slogan was that worthy candidates were put by,[102] and the worst principled men were chosen.[103] These pamphlets, therefore, illustrate how a Court–Country division existed in what is usually described as Whig and Tory literature.

The suggestion that an anti-Court sentiment still held sway over the succession issue should not be surprising if the election is placed in its political context. The 1679 session had tenaciously pursued an investigation into the numbers and names of Danby's Court pensioners,[104] but before this could be completed Parliament had been dissolved in July, despite the opposition of privy council.[105] A week after the dissolution had been announced the repeatedly postponed trial of Sir George Wakeman, the Queen's physician accused of attempting to poison the King, had finally been held. Charles, who not unreasonably saw Wakeman as a proxy for his wife, may have wept tears of joy at the outcome,[106] but the verdict of not guilty provoked accusations of a political fix from a press anxious to test its new freedom.[107] The acquittal stirred popular anti-catholic outrage nationwide,[108] and proved, as Ralph Montagu remarked, 'much better for us Mutineers' than for the Court.[109] Moreover, fears of popish influence raised by the trial went hand in hand with fears about encroaching arbitrary power. Charles was rumoured to be contemplating establishing a body of 200 officers, commonly believed to be

---

[99] *England's Great Interest in the Choice of the New Parliament* (1679), p. 3; *The Character of Popery and Arbitrary Government* [1679], p. 6.

[100] *The Nation's Aggrievance* (1679), p. 1.

[101] *Advice to the Nobility, Gentry, and Commonalty of this Nation* (1679), p. 1.

[102] Ibid., pp. 1–2.

[103] *The Moderate Parliament Considered* (1679), p. 2.

[104] Haley, *Shaftesbury*, p. 519; Jones, *First Whigs*, p. 73.

[105] HMC *Ormonde*, iv. 530–1; All Souls, MS 242, f. 504, newsletter, 11 July 1679.

[106] HMC *Ormonde*, v. 158.

[107] Kenyon, *Popish Plot*, p. 202; Crist, 'The press after the expiration of the Licensing Act', pp. 52–3. *The Domestick Intelligence*, no. 5, 22 July 1679, reported the case and printed the names of the jury who had brought in the verdict.

[108] 'The Country as well as the City do much resent the verdict' (Congress newsletter 6/249, 24 July 1679). Alderman Bathurst, one of the jury, 'was hissed off the Exchange' (Congress newsletter 6/250, 16 July 1679).

[109] *Diary of Henry Sidney*, i. 33–4, 37.

nothing 'but a foundation of a standing army',[110] and the King had ominously posted troops to several of the towns near London.[111] Some feared that Charles would attempt to rule without Parliament,[112] or that if Parliament did meet it would not be at the time proposed, and would not be for long.[113] Never did Country fears of the Court seem more justified.

The elections themselves reinforce the idea that the 'great antipathye ag[ains]t the Court party' was more important than an exclusionist/anti-exclusionist divide.[114] At Windsor, despite, or perhaps because of, the presence of the Court, the inhabitants shouted 'No Courtier, No Pensioner';[115] and at Lichfield Thomas Thynne had to promise the electors that his friend 'Mr Finch should not be a courtier.'[116] John Verney considered Sir Francis Clerke to be the wisest candidate standing at Rochester, but remarked that 'his fault as they call it is that he votes for the Court',[117] though even Sir Ralph Verney's friend, John Stewkeley, wished that 'the former pensioners may be so well knowne as not to be chosen'.[118] Samuel Jeake of Rye declared that he was 'for noe Courtiour nor pensioner but a Countrie Gent[leman]'.[119] There are, by contrast, very few documented instances where a candidate's position on exclusion was used against him. In June the news that Boroughbridge's two MPs had voted 'for the innocent Duke' (even though one had abstained on the division for the bill's second reading) had been 'received even w[i]th a hissing', and in Durham one of the candidates addressed the electorate before they polled about the jails, Inquisition, and French mercenaries that a catholic King would employ against protestants.[120] In Suffolk Sir Charles Gawdy was allegedly called a papist and voter for duke of York by Henry Edgar, one of the rival candidate's electoral agents, though Edgar

---

110 *Diary of Henry Sidney*, i. 35. One newswriter described the intended guard as 'a nursery of officers to head an Army, upon any occasion' (Bod., MS Don. C. 38, Fleming newsletters, 26 July 1679).

111 All Souls, MS 171, f. 48, newsletter, 26 July 1679.

112 PRO, 31/3/143, f. 42, Barrillon dispatch, 14/24 July 1679.

113 Chatsworth, Devonshire Collection, Group 1A, Roger Jackson to Devonshire, 12 July 1679; Bod., MS Carte 243, f. 392, Sir Nicholas Armorer to Arran, 6 September 1679.

114 Congress newsletter 6/262, 21 August 1679.

115 *English Intelligencer*, no. 7, 23 August 1679.

116 Bod., MS Carte 243, f. 383, Nicholas Armorer to Arran, 16 August 1679. Thynne wrote to Finch that 'the prejudices against courtiers are pretty strong' (*History of Parliament*, i. 385).

117 Bucks. RO, Verney mss, M11/33, John Verney to Sir Ralph Verney, 4 August 1679.

118 Bucks. RO, Verney mss, M11/33, Stewkeley to Verney, 28 July 1679.

119 *An Astrological Diary of the Seventeenth Century: Samuel Jeake of Rye 1652–99* ed. M. Hunter and A. Gregory (Oxford, 1988) p. 30.

120 Leeds AO, Mexborough mss, Reresby 14/75, E. Morris to Reresby, 8 June 1679; Guildhall Library, Durham County Poll 1679. The speaker at the latter was presumably either William Bowes or Thomas Fetherstonhalgh, the elected MPs.

vigorously denied speaking the words;[121] in Hertfordshire the exclusionist Sir Robert Peyton spread the rumour that Titus, his fellow exclusionist, and Sir Charles Caesar had voted against the bill,[122] though Peyton's puzzling tactics probably only strengthened Titus's resolve to stand elsewhere;[123] and in Somerset the bishop of Bath and Wells thought that if Sir Hugh Smyth lost the vote it would be 'because he was against the Bill concerning the D[uke] of Yorke', though in fact Smyth decided not to stand at all.[124] Elsewhere however (with the important exception of London and its environs, which will be discussed later), if exclusion was an issue, there is a dearth of evidence that people considered it as such in the localities.

Sir Hugh Smyth's reluctance to stand at the poll raises the possibility that exclusion was not talked about because opponents of the bill had been deterred from standing. The evidence suggests, however, that the controversy did not generally deter MPs from seeking re-election: of the 128 MPs who voted against the bill only thirty at most did not stand again,[125] and there were relatively few of them for whom the exclusion issue was the overriding factor in their decision. For example, Samuel Pepys and Sir Anthony Deane had wanted to stand again, but the attack on them over naval affairs made their candidature imprudent; Sir Thomas Littleton could not find a seat;[126] and Sir Robert Eden and John Tempest probably desisted in Durham because of the charges that they had used corruption to obtain their election earlier in the year.[127]

It might nevertheless be argued that, although exclusion was not publicly voiced as the central issue at stake, the candidates themselves recognised it to be so and aligned themselves on exclusionist lines. If so, this should be most clearly evident in contested elections, but exclusion seems to have played a minor role even in those. A mobilisation of 'Country', rather than 'Whig', forces seems to be the correct explanation of many of the results. This can be seen by examining contests that have been claimed as 'Whig' victories, such as

---

[121] P. Murrell 'Suffolk: The Political Behaviour of the County and its Parliamentary Borough from the Exclusion Crisis to the Accession of the House of Hanover' (Newcastle, Ph.D., 1982) p. 42; Essex RO, D/DBy/C22, f. 122, Edgar's testimony on oath, 30 April 1680.

[122] Grey, *Debates*, viii. 140. The county 'resolved against Titus … for his ill behaviour in the matter of the D[uke]' (*HMC Fitzherbert*, p. 20). Peyton was soon to attempt a reconciliation with the duke of York.

[123] *History of Parliament*, i. 269. As early as 12 July his partner, Sir Charles Caesar, believed Titus would be opposed if he stood in Hertfordshire.

[124] BL, Longleat mss, M/863, reel v, Coventry papers vol. vii, bishop of Bath and Wells to Secretary Coventry, 27 August 1679; *History of Parliament*, iii. 442.

[125] It is not known if three MPs (Sir Roger Norwich, Sir Henry Pickering and Sir John Clopton) sought re-election.

[126] *History of Parliament*, ii. 751.

[127] *History of Parliament*, i. 226.

the highly publicised struggle in Essex.[128] Sir Eliab Harvey and Colonel Mildmay, the country MPs in the first election of 1679, had both voted for the exclusion bill; but at the start of the campaign Harvey had been persuaded by the duke of Albemarle, the lord lieutenant, to stand with the more moderate Sir Thomas Middleton against Mildmay. The latter, after attempts at reconciliation with Harvey had failed,[129] found a radical partner, John Lamotte Honeywood, with whom he obtained a clear victory. The exclusionist Mildmay thus defeated the exclusionist Harvey. More important than the issue of the bill had been the challenge to Albemarle's local interest by the gentry headed by Lords Grey and Chandos. A Court–Country conflict is also a more accurate explanation of the heat aroused in the Buckinghamshire elections.[130] At the county election the most prominent issue of the election was the corruption of Courtiers. Although there was no contest at the polls, Sir Richard Temple, who had been one of Danby's pensioners, and his partner Lord Latimer, who was Danby's son, became the target of abuse, since they were standing in the Buckingham town election. The opposition to them raised election cries of 'No Traitor's Son! No Pensioner!', not 'No opponent of Exclusion!'[131]

A third, and most interesting, election case is that of the borough of Shaftesbury, not only because of the obvious association with the earl, but also because poll records survive for the first two elections of 1679.[132] These reveal that in the autumn election the combination of Thomas Bennett and Henry Whitaker, which had been successful in the earlier election, collapsed in a similar way to the pairing of Mildmay and Harvey in Essex. Both Bennett and Whitaker had voted for exclusion, and Bennett's importance in the Commons has already been noticed; but he was apparently prepared to drop an alliance of like minds for reasons of local electoral politics to side with Sir Matthew Andrews, a candidate of undistinguished personality and views, who was probably responsible for the doubling of the borough's electorate between the two 1679 elections.[133] Bennett gained 119 votes from the newly

---

128 Jones, *First Whigs*, pp. 97–8; *Essex's Excellency* (1679); *A Faithful and Impartial Account of the Behaviour of a Party of the Essex Freeholders* (1679); *History of Parliament*, i. 229.

129 All Souls, MS 171, f. 51, newsletter, 16 August 1679.

130 For accounts of the elections see *A True Account of what Past at the Election ... of Bucks* (1679), *The Answer of the Burgesses and Other Inhabitants of Buckingham* (1679), and *A Letter from a Freeholder of Buckinghamshire* (1679).

131 *History of Parliament*, i. 136. Temple was also accused of being a papist (Bucks. RO, Verney mss, M11/33, Sir Ralph Verney to John Verney, 25 September 1679), and was denounced as 'an Original Sinner in the Muster Roll of the Club of Unanimous Voices' (*A Mild but Searching Expostulatory*, p. 1), a reference to his inclusion in the *A List of One Unanimous Club of Voters*.

132 Wilts. RO, Bennett Papers 413/435.

133 *History of Parliament*, i. 220. Andrews was a Court Whig after the Revolution.

created electorate, 80 per cent of whom gave their second votes to Andrews, and eighteen of Bennett's earlier voters switched their votes away from Whitaker. Interest not exclusion was the issue, and can be shown in many other places besides Shaftesbury. At Westminster Sir William Pulteney broke his alliance with the exclusionist Sir William Waller;[134] at Abingdon the exclusionist Sir John Stonhouse was opposed by Major Dunch, the son-in-law of one of the leaders of the opposition peers, Lord Wharton;[135] at Stockbridge three MPs who had supported the bill contested the same seat;[136] and at Aldborough Sir Brian Stapylton, an opponent of exclusion, joined with an exclusionist, Sir Godfrey Copley, forcing the Courtier Sir John Reresby (who had himself tried to ally with Copley) to withdraw on the eve of the poll.[137]

But although expediency often prevailed over principle in the elections, they were not devoid of ideology because of the anti-Court, anti-corruption rhetoric and because the interest of the nonconformists often lay in supporting opposition candidates. Nonconformist support for some Country candidates had been apparent in the elections earlier in the year, but religious division became much more evident in the election propaganda printed in the autumn. One pamphlet, *An Impartial Survey*, drew categories of presbyterian, independent, anabaptist, papist, quaker, brownist, and fifth monarchist, and warned that such factions would 'turn all into confusion'.[138] The author of *The Moderate Parliament* also saw a conspiracy against episcopacy as well as against monarchy,[139] and *The Cloak in its Colours* advised against electing nonconformists in a vitriolic attack on presbyterianism, which suggested that the tenets of Calvinism were anti-monarchical.[140] In reply the 'Country' electioneering pamphleteers attacked the 'idle, covetous and sycophant men who cr[ied] up the Prince like an Angel, so long as he will be their Executioner, to whip, imprison, or hang all that are not of their flock'.[141] *The Freeholders Choice* similarly castigated the 'high flown Ritualists and Ceremony mongers of the clergy' who traduced all 'worthy men' as fanatics or favourers of them, and the author urged voters not to follow the recommendations of such men.[142] *England's Great Interest*, written by the quaker leader William Penn, not surprisingly pleaded 'that Protestant

---

[134] Ibid., i. 316. [135] Ibid., i. 129. [136] Ibid., i. 257.
[137] Ibid., i. 471–2; Leeds AO, Mexborough mss, Reresby 14/172e, Edward Morris to Reresby, 24 August 1679.
[138] *An Impartial Survey of ... Candidates* (1679), pp. 1–2.
[139] *The Moderate Parliament Considered* (1679), p. 2.
[140] *The Cloak in its Colours: or the Presbyterian Unmask'd* (1679), pp. 7, 12. It was a reply to *The Countries Vindication*.
[141] *The Character of Popery and Arbitrary Government* (1679), p. 4.
[142] *The Freeholders Choice* (1679), pp. 2–4.

Dissenters be eased',[143] and *London's Choice* remarked that for loyalists the dispute was 'no longer [between] Papist and Protestant, but Fanaticks and Church of England Men'.[144]

The religious conflict portrayed by the propagandists was reflected in the election campaigns themselves. Although the idea was eventually rejected, the clergy in Norfolk had contemplated imposing an oath on the supporters of Sir John Hobart and Sir Peter Gleane, 'that they should swear they had been at Church and received the sacrament according to the usage of the Church of England'.[145] The bishop of Chichester wanted to use the weapon of excommunication against the MP Colonel Braman,[146] and nonconformists' support for opposition candidates was frequently observed.[147] The extent of the religious polarisation must not, however, be exaggerated. Firstly, there is a danger in seeing a nonconformist interest as being too coherent and focused, or at least of being stronger than other ties of loyalties. At Colchester, local factors meant that two leaders of the dissenters polled on different sides, and Margaret Child found that in Durham there was little overall correlation between Whig voters and dissenters indicted for nonattendance.[148] Secondly, not all the clergy supported the 'Court' candidates. Over forty clerics from Kent supported the exclusionist Edward Dering,[149] and at Middlesex the Cavalier Sir Francis Gerard complained to Sancroft that not many of the clergy appeared for him, whilst one had even dared to oppose him.[150] At Gloucester a minister named Vernon was observed to be 'very busie running from house to house to make voices' against the candidate supported by the

---

143 *England's Great Interest in the Choice of the New Parliament* (1679), p. 1.
144 *London's Choice of Citizens* (1679), p. 3.
145 *Domestick Intelligence*, no. 19, 9 September 1679. Voters were turned away at Ludlow merely for being 'supposed Fanaticks and Nonconformists', (Staffs. RO, D/1788/18/1, 'The case for the election of Burgesses'). In 1681 Sir Francis Pemberton gave his legal opinion that the oaths should not be tendered with the purpose of preventing a man from voting (*CSPD 1680–1*, p. 118).
146 Bod., MS Tanner 149, f. 139, Bishop Carleton of Chichester to Sancroft, 20 July 1679; *HMC Verney*, p. 474. Excommunication was also considered as a way of preventing nonconformists from voting (All Souls, MS 171, f. 48, newsletter, 26 July 1679; Newdigate newsletter Lc.816, 28 July 1679). In Hertfordshire quakers were refused a vote because they could not swear they had 40 shillings a year (Newdigate newsletter Lc.830, 2 September 1679). *A Sober Discourse of the Honest Cavalier* (1680), p. 21, suggested that only Churchmen should vote.
147 Lacey, *Dissent and Parliamentary Politics*, pp. 112–20; *The Diary of Ralph Josselin*, p. 623; G.R. Cragg, *Puritanism in the Period of the Great Persecution* (Cambridge 1957), p. 24.
148 T. Glines, 'Politics and Government in the Borough of Colchester, 1660–1693' (Wisconsin Ph.D., 1974), p. 174; Child, 'Prelude to Revolution', p. 327. Child speculates that nonconformist congregations increasingly drew support from the lower orders and that consequently many dissenters may not have been qualified to vote. It would be helpful to have more studies of polls in terms of religious allegiance in order to analyse the coherence and strength of the 'dissenting interest' for the pre-Revolution period.
149 *Domestick Intelligence*, no. 23, 23 September 1679.
150 Bod., MS Tanner 38, f. 80, Gerard to Sancroft, 9 September 1679.

Court, and at Chichester Colonel Braman, a veteran 'agitator' of the Putney debates, was even supported by Dr Thomas Briggs, chancellor of Chichester diocese, who took advantage of the situation to pursue his running battle with the bishop.[151] Nor did opposition candidates rely solely on dissenting votes. Although in London Sir Thomas Player attracted the support of nonconformists, he had enough anglican voices to carry his election even if those of dissenters were discounted, and two 'eminent' anglican divines were said to have supported him.[152] Similarly in Warwickshire Sir Richard Newdigate bet £1,000 that he could outvote his loyalist competitors on anglican votes alone.[153]

The second general election of 1679 had gone 'generally against the humor [of the Court], and itt seemes to me', wrote one gloomy observer at the beginning of September, 'that the spiritts of the people rise higher and higher so that if itt should come to an other election the country must be driven out of the field by force and if the people should be oposed the nation might goe together by the Eares'.[154] The campaign had been marked by a swelling, if not yet ripe, division between anglicans and nonconformists, with local interest outweighing the national issue of exclusion and a consequent haziness of party organisation and discipline. Above all, it demonstrated a Court–Country divide, where 'not only inclination, but even moderation towards the Court seem[ed] to be grown matter of accusation'.[155] The bill can only be seen as *the* issue of the campaign, if it is assumed that the Court–Country conflict hid an exclusionist–anti-exclusionist divide which people knew to be more important, but which they preferred to approach indirectly. This assumption is generally unsubstantiated. Whilst there was evidently a correlation between support for the bill and success at the polls, it does not follow that just under half of those who opposed the bill were rejected *because* of their vote on this single issue. For that to have been the case the whole electorate would have had to have known how candidates had voted on the bill, or if they had not previously sat, how they would vote on it; and only one issue would have had to have been at stake. The available evidence, however, suggests otherwise.[156] MPs and candidates were rated on a broader list of attitudes towards popery and arbitrary government, and hostility to the

[151] BL, Longleat mss, M/863, reel iv, Coventry papers vol. vi, f. 189, mayor and corporation of Gloucester to Secretary Coventry, 15 December 1679; Bod., MS Tanner 149, f. 139, to Sancroft, 20 July 1679.
[152] *HMC Lindsey*, p. 33; *London's Choice of Citizens* (1679), p. 3.
[153] *CSPD 1679–80*, p. 395.
[154] BL, Longleat mss, M/863, reel iv, Coventry papers vol. vi, ff. 127–8, 'W.F' to Secretary Coventry, 5 September 1679.
[155] *HMC Ormonde*, iv. 535.
[156] Fifty-five per cent of those who voted against the bill were returned at the election for the same constituency (Browning and Milne, 'Exclusion bill', p. 207).

Court was based primarily on the lack of independence exhibited by its supporters, who allegedly sold their own honesty, religion and integrity, as well as the liberties of the nation. Nor does it follow that because many MPs who were returned at the elections allowed the bill to pass the House in 1680 (and in the absence of a later division we do not know how precisely many actually supported it then), they must have stood on an exclusionist ticket at the polls. This would be to analyse 1679 anachronistically in terms of what happened later.

Moreover, although I have argued that a Court–Country conflict was seen by contemporaries as the most important line of division, the Court cannot simply be identified with an anti-exclusionist position because of a number of factors that were working to blur even this distinction. Shaftesbury remained lord president of the council throughout the election period, and thus still held office even though he did not go near the Court.[157] Although his followers were not singled out for criticism by Country pamphleteers, no attempt was made to exempt them from the castigation doled out to courtiers in general, and this ambivalence precluded any clear-cut party divisions during the elections.[158] Similarly, Charles's retention of Shaftesbury's services until after the polls had closed compromised the clarity of the Court's stance, a source of confusion deepened by the King's own attitude.

Finally, there were certain ambiguities within the Country message that makes it difficult to define as either exclusionist or anti-exclusionist. Prominent opposition candidates did not always live up to the ideal of free elections depicted by the Country pamphleteers, who attacked the large sums of money lavished on voters and urged the emulation of places where the candidates had been put to no charge.[159] The exclusionist George Treby was assured that the support of the 'meaner sort of the electors' at Plympton Erle would be secured 'by some expenditure in good ale';[160] at Dover the exclusionist Papillon's supporters organised a rival and better feast for the electors than that which had been laid on by the Governor;[161] and Algernon Sidney was accused of bribery when he left £10 with one of the overseers of the Amer-

---

[157] *HMC R.R. Hastings*, ii. 388. Shaftesbury left London in mid August (*Domestick Intelligence*, no. 14, 22 August 1679).
[158] Southwell, however, believed Shaftesbury laboured 'openly in the new elections to have them men of his own mind' (*HMC Ormonde*, iv. 535).
[159] *The Character of Popery and Arbitrary Government* (1679), p. 6; *England's Great Interest in the Choice of the New Parliament* (1678), p. 3; *Essex's Excellency*, p. 8; *Domestick Intelligence* no. 16, 29 August 1679; *Plain Dealing* (1681), verso. See also George, 'Elections and Electioneering 1679–81', [*EHR*, xlv (1930)], p. 571.
[160] *History of Parliament*, i. 206.
[161] *Domestick Intelligence*, no. 30, 17 October 1679.

sham election,[162] an election at which one contemporary swore 'hee never saw, soe many men, soe very Drunke, in his Life'.[163] Neither did following 'Country' advice always secure the return of opposition MPs. For example at Ludgershall a group of electors engaged themselves to oppose all who tried to win election by entertainments, bribery or excessive drinking, but returned two loyalist MPs, prompting the remark that the electors had made 'a worse choice sober than perhaps they had ever done, stark mad'.[164] Thus although it has been claimed that the attack on electoral spending was directed primarily against Tory aristocrats,[165] concern at the excessive cost of, and abuses during, elections cut across 'party' lines. Courtiers, as well as their opponents, showed an awareness of the need to limit opportunities for spending. The lord chancellor wrote to the loyalist earl of Yarmouth complaining that, by delaying sending the writ to the sheriff, Yarmouth would cause 'very great charges' to candidates;[166] and lord chief justice North praised the Wiltshire Grand Jury when it complained that there had been 'much debauchery, Drunkenness and Excess in electing members'.[167] Similarly, there were those both amongst the loyalists and their opponents who thought electoral entertainments were inevitable, and therefore tried to raise subscriptions to cover expenses.[168]

The second election of 1679 was thus considerably more complex than some have thought. The prominence given to exclusion as the single issue over which lines were drawn is an oversimplification of attitudes and concerns.

---

[162] *History of Parliament*, i. 137–8. For Sidney's tactics at the election at Bramber in 1679 see *Diary of Henry Sidney*, i. 115–16.

[163] Bucks. RO, Verney mss, M11/33 Sir Ralph Verney to John Verney, 7 August 1679, quoting the observation of Harry King.

[164] *History of Parliament*, i. 451. *The Domestick Intelligence* no. 11, 12 August 1679 claimed that there had been great excess of drinking there.

[165] Ashcraft, *Revolutionary Politics*, p. 235.

[166] BL, Add. 27,447, f. 421, Finch to Yarmouth, 14 August 1679.

[167] *Domestick Intelligence*, no. 11, 12 August 1679; UCNW, Mostyn MS 9089, f. 166, newsletter, 12 August 1679.

[168] Lords Windsor and Coventry raised £500–800 for the loyalist candidate contesting the Worcestershire county election (*Smith's Protestant Intelligence*, no. 9, 19 February 1681; *History of Parliament*, i. 462). Lord Cholmondeley hoped the gentry would confederate together on their charges to counterbalance his rival Booth's election expenses (*History of Parliament*, i. 151). It was thought that the Court bore the election costs of courtiers who stood in the second election of 1679 (Bucks. RO, Verney mss, M11/33, John Stewkeley to Sir Ralph Verney, 4 August 1679). On the opposition side it was rumoured that Blount's election expenses at Buckingham were 'defrayed by a Clubb of their party', presumably the Green Ribbon Club of which Blount was a member, though Verney was sceptical about the validity of the report (Bucks. RO, M11/35, Edmund Verney to Sir Ralph Verney, 21 April 1681). A subscription was raised in Norfolk to which Sir John Holland pledged £20 (J.M. Rosenheim, 'Party Organisation at the Local Level: the Norfolk Sheriff Subscriptions of 1676', *HJ*, xxix [1986], p. 722). Sir William Hickman believed the opposition in Nottinghamshire had 'the greatest part of the expenses … born for them' (BL, Althorp MS C2, Hickman to Halifax, 13 September 1679). One loyalist pamphlet, *England Bought and Sold* (1681), p. 9, did justify election expenses, but only because the author, John Nalson, insinuated that the opposition's election expenses were paid underhand.

Voters took account of a candidate's whole stance towards the Court, and were particularly agitated about Members who had been pensioners, corrupt in their relationship with government and the electorate, or who were thought not to be capable of independent action to safeguard religion and liberty; and complicating the picture further were a host of local and personal factors which could cut across expected behaviour. In general, however, a candidate's general attitude towards popery and arbitrary government was more important than his record on the specific issue of the succession.

THE RADICALISATION OF LONDONERS

Although I have stressed that exclusion was not *the* issue in most of the elections, there was, by late September, a propaganda war over the succession.[169] This printed controversy took place after the close of the vast majority, but not all, of the polls.[170] Most importantly, London and Southwark, did not elect their Members until early October, and one tract, apparently designed for the London electorate, did urge the election of men of tested principles in relation to a popish successor, and arbitrary government.[171] Inhabitants of the capital were therefore likely to have been influenced by the debate, though its impact was far more subtly intertwined with other issues than appears at first sight.

The origins of the controversy lay in Charles's illness in late August. It is possible that the King, whose powers of dissimulation were amongst his most developed talents, deliberately played up his sickness in order to secure the return of his brother and an agreement with the French. Negotiations with France had reached a state of near completion, and only a few days after Barrillon had been told that James's return would secure the deal, Charles conveniently took to his bed and Sunderland, who had been dealing with the ambassador, sent a messenger to fetch the duke.[172] Observers of the Court made remarks suggesting that at the least the severity of the illness had been exaggerated, though how near the King came to dying will probably never be known.[173] What is clear is that the incident raised the stakes by making a

---

169 BL, Add. 29,557, f. 260, Henry Fanshawe to Lord Hatton, 30 September 1679. *A Letter on the Subject of the Succession* (1679), which attacked exclusion, has a printed date of 18 September.

170 Elections had generally taken place in August, but forty-two out of the 267 constituencies held them on or after 15 September 1679. Many of these were in far-flung areas of the country such as Cornwall, Devon and Wales.

171 *A Most Serious Expostulation* (endorsed 'October 1679' on Cambridge Univ. Lib. Sel. 2. 116. 11). Three other Surrey constituencies and seven of the Cinque Ports voted in October.

172 PRO, 31/3/143, ff. 50–7, Barrillon dispatch, 21/31 August 1679; Clarke, *James II*, i. 564–5. The talks had taken place in the apartment of the duchess of Portsmouth, Sunderland's ally at Court, and she restricted access to the King during his 'illness' (Bod., MS Carte 72, f. 520, articles of impeachment against her).

173 Reresby, *Memoirs*, p. 187; Temple, *Memoirs*, p. 342; *The Impostor Expos'd* (1681), p. 143.

succession crisis appear more imminent. 'There is no extremity of disorder to be imagined that we might not have fallen into if the King had died', wrote Algernon Sidney.[174]

Yet at first, James's return was met in London with calmness and even some signs of support, rather than unrest.[175] James was 'offer'd so many bended knees that it's beleeved for three days past [there] has bin more kneeling ... than in four months before'. The duke himself informed William of his joy 'to find I have so many friends left' and that the City was quiet, with 'most of the rich men' pleased with the turn of events.[176] Enthusiasm for York's return was not shared by all – a bonfire celebrating it in the Strand was kicked out by some 'yong men'[177] – but the muted reaction confirms the invalidity of raising exclusion to an all-important level at this stage. It was York's subsequent struggle to have Monmouth, the 'Protestant duke', sent into exile that intensified what at this time should be termed a London-orientated succession crisis. Monmouth's popularity was at its zenith. Ralph Montagu 'and all the Presbyterians and dissenting people' tried to persuade Monmouth to disobey his father and stay;[178] but 'besides the young hot-headed fellows and all the Presbyterians, there were [also] many of the serious and moderate men for him', and, after the news that he was to be sent abroad had spread through the City 'like gunpowder set on fire', Londoners were dismayed at the prospect of his departure.[179] The 'rancour and partiality' that was observed in London was thus due to popular agitation about whether or not both the protestant Monmouth and catholic James should leave the country.[180] The decision to exile Monmouth created a fear that popery was prevailing at Court, and, whilst there undoubtedly was an element of exclusionist sentiment in the unrest,[181] it is important not to see all anti-popery as being simply translatable into support for the bill. Despite growing links with City radicals, Monmouth was not yet seen as a factious figure, partly because Charles was, publicly at least, still on good terms with him. The moderate Sir Ralph Verney was amazed at the decision to banish Monmouth, took no exception to the popular demonstrations in favour of him (even though his son was stopped by one crowd which demanded money) and disliked the increase in York's power; but there is no evidence allowing us to describe him as an exclusionist

[174] *Sidney Letters*, p. 97.
[175] Longleat, Muddiman newsbook, 2 September 1679; UCNW, Mostyn MS 9067, f. 55, J. Lloyd to Thomas Mostyn, 2 September 1679.
[176] BL, Add. 32,680, f. 119, Mountstevens to Sidney, 6 September 1679; Dalrymple, *Memoirs*, ii. 247.
[177] Newdigate newsletter, Lc. 831, 4 September 1679.
[178] Dalrymple, *Memoirs*, ii. 248–9.
[179] *HMC Lindsey*, p. 64; *Hatton Corresp.* i. 194.
[180] *HMC Ormonde*, v. 204.
[181] Longleat, Thynne mss, vol. 41, f. 177, newsletter, 9 September 1679.

and some to suggest that he opposed the bill.[182] Moreover, if exclusion had been the main issue at this stage, and Shaftesbury the exclusionists' leader, it is hard to explain why the earl did not hurry up to London, but instead remained on his estates at a discreet distance from the events in London.[183]

Indeed, it was the duke of Buckingham who played the more important role at this time, as he sought to exploit the unrest for his own purposes. Buckingham was a 'flashy and vain' character who loved to cut a figure at the elections in London, and Middlesex, and courted popularity; but he may also have been seeking revenge for a snub offered to him by the Court. He had gone to Windsor in the first week of September and been refused access to Charles because the King said he would speak to no one who electioneered so vigorously against him, with the result that Buckingham was described as being 'like a woeman that railes upon her lovers for no other reason but because the[y] discontinue their visitts'.[184] Buckingham opposed Shaftesbury because he was a rival for power, and he did not favour Monmouth's pretensions to the throne, possibly because he bizarrely believed himself to have an equally valid claim to the Crown through his mother's line;[185] yet, together with Francis Jenkes, Sir Thomas Player 'and the rest of that gang in the city', Buckingham met with Monmouth's right-hand man, Sir Thomas Armstrong to discuss, it was said, a plan to create a common council of men who had not taken the corporation oaths, thereby ensuring that the City was in 'a good posture'.[186]

The rumour is significant because it shows how national politics were interacting with City politics, religious disputes, and Buckingham's eccentric personal motives. Buckingham had been boasting about his power over London to Barrillon since the summer, and now saw a chance to place himself at the head of the City radicals by backing the candidature of his friend Jenkes in the London shrieval election.[187] Sir Thomas Player also seems to have tried to promote Jenkes's chances by making a speech on 13 September, just before the poll, in which he asserted that James's religion had encouraged the Popish Plot.[188] Player's comments were 'very ill lookt upon' by moderates – Lady

---

182 Bucks. RO, Verney mss, M11/33, Sir Ralph Verney to John Verney, 18 September, 22 September 1679; *HMC Verney*, p. 475; *History of Parliament*, iii. 635.

183 Haley, *Shaftesbury*, p. 547.

184 *Ailesbury Memoirs*, i. 13; UCNW, Mostyn MS 9089, f. 172, newsletter, 9 September 1679; Longleat, Thynne mss, vol. 41, f. 177, newsletter, 9 September 1679.

185 PRO, 31/3/143, f. 38, Barrillon dispatch, 3/13 July 1679; Dalrymple, *Memoirs*, ii. 288.

186 Longleat, Thynne mss, vol. 41, f. 177, newsletter, 9 September 1679; *CSPD 1679–80*, p. 240; Bod., MS Carte 232, f. 55, Longford to Arran, 16 September 1679; Bod., MS Don. C38, Fleming newsletter, 16 September 1679.

187 PRO, 31/3/143, f. 61, Barrillon dispatch, 4/14 September; ff. 75–6, Barrillon dispatch, 22 September/2 October 1679. Barrillon described Jenkes as a fanatic.

188 *An Account of the Proceedings at the Guildhall* (1679); *The Vindicator Vindicated* (1679), p. 2. Player, who was accompanied by 'an hundred persons at his heels', had moved for the exclusion bill in the last session (*An Answer to the Excellent and Elegant Speech made by Sir Thomas Player* (1679), p. 1; *History of Parliament*, iii. 251).

Gardiner, for example, thought that only a miracle could now prevent a civil war between the loyalists, on the one hand, and the papists and republicans on the other – but his speech was 'not commended' even 'by his own party', who thought it 'done only to get fame amongst the people' to support his own election to Parliament.[189] The succession was thus being used in local factional disputes just as much as at a national level. Moreover, Player's demand that the City guard be doubled was rejected by the court of aldermen, which instead went to Windsor to congratulate the King on his recovery; and as a further indication that London was not yet an opposition stronghold, Jenkes failed to secure election as sheriff. Buckingham, under threat of prosecution for having accused lord chief justice Scroggs of having secret orders to favour papists, found it prudent to abscond abroad.[190] Bonfires and bell-ringing greeted the King's return to Whitehall, and it was remarked that London thereafter seemed 'more calm and undisturbed than any place else' as 'the temper of the people began to coole'.[191] The only consolation for the radicals was the election as lord mayor of Sir Robert Clayton, a cautious politician who nevertheless made a speech on 29 September in favour of the unity of protestants.[192]

The dispute over London politics, and Monmouth's fate, had helped polarise opinion in the City between the 'mobile', or mob as it was soon called, who were observed to have 'noe great affection' for James, and the 'nobility and gentry' who 'highly caressed' the duke.[193] The lord mayor had voiced his disapproval of the crowd which had followed Player, requesting that 'they would not be so numerous in their address, since they might as well make known their minds by a few as by many'.[194] Increasingly, the dispute in London was becoming one fomented by a faction, led by Player and others, that appealed to popular support, and especially to dissenters. John Verney thus observed that the City was 'strangely divided between the mad

---

[189] Bucks. RO, Verney mss, M11/33, Gardiner to Sir Ralph Verney, 15 September 1679; *HMC Verney*, p. 475; Congress newsletter 6/271, 6/273, 16, 20, September 1679; *CSPD 1679–80*, p. 244. Jenkes was also said to have ambitions for a seat in Parliament.

[190] BL, Add. 62,585, f. 96, Bulstrode memoirs; Bucks. RO, Verney mss, M11/33, Lady Gardiner to Sir Ralph Verney, 22 September 1679. At the beginning of October Buckingham was thought to have had a private conference with Jenkes (Newdigate newsletter Lc.844, 2 October 1679), and re-appeared in early November, suspected of having been dealing with Louis XIV 'in behalf of the people in England' (*HMC Ormonde*, v. 242). *The Second Part of the Growth of Popery* (1682), p. 266, claimed that Buckingham had 'worked himself so far into the secrets of the French King' that 'the money aimed at to be paid us from France came to nothing'.

[191] Chatsworth, Devonshire Collection, Group 1B, newsletter 20 September 1679; *HMC Ormonde*, iv. 536; BL, Add. 29,557, f. 260, Fanshawe to Hatton, 30 September 1679.

[192] *The Speech of Sir Robert Clayton* (1679), p. 3. Clayton 'valued himself very much on his being of no faction and never to have been in a conventicle' (*CSPD 1680–1*, p. 491).

[193] UCNW, Mostyn MS 9089, f. 174, newsletter 20 September 1679.

[194] *An Account of the Proceedings at the Guildhall* (1679), p. 3.

separatists and the Church of England men', and Secretary Jenkins referred to the contest as being one between the 'conformists or nonconformists'.[195] Dissenters may have been attracted in part by the vehemence of the City faction's passionate belief in the catholic plot at a time when some were questioning its veracity and continuing relevance.[196] A significant part of Player's speech on the 13 September had been devoted to highlighting how some people tried to 'lessen the Plot, and some would make it no Plot at all; others say that it was a Plot made by the Protestants, and then cast upon the Papists; others would have it to be altogether a Protestant Plot'; those in the last category 'were the most dangerous, and had been deservedly styled Protestants in Masquerade'.[197] Credulity in the plot, or in its continuing threat, was evidently waning, to the consternation of zealous protestants, who saw a division between themselves and less vigilant protestants or crypto-catholics.

Contemporaries discerned the legacy of the 1640s in the resurgence of crowd politics and the activity of the dissenters, and the rancour of the press seemed to confirm the parallels. One writer, who opposed Jenkes's candidature as sheriff, asked readers to 'consider the danger and inconvenience that ariseth from the multitude of pamphlets that are published every day, filled with lies and falsehood', and urged citizens to slight them 'instead of reading them with delight and complacency'.[198] The author of *The Present Great Interest* also regretted that the Green Ribbon Club let 'fall doubtful Intelligence at each coffee house' and that so many should 'Libel and Lampoon' the duke of York. He suggested that if the penal laws against catholics and sectaries had been strongly enforced there would be no crisis, and thought it was 'time for some of the most prudent among the nobility and gentry, to arise on behalf of God, religion and the laws, that our King and we perish not together'. He proposed an eight-point course of action, consisting of a purge of Courtiers 'to reform the swearer, the blasphemer, the flatterer, and the Lyer'; the appointment of JPs only 'of very unquestionable loyalty, and firm to the Church of England'; closer supervision of conventicles; the suppression of those 'nurseries of sedition and rebellion' the coffee houses; a register of popish families; strict visitations of the dioceses; and the presentation of an address from 'the most noble personages of the kingdom' to inform James of the fears aroused by his popery. The tract ended with an exhortation 'that all honest and loyal hearts would joyn unanimously together to support the

---

195 *HMC Verney*, p. 475; *CSPD 1679–80*, p. 565.
196 A catholic tract published in late September ridiculed the idea of the plot (Luttrell, *Brief Relation*, i. 21–2). Some of the clergy apparently gave credence to the idea of a protestant plot [*A Letter from a Gentleman of the Isle of Ely* (1679), pp. 2–3].
197 *An Account of the Proceedings at the Guildhall* (1679), p. 3.
198 *Venn and his Myrmidons* (1679), pp. 2, 5.

interest of the king and the Church'.[199] This manifesto of loyalism, with its emphasis on strict anglicanism pursuing the middle way between popery and dissent, contains many of the ingredients conspicuously followed by the government in 1681, even though it was tinged with a pious critique of Court morality that Charles would always ignore. With a consensus even in London amongst all but the most radical about the need for moderation, the ingredients for a loyalist reaction appeared to be present.

There were even signs that such a sea-change in the political climate might occur. The government tried to restrain the press as part of an attempt to deprive 'seditious' opinion of publicity. On 24 September L'Estrange was finally empowered to seize seditious books, and in mid October a number of distributors of tracts offensive to the government were arrested.[200] On 31 October the King issued a proclamation, offering a £40 reward for the discovery of the author or printer of any seditious tract, and lord chief justice Scroggs waged a personal crusade against anyone who criticised him in print.[201] The King, as we saw earlier, simultaneously began to form a resolute Court, and urged the London City authorities to 'have a care of those that are enemies to the Church of England, which gracious expression ... extreamly delighted all the hearers'.[202] This effectively silenced rumours that he had been intending 'to grant an indulgence from the Church of England'.[203]

Yet the hoped-for loyalist reaction did not materialise. In part, this was due to continued suspicions about James. On 21 October he assured a thin representation of the Artillery Company that he would maintain the protestant religion and property if he became King, and would defend the City and the nation; but the event was perceived as a mere propaganda exercise 'to retrieve a little in the eye of the nation, that reputation of the York-interest lost in the late choice of Parliament men', and a crowd, incited by Oates and Bedloe from a balcony owned by the 'blink-eyed bookseller' Thomas Cockerill, gave the duke a fairly hostile reaction as he returned from the feast.[204] However, more was at stake than the succession. York's attempts to

---

[199] *The Present Great Interest Both of King and People* (1679), printed date of 16 September 1679.

[200] PRO, PC.2/68, ff. 371, 390, privy council minutes.

[201] PRO, PC.2/68, ff. 390, 399, 424, privy council minutes; A.F. Havighurst, 'The Judiciary and Politics in the Reign of Charles II', *Law Quarterly Review*, lxvi (1950), 236; Crist, 'Government Control of the Press', pp. 55–60.

[202] Congress newsletter 6/286, 21 October 1679.

[203] Newdigate newsletter, Lc.850, 16 October 1679; All Souls, MS 171, f. 74, newsletter, 17 October 1679.

[204] Newdigate newsletter, Lc.853, 23 October 1679; All Souls, MS 171, f. 77, newsletter, 22 October 1679; *A True Account of the Invitation and Entertainment of the Duke of York* (1679), p. 2; Wood, *Life and Times*, ii. 467 n. 1. A paper pinned over the door of the hall where the feast was held threatened to make a list of all who dined there 'under the abominable name of Yorkists' (Bod., MS Don. B.8, f. 597, newsletter, 21 October 1679).

have Parliament's meeting postponed, culminating in the decision to prorogue on 17 October, dashed hopes of security for religion, and increased
suspicions of French influence at Whitehall. Contemporaries were aware that
they were also witnessing a crisis of Parliaments. 'I doe realy think this will be
eyther a happy meeting, or else the last Parliment that I shall live to see', wrote
one prospective MP,[205] and it was said at the end of October that 'the people
talke very loude of these often putting off of Parliam[en]ts & seeme to be
much discontented'.[206] A document probably drawn up at about this time
outlined how MPs might act in a new session, and directed that an address be
made to the King 'that the Parliam[en]t may sitt some competent time to
dispatch the weighty affaires of the kingdome', presumably as part of an
attempt to forestall the King's tactic of dismissing MPs whenever they became
inconvenient.[207] Once more concerns about the survival of Parliaments
became the most important issue.

The pressure for MPs to sit was heightened by the discovery at the end of
October of the Meal Tub Plot, the attempt by the catholic Mrs Cellier to
fabricate a protestant plot, based on information that her agent Thomas
Dangerfield had gleaned from the coffee houses. Dangerfield may have invented less than it appeared at the time, for the lists he compiled of City
radicals correspond fairly accurately with the known membership of the
Green Ribbon and other clubs in London, and he gave the government
information about their activities that can be corroborated or which seems
too detailed to have been wholly fabricated, though he evidently built on fact
to give credence for his unsubstantiated claim that the meetings discussed
rebellion.[208] The effects of the Meal Tub Plot on public opinion were dramatic. Just at the time when belief in the threat from plotting papists appeared
to be diminishing, the new evidence of catholic treachery once more revived
the anti-popish hysteria which Oates's revelations had aroused in 1678.
Consequently, huge crowds attended the London pope-burning processions
on 5 and 17 November. Moreover, the exposure of the catholics' activity
seemed to confirm Player's claim that there was a deliberate attempt to cast a
plot upon protestants. The Meal Tub Plot therefore destroyed any widespread reaction in favour of the Court by projecting its critics as the innocent
victims of popish machinations. This anti-popery was not simply exclusionist
in nature. At the pope-burning processions in November, the displays focused

---

[205] NLS, MS 7008, f. 219, Sir James Hayes to earl of Tweeddale, 11 September 1679.
[206] *The Pythouse Papers*, ed. W.A. Day (1879), p. 74.
[207] Longleat, Coventry mss, vol. vi, ff. 248–51, 'Severall Usefull and Indispensibly necessary
Cautions and Instructions'.
[208] See chapter 6. For Dangerfield's information to the government about the activities of Player,
Jenkes, Col. Blood, Sir William Waller, Disney and Mason see Col. Mansell's *An Exact and
True Narrative of the Late Popish Intrigue* (1680), pp. 18–27. Mansell, p. 7, claimed he
could not 'pick out half a dozen presbyterians' from the names listed by Dangerfield.

on the events surrounding the murder of Sir Edmund Berry Godfrey and on the Pope and his minions, with no reference being made to James. But fear of catholic plotting sharpened an already present desire to see MPs assemble to discuss the dangers which the nation faced. As Sir Robert Howard remarked, the Meal Tub Plot made 'most men of the modestest principles eager for a Parliament ... the City is with those that think it necessary for a Parliament to sit in January, and I believe this opinion is so universal that it will come with more weight to the King than can be conveniently resisted'.[209] It was this sentiment that created the conditions necessary for the launch of mass petitions calling for Parliament to sit.

CONCLUSION

The year 1679 was dominated by Charles II's use of his prerogative powers to prorogue, dissolve and summon Parliament, and each dismissal of MPs provoked anger, especially in London, to the extent that some feared riot or rebellion. Parliament's sitting was thus an issue which agitated nearly every sector of society and focused fears about the intended introduction of arbitrary power. One expression of the frustration with the King's policy of avoiding Parliament's advice was the repeated attempt to petition for the assembly of MPs; another was the rejection at the polls of any candidate connected with the Court. The general elections of 1679 were, despite claims that the autumn polls were fought over the national issue of exclusion, characterised by antipathy to the Court, popery and arbitrary government, though increasingly attitudes towards dissent and the actions of the nonconformists helped shape the contests. Strong calls had been made for the greater unity of protestants, but these demands led to a division between those who were prepared to relax insistence on dogma in order to broaden the church, and those who saw any concession as the prelude to the church's destruction. The rebellion by the Scottish covenanters in June 1679 helped make this division clearer, and although religious polarities were still to a large extent hidden by a shared anti-popery, the perceived waning of the catholic threat began stirring loyalist reactions against dissent. This movement of opinion was most apparent in London, where disputes were fomented by the duke of Buckingham's interventions in City politics, and where some form of resurgent loyalism seemed about to emerge. That reaction nevertheless failed to materialise, largely because the discovery of the Meal Tub Plot reinvigorated anti-popery and fuelled demands for Parliament to sit. Thus in 1679 the country was still not divided along exclusionist, or Whig and Tory lines, and, before we can talk in terms of party politics, required a catalyst both in the process of accelerating polarisation and exposing it.

[209] *HMC Ormonde*, v. 238.

8

'The popular humour of petitioning'[1]: public opinion, 1679–80

The winter of 1679–80 was to prove an important turning point in the political crisis. It witnessed a deliberate attempt to use the weight of popular opinion to influence national politics, a tactic that altered the character of the conflict by mobilising extra-parliamentary dissatisfaction and escalating a propaganda war. Significantly, the issue at stake was not the narrow one of the exclusion bill *per se*, but the wider concern, which had been obvious throughout 1679, that Parliament should be allowed to sit in order to discuss the nation's grievances and to settle its fears. The urgency of those needs deepened the matter into a constitutional struggle over the King's prerogative powers, and raised fundamental questions about the nature of government and obedience. Moreover, it focused controversies about the origins of royal authority, the role of Parliament and the rights of the people into a single demand which represented the crux of fears about popery and arbitrary government and which had repeated political relevance because Charles relied on his powers to summon and dismiss MPs as the principal means to cut the ground from under the feet of his critics.

The effect of the Meal Tub Plot in re-animating anti-catholic feeling and fuelling demands for Parliament to sit, convinced Shaftesbury that popular pressure could be harnessed to force Charles to concede to all his demands.[2] Rather than return to office, as he had done fruitlessly in April 1679, the earl deliberately placed himself at the head of the unrest and embraced an alliance with the people, hoping to frighten the King into submission.[3] Moreover, reports in newsletters which claimed that Charles had made an agreement with France for three years may have strengthened Shaftesbury's new belief

---

[1] Bod., MS Tanner 129, f. 52, Samuel Crossman to Sancroft, 21 January 1680.
[2] The following paragraphs are a summary of Knights, 'London's "Monster" Petition of 1680', *HJ*, xxxvi (1993), 39–67.
[3] Barrillon recognised Shaftesbury's policy as new (PRO, 31/3/143, f. 111, Barrillon dispatch, 1/11 December 1679). Shaftesbury told Charles that if he was not believed or trusted there would no longer be peace in England (L. Von Ranke, *History of England* [1875], iv. 95, quoting the Venetian Ambassador's report of 1 December 1679).

that only popular pressure could force the King's hand.[4] Such pressure was to take the form of petitions calling for Parliament's sitting.[5] On 11 November, two days after Charles's refusal at a privy council meeting to discuss Parliament's assembly, Sir Robert Southwell warned Ormonde about an imminent petitioning campaign.[6] A fortnight later he reported that the Court's critics planned to send some of the nobility to wait on the King to press for a Parliament, and, if that failed, to offer a petition 'by which precedent many others are like to be made from different parts of the Kingdom, which is thought a method irresistible'.[7] Charles's proclamation on 11 December further proroguing Parliament only seemed to make such action all the more necessary.

The request for Parliament to sit on 26 January 1680, the earliest date conceived by the King, became the 'chief discourse' of contemporaries,[8] and could have been expected to unite all groups, since a meeting would offer radicals another chance to press the issues pursued in the earlier session, moderates a thorough investigation of catholic plotting, and loyalists the possibility of granting the King the money which he still needed.[9] There was even speculation that the bishops would join an address to be signed by the nobility.[10] Initially, then, petitions were to represent a universal plea to a Court that was increasingly suspected of being dominated by a French, catholic faction.[11] Signing a petition was to be 'but a discriminatory Act or test between Papists and Protestants'.[12]

---

[4] UCNW, Mostyn MS 9089, f. 191, newsletter, 13 November 1679; All Souls, MS 171, f. 86, newsletter, 11 November 1679; BL, Longleat, M/863, reel vii, vol. xi, f. 443, newsletter, 15 November 1679; Bucks. RO, Verney mss M11/33, Cary Gardiner to Sir Ralph Verney, 20 November 1679; PRO, 31/3/143, ff. 102–3, Barrillon dispatch, 27 November/7 December 1679. It was reported that the duke of York had also come to an agreement with France (PRO, Kew, FO.95/565, d'Avaux dispatch, 20/30 November 1679).

[5] *A Word to the Approaching Parliament* (1679), had argued, p. 3, that if the King broke the fundamental laws 'it should be the first attempt of the subjects to labour to persuade the Prince from his intentions by Petitions and Remonstrances'.

[6] *HMC Ormonde*, iv. 558.

[7] *HMC Ormonde*, iv. 560.

[8] *The True Domestick Intelligence*, no. 53, 6 January 1680.

[9] For the belief that Parliament offered the only prospect of relief for the ailing national finances see *Hatton Corresp*. i. 214.

[10] *HMC Ormonde*, iv. 560.

[11] Bucks. RO, Verney mss, M11/33, Cary Gardiner to Sir Ralph Verney, 20 November and 7 December 1679.

[12] Longleat, Muddiman newsbook, 8 April 1680, reporting on the prosecution of Thomas Dare, a petitioner. Two people were examined before the privy council for saying 'that they were all Papists that refused to subscribe to the Petition for the sitting of the Parliament' (*Mercurius Anglicus*, no. 23, p. 74). In Bristol the promoters of a petition there went round 'alledging they were Papists, or popishly affected, who were ag[ain]st it' (Bod., MS Tanner 129, f. 52, Samuel Crossman to Sancroft, 21 January 1680). *A Vindication of Addresses in General* (1681), p. 2, claimed that the Petitioners 'had given the stamp of Papist, and Popishly affected, upon all Non-Petitioners'.

Yet petitioning, far from being a demonstration of unity, exacerbated many of the tensions apparent in the precarious alliance of anti-catholic forces. One split began to emerge when it was clear that the campaign was being driven by a faction of peers, consisting of Shaftesbury, Grey, Howard, North, Huntingdon, Chandos, Kent, Clare and Wharton.[13] Their aim was twofold: first, to put pressure on the King to force him to make concessions and, second, to do so in a way that secured the maximum impact on public opinion. The peers, however, needed time to prepare for a nationwide campaign, and to make attempts, which proved unsuccessful, to persuade lord mayor Clayton to call an extraordinary common council, which they hoped would petition the King.[14] It was not until 7 December that the peers' petition was presented, and even then it had only sixteen signatures.[15] The number of peers who subscribed must have been disappointing for Shaftesbury, for Andrew Swatland's analysis of the House of Lords in the period has revealed a fairly regular opposition group of at least thirty lords, a turn-out which suggests that Shaftesbury's power and influence, even at their height, need to be assessed cautiously.[16] Moreover, the subscribers were now exposed as a listed faction.

The peers' petition is also important for the change it brought about in the status of the duke of Monmouth. The delay in presenting the petition may have been designed to allow him time to return from exile.[17] He had left Holland by 25 November,[18] acting in concert with William of Orange if the

---

13 *CSPD 1679–80*, p. 296; *Hatton Corresp.*, i. 206–7. These Lords were present at Oates's trial for buggery (*HMC Ormonde*, iv. 561), though Halifax, Paget, Cavendish and the bishop of London had also attended (*The True Domestick Intelligence*, no. 42, 28 November 1679).

14 *Hatton Corresp.* i. 207–8.

15 It was signed by sixteen peers: Bedford, Saye and Sele, Clare, Stamford, Shaftesbury, Rockingham, Kent, Eure, Holles, North, Chandos, Grey, Howard of Escrick, Herbert of Cherbury, and Delamere. Roger Morrice included Lord Townshend (Dr Williams's Library, MS 31.P, Ent'ring Books, vol. i, f. 241, 9 December 1679), but the list of signatures (Huntington, HA Parliament Box 4 [20]) does not include him. Prince Rupert introduced the petitioning lords to Charles's presence (UCNW, Mostyn MS 9089, f. 180, newsletter, 9 December 1679). The peers' petition was printed in the *Domestick Intelligence*, no. 45, 9 December 1679.

16 Swatland, 'The House of Lords', pp. 263–4. Simms ('Organisation of the Whig Party', pp. 401–6) lists forty-two peers as having sided with Shaftesbury. Holles told Barrillon that he had signed the petition in order to keep his credit with the people 'and to prevent the excluding of the Duke of York' (quoted by Lacey, *Dissent and Parliamentary Politics*, p. 136).

17 James claimed that Monmouth's return was concerted with the petitioning lords (*Original Papers*, p. 98), a belief shared by D'Avaux (*Négociations de Monsieur le Comte d'Avaux en Hollande depuis 1679* (1752), i. 65; PRO [Kew], FO.95/565, d'Avaux dispatch, 12/22 December 1679).

18 *Diary of Henry Sidney*, i. 194–5. There had been rumours that he would leave for England as early as 16 October (Congress newsletter 6/284; Newdigate newsletter Lc.850).

French Ambassador at the Hague is to be believed,[19] and reached England *incognito* on 27 November.[20] His reappearance in London sparked more bonfires than at any time since the Restoration, with at least sixty between Temple Bar and Charing Cross.[21] Charles's immediate fear was that an insurrection was intended: Monmouth was therefore told to leave, was relieved of his right to issue military orders, and his right-hand man, Sir Thomas Armstrong, was turned out of the Guards.[22] When he refused to return into exile Monmouth was stripped of his remaining offices, and attempts to reconcile father and son failed.[23] Although not a signatory of the peers' petition, Monmouth was driven further into the arms of the associating lords, who no doubt welcomed the additional popularity that his support lent their cause;[24] but his return forced him to make his ultimately fatal choice of open opposition to his father's wishes. This heightened the political tension. On the day of his public reappearance a pamphlet upholding his legitimacy had been published,[25] and it was believed that those who supported him did so 'only in opposition' to the Duke of York.[26] If this was so, the large number of people who visited Monmouth, and the rumours that Parliament would set up Monmouth as heir when it sat, must have alarmed

[19] D'Avaux, *Négociations*, p. 65. Monmouth and William had a very friendly meeting just before his departure (PRO [Kew], FO.95/565, d'Avaux dispatch, 20/30 November 1679) and Col. Fitzpatrick told d'Avaux that William probably knew about the plan to petition, since Bentinck talked about it only two days after Monmouth left for England (ibid., 5/15 December 1679). A Dutch minister, however, showed surprise when Fitzpatrick told him that mass petitioning was illegal (ibid., 28 November/8 December 1679). Sir William Temple had advised William to ally with Monmouth (*Diary of Henry Sidney*, i. 186). Monmouth and William supported the suggestion of a meeting of Parliament (*HMC Ormonde*, iv. 565). William felt it necessary to send Charles a letter in which he cleared himself from having advised Monmouth to return, but in which he also took the opportunity to urge Charles to unite with his Parliament (Bod., MS Carte 228, f. 140, Henry Sidney to Thomas Wharton, 7 January 1680). Charles remained convinced that Orange had contacts with the English malcontents (PRO, 31/3/143, f. 137, Barrillon dispatch, 19/29 December 1679).

[20] Newdigate newsletter Lc.867, 27 November 1679.

[21] *Hatton Corresp.*, i. 204; *HMC Verney*, p. 478; Newdigate newsletter Lc.868, 29 November 1679; *CSPD 1679–80*, p. 295; *HMC Ormonde*, v. 244. The Green Ribbon Club ordered one of the bonfires to be lit (Pepys Lib., MS 2875, f. 478, minutes, 28 November 1679).

[22] *Original Papers*, p. 99.

[23] The earl of Anglesey tried unsuccessfully to bring about a reconciliation (BL, Add. 18,730, f. 63, diary, 30 November 1679). Intermediaries (including Capt. Godfrey, lords Fauconberg, Macclesfield, Gerard, Monmouth's wife and Nell Gwyn) tried to obtain an audience for Monmouth with his father, (*Original Papers*, p. 99; Clarke, *Memoirs* i. 579).

[24] Monmouth's popularity was probably at its peak at this time (*HMC Ormonde*, v. 245).

[25] Southwell described it as 'proving the right of succession to the Crown and the solemnity of a marriage' with Monmouth's mother (*HMC Ormonde*, iv. 562). cf. *Original Papers*, pp. 99–100.

[26] Bucks. RO, Verney mss, M11/33, Cary Gardiner to Sir Ralph Verney, 1 December 1679.

the Yorkists.[27] There was also speculation that William of Orange would come over 'to gett an Interest in England',[28] and that James would return from Scotland.[29] Petitioning had thus precipitated another round of the succession crisis.

The petition offered for mass subscription in London nevertheless made no reference to exclusion, concentrating instead on reaping support from more general fears of popery and by calling for Parliament to sit on the 26 January 1680, the date to which it had been prorogued. It was accordingly drafted in moderate language so as to win as much support as possible. Yet instead it attracted the charge of being seditious, for it was promoted against the wishes of the King, and many of London's most prominent religious and political radicals helped organise, as well as sign, it. Nonconformist preachers and their congregations, men involved in the production of 'seditious' literature, and those who later actively plotted against the government in 1683 and 1685 all signed the roll-call of the discontented.[30]

I have elsewhere discussed the petitioning campaign in London and the possible effect it may have had on shaping the political theory of one of its subscribers, John Locke.[31] This chapter will therefore consider the national context of the campaign, and examine the success or failure of petitioning outside the capital in order to try to assess the overall impact on public opinion. To do so will also involve a closer inspection of the ideological debate conducted at this time concerning the nature of Restoration government, making it possible to highlight positions that were later to develop into 'Whig' and 'Tory' maxims. Finally, by studying the pamphlets published in the autumn and winter of 1679–80 in terms of the political theories they espoused and the form of discourse they employed, it is possible to show that their language and concerns are strongly reflected in Locke's work, raising questions about the extent to which he was writing to justify resistance for Shaftesburian radicals or a more theoretical right of resistance.

27 *HMC Ormonde*, v. 246; Bucks. RO, Verney mss, M11/33, Cary Gardiner to Sir Ralph Verney, 1 and 7 December 1679.
28 Bucks. RO, Verney mss, M11/33, John Verney to Edmund Verney, 8 December 1679; PRO, 31/3/143, f. 108, Barrillon dispatch, 1/11 December 1679; Newdigate newsletter Lc.871, 6 December 1679.
29 *HMC Ormonde*, iv. 564; *CSPD 1679–80*, p. 295. Barrillon speculated that Shaftesbury may have supported Monmouth's return precisely to force the return of the duke of York (PRO, 31/3/143, f. 107, Barrillon dispatch, 1/11 December 1679).
30 This is a summary of my detailed examination of the petitioning campaign in 'London's "Monster" Petition'.
31 Knights, 'Petitioning and the Political Theorists: John Locke, Algernon Sidney and London's "Monster" Petition of 1680', *Past and Present*, 138 (1993), 94–111.

PETITIONING IN THE PROVINCES

Although none of the mass petitions promoted outside London appear to have survived, so that evidence about the provincial campaign is not as good as that for the capital, some idea of the scope of activity in the boroughs and shires can be derived from comments in newsletters, newspapers, correspondence and pamphlets. From such sources we know that two different forms of petitions existed for use in the country.[32] One, to be signed by the 'Country gentlemen', was more forthright and antagonistic to the King than the version promoted in London, since, unlike the latter, it reminded Charles that 'by the known laws of this realm (which your majesty has obliged your self by your coronation oath to observe) your majesty is to use the advice of your great council, the Parliament, for redressing grievances and providing extraordinary remedy against unusual and eminent dangers'; it also referred to Charles's promise in April 1679 'to consult with and be advised by Parliaments in all your majesties weighty and important affairs'. Unlike the London petition, which made no mention of exclusion or the duke of York, the 'country' petition repeated the resolution of the Commons that the Popish Plot had been encouraged by the hopes of a popish successor, though it stopped short of demanding any specific action against James and a reference to a popish successor was contained in square brackets as though its inclusion was uncertain and could be deleted. The petitioners claimed to 'have been awakened to a greater sense of our danger and of the narrowness of our destruction' by the King's recent illness, and pointed out that the Meal Tub Plot was evidence of the continued restlessness of the papists. The petition concluded by requesting, like the London text, that conspirators be dealt with and that Parliament should meet on 26 January, though it differed by adding that MPs should be allowed to sit 'till they have accomplisht those great ends which will render your majesty the most beloved of princes, will make your name glorious to posterity, and your subjects most happy under your reign', leaving the impression that unless he agreed to Parliament's demands, the King would continue to meet with disaffection.[33] A second and milder version, with the same title but ostensibly from the 'baronets, knights, gentlemen and yeomen', emphasised the importance of investigating the Plot, of pursuing the impeachments and of protecting the country against the threat from France. Regarding Parliament as the 'most apt means to discover the depth and soul of the said conspiracy, try those who are impeached, and provide future security', the petition duly requested its sitting on 26 January 1680.[34]

---

[32] *Mercurius Anglicus*, no. 6, 6–10 December 1679, p. 27; HMC *Verney*, p. 496; *CSPD 1679–80*, p. 307.

[33] *Mercurius Anglicus*, no. 6, 6–10 December 1679.

[34] Bod., Nichols. Newspaper IB/467, *To the King's Most Excellent Majesty* (1680).

In the absence of the petitions themselves, it is not clear which form of wording was adopted in any region, though we do know that in Leicester it was the London style that found favour.[35] This was also the case in at least one county, Somerset, where a printed copy of the text used in London was sent there by the Green Ribbon Club member Hugh Speke, with promises to send fifty more by the next coach; he also added that 'the easiest and best form' was 'what London and Middlesex both subscribe to ... the other larger form will not pass'.[36] Speke's comment suggests that only a moderate form of words, which did not refer to the succession or to the King's obligation to be advised by Parliament, would attract mass support.[37] Anti-popery was what attracted the crowds, rather than radical ideology or attacks on the duke of York. Speke added that he would have the petition specially 'printed as for our own county and in a larger character and in the same form as this, after which I would have you get all the best of the gentry to subscribe'. The aim was thus to attract the support of the upper as much as the lower orders, though the promoter of the Suffolk petition had a policy to 'refuse no man's hand whither he be a freeholder or not, the more hands bee to it the better'.[38]

L'Estrange's *Seasonable Memorial*, published a week before Parliament was due to sit, attacked the printed texts sent down from London into the country by asserting that they 'were not the petitions of the subscribers, but of those that set them on ... and that which was taken and imposed on the sense of the nation was only the project and dictate of the caball'.[39] There was evidently some truth in the charge; but even so, L'Estrange underestimated the independence of action in the localities. Indeed, pressure from the provinces to organise a petitioning campaign in the autumn had been evident as early as the end of October, before any talk could have filtered out of London. George Treby, soon to be appointed London's recorder in place of the infamous Sir George Jeffreys, had received a letter from a country correspondent who claimed that 'many would wish a petition to be presented first from London, and then from all the counties, that Parliament may sit in January and continue sitting until some terms are made about the King's person, and the Protestant Religion'.[40] The provinces, rather than being imposed on by

---

35 *Records of the Borough of Leicester 1603–1688* ed. H. Stocks (Cambridge, 1923), pp. 554–5. The text of the Kent petition was also slightly different since it included mention of the subscribers' fear of French power (*Domestick Intelligence*, no. 57, 16 January 1680).

36 *CSPD Addenda 1660–1685*, p. 478.

37 The radical Col. Scott had redrawn the London petition in more moderate and submissive language for precisely this reason (Knights, 'London's "Monster" Petition', pp. 44–5).

38 BL, Longleat mss, M/863, reel vii, vol. xi, f. 453, Sir Samuel Barnardiston to Sir William Spring, 6 December 1679.

39 *Seasonable Memorial in some Historical Notes* (1680), p. 19.

40 *HMC Fitzherbert*, p. 21.

the London cabals, had wanted to be led by the capital, where in any case clubs met to discuss county affairs.[41]

Thus although London was to lead the dance, it may well have been to the tune of the provinces. Certainly, once launched the campaign involved local men in gathering names. Southwell remarked that the petitions were 'confided to certain gentlemen ... to go from parish to parish' collecting subscriptions, and Roger North observed that the petitions were 'put into the Hands of Agitants and Sub-agitants in the Counties ... and these Agitators, being choice Party-Men and well instructed, went to every free voter, and indeed every one, as they came in their way, demanding their Hands to the Petition'.[42] Moreover, the campaign in the provinces seems to have begun before that in London, and even before the peers presented their petition on 7 December. By 6 December it was reported that one in Essex already had almost 8,000 hands to it,[43] and Sir Samuel Barnardiston wrote to his fellow Suffolk MP to begin the campaign there using the Essex petition as a model.[44]

Despite the numerical success in gathering subscriptions in London, the petitioning campaign nevertheless failed nationwide, both as propaganda and in securing its political objectives. In part this was due to the King's hostile reception of the capital's petition when it was presented on 13 January 1680 by Sir Gilbert Gerard and a party of nine others.[45] When one of them 'offered to read it, and began some part of it ... His Majesty told the petitioners to this effect, That he well knew the Contents of it, and as the Supream Head of the Gov[ernmen]t would take care of it.'[46] After this

---

[41] Dangerfield claimed that Col. Blood's club was in touch with Huntingdonshire, and that Waller's discussed affairs in Dorset, Devon and Cornwall (BL, Longleat mss, M/863, reel vii, Coventry papers vol. xi, ff. 441–2, n.d. endorsed 'Mr Willoughby's remarks'; Willoughby was an alias for Dangerfield).

[42] *HMC Ormonde*, iv. 565; North, *Examen*, p. 542. The term 'agitator' is used in reference to petitioners by Andrew Pascall in a letter dated 18 April 1682 (Bod., MS Aubrey 13, f. 49).

[43] *HMC Ormonde*, iv. 565. On 9 December it was said to have 20,000 names (UCNW, Mostyn MS 9089, f. 180, newsletter), and over 40,000 by the end of the month (Newdigate newsletter Lc.881, 30 December 1679).

[44] BL, Longleat mss, M/863, reel vii, vol.11, f. 453, Barnardiston to Spring, 6 December 1679.

[45] They included Francis Charlton, John Ellis, Thomas Johnson, Ellis Crispe, Anthony Selby, Henry Ashurst, Aaron Smith and Thomas Smith (*Domestick Intelligence*, no. 56, 16 January 1680; Newdigate newsletter Lc.887, 17 January 1680; Bucks. RO, Verney mss, M11/34, John Verney to Sir Ralph Verney, 14 January 1680). Charlton had been active in promoting the petition of May 1679 (Browning, *Danby*, ii. 82). Charlton and Johnson were 'well known for a dissatisfaction to the p[rese]nt government, Johnson having been in armes ag[ains]t the K[ing]' (Congress newsletter 7/6, 13 January 1680). According to this report Mr Smith had been 'a captain in the parlia[men]ts armie & Mr Ellis p[rese]nted a petition to the K[ing] in the name of severall thousand his Maj[esty's] subjects of London and Westminster'. A John Ellis signed the petition on the page headed by Mansell's name (Huntington Lib., MS HM 68 sheet – [176]).

[46] *Mercurius Anglicus*, no. 16, p. 59, 13 January 1680.

outburst, the promoters of the county petitions were understandably reluctant to present them until London's common council had led the way.[47] The success of the national campaign therefore depended on official sanction from the City's elective body. When this was not forthcoming at the meeting of the common council on 13 January, the Court was understandably 'very pert upon this unexpected good success',[48] and one observer thought the defeat marked the end of petitioning.[49]

Indeed, only six provincial petitions were presented and most received very short shrift from the King. Essex's had been the first to be promoted, and accordingly received the most angry response from the King.[50] Due to the influence of the duke of Albemarle, neither the Essex nor the Wiltshire petition had been endorsed by the assizes, and Charles consequently sought to exploit the fact that the petition did not have the sanction officially required by the law. 'Being demanded whether it came from the Grand Jury, the [presenters] made answer, It did not. Whereupon his Majesty was pleased to reply, That then it was not the petition of the County of Essex ... [and] wonder'd that Gentlemen of their Quality and Estates should concern themselves in such a Petition.'[51] According to one newswriter, Charles also told them 'that he believed some of those that subscribed meant well but they were abused by those that did not'.[52] This belief that an evil faction had led men astray may explain the King's more moderate reaction to the presenters of the Berkshire petition, to whom he offered to reconcile matters 'over a cup of Ale'.[53] But generally Charles was hostile to the petitions, which he regarded as an invasion of his prerogative powers to summon Parliament whenever he wanted. He told Thomas Thynne, the presenter of the Wiltshire petition, that he was 'an Impertinent foole to meddle with what did not concerne him', and is also reported to have asked

---

[47] PRO, 31/3/144, f. 49, Barrillon dispatch, 19/29 January 1680. On 17 January it was noted that petitioning languished in several counties (HMC Ormonde, iv. 576). Newdigate newsletter Lc.890, 20 January 1680, noted that 'it's said some of them [county petitions] are discouraged & have Retracted their Intentions upon his Ma[jes]tyes ill Resentment of the late London Petition'.

[48] Diary of Henry Sidney, i. 248.

[49] Cheshire RO, DCH/k/3/2, Edward Cholmondeley to Mr Adams, 20 January 1680.

[50] Mercurius Anglicus, no. 20, 24–6 January 1680, p. 67. Sir Gower Barrington, Col. Mildmay, Sir Robert Wight, Sir Robert Rich, Mr Hanwood, Mr Traford and Mr Atwood presented it (Newdigate newsletter Lc.892, 24 January 1680). Congress newsletter 7/10, 24 January 1680 claimed that John Lamotte Honeywood helped the presentation. See also The Essex Ballad (1680).

[51] Leeds AO, Mexborough mss, Reresby 15/71 newsletter, 17 January 1679/80; Mercurius Anglicus, no. 20, 24–8 January 1680.

[52] Congress newsletter 7/10, 24 January 1680.

[53] Leeds AO, Mexborough mss, Reresby 14/97 newsletter, 24 January 1679/80. It was presented by 'Sir John Stonehouse, Mr Barker, Wood &c most of them honest gentlemen' (Original Papers, p. 101). Barker was MP for the county, Stonhouse MP for Abingdon. According to Newdigate newsletter Lc.892, 24 January 1680 Lord Lovelace also presented the petition. It was printed in Domestick Intelligence, no. 57, 20 January 1680.

What doe you take me to be and what doe you take yo[u]rselves to be ? I admire Gentlemen of your Estates should animate People to Mutiny and Rebellion. Why do you say the County sent you ? had you these directives from the Grand Jury ? Mr Thynne replyed no; no indeed, says the King, you came from a company of late and disaffected people, who would faine sett us in troubles.[54]

Charles was also outraged by the presentation of the Somerset petition on the steps of Parliament just as he was about to announce a further prorogation, but when he asked its presenter 'how he dared do that?' Thomas Dare fell back on the justification of his surname.[55] Petitions were also presented from Hertfordshire[56] and York, the only provincial city to carry through the campaign,[57] but many more had failed to attract sufficient support, especially from grand juries. They are known to have been unsuccessfully set on foot in Bridgwater, Oxford and Wells, as well as in a number of other counties such as Kent, Norfolk, Suffolk, Lancashire, Yorkshire, Cumberland, Buckinghamshire, Monmouthshire, Dorset, Derbyshire and the London Inns of Court.[58]

---

[54] Leeds AO, Mexborough mss, Reresby 14/97, Edward Reresby to Sir John Reresby, 24 January 1680; Bulstrode newsletter, 23 January 1680; BL, Add. 29,569, f. 227, [Anne, wife of the earl of Manchester] to Lord Hatton. n.d.; *CSPD 1679–80*, p. 377. According to the Dowager Countess Sunderland, Sir Walter St John and Sir Edward Hungerford accompanied Tom Thynne in presenting it (*Diary of Henry Sidney*, i. 252). *The Wiltshire Ballad* (1680) claimed the petition was drawn up by three MPs, including the two knights of the shire, and that Sir Thomas Mompesson was the first to sign it and promote it (*POAS*, ii. 313). Alexander Thistlethwayte and Sir Richard Grobham Howe are also suggested as promoters. The petition was said to have attracted 30,000 signatures (*CSPD 1679–80*, p. 377), though it was also reported that it was 'sub[scribe]d by a few Gentlemen & some others of the County of Wilts[hire]' (Congress newsletter 7/9, 22 January 1680). *The Domestick Intelligence* claimed that 'many of the Justices of the Peace and the considerablest Gentry in the Countrey' had signed it (no. 57, 20 January 1680).

[55] Longleat, Muddiman newsbook, 27 January 1680; North, *Examen*, p. 543. The petition was presented by two Green Ribbon Club men, Thomas Dare and Mr Parsons, for which they earned their fellow members' thanks (Pepys Lib., MS 2875, f. 480, minutes, 26 January 1680). According to this source many 'great Men' had refused to present it. According to the Somerset grand jury of 20 April 1680, the petition had been promoted 'by disloyal and turbulent persons in a clandestine and unlawful manner' (*CSPD 1679–80*, p. 440). John Oldmixon claimed it had 2,000–3,000 signatures: *History of Addresses* (1709), i. 18).

[56] The Hertfordshire petitioners came to London to see 'Sir Thomas Byde & their other Knight of the Shire [Sir Jonathan Keate] to consult with them ab[ou]t presenting their petition' (Newdigate newsletter Lc.882, 1 January 1680). Byde and Sir William Cowper presented the petition (*The Domestick Intelligence*, no. 52, 2 January 1680). Congress newsletter 7/1, 1 January 1680, claimed there were 10,000 signatures to it.

[57] 'The Yorkshire petition was not presented in Council as proposed' (*Original Papers*, p. 101). It was eventually handed over by Sir John Hewley (*Mercurius Anglicus*, no. 20, 24–8 January 1680, p. 68; Newdigate newsletter Lc.893, 27 January 1680). The names of the archbishop of York's cook, coachman and other servants had reputedly been inserted without their knowledge by the constable of the city 'for he thought it was so good a work that no body would refuse it' (*True Domestick Intelligence*, no. 60, 30 January 1680). In York it was reported that there were 'but 19 of any credit who have not subscribed it' (All Souls, MS 171, f. 105, newsletter, 3 January 1680).

[58] Bod., MS Carte 228, f. 140, 'W.T' to Thomas Wharton, 7 January 1680 re York; Lancs. RO, Kenyon MS DDKe/6/21 re Lancashire and Cumberland; Longleat, Muddiman newsbook, 19

An insight into both the organisation of, and the difficulties encountered by, the regional campaigns can be gained from a report by Roger Kenyon describing petitioning in Lancashire.[59] Whereas the political élite seems to have been in a state of paralysis in Bristol, where the city's MP Sir Robert Cann 'very far endeavour'd to serve the government' but found 'too few ... standing by him',[60] attempts to obtain gentry support in Lancashire for a petition at the quarter sessions prompted swift, forestalling action from the county's leaders. The promoters of the petition there were William Spencer, MP for Lancaster and a nephew of Shaftesbury's,[61] and the Hon. Charles Gerard of Brandon, the knight of the shire,[62] assisted by Serjeant Edward Rigby, MP for Preston and a King's counsel,[63] and William Kerby, surveyor general for the customs in the North. Unable to persuade the Lancaster Session to sign, the petitioners had turned their attention to the Preston Sessions, but, despite a letter from Lord Brandon to promote the petition, the mayor of Preston refused to have anything to do with it, and declared 'that his head should sooner be had than his hand'. He further ordered that the King's proclamation against tumultuous petitioning be fixed to the door of the Town Hall, and 'all was Put to a stand by my L[or]d of Darbyes appearing flatly against any manner of concurrence'. Opposition to the petitioning was also encouraged by an anonymous paper called 'Reasons ... ag[ains]t the addressing the King with a Petition' which, according to Kenyon, 'did much satisfy some gentlemen that read them'.[64] The experiences of Lancashire was that petitioning helped divide the county community, but also that it had stirred some loyalists into action.

January 1680 re Sarum; *London Gazette*, no. 14830, 22–6 January 1680 and Luttrell, *Brief Relation*, i. 32 re Bridgwater, Oxford and Canterbury: ibid. i. 31 re Wells, Salisbury, Dorset, Derbys.; Newdigate newsletter Lc.884, 27 December 1679 re Inns of Court; *Original Papers*, p. 101 re Norfolk; BL, Longleat mss, M/863, reel vii, vol. xi, f. 453, Barnardiston to Spring, 6 December 1679 re Suffolk; Newdigate newsletter Lc.890, 20 January 1680 re Kent; Congress newsletter 7/7, 17 January 1680 re Bucks; *CJ*, ix. 658 re Monmouthshire. Humphrey Prideaux remarked that in Oxford the townsmen 'all subscribe like mad' (*Prideaux Corresp.*, p. 75). Wood observed that the Oxford petition was then presented to the grand jury by Brome Whorwood, William Wright and Sir Thomas Horde, but 'not three parts of the grand jury consented to it' (Wood, *Life and Times*, ii. 476).

59 Lancs. RO, Kenyon MS DDKe/6/21.
60 Bod., MS Tanner 129, f. 52, Crossman to Sancroft, 21 January 1680.
61 Spencer visited Shaftesbury in London. Evidently hot-blooded, Spencer threatened the parson of Lancaster that he would 'run him through for drinking the Duke of York's health & declareing ag[ains]t [petitioning]' (Lancs. RO, Kenyon MS DDKe/6/21).
62 According to Kenyon, Gerard had 'received soe much grace & intimacy from his Majesty as any Younge Man about Whitehall'.
63 Rigby was later Chairman of the Commons Committee into abhorring petitions. Kenyon reported him to be 'a declared Enemy to the Duke' of York. Rigby was the son of Alexander Rigby, one of the most active parliamentarians in the North.
64 This was printed as *Reasons offered by a Well-Wisher* (1680). cf. 'Reasons Offered by a Person of Honour at a meeting of the Gentlemen of Gloucestershire', printed in *HMC Hodgkin*, pp. 316–17, which is the identical text misdated as '1 Jan. ?1676'.

The petitioners had grounds to be disappointed about the extent to which they had swayed public opinion. As the Countess of Sunderland remarked, 'the petitions fell flat to what was expected',[65] and even Burnet thought the campaign had shown 'rather the weakness than the strength of the party'.[66] The reasons for the failure are not hard to find. By adopting extra-parliamentary action the petitioners were bound to appear factional to a nation which 'naturally loves a parliamentary cure, but is jealous of all other methods'.[67] Petitioners thus laid themselves open to the charge that they had tried to 'muster a Party & manage them to some ill purpose'.[68] The names of those who refused them had been noted down, sometimes physically as well as mentally,[69] whilst those who signed had listed their allegiance to the opposition. Attitudes to petitioning became a touchstone for determining political allegiance, so that Burnet believed that, if Charles dissolved Parliament again, those who had promoted them would be chosen, 'for the inferiour sort of people are mighty set on them and make their judgments of men by their behaviour in that matter'.[70] As Roger North remarked 'a perfect Distinction was form'd of Petitioner and Anti-petitioner', and it is no coincidence that it was during the campaign that projects for an Association of Protestants were again mooted.[71]

[65] *Diary of Henry Sidney*, i. 252.

[66] Burnet, *History*, ii. 249.

[67] Burnet, *History*, ii. 249. *A Caution against Tumultuous Petitioning* (1680), p. 2, argued that MPs had 'no lawful authority when out of the House'.

[68] Longleat, Muddiman newsbook, 13 January 1680. It was alleged that in Bristol, 'where some have modestly refused to sett their hands, the promoters of those petitions have menac'd they were better to do it voluntarily now than be compelled (as they would be afterward) to do it with shame' (Bod., MS Tanner 129, f. 52, Crossman to Sancroft, 21 January 1680).

[69] *HMC Ormonde*, iv. 565. An ensign of the trained bands refused to sign because he did not see his Captain's hand there, prompting the promoter of the petition to remark that 'he would putt him in the black book'; the privy council was informed and the ensign examined, but 'the Gentleman said it was only a drolling expression and so was discharged' (Congress newsletter 6/313, 25 December 1679). The *Loyal Protestant*, no. 23, 24 May 1681, claimed that Samuel Harris, a baptist promoter of petitions, had threatened to enter the names of those who refused to sign in a black book. For further details about Harris see Knights, 'London's "Monster" Petition', p. 51.

[70] Bod., MS Add. D. 23, f. 5, Burnet to Charles, 29 January 1680.

[71] North, *Examen*, p. 544. Kenyon (Lancs. RO, Kenyon MS DDKe/6/21) reported that an association in Lancaster was 'hotly discoursed of ... nay they have been soe forward there as to discourse of Raysing of Men, nominating Captains & Officers whereof one Mr Dodding the sonne of a Parliament Coll. was to bee chiefe and all this without any commission, and has beene in agitation for some weekes amongst them'. Southwell also heard of a plan for an association (*HMC Ormonde*, iv. 566). The duke of York referred to the petitions as 'Lord Shaftesbury's association' (*HMC Dartmouth*, i. 48). Two pamphlets published in 1679 raised the possibility of an Association: *The Instrument or Writing of Association, The Act of Parliament of the 27th of Queen Elizabeth to Preserve the Queen's Person*, and *To the Right Honourable the Lords and Commons* (the latter is undated but a MS note on the Bodleian copy dates it as 1679). *The True Domestick Intelligence*, no. 45, 9 December 1679, referred to the petitions as 'a form of an Association'.

The petitions fostered two apparently paradoxical developments that helped to determine the future conflict and were ultimately to polarise the nation. The first was that Charles's refusal to let Parliament sit further alienated the discontented, who were now forced into challenging the King rather than, or as well as, his brother. As Burnet bluntly told Charles:

most people grow sullen and are highly dissatisfied with your M[ajesty] and very distrustfull of you; formerly your ministers and his R[oyal] High[ness] received the blame of things which were ungratefull but now it falls upon your selfe and time, which cures all other distempers, Increaseth this'.[72]

Petitioning thus helped resolve the crisis into one about the present government of Charles as much as about the future and only possible administration of his brother. Second, the situation brought about by Charles's policy was also ironically one in which the King could begin to recruit support. The gathering of mass subscriptions had frightened many observers. This was, remarked Henry Muddiman, 'the old approved way of fomenting a new rebellion', and Anthony Wood compared the petitions to those of 1641.[73] Not only were these the steps to disorder, but unrest seemed imminent.[74] On 23 December 1679 Henry Coventry doubted 'whether any water will quench the flame of the rabble',[75] and a few days later he observed that the people were 'full of jealousies'.[76] The country appeared to be on the verge of chaos. On the day the London petition was presented, Humphrey Prideaux wrote a distraught letter to John Ellis in which he claimed that the King seemed 'to all ends and purposes to be an undon man ... and therefore I give all for lost'.[77] Two days before Parliament was due to sit Coventry reported that 'fears and jealousies [were] as high as ever'.[78] The petitioners had succeeded in raising the spectre of civil war, and part of the nation had recoiled. Since fear of disorder was at least as strong as a fear of popery and arbitrary government, this was a reaction that the King could, and ultimately did, exploit to his

---

[72] Bod., MS Add. D. 23, f. 5, Burnet to Charles, 29 January 1680.
[73] Longleat, Muddiman newsbook, 12 December 1679; Bod., MS Top.Oxon.e.102, f. 136, Wood to Fullman, 12 December 1679. The mayor of Chichester remembered 'that they began the rebellion much as they are about to do, by Petitioning the King for Parliament' (quoted by C. Price, *Cold Caleb: Ford Grey, First Earl of Tankerville 1655–1701* [1956], p. 50). Barrillon thought Shaftesbury managed the republicans who hoped for a new civil war (PRO, 31/3/144, f. 29, Barrillon dispatch, 5/15 January 1680). For other comments about petitioning and civil war see *Reasons Offered by a Well-Wisher* (1680), p. 3; *A Letter to a Friend Reflecting upon the present Condition of the Nation* [1680], p. 3; *Goodman Country* (1680), p. 3; *Petition to the Petitioners* (1680), p. 2; *A Caution against Tumultuous Petitioning* (1680), p. 1.
[74] All Souls, MS 116, f. 59, 'A Petition for the Presbiters'.
[75] *HMC Ormonde*, v. 259.
[76] BL, Eg.3680, f. 152, Coventry to Bulstrode, 29 December 1679.
[77] *Prideaux Corresp.*, p. 75.
[78] *HMC Ormonde*, v. 266.

own advantage. Moreover, men were also beginning to point out that the principles behind attempts to bar James from the throne meant that 'an actual Prince may be depos'd with as much Justice as an Heir can be excluded the succession, and so (for ought we know) his R[oyal] H[ighness] being once remov'd and out of their way, the next attempt will be against His Majesty'.[79] Thus, the very focus of discontent, demonstrated by the petitioning campaign, on Charles's arbitrariness coincided with fears that the attack on James was a smoke-screen for the destruction of the monarchy.

Alongside the idea that the country was drifting towards civil war came the belief that the good old cause had been revived in terms of personnel as well as tactics and principles. L'Estrange claimed that if men examined the present disturbers of the state they would find 'the old Republicans to be the Ringleaders',[80] and that the 'same Faces [were] now at work again'.[81] The author of the *Advice to the Men of Shaftesbury* (1681) noted that some of the opposition had been active in 1640,[82] and *An Apostrophe from the Loyal Party* (1681) warned the King that 'those men by whom your Royal Father fell, and pursued you to Banishment ... are the men, Sir, who strike so boldly at your Crown'.[83] The signatures on the London petition can have done nothing to quieten these fears. The author of the 'Reasons against the Addressing the King with a Petition' wrote that not one of the peers who had petitioned could 'claime to any honorable service performed either to this King or his father during the late Rebellion ... and if the late warre were begun w[i]th petitions, & by these very men & their fathers it can not but bee adviseable by all loyall Gentlemen what may be the end of these petitions'.[84] Any former Royalists that signed, the author claimed, did so because they had voted for exclusion or because they were 'waspish they are not better preferrd'. The author of *A Letter to a Friend Reflecting upon the Present*

---

[79] *Captain Thorogood His Opinion* (1680), p. 8. cf. *Great and Weighty Considerations* (1679?), p. 7: 'by whatsoever power or pretence the Parliament can depose the Presumptive Heir, by the same they may depose the actual possessor of the Crown'.

[80] *Citt and Bumpkin* (1680), p. 28. The reappearance of republicans in active politics is a noteworthy feature of the period, though they suffered from a crisis of leadership. The duke of Buckingham, who had most links with them, was thoroughly unreliable. In May 1680 he offered to turn informer to 'discover such contrivances ag[ain]st the King & governm[en]t as shall cause some great men [to] lose [their] heads' (Congress newsletter 7/50, 13 May 1680, and see also chapter 5).

[81] *A Word Concerning Libels* (1681), p. 11.

[82] *Advice to the Men of Shaftesbury* (1681), p. 3.

[83] *An Apostrophe from the Loyal Party* (1681), p. 3. cf. *A Letter from an Impartial Hater of the Papists* [1679?], p. 1.

[84] Lancs. RO, Kenyon MS DDKe/6/21. Its accusation was not unfounded: of the 16 peers that petitioned only 2, Rockingham and Chandos, came from Royalist backgrounds.

Condition observed 'many of these Petitioners to be old Colonels',[85] and Muddiman thought they were promoted by 'those of the Old Leaven'.[86]

The petitioners had sought to use the pressure of public opinion to force Charles to capitulate;[87] instead they had 'alienated many sober and well-meaning men from all the councells that were carried on in such a manner, for they began to think that the Protestant Religion was under a pretence to alter the Government, or to help the Duke of Monmouth into the Throne after the King's death'.[88] An interesting case study of the shift in moderate opinion at this time is the Buckinghamshire gentleman, Edmund Verney. In June 1679 he had approved of petitioning against Parliament's prorogation, and had supported Thomas Wharton and John Hampden, both strong supporters of the exclusion bill, for knights of the shire. As late as the end of September Verney was dining with another supporter of the bill, Sir Francis Drake, and with Charles and Thomas Pope Blount, two members of the Green Ribbon Club. Yet Verney had been alarmed by Monmouth's return, and evidently feared unrest. He did not think petitioning was illegal 'if it be done with such a decorum as it ought, for if the subject in generall or particular bee oppressed, and must not for all that represent theyr grievances to his Majesty, certainly wee are in a miserable condition, beyond the Turkish Slavery, w[hi]ch is beneath the English Spirit to endure'. But, he added, 'I doe not speake this out of any designe to sett my Hand to any such Petition, for I resolve on the contrary, as yet, seeing no present need.' Moreover, it was at precisely this time that he seems to have formulated his position against radical exclusionist sentiment, whilst reserving a willingness to recognise a *de facto* exclusion. He believed that 'the Duke of York is the undoubted Right Heire to the Crowne if the King (whom God long preserve) Dye without Issue ... therefore to Endeavour an Alteration of the Line, w[hi]ch I am sure cannot bee Legally Done without our good King's consent, which hath Declared Hee will never Give, is to Entayle a warr upon Posterity'. Only if Parliament and the King agreed to alter the succession would the people, and Verney, submit to the change.[89] The campaign was thus highly important for detaching moderate

[85] *A Letter to a Friend Reflecting upon the Present Condition of this Nation* [1680], p. 3. *Goodman Country* (1680), p. 3, calls the petitioners 'quondam committee men, and sequestrators'.

[86] Longleat, Muddiman newsbook, 17 January 1680.

[87] It was believed that Charles would not hazard his Crown for the sake of his brother (PRO, 31/3/143, f. 70, Barrillon dispatch, 15/25 September 1679).

[88] BL, Add. 63,057B, Burnet's ms history, f. 54.

[89] Bucks. RO, Verney mss, M11/33, Edmund Verney's letters dated 2 June, 30 July, 25 September, 3 December, 10 December and 18 December 1679. For similar sentiments about petitioning see *A Letter to a Friend about the late Proclamation on the 11th December* (1679), pp. 7, 11.

'Country' opinion from the exclusionist cause and from a radical or factious opposition.[90]

The petitions pressing Charles to let Parliament sit on 26 January 1680 are an indication of the opposition's ability to organise, but only in London and a handful of other counties, many of which were near the capital. The London petition offers clear evidence of Shaftesbury's encouragement of the petitioners, but the campaign also marks a turning point in Shaftesbury's position. As in the 1679 Parliament, he had taken advantage of an agitation that already existed but which he stirred further and to which he gave direction. Yet this reliance on popular pressure alienated moderates and raised fears that he sought civil war; and that reliance made him appear weak in the coming months when popular agitation subsided. Paradoxically, the campaign shows the strengths and the weaknesses of Shaftesbury's political tactics. He had finally stirred the King into resolution, and shown not so much how indispensable he himself was to the political process, as how difficult it would be for Charles to work with anyone whose strength depended on popular opinion.[91] Moreover, Shaftesbury had begun a struggle to show who truly represented the will of the nation, a challenge to the loyalists that ensured a continuation of the struggle between petitioners and their opponents.

THE PRESS AND POLITICAL THEORY

Before considering the struggle to represent the will of the nation, we need to take an overview of the period between the late summer elections and the petitioning campaign in terms of political theory, for if the winter of 1679–80 marked a political turning point we might expect to see new ideological developments to match. We might also expect to find the newly liberated press providing a vehicle for vigorous debate, and to be able to use the propaganda published at this time to explore the emergence of divided opinion. This section will therefore study the themes and issues debated in the literature in order to reconstruct the positions that separated writers, and hence examine the embryonic programmes adopted by loyalist and opposition controversialists.

By October 1679 the press took 'an inexcusable liberty of imposing anything that might be thought vendible on the people',[92] and 'afforded such flames as if all the Beacons of England were set on fire'.[93] One of the contributions to the debate about popery and arbitrary government was a reprint of Henry Parker's *Political Catechism* of 1643, which used Charles I's

---

[90] Even some of those who supported the exclusion bill opposed the campaign (Knights, 'London's "Monster" Petition', p. 45).

[91] PRO, 131/3/144, f. 46, Barrillon dispatch, 5/25 January 1680.

[92] Longleat, Muddiman newsbook, 14 October 1679.

[93] *HMC Ormonde*, iv. 546.

answers to the Nineteen Propositions to argue for a limited monarchy.[94] Parker had stated that the Commons must have a share in government, that the King was not above the law and that to resist his transgressions was not wrong. The tract also declared – aptly in view of the situation in 1679 – in favour of frequent parliamentary sessions because

it was not intended in the constitution of this government that the King in the greatest matters of importance for public benefit should only hear what [MPs] say and then follow it or reject it merely at his own pleasure; for this may be as well done in an absolute monarchy.[95]

The publication so infuriated the government that on 15 October it ordered the arrest of the tract's distributors. At the same time, those who had dispersed *An Appeal from the Country to the City* were also arrested. This pamphlet had graphically portrayed the massacre of protestants by a popish successor and suggested Monmouth as the fittest candidate for the throne. L'Estrange published a reply, which claimed that 'the whole kingdom ... is again split into two parties; the one consisting of mutineers and schismatiques, the other of loyal servants and subjects of the Crown'. He alleged that the *Appeal* was a call to rebellion against 'the King that now is', and, perhaps with reference to *A Political Catechism*, that the principles being advocated in the City were nothing 'but the venom of the old cause swallow'd and spew'd up again'. L'Estrange tried to convince the City that its security lay 'betwixt the two extremes of Popery, on the one hand, and Libertinism on the other'.[96]

The publication of the *Political Catechism* and *An Appeal* is further evidence that the succession issue reinjected life into an older debate that streched back at least to the 1640s about the nature of government and the allegiance of the subject. The legality of exclusion rested on the doctrine of the supremacy of Parliament over the King and his prerogatives, and raised questions about the obligation men owed to rulers, and when, if ever, these bonds could be broken. Much of the legacy of mid seventeenth-century ideology, which Jonathan Scott has quite rightly wished to emphasise as still relevant to the period 1679–80, is, ironically, most visible in the small core of material about the succession which he slights.[97]

Pamphlets debating the succession issue in the second half of 1679 showed a remarkable sophistication in their discussion of the origin of government

[94] The tract may have been published because *The Reasons and Narrative of Proceedings Betwixt the two Houses* (1679), which referred to the propositions, had appeared in May.

[95] *Political Catechism* (1643), pp. 2–5. Wing lists the reprint as ?1683, but the evidence for its publication in 1679 seems unquestionable.

[96] *An Answer to the Appeal from the Country to the City* (1679), pp. 13–15, 37. L'Estrange made similar arguments in *The Case Put Concerning the Succession* (1679), of which Pepys received a copy in late October (*Letters and Second Diary of Samuel Pepys*, ed. R.G. Howarth [1932], p. 102).

[97] Scott, *Restoration Crisis*, p. 21.

and the extent of political obedience. Supporters of the bill claimed that the duke of York was 'no more than the meanest persons in the kingdom', and that the collective power of all the people as represented in Parliament was the source of the King's authority: 'thus a King is not for [hi]s own sake, but [hi]s Subjects sake only; and we have in truth rather title &c to him than he to us'.[98] In other words, the monarchy had been created by the people, who held sovereign power through their representatives in Parliament, and not by divine right perpetuated by hereditary succession. The refutation of *jure divino* ideas had begun in earnest during the second election campaign of 1679. As discussed in the last chapter, summer election tracts as *The Free-holders Choice* and *The Character of Popery and Arbitrary Government* contained bitter denunciations of high-flying clergy for corrupting the mind of the Prince with arbitrary and unmanly maxims of government, setting up 'absolute monarchy to be *jure divino*' and teaching that men had 'no property either in their lives or goods, but during the prince's pleasure'.[99] Subsequent propaganda followed a similar vein, and developed the case against the divine right theorists. *The Case of Succession to the Crown* attacked men who justified introducing 'absolute tyranny under the title of divine right, which consists neither with the Law of God, nor Nature', and again asserted that all men were represented in Parliament. It also gave an account of the evolution of society in order to explain how the people had first come to be ruled by law and by a legislature:

Men at first, before they were associated in societies, had no particular Laws to be ruled by but the law of nature and of reason, which is all one, which lex natura leaves all things common, which is status belli and gives a man right to what he can get, there being no public laws to distinguish and defend properties.

Men therefore entered society to restrain the stronger from invading the weaker, and for mutual love and protection, choosing arbitrators to determine controversies. The law, the author claimed, was 'for the good of them for whom it is instituted', and 'all laws that tend not to the public good, nor preserves that right due to the commonalty, are unjust and void'. The author had tried to convince his readers that 'here you see that monarchy is far from being *jure divino*, or by the law of nature, but ariseth by consent; so that the

---

[98] *A Plea to the Duke's Answers* [1679], pp. 2–3. It was referred to by *The Case Put Concerning the Succession*, which, as already noted, was published in the autumn of 1679.

[99] *Freeholders Choice* (1679), p. 2; *The Character of Popery and Arbitrary Government* (1679), p. 4. The latter also argued that original institution of Parliament was for the preservation of the people, and that in the rest of Europe such representative institutions had been undermined. *The Character of Popery and Arbitrary Government* (1679) also (p. 5) argued that Parliaments were corrupted when 'either they sit too long, too seldom, or are too frequently dissolved', an attack on Charles's use of his power to summon and dissolve Parliaments. The author may have been Henry Care, since much of the argument was later incorporated into *English Liberties* (1681), which has been ascribed to him.

succession is transferable, when the public safety requires it, and so all statutes tending to the public safety are good'. 'The means and way to preserve the common good and safety is by Parliaments', and the concept of *jure divino* 'throws out this well constituted government, and brings in absolute tyranny, giveing power to invade any man's life and property at pleasure'. Furthermore, the author suggested that divine right succession must have been broken by the Norman Conquest.[100] Nearly all the essential elements of radical 'Whig' thought are present in this pamphlet: a belief in the law of nature, the idea of society by consent founded to preserve property, the importance of the legislature as sovereign, the advocacy of the argument that only laws which tended to the public good were just and an attack on tyranny and on the doctrine of divine right succession.

Yet the debate on the succession was rather one-sided. Most publications on the issue attacked, not supported, the exclusion bill and the principles perceived to lie behind it. L'Estrange's pen, in particular, was extremely busy, and in *The Free-Born Subject* (1679) he tackled a number of opposition maxims. Kings, he claimed, had the right of dominion and the right of property, and were bound to obey the law by honour and conscience, 'but no further', otherwise they would not have sovereign power. The law thus chalked out the subjects' rights 'in case they be invaded', but if the King broke the law the people could only resort to legal remedies, and no violence could be offered against him, 'for popular commotions are the most criminal and dangerous of all sorts of oppressions'. In short, he argued, 'we are to help ourselves by law if we can; but if the law will not relieve us, we must be patient'. Making the same argument in another pamphlet, L'Estrange queried who was to decide when a prince failed in his duty,[101] and attacked the idea of popular sovereignty, a theme that he took up again in *Citt and Bumpkin*, written in the wake of the petitioning campaign. In it he claimed that the doctrine of 'the ultimate sovereignty of the people' led to the subversion of government. One of the characters in his dialogue asks 'what if a King will transgress all the laws of God and Man? May not the People resume their trust?'. The answer, given by another character (significantly called Trueman) was

No ... who are these people? if a representative, they are but trustees themselves ... where are we next then? for if it devolves to the loose multitude of individuals (which you will have to be the foundation of power) you are then in an anarchy, without any

---

[100] W.G., *The Case of Succession to the Crown* (1679), pp. 3–14. *A Word Without Doors* (1679), p. 1, argued that there was no one divinely instituted form of government; the tract was probably printed in 1679, since it was referred to by *A Coffee House Dialogue* (1679?), p. 2, and by *Captain Thorogood His Opinion* (1680), and itself attacks *Great and Weighty Considerations* (1679?).

[101] *The Case Put Concerning the Succession* (1679), p. 21.

government at all ... if you make the government accountable upon every humour of the people, it lapses again into confusion.

Trueman asserted that there was no remedy against tyranny but patience, and refused to allow an appeal to the laws of nature or self preservation because it made the people judges, and would dissolve government.[102]

L'Estrange was not alone in thinking that the publication of *A Political Catechism* recommended 'the doctrine of 1642 to the practice of 1679' or in attacking the ideas of popular sovereignty and the right of resistance against a tyrant.[103] *The King's Prerogative*, a tract written by David Jenkins, a contemporary critic of Parker's work, was published on 20 January 1680, in order to declare that the King could not be judged because he was above the representative body of the realm: the King did not hold his crown by allowance from the people 'but by inherent birthright', and did not derive his power from the people. Other writers took refuge in patriarchalism, the idea that political power mirrored and stemmed from paternal power, to attack the notion of popular sovereignty. *A Letter from a Gentleman of Quality in the Country to his Friend*, which argued that the laws of God and nature forbade the alteration of the succession, cited the patriarchal theory of power, stating that 'by the law of nature the father had rule over his children; and the king over his subjects'. After a digression about conquest and usurpation, the tract concluded that the heir 'derives not the Crown from his predecessor, or the people, but immediately from God'. Another publication in 1679 asserted *The Divine Right of Kings*, arguing that 'kings are *jure divino*, by divine right to be obeyed and not by violent force to be resisted, although they act wickedly'.[104] The title of another tract, *A Letter to a Friend shewing from Scripture and Reason how false that State-Maxim is, Royal Authority is Originally and Radically in the People*, fully reflected its content. The author felt an obligation to refute the 'Leviathan' principle that King and Parliament derived their authority from the consent of the people in the first constitution of the government. He declared that: 'God is the immediate author of sovereignty in the king, and that he is no creature of the people's making.' He also attacked the other 'false state maxim ... that everyone is born a free man', arguing that such a state of equality had never existed and was in any case 'contradictory to the word of God, which teacheth that God did fix government in Adam'. Every man could not be born free because he was born subject to his father and other superiors; neither was every man rational, and certainly not equally rational. In a blistering attack on principles espoused since 1641, the author listed a number of seditious maxims, including the

---

[102] *Citt and Bumpkin* (1680), pp. 37–8.
[103] *The Case Put Concerning the Succession* (1679), p. 25.
[104] *The Divine Right of Kings Asserted* (1679), p. 1.

idea that 'sovereignty is derived from the people by communication, so that they may resume it in some cases'.[105]

The denial of popular sovereignty was made in a host of other publications. *A Word to the Approaching Parliament*, published in October 1679, argued that God created men unequal, and that it was 'this order proceeding from the wisdom of God, that had subjected the multitude to one man'. God made obedience a religious duty, and men should not resist their magistrates, partly because 'subjects cannot understand the true condition of affairs'. Moreover, the tract continued, the kingdom was the Prince's inheritance, not the subjects. *A Letter on the Subject of the Succession*, which had a printed date of 18 September, agreed that nothing could justify rebellion, a view endorsed by *A Seasonable Memento both to King and People*, which denied that the Crown had been established by any 'pact or covenant', and suggested that the people were prone 'to be easily led and perswaded into rebellion under the false show of recovering liberty'.[106] *Great and Weighty Considerations Relating to the D[uke]* enlarged the arguments against deposing a king, stressing the need to trust to providence, even when the nation was persecuted by its Prince. The power of Parliament, the author continued, came from the King, who derived all his authority from God alone, not from the people; therefore 'how can the People deprive their Prince of that which they have no power to give?'. The tract warned of the tyranny of Parliament, and suggested that the 'grand principle' that government was made for the good and welfare of the people, or *salus populi suprema lex est* in Latin, was 'the groundwork of all Anarchy and rebellion'. Comparing the 1679 Parliament with the Rump, it argued that 'these cunning politicians now will have a new model of government', which gave MPs 'an absolute power and independent power, not only over mean subjects, but also over the royal family', including the present King.[107] The writer of *A Letter to a Friend Reflecting upon the Present Condition of this Nation* similarly agreed that Parliament threatened the true notion of liberty and property.[108]

---

[105] *A Letter to a Friend, Shewing from Scripture* (1679), pp. 3–9. *A Word to the approaching Parliament* (1679), p. 3, similarly argued that God made men unequal and subjected the multitude to one man's rule. For the opposite argument that men were by nature equal and that in a civil society man was exempt from the law, see Locke, *Second Treatise*, paras. 4, 94.

[106] *A Letter on the Subject of the Succession* (1679), pp. 7–8; *A Seasonable Memento* (1680), pp. 3–4, 10. The latter (p. 5) nevertheless parted from other loyalist tracts in arguing that subjects had acquired the right to property, which could not be taken from them without consent.

[107] *Great and Weighty Considerations* (1679), pp. 2–8. The tract claimed to have been written on the last day of June 1679.

[108] *A Letter to a Friend Reflecting upon the Present Condition of this Nation* (published by 10 February 1680), pp. 4–5.

The loyalist arguments were taken in a new direction by *Captain Thorogood His Opinion of the Point of the Succession*, which has a printed date of 3 January 1679/80. Some of the author's beliefs were commonplace: he denied that the King was only a supreme governor, though he did talk in terms of the trust reposed in a king, and asserted that monarchy was *jure naturae*, not 'changeable at the will and pleasure of the people'. But he also pointed to one of the crucial problems with his opponents' theory by asking how the will of the people could be known. The people's will, he argued, was only apparent in Parliament, but MPs were not truly representative because the electorate was so small and the constituencies were unfairly distributed. He concluded that 'the supposition of the Parliament's representing the people is a fiction of law'. Granting for the sake of argument that sovereignty did rest with the people, the pamphlet suggested that, since the ruin of society was a common concern, it had to be left to everyone 'to be weighted by their own judgment' because 'as everyone was actually aiding by his choice and agreement in erecting such a dominion, so it's necessary he should by the same means concur to its change and destruction'. Even if Parliament was representative of the people, the author continued, the power of calling the legislature still belonged to the King.[109]

The defence of the King's prerogative to summon and dismiss Parliament at his pleasure pushed the loyalist argument further.[110] *The Inconveniencies of a long continuation of the same Parliament*, published on 28 January 1680 (only two days after the prorogation), regarded frequent dissolutions as necessary 'for the preservation of monarchy'. The 'long continuance of one and the same Parliament, or the same Members in parliament, which are both alike, is the most pernicious thing imaginable both to King and people', and the frequent use of prerogative power showed the people where sovereign power lay. The author denied the validity of Edwardian statutes requiring annual Parliaments, claiming that the King only was to judge when to exercise his authority; if he had admitted the advice of Parliament as necessary, then sovereignty would be 'divided amongst the many'. Frequent dissolutions prevented attempts by the people to 'grapple with the King for a share of the sovereignty'. In his account of the origin and ends of government, the author explained that the word commonwealth had wrongly been used as denoting the rule of the many, and really meant

a lawful government of many families, and that which unto them in common belongeth; and the end and design thereof is, that the wicked be punisht, and the good and just protected. So that it is ... more to the common good when the government is in the hands of one man, than in the hands of many ... Yet the dissolution or

---

[109] *Captain Thorogood His Opinion* (1680), pp. 2–7. Compare pp. 3–4 with Locke, *Second Treatise*, paras. 157–8.

[110] See also Knights, 'Petitioning and the Political Theorists', pp. 99–103.

prorogation of Parliament hath been of late lookt upon to be so high a violation of right, and so great a point of mis-government as if thereby our liberties were lost, and our lives and estates subjected to the arbitrary power and pleasure of our king.

The author hoped that when the present or a new Parliament met 'they may remember it is a great grace and favour in the King to advise or consult with them at any time, and therefore may they not insist upon what belongs not to them'.[111]

It is easy to see how Filmer's *Patriarcha* was published as part, or indeed as the embodiment, of this loyalist attack in the autumn and winter of 1679–80 on the theory of popular sovereignty and the right of resistance. Its account of God's investure of royal power in Adam and his descendants supplied an intellectual alternative to the explanation of political power created by the people, and chimed with the chorus of *jure divino* that loyalist pamphleteers were singing.[112] It was also part of a re-examination of material written in the 1640s that was relevant to the current crisis.[113] Sir John Monson's *Discourse Concerning Supreme Power and Common Right*, originally written in 1641, was published by 2 February 1680, and argued, like Filmer, that power was never originally in the people, that God gave Adam paternal power, and that 'all just power, especially the government of Kings, derives its pedigree from paternal, and is an ordinance of God'; resistance was never lawful.[114] In part, the revival of old works of political theory had been initiated by the repub-lication of Parker's *Political Catechism*, but it must also have drawn steam from the numerous assertions of L'Estrange and others that the principles of the good old cause were being revived and leading the country towards a second civil war in which Charles as well as James stood to lose his crown.[115]

---

[111] *The Inconveniences of a long Continuance of the same Parliament* (1680), pp. 1–3. cf. Locke, *Second Treatise*, paras. 13, 132–4.

[112] See also *Truth and Honesty in Plain English* (1679), chapter 1, which claimed monarchy was a government 'founded in paternity'. For other expressions of Filmerianism see *God and the King* (1680), *Three Great Questions Concerning the Succession* (1680), *The Power of Parliaments in Case of Succession* (1680), *Protestant Loyalty Fairly Drawn* (1681) and *The True Notion of Government* (1681). W. Kennett, *A Letter from a Student at Oxford* (1681), p. 14 praised Filmer. Another edition of *Patriarcha* was published by 15 April 1680 and advertised in the *London Gazette* no. 1503, 12–15 April 1680. Luttrell (*Popish Plot Catalogues*, p. 10) noted that Filmer's *The Power of Kings* (a reprint of his *Necessity of the Absolute Power of Kings*, first published in 1648) had been published by 13 April and condemned it as 'a piece highly advancing the king's prerogative to the perfect abridging the subjects liberties'.

[113] *A True Narrative of the Popish Plot against Charles I* (1680), *The earl of Strafford's Letter (1641)*, *The Last Speech and dying words of Thomas ... Pride* (1680) and *A Panegyrick Upon Monarchy, Written 1658* were printed at the turn of the year.

[114] *Discourse Concerning Supreme Power* (1680), pp. 2–8.

[115] *The Case Put Concerning the Succession* (1679), pp. 19–22; *A Letter on the Subject of the Succession* (printed date 18 September 1679), p. 5. L'Estrange's *Seasonable Memorial in some Historical Notes* (1680) was written to 'lay open the misery and method of the late rebellion; and so to expose it, that the same Project and model may not be made use of for another' (p. 37).

We have already seen how much contemporaries feared civil war at this time, and how it was claimed that the same principles and men involved in the 1640s were now at work again.

In the autumn and winter of 1679–80 the loyalists thus attacked the ideas of the equality of man, the formation of government by popular consent, the representative nature of Parliament, the people's right to a Parliament and their right to resist, suggesting that the principle of *salus populi* led directly to civil war; they asserted instead that the King derived his power solely from God, that he exercised a patriarchal authority with prerogative powers and that he should not be resisted. The frequency and vigour of the loyalist attack called for a reply that rebutted the arguments used to deny popular sovereignty and the right of resistance. A lawyer named Thomas Hunt attempted to do so in his *Great and Weighty Considerations ... Considered*, in which he argued that power was exercised for the good of those that are governed, and that the power of Parliament was unrestrained and unlimited. 'Men make governments and God commands us to obey them', he asserted, and the forms of government were decided by men not God. 'Every form of government is our creation and not Gods ... and was never intended unalterable.' Both King and Parliament 'derived their authority from the consent of the people in the first constitution of the government'.[116] But, effective as Hunt's tract may have been, a work of more intellectual substance was needed to refute the persuasive pens of L'Estrange and others, and to assert positively the doctrines that were now so obviously under attack. It was this need, as well as to justify the ideas behind the petitioning campaign, that may have forced Locke to begin writing his *Second Treatise of Government*.

JOHN LOCKE AND THE *SECOND TREATISE*

The suggestion that Locke wrote, or at least began, his *Second Treatise* at this time has recently become a controversial one. Peter Laslett used bibliographical evidence to show that Locke was drafting part of his *Two Treatises* in the autumn and winter of 1679–80, arguing that his theory for a contractual form of government and for the justification of resistance was 'an Exclusion tract, not a Revolution pamphlet' as had for long been thought.[117] More recently, however, Richard Ashcraft has suggested that 'both Locke's argument and the specific language he employs ... state the position to which Shaftesbury and the radical Whigs had arrived following the dissolution of the Oxford Parliament' in March 1681.[118] The discrepancy in dating is

---

[116] *Great and Weighty Considerations ... Considered* (1680), pp. 4, 8, 20. Hunt also asserted (p. 29) that there were no laws safeguarding property in a state of nature.

[117] Locke, *Two Treatises of Government*, ed. P. Laslett (Cambridge, 2nd edn 1967), pp. 61, 65.

[118] Ashcraft, *Revolutionary Politics*, p. 315. His arguments are put forward in detail in chapter 7.

important in terms of how we interpret Locke's work. To follow Ashcraft's line is to accept that Locke was inspired to write his work as a justification for revolution planned by the radicals in the Shaftesbury circle. Locke thus emerges as a revolutionary in his own right. To accept Laslett's dating still requires considerable re-adjustment to the old view that Locke did not personally sully his hands with day-to-day politics, but, if he was writing to refute Filmer's *Patriarcha* rather than justify revolution, it does not place Locke in quite such an extreme camp. This section will therefore re-examine the political context of Locke's work and suggest that Ashcraft's own technique of relating Locke's theory to contemporary pamphlet literature actually supports Laslett's dating. If we narrow our study from all the material printed between 1679 and 1683 to those tracts published between September 1679 and February 1680 we shall find many of the arguments to which Locke was replying.[119] Of course, such arguments were themselves not particularly novel, and replies to them did increase in volume as the crisis developed; but the juncture of the petitioning campaign, the succession crisis and a free press did provide new conditions in which controversy could flourish. It is thus as a contribution to this vibrant pamphlet debate, of which Filmer's work was a part, as well as a justification of the petitions' demands for Parliament to sit, that Locke's own thoughts may have been first intended;[120] certainly, both the language and the arguments he uses were part of this exchange of ideas.

Locke claimed, in a passage that may be considered as a paraphrase of the arguments used by L'Estrange and other loyalists, that even to ask what were the boundaries of allegiance to an absolute king had become a question that

can scarce be born. They are ready to tell you, that it deserves Death only to ask after Safety. Betwixt Subject and Subject, they will grant, there must be measures, laws and judges for their mutual peace and security: but as for the ruler, he ought to be absolute, and is above all such circumstances ... to ask how you may be guarded from harm or injury on that side where the strongest hand is to do it, is presently the voice of faction and rebellion.[121]

Locke, however, did dare to ask the question, and it is clear that his thesis answered almost every point raised by loyalist pamphleteers in the autumn and winter of 1679–80, giving the impression that they, as well as Filmer,

---

[119] The most important notes on the dating of the publications are those made by Luttrell, who accumulated a very large collection of ephemera, and it is worth noting that this library was kept where Locke and Shaftesbury studied (*Hearne's Remarks and Collections* [Oxford Historical Society, lxxii, 1921], xi. 96). The argument that Locke was not influenced by tracts which were not in his own library is therefore suspect. If Locke did have access to Luttrell's collection, he had pamphlets before him almost as soon as they came off the presses.

[120] M. Goldie, 'John Locke and Anglican Royalism', *Political Studies* xxxi (1983), 61–85, also argues that Locke was attacking others besides Filmer, but focuses on the anti-clerical context of Restoration royalist ideology.

[121] Locke, *Second Treatise*, para. 93. cf. para. 203.

were his targets.[122] Starting from the premise that every man is free, and equal to one another, Locke believed that the law of nature or reason set the bounds to natural freedom. He asserted that in a state of nature, the right of governing and power to govern, is a fundamental, individual, natural right and power; but that in a state of nature property, which was the fruit of a man's labour as well as the broader idea of his life and liberty, could not be protected. Men therefore entered society by joining together to set up judges to decide disputes, and political power was derived from the community of individuals, who empowered a public body to exercise the law of nature and defend his property. This social compact established a legislative power, able to establish rules which a distinct executive power enforced. When an individual was within the community he must accept its rules and rulers; but if the end for which the government was established was abused, the government was dissolved and the power devolved again to the people. It was for the people to decide whether or when their governmental trustees acted contrary to the trust placed in them; if the governors resisted such a judgment, then the state of nature would return. Such a situation would not, Locke believed, happen very often, for the people would not easily react in this way; but if it did, the ultimate appeal was to heaven.[123]

It is evident from this short analysis of Locke's argument in the *Second Treatise* and of the content of the pamphlet literature, how carefully he was refuting the theories offered by loyalists in the autumn and winter of 1679–80 and how closely he was paralleling those offered by writers who justified popular sovereignty in Parliament. Many of their themes, and the type of language they employed, mirror Locke's. The attack made by *The Character of Popery* on the sycophancy of clergy who 'set up absolute monarchy to be *jure divino*' finds an echo in Locke's opening castigation of 'a generation of

---

[122] He refers to 'some men' and 'flatterers', rather than Filmer alone, when he discusses absolute monarchies, and attacks what 'they' say (ibid, paras. 90–4). In para. 103 he seems to directly refer to those pamphleteers who investigated the origin of government in order to attack the legitimacy of exclusion, and warns them that the debate they engaged in would be 'little favourable to the design they promote, and such a power as they contend for'. *Captain Thorogood His Opinion* (1680), p. 8, and *Great and Weighty Considerations* (1679), pp. 6–7, had discussed the alterations in the Jewish commonwealth to deny that monarchy was elective, but in paras. 108–9 Locke cited Jewish precedent to show that monarchy was elective. Filmer was not the target in paras. 113–14 where Locke discussed the 'objection I find urged against the beginning of Polities, in the way I have mentioned... viz. that all Men being born under Government, some or other, it is impossible any of them should ever be free, and at liberty to unite together, and begin a new one, or ever be able to erect a lawful government'. Locke may here have been referring the points made by Robert Brady's *The Great Point of Succession* (1681), p. 27. If so, this would support Laslett's suggestion (*Two Treatises*, pp. 348–9) that chapter viii was revised in 1681. On the other hand, the objections listed by Locke are remarkably similar to those stated in *A Letter to a Friend, Shewing from Scripture* (1679), pp. 6–7. Locke's comment shows that he was aware of loyalist attacks on a position that had already been established before he was writing.

[123] See Laslett's introduction to the *Two Treatises* for an excellent discussion of Locke's theory.

men ... who would flatter princes with an Opinion that they have a Divine Right to absolute Power'.[124] Similarly, Locke's concern to root his theory in a defense of property rights reflected the concerns expressed in Penn's election pamphlet, *England's Great Interest*, which argued that a man's property (his right to his life, liberties and estate) made him 'a sort of little sovereign to himself. No man has power over his person to imprison or hurt it, or over his estate to invade or usurp it ... now the law is umpire between King, Lords, and Commons.'[125] That idea of the law as umpire is expressed in Locke's argument that civil society was a state 'from whom the state of war is excluded by the Umpirage which [citizens] have provided in their Legislative', and that anyone who took away law 'takes away the Umpirage which every one had consented to'.[126] The essential elements of Locke's work were already present in *The Case of Succession*, which not only gave an account of the evolution of society in remarkably similar terms,[127] but also attacked divine right doctrine and tyranny, and stressed the importance of the legislature. The only major element missing was the justification of resistance, and it is the apparent absence of such ideas in the literature at this time that seems to make 1681, when rebellion was under more active consideration by some radicals, the more likely date for Locke's writing. Yet apart from the fact that such an approach assumes that he was writing to justify an actual intended rebellion rather than a more theoretical defence of the people's rights, one tract did, like Locke, suggest that the prevention of Parliament's sitting dissolved the government and justified an appeal to heaven. *England's Alarm*, published with the date 1679 and published towards the end of the year, argued that without Parliament

it may be said that the people and nation of England (during that casma and gulf of dissolution) have also no being ... and if bad counsel, or thwarting providence, or Romish policy should either prorogue your [MPs'] time or dissolve your being once more, 'tis past peradventure feared, we nor you should live any longer ... so say I to you, if through fear, cowardice or sloath, you should outsleep three quarters of a year more, our Petitions will end, and your work will be finished: Yet will God raise up others yet invisible to deliver his redeemed'.[128]

---

124 *First Treatise*, para. 3.
125 *England's Great Interest in the Choice of the Parliament* (1679), p. 2, which also emphasises the people's power of making laws. Scott, *Restoration Crisis*, pp. 135–6 also notes the importance of the pamphlet in terms of political theory, and suggests (*Sidney and English Republic*, p. 217) that Sidney helped write it. For the loyalist use of the property argument see *Fiat Justicia* (1679), p. 2: 'if it were such a crime to be of this or that opinion so high as to make a man liable to be disinherited, how could any one be sure of what he has?'
126 Locke, *Second Treatise*, paras. 212, 227.
127 Locke's work was subtitled 'an essay concerning the true original, extent and end of civil government'.
128 *England's Alarm* (1679), pp. 4–8. The tract ends with a puritanical attack on the debauchery of London. A warrant, dated 26 November 1679, was issued to seize it (PRO PC2/68. f. 450, privy council minutes). On the same day another was issued against *The Sighs and Groans of the People*, of which no copy appears to have survived, though its title suggests that its content was of a similar nature.

Locke did not employ such religiously apocalyptic language, but the sentiment is similar and it is perhaps significant that his justification of resistance is deliberately couched in terms of an appeal to heaven.

Locke's *Second Treatise* provided a comprehensive rebuttal of the loyalists' arguments put forward in the autumn and winter of 1679–80. In it, he not only re-asserted the doctrine of popular sovereignty, but also showed that its corollary, the people had a right to resist, was not destructive of society and did not lead to anarchy, as many loyalists had asserted. If Locke's work is seen as a contribution to the pamphlet debate that winter, the tension between the radical and conservative elements in his thought may be more explicable, since the work would have been the product of, on the one hand, the need to assert popular sovereignty and, on the other, the need to refute arguments that this doctrine led inevitably to anarchy and rebellion. Thus, having asserted the right of appeal to heaven, Locke was concerned lest 'any one think, this lays a perpetual foundation for disorder; for this operates not, till the inconvenience is so great, that the majority feel it, and are weary of it, and find a necessity to have it amended'.[129] The charge that the doctrine of the good of the people led to anarchy and rebellion was thus flatly contradicted by his insistence that '*salus populi suprema lex* is so just and fundamental a rule, that he who sincerely follows it cannot dangerously err'.[130]

There is one further reason why Laslett's original dating of the *Two Treatises* still seems to be valid. Laslett noted Locke's fascination with Hobbes, but thought that 'it cannot be shown that when he wrote Locke had any recent contact with *Leviathan* or with any other work of Hobbes at first hand'.[131] If, as we now take for granted, Locke was far more aware of events and pamphlets than was once thought, he cannot have been unaware that Hobbes died on 4 December 1679, and that several tracts about Hobbes and his views were published soon after.[132] More importantly, his *History of the Civil Wars*, or *Behemoth* as it is more commonly known, had been printed by early September 1679, and had alarmed the privy council into conducting an enquiry into its publication.[133] Since Shaftesbury was still nominally head of

---

[129] Locke, *Second Treatise*, paras. 158, 168. In his final chapter Locke specifically answered the objection to his theory that it 'lays a ferment for frequent rebellion' by suggesting 'quite the contrary. People are not so easily got out of their old forms as some are apt to suggest' (ibid. para. 223). He even claimed his ideas were the best means to prevent rebellion (ibid. para. 226). Locke refuted the loyalists by stating that 'the end of government is the good of mankind' and that the people were 'more disposed to suffer than right themselves by resistance' (ibid. para. 230). Such a right to resistance, although it 'hath of late been denied' nevertheless existed (ibid. para. 231).

[130] Ibid. para. 158. cf. para. 135.

[131] Laslett, *Two Treatises*, p. 71.

[132] *The Last Sayings* (1680), *The Life of Thomas Hobbes* (1680), *An Historical Narration concerning Heresy* (1680).

[133] PRO, PC2/68, f. 364, privy council minutes.

the council at this time, it is not inconceivable that he should have drawn Hobbes's writings to his client's attention. It may also be significant that Anthony Wood noticed that *Leviathan* itself was reprinted in 1680 'with the old date', a safeguard presumably designed to avoid censure.[134] Whether prompted by such reprints or not, Locke would surely have been driven back to consider the work of Hobbes by the discussion on the state of nature, for at least one controversialist attacked his opponents as 'Hobbeans', and referred to one tract's advocacy of doctrine of the original power of the people as 'our author's Leviathan'.[135]

Ashcraft skilfully uses pamphlet evidence and political circumstance to suggest that Locke wrote his tract in 1681–3; but whilst accepting that this large body of propaganda had relevance to Locke's concerns, we do not have to accept that Locke must therefore have begun writing in response to the height of the printed debate in 1681. If we are looking for what prompted Locke to start his work, we need to find the catalyst for his ideas. I have suggested elsewhere that his involvement in the petitioning campaign may have first set him thinking about his treatise; and I have argued here that such a work was also needed to counteract an aggressive pamphlet campaign by loyalist writers attacking the maxims of popular sovereignty and the right of resistance. By studying the printed controversies of the autumn and winter of 1679–80 in some detail, it is possible to show that Ashcraft was too hasty in dismissing the language of this period as un-Lockean, and that, far from being concerned with other issues, there was a debate about the origin of government and the nature of political allegiance which precisely echoes the themes of Locke's work. And if we suspect that Locke may have begun writing in response to the intellectual controversy in the autumn and winter of 1679–80, then we must retreat from regarding his work as, initially at least, a manifesto for revolution, and see it, as Laslett does, as a contribution to a debate about the nature of government and the extent of political obedience. Filmer's work was chosen as a target because it was the epitome of a set of arguments that were already being aired in print as a result of the debate over the succession and the petitioning campaign. Given Laslett's unrefuted bibliographical arguments for the dating of the second treatise in the autumn and winter of 1679–80, and the influence of the contemporaneous petitioning campaign on Locke's thought, the evidence suggests that Locke may well have begun his work then, even if he revised it later, and, if so, that he aimed to rebut the torrent of loyalist propaganda that, in attacking the exclusion bill, denied the sovereignty of the people. Championing the right of resistance was a logical conclusion from the arguments Locke employed, but it may not initially have been his primary aim. Only later, perhaps, between 1681 and 1689, did

[134] Wood, *Life and Times*, ii. 475.
[135] *A Letter to a Friend, Shewing from Scripture* (1679), pp. 4, 6.

the revolutionary character of the work assume a growing importance. In other words Locke was a radical who became a revolutionary. If he was formulating the reasons why the people might rebel in 1679–80, he was writing, not to urge them to take up arms, but to explain why they would be within their rights if they did so.

CONCLUSION

The winter of 1679–80 was dominated by the campaign to gather support for petitions calling on Charles to allow Parliament to sit in order to discuss the security of the people. The petitioners focused their demands, not on the succession, but on the prosecution of the plot and the need to call Parliament in a time of danger, suggesting that popery and arbitrary government were still the principal concerns. Yet, although the campaign in London represented a high-point of opposition organisation, the national picture revealed the limits of the cabals' powers. They had mustered the signatures of only sixteen peers, and presented only six regional petitions, whilst many more that had been set on foot elsewhere had met with failure. The campaign nevertheless marked an important political and ideological watershed. By siding with the petitioners, and by returning to England against his father's orders, Monmouth had embarked on his ultimately fatal course of appealing to popular support to win his crown rather than rely on the King's favour. More generally, petitioning forced many men at a personal level to commit themselves either to the 'discontented' or to those who saw in the maintenance of the status quo the only refuge from chaos. Petitioning therefore focused dissatisfaction on Charles's 'arbitrary' deferral of Parliament, rather than, or as well as, on the popery of his brother, and at the same time alienated those who saw in the appeal to popular opinion the road to renewed civil war, thereby detaching from the opposition an important section of society which the Court could ultimately woo over to its side. The dubious legality of the petitions, and their parallel with those promoted in the early 1640s, rendered their supporters open to the charge of trying to awe the King into submission and of adopting the tactics of rebels intent on invading the royal prerogative.

Such allegations, on top of the simmering succession crisis, provoked a lively debate over the nature of a subject's obedience and obligation to his Prince and over the constitutional role of Parliament and the people. Loyalists argued aggressively in favour of divine right monarchy, patriarchalism, the supremacy of the King's prerogative powers, sovereignty in the monarch, passive obedience and submission to providence; and against ideas of popular sovereignty, the equality of man, appeals to the law of nature or self preservation or the good of the people, the creation of pacts with the people and against a right of resistance. In order to refute the loyalist position, as well as to answer Filmer's *Patriarcha*, Locke may well have began writing his *Second Treatise*, the arguments and language of which were mirrored in the vigorous press debate and in the controversy aroused by the petitioning campaign and the succession issue. In any case, ideological lines were being drawn that would ripen into opposing political creeds; but before the process of polarisation could continue a number of factors needed to be present. One was the shift from neutrality or hostility to support for the Court, another was for the loyalists to challenge what constituted the will of the people, and another was the deepening of a religious crisis about the role of dissent and the heightening of tension about the succession.

9

Petitioners, abhorrers and addressers: public opinion, February 1680–February 1681

Whereas the winter of 1679–80 helped change attitudes towards the Court's opponents, the period between February 1680 and 1681 contains important shifts in political resolution and activity. Although loyalists had mostly avoided direct confrontation with those petitioning for a Parliament, by early 1681 they were conducting their own campaign, albeit on a small scale, and employing their opponents' own tactics in order to challenge their position. This emerging loyalist vigour explains why divisions strengthened in 1681. But it was not just the loyalists who underwent some transformation over the period. The character of the opposition also underwent a develop-ment, or rather, some of its characteristics that had remained hidden in 1679 were exposed. In the light of the near collapse of Shaftesbury's power in the spring of 1680, and the prominence of local initiative in the addresses presented to MPs during the 1681 elections, the claim that Shaftesbury led and organised a consistently strong exclusionist party nationwide must be questioned. This chapter therefore seeks to show the role that petitioning, abhorring and addressing had in encouraging confrontational politics, and also to chart changes in, and characteristics of, public opinion and political organisation.

A LOYALIST SPRING

During the petitioning campaign of December 1679 and January 1680 the loyalist response had been muted. In December 1679 there had been 'some talke of a Petition of the Loyall Party, to be handed about in each Parish esteeming all enemies to the government that are of, or side with, the Adverse party',[1] and a blank address to this effect, entitled *The Loyal Protestant*

---

[1] UCNW, Mostyn MS 9089, f. 206, newsletter, 23 December 1679; *Mercurius Anglicus*, no. 11, 24–7 December 1679.

Association, had been printed,[2] but never actively promoted.[3] In the absence of a proper channel through which to vent their frustration, some loyalists had pursued spoiling tactics against the opposition's petitions. One navy captain had walked off with a petition which had been circulated in the Amsterdam Coffee House, though he had later been prevailed on to return it.[4] Less obliging were three men who had gone to sign a petition promoted by William Horsley in the Strand and who 'immediately tore it in pieces, and threw it towards the fire', though the culprits soon found themselves before an unsympathetic Grand Jury.[5] Another petition had been burnt at the Sun Tavern,[6] and the idea of a fire had evidently appealed to the opponents of the petition, since they had also lit a bonfire by Bow Church in Cheapside.[7] But the discontent which these actions represent had not been widespread. They had amounted to piecemeal action, often taken by individuals or small groups rather than by a crowd, and had little or no support from members of the City hierarchy, or from the Court. The opposition to petitions had not extended outside London as far as encouraging a rival campaign. Although it was reported on 17 January 1680, that the Somerset Assizes were 'sending up representations to His Majesty of their dislike and aversion' to petitioning,[8] and in Norfolk 'instead of presenting the petition to the Justices of the Session [the grand jury had] presented the promoters thereof',[9] a nationwide campaign of condemning the petitions had not spread throughout the country.

Such a campaign only occurred after a brief revival of cohesion at Court under the Chits ministry, composed of Sunderland, Hyde and Godolphin. Three strands of their policy were especially important in encouraging an incipient loyalist reaction.

---

[2] For a copy ready for signatures see Bod., Ashm. 1680 (2). *The True Domestick Intelligence*, no. 45, 9 December 1679, carried a story about the organisation of a loyal association for the defence of the King's person. As a result, Claypool, the paper's author, was arrested for 'being suspected to be concerned in drawing up the pretended petitions' (*CSPD 1679–80*, p. 307). This is probably the Claypool whom the privy council ordered to be arrested for writing seditious pamphlets (PRO, PC.2/68, f. 472, privy council minutes 10 December 1679).

[3] 'This Petition or Rather protestation takes not with the people neither is there yet any account of subscriptions' (Newdigate newsletter Lc.884, 27 December 1679).

[4] Newdigate newsletter Lc.882, 1 January 1680. *Domestick Intelligence*, no. 53, 6 January 1680, identified him as one Whiston, a captain of a frigate.

[5] *The Domestick Intelligence*, no. 57, 20 January 1680; *An Account of the Proceedings for the Sessions for the City of Westminster* (1680). According to UCNW, Mostyn MS 9089, f. 223, newsletter, 10 February 1680, Jeffreys gave Whitbread, who led the three, £5 to drink the King's health 'and told him hee would bee his councell att any time for nothing'. This claim was repeated in Parliament (Grey, *Debates*, vii. 466–7). Another of the three accused men, named Smallbone, a woodmonger near Charing Cross, was nominated for the new commission of the Lieutenancy in April 1681 (*CSPD 1680–1*, p. 237).

[6] *The True Domestick Intelligence*, no. 55, 13 January 1680.

[7] *CSPD 1679–80*, p. 376.

[8] *HMC Ormonde*, iv. 576.   [9] *Original Papers*, p. 101.

The first was the purge of the commission of the peace, and other local offices, a process initiated in December 1679 and executed in early 1680.[10] The maxim behind the purge was that 'non are to be suffered to officiat that office but such as are well affected both to Church & State',[11] and support for petitioning became one of the criteria for removal. One loyalist recognised the value of petitions as lists of the government's opponents, and suggested to the secretary of state that the oaths of allegiance and supremacy be tendered to all signatories.[12] Although this was impractical, the government certainly used evidence of petitioning against subscribing JPs.[13] When Thomas Thynne requested the return of the Wiltshire petition which he had presented, 'his Majesty told him he would take care of it, and departed to another room', with the result that all the Wiltshire MPs, except Thistlethwayte, who had been involved in the petitioning campaign, were left out of the new commission.[14] Whether the petitions were examined name by name is unknown; but when the King established a committee to consider the commission of the peace, observers noted that it struck off 'all who would not understand, or which is all one, would not obey His Majesty's Proclamation, prohibiting tumultuous and seditious Petitions'.[15] Contemporaries ascribed the purge of Sir James Hayes and Brome Whorwood (MP for Oxford) from the commission of the peace, Lord Herbert of Cherbury's company from the guards, and Lord Huntingdon from his office as custos rotulorum of Warwickshire, directly to their involvement in the campaign;[16] and Judge Atkyns was removed 'for his too publicly giving countenance to the petitions'.[17] Two Lancashire JPs, whom Roger Kenyon noted as having been involved in petitioning, were dismissed, and all the MPs who signed the London petition

---

[10] PRO, PC.2/68, f. 470, privy council minutes 5 December 1679; *HMC Ormonde*, iv. 574; Newdigate newsletter Lc.897, 5 February 1680; ibid. Lc.909, 4 March 1680; BL, Althorp MS C2, Sir William Hickman to Halifax, 18 April 1680. For analysis of the purge see L. Glassey, *Politics and the Appointment of Justices of the Peace 1675–1720* (Oxford, 1979), pp. 45–52, and N. Landau, *The Justices of the Peace 1679–1760* (California, 1984), pp. 73–5.

[11] Congress newsletter 7/43, 20 April 1680.

[12] All Souls, MS 239, f. 204, 'Advantages w[hi]ch may be made by the factious petitioning of his Majesty', signed Thomas Rowe. He also suggested that the petitioners' religious sympathies should be analysed.

[13] *HMC Lords 1678–88*, pp. 186, 193.

[14] *CSPD 1679–80*, p. 377; *Wiltshire Ballad (POAS*, ii. 312–18); *HMC Lords 1678–88*, p. 191.

[15] *Diary of Henry Sidney*, i. 253. cf. Luttrell, *Brief Relation*, i. 37; *The True Domestick Intelligence*, no. 56, 16 January 1680. Ormonde was later informed that in most cases the abhorrers had ousted petitioners (*HMC Ormonde*, v. 502).

[16] Wood, *Life and Times*, ii. 476–7; *Diary of Henry Sidney*, i. 253, 282; *HMC Ormonde*, iv. 574 Bulstrode newsletter, 20 February 1679[80]; Corpus Christi College, Oxford, MS 310, Wood to Fullman, 13 March 1680.

[17] *HMC Ormonde*, v. 273. Atkyns had justified petitioning as a right of the people in response to Scroggs's statement at a sessions dinner that petitioning resembled the tactics of 1641, and Scroggs appears to have informed the King of the remark (*CJ*, ix. 691).

were deprived of their local offices.[18] Although the purge did not remove all critics of the Crown from local influence, and was by no means a simple purge of exclusionists,[19] it undoubtedly favoured and encouraged the loyalists.[20]

They were also heartened by a second government initiative: the enforcement of the Corporation Act as part of a wider policy to appeal to the Church interest. On 12 March 1680 Charles sent a circular letter reminding corporations about the law's requirements, and took active measures to follow it up.[21] Thus on 7 April the privy council ordered the mayor and aldermen of Bedford to appear before them for not enforcing the Act;[22] and the next day secretary of state Jenkins wrote to the mayor of Newcastle hinting that there would be 'inconveniencies and trouble' for some corporations that failed to comply.[23] The implication was that corporations' charters were at risk. Indeed, Charles had already asked the privy council if York had made any slips that could justify the loss of its charter,[24] and in June the deputy lieutenants of Devon suggested that Tiverton be granted a new one because of the borough's failure to enforce the Corporation Act.[25] It is also clear from a series of letters in the Papillon papers relating to Dover that the government was using the threat of revoking charters to force corporations into quiescence, and that Papillon saw the manoeuvre as a means to regulate his borough's magistracy, and hence its election of MPs.[26]

As the enforcement of the Corporation Act shows, the loyalist spring of 1680 drew much of its inspiration from an aggressive attitude towards dissent.[27] In February there was 'great discourse of setting on the execution of the Laws against Non-conformists, and that the King had said of late that

---

18 Lancs. RO, Kenyon MS DDKe/6/21, letter dated 25 February 1679[80]; *HMC Lords 1678–88*, p. 182. Glassey, *Appointment of JPs*, p. 51, remarks on the similar removal of Kent petitioners. For the signatures of the MPs on the London petition see Knights, 'London's "Monster" Petition', pp. 55–6.

19 Glassey, *Appointment of JPs*, p. 50; Challinor, 'Restoration and Exclusion', p. 373.

20 Van Prinsterer, *Archives*, v. 393.

21 PRO, PC.2/68, f. 601, privy council minutes, 12 March 1680; BL, Althorp MS C2, Sir William Hickman to Halifax, 23 March 1680. Charles personally attended the committee set up to purge the corporations (Newdigate newsletter Lc.955, 29 June 1680).

22 PRO, PC.2/68, f. 632, privy council minutes, 7 April 1680.

23 *CSPD 1679–80*, p. 434.

24 *HMC Ormonde*, v. 288.

25 *CSPD 1679–80*, pp. 499–500. Interestingly the legal opinion cited is that of Henry Pollexfen, the 'Whig' lawyer who was later to defend London's charter. The type of charter emerging from the process of review was evident in the case of Hertford, where power was specifically reserved to men who were conformable to the Church of England (V. Rowe, 'Hertford's Borough Charters of 1680 and 1688', in *Hertfordshire in History* ed. D. Jones-Baker [1991], p. 176).

26 Kent A.O., U1015/O25/2–48.

27 For a discussion of this in its local context see C. Lee, '"Fanatic Magistrates": Religious and Political Conflict in Three Kent Boroughs 1680–1684', *HJ*, xxxv (1991), 43–61.

their carriage this last year has been such that they have no reason to expect any favour from him, and that he will take all the advantage against them the Law will give him'.[28] These official noises further encouraged pamphleteers to vent their spleen against conventiclers. The author of *A Letter to a Friend in the Country Touching the Present Fears* summed up the mood of many other tracts printed at this time when he argued that the 'present jealousies which do possess the minds of the people, especially the vulgar sort, may solely be attributed to the great increase of sects and factions amongst us ... I desire you only to peruse the records of 40 and 41 and thereby you will plainly see their pretence to religion and reformation, and their intention to rebellion'.[29] The association of opposition to the Court with dissent and rebellion was made frequently and sharply. As one discontented pamphleteer complained, 'if a man believes it is his duty [to] serve God, his King and Country faithfully, [they] cry him down as a person dangerous and disaffected to the government, to which end they traduce them as fanaticks, schismatics or favourers of them'.[30] The increasingly strident tone adopted by pamphleteers against nonconformists was even reflected by clergymen who had hitherto been considered moderates and reconcilers. On 2 April John Tillotson, dean of Canterbury and an ally of both Shaftesbury and exclusion, preached a sermon that one critic thought was 'downright Hobbism', in which he argued that no-one should affront an established religion, and draw men away from it, on the pretence of conscience unsupported by divine revelation. Although Tillotson's words offended anglicans as well, the dissenters were disturbed by his attack on nonconformity, and one leading divine, John Howe, remonstrated with him until the dean broke down weeping and retracted his view.[31] Less easily persuaded, more outspoken, and consequently more vilified in print, was Edward Stillingfleet, who on 11 May delivered a sermon printed with the provocative title *The Mischief of Separation*. This, as Robert Beddard has pointed out, was widely interpreted as an attack on the existence of nonconformity because Stillingfleet argued that a union of protestants was impossible while nonconformity continued.[32] In other words, he had sided with

---

[28] *Burnet Letters*, p. 8. In April the Bishop of Exeter reported that conventicles had been suppressed, meeting houses pulled down and a preacher named Hallet forced to flee (Bod., MS Tanner 37, f. 17, to Sancroft, 24 April 1680).

[29] *A Letter to a Friend in the Country Touching the Present Fears*, p. 1. The tract was published on 10 February 1680. Luttrell noticed in February how many other libels turned 'all to 41' in their warnings of the danger of civil war (*Brief Relation*, i. 36).

[30] *Answer to the Pretended Letter to a Friend in the Country* (1680), p. 2.

[31] Birch, *Life of John Tillotson*, pp. 66–7. The sermon was printed, on the King's order, as *The Protestant Religion Vindicated*. The logical extension of Tillotson's argument, as Howe pointed out, was that the Reformation had been wrong.

[32] R. Beddard, 'Vincent Alsop and the Emancipation of Restoration Dissent', *Journal of Ecclesiastical History*, xxiv (1973), pp. 163–4. In the dedication, Stillingfleet nevertheless claimed that he 'was so far from intending to stir up the magistrates and judges to a persecution of dissenters, as some ill men have reported, that my only design was to prevent

those who saw in the separation of dissenters a means by which the papists could undermine protestantism. The concern of both Tillotson and Stillingfleet to steer a narrower middle way between popery and dissent reflected how far the idea of comprehension had receded from the heady days of the previous spring, when fear of popery had suggested the need for a second reformation of the established church.

At the same time as loyalist propaganda was becoming increasingly combative, attempts were made to curb the excesses of opposition prints. Thus the third strand in the Chits' domestic policy to quieten the nation consisted of trying to muzzle the press through prosecutions of publishers and writers. The proclamation of 31 October for the suppression of seditious books had proved an almost total failure, and the government had grown increasingly concerned about the involvement of newsmongers in the petitioning campaign, prompting a number of arrests in the winter.[33] The loyalist newswriter Muddiman thought in December 1679 that it was high time for a 'severe inquisition' into the press, and on 28 January 1680 the privy council duly ordered the judges to consider means of suppression.[34] As a result, important opposition publishers such as Benjamin Harris, Francis Smith and Langley Curtis's wife Jane were all successfully prosecuted in February,[35] and, following a proclamation on 12 May which banned all unlicensed newsbooks and pamphlets 'as manifestly tending to the breach and disturbance of the peace', over a dozen newspapers 'left off' publication.[36] The rate of production of tracts appears to have slowed during the spring and summer and, despite a brief surge in July for reasons that will be discussed later, it only regained its former levels in November, once Parliament was sitting again, when the sixth edition of *The Weekly Advertisement of Books* ran to three sides instead of its usual one.[37]

Loyalists drew encouragement from the initiatives concerning the press, corporations and local officeholding, which combined with a decline of the organisational capabilities of the opposition after the high-point of the

any occasion of it by finding out a certain foundation for a lasting union'. At the end of the year Stillingfleet made his position still clearer with the publication of *The Unreasonableness of Separation*. For a discussion of Locke's reply to this see Ashcraft, *Revolutionary Politics*, pp. 490–97.

33 Knights, 'London's "Monster" Petition', pp. 58–9.
34 Longleat, Muddiman newsbook, 12 December 1679; PRO, PC.2/68, f. 530, privy council minutes.
35 Luttrell, *Brief Relation*, i. 33, 35; *Domestick Intelligence*, no. 63, 10 February 1680.
36 *Popish Plot Catalogues*, pp. 20–1; Bucks. RO, Verney mss, M11/34, John Verney to Sir Ralph Verney, 22 May 1680.
37 This is the impression conveyed by Luttrell's *Popish Plot Catalogues*. In January 1680 he collected sixty-nine pamphlets, sixty-three in February, forty-six in March, forty-five in April, forty-six in May, forty-three in June, fifty-one in July, thirty-six in August, thirty-eight in September and thirty-nine in October. As late as 25 October William Lawrence referred to 'this tyme of interdiction of the press' (PRO, 30/24/6A, pt 1, f. 179, Lawrence to Shaftesbury, 25 October 1680).

petitioning campaign. They were also heartened by London's favourable reaction to the duke of York's return from Scotland in late February, when James was greeted with bell-ringing and bonfires, even though Charles told the lord mayor to suppress them on the grounds that they might imply that his brother had left under royal displeasure.[38] One bonfire at Temple Bar even set light to a hat with a green ribbon in it, a symbolic rejection of the Club's recent activities.[39] Some of the bonfires provoked counter-demonstrations of support for Monmouth, and some were promoted from above – the duke of Lauderdale was said to have stumped up £150 for two of them[40] – but their number suggests some indication of genuine popular support. The diplomat Gabriel Sylvius, who had recently arrived in London, was certainly surprised at the warmth of the reception, and there were reports of similar, albeit organised, expressions of joy occurring at Portsmouth, Barham Downs and Canterbury.[41] Moreover, amidst (unfounded) speculation that James would reconvert to protestantism, and that he would be reconciled with Monmouth, the lord mayor and aldermen went to kiss York's hand, an occasion when James specifically thanked them for rejecting the petition in December.[42] The duke even pardoned Sir John Coventry, who had drunkenly accused James of popery, and this 'moderate carriage, even to those who have beene most his Enemys', was observed to 'gaine upon some ill natures'.[43] Accordingly, when the royal brothers went to dine in the City, the balconies along their route were said to be 'filled with people' and the pair were cheered by 'a numerous strayne of people following from the City with Acclamations to the gates of Whitehall'.[44] Not surprisingly, the King and duke were 'delighted with their reception'.[45]

February and March 1680 were very quiet and peaceful months, making it impossible to describe the unrest of the crisis as consistent or continuous. The newswriter Muddiman warned the recipients of his letters not to expect 'so ample accounts as usually' because of the 'vacancy of businesse at home', and the coffee houses were said to find very little to discuss.[46] Seeking to fill the

[38] *HMC Ormonde*, iv. 580; *Currant Intelligence*, no. 5, 24–8 February 1680.

[39] *The True Domestick Intelligence*, no. 68, 24–7 February 1680.

[40] Newdigate newsletters, Lc.905, 24 February 1680.

[41] *Diary of Henry Sidney*, i. 285–6; Longleat, Muddiman newsbook, 2 March 1680; *Currant Intelligence*, no. 7, 28 February–6 March 1680 (the entertainments were organised by Sir Thomas Peyton and Lord Strangford, the latter a suspected catholic).

[42] Newdigate newsletters Lc.904, 906, 908, dated 21, 26 February, 2 March 1680; Congress newsletter 7/26, 2 March 1680; *CSPD 1679–80*, pp. 399–400; *HMC Kenyon*, pp. 115–16.

[43] Bod., MS Carte 243, f. 441, Nicholas Armorer to Arran, 2 March 1680; ibid., f. 442, Thomas Fairfax to Arran, 6 March 1680; Bod., MS Don. C.38, Fleming newsletters, f. 280, 2 March 1680.

[44] Longleat, Muddiman newsbook, 8 March 1680.

[45] NLS, MS 14407, f. 64, Lord Fauconberg to earl of Tweeddale, 28 February 1680.

[46] Longleat, Muddiman newsbook, 16 March 1680; BL., Althorp mss, C2, Sir William Hickman to Halifax, 16 March 1680.

vacuum, loyalism to church and state showed signs of a new assertiveness. The bishop of Chichester gleefully reported that 'things appear with a better aspect th[a]n not long since they did; they tell me the dissenting partye in all parts of this country are more crestfallen since his Ma[jes]ty began to act like himself, like a King and to lett the people know they are but subjects'.[47] The Chits' policy of appealing to the Church interest, by presenting a strong line against both papist and dissenter, appeared to be the way to win support. Sometimes, though, the support was of the wrong sort, for in late March London was disturbed by reports of a plan by apprentices to burn the Rump, and pull down conventicles and bawdy houses.[48] Yet their leader, Thomas Alford, was only taking government policy to the streets when he told his supporters that they should stand for protestantism 'as it is now established by law, and we'll drink the king's good health to the confusion of both papists and presbyterians'.[49] The conspiracy was accused of having had catholic instigators, but neither this, nor Shaftesbury's claims about the existence of a plot in Ireland, revived anti-catholic hysteria.[50] Only an assassination attempt in mid April on the anti-catholic JP, John Arnold, temporarily re-awakened 'men's fears and apprehensions of the plot, which were pretty well asleep', and even that did not generate anything like the alarm triggered by Godfrey's murder in 1678.[51] Belief in the popish threat was increasingly being confined to a radical minority of zealous protestants, and no longer held sway over the public's imagination.[52] One writer thought that even in London it was difficult to find anyone who did not believe 'that the plot was only a piece of state pageantry, & noe reall thing, & that mischief, if true, was fully satisfyd in the death of those few miscreant martyrs they have payd the penaltyes'.[53] There was a great deal of truth in Hyde's statement in April that everything was 'wonderfully quiet, to the great dissatisfaction of some very few that doe all they can every day to make it otherwise'.[54] It was precisely at this time, as we saw earlier, that Shaftesbury's power was thought to be collapsing. Attempts to disturb the peace were therefore seen as factious, and failed to capture popular support. Significantly the government felt strong

---

[47] BL, Longleat mss, M/863, reel v, Coventry papers vol. vii, Chichester to Coventry, 12 March 1680.

[48] *CSPD 1679–80*, p. 423.

[49] *Mercurius Civicus*, no. 2, 24 March 1680.

[50] Bod., MS Carte 243, f. 454, Armorer to Arran, 3 April 1680.

[51] Van Prinsterer, *Archives*, v. 395; BL., Althorp MS C4, Sir William Coventry to Halifax, 20 April 1680.

[52] For attempts to boost belief in the plot see *A Full and Final Proof of the Plot* (1680), *The Plot Revived* (1680).

[53] UCNW, Mostyn MS 9090, f. 22, letter to Thomas Mostyn, 22 May 1680.

[54] BL, Add. 32,680, f. 332, Hyde to Sidney, 6 April 1680.

enough in late April to discredit the story of Monmouth's legitimacy by investigating the sources of the rumour that Charles had married his mother.[55]

Capitalising on the resurgence of loyalty to the Court, attempts were made to present addresses against the winter's petitions.[56] Thomas Dare, who had presented the Somerset petition, was himself presented on 29 March for seditious words, and the prosecuting grand jury took the opportunity to disown the roll of names which he had handed to the King.[57] In April another key petitioner, Francis Jenkes, was prosecuted for seditious words,[58] and Essex and Somerset, both areas affected by the petitioning campaign, made declarations 'to remove the Reproach by disowning their ill doings & declareing that it was not the Bodys of the Counties but some evill men who by undue practices had prevailed upon the unworthy sort of people'.[59] On 17 April Francis Withens presented Westminster's address testifying the city's 'dislike and abhorrence of the late petitions for a Parliament that were carried on there',[60] and although it was reported that at first they 'wanted nothing to do with it', Middlesex followed suit with an address that not only abhorred petitioning, but also swore loyalty to the King's lawful successors.[61] Similar addresses were presented in Lancashire and Berkshire, the latter asserting that 'the power of calling, proroguing and dissolving of Parliaments is his Majesties only Inherent and undoubted right', a declaration which prompted Robert Yard of the secretary of state's office to comment that 'the humour of the people seems very much changed of late'.[62] In May King's Lynn and

---

[55] *CSPD 1679–80*, pp. 447–451, 460. The action was necessary in part to counter the assertions of *The Popish Massacre*, printed to champion Monmouth's legitimacy (*CSPD 1679–80*, p. 460).

[56] Ralph, *History of England* (1744), i. 494, suggests that they followed the declaration of the Scottish Privy council on 28 February 1680, which expressed a 'just abhorrence' of the petitions.

[57] *CSPD 1679–80*, pp. 425, 440; Latimer, *Annals of Bristol*, p. 399. According to a report of the House of Commons the jury was composed 'of persons that had highly opposed petitioning for the sitting of this Parliament' (*CJ*, ix. 691).

[58] *Currant Intelligence*, no. 21, 23 April 1680.

[59] Longleat, Muddiman newsbook, 10 April 1680. *Currant Intelligence* no. 15, 2 April 1680.

[60] Luttrell, *Brief Relation*, i. 41; *The London Gazette*, no. 1504, 15–19 April 1680; *Currant Intelligence*, no. 20, 17–20 April 1680.

[61] Nottingham University Library, DDSR 19/14, L. Champion to Halifax, 24 April 1680 (the letter is in French); *Mercurius Anglicus*, no. 49, 5–8 May 1680, p. 126; *The London Gazette*, no. 1509, 3–6 May 1680. It was promoted by Thomas Rowe, possibly the same Thomas Rowe who had suggested that the petitions be analysed by the government.

[62] *The London Gazette*, no. 1511, 10–13 May 1680 (Lancashire's abhorrence, 22 April 1680); ibid., no. 1509, 3–6 May 1680 (Berkshire abhorrence); *Mercurius Anglicus*, no. 49, 5–8 May 1680, p. 126; Luttrell, *Brief Relation*, i. 43; Bulstrode newsletter, 30 April 1680. A petition for Parliament to sit was delivered to the Berkshire court of sessions but the next day several JPs desired its removal from the rolls of the court (Grey, *Debates*, viii. 72).

Norwich combined their address abhorring the petitions with a message of congratulations to the court on the return of the duke of York.[63] 'Thus the Petitioners', remarked one newswriter, 'whoe had once theire time, see themselves run downe and their proceedings decryed.'[64] Charles even objected to the election in April of Lord Chandos as Ambassador of the Turkey Company, on the grounds that he had been involved in petitioning; Chandos, sensing which way the political tide was flowing, acknowledged his fault, and declared 'that now he abhorred all such practices'.[65]

Although the loyalist newswriter Muddiman wrote that addresses of abhorrence would doubtless 'be the sentiment of all other Corporations when the Act of Parl[iamen]t for perging them of current members shall be put in execution',[66] the momentum of the abhorring movement had nevertheless largely evaporated by the end of May.[67] The addresses had often depended on a few energetic courtiers, such as the earl of Albemarle in Essex, Lord Paston and the earl of Yarmouth in Norfolk and Sir George Jeffreys in London, or on the judges on their circuits.[68] They had not affected many areas of the country, nor invited mass subscriptions. The main value of the addresses, like the petitions they abhorred, was as propaganda, and they were therefore

---

[63] Luttrell, *Brief Relation*, i. 43. For the Norfolk address see BL, Add. 41,656, f. 57; *The London Gazette* no. 1510, 6–10 May 1680, which states that the recorder of Norwich was replaced because of his opposition to the abhorrence. It was presented by the earl of Yarmouth. Yarmouth's son, Hon. William Paston, who presented the King's Lynn address, together with John Turner and Simon Taylor, Kings Lynn's MPs, were denounced as abhorrers in November 1680 (*CJ*, ix. 644). Newdigate newsletter Lc.934, 13 May 1680, also records an address from Lincoln brought by Mr Bertie 'declareing they will stand by his Ma[jes]tye & his lawfull Successors'.

[64] Bulstrode newsletter, 7 May 1680.

[65] Luttrell, *Brief Relation*, i. 42. Newdigate newsletter Lc.946, 10 June 1680, reported that Chandos had recanted his recantation.

[66] Longleat, Muddiman newsbook, 5 May 1680. Dare had been removed from the Bristol Corporation, and the bishop of Bath and Wells remarked that he wished every charter had a clause allowing such a purge (*CSPD 1679–80*, p. 428).

[67] But in June Sir William Danson presented an address from Ripon, thanking Charles for his declaration that he had not been married to Monmouth's mother (UCNW, Mostyn MS 9090, f. 39, newsletter, 22 June 1680), and in July the Herefordshire grand jury refused an abhorrence of petitions (BL, Add. 70,233, unfol. Sir Edward Harley to Robert Harley, 30 July 1680).

[68] BL, Add.32,680, f. 332, Hyde to Henry Sidney, 6 April 1680. Oldmixon claimed (*History of England*, p. 644) that the abhorrences were the products of menaces and frauds. One case may lend some credence to this charge. Sir William Jones thought that the Somerset address had been 'framed by others, and sent to them' and that the under-sheriff had manipulated a grand jury that would pass it (Grey, *Debates*, viii. 33). Sir William Portman pointed out that it 'was not the Gentlemen of Somersetshire that abhorred; it was only the Grand Jury' and Thomas Thynne claimed the bishop's influence there had been behind some of the signatures (ibid., vii. 371).

printed in the *Gazette*. The abhorrences were also influenced by considerations of foreign policy, being printed in order 'to recover the prejudices
which were brought on the King's Affairs in Foreign parts'.[69] From February
onwards the government had been committed to seeking a defensive alliance
with the Dutch against France, and therefore had to show that the King was
strong in his own country; ironically this stand was made by attacking
petitioning, which William of Orange had shown signs of supporting.

As in the autumn of 1679 there were signs in the spring of 1680 that the
loyalists were gaining the upper hand. Even more than the year before,
moderate opinion was being wooed by the policy of steering a middle course
between popery and dissent, even though the enforcement of the Corporation
Act, the purge of local officeholders, and the 'abhorrences' all suggested that
the initiative still had to come from above. The neutralising of the panic
inspired by the Plot had left the majority of the nation slightly directionless,
resenting factious attempts to disturb domestic peace but as yet still to be won
over by the Court and animated into action on its behalf. And in May events
threatened to derail that process altogether.

THE REVIVAL OF PETITIONING

On 13 May Charles again fell ill, thereby once more reviving fears for the
security of religion and liberties. The 200–300 MPs who had gathered for the
prorogation of Parliament on 17 May were reported to have resolved to
remain assembled if his illness continued, and cabals, attended by Monmouth, met at Shaftesbury's house.[70] It was presumably no coincidence that
on 15 May *A Letter to a Person of Honour ... concerning the Black Box*,
which stated that Charles had married Monmouth's mother, was published
'by stealth' and zealously distributed both in London and in the country.[71]
Charles recovered his health, and in reply made a declaration on 2 June
repeating the affirmation he had made in March that he had only ever been
married to the Queen;[72] but the announcement was thought to have been
made in response to pressure from James, and, according to one observer,
'rather animated than discouraged the party'.[73] One sign of this revitalised

---

[69] *Burnet Letters*, p. 21.
[70] PRO, 31/3/145, f. 55, Barrillon dispatch, 20/30 May 1680; ibid., f. 80, 10/20 June 1680.
[71] *Popish Plot Catalogues*, p. 15; HMC *Ormonde*, v. 329; *CSPD 1679–80*, p. 487; Newdigate
     newsletter, Lc.939, 25 May 1680. The tract was written by Robert Ferguson (Ferguson,
     Ferguson the Plotter, pp. 46, 55) For a reply to it see *The Impostor Expos'd* (1681).
[72] *CSPD 1679–80*, p. 502.
[73] HMC *Ormonde*, v. 561. cf. *Burnet Letters*, p. 35: it was 'generally thought that the Duke has
     lost more than he has gained by Procuring the Declaration'.

discontent was the publication of *A Letter to a Person of Honour concerning the King's [Declaration]*, which slighted credibility in the King's protestation, arguing that he had broken his word so many times before that he was hardly to be trusted now. It continued with an attack on James as a papist and a favourer of arbitrary power who ought to be tried in Parliament for his treason.[74] Yet it was a testament to how far the Chits ministry had regained public opinion that, as Barrillon observed, the King's illness did not stir the London population as the cabals had expected;[75] and Sir William Temple had never seen such a large crowd at the duke of York's levee.[76] Outside London the events may only have encouraged further action against dissent. By early June it was reported that 'the penall laws are put in full execution ag[ains]t Nonconformists all over England'.[77] Later that month it was said that over 700 'fanatics' would be prosecuted at the Leicestershire assizes as recusants, and in July that 'they prosecute the Fanaticks very much in the west, endeavouring to hinder [their] meetings'.[78] In the same month, an anglican wrote to archbishop Sancroft urging an attack on both conventiclers and papists, the moral reform of the clergy, and the exclusion of presbyterians from Parliament.[79]

On the other hand, the political initiative was passing out of the government's hands back to its radical critics. As one writer put it, 'there never was such a delirium as this at present in the worlde knowne ... for though the fire lye still, the flame must burst forth, either to consume or purge us of our drosse'. The flames, in London at least, were now deliberately fanned by Shaftesbury. The twin issues of petitions and Parliament's assembly had been relegated in importance during the spring, but they had never entirely been absent. Plans to revive petitioning, including an address from London's common council in order to threaten a recall of loans to the King if the nation's grievances were not redressed, had ignominiously fallen flat in late January and February 1680;[80] but Barrillon reported in April that Shaftesbury still hoped to persuade a London common council to petition for a Parliament.[81] The 'abhorrences' of the petitions had demanded some

---

74 *A Letter to a Person of Honour Concerning the King's Disavowing the having been married to the Duke of Monmouth's Mother* (1680), pp. 5, 9, 15, 23.
75 PRO, 31/3/145, f. 80, Barrillon dispatch, 10/20 June 1680.
76 *Diary of Henry Sidney*, ii. 53–4.
77 Newdigate newsletter Lc.942, 1 June 1680.
78 Newdigate newsletter Lc.995, 29 June; ibid. Lc.963, 20 July 1680. For the bishop of Exeter's repression of conventicles see Bod., MS Tanner 37, f. 17, letter to Sancroft, 24 April 1680.
79 Bod., MS Tanner 37, f. 75, anonymous paper handed to Sancroft, 21 July 1680.
80 *Burnet Letters*, p. 8; PRO, 31/3/144, f. 78, Barrillon dispatch, 12/22 February 1680; Lancs. RO, DDKe 6/21, letter dated 25 February [1680]; Newdigate newsletter Lc.896, 3 February 1680. Burnet wrote to the King on 29 January that petitions were under consultation and that many were inclined to promote them (Bod., MS Add. D.23, f. 5, Burnet to Charles, 29 January 1679/80).
81 PRO, 31/3/145, f. 29, Barrillon dispatch, 22 April/2 May 1680.

response, and although lord mayor Clayton resisted pressure to summon the council,[82] the June shrieval elections gave the opposition a new public platform for their views. After the election of Slinsgby Bethel and Henry Cornish, both subscribers of the London petition presented in January, a petition calling for a Parliament to sit was handed to one of the old sheriffs. The Hall rang with cries of 'Petition, Petition, Parliament, Parliament; in which they were so unanimous', one pamphleteer claimed, 'that by the best observation it is supposed there were not Forty men in the whole Hall that appeared against it'.[83] At the same time a similar petition was prepared by one of the three Grand Juries of Middlesex which was composed of 'very vigorous men'. It was to this jury that Shaftesbury and his followers came to present the duke of York for recusancy, 'in order to mix the two affairs together and to make the people who wanted a Parliament more eager to sustain the accusation against the Duke of York'.[84] Scroggs dismissed the jury, and the petition was temporarily lost, but maximum publicity had been extracted from the occasion,

---

[82] Nottingham University Library, DDSR 219/14, L. Champion to Halifax, 28 March 1680 (the letter is in French). Champion reported that the lord mayor expressed the wish that common council would relieve him of the burden of deciding when to call it by passing an act by which all future mayors would be obliged to call common council once a month. The parallel with the King's prerogative to summon Parliament when he liked must have been obvious to City radicals (for a discussion of the mayor's powers in this respect see G. De Krey, 'The London Whigs and the Exclusion Crisis Reconsidered', in *The First Modern Society*, eds. L. Beier, D. Cannadine and J. Rosenheim [Cambridge, 1989], p. 471).

[83] *A True Account of the Proceedings at the Common Hall* (1680). Sir John Hobart remarked that the petition was 'unanimously' agreed on by the 5,000 who attended (Norfolk RO, KC/7/6/51, Hobart to William Wyndham, 26 June 1680). The King had warned the mayor to prevent the promoting of the petition (Newdigate newsletter Lc.952, 24 June 1680; Leeds AO, Mexborough mss, Reresby 15/38, newsletter, 24 June 1680). According to All Souls, MS 171, f. 119, newsletter, 24 June 1680, two petitions were addressed to the King instead of one to the sheriff and one to the King, and the sheriff therefore refused to read them.

[84] PRO, 31/3/146, ff. 10–11, Barrillon dispatch, 28 June/8 July 1680. The names of the subscribers on the Middlesex Grand Jury were: Charles Umphreville, John Hartopp, John Smith, Arthur Barnardiston, Samuel Harwer, John Roberts, John Pargeter, Michael Caston, John Green, Richard Stevens, Robert Treden, Henry Gerard, John Tuber, Edward Probert, Martin James, Nathanial Grimes, Thomas Evans, William Cleeves and John Keeling (PRO [Kew], Adm.77/1/54, newsletter, 24 June 1680). The Duke of York described the petition as coming from the 'disaffected party' in the City (Van Prinsterer, *Archives*, v. 408). One newswriter described Umphreville as 'a person whose principles are very well knowne, and most of the rest were shopkeepers' (Bulstrode newsletter, 25 June 1680). The sheriff was reprimanded by the lord chancellor for choosing such factious men (Newdigate newsletter Lc.955, 29 June 1680; Congress newsletter 7/67, 26 June 1680). The petition was disowned by the Grand Jury for the Western parts of Middlesex which was sitting at this time (Bulstrode newsletter, 28 June 1680; Newdigate newsletter Lc.953, 26 June 1680; Longleat, Muddiman newsbook, 26 June 1680). According to one report Cornish was foreman of this (Newdigate newsletter Lc.955, 29 June 1680), and John Verney, writing to Sir Ralph Verney, described both Bethel and Cornish as 'great Petitioners, the last being the second man that subscribed the late Petition' (Bucks. RO, Verney mss, M11/34, 1 July 1680). According to Verney, Lord Cavendish went to Windsor where 'he spoke about the sitting of the Parliament; but his Majesty in great anger turned away and went from him' (*HMC Verney*, p. 479).

including a pamphlet which set out the reasons for York's indictment.[85] Shaftesbury appeared to have given up all attempts at compromise and resolved to force Charles to capitulate. The earl's extreme language at this time gave more scope than ever for his followers to be represented as rebels, and it was perhaps for this reason that rifts appeared amongst the bands of radicals.[86] The indictment further alienated moderates such as Sir William Temple, and undermined Shaftesbury's own position by making it appear that his ideological stance was a threadbare cover for a personal vendetta.[87]

Opposition groups in London, however, continued to work for a petition. Although at the prorogation on 1 July the King told the judges to assure the nation that Parliament would sit in November,[88] rumours soon circulated that Middlesex would petition for Parliament to sit immediately.[89] The petitioners were given another opportunity to promote their designs when the disqualification of Bethel and Cornish for noncompliance with the Corporation Act forced a re-election on 14 July. At a stormy gathering, the pair were rechosen on a show of hands, but when a petition for Parliament to sit was suggested the idea was immediately drowned by Court sympathisers who demanded a poll.[90] Recorder Jeffreys, whose unsavoury reputation had already earned him the nickname of 'the foul mouth of the City', had orders to threaten the crowd with the revocation of London's charter, but he was hissed and interrupted.[91] The election of occasionally conforming sheriffs in London, occasioned perhaps by the need to control the political arm of the law in order to prevent it being used against dissenters, signalled a new confidence amongst London's religious radicals.[92] Jenkins thought the

---

85 *Reasons for the Indictment of the Duke of York* (1680). There were rumours in early July that the 'associated noblemen and gentry' would repeat the attempt at Hick's Hall, Middlesex, and at Reading (Bucks. RO, Verney mss, M11/34, John to Sir Ralph Verney, 5, 8 July 1680; UCNW, Mostyn MS 9090, f. 54, newsletter 17 July 1680). For radicalism at Reading at this time see *CSPD 1679–80*, p. 592.

86 *Russell Letters*, pp. 131, 133.

87 Temple, *Memoirs*, p. 350.

88 Charles had told the lord mayor on 24 June that Parliament 'should for certain meet' (Leeds AO, Mexborough mss, Reresby 15/38, newsletter, 24 June 1680). Sir James Hayes reported the same thing, which he had heard from 'a person in very Eminent places who was yesterday long with the King in private' (NLS, MS 14407, f. 67, letter to Tweeddale, 25 June 1680). For Charles's directions to the judges see BL, Althorp MS C5, Thynne to Halifax, 1 July 1680).

89 *Burnet Letters*, p. 39.

90 Leeds AO, Mexborough mss, Reresby 15/73, newsletter, 15 July 1680. A Mr Johnson, a jeweller in Cheapside, had 'opposed the petition when the sheriffs were chosen' (*CSPD 1680–1*, p. 237).

91 Bod., MS Locke B.4, ff. 55–6, copy of letter to Jeffreys, 17 July 1680; *CSPD 1679–80*, p. 554; All Souls, MS 171, f. 121, newsletter 14 July 1680; Bucks. RO, Verney mss, M11/34, John Verney to Sir Ralph Verney, 15 July 1680; BL, Althorp MS C5, Thynne to Halifax, 15 July 1680.

92 The religious implications of the elections were apparent in the enforcement of the corporation act for livery men (Newdigate newsletter Lc.954, 1 July 1680; All Souls, MS 171, f. 121, 19 July 1680; *CSPD 1679–80*, p. 560).

contest in London a purely local affair, rather than a trial of strength between the King and his critics, but he recognised that the slates of candidates represented 'the conformists or non-conformists';[93] and Bethel, with his history of activity under the Commonwealth and abjuration of the Stuarts, symbolised the loyalists' greatest fears of a resurgent republican-dissenting alliance that would turn all to confusion.[94] Nevertheless, the declaration on 29 July of the results of the poll allowed the presentation to the lord mayor of a petition asserting London's loyalty '& at the Tayle of it a Panegyrick for the sitting of the Parl[iamen]t'.[95] This was read, despite opposition from some aldermen,[96] and 'halloed up' before being 'cheerfully' accepted by the lord mayor.[97] The petition was in print by the next day,[98] and shortly afterwards Clayton formally presented it to the King. The Court, though angry at the turn of events,[99] could perhaps count itself lucky that a more aggressive petition drawn up by Papillon had been 'waved and another presented in Lieu thereof', since this other draft claimed that there had for many years been a popish plot to destroy protestantism and the established government, and concluded that only the King in Parliament could make suitable provision to safeguard the nation.[100] Even so, the King pointed out that the petition with which he was presented omitted a declaration of loyalty to the church as it was then established.[101]

Outside London the petitioners once again had much less success. 'The Petitioning humor is not so high in the Country as it was of late in the City', remarked Jenkins,[102] who nevertheless feared that the petitioners' activities

---

93 *CSPD 1679–80*, pp. 564–5. Nonconformist ministers were reprimanded in mid July for having 'been busy promoting petitions' (*HMC Verney*, p. 479).

94 Bod., MS Eng. Lett. D.72, O. Wynne to Bulstrode, 19 July 1680.

95 Longleat, Muddiman newsbook, 29 July 1680.

96 Notably Sir Robert Vyner and Sir George Waterman (*CSPD 1679–80*, p. 581).

97 Leeds AO, Mexborough mss, Reresby 15/108a, newsletter, 29 July 1680; Longleat, Muddiman newsbook, 29 July 1680. Jenkins referred to the petition as 'stale and ridiculous after so many declarations of His Majesty that he intends the Parliament shall sit in winter' (*CSPD 1679–80*, p. 579). According to Bulstrode newsletter, 30 July 1680, the lord mayor had remarked that he 'could have wished the clause relating to the Parliament had been omitted'.

98 *CSPD 1679–80*, p. 580.

99 PRO, 31/3/146 f. 50, Barrillon dispatch, 5/15 August 1680; Bod., MS Carte 222, f. 228, newsletter, 7 August 1680.

100 Kent AO, U1015/07/4, 'Petition of Common Hall' (printed in *The Memoirs of Thomas Papillon of London 1623–1702*, ed. A.F.W. Papillon [Reading 1887], pp. 158–9). Though this draft was rejected Papillon still presented the other petition (Bulstrode newsletter, 6 August 1680).

101 Newdigate newsletter Lc.969, 5 August 1680.

102 PRO, SP.104/68, f. 9, letter to Hyde, 10 August 1680.

augured civil war.[103] A Petition begun in Exeter 'went not far',[104] and when a petition was presented to the York Grand Jury which had just acquitted the catholic Lady Tempest, it was torn up by a Mr Darcy. Sir John Reresby was then approached by fifty gentlemen who desired him 'to draw up something to expresse an abhorrence of such proceedings'.[105] The revival of petitioning had thus provoked a renewal of the abhorring campaign. At Durham the Grand Jury presented an address thanking the King for his care of the people and religion, assuring him that there had 'not been the least offer made for promoting any petition in the county', an address which so pleased the King that he ordered it to be published 'totidem verbis'.[106] Kent's and Devon's grand juries also renounced petitioning,[107] though the Carlisle grand jury, whilst refusing a motion of one of its members for a petition for Parliament to sit, 'would not condemn other Grand Jurys that had petitioned believing they designed the nation's good'.[108] This second round of abhorrences, as Reresby's comments illustrate, seems to have owed more to local initiative, though their small number suggests that their value was once more greater as propaganda than as a guide to the political disposition of the country.

The attempts to indict York and to petition for a Parliament showed that Shaftesbury had once again put himself at the head of public discontent; but although this had the effect of making him look powerful, Secretary Jenkins observed that the malcontents 'are not either in number or quality what they pretend to be, & the bulke of the nation is in a far better temper than it was 6 or 8 months agoe'.[109] It was not long, he felt, before the 'moderate sort of men ... [see] how far they have been hurried on beyond their just measures by an unreasonable jealousy of their governors'.[110] The government was quietly confident that the majority of the nation were no longer prepared to join with the opposition. Even London returned quickly to a state of calm after the shrieval elections; and the prorogation on 22 July was heard by only a thin

103 *CSPD 1679–80*, p. 567.
104 *CSPD 1679–80*, pp. 566–7. The petition was organised by Sir William Courtenay, Sir Francis Drake, Harris, Glyde and others who met at the Bear Inn. Newdigate newsletter Lc.969, 5 August 1680, reported news from Devon of several people who had signed a paper 'promising to stand by one another in petitioning' for a Parliament.
105 Newdigate newsletter Lc.970, 7 August 1680; Reresby, *Memoirs*, p. 199; Longleat, Muddiman newsbook, 10 August 1680; UCNW, Mostyn MS 9090, f. 62, newsletter, 10 August 1680. Newdigate newsletter Lc.970, 7 August 1680, blamed Sir John Kaye for tearing the petition.
106 *CSPD 1679–80*, p. 605; J.S. Cockburn, *A History of English Assizes 1558–1714* (Cambridge, 1972), p. 251; Durham University Library, Old Library MS E.i.9, f. 146, Durham address.
107 *CSPD 1679–80*, p. 607; *The London Gazette*, no. 1537, 11 August 1680; Luttrell, *Brief Relation*, i. 53; Newdigate newsletter Lc.968, 3 August 1680. Bulstrode newsletter, 2 August 1680, carried advance notice of the presentation of the Kent address.
108 Newdigate newsletter Lc.878, 31 August 1680.
109 PRO, SP.104/67, Jenkins to William, 29 June 1680.
110 *CSPD 1679–80*, p. 587.

House, 'just the fatall number of 41' according to one source.[111] By mid August the newswriters could again find very little to report, and even as Parliament's sitting drew near there was 'no extravagance either in town or country'.[112] Yet this quietness was part of the government's problem. Although not so anti-Court as they had been, the provinces were generally still unprepared to move on to the offensive against the court's enemies, since such action would disturb the tranquillity. The new round of addresses had suggested that this attitude was beginning to change, at the same time as highlighting how far the loyalists had yet to go to persuade the nation of their cause. A spirit of cautious neutrality still seemed to pervade.

Moreover, the nearer Parliament approached and the more aggressive the opposition cabals became, the less the government felt able to employ its most effective weapon, the enforcement of laws against dissent. The attempt to purge the corporations of nonconformists had helped polarise the conflict in religious terms, but it may also have heightened tensions between loyalist corporations and freemen bodies where dissent was rife, and in any case the initiative to enforce the Corporation Act was now threatened by the need to conciliate opinion before MPs assembled. Charles told the circuit judges in July to enforce the laws against the papists, but to spare 'moderate peaceable dissenters', an abandonment of the twin-track campaign to prosecute both catholic and protestant nonconformity that disillusioned many episcopalians and strict Churchmen.[113] At about this time, lord privy seal Anglesey informed the mayor of Gloucester, who had complained about a noncon-formist preacher, to emulate the King's clemency towards protestant dis-senters; and a prosecution against Sir Patience Ward for failing to take the sacrament was halted by the attorney general. Jenkins wrote that there were no prosecutions of conventiclers in and around London, for 'certainly the true season to suppress sectaries has been long since lost. They have put us now on the defensive.'[114] The swing back towards tenderness for nonconformity was symbolised by the publication just before Parliament sat of *The Naked Truth. The Second Part*, which was considered 'so severe a book against the B[isho]ps' that its author, Edmund Hickeringill, was in danger of arrest; significantly he had in May preached a strong sermon called *Curse ye Meroz* 'ag[ains]t the fanaticks' only a few days before Stillingfleet's attack on separatism. The contrast in tone indicated just how far the tide had turned.[115] Stillingfleet, too, was preparing a more conciliatory book, which made

[111] PRO, SP.104/68, f. 8, Jenkins to Sidney, 6 August 1680; Leeds AO, Mexborough mss, Reresby 15/39a, newsletter, 22 July 1680.
[112] All Souls, MS 171, f. 123, newsletter, 31 August 1680; BL, M/904 reel viii, Longleat (Thynne) mss, vol. xv, f. 16, Halifax to Thynne, 18 October 1680.
[113] BL, Althorp MS C5, Thynne to Halifax, 1 July 1680; PRO, 31/3/146, f. 17, Barrillon dispatch, 5/15 July 1680.
[114] *CSPD 1680–1*, pp. 45–6; Bulstrode newsletter, 24 September 1680.
[115] Newdigate newsletter Lc.996, 19 October 1680; *Popish Plot Catalogue*, p. 20.

specific proposals of how the Church might make concessions to comprehend moderate nonconformist sensibilities.[116]

Further evidence that the government had been wrong-footed came from the reaction to Monmouth's summer tour of the west country where he 'was suffered without check to go from place to place and county to county and was met and caressed like an heir apparent, whilst some thought the king being so passive at it was not therewith displeased'.[117] Once again Charles's unwillingness to act thus confused and undermined a coherent Court policy. Despite the declaration denying Monmouth's legitimacy, Monmouth appealed for popular support, and was greeted with large crowds and a rash of pamphlets supporting his cause.[118] Although some of these were answered in print there was no loyalist press campaign to prepare public opinion before Parliament sat, and it was reported in August that L'Estrange had been told by the King 'to forbear writing such papers as tend to division'.[119] The prospect of Parliament's assembly had pushed the government, like much of the public as a whole, into a passive neutrality. The path was therefore clear again for the radicals to assume the direction of affairs.

PETITIONING AND PARLIAMENT

The day before Parliament met on 21 October, London's common council voted an address to the departing lord mayor Clayton, thanking him for 'his asserting the right of petitioning his Ma[jes]ty for the calling and sitting of a Parliam[en]t, notwithstanding all opposition to the contrary'.[120] The abhorrences against petitions were also still fresh in the minds of MPs, and were referred to as a grievance in the debate on 26 October, when the House also re-affirmed its commitment to preventing a popish successor.[121] The next day Sir Gilbert Gerard, the presenter of the London petition in January, moved that it was the subject's right to petition, and found unanimous support.[122] The matter was pursued further by a vote which declared that 'to traduce such Petitioning is a violation of duty', and that to represent it to the King as seditious was to betray the liberty of the subject, subvert the constitution and introduce arbitrary government.[123] A committee was appointed to

116 *The Unreasonableness of Separation* (1680), published in December. For a discussion of the tract see Spurr, *Restoration Church*, pp. 155–8.
117 *HMC Ormonde*, v. 561.
118 *A Letter to his Grace the D. of Monmouth* (1680), *A True Narrative of the Duke of Monmouth's late Journey* (1680), *His Grace the Duke of Monmouth Honoured* (1680), *The Obscured Prince* (POAS, ii. 257–60).
119 *CSPD 1679–80*, p. 596.
120 CLRO, common council Papers 1680, minutes of the meeting 20 October 1680.
121 Grey, *Debates*, vii. 362–3.
122 Ibid., vii. 369–70. The vote was printed by Francis Smith as *Wednesday Octob. 27 1680 Two Unanimous Votes ... concerning the Subjects right in Petitioning*.
123 Ibid., vii. 371–2.

enquire into abhorrers with only three of its forty-eight nominated members of a doubtful anti-Court sentiment.[124] Indeed it included a number of men, such as Edward Rigby, Sir John Hartopp, Thomas Papillon and Thomas Horde, who had taken an active part in the campaign.

Petitioning was an important issue for the opposition for two main reasons. First, it was an issue that maintained the momentum for redress of grievances in the House of Commons even after the exclusion bill had been passed. Second, the attack on abhorrers, who were castigated as the betrayers of liberties, acted as a springboard for wider attacks on government officials and supine judges. More immediately it led to the expulsion of two MPs who supported the Court, and thereby cowed other loyalists.[125] One of the MPs expelled was Sir Francis Withens, MP for Westminster.[126] He had presented an abhorring address and, despite an abject confession of the people's right to petition, was turned out of the House with the Speaker's condemnation ringing in his ears that he had committed 'a crime against those unborn'.[127] Withens was singled out because his address had 'led the dance' of ab-horring,[128] but it was no coincidence that the charge against him was pro-moted by Sir William Waller, the energetic hunter of papists and 'great man for petitioning',[129] who had unsuccessfully contested the Westminster elec-tion with Withens and who gained the seat after Withens's expulsion; or that one of the witnesses against Withens was Aaron Smith, an active petitioner.[130]

One of the reasons why the Commons had added the vote about pursuing abhorrers was, as both Winnington and Sir Robert Howard hinted, to punish those responsible for the proclamation in December 1679 which had con-demned tumultuous petitioning.[131] The principal targets of the inquisition on abhorring were therefore the two Court advisers, Sir George Jeffreys and

[124] *CJ*, ix. 640.
[125] Sir Robert Cann was expelled for declaring disbelief in the plot (*History of Parliament*, ii. 6), but Ailesbury ascribed the real reason to Cann's involvement in abhorring (*Ailesbury Memoirs*, i. 47). For Cann's opposition to petitioning in Bristol see chapter 8. Algernon Sidney thought six or seven MPs would be expelled for 'abhorring' (*Sidney Letters*, p. 101). Roger North claimed (*Lives of the Norths*, i. 366), that Sunderland used the attack on abhorrers to try to ruin other ministers, notably Francis North.
[126] Titus later claimed the credit for his expulsion: *Killing no Murder* (1689), unpaginated first sheet.
[127] Grey, *Debates*, vii. 378–9, 385–91. Withens had also been responsible for returning the grand jury to hear the duke of Buckingham's case (ibid., vii. 379). North (*Examen*, p. 550) claimed that Withens would have been supported if he had stood up for what he had done, but his submission 'so disgusted even his friends, that they joined all with the Country Party and with one common Consent *Nemine Contradicente* kicked him out of the House'.
[128] Grey, *Debates*, vii. 390.
[129] Wood, *Life and Times*, ii. 484.
[130] Grey, *Debates*, vii. 385–91; Newdigate newsletter Lc.1001, 29 October 1680. Smith testi-fied that Withens said that 'Peticioning was the seed and Spawne of Sedition after the King had forbidd it' (Bulstrode newsletter, 5 November 1680). For Smith's petitioning activities see Knights, 'London's "Monster" petition', pp. 53–4.
[131] Grey, *Debates*, vii. 363, 369.

Francis North. Jeffreys had wanted a proclamation that would have allowed JP's to prosecute anyone who petitioned,[132] and his uncompromising line as recorder of London, together with his association with James, had long made him unpopular with a group of City radicals.[133] Indeed, just before Parliament sat Bethel had attempted to prosecute the Recorder and pack a jury to secure his conviction.[134] It is therefore not surprising that it was Pilkington, himself a subscriber to the petition promoted in London the previous winter, who on 27 October delivered the City's address against Jeffreys for threatening petitioners and jurors.[135] Condemning him for his part in 'murdering Petitions', the House resolved on 13 November that he had betrayed the rights of the subject and an address was passed requesting his removal from all public offices,[136] with the result that he quitted his recordership 'in fear'.[137] Moreover, the attack on abhorrers became an important vehicle for the condemnation of Charles's judges.[138] Lord chief justice North, who had drawn up the December proclamation, accordingly found himself the subject of an impeachment.[139] On 23 November a debate on petitioning turned into an assault on Sir William Scroggs,[140] and Justice Jones was ordered to be impeached for his severe treatment of the petitioner Thomas Dare.[141] There are signs, however, that the investigation of 'abhorrers' lost the Commons

[132] North, *Examen*, p. 544.

[133] 'Sir Geo Jefferyes has had a very uneasy time in the citty since his being the Duke [of York]'s solicitor' (BL, Add. 29,557, f. 85, William Longueville to Lord Hatton, 21 January 1678/9).

[134] Congress newsletter 7/111, 16 October 1680. When the new sheriffs were sworn in 'a Petition was put up for removing the Recorder' (Newdigate newsletter Lc.989, 30 September 1680). The attack was prepared by 'many cabals' (Longleat, Muddiman newsbook, 19 October 1680), and Jeffreys objected to the jury 'sayeing that most of them wer knowen dissenters'. Cornish refused to become involved in the dispute and the jury was discharged. Newdigate newsletter Lc.995, 16 October 1680, claimed that Jeffreys accused the jury of being composed of 'men prejudic'd ag[ains]t him'.

[135] Grey, *Debates*, vii. 373.

[136] Ibid., vii. 460–71. In this debate Ward informed the House that Jeffreys had given the lord mayor and aldermen advice in December 1679 that petitioning 'was bordering upon treason, and the beginning of Rebellion, and promoting sedition'.

[137] BL, Add. 32,578, f. 5, notes made by North. Charles quipped that Jeffreys 'was not Parliament proof' (North, *Examen*, p. 551).

[138] On 27 October Sacheverell had said that if the judges could persuade the King to issue the proclamation against petitioning 'they are master of the whole government, and the King shall never know what is wrong, and consequently cannot do us right' (Grey, *Debates*, vii. 370). cf. Harbord's speech on 29 October (ibid., vii. 387). Titus remarked that 'as long as Judges hold their places *durante bene placito*, they will do what they please, and there is an end of your Justice' (ibid., viii. 58).

[139] Grey, *Debates*, viii. 61–71. The attorney-general, Creswell Levinz, revealed that North sent him a draft (North, *Examen*, pp. 551–2). The usually moderate Hickman, a friend of Halifax, supported the impeachment of North.

[140] Grey, *Debates*, viii. 53. See *A Collection of the Substance of Several Speeches and Debates* (1681), p. 3, for Winnington's verdict on the judges that 'twas not Petitioning but Parliaments they Abhorr'd'. All Souls, MS 242, f. 255, is a slightly different version of the same speech.

[141] North, *Examen*, pp. 562–3; *CJ*, ix. 691–2.

some public support. The committee ordered a number of opponents of petitions to be taken into custody, but these arrests raised questions about the extent of the Commons' jurisdiction outside the House.[142] When Ralph Stawel, the foreman of the Exeter grand jury that had abhorred petitioning, refused to submit to arrest, the committee found itself powerless to act,[143] and its activity was later used as evidence that the greatest threat to the liberties of the subject came from Parliament itself.[144] The issue had helped tarnish Parliament as an arbitrary institution that threatened, rather than protected, individual freedoms.

The consideration of petitioning had also stirred the City into renewed activity. The exclusion bill had not been carried up immediately to the Lords after its passage in the Lower House partly in order to allow the weight of London's opinion to awe those peers who were undecided, and on 12 November a common council considered making 'some kind of addresse to his Ma[jes]tie in this great conjuncture of passing the bill'.[145] The text, drawn up by Clayton, Player, Pilkington and Dubois, requested the King to 'hearken and Incline to the Humble Advice of ... your great Councel of Parliment' and to allow it to sit until it had perfected its business; but Charles told its presenters 'that they should meddle with those things that concerned them; he knew what he had to do without their advice'.[146] To emphasise the union of

---

[142] *Ailesbury Memoirs*, i. 47. Those taken into custody included the foremen of the Devon and Somerset grand juries, the clerk of Westminster assizes, the clerks of the peace and under-sheriffs for the above counties (seventeen names are printed as *A List of Abhorrers* [1681]). The 'abhorrers' Sir Brian Stapylton and Sir Thomas Mauleverer were untouchable because of Sir John Reresby's careful wording of the York address (Reresby, *Memoirs*, p. 202; Grey, *Debates*, vii. 393). In Oxford at the beginning of October John Pratt toasted 'the confusion of all Popish Princes', and when four dons reproved him Pratt complained about them for 'talking against petitioning' (Wood, *Life and Times*, ii. 498). Bod., MS Wood F.39, f. 35, A. Allum to Anthony Wood, 12 November 1680, gives information about the Oxford ab-horrers: Harding of Trinity, Mills of Queens, James and Trelawney of Christ Church, Slaughter and Ellwood of Corpus Christi, Crimes of Exeter, Thornton of Wadham, and Davenport of Oriel. Their accuser was a Fellow of Wadham, 'Prat's sonn', a member of the Green Ribbon Club who supported Monmouth. Sir John Kaye and Charles Bertie were said to have wanted to go abroad before Parliament sat to prevent interrogation about their abhorring activities (*CSPD 1679–80*, p. 596).

[143] North, *Examen*, p. 561.

[144] see chapter 10. *A Letter from a Person of Quality to His Friend* (1681), p. 5, defended Parliament by arguing that 'the power of that House concerning the taking men into custody has not yet received an exact adjustment'. *A Just and Modest Vindication* (1681), p. 15, argued that abhorrers had infringed Parliament's prerogative. *The Lawyer Outlaw'd* (1683), p. 17, questioned the right to imprison for such offenses.

[145] PRO, SP.104/67, ff. 17–18, Jenkins to William, 12 November 1680. The text was printed as *To the King's Most Excellent Majesty* (1680).

[146] CLRO, common council papers 1680, minutes of meeting of 12 November 1680; *The Humble Petition and Address* (1680); *Letters of Pepys*, p. 107; Luttrell, *Brief Relation*, i. 60. Sir John Lawrence and Michael Godfrey had also been named to help draft the address. According to Barrillon (PRO, 31/3/147, f. 30, 15/25 November 1680), 300 had attended the meeting, which also voted to place an inscription on the Monument declaring papists to have been responsible for the Great Fire. The text for this was approved on 17 June 1681.

City and Parliament, a long address from the Commons was presented the same day, though again Charles was observed to show great impatience when 'the part w[hi]ch mentioned the ill counsels w[hi]ch had been given for dissolving & proroguing of Parl[iamen]ts' was read, and the King stomped off without a word.[147] Undeterred, at the end of November a London Grand Jury accepted not only another indictment of the duke of York for recusancy, but also an address which thanked the King for letting Parliament sit and desired that he might listen to its advice and not dissolve it.[148] The addresses were evidence of the strengthening alliance between Parliament and the City, where many MPs had taken lodgings at the beginning of the session, and of the continuing importance of the King's control of the length and timing of parliamentary sessions.[149] It was increasingly apparent that a polarisation between abhorrers and petitioners had emerged both inside and outside Westminster. On 17 November pictures of abhorrers, including Jeffreys, had been burnt with the Pope (see print),[150] and it was reported that, at the election for London's common council in December, abhorrers or those who had hindered petitioning were rejected.[151] Indeed some even seem to have welcomed the label abhorrer as a mark of loyalty. 'Shabby' Rawlins, a former corrector of the press, made a dramatic declaration in Richard's coffee house, in which he attacked the House of Commons and boasted that he was an abhorrer of petitions; when asked if he were mad he replied 'if I am Mad, I am qualified for a Parliament man'.[152] It was in this atmosphere of bitterness that on 10 January 1681 Charles prorogued Parliament, though not before a motion had been made that Parliament should retire to the City, and that it should only be prorogued by a commission of the privy seal.[153]

[147] J. Rylands Library, Legh mss, Richard Sterne to ?Richard Legh, 13 November 1680.

[148] Dr Williams's Library, MS 31.P, Morrice Ent'ring Books f.280, 30 November 1680; Longleat, Muddiman newsbook, 29 November 1680. 'The Court tooke it but withal lett them know they stood not obliged to it', and the address was published on 8 December (Bod., Nichols Newsp. 2B/313).

[149] *CSPD 1680–1*, p. 62: PRO, 31/3/146, Barrillon dispatch, f. 107, 7/17 October 1680; ibid., f. 109, 11/21 October 1680.

[150] PRO, 31/3/147, Barrillon dispatch, f. 48, 22 November/2 December 1680. *Jesuite in Masquerade: or the Sheriff's Case Uncas'd* (1681), p. 6, remarked that 'a man may suffer Martyrdom in Effigie upon Queen Elizabeth's day for being an Abhorrer'. See p. 149.

[151] *CSPD 1680–1*, p. 106. *A Seasonable Momento for all that have Voyces* (1681), p. 1, advised voters in the general election to beware of abhorrers. A.G. Smith, 'London and the Crown 1681–5' (University of Wisconsin, Ph.D. 1967), p. 24, has argued that slightly more 'Tories' than 'Whigs' were elected.

[152] *The True Protestant Mercury*, no. 1, 28 December 1680. 'Shabby' Rawlins was one of the authors of *Heraclitus Ridens*, which began publication in 1681 (T.F.M. Newton 'The Mask of Heraclitus: A Problem in Restoration Journalism', *Harvard Studies and Notes in Philology and Literature* (1934), pp. 154–5). Newdigate newsletter Lc.1054, 15 March 1681, claimed Rawlins lost an eye in a coffee-house brawl after making disparaging remarks about the Oxford Parliament.

[153] PRO, 31/3/148, Barrillon dispatch, f. 19, 10/20 January 1681; ibid., f. 21, 13/23 January 1681. In December d'Avaux reported that the republicans claimed they were resolved to

The year 1680 had witnessed a see-saw of petitioning and addressing movements. The loyalist reaction to the previous winter's campaign for Parliament to sit had taken the form of addresses presented to Grand Juries 'abhorring' the petitions, but the promotion of 'abhorrences' had been most energetic when provoked by new attempts in the summer of 1680 to foster petitions to call Parliament, and even then the loyalist effort had been limited in vigour, often relying on central direction rather than local initiative. Nevertheless, the abhorrences had been considered by most MPs to have been an affront to the subject's right to petition, and when Parliament sat in October those who had promoted them were pursued by a parliamentary committee. The activities of this committee had further polarised the division between petitioners and abhorrers. The petitions and addresses partly reflected swings in national opinion, but they also symbolised a struggle for the control of propaganda as each side sought to represent the national will. This struggle was now about to enter a new phase of intensity.

THE GENERAL ELECTION OF 1681

Soon after the prorogation, attempts were made to prevent Charles from dissolving Parliament. A group of citizens drew up a petition requesting the lord mayor to summon common council,[154] and when it met on 13 January, the assembly agreed to a petition presented by a prominent nonconformist, Alderman Hayes, requesting that Parliament should sit until grievances had been redressed, and should continue to do so 'till they were freed of the fears of popery & Arbitrary Gov[ernmen]t'.[155] The petitioners claimed that they knew 'no way (under heaven)' to secure the nation from ruin than 'the speedy sitting of this present Parliam[en]t (the surprizing prorogation of which greatly adds to, and increases, the[ir] just fears and jealousies)'. As with the petition promoted the previous year, the succession was not mentioned as a particular grievance, though it is interesting to note that in the revision of the text undertaken by Player, Treby and Clayton before its presentation to the King, a reference was inserted about the encouragement the papists had received from 'hopes of a popish successor'.[156] Once again the question of

remain assembled even when Charles wished to prorogue or dissolve them (PRO [Kew], FO.95/566, 23 December 1680/2 January 1681).

154 *The True Domestick Intelligence*, no. 87, 11 January 1681; *CSPD 1680–1*, p. 131.

155 Congress newsletter, 7/147, 13 January 1680. For the original text and record of a debate about it see CLRO, Common Council Papers 1681, item 15 and minutes of 13 January 1680. *The True Domestick Intelligence*, no. 89, 18 January 1681 reported that 'a certain huffing Coxcomb', who reflected on the common council for the address, was set upon by the crowd. Roger Morrice thought 'nobody opposed the petition' (Dr Williams's Library, MS 31.P, Ent'ring Book, f. 273), which was printed as *The Humble Petition of the Right Honourable the Lord Mayor* (*Somers Tracts*, viii. 143–5).

156 *Somers Tracts*, viii. 144. The petition was drafted by Sir John Lawrence, Sir Robert Clayton, Thomas Player, George Treby, John Dubois, John Ellis and Michael Godfrey. A newsletter (*HMC Kenyon*, p. 125), claimed it was accepted 'with small alterations in the forme but not

Parliament's assembly had become the focus of discontent about popery and arbitrary government. When the petition was presented to Charles the next day he told them 'that he doubted not of the fidelity & affection of the Citty of London; that he wished them to beware of those men that would putt them upon such things as they had nothing to doe with' and that the address seemed 'rather to advise th[a]n Petition'.[157] Charles was probably even more angry than his comments suggest, since the petition was later used as one of the grounds for the forfeiture of the City's charter. A second petition, from Exeter, demanding that the Parliament sit at the time appointed, was signed by 4,000 people; and a third, from Honiton, was reported to have 6,000 signatures.

These petitions were about to be presented when Prince Rupert told the organisers that 'it was too late, for his Majesty had resolv'd to dissolve Parliament'.[158] As had so often happened in 1679, the petitioners' demands had been made irrelevant by the march of events. On 18 January Charles told his privy council, 'without asking (yea refusing to take) their advice, his dreadful resolution of dissolving the Parliam[en]t' and calling a new one to sit at Oxford, in order to 'prevent the petitioning of the City of London and the caballing of them and the City together'.[159] The dissolution 'vexed a great many' people, who expressed their resentment so openly that one keen observer thought that parliamentary freedom of speech 'continued even without doors'.[160] The capital's inhabitants were said to be 'ready to eat their nails for anger that the Parliament must meet at Oxford', and rumours

in the matter', but glossed the text as calling for exclusion. Michael Warton, MP for Hull, described it as 'long drawn but very well' (Hull RO, MS L993, letter to the Mayor, 15 January 1681).

157 PRO, SP.104/67, f. 27, Jenkins to William of Orange, 14 January 1681; Bulstrode news-letter, 14 January 1681; BL, Add. 28,938, f. 54, 'the King's answer to the City's petition', n.d. Several aldermen and common councilmen 'that were no friends to it, were, notwith-stand[in]g, appointed to attend the delivering of it' (BL, Add. 32,681, f. 140, Jenkins to Henry Sidney, 14 January 1681; Congress newsletter 7/148, 15 January 1681). For the names of those ordered to present it see CLRO, common council papers 1681, minutes of the meeting on 13 January 1681.

158 *The True Protestant Mercury*, no. 8, 18–22 January 1681. According to Newdigate news-letter Lc.1231, 18 January 1681 it was the duke of Albemarle who met the petitioners. However, one newswriter reported that they did present the petition to the King, and that the presenting party included Sir William Courtenay, Sir Walter Yonge 'and divers members of the West of England' (*CSPD 1680–1*, pp. 137–8). According to All Souls, MS 171, f. 131, newsletter, 18 January 1681, a third petition from Devon came from Ashburton. This report also says that the petitioners did not actually present it.

159 BL, Add. 18,730, f. 80, diary, 18 January 1681; Luttrell, *Brief Relation*, i. 64. Ironically it was Titus Oates who seems to have started a rumour in October 1680 that Parliament would be adjourned to Oxford (*CSPD 1680–1*, p. 52; PRO, SP.104/67, f. 13, Jenkins to William of Orange, 5 October 1680; PRO, 31/3/146, Barrillon dispatch, f. 107, 7/17 October 1680; *HMC Le Fleming*, p. 172). Lord Grey nevertheless claimed that Shaftesbury contemplated not going to Oxford and remaining in London on the grounds that a large number of MPs were resolved to adjourn there if Charles dissolved the new Parliament (*The Secret History of the Rye House Plot* [1754], pp. 6–9).

160 Bulstrode newsletters, 21 January 1681.

circulated that money had recently been sent from France to the King.[161] Certainly the dissolution was said to have destroyed the hopes of the European protestants, and fear was widespread that France could now dominate Flanders.[162] Popery and arbitrary power were again looming large.

These were the conditions in which the third general election of the period took place. The 1681 polls have been depicted as having been dominated by the exclusion issue and by an exclusionist party led by the earl of Shaftesbury.[163] It will be suggested here, however, that, although the issue of exclusion had undoubtedly grown in importance since 1679, it still did not play an all-encompassing part; that the 'instructions' presented to MPs at the elections showed broader concerns and provoked a much more vigorous loyalist reaction than has previously been admitted; that religious division was increasingly important; and that the period witnessed a bitter paper war between rival pamphleteers and propagandists that both polarised opinion and split moderates further away from the Court's radical critics.

An analysis of the propaganda produced for the 1681 elections shows the continuity and change in attitudes since 1679. Eight tracts were published specifically to advise the electorate on the choice of MPs for the Oxford Parliament in 1681.[164] The succession was certainly a more pervasive issue than it had been in the previous election. *The Advice to the Freemen of England*, for example, asked voters to consider a candidate's opposition to a popish successor;[165] *The Certain Way to Save England* advised readers to 'observe those well that are mighty zealots for a Popish Successor';[166] and *A Seasonable Momento for all that have Voyces* warned about the fate of landholders if a popish king succeeded.[167] But the succession was one factor among many, and propagandists advising the electorate did not cease to think in terms of Court and Country after the 1679 elections; indeed, they continued to try to dissuade voters from electing pensioners or Courtiers. Thus *Plain Dealing* attacked pensioners and talked slightingly of a Country MP who also voted now and again for the Court,[168] whilst *A Dialogue between Two Burgesses* advised its readers not to choose Mr Sweetlips the Courtier, or

---

[161] *CSPD 1680–1*, p. 139; PRO (Kew), FO95/567, d'Avaux dispatch, 20/30 January 1681; *Savile Corresp.* p. 181.

[162] Hull RO, L996, M.Warton to mayor of Hull, 20 January 1681.

[163] Jones, *First Whigs*, pp. 159, 211; Jones, 'Parties and Parliament', pp. 57–8; Speck, 'The Electorate in the First Age of Party', p. 45.

[164] *A Most Serious Expostulation* may also have been printed in 1681, though it is listed as 1680 by Wing. *Considerations Offered to all the Corporations* (1681) was an idiosyncratic election tract that concentrated purely on how the elections would affect trade.

[165] *The Advice to the Freemen of England* (1681), p. 1. It was reprinted as part of *The Protestant Mercury*, no. 11, 29 January–1 February 1681.

[166] *The Certain Way to save England* (1681), p. 16.

[167] *A Seasonable Momento for all that have Voyces* (1681), p. 2.

[168] *Plain Dealing* (1681), verso.

Mr Sell-Trust the pensioner. *A Letter to a Friend* hoped there would be no pensioners elected or 'Fellowes that love their Pockets better than their Countrey'.[169] *The Certain Way to Save England* advised the electorate to choose 'No Bribers, or Sellers of Places in Church or Commonwealth; Much less Honours and Places about the King', and no pensioners.[170] The pamphlet had lifted these passages from Penn's *England's Great Interest* which, as we have seen, had been published to influence the 1679 elections. Similarly *An Address to the Honourable City of London* was a reworking of *The Character of Popery and Arbitrary Government*, which had originally been printed for the second election of 1679. The revision retained the earlier tract's castigation of any 'who in their Profess[i]on or near Relations have any dependency upon the Court',[171] and the pamphlet was so popular that it was reprinted again in 1681 as part of a larger work called *English Liberties*.[172] So widespread was the attack on pensioners that Colonel Whitley, who had been named on a recent list of them, but who had voted against the Court, had to be cleared as suitable for election by *Smiths Protestant Intelligence* as a 'worthy Gentleman'.[173] It could be argued that the attack on pensioners and Courtiers was little more than a cover for an attack on opponents of exclusion; but the cover itself is significant, with Country prejudices against Court manipulation, rather than an open confrontation over the policy of exclusion, characterising the campaign.

The elections themselves reinforce the suggestion that exclusion has been exaggerated as the issue over which candidates fought. Although at Colchester Oates accused Sir Walter Clarges of being 'well affected to the Duke and having voted for him', at Lichfield George Bridges concentrated on asserting that Daniel Finch had voted for the Irish Cattle Bill as a means of undermining his rival.[174] Sir Ralph Verney, who was standing with the Country-turned-Courtier Sir Richard Temple at Buckingham against two opposition candidates, Sir Peter Tyrrell and Charles Blount, nevertheless recommended that at the county election his friends should vote for the exclusionists Wharton and Hampden.[175] The vagaries of Sir Richard Temple's attitude to the electors of Buckingham are particularly illuminating.

---

[169] *A Letter to a Friend Concerning the next Parliament's sitting at Oxford* (1681), p. 1.
[170] *The Certain Way to save England* (1681), pp. 6, 13.
[171] *An Address to the Honourable City of London* (1681), p. 8.
[172] In this form it was reprinted in 1682, 1691 and 1700.
[173] *Smith's Protestant Intelligence*, no. 11, 24–8 February 1681.
[174] Nottingham University Library, DDSR/219/14, L. Champion to Halifax, n.d (but c. 17 February 1681); *The Manner of the Election of the Honourable and Approved Patriots* (1681), p. 1; *History of Parliament*, i. 385.
[175] Bucks. RO, Verney mss, M11/35, Sir Ralph Verney to Coleman, 27 January 1681. A few days later Temple informed Verney that Wharton and Hampden had pressed the sheriff to give the election precept to Sir Peter Tyrrell, a rival candidate (ibid., Temple to Verney, 3 February 1681).

In the first election of 1679, when it seemed that his opponents Lord Latimer and Sir Peter Tyrrell might win, he had threatened to ignore the claim of the burgesses that the right of the election lay in them, and 'to bring it to a popular Election'; admittedly Temple had doubts about the wisdom of this course of action, but these were largely on the grounds that a popular election 'would be more chargeable'.[176] The idea of a popular election was nevertheless soon taken up by his opponents. In 1680 a burgess, Henry Robinson, broke into the town's chest in an abortive attempt to make public the terms of the town's charter to justify a popular election.[177] In the 1681 elections, therefore, Temple's opponents, Tyrrell and Blount, set up on a popular ticket, relying on the discontent that the rule of seven burgesses had aroused. That it was more of an electoral tactic than a principle can be seen in the fact that Tyrrell was initially reluctant to rely on the popular vote, and only espoused it when he saw that he would lose on the burgess vote.[178] Tyrrell's rivals held equally flexible views. Although Sir Ralph Verney initially declared he was 'absolutely resolved not to renounce the Burgesses, nor side with the Populace to deprive them of their Right', his agents were at the same time collecting subscriptions for votes among the populace.[179] His partner Temple employed somebody to walk through the town crying 'A Temple, A Temple',[180] and, as soon as he saw the popular vote swing in his favour, used his influence to have the election called immediately.[181] At a local level, therefore, tactics were sometimes more important than principle, both in terms of national issues and the franchise.[182]

Moreover, there is little evidence of a disciplined, centrally organised, exclusionist party in the 1681 elections. In Oxfordshire four 'very worthy men' competed against each other, causing Shaftesbury to intervene on the behalf of the sitting members, though with the result that only one of the challengers would stand down; and the earl's wish to see one of his lawyers, who was 'a mighty man with Dr. Oates and that club', chosen for Gloucestershire apparently failed to sway the electorate there.[183] Shaftesbury's

---

[176] Bucks. RO, Verney mss M11/32, Sir Ralph Verney to John Verney, 10 February 1679; ibid., Edmund Verney to Sir Ralph Verney, 21 April 1679.
[177] Huntington Library, Stowe MS STT 246, William Chaplyn to Sir Richard Temple, 2 May 1680; Bucks. RO, Verney mss, M11/35, Verney to Temple, 7 February 1681.
[178] Bucks. RO, Verney mss, M11/35, Temple to Verney, 3 February 1681.
[179] Bucks. RO, Verney mss, M11/35, Verney to Temple, 4 and 5 February 1681.
[180] Bucks. RO, Verney mss, M11/35, Coleman to Verney, 4 February 1681.
[181] Bucks. RO, Verney mss, M11/35, Coleman to Verney, 7 February 1681.
[182] Coleby, *Central Government and Localities*, p. 210 ('on closer inspection Whig populism looks more like electoral opportunism'); Jones, 'Parties and Parliament', p. 54. cf. the cases of New Windsor, Great Marlow, Montgomery Boroughs and Tamworth (*History of Parliament*, i. 131, 144, 319, 390–1).
[183] *History of Parliament*, i. 236–7, 357; Haley, *Shaftesbury*, p. 625; Jones, *First Whigs*, pp. 165–6 (I am grateful to Stuart Handley for drawing the Gloucestershire case to my

credibility as the leader of an exclusion party is also rendered suspect by his attempt to oust Maurice Bockland, MP for Downton, who had shown himself to be 'against Popery and a Popish Successor as much as any man', but who had upset the proud earl over 'one or two private causes'.[184] In the borough of Shaftesbury the issue of exclusion still played a subordinate role in 1681 as the Bennett–Andrews combination, forged in the second 1679 election, outvoted the exclusionist Whitaker; the latter was unsupported by Bennett's exclusionist friends, Sir John Coventry, Thomas Freke and Thomas Thynne, even though they had been ready to attend the election if Bennett's own success seemed doubtful, and even though Shaftesbury had recommended that Whitaker was fit to serve in Parliament.[185] Whitaker does not seem to have been embittered by the lack of help shown him by his fellow exclusionists since he dined after the poll with Bennett's uncle (who had acted as his electoral agent) and the son of John Bowles, a rival candidate, 'very merry and friendly all together'.[186]

Further evidence of large cracks in party loyalty comes from voting patterns. The loyalist Sir John Kaye experienced problems with voters who had promised to vote for him and who then 'proved knaves';[187] and forty-one of Sir Richard Temple's voters at Buckingham polled their second votes for his main rival, Sir Peter Tyrrell, when his electoral partner, Sir Ralph Verney, did not appear at the election due to ill health.[188] Poll books survive for the corporation of Reading's elections of February 1679 and February 1681,[189] and these show that although there was only a difference of eighty-one votes between the exclusionist John Blagrave's total poll on both occasions, only half of those who voted for him at the first election polled for him at the second.[190] Similarly, although 159 of William Kenricke's 386 voters in 1679 gave their other vote to Blagrave, and 157 of Kenricke's 1679 voters polled for Blagrave in 1681, only eighty-one of Kenricke's 1679 voters polled

attention). At a by-election held at Newcastle-under-Lyme as a result of Leveson Gower's preference to sit for Shropshire, the rival candidates both supported the exclusion bill (*History of Parliament*, i. 388).

184 *History of Parliament*, i. 672.

185 *The Pythouse Papers*, pp. 89, 96–7.

186 *History of Parliament*, i. 221.

187 Leeds AO, Mexborough mss, Reresby 15/48, Kaye to Reresby, 17 February 1680[1]. cf. BL, Althorp MS C2, Hickman to Halifax, 20 August 1679: 'I cannot say til the Election is over [that] mine is pass'd doubt.'

188 Bucks. RO, Verney mss, M11/35, Temple to Verney, 10 February 1681. Two burgesses promised to give their first votes to Tyrrell and their second to Verney (Huntington Library, MS STT 2450, Sir Ralph Verney to Sir Richard Temple, 7 February 1681).

189 Berkshire R.O., Reading Corporation, uncatalogued mss.

190 In 1679 Blagrave polled 944 votes (*History of Parliament*, i. 132 gives a figure of 927) and 863 votes in 1681. Comparison of the polls shows that only 476 of his 1679 voters voted for him again in 1681. (This has been calculated by hand; computer analysis of the polls would shed further light on voting behaviour.)

consistently for Blagrave in both elections. These figures suggest a high turnover of voters, but also shifting loyalties.[191] One feature of this shift seems to have been of the gentry away from support for the opposition MP Blagrave. In 1679 he polled thirty-four 'gentry' votes, but only seventeen in 1681,[192] and elsewhere gentry support for the opposition seems to have flagged,[193] suggesting that the government was right to be confident that it had gained 'a Majority among the substantial wealthy men.'[194]

Indeed glimpses of the loyalist reaction, that became obvious to most contemporaries only after the dissolution of the Oxford Parliament, can be seen in the 1681 elections themselves. The strength of this reaction was not evenly distributed throughout the country, and sometimes remained un-tapped, such as in Wiltshire where several gentlemen apparently told the earl of Clarendon that 'the King should be served, if they knew which way to do it, but they know not from whom to take their aim'.[195] Nevertheless in certain areas the election results were encouraging for the Court. In Middlesex its sympathisers, Hugh Middleton and Sir Charles Gerard, significantly in-creased their share of the vote;[196] and in Norfolk the majority of the Court's opponent Sir John Hobart over the loyalist candidate was reduced from 808 in 1679 to ninety-eight.[197] At Derby the return of opposition MPs George Vernon and Anchitell Grey was uncertain because Parliament's proceedings

[191] On the other hand, in the borough of Shaftesbury, where there was a much smaller electorate, voting was much more consistent (of Bennett's ninety-six voters in the first election only four defected in the second, and only three of Sir Matthew Andrews' ninety-five voters did likewise). P.J. Challinor has found that only 3 per cent of voters in Cheshire split their votes between candidates ('Restoration and Exclusion', p. 379). I hope to be able to make a computer analysis of the large electorate of Durham city and county to determine the consistency of voting patterns. The polls are discussed by M. Child in her excellent thesis 'Prelude to Revolution'.

[192] The identification of 'gentry' has been made from the annotation on the polls. It is therefore possible that a different definition was used in the two polls; certainly two men, Robert Terrell and William Beisley, were given different epithets. Much more work would be needed on Reading archives to test the validity of the labels.

[193] At Shaftesbury six of the gentry who had voted for the opposition candidates in the first 1679 election did not vote in the autumn (Wiltshire RO, 413/435 Polls). Coleby has found that only fourteen of Hampshire's sixty resident JPs voted for opposition candidates in the 1681 election (*Central Government and the Localities*, p. 162). Child also found that gentry support for the opposition candidate Christopher Vane diminished at Durham ('A Prelude to Revolution', p. 58).

[194] PRO, SP.104/190, Jenkins to Sir Richard Bulstrode, 20 May 1681. cf. Van Prinsterer, *Archives*, v. 423: 'the rich sober men of the nation desire to be quiet and preserve the government'.

[195] *CSPD 1680–1*, p. 165.

[196] *History of Parliament*, i. 308.

[197] Ibid., i. 322. cf. Bod., MS Tanner 37, f. 255, Lawrence Womock to Sancroft, 23 February 1680/1, predicting that the loyalist vote on the Isle of Ely would have doubled since the last election.

had been so much disparaged there;[198] whilst at Salisbury the opposition MP Sir Thomas Mompesson was replaced by John Wyndham, a strong supporter of the Court, and it was reported that the votes of the last Parliament had been burnt.[199] At Southwark the radical sheriff of London, Slingsby Bethel, and his partner Smyth were defeated despite the large electorate there and 'for all the Duke of Buckingham & Lord Gray's rideing before on their manag'd horses through the towne'.[200] On the basis of the election results Jenkins remarked that 'one would imagine that the humour does something abate'.[201]

The growing vigour of the loyalists was shown clearly at Bristol, the fiercest contest of the elections.[202] The central issue in the election was not exclusion – an election pamphlet supporting the Country candidates Atkyns and Knight did not even mention the subject – but religion.[203] The dissenters had 'got a By-word, or Proverb amongst them, to ask, will you have an English or a Latin Bible, alluding to the words of some body there, who spoke in favour of the latter'.[204] The clergy, however, were solidly behind Hart and Earle, and ordered the doors of all churches to be locked to stop bell-ringing for Atkyns, who faced a riot on his entry into the City, incited by the loyalist Artillery Company.[205] Hart complained that Sir John Knight was 'very much countenanced by all the Dissenters',[206] and the archbishop of Canterbury was informed that quakers and dissenters were Atkyns's chief supporters.[207]

Elsewhere, too, the survival of the Church of England was increasingly seen to be at stake, threatened by popery and dissent alike. The newswriter Henry

---

[198] *Smith's Protestant Intelligence*, no. 3, 8 February 1681.

[199] *CSPD 1680–1*, pp. 159–60; *History of Parliament*, i. 457.

[200] Leeds AO, Mexborough mss, Reresby 18/44, E. Reresby to Sir John Reresby, 12 February 1680[1]. The poll result was, however, disputed (Congress newsletter 7/165, 5 March 1681). Opposition candidates were defeated at Southwark in all three elections of the period, though the contest in 1681 was the fiercest.

[201] *HMC Ormonde*, v. 584.

[202] *History of Parliament*, i. 238–9; F.J. Nicholls and J. Taylor, *Bristol Past and Present* (1881), iii. 80.

[203] *History of Parliament*, i. 239; *Reasons for Chusing Sir Robert Atkyns and Sir John Knight* (1681). This was probably one of the 'reflexive papers set up in the night at our Gates' referred to by Samuel Crossman (Bod., MS Tanner 37, f. 296, Crossman to Sancroft, 7 February 1680/1). The petitioning and addressing campaigns of 1679–80 were also an issue: Hart and Earl were 'abhorrers' of petitions, and Atkyns and Knight were petitioners (Nicholls and Taylor, *Bristol*, pp. 78, 80).

[204] *The True Protestant Mercury*, no. 19, 26 February/2 March 1681.

[205] *The Loyal Protestant*, no. 3, 15 March 1681; *Smith's Protestant Intelligence*, no. 20, 4–7 April 1681.

[206] *CSPD 1680–1*, p. 163.

[207] Bod., MS Tanner 37, f. 246, Crossman to Sancroft, 7 February 1680/1. *Reasons for Chusing Sir Robert Atkyns and Sir John Knight* (1681), side 1, noted that both candidates were 'always known to be of the Church of England'. Lacey, *Dissent and Parliamentary Politics*, p. 114, quotes a Quaker source which believed the sect was prosecuted in Bristol because they had 'joined with presbyterians to choose Parliament men'. Ironically the ultra-loyalists had approached the Quakers for support in return for non-prosecution (Latimer, *Annals of Bristol*, p. 400).

Muddiman prayed that the choice of MPs 'be such that ... the Religion of the Church of England [be] more and more established, that neither Popery nor Fanaticisme may again make their prey upon that Flock but the woolfe may be destroy'd and the sharp biter muzzled'.[208] Nonconformity, which by 1681 appeared to some to be the greater of the two religious threats, was openly made the key issue at some elections. According to one report, the candidate in the Leicestershire election, Sir John Hartopp, a member of Owen's Independent congregation in London, nearly lost his life when his neighbour 'discharged a Pistol with a brace of Bullets at him, which missed hi[s He]ad very narrowly, swearing that all Fanaticks should be sent to the Devill with Bullets ere long'.[209]

The loyalist reaction depended to a large extent on the assertiveness of Churchmen at a local level, though the church hierarchy did all they could to encourage it. In Somerset the bishop exhorted 'his clergie to make what opposition they could, in so much there were never so many of the clergy ever seen at any county election', though they were apparently insufficient to overcome the interest of 'the greatest fanatick of a fool this day in England', George Speke.[210] The bishop of Bath and Wells was said to have commanded persons 'to make Parties in new Elections',[211] and at Durham Dean Granville told his congregation at morning service to vote for their former members who were good churchmen, though he was interrupted by a dissenter, who claimed the MPs were 'neither Protestants nor enemies to Popery'.[212] Two proposals, drawn up and sent to Court in January 1681 just before the elections, both suggested that the parish clergy ought to be allowed to sit in the House of Commons to counter the 'faction'.[213]

The increase in religious conflict is not hard to explain. During the 1680–1 Parliament, the reading public had been had been deluged with pamphlets arguing about the status of the dissenters, and the measures taken by MPs towards comprehension and indulgence are well known; less well known, but equally important in terms of public opinion, are MPs' attempts to repeal part of the penal code.[214] On 6 November 1680 Members had

---

208 Longleat, Muddiman newsbook, 22 January 1681.
209 *Smith's Protestant Intelligence*, no. 12, 7–10 March 1680/1.
210 Bod., MS Wood F.40, f. 293, 'H' to Wood, 15 March 1681.
211 *Advice from Parnassus*, no. 3, 31 February 1681.
212 *History of Parliament*, i. 226; *CSPD 1680–1*, p. 386. Margaret Child found that virtually every clergyman in the county of Durham supported the loyalist candidate William Bowes ('Prelude to Revolution', p. 500). cf. *Plain Dealing* (1681), verso: 'Our Parson says I am bound in conscience to vote for those that are for Absolute Obedience to Prince and Prelate.'
213 All Souls, MS 242, ff. 263–72; All Souls, MS 242, f. 274, dated 30 January 1681, though received by Jenkins 15 April (this is a copy of Bod., MS Tanner 37, f. 221, anonymous letter, ostensibly from Copenhagen, to Sancroft, 28 December 1680). *Certain Material and Useful Considerations* (1680), p. 2, observed that the House of Commons did not include the clergy 'who are a considerable part of the Kingdom'.
214 Horwitz, 'Protestant Reconciliation', pp. 204–5, 214.

demanded clarification of the laws against dissenters in the light of Charles's earlier announcement to the circuit judges not to enforce them. Capel had urged that 'we are now to enlarge the church as far as we can', and had secured a resolution that the Elizabethan and Jacobean statutes had not been intended against protestant dissenters. Sacheverell had then proposed a bill to repeal the act of 35 Elizabeth cap.1, a statute which, though seldom used, specifically punished protestant recusancy, and the House had agreed to bring in the necessary legislation.[215] The bill had duly passed, and been approved by the Lords, after amendments which included the removal of its preamble.[216] In reaction to the government's enforcement of the law earlier in the year, MPs had also resolved on Christmas eve to repeal the Corporation Act, which Jenkins believed was one of the 'corner-stones w[hi]ch I hope I shall not see remove'd in my dayes'.[217] The preamble to the bill insisted that the Act had nevertheless 'proved manifestly inconvenient and destructive to the good government of corporations by disabling and incapacitating persons of sufficiency and ability'.[218]

The repeal of the Corporation Act had been lost at the prorogation, and barely two days after the end of the session the government had reminded London's rulers to enforce it, though the common council narrowly voted to delay reading the order.[219] The act to repeal the severe Elizabethan law against nonconformity had also failed to reach the statute book as a result of a piece of royal chicanery when Charles simply ordered the clerk of the House not to present the bill for his approval.[220] This breach of etiquette, if not the law, was investigated when Parliament sat again, and in the meanwhile provoked a sharp pamphlet exchange about whether the law was still valid. Moreover, there was plenty to argue about concerning the House's tenderness for protestant dissenters, symbolised by its vote on 10 January that the enforcement of the penal laws against them encouraged popery and was a danger to peace.[221]

By the beginning of 1681 both dissenters and strict Churchmen had adopted aggressive and resolute positions that inevitably led to conflict. Some dissenters crusaded with a reforming zeal. At the end of February a presentment, inspired by sheriff Slingsby Bethel, was made against the churchwardens at All Hallows, Barking, for allowing a wooden image of an angel in

[215] Grey, *Debates*, vii. 422–5; *CJ*, ix. 647; Burnet, *History*, ii. 278.

[216] *HMC Lords 1678–88*, p. 214.

[217] *CJ*, ix. 692; BL, Add. 32681, f. 127, Jenkins to Sidney, 28 December 1680. The bill had its first reading on 3 January 1681 and a second reading three days later.

[218] NLW, Trevor-Owen mss, MS 147, 'preamble'.

[219] *CSPD 1680–1*, p. 132; *HMC Kenyon*, p. 125.

[220] Burnet, *History*, ii. 278–9.

[221] An address to the king not to prosecute dissenters had almost passed the House 'but at last upon consideration that this was to addresse to the kinge in effect to putt forth another Declaration [of indulgence], they left it out' (*HMC Finch*, ii. 102).

their church. The prosecution for idolatry had evidently been meant to cowe George Hickes, the former chaplain of the duke of Lauderdale, who had preached against dissent, and serve as a warning to others 'not to suffer such seducing trinkets and small preparatories for popery to continue'.[222] At the same time Edward Whitaker, the duke of Buckingham's lawyer and the author of a number of tracts about the penal statute of 35 Elizabeth, indicted the bishop of London for holding a court in his own name.[223] Anglicans were frightened by such offensive behaviour. Sir John Kaye thought his friend Reresby could not 'imagine to what a height the dissenting party are grown to', and feared that if Parliament granted them liberty then 'farewell Church of England'.[224] Despite instructions to the judges to again be 'very tender as to the dissenters', they were allegedly presented 'as vigorously ... as ever', including sixty at Salisbury and a number in Norwich, Chichester and Chelmsford.[225] The church hierarchy believed that dissenters were 'the very nerves and sinews' of the opposition and that 'if the laws were strictly put in execution there's no doubt they would shrink up'.[226] It was a sentiment that Charles was personally encouraging, no matter what his public statements. On 12 March a group of loyalist MPs were entertained at Whitehall by Chiffinch and the King dropped in for a private pep-talk. He told them that 'he would go as far as any man (this was his expression) for the preservation of the protestant religion as by law establish'd, and the utter extirpation of popery, whereupon Sir Thomas Vernon said "Amen and Presbytery too", to which the King rejoin'd "with all my heart for I have smarted from those

---

[222] *The True Protestant Mercury*, nos. 19, 26 February–2 March; ibid., no. 21, 5–9 March 1681; Bod., MS Eng. Misc. e.4, f. 14. account by Hickes, which notes that the bookseller Walter Kettilby aided him. For the Hickes controversy see *A Narrative of a Strange and Sudden Apparition* (1681), *A New Narrative of a Fiery Apparition* (1681), *The Sham Indictment Quashed* (1681) and *The Birth and Burning of the Image called St Michael* (1681). For a slightly earlier pamphlet attack on images see *A Letter wherein is shewed first, what Worship is due to Images* (1680), and see also J. Spurr and M. Goldie, 'Edward Fowler and the Struggle for St Giles Cripplegate' (*EHR*, forthcoming) for Fowler's destruction in 1679 of an idolatrous window. The following year John Tillotson took down a 'sun over the screen behind the communion table' (Birch, *Life of Tillotson*, p. 80).

[223] Newdigate newsletter Lc.1046, 24 February 1681. Whitaker's publications included *A Short History of the Life and Death of the Act made the 35th of Elizabeth* (1681), and *A Justification of the Paper, Entituled A Short History* (1681). According to Verney, Whitaker had been 'a broken upholsterer, turn'd Atturney or solicitor for the Factious' (endorsement on CUL, Sel. 2. 118. 58). He acted as lawyer for the 'Protestant Joiner', Stephen College, in the summer, and became solicitor to the admiralty after the Revolution.

[224] Leeds AO, Mexborough mss, Reresby 16/6, Kaye to Reresby, 16 January 1681.

[225] Nottingham University Library, DDSR/219/14, L. Champion to Halifax, 19 February 1681; *Domestick Intelligence*, no. 97, 15 February 1681; *The True Protestant Mercury*, no. 15, 12–16 February 1681; *Smith's Protestant Intelligence*, no. 7, 19 February 1681 and no. 14, 15 March 1681; Newdigate newsletter Lc.1067, 19 March 1681. Judge Weston told the Hertford grand jury to prosecute dissenters (*Domestick Intelligence*, no.103, 2 Mar. 1681).

[226] Bod., MS Tanner 37, f. 255, Womock to Sancroft, 23 February 1681.

people allready"'.[227] Even within Parliament the tide of opinion was thought to be turning against dissent, for one observer calculated that there were fewer MPs in the new Parliament in favour of repealing the Elizabethan legislation and that it had lost support because it had been 'so hotly pursued before'.[228]

'GREAT AND DANGEROUS INNOVATIONS':[229] THE INSTRUCTIONS PRESENTED TO MPS

The second general election of 1679 and the election in 1681 had much in common. National issues played a much greater role in 1681 than they had done before, and a candidate's views on the bill were significant; but they were part of a broader range of concerns, and not in themselves of paramount importance for the electorate. Seventy-eight MPs (roughly a quarter of the Members who sat in all three Parliaments[230]) opposed exclusion, and a large number of constituencies returned one loyalist and one opposition MP in 1679 and 1681,[231] suggesting either that local interest or local factors were still very important, and/or that opposition to exclusion was not as unpopular as it is often assumed to have been.[232] Attitudes towards dissent had assumed greater importance since 1679, and the most significant difference between the two elections was the increased vigour in 1681 of the loyalists. Nevertheless, with a sharp drop in the number of contests at the polls,[233] it is not the elections themselves, so much as the instructions presented to MPs, that have been used to portray a highly organised Whig party machine directed by Shaftesbury.[234] Does the evidence justify such a claim?

There are serious problems with the idea that the addresses made to MPs were based on the draft 'instruction' in the Shaftesbury papers, which demanded exclusion, annual Parliaments sitting until they had finished their

---

227 NLW, MS 6272C, f. 28, Mutton Davies to Sir Thomas Edwards, 12 March 1681.
228 *HMC Ormonde*, v. 619.
229 PRO, SP.104/189, Jenkins to Henry Savile, 28 February 1681.
230 26 per cent of the 300 MPs who sat in all three Parliaments.
231 Kishlansky, *Parliamentary Selection*, p. 174.
232 Harris (*London Crowds*, chapter 6) has argued for the existence of a popular toryism. Of the sixty new members in 1681, twenty-five were MPs who supported the Court (*History of Parliament*, i. 78). This figure relates to MPs who sat in Parliament for the first time, though there were 110 MPs elected to sit at Oxford who had not sat in the previous Parliament (*A New Catalogue of ... the Parliament Assembled at Oxford*, appended to *Vox Patriae* [1681]).
233 *History of Parliament*, i. 106. MPs had met together in London to reduce the number of contests (Bulstrode newsletters, 21 January 1681).
234 Jones, *First Whigs*, pp. 167–73; Feiling, *The Tory Party*, pp. 176–7. Jenkins commented that the addresses were organised 'by the Great Cabal in London' (PRO, SP.104/189, Jenkins to Sir Henry Goodricke, 13 March 1681). Professor Sutherland also sees in the 'Shaftesbury draft' a common origin for the addresses (*Restoration Newspapers*, pp. 168–9). For a discussion of the 'instructions' see George, 'Elections and Electioneering', pp. 572–5.

business, freedom from mercenary soldiers, and that no money be granted until the people's liberties were secured.[235] A simple comparison of the draft with the addresses, only twenty-three of which were ever presented to MPs, reveals significant differences.[236] Most obviously, none of the presented 'instructions' instruct; at most they give 'directions' or 'recommend' policies. The term 'instruction' was used as a term of abuse by loyalists such as Jenkins, who employed it in propagandist letters sent abroad to foreign envoys intended to show the activities of the opposition in the most conspiratorial light possible.[237] I shall therefore refer to the texts as addresses. A more important difference is that of the draft's three instructions only the insistence on exclusion was widely made in the addresses presented to MPs, and even then they were not, as has been claimed, simple mandates for the bill.[238] The Westminster address, for example, referred only to 'those Just, Legal and necessary Expedients' needed to secure religion,[239] a phrase that could be interpreted as support for the expedients to settle the succession that Charles promised to offer the Oxford Parliament. Dover's address to its MPs referred vaguely to the 'perfecting of those good Bills that were before you in the last parliament'.[240] Kent's and Nottinghamshire's did not even mention the succession at all,[241] and even where exclusion was specifically desired, it often came after a call for measures to safeguard Charles's safety and for the further investigation of the Popish Plot.

Moreover, other demands made by the addresses rivalled that of exclusion. Whereas the draft instruction did not mention the religious legislation to ease the state of nonconformists, sixteen of the actual addresses reminded Members of the need for a union of protestants, a sign of strong support for the bills of comprehension and indulgence which had been debated in November and December 1680 for the indulgence and comprehension of dissenters. The third directive of the draft, which called for the nation's freedom from guards and mercenary soldiers, was voiced by only one

---

[235] Printed in Christie, *Shaftesbury*, ii. cxi–ii.

[236] They were from London, Westminster, Chichester, Colchester, Bedfordshire, Suffolk, Hertford, Essex, Surrey, Leicestershire, Yorkshire, Bridgwater, Nottinghamshire, Berkshire, Dover, Newcastle-under-Lyme, Sussex, Cheshire, Northamptonshire, two from Taunton, Winchelsea and Kent. The latter was not printed in *Vox Patriae* (1681), which gathered most of the addresses, but is printed in the *The True Protestant Mercury*, no. 22, 9–12 March 1681.

[237] PRO, SP.104/189, Jenkins to Henry Savile, 28 February 1681, and ibid. Jenkins to Goodricke, 13 March 1681.

[238] Jones, 'Parties and Parliament', pp. 57–8. One observer nevertheless commented that the electorate 'generally article their Members to insist upon his exclusion' (BL, Add. 28,875, f. 175, Samuel Ellis to John Ellis, 8 March 1681).

[239] *Vox Patriae* (1681), p. 9.

[240] *Vox Patriae* (1681), p. 16.

[241] *The Protestant Mercury*, no. 22, 3 March 1681; *Vox Patriae* (1681), p. 15.

address, that from Middlesex;[242] and although the draft 'instruction' finished by assuming that money would be withheld from the King until grievances had been resolved, only half of the presented addresses actually carried such a threatening phrase. If the draft 'instruction' was ever intended as a model for others to copy it is difficult not to conclude that it was remarkably unsuccessful. It is nevertheless significant that ten of the addresses urged members to continue to maintain the right to petition, a plea that reflected the depth of feeling aroused by the petition-abhorring controversy and suggests that the thrust for the organisation of the addresses came from those involved in earlier petitioning campaigns.[243] Shaftesbury had been influential in such activity, and no doubt still remained so; but we have seen earlier how the petitioning movement had acquired its own momentum and it is unnecessary to see his hand behind all opposition. We must therefore study how the addresses came about in order to better understand their character.

The addresses had their origin in the petitions promoted in response to the dissolution of the Westminster Parliament. Reaction to the announcement had been swift, for in the space of twelve hours 6,000 signatures were said to have been gathered on a petition from Warwickshire for the sitting of the new Parliament.[244] This reaction may have prompted Charles to make it clear that Parliament would sit at the appointed time,[245] but the spontaneity of the petitions no doubt encouraged sixteen peers, including Shaftesbury, to sign their own petition which was presented to the King by the earl of Essex on 25 January 1681.[246] This reminded Charles of the dreadful consequences of Parliaments previously held in Oxford, asked for the meeting to be held

---

[242] Oxford common council nevertheless voted not to quarter any of the guards, and a Westminster grand jury with Sir William Waller as its foreman was reported to have presented them as 'riotous and dangerous to the kingdom and the protestant religion' (Newdigate newsletter Lc.1034, 27 January 1681; Nottingham University Library, DDSR/219/14, L. Champion to Halifax, 1 February 1681; *CSPD 1680–1*, p. 151). Jenkins reported that 'the faction is deliberating at this time how to make the guards an illegal institution' (PRO, SP104/189, Jenkins to Savile, 7 February 1681. cf. *HMC Ormonde*, v. 575). *The Intrigues of the Popish Plot Laid Open* (1685), p. 30, alleges that Shaftesbury halted such attempts because the guards helped impoverish the King; if true, this evidence raises doubts about the earl's authorship of the draft 'instruction'. For the problems of its provenance see also Haley, *Shaftesbury*, p. 627, n. 3.

[243] Jones (*First Whigs*, p. 168) points out the link with petitioning, and the organisation developing out of the earlier campaign.

[244] Newdigate newsletter Lc.1032, 20 January 1681.

[245] BL, Add. 32,681, f. 167, Jenkins to Henry Sidney, 11 February 1681.

[246] It is printed in *Vox Patriae* (1681), p. 5. The petition was presented the day after Essex had been turned out of the privy council (PRO, PC.2/69, privy council minutes, f. 192, 24 January 1681). Five of the sixteen subscribers (Monmouth, Salisbury, Essex, Mordaunt and Paget) had not signed the petition of December 1679. Say and Sele, Rockingham, Holles (dead), North and Chandos who had signed the earlier petition did not sign in 1681. Although they did not subscribe, Lord Strafford and the bishop of London both regretted Parliament was to sit at Oxford (BL, Althorp MS C3/67, Strafford to Halifax, 18 February 1681; Kent AO, U1713/C2, f. 24, Charles Dering to Southwell, 20 January 1681).

in London, condemned the stifling of investigations into the Popish Plot which the prorogations and dissolutions since 1678 had caused, and claimed that the presence of the guards, too many of whom it was alleged were papists, would restrict the freedom of debate.[247] When the King received the petition he 'told them he loockt upon itt, as their private opinion, and that his own was contrary to it', and gave Essex the evil eye as he asserted that 'some of them were of a contrary opinion but a year ago'.[248]

The peers had once again taken the lead in petitioning, as they had done in 1679, and it seems likely that in 1681 Shaftesbury and his allies thought a repetition of the tactic would produce similar results and initiate a nationwide petitioning campaign. Among Shaftesbury's papers is a draft petition calling for the Parliament to be held in London, and for Charles to listen to its advice.[249] But, although the peers' petition received widespread attention in the newspapers[250] and became the focus of an exchange of pamphlets,[251] the example of the Lords was not followed. The Westminster petition that was to have emulated the peers' demands never appeared,[252] and although efforts were made to stir up the seamen, watermen, hackney coachmen and suburbs men to petition for a London Parliament 'the faction [was] enraged that the bulky [or] wealthy part of the city [was] not more forward in imitating & writing after the Lords Petitioners'.[253] As Secretary Jenkins observed, 'it appeares the citty is not so forward in violent things, as some of the restlesse

---

247 The petition's organisation was slightly haphazard. It was signed when the peers dined together at Clare House the previous evening (BL, Add. 28,053, f. 230, Arlington to Danby, 25 January 1681) but when Lord Townshend was asked to sign it, he refused to do so, and even hindered several others from subscribing (*Original Papers*, p. 116). Moreover, one un-named peer, described as 'one of the great pillars of the protestant interest' who wanted to sign, is reported to have been forced to run after it as it was being taken for presentation (Nottingham University Library, DDSR 219/14, L. Champion to Halifax, 26 January 1681).

248 Nottingham University Library, DDSR 219/14, Champion to Halifax, 26 January 1681. Charles sent for one of the subscribers, Lord Mordaunt, who confessed that he had signed mainly because Charles had not given him command of Lord Plymouth's regiment.

249 PRO, 30/24/6B/392. The earl of Strafford, who sympathised with the petitioners' demands, heard 'there wilbe such petitions as soone as the Par[liament] meets at Oxford as some beleeve the K[in]g will be content to have it at London' (BL, Althorp MS C.3/67, Strafford to Halifax, 18 February 1681).

250 *The Domestick Intelligence*, nos. 91, 25 January 1681, and 92, 29 January 1681; *True Protestant Mercury*, no. 10, 25–9 January 1681. Bulstrode newsletter, 21 January 1680/1, also reported the petition, whilst the government's *London Gazette* pointedly ignored it.

251 The Lords' petition was printed, but without the King's reply (Nottingham University Library, DDSR/29/14, L. Champion to Halifax, 26 January 1681). On 28 January *A Letter to a Noble Peer of the Realm about his late Speech and Petition* was published, reputedly written by Roger L'Estrange and printed by Nathanial Thompson (*CSPD 1680–1*, p. 151; *The Domestick Intelligence*, no. 97, 15 February 1681). *Jesuita Vapulans* (1681), pp. 1–2, defended the petition.

252 *The Domestick Intelligence*, no. 92, 29 January 1681.

253 HMC *Ormonde*, v. 570. *True Protestant Mercury*, no. 10, 25–9 January 1681, reported that 'near 1000 watermen' had signed a petition requesting Parliament to sit at Westminster 'otherwise they and their Families will be exposed to Ruine'.

spirits would have it'.[254] Much of the impact of the peers' petition had been lost by the time common council sat on 4 February,[255] with the result that the peers had to be content with an address of thanks.[256]

Although the common council's address did not follow the peers' demand that Parliament should sit at Westminster, the lead from London was highly influential. Widening the tactic, which had been employed by York and Shropshire even before the prorogation of the Parliament,[257] of thanking MPs for their services, the London address thanked its Members for searching into the Plot, preserving the King's person, preserving protestantism, securing the meeting of Parliament, promoting unity of religion, endeavouring to repeal the Act of 1593 against sectaries and the Corporation Act, and 'especially for what progress hath been made towards the Exclusion of all Popish Successors, and Particularly of James Duke of York'; it was sure that until they had been secured against popery and arbitrary power no money would be granted, and finally resolved to stand by the MPs with lives and fortunes.[258] London's text thus became the model for others to emulate. 'The example of the Citty of London in makeing addresses to the persons they choose, concerning the future proceedings in Parliament is now followed in many places', commented one newswriter,[259] and the Hertford address readily admitted its debt to the City's example.[260] Since one of Hertford's MPs was Sir William Cowper, a zealous supporter of Shaftesbury, the discontented earl's control over the campaign seems slight. The earl no doubt supported it, perhaps even encouraged it, but there is little evidence that he organised it, and even sparser evidence that the country was at the behest of a party machine controlled by him. Indeed the view that Shaftesbury must be seen as the driving force behind the opposition throughout the country has obscured the local character of the campaign and the role of local initiative.

Although the City's address stated the basic issues considered important by later addresses, local factors helped shape the campaign. The need for sensitivity about local opinion is clearly evident in a speech made by Sir James Johnson to the electors of Great Yarmouth, in which his predominant theme

254 PRO, SP.104/67, f. 28, Jenkins to William of Orange, 28 January 1681.
255 The meeting had been delayed because the lord mayor was ill (Congress newsletter 7/153, 1 February 1681; Nottingham University Library, DDSR 219/14, Champion to Halifax, 29 January 1681 and 1 February 1681).
256 The two sheriffs, Bethel and Cornish, presented the address to Essex (*The Domestick Intelligence*, no. 95, 4 February 1681). Sir Gilbert Gerard successfully beseeched a Middlesex grand jury to give thanks to the peers (*HMC Ormonde*, v. 579; *The Domestick Intelligence*, no. 97, 15 February 1681).
257 *Vox Patriae* (1681), p. 2; *True Protestant Mercury*, no. 4, 4–8 January 1681.
258 *Vox Patriae* (1681), pp. 8–9. The London address was published on 5 February 1681 in *A True Narrative of the Proceedings at Guildhall* (Bod., Nichols Newspapers 3A/52).
259 Bod., MS Carte 222, f. 250, newsletter, 25 February 1681.
260 *Vox Patriae* (1681), pp. 11–12. Other addresses closely modelled on the London address are Chichester and Leicestershire (ibid., pp. 9, 13–14).

was a desire to act for the well-being of the town 'and if it were possible, for every individual in it'.[261] In some cases the addresses owed something to the need of localities to represent their views to MPs who, in order to avoid expense on travel and electoral entertainments, had not returned to their constituencies for the elections, a practice that had been encouraged by the press.[262] Even a borough as near to London as St Albans 'having notice their two late Members designed to come down from London thither, and judging it might be some charge and trouble to them, called a Hall the day before, and immediately proceeded to Elect them'.[263] The Bridgwater, Winchelsea and Newcastle addresses were all presented to MPs who were absent from their elections, and apparently derived from local sentiment. Thus at Newcastle the address came from the Mayor Ralph Wood, the alderman and two JPs, Nathaniel Beard and William Middleton, and had been signed by 200 inhabitants;[264] whilst the Bridgwater address was agreed on when the electors repaired to an inn at the request of the mayor and Deputy Recorder George Musgrave.[265] Even when the elected Members were present it was often only for the election itself, and the addresses must therefore have been seen as a useful way of conveying the prevailing opinions and grievances of their constituents.

Although the presence of active MPs in the localities undoubtedly gave encouragement to the promoters of addresses, the initiative could still come from the localities rather than the Members themselves. Sir William Pulteney added his own verbal resolution 'never to live to see a Popish successor' to the Westminster address, a move which suggests that he had taken little or no part in its original drafting.[266] In October 1681 the Northampton Grand Jury inquired into those who had presented the address to Parkhurst and Fleetwood and found that its promoters dined together every Saturday at the Swan in Northampton.[267] Indeed the local origins of the first address made in the exclusion crisis to MPs about national grievances is well documented: after the Middlesex election in February 1679 'whilst the great ones were at dinner some of the freeholders said they would dine by themselves', with the result

---

[261] Cited by P. Gauci, 'The Corporation and the Country: Great Yarmouth 1660–1722' (Oxford D.Phil., 1991), pp. 192–3.

[262] *Plain Dealing* (1681), p. 2: 'Let us chuse them [i.e., MPs] without the expense of a penny, or the trouble of a journey'.

[263] *Smith's Protestant Intelligence*, no. 3, 4–8 May 1681. The successful candidates were also absent at Derbyshire, Beverley, Maidstone, Harwich, Pembroke, Hull, and Monmouthshire (*History of Parliament*, i. 188, 233, 318, 473, 477; *The Domestick Intelligence*, nos. 94, 1 February 1681 and no. 106, 16 March 1681).

[264] *Vox Patriae* (1681), p.17. A Maximilian Beard presented the Middlesex address (*Smith's Protestant Intelligence*, no. 14, 4 March 1681.)

[265] *The Domestick Intelligence*, no. 102, 4 March 1681.

[266] *True Protestant Mercury*, no.14, 8–12 February 1681.

[267] *CSPD 1680–1*, p. 543.

that an address was presented to Sir Robert Peyton and Sir William Roberts signed by fifty gentlemen, which urged the new members to press for better security for the King, the maintenance of liberty and property, the preservation and union of protestantism and a bill for widening the scope of Habeas Corpus.[268] In March 1679 the quakers at York had presented newly elected MPs with grievances which they wished redressed; in April of that year a paper of instructions for Bristol's representatives had been drawn up by the city's council to urge Members to seek a revision of the statute prohibiting the import of Irish cattle; and in early November 1680 Treby had been sent a paper of 'advice from friends in the country' telling him how MPs should proceed.[269] These examples emphasise a greater local initiative than has previously been recognised,[270] and question the assumption that the addresses were the product of a Whig central party machine that dictated to the provinces.

The influence of the localities was also evident in the growing radicalism of demands, as each address added new grievances to those that had gone before. The sheer variety of wording suggests that they were not slavishly copied from a single source, as even the petitions of 1679–80 had been. The Essex address, presented on 22 February, asked that the fleet and garrisons should be entrusted to men of known loyalty and religion. Surrey, on 23 February, wanted a bill for regulating elections and the frequency of Parliaments, and also a bill for preventing pluralities of church livings, nonresidency and scandalous behaviour among the clergy. Sussex wanted a 'firm and Legal Association' to secure Charles's person and a commitment to seek justice against the pensioners of the Cavalier Parliament. Taunton, on 11 March, desired action 'to give a check to Prophaneness and Debauchery', whilst the town's 'young Men' in a separate address wanted investigation of the arbitrary actions of the ecclesiastical courts, as well as the removal of oaths and tests barring dissenters from office. Winchelsea urged that land should be put 'under a Voluntary Register, that thereby this Kingdom may be a just and Honourable Fund, whereby Monies may be taken upon all urgent occasions', requesting in addition an investigation into the Navy.[271]

This increasing catalogue of demands suggests that instead of following a static list of requests issued by a central party organisation, it was the

---

268 Bod., MS Carte 228, f.147, newsletter, 25 February 1679; All Souls, MS 171, f.26, newsletter, 27 February 1679; Newdigate newsletter Lc.752, 27 February 1679.

269 Bod., MS Wood F.40, f.264, Godfrey Bosseville to Mr Allum, 10 March 1678/9; Latimer, *Annals of Bristol*, p.393; HMC *Fitzherbert*, p.23.

270 B. Kemp, *King and Commons 1660–1832* (1957), p.44, claims the addresses 'did not originate with the constituents who put it forward'. cf. Jones, *First Whigs*, p.172: 'there was no question of the [whig leaders and organisers] allowing policy to be determined by the freeholders or people'.

271 *Vox Patriae* (1681), pp.12, 13, 17–20.

localities which added the new grievances to be redressed. Any similarities between the wording of the addresses can be explained by the fact that they were regularly printed in the newspapers, most notably in Benjamin Harris's *Protestant Domestick Intelligence*, Curtis's *True Protestant Mercury* and *Smith's Protestant Intelligence*, which therefore offered the basic form on to which other grievances could have been grafted. Although the newspapers were sympathetic to Shaftesbury there is little evidence that he had any editorial control over what they printed or that he ordered them to report the campaign so assiduously. As was shown earlier, contemporaries could draw on a large amount of printed and manuscript information from which they were able to draw their own opinions.

The news available in the provinces was, however, interpreted in a different way by loyalists, who sought to counter the addresses to MPs with demands of their own. This willingness to copy the tactics used by their opponents, increasingly evident in the last days of the parliamentary session,[272] represents a significant development, marking a move away from the aloof condemnation of the 1679/80 petitioning campaign. It was a development, one newspaper claimed, that was forced upon the loyalists by necessity,[273] but it is significant that they were prepared to take up the challenge apparently without Court backing or encouragement. Once again the counter-addresses highlight a local rather than a central reaction, and suggest that the passivity of 1680 was increasingly being dispelled.

At least nine such addresses were drawn up, though three of these were rejected and not presented.[274] The addresses shared some of the concerns of their opponents: the Cricklade address, for example, asked for its MPs to preserve the subjects' rights, preserve the King's person and further investigate the Popish Plot; and the Chester, Cheshire, Southwark and Maldon addresses made similar demands. But the loyalist addresses distinguished

---

[272] Bod., MS Tanner 37, f. 221, letter to Sancroft dated 28 December 1680, urging the loyalists to 'beat the ringleaders of sedition at their own weapon of popularity'; Birch, *Life of Tillotson*, p. 82, indicating that the clergy contemplated an address in response to Charles's speech on 4 January 1681 rejecting exclusion.

[273] *The Loyal Protestant*, no. 5, 22 March 1681, claimed that the Southwark address was 'not occasioned by the least apprehension we have of any necessity of our giving you directions' but insisted that the other ill instructions 'have forced upon us this way of declaring our minds'.

[274] Cambridgeshire (*Observator*, no. 8, 30 April 1681); Bristol (*Observator*, no. 6, 26 April 1681, printed as *The Bristol Address*); Maldon (*Loyal Protestant*, no. 3, 15 March 1681); Southwark (*Loyal Protestant*, no. 5, 22 March 1681); Norwich (*Strange and Wonderful News from Norwich* [1681]), cf. Evans, *Seventeenth Century Norwich*, pp. 272–3; Cheshire (*True Protestant Mercury*, no. 21, 5–9 March 1681; the address also came from the 'orthodox clergy'); Chester (NLW, Wynnstay MS C37); Exeter (All Souls, MS 242, f. 33); Cricklade (*Domestick Intelligence*, no. 105, 15 March 1681; the address was printed separately as *Certain Proposals Humbly Offered by the Bailiff* [1681]). Jones, *First Whigs*, p. 172, and Lipson, 'Elections 1679–81', p. 69, discuss some of the loyalist addresses.

themselves from their rivals in two ways. First, they voiced support for the Church of England. The Cheshire loyal address wanted the preservation of the church 'in Doctrine and Worship, ordering of Priests, administration of Sacraments, and other Rites as they are at present by Law established',[275] and the Bristol loyal address recommended its MPs not to repeal any of the laws against dissenters, but to pass new legislation against papists and fanatics.[276] Second, by their willingness to grant the King money, the loyal addresses directly refuted the tactic of starving the Court of money which had been used by the Commons in the previous Parliament to exert pressure on Charles. The Exeter address 'utterly discountenance[d] the part of the Bedfordshire address wherein noe money is to be given to the King till their petition be granted for tis in effect to say that we cannot trust our soveraigne as to the keeping out of Popery and Arbitrary Power'. Other loyal demands included measures to secure the subjects' rights from illegal imprisonments[277] and legislation to curb the insolences of the press after the lapse of the licensing law in 1679. Chester thus recommended 'that the Act for preventing abuses in printing seditious Treasonable Unlicensed Books and Phampletts may bee revived and care taken that men of sound Judgm[ent] & known integrity may bee apoynted Imprimaturs'. Only three of the loyal addresses, those from Exeter, Chester and Cheshire, tackled the succession question, the first of these leaving the whole matter to the King, with a reminder of the usual anti-exclusionist argument of not doing evil that good may come of it, whilst Cheshire's asked its MPs to 'embrace with thankfulness his Majesty's most gracious Intimation of his Royal assent to secure us ag[ai]st the danger of a Popish successor'. This indicates some support at least among loyalists for the policy of limitations on a popish successor promised by the Court.

There is evidence that some loyalists wanted to see the counter-addressing campaign spread nationwide. In February 1681 Archbishop Sancroft received a paper stating that, although the country gentry did not want to emulate the City of London's example of making recommendations, they would petition if Charles so wanted.[278] It might, the author argued, 'bee of great use at this time to have their thoughts concerning the Meanes to preserve the Religion Established in these nations under a successor supposed to be of another persuasion'. The author of the document therefore suggested that a letter be sent to grand juries and JPs telling them to address the King with their opinions about the bill for uniting protestants, about petitioning and the imprisonment of abhorrers, and about a general toleration for all

---

[275] *True Protestant Mercury*, no. 21, 5–9 March 1681.
[276] *True Protestant Mercury*, no. 24, 16–19 March 1681.
[277] This was an attack on the parliamentary inquiry into the abhorrers of the petitions of 1679–80 which had resulted in the arrests of non-members. The Bristol address demanded preservation against the imprisonment of subjects 'least we be enslaved'.
[278] Bod., MS Tanner 37, f. 254, 'E.B' to Sancroft, 18 February 1680/1.

except papists; the Court for its part was to give an undertaking that no one would be imprisoned for their views, 'without which they will be unwilling to speake their mindes freely'. This advice suggests both a confidence that the true sense of the nation was loyalistic, and a frustration that the Court was unable to protect the expression of its real sentiment, and it is ironic, though also symptomatic of shifts in opinion, that tactics which had been so strongly condemned after the petitioning campaign of 1679–80 should be advocated in the beginning of 1681 to determine the will of the gentry throughout the country.

The loyalist addresses indicate a growing resolution of opinion as well as a certain dissatisfaction with the lack of firm central direction from the Court, two characteristics that can also be seen in the attack made on the rival addresses made by an increasingly strident loyalist press. Nathanial Thompson's newspaper, *The Loyal Protestant and True Domestick Intelligence*, reported that the mayor, aldermen and common councillors of Colchester knew nothing of the Essex address 'till it came down in Print',[279] and that Chichester,[280] Bristol and Norwich made similar protestations.[281] One loyalist pamphleteer claimed that the addresses were the invention of the opposition publishers Smith and Harris '& some other of these true intelligencers, as 'twere easy to prove in severall particular instances were it necessary'.[282] On 16 April Thompson's newspaper pointed out that the addresses could not be representative of the nation since only twelve out of fifty-two counties and eleven out of 250 boroughs had presented them;[283] and L'Estrange concluded that the addresses acted 'in the Name of the People, without the People's Commission'.[284] The loyalists therefore challenged the claim that the addresses truly represented the nation.[285] Sir John Reresby claimed that the Yorkshire address was the work of 'only six or seven factious persons ... though it passed for a more general thing',[286] and Jenkins claimed

---

[279] *The Loyal Protestant*, no. 3, 15 March 1681. *A Seasonable Address to the Houses* (1681), p. 19, claimed that Benjamin Harris had invented the Colchester address, and a declaration to that effect was entered into the borough's assembly book (Glines, 'Politics and Government in Colchester', p. 178), but see *Vox Patriae* (1681), p. 10, for the claim that the retraction was forced on the corporation by the mayor.

[280] For the text see *CSPD 1680–1*, p. 282.

[281] *The Loyal Protestant*, no. 8, 2 April 1681.

[282] Bod., MS Jones 17, f. 216 verso.

[283] *The Loyal Protestant*, no. 12, 16 April 1681.

[284] *The Observator*, no. 5, 25 April 1681.

[285] Their fears were probably increased by Clayton's reference to the addresses from London to justify introducing the exclusion bill on 26 March 1681 (Grey, *Debates*, viii. 309). Sir Richard Temple opposed the printing of votes in 1689 in a speech in which he referred to the 1681 addresses (Grey, *Debates*, ix. 144, quoted by G. Davies, 'The Political Career of Sir Richard Temple', *HLQ*, iv [1940], 79).

[286] Reresby, *Memoirs*, p. 219. A copy of the address (BL, Stowe 746, f. 16), is endorsed 'Capt. Pickerings'. The address is printed in *The Parliamentary Representation of York 1258–1832*, ed. A. Gooder (*Yorkshire Archaeological Society Records Series*, xcvi [1937]), 173–4.

that 'those addresses & Instructions are the contrivances of a very few ... & are meerly imposed upon the People by artifice and surprize'.[287] *Heraclitus Ridens* maintained that at Hampstead Heath the electorate's 'consent was never askt till they hear[d] it read, and then half a score bawling schismaticks cry Ay, ... and this goes for the consent of the Freeholders. This makes the party look great and formidable'.[288]

These aspersions provoked defences from the advocates of the addresses. Thus the *True Protestant Mercury* was forced to admit that, although Sir Thomas Smith had made 'a very Rhetorical speech to the Knights elected', he had not been 'pitch't upon to be the mouth of that vast Body of Freeholders' and had not therefore presented the Suffolk address, which had called for exclusion, frequent Parliaments and the union of protestants; but the newspaper still insisted that, although twenty or thirty others might be found who opposed it, the address 'was approved by the Gentlemen of the best Quality in that Country'.[289] *The Impartial Protestant Mercury* similarly pointed out that, although the Taunton address had been condemned by some magistrates, seven had not disowned it, four lived outside the borough, one had actually given his assent to it at the time of the election and eight others had been in arms during the Civil War, leaving only four 'young Tools'.[290] *Smith's Protestant Intelligence* also tried to save face for the opposition addresses by reporting that a prosecution of the Essex address as a seditious paper had been dropped when some gentlemen remarked to the loyalist 'that in case they had been at the Election, they would have appeared but a very Small Body, in Comparison with those that made it'.[291] The newspaper also questioned whether the Cambridgeshire loyal address 'be owned by one Freeman of the County ... and although it bears the name of the county and Isle of Ely, which is at least a third part of the county, there was not one Inhabitant in the Isle of that Jury' which made the address.[292] Although the addresses had not relied on mass signatures,[293] they did claim to represent the voice not just of the meaner sort, but of the gentry and freeholders of the nation, and a unanimous voice at that. The Essex address boasted that

being openly read to the Representatives and confirm'd by the Unanimous and Loud Acclamations of the Freeholders, for further demonstration that it was the sense of

---

[287] PRO, SP.104/189, Jenkins to Sir Henry Goodricke, 13 March 1681.

[288] *Heraclitus Ridens*, no. 7, 15 March 1681. The criticism of ratification by popular clamour ignored the fact that the loyal Maldon address was ratified in a similar way, 'with three Hussas of great Joy' (*The Loyal Protestant*, no. 3, 15 March 1681).

[289] *True Protestant Mercury*, no. 27, 26–30 March 1681. For Smith's disavowal see *CSPD 1680–1*, p. 183.

[290] *Impartial Protestant Mercury*, no. 6, 12 May 1681. For the mayor and aldermen's signed disavowal of the address see PRO, SP.29/415/80.

[291] *Smiths Protestant Intelligence*, no. 14, 14–17 March 1681.

[292] *Smiths Protestant Intelligence*, no. 15, 17–21 March 1681.

[293] Except Surrey's, which claimed to be signed by 2,000.

each Individual person in that numerous Assembly, it was offered, that so many as agreed to it, should say Ay; upon which they all cried out Ay, Ay. And if any there were otherwise minded, they were desired to express their Dissent by saying No; At which there was Altum Silentium, not one to be heard saying No.[294]

The Yorkshire address similarly claimed to be 'fully consented to by the whole Assembly by a general Acclamation';[295] and every article of the Stamford address 'was read to the Electors severally, and they gave their consent by Loud Acclamations'.[296] The debate had effectively degenerated into claim and counterclaim made by the different factions of the press, although the controversy had focused attention on which group truly represented the people, as well as on the position of the MP as a delegate or representative.[297]

The campaign also had an important role in heightening fears that the country was drifting towards civil war, for the resolution of many addressers to support MPs with their lives and fortunes was castigated by the loyalists as evidence that a party was preparing to engage in rebellion. One anonymous commentator complained that the Northamptonshire address failed to define the 'common enemy' it talked of, a term by which 'for ought that appears may be intended the King and the Church'; worse still, the author thought, the address promised to stand by MPs no matter what their actions, 'without an exception to a downright rebellion' or the establishment of a republic.[298] *Heraclitus Ridens* queried 'whether promising to assist any persons whatsoever with life and fortune, without the express consent of his Majesty first had and obtained, be not a constructive levying war against his Royal Authority, within the meaning of the Act for settling the whole and intire power of the militia in his Majesty'.[299] The smear that the addresses incited rebellion was

---

[294] *Vox Patriae* (1681), p. 12. *True Protestant Mercury*, no. 18, 23–6 February 1681, gives a similar account.

[295] *Vox Patriae* (1681), p. 14.

[296] *Smiths Protestant Intelligence*, no. 10, 28 February–3 March 1681. At Newcastle everyone threw up their Hats 'as a Testimony of their concurrence' (*True Protestant Mercury*, no. 22, 3 March 1681).

[297] *Democritus Ridens*, no. 1, 30 May 1681, argued that although the electorate conferred full power to its representatives, they remained judges of their actions. Penn's draft of the Fundamental Constitution of Pennsylvania, drawn up probably in the summer of 1681, required annually elected deputies to bring to the assembly signed instructions from their constituents which none were to exceed; the 1676 New Jersey Concessions and Agreements made similar provisions (*Papers of William Penn*, ed. M. and R.S. Dunn, ii. 144–5; i. 404). Algernon Sidney, for whom Penn worked as an electoral agent in 1679, wrote in his *Discourses Concerning Government* that MPs were accountable to the electorate, and talked about instructions to delegates (pp. 423, 453). For the relationship between Sidney and Penn see Scott, *Algernon Sidney and the English Republic*, p. 216; Scott, *Restoration Crisis*, pp. 127–38, 164, 181–3.

[298] *CSPD 1680–1*, p. 203.

[299] *Heraclitus Ridens*, no. 7, 15 March 1681. *The Observator*, no. 8, 30 April 1681, compared the Taunton address to those made from the same town in 1640 and 1647.

particularly damaging for the opposition at a time when Edward Fitzharris was arrested for writing a pamphlet that was a call to arms,[300] and when large armed retinues accompanied MPs to Oxford, a propaganda tactic designed to show strength that backfired when it was later used to reinforce allegations that the opposition had intended to seize the King.[301] Part of the indictment against Shaftesbury after his arrest in July related to words he had allegedly spoken on 18 March to the effect that, if the King refused to pass the exclusion bill, the repeal of 35 Elizabeth and a comprehension bill, his supporters had 'provided strength to compel' him. At the same time, Shaftesbury was supposed to have said 'he would never desist until he had brought this kingdom into a commonwealth without a king', and was accused of planning an association of protestants commanded by Parliament.[302] All these allegations were part of a concerted attempt by the government to cast MPs in the role of rebels under Shaftesbury's leadership, when in fact the cavalcade of armed supporters had been thought necessary to defend Parliament against the troops stationed by the King around Oxford.[303] Distrust of Charles's intentions had reached its height. The struggle between Parliament and the King seemed to have resolved itself into an armed contest similar to that of the 1640s.

CONCLUSION

Loyalist fortunes fluctuated during 1680–1 between the high point of the spring and early summer to the nadir of the autumn. In the early months of 1680 the Chits ministry purged the commission of the peace, enforced the Corporation Act and put an end to the excesses of the press, all policies aimed at rendering troublesome elements ineffectual. Loyalists drew encouragement from these initiatives, which had relied on an appeal to a strong Church interest, though the motive behind the stricter approach to dissent owed much to a desire to rid the country of factiousness in its broadest sense. The ministry partly achieved its aim, since those who had been active in promoting petitions during the previous winter became a broken and weak group. The consequent period of calm was itself important because thereafter discontent inevitably appeared factious and designed to wreck the fragile stability. Moreover, it became easier for rigid Churchmen to claim that

---

300 Haley, *Shaftesbury*, pp. 629–30.
301 Luttrell, *Brief Relation*, i. 121. Muddiman referred to the cavalcade as a 'new way of licking in volunteers' (Longleat, newsbook, 15 March 1681). For evidence that loyalist crowds wished to accompany their MPs to Oxford see *CSPD 1680–1*, pp. 202–3.
302 *The Proceedings at the Sessions House in the Old Baily ... on Thursday 24th of November 1681*, pp. 10–11, 18.
303 Dalrymple, *Memoirs*, ii. 297. Warcup reported that 'the Lords intend to address about insecurity at Oxford' (All Souls, MS 239, f. 96, 'Coll. Warcup's paper', received 28 February 1681).

nonconformity as much as popery threatened the church, and to equate political with religious dissent and thereby remove its legitimacy.

Capitalising on the resurgence of loyalty, addresses abhorring the winter petitions were promoted in late spring, though they were few in number and their main value was as propaganda. The half-hearted nature of the campaign suggests that loyalist opinion was not yet animated, and that moderate opinion had still to be won over by the Court. Yet the increasingly long prorogation of Parliament played into the hands of the opponents of the Court, by reviving fears of arbitrary government, and highlighted the fact that problems had been shelved rather than solved. Taking advantage of the heightened tension in London caused by the shrieval election, Shaftesbury and a small group of followers tried to indict the duke of York for recusancy and to renew the petitioning process. This action further alienated moderates, with the result that the unrest did not spread outside the capital, nor remain at fever pitch for long even there. Nevertheless, the pressure of the approaching session of Parliament awed the ministry into timidity, making it wary of positive action, particularly against dissent, thereby depriving loyalists of a lead and allowing opposition groups to regain the initiative.

One of the main issues taken up when MPs met was the people's right to petition, indicative of a polarisation between petitioner and abhorrer as well as the broader ideological divide over the legitimate extent of popular partici-pation in government. The investigation into the abhorrences maintained the momentum for the redress of grievances, including the succession, in the Lower House and further cowed the loyalists into quiescence, even though the arrests MPs ordered were later used to justify allegations that it was Parliament rather than the King or his brother who acted arbitrarily. The prorogation in January 1681 was met by further petitions requesting that MPs be allowed to sit, and after the subsequent dissolution yet more ad-dresses were presented, this time to Members at the time of their election. These were not, as has sometimes been suggested, simple mandates for exclusion organised from above, but are evidence of the large catalogue of opposition demands and, with the nine counter-addresses they provoked, of an increasingly important local dimension to the crisis. The loyalists indicated a growing willingness to copy opposition tactics and to regain the means of representing public opinion, and their increased vigour was also discernible in the elections themselves, even though the result was largely the return of sitting Members. Although the succession played a much more important role than it had done at previous polls, a Court–Country polarity still prevailed to a surprising degree, together with a stronger awareness of religious tensions. With the survival of the church at stake, loyalists increasingly saw the time as ripe for action. As John Kaye put it, this is an age wherein all friends and true-hearted and honest-principled men ought to stick close to each other; and soe long as they transgress not the laws of the land, but make them, loyalty to our sovereign and the protestant religion as wee have itt now by law happyly established amongst us, the rules of our actions, we may bidd a defiance to all Popish fooleryes and fopperyes, and Phanaticall and Enthusiastick treacheryes and perfidiousness.[304]

[304] Leeds AO, Mexborough mss, Reresby 15/69, Kaye to Reresby, 20 November 1680.

'The scene begins to turne'[1]: propaganda and ideology in 1681

Although the elections for the Oxford Parliament had offered some signs of renewed strength in the country, the loyalists had nevertheless lost their third election in two years. The period immediately before and after the short-lived 1681 Parliament therefore saw a second great wave of loyalist attacks on MPs' actions and their claim to represent the will of the nation, an assault which in many ways mirrored the previous spring's incipient reaction, but this time took off in a way that the abhorring campaign had not. This chapter will focus on propaganda and opinion in the first half of the year, when the loyalists lost at the polls and on the floor of the House of Commons, but gained control of the press and the addressing movement, the major public platforms for the expression of public opinion. It was victory in these areas that proved the most important since, once Parliament had been dissolved, opposition groups were left without an effective voice, except in the City of London. The period witnessed the predominance of the loyalist interpretation of the security of religion, as well as their successful questioning of Parliament as the true expression of the country's wishes and as the guardian of liberties and property. However, the loyalists achieved their propaganda coup partly by emulating their opponents' tactics, which they had once condemned, and partly by usurping many of their most important rallying cries. Whilst this process helped to divide, it also neutralised much of the opposition to the Court, often leading to acquiesence in, rather than genuine support for, a loyalist reaction.

THE REPRESENTATION OF THE PEOPLE AND THE TYRANNY OF PARLIAMENT

On 28 February Secretary Jenkins received a paper of proposals and observations, written by Colonel Warcup, a JP who had once been an ally of the Country opposition and had taken many of the depositions of the witnesses of

[1] Bulstrode newsletter, 13 June 1681.

the Popish Plot.[2] At one level the document shows the alienation of moderate, anti-catholic opinion from extreme actions taken by radicals. Warcup gave a horrified account of a group led by Sir William Waller and John Wildman, who had recently attempted to persuade a Westminster grand jury to indict the duke of York for recusancy, the King's guard as a riotous assembly and the clerks of the House of Commons for 'smothering' the bill to repeal the statute of 35 Elizabeth against protestant dissenters.[3] Warcup proposed that in order to provide for the King's safety, Charles 'should have none about him, but Loyall sons of the Church of England', and that James should return to counterbalance the influence of Monmouth. In addition, those who spread false news should be prosecuted, and London secured in case of unrest. Warcup also wanted to see a prosecution for conspiracy over Shaftesbury's allegations of an Irish Plot, an action that would 'ease the minds of Loyall People from feares and Jealousies fomented by the Phanaticks'. The government was later to pursue policies remarkably similar to those advocated by Warcup, whose comments suggest a strengthening of resolve to assert loyalty to church and state, even by those who had previously been fired by anti-catholicism. But perhaps Warcup's most interesting comments concerned the sitting of the Oxford Parliament itself. He suggested that

the severall pamphlets sold since the dissolution of the last Parl[iamen]t ought to bee inspected: Tis supposed that thereby will appeare that the present Parl[iamen]t is *not* a free *Parl[iamen]t* as it ought to bee, therefore not legall, becaus at the severall elections instructions were given by word of mouth or in writing to Members elected ... these instructions being printed in the Pamphletts is an Awe upon all the Members.[4]

Warcup thought a prorogation would be dangerous 'becaus then the members returne home, dignifyd as Members, by that they may assemble their Representatives ... [and] in a manner sett up a popular government'; but if dissolved, 'the Members could not justify caballing and assembling ... nor make resolves equal to votes and the Loyall Party men out of danger of Parl[iamen]ts priviledges, will show themselves true to the Governm[en]t'. Although throughout 1679 and even much of 1680 Parliament had seemed an essential bulwark against popery and arbitrary power, Warcup was suggesting that it was no longer free and had itself become a grievance to all loyal people.

The charge that Parliament was becoming arbitrary was echoed elsewhere. Although the addresses presented to MPs had been presented after the choice

---

2 All Souls, MS 239, f. 96, 'Coll. Warcup's paper'. This supplements what we know of Warcup's activity from a diary he kept ('The Journal of Edmund Warcup', ed. K. Feiling and F. Needham, *EHR*, xl [April 1925], 235–60).

3 For details of the presentment of the duke see All Souls, MS 243, f. 172, 'The Case of Vindicating his Royal Highness', 28 February 681; Clarke, *James II*, i. 666; *Original Papers*, pp. 114–6.

4 The Winchelsea address was printed in *The True Protestant Mercury*, no. 26, 23–6 Mar. 1681, which was published even whilst Parliament sat.

of candidates, their promoters laid themselves open to the charge of imposing a programme on Parliament. What could be more arbitrary, asked the *Observator*, 'than for your Voxes Populi and Patriae to set Rules to King, Lords and Commons what bills to Prepare and offer, and what to pass'.[5] Consequently, L'Estrange said, 'the Parliament is not a free Parliament'.[6] Another loyalist pamphleteer complained that 'we do indeed still please ourselves with the name of a free Parliament and free elections, w[he]n alas there is no such thing'.[7] John Nalson's *England Bought and Sold* argued that the opposition's publication of *The Certain Way to Save England*, a tract which advised freeholders how to vote, violated the privilege of the people to choose without restriction.[8] The elections therefore, as one pamphleteer put it, did not truly 'feel the Pulse of the Nation'.[9] Ironically the tactics of the opposition had pushed loyalists into claiming to defend what the opposition had long claimed to cherish, a free Parliament.[10] They had usurped the main anti-Court rallying cries of 'liberty' and 'arbitrary power', and tapped the same powerful resentment of infringement on the independence of MPs which had fuelled the attack on the Court's earlier bribery of Members. The political climate had changed so rapidly that Charles was able to open the new Parliament with a speech condemning the 'unwarrantable proceedings' of the last meeting, and an announcement that as he would 'never use arbitrary government' himself, he was 'resolved not to suffer it in others', a warning that MPs had to keep within the 'known and established Laws of the land'.[11]

Loyalists successfully alleged that the nation's true interest could be perverted equally by corruption and by being overawed by a faction. Indeed, in their concern to cast doubt on the validity of Parliament as the true representative of the nation, some loyalists voiced criticisms of the way MPs were chosen, and the type of Member accordingly returned by an unrepresentative system. One tract supportive of the government attacked MPs as out of touch with the real sentiment of the nation because Parliament contained a preponderance of the gentry over traders. This meant that the country was full of 'needless and imaginary fears and apprehensions from higher powers' because Members did not fully understand the true situation.[12] Moreover, it was the radical loyalists rather than their opponents, who pointed out the

---

[5] *The Observator*, no. 41, 10 August 1681.
[6] *The Observator*, no. 5, 25 April 1681.
[7] Bod., MS Jones 17, f. 231, 'an Answer to a Vindication'.
[8] *England Bought and Sold* (1681), p. 2. cf. All Souls, MS 240, f. 363, 'the Scheme of a Paper', n.d.
[9] *The True Englishman* (1681), p. 8.
[10] Harris, *London Crowds*, pp. 133–44, shows how 'tories' reinterpreted tyranny and popery against the nonconformists.
[11] *LJ*, xiii. 745.
[12] *Considerations Offered to all the Corporations* (1681), pp. 1–6.

iniquities of a narrow franchise, even though it is generally claimed that it was the opposition to the Court who argued for election on a wide electorate.[13] One tract, published at the beginning of 1680 to champion the rights of the duke of York, had argued that MPs were not representative of the people since

> they did not derive their power from a third part of the Nation ... none have votes in Elections, but Freeholders of at least forty shillings a Year, and Citizens and Burgesses ... [and] the whole number of Labourers, Servants, Artificers and Tradesmen, not residing in, or at least free of cities and Boroughs are totally excluded ... And what can be more unequal not to say unjust, then that a numerous and upon due computation the far greatest part of the nation ... should be debarred their right of choosing a Master or Pilot [?]'[14]

These arguments were taken up by loyalists with vigour in 1681. The *Observator* remarked that the Commons did 'not represent a 50th part of the Nation',[15] and another writer noted that the electorate did not consist of 'above the 10th part of the Kingdom, if so much'.[16] Yet another loyalist pamphleteer remarked that since

> the members of Parliament are chosen by the men of money, the freeholders, the least part of the nation at this day ... [and] those that are under [the 40 shilling qualification] may truly say they have given them no manner of commission on their part, which destroys the foundation of the generall binding power of a vote of the commons.[17]

This strain of thought sat very uneasily with a conservative strand within loyalist opinion which argued that voting was not a natural right, or that a wider franchise was undermining the power of landed men.[18] Indeed, the

---

13 For discussion of this subject see J.H. Plumb, 'The Growth of the Electorate in England 1660–1715', *P&P*, xlv (1969), 108–9; *Ailesbury Memoirs*, i. 48; BL, Longleat mss, M/863, reel v, Coventry papers vol. vii, ff. 148–9, bishop of Bath and Wells to Henry Coventry, 22 February 1679; H.T. Dickinson, 'The Precursors of Political Radicalism in Augustan England', in *Britain in the First Age of Party*, p. 75. For a discussion of the loyalist propaganda see also Ashcraft, *Revolutionary Politics*, pp. 237–8. It is worth noting that even radical critics of the Court did not always favour a wide franchise where their interest cut against it: see Bethel's election at Southwark (*Smith's Protestant Intelligence*, no. 6, 15–18 February 1681). Algernon Sidney said that 'of common right those only ought to have voices in elections who pay scot and lot' (*History of Parliament*, i. 138).
14 *Captain Thorogood* (1679), p. 3. cf. *Three Great Questions* (1680), p. 12; BL, Add. 32,518, f. 51, notes made by Francis North.
15 *Observator*, no. 25, 20 June 1681.
16 *Antidotum Britannicum* (1681), p. 66. cf. *The Impostor Expos'd* (1681), p. 91.
17 All Souls, MS 242, ff. 314–51 (f. 51 of the tract).
18 *Heraclitus Ridens*, no. 16, 17 May 1681, argued that 'if it were a Natural Right, all persons who are born in England would have a vote at Elections', and could call Parliaments as often as they liked. The earl of Ailesbury complained that MPs were chosen 'contrary to the genius of a great part of the men of most worth in their several counties ... because the common, unthinking people have a voice equal to a man of the best estate', (*Ailesbury Memoirs*, i. 59–60) or, as one pamphleteer put it, 'every little 40s. man hath as much power in electing two

[*continued overleaf*

suggestion of the need for a narrower franchise found resonance within the Country opposition. The 1679 bill to regulate elections, for example, a measure promoted by the critics of the Court, had stipulated that electors be householders, resident for a year before the election, payers of scot and lot and, if they lived in the country, worth over £200.[19] These clauses would have disabled 'all the 40s. men from being electors', and have drastically reduced the size of the electorate.[20] The overlap on the franchise question between radical loyalists and Country opinion shows a blurring of 'party' distinctions, as well as how the supporters of the Court could usurp the stance, or at least the language, of their rivals.

Some loyalists also claimed that the rights of the electorate were being infringed by the unequal geographical distribution of seats. The theme of the reform of the geographical distribution of seats, first raised by a loyalist tract the previous year,[21] was taken up at the end of 1680 by another loyalist who suggested that Parliament was not a true representative of the people because of the shortcomings of the electoral system itself, and proposed that the King remove the burden of choosing MPs 'from those Towns that desire it, & place it upon others more fitt for the Honour, & that the great Cities of London and Bristol & the like should have their Number of Parliament men increased'. Under the author's scheme, every Welsh county was to have three seats, and every English county four, with the exceptions of Yorkshire which was to have six and Ely and Lincolnshire which were both to have five.[22] The similarities between these suggestions and some of the more radical proposals of the Court's critics are striking. The 1679 bill for regulating elections had provided that any city where corruption took place during elections 'shall from that time forfeit their Priviledge of sending members to Parliament', and their seats would be redistributed within the county as directed by the House of Commons.[23] Most interestingly, the champion of the Whig cause, John Locke, espoused the need for geographical redistribution in terms remarkably

members as a country gentlemen of £2000 per annum' (*Religion and Loyalty* [1681], p. 6). An undated document amongst the papers of Robert Hooke, called 'a Project to regulate Elections', complained that 'a Freeholder of 40s. a yeare has a vote in the Election of K[nigh]ts of the Shire; & a Gentleman or K[nigh]t of £10,000 a yeare has no more'; the scheme therefore would have given extra votes to men of large estates (Guildhall Library, MS 1757, no. 14). On 1 August 1679 Hooke noted 'Rules for chusing parliaments' in his diary (*The Diary of Robert Hooke*, ed. H.W. Robinson and W. Adams [1968], p. 419).

19 This had been the figure implemented in 1653 (J. Cannon, *Parliamentary Reform*, pp. 14, 19). *A Safe and Easy Way* (1680) recommended that the electorate should consist of all scot and lot voters.

20 All Souls, MS 240, f. 363, 'the Scheme of a Paper'.

21 *Captain Thorogood* (1680), p. 4.

22 Bod., MS Tanner 37, f. 221, anon. to Sancroft, 28 December 1680. A copy of this appears to have been forwarded to Jenkins (All Souls, MS 242, ff. 263–72). The document hinted that a remodelling of the corporation charters, along the lines of that actually pursued soon after, would reduce the Commons to its proper place in the constitution.

23 *The Bill for Regulating Abuses in Elections* (1679), p. 2.

similar to those of the more radical loyalists.[24] The sincerity with which the latter articulated their reforms of the system may be doubtful, and their proposals may well have been driven by the experience of defeat and the need to depict Parliament as unrepresentative, but the shared rhetoric was an interesting development showing that language was sometimes as important as conviction.

Nor was it just that loyalists claimed the elections had not been free, for they reinterpreted the rallying cry of arbitrary government by suggesting that Parliament's actions had shown it to be the greatest tyrant. A reply to the peers' petition presented by the earl of Essex in January attacked Parliament for invading liberty and endeavouring 'to monopolise Arbitrary Power', and the paper sent to Sancroft had likewise warned that MPs sought to make themselves absolute.[25] In February 1681 at Chichester a parson preached 'that our enemies did once design to destroy us, by blowing up our Parliament; but now we are like to be blown up by our Parliament and their destructive counsels'.[26] *A Dialogue betwixt Sam the Ferriman* attempted to portray the ordinary man's belief that Parliament, both at Westminster and the 'little-arsed one' at Oxford, had been 'worse than mad'. MPs, it suggested, had used bribery to win their seats, and acted arbitrarily:

they call that power which they themselves both do and act by and would govern all by, the liberty of the subject, tho no subject, but a few Members, have any liberty at all; but if his Majesty, God bless him, should act by the same power, and do the same things which they do, then they call the very same power flat down-right tyranny.[27]

Parliament was represented as popish and arbitrary because it attacked the church and acted tyrannically. *A Seasonable Address to both Houses*, written to influence opinion at Oxford, insisted that instead of running into popery and arbitrary government, the country was heading for presbytery and a commonwealth, and revealed that the opposition maintained links with the nation's enemy, France. Having listed Parliament's actions, the author (sometimes but probably inaccurately said to be the earl of Halifax[28]) exclaimed 'if these be not odd and arbitrary proceedings I know not what are'. By contrast, he asked, 'what one illegal arbitrary act had [the king] done in his twenty years reign?'[29] Concomitant with the challenge of arbitrariness was the assertion that Parliament and the people had no right to meddle with the King's actions. White Kennett's *Letter from a Student at Oxford* put such a view so eloquently and forcefully that MPs would have reprimanded him had

---

[24] Locke, *Second Treatise*, paras. 157–8. cf. Ashcraft, *Revolutionary Politics*, pp. 238–9.
[25] *A Letter to a Noble Peer* (1681), p. 2; Bod., MS Tanner 37, f. 221, anon. to Sancroft, 28 December 1680.
[26] *Smith's Protestant Intelligence*, no. 10, 27 February 1681.
[27] *Harleian Miscellany* (ed. W. Oldys and T. Park, 1809), ii. 113, 120–1, 127.
[28] Foxcroft, *Halifax*, ii. 532–3.
[29] *A Seasonable Address to both Houses* (1681), pp. 5, 7–8, 11.

the Oxford Parliament lasted longer.[30] Having praised Filmer, he asserted that the King's power was by divine right and that subjects had 'no privilege to question their sovereign's authority'; Parliament therefore had no right to try to alter the succession.[31]

The charge of arbitrariness was nevertheless refuted by Parliament's supporters prior to, or soon after, the Oxford Parliament, by a re-assertion of the doctrine of popular sovereignty in the legislature.[32] *The Character of a Popish Successor*, probably written by Elkanah Settle, defended attempts to exclude James on the grounds that the people had a right to protect their own liberties and privileges, and that Parliament had frequently determined the course of the succession in the past. Monarchy had been instituted either by conquest, in which case the argument about hereditary right was meaningless, or by the consent of the people, in which case Kings were 'made for the people and not the people for the kings'.[33] These same arguments were repeated by *A Dialogue at Oxford* which defended the last Parliament held at Westminster, claiming that a vote of the House could not be illegal and that the series of provocative resolutions on the day of the prorogation had been 'chiefly intended (as an argument) to persuade the sitting of a Parliament during the distress and hazards of the kingdom'. The author also suggested that the people had originally set up their magistrate by consent, that they were represented in Parliament and that the law determined the frequent meeting of MPs. Thus, far from acting arbitrarily, MPs had the right to punish those who struck 'at the very root of Parliaments themselves', a reference possibly to the arrests of those who had abhorred the petitions calling for Parliament's sitting.[34]

The theme of the King's control over Parliament's sitting was taken up shortly before the Oxford Parliament by an important tract, *Vox Populi*, which claimed that King Alfred had ordained that Parliaments should sit 'twice a year or oftener if need be', and that Parliaments 'ought frequently to meet for the common peace, safety and benefit of the people' at a fixed time.[35] It argued in Lockean terms that Parliaments were 'lay'd in the essence of government' and were 'the bulwark of our liberty'. Since they were a necessary part of the constitution, 'they must have their certain stationary times of session and continuance', and

---

[30] Wood, *Life and Times*, ii. 520–1.

[31] *A Letter from a Student at Oxford* (1681), pp. 12, 15–16.

[32] For comments about the large output of opposition propaganda at this time see *CSPD 1680–1*, p. 139; Longleat, Muddiman newsbook, 22 February and 5 March 1681.

[33] *The Character of a Popish Successor* (1681), pp. 24, 27, 33.

[34] *A Dialogue at Oxford* (1681), pp. 5–18. cf. the attack on abhorrers in *Popery Display'd* (1681), p. 5.

[35] *Vox Populi* (1681), p. 3, 5. cf. *A Just and Modest Vindication* (1681), p. 1; Christie, *Shaftesbury*, ii. appendix vii/3 (second directive of the 'instruction' found amongst Shaftesbury's papers).

ought frequently to meet for the common peace, safety and benefit of the people, and support of the government ... so that not to suffer Parliaments to sit to answer the great ends for which they were instituted, is expressly contrary to the common law, and so consequently the law of God as well as the law of nature, and thereby violence is offered to the government itself, and infringement of the people's fundamental rights and liberties.[36]

The implications of such ideas were pointed out in a reply written by John Nalson, who believed that the argument about the people's right to call Parliament 'by clear consequence strikes directly at the king, as an oppressor'. He refuted the doctrine that a king was only king when he ruled well, suggesting that this was 'a charge of misgoverning slily thrown upon his Majesty', and that 'the poysonous dregs and lees of the late horrid and unnatural rebellion begin again to rise', an assertion that carried conviction when Nalson pointed out that *Vox Populi* was merely a compendium of the trial of Charles I 'beaten a little thinner'. The only comfort Nalson drew from his opponent's allegations was that Charles II could not 'be taxed with so much as one arbitrary action'. Ideologically then, the survival of Parliament seemed to be worked out with reference to earlier seventeenth-century ideas about popular government and Parliament's essential role in the constitution.

This debate points to a fundamental tension within the exclusionist argument which the loyalists did all they could to exploit. On the one hand, exclusion had been justified in Parliament and elsewhere as the means by which monarchy could be preserved. *The Character of a Popish Successor* had argued that in struggling to prevent the tyranny of a popish successor the people had grown 'jealous of monarchy', and that it was therefore better 'to take out one link of the whole chain of succession, than, by preserving that, to break the whole to pieces'.[37] Similarly, *Reasons for His Majesties Passing the Bill of Exclusion*, ascribed to Lord Cavendish, appealed to Charles's self interest by arguing that agreement with the people by conceding exclusion would make him powerful, whilst limitations on royal authority would not.[38] The earl of Huntingdon even went as far as saying that there was not a supporter of the bill who was not 'most zealous for the support of this monarchy and the King in his royal prerogatives'.[39] Yet, on the other hand, the principle that Parliament could alter the succession, a maxim which had to be supported if exclusion was legal, implied that power lay originally in the people and undermined the prerogative powers of all Kings, including

---

[36] An appendix to the tract, called *Vox Regis* (1681), used speeches made by James I in 1603 and 1609 to show that previous kings acknowledged that all but tyrants put themselves within the law.

[37] *The Character of a Popish Successor* (1681), pp. 17, 23.

[38] *Reasons for His Majesties Passing the Bill of Exclusion* (1681), p. 5.

[39] *HMC R.R. Hastings*, iv. 303.

Charles II. There was thus a paradox between the professed ends, and the means and ideology by which those ends could be achieved. Whilst there were some radicals who believed that Charles's abuse of his powers of summoning and dismissing Parliament had subverted the rights of the people, most hesitated to openly accuse the present King of arbitrary government – Charles was, after all, the only person standing between the nation and a popish king – though the continued attacks on his ministers indicated MPs' mistrust of him. There was thus a tension between moderates, who preferred to attack the prospect of a popish king, and extremists, or 'true Whigs', who attacked Charles's actions. For a long while, the fear of popery and the prosecution of Danby had hidden this split, but as the Court's critics began to attack the present King more openly, support for the opposition dried up, leaving it to shrink to its radical core. Once the loyalists could insist that the opposition aimed not at the security of the nation, but at the overthrow of monarchy and at rebellion, they had effectively won the argument about the succession.

Similarly, the loyalists could also dominate over their opponents if they could show that, far from wanting to reform the church, the dissenters and their allies wanted to destroy it. Such accusations forced critics of the established church and state on to the defensive. Henry Booth, later Lord Delamere, for example, felt the need to clear his name from the imputation that he was 'an evil man as to the King and Church', by declaring that he was in favour of the church 'as it is now established under episcopacy ... [but] I am for bringing in Protestants'.[40] Yet although the attack on dissenters and their allies within the church was blunted by Parliament's re-assembly, and John Cheney complained that the prospect of the Oxford Parliament knocked the bottom out of the market for tracts advocating conformity to the Church of England,[41] the lull was only temporary, and demands for a reformed protestant church to fight popery were soon drowned out by the noise of those clamouring against dissent. Throughout 1680 and 1681 the pressure on the church from popery had forced it to try to seek a united front. It did so by making its own interpretation of the call for the unity of protestants the loudest. A spate of pamphlets urged nonconformists to join the Church of England as it stood, and defended its structure against the criticisms of the dissenters, who were castigated as being in league with the papists.[42] Thus

---

[40] *The Speech of the Honourable Henry Booth* (1681).

[41] Bod., MS Tanner 37, f. 234, John Cheney to Sancroft, 21 January 1680/1. cf. *Reliquiae Baxterianae* (1696), pt iii, p. 190: 'the times were so bad for selling books that I was fain to be myself at the charge of printing my *Methodus Theologiae*' (published in 1681).

[42] The identification of dissenters as papists which Harris found in the more popular forms of propaganda (*London Crowds*, chapter 6) was thus repeated in longer, more sophisticated and more expensive literature.

A Parallel between Episcopacy and Presbytery, which had appeared in the summer of 1680, defended episcopal government and told the presbyterians to unite by joining the church 'as it is expressed in the thirty-nine articles'.[43] *A Word in Season for Christian Union* (1680) similarly appropriated the language of unity in favour of the argument for strict conformity, and John Nalson once again took the argument a stage further by suggesting not only that all good protestants should unite in the established church, but also that 'the chief rise and original of our unhappy divisions and separations is to be fetched from the devilish policy of the papists counterfeiting a design to advance the reformation of the protestant religion to a greater purity'.[44] *The Moderation of the Church of England* (1679) suggested that moderation, like unity, was 'the word in fashion, which all divided parties among us use to sanctify their appeals', but that the established church was truly moderate and that the dissenters preferred to unite with the papists than 'come into entire union with our excellent reformed church'.[45] *A Serious Enquiry into the Means of an Happy Union* (1681) argued that schism was a sin of which all nonconformists were guilty, and that conventicles must therefore be suppressed; 'when all is done, the only probable way of an Happy Union is by setting aside all thoughts of toleration or comprehensions upon any other principles than the word of God', and by insisting on strict conformity.[46] *Of the Unity of the Church* (1681), as its title suggests, also urged unity to the established church and condemned schismatics. Having identified the church as standing between what one pamphleteer described as the Scylla of popery and the Charybdis of dissent,[47] and having usurped the rhetoric of unity, its supporters increasingly called for the prosecution of nonconformists once the threat from popery had receded. The author of *A Letter to a Noble Lord* (1681) claimed he had spent the last two years supporting the attack on the papists, but now 'for the same consideration am now as much for opposing the seditious fanaticks' who 'side with the Pope to overthrow the mitre and

---

43   *A Parallel*, p. 3. *Omnia Comesta a Bello*, a fierce attack on bishops, was originally printed in 1667 but reprinted in 1679. cf. *A Disputation proving that it is not convenient to grant unto Ministers Secular Jurisdiction* (1679); *Episcopal Government* (1679). For the controversy about bishops, and the role of anti-clericalism see M. Goldie, 'Danby, the Bishops and the Whigs', in Harris *et al.*, *Politics of Religion*, 75–105; Goldie, 'Priestcraft and the birth of Whiggism', in *Political Discourse in Early Modern Britain*, ed. N. Phillipson and Q. Skinner (Cambridge, 1993), pp. 209–31.

44   *Foxes and Firebrands* (1680), p. 22. As early as February 1679 Nalson had argued in *A Letter from a Jesuit* that a comprehension or toleration of dissenters was the best way to ruin the church and let the papists in.

45   *The Moderation of the Church of England* (1679), To the Reader, p. 2.

46   *A Serious Enquiry into the Means of an Happy Union* (1681), pp. 4, 31, 38, 46. cf. *A Short Defence of the Church and Clergy of England* (1681) and *The Zealous and Impartial Protestant* (1681).

47   *The Cloak in its Colours* (1679), p. 3.

the Crown'.[48] From being seen as possible supports to protestantism, the dissenters had become to be perceived by many vocal critics to be at least as great a threat to true religion and the state as popery. As Joseph Glanvill pointed out in *The Zealous and Impartial Protestant*, the church was now 'twisted with our Monarchy, and the whole frame of our civil government; so that the overthrow of one will be the destruction of both'.[49]

The loyalists had succeeded in using opposition rallying cries to their own advantage. Tyranny, liberty, popery, unity, arbitrariness, the representation of the people: all these now had rival interpretations. It is this overlap of claims, beginning to become defined most clearly by early 1681, that helps explain the emergence of two sides, each struggling to persuade the nation that it was the sole champion of rights and liberties, security and religion. But Charles now needed to press home and accelerate the inroads the loyalists were making into the ideological support for his parliamentary critics. His answer was to do away with Parliament and appeal directly to the people.

THE KING'S *DECLARATION*

On 28 March 1681 Charles surprised MPs by appearing in his robes and dissolving their assembly. On his way out he justified his action to the young, and enthusiastically loyal, Thomas Bruce by remarking that he had better have one King than five hundred,[50] a phrase echoed in a poem which depicted the kingdom as groaning under '500 kings' and which supported the dissolution because it showed that 'Charles is in the throne / and by the Grace of God will Reign alone.'[51]

As the verse suggests, the dissolution of the Oxford Parliament was seen by some loyalists as a defiant gesture by the King that would finally stem the tide of disorder. One gleeful pamphleteer rejoiced at the sight of the dissolved Members, and could not help 'but laugh to see how silly and sneaking they lookt, with their Heads hanging downwards, and their Hats flapping about their Ears, their hopes frustrated, and their Designs infatuated; when in their setting out they appeared brisk and airy.'[52] Another poem described the gloom of those who supported MPs' actions, lamenting that

> They are dissolved, and with them all our hopes,
> Prepare for Smithfield fires, for Racks and Ropes;
> For that's the pleasing Exercise of popes.[53]

[48] *A Letter to a Noble Lord* (1681), first side.
[49] *Zealous and Impartial Protestant* (1681), p. 3.
[50] *Ailesbury Memoirs*, i. 57.
[51] *The Parliament Dissolved at Oxford March 28 1681* (1681), printed in *POAS*, ii. 411–13.
[52] *Obsequium et Veritas* (1681), p. 2. Col. Edward Cooke thought that the 'distractions' caused by the 'surprising dissolution' surpassed those of a routed army (*HMC Ormonde*, vi. 9).
[53] *The Tune to the Devonshire Cant* (1681).

Some nevertheless feared that despondency would give way to mutiny. There were those who thought 'ther would have been some stirs or riseings in London upon it',[54] and when the news of the dissolution reached Chichester one James Lander, who had been gathering names to a petition requesting that Parliament should be allowed to sit 'til they had done their work', announced publicly that those who had voted in the elections should go to Oxford, 'to make good what we have done'.[55] Certainly Charles took no chances, and 'went in all speed away from Oxford the same day' as the dissolution was announced.[56] The King need not have been quite so anxious for, as one newswriter reported, men were generally dissatisfied with Parliament's proceedings, especially those relating to Edward Fitzharris, an unsavoury and double-dealing spy who had been impeached by the Commons in an attempt to plumb, or create, a further branch of the Popish Plot.[57]

It was essential for the Court to follow up the early signs of loyalist revival, evident in the early months of 1681, by persuading the nation that the King's actions had not been arbitrary or influenced by popish counsel, and that the dissolution had been necessary to maintain the King's prerogatives and the peace of the Kingdom. The Court needed to build on the disillusionment with Parliament, and to establish beyond question the argument that MPs, rather than the King, posed the threat to protestantism and liberty. Something was needed to persuade moderate men that the threat to liberty, religion and peace was now greater from the opposition than from the Court; something was needed to encourage the growing signs of a rebirth of loyalist strength; and something was needed to refute the propaganda that the opposition press would undoubtedly produce to attack the decision behind the dissolution. *His Majesties Declaration to all his Loving Subjects touching the Causes and Reasons that moved him to dissolve the two last Parliaments*, given at Whitehall on 8 April 1681 to be read in all churches and chapels by order of the King, was the solution.

Such a declaration had been in the minds of Courtiers for some time. Danby had clearly expected one on the dissolution of the 1679 Parliament. Writing to the earl of Bath from the Tower on 3 June 1679 he had 'wondered there is no news of a declaration, when there is so much need of one, and so good

---

[54] Reresby, *Memoirs*, p. 222. Francis Gwyn nevertheless noted on 5 April that the City was 'in very good order', and Arran made a similar observation a few days later (*HMC Ormonde*, vi, 27–8).
[55] *CSPD 1680–1*, pp. 227–8.
[56] Reresby, *Memoirs*, p. 222–3; *HMC Ormonde*, vi. 21.
[57] Bulstrode newsletter, 1 April 1681.

grounds for the King to make one upon'.[58] The bishop of Exeter had likewise wished 'that some vindication were published' to put the Court's case,[59] and Sir Thomas Thynne had also thought that a 'declaration of the causes of the dissolution, with a narrative of the King's offers and [Parliament's] proceedings' was advisable.[60] As the 1680 Parliament drew nearer its end the archbishop of Canterbury had been advised to procure 'a Remonstrance of the just and necessary causes' of its dissolution.[61] In January 1681 the government's committee of intelligence had debated publishing a declaration to this effect, though 'nothing was agreed upon'.[62] This discussion may well have been held in response to a memorandum drafted by Danby, which suggested that in preparation for a declaration the Commons' Journal should be searched to find evidence that the House had exceeded its powers.[63] Whether deliberately leaked or not, a newsletter reported the debate at the committee,[64] and in February the earl of Clarendon reported that the gentry in Wiltshire expected a declaration from the King.[65] Despite these calls for a statement from the King, the Court may have avoided such action because of fears that any declaration would be compared to one drafted by the catholic plotter and one-time secretary to the duke of York, Edward Coleman, whose letters to Father La Chaise had caused such an outcry in 1678.[66] Indeed, even in 1681, when the declaration was published, the parallels with Coleman's intended propaganda were made.[67] Nevertheless, the decision after the Oxford Parliament to appeal to the people is a further indication of the change of mood in loyalist circles.

The wording of the *Declaration* gives an insight into the government's

[58] Browning, *Danby*, ii. 85. See BL, Eg.3345, ff.76–7, 'Minutes for a declara[tio]n', and ff.78–81, 'draft declaration of vindication'. Southwell reported talk of a declaration at this time (*HMC Ormonde*, iv. 519).

[59] Bod., MS Tanner 38, f.45, Dr Thomas Lamplugh to Sancroft, 14 June 1679.

[60] BL, Althorp MS C5, Thynne to Halifax, 12 July 1679.

[61] Bod., MS Tanner 37, f.221, anonymous letter to Sancroft, 28 December 1680.

[62] BL, Add. 15,643, f.93, minutes for 25 January 1681.

[63] BL, Add. 28,042, f.19, undated memorandum. BL, Add. 28,043, f.23, appears to be extracts from the *Journal of the House of Commons* to this effect.

[64] Newdigate newsletter Lc.1033, 25 January 1681.

[65] *CSPD 180–1*, p.164. Barrillon reported that a declaration would be issued before the Oxford Parliament sat to explain the expedients that the King intended to offer MPs (PRO, 31/3/148, f.41, dispatch, 1/10 February 1681).

[66] Bod., MS Carte 72, ff.447–50, 'declaration prepared by Mr Coleman'. Ronalds, *Attempted Revolution*, p.15, notes that it was printed in the account of Coleman's trial. *The Protestant Antidote* (1680), p.1, referred to this printed version, and quipped that its author could well have been 'the late Intelligencer of Fetter Lane'. Coleman's declaration had been intended to defend a dissolution of the Cavalier Parliament. Having first traced the Parliament's turbulent history since 1672, it attacked the 'forwardnesse of some few tumultuous heads' who designed to alter church and state, compared this with the troubles experienced by Charles I, and ended with a threat to prosecute anyone who spoke 'seditiously slightly or irreverently' of the dissolution.

[67] *A Just and Modest Vindication* (1681), p.4.

policies, and into the deliberate attempt to turn the opposition's slogans back on themselves. Its main thrust of argument was that despite expectations of doing good, the Parliaments had consistently failed to live up to hopes; the offer of assent to any measure of security except exclusion had been ignored and instead the Crown had received remonstrances rather than answers, illegal votes and arbitrary proceedings. The votes of 7 and 10 January, prohibiting the King from raising any money and attempting to suspend the penal laws against the dissenters, were singled out for particular abhorrence, and it was argued that exclusion, if granted, would have led to another civil war and important changes in the monarchy. The King also tried shifting blame for the dissolution of the Oxford Parliament by citing the votes of 26 March 1681 to show the incompatibility between the two Houses. The *Declaration* concluded that the King was resolved to call frequent Parliaments, and loyal men were urged to prevent a relapse into the confusion of 'the late Troubles'. In other words, the actions of Parliament, not those of the King or the possible and future ones of his brother, threatened to plunge the nation into chaos.

There is evidence that the *Declaration* was one of a number of manifestos drawn up for consideration by the King and council. An undated and unsigned manuscript version of a declaration is bound with Danby's parliamentary papers,[68] and the earl's authorship of this is accepted by his biographer Browning, even though the paper is dismissed by him as 'the most unconvincing paper of its kind which Danby ever drew up'.[69] Browning argued that it was an attempt by an old minister to regain some influence, 'only to have the mortification of seeing it rejected in favour of a much shorter manifesto composed by Chief Justice Sir Francis North'. It might be possible to support this view were it not for the existence of a further undated manuscript draft declaration justifying the recent prorogations and dissolutions. It is bound in the Wynne collection of manuscripts at All Souls which contain the papers of Secretary of State Sir Leoline Jenkins,[70] and is endorsed 'Dr[af]t of a Declar[atio]n by Anonymous Ab[ou]t settling of Peace & Quietnes in the Land'. The arguments it uses are similar to those expounded in Danby's draft, a similarity which suggests that the fallen minister was by no means isolated in his political viewpoint; that Danby's draft, rather than being a bid to regain favour at Court, was part of a wider consultation of

---

[68] BL, Add. 28,091, ff. 89–101. It will be referred to hereafter as Danby's draft.
[69] Browning, *Danby*, i. 346, and note 4. Browning's attribution of the published *Declaration* relies on the evidence of Roger North. According to Barrillon the lord chancellor worked with the secretaries of state to draw up the declaration (PRO, 31/3/148, f. 104, Barrillon dispatch, 4/14 April 1681). *The Second Part of the Growth of Popery* (1682), p. 295, claimed that 'L[ord] H[alifa]x' was responsible for it.
[70] All Souls, MS 240, ff. 438–43, hereafter referred to as the 'anonymous' draft.

advisers; and that the rejection of both drafts shows Charles's wish for a declaration that would unite rather than divide.

The draft declarations are different from each other in style and content. Danby's draft analyses all three Parliaments of the period, giving detailed instances of breaches of prerogative or antagonistic behaviour on the part of the Commons. The 'anonymous' draft, on the other hand, treats the subject of the dissolutions and prorogations in a far more general way, avoiding detailed criticisms of the Parliament's proceedings, concentrating instead on underlying causes of unrest, and on comparisons with the problems of Charles I. Nevertheless there are so many similarities between them that if Danby's draft is to be described as 'unconvincing', the term must also be applied to the 'anonymous' draft.

The most striking similarity between the manuscripts is the reliance on the memory of the civil war, which forms a major plank in their defence of the King's actions and their attack on his opponents. Both are concerned to show that the same methods that had brought about the civil war were now on foot again. Danby's draft compares the printing of votes, the address to alter the personnel of the armed forces, and the trial of Stafford to 'the fatall Parliament of 1640'. It argues that the King was 'willing to hope that the intentions were not the same in that Parliament in 1680; but the actions did so nearly resemble one another, that itt cannot be thought unreasonable in us ... to bee apprehensive that from such like beginnings might proceed the like effects'. Similarly the 'anonymous' draft broke its promise to 'say nothing of those unparliamentary agitations' of the civil war by asking 'how did the Methods of Forty one succeed? No otherwise than as the same Methods would have succeeded also with us' if Charles had not dissolved the Parliament. It continued with a lengthy analysis of the events of over twenty years before: 'this being likewise our Case we have great reason to provide against those dreadfull Events which took their Rise, under Our Dear Father, from These beginnings'. Both drafts therefore support the idea that the crisis of 1679–81 has to be set in the context of the unrest earlier in the century, though we should be careful to realise that the parallels were also being used for propaganda purposes.

The draft declarations went some way beyond merely paralleling the crisis of 1679–81 with that of 1641–2, to suggest that the situation needed a vigorous response. Danby's draft hoped that 'instead of such Associations as have been preached of late by ill men, all good men ... will associate together to promote those good ends [of putting the country into order] by incouraging one another in their severall counties, and by being unanimous in their Execution of the lawes wherein they shall receive the utmost of our Assistance'. This was in effect to suggest the formation of a rival Association to that which had been proposed in the 1680 Parliament. The 'anonymous' draft was less direct but seems to have adopted a similar idea: nothing, it argues, could 'be more pertinent to Our purpose than the Remarques of Our Royal Father, in His Declaration of Aug[ust] 12 1642, concerning the Fountain of his troubles'. By comparing the 1681 *Declaration* with that issued by Charles I when he raised his standard at Nottingham, the author can have left his intended readers in no doubt that similar tough measures were necessary.

Both drafts set the political crisis in a religious framework and were concerned not only to tie the problems to the presence of dissenters from the Church of England, but also to threaten them with retribution. Danby's draft declared the King's resolution 'of renewing our steadfast resolutions to ... maintain with our Life & all that is dear to us the True Protestant Religion as itt is now Established by Law, ag[ains]t all the opposers of itt', and made it clear that although the King had been 'willing to show indulgence towards the dissenters ... wee are not affeared to acknowledge our Error in itt'. The 'anonymous' draft similarly pointed out that 'we have not taken any Advantage upon Dissenters ... but suffered the Laws against them to Sleep, without forcing the severity of their Execution ... But if they shall so presume upon our Lenity ... [we shall] strictly command the putting of all Laws in execution against such offenders.'

The drafts also insisted that the electorate should choose suitable men to sit in Parliament in future. The 'anonymous' draft regarded tumultuous elections as the source not only of the Great Rebellion but also of the present unrest; therefore 'there need no more under Heaven to make This a Happy Nation, then only a Choyce of Protestant members of the Church of England, as it is established by Law, for the People's Representative'. Danby's draft also warned the electorate to 'bee circumspect in the choice of such men to represent them in parliam[en]t as are moderate in their tempers, and so fitted in their principles to the present Government (both in Church and State) that they may not come thither with minds busied how to lay new foundations, but how to confirm and Establish the old ones'. The election of worthy anglican men thus lay at the heart of their solution.

The drafts cannot have been rejected on the grounds that they were out of touch with public opinion, for the addresses that were presented to the King in the spring and summer echoed many of their sentiments. The issue of the civil war, for example, was a significant theme in many of the addresses of thanks. About a quarter of them contained overt references to the 1640–60 period, either to prove past loyalty or to express fears that the nation was once again treading the same path to chaos.[71] Pontefract's address referred to the medals coined in honour of the proclamation of Charles II as King on his father's death, offering the 'once Princely, now ruined Castle, our present

---

71 They were printed in *Vox Angliae* (1682), *The London Gazette*, and sometimes individually.

demolished Parish Church, shattered Houses, bare and tottering Walls, to be the Testimonies of our past, and Obligations to our future Loyalty'.[72] Surrey's address paralleled the 1681 campaign of loyal addresses to the petitions made by the Surrey gentry during the wars, which had been performed 'to their utmost hazard and with the loss of some of their Lives'.[73] The addresses from Gloucester, Reading, Barnstaple, Derby, Coventry, Deal, Essex and Huntingdon all expressed fears that a second rebellion was planned,[74] and Okehampton admired Charles's wisdom for 'so calmly suppress[ing] those threatening Flames which were breaking forth'.[75] Durham had 'expected scarce anything less than confusion'.[76]

The idea of rallying to the royal flag was voiced by other loyalists. *A Dialogue between the Pope and a Phanatick* (1680) was interrupted by the entry of a Cavalier who said 'it is evident enough by your Plotts and Petitions that you design another war ... we do therefore declare that we will speedily furnish ourselves with Arms ... and upon the first notice of a Rebellion, we will repair to the Royal Standard'.[77] The city of Hereford's address of thanks for the *Declaration* made a pledge to defend Charles and the succession 'with the last drop of our Blood, and penny of our Fortunes',[78] and the Northampton address of thanks promised that its inhabitants 'will be ready at any time when your Majesty shall command us, to march out and Fight against any Rebels' that appeared against the King and his lawful successors.[79] The tone of the draft declarations would therefore not have appeared unconvincing to the more militant loyalists.[80] This was especially true in terms of religion. Rumours circulated almost immediately after the dissolution that the laws against dissenters, including the Elizabethan statute, would be enforced.[81] One circuit judge made it clear that although he was unwilling 'to whet the edge of the law' of 35 Elizabeth, it would be enforced against those 'sort of peopell who wold break through the Church to distroy the state'.[82] The identification, made by the draft declarations, between loyalty to the

---

[72] *Vox Angliae* (1682), pp. 18.   [73] *Vox Angliae* (1682), p. 40.

[74] *Vox Angliae* (1682), pp. 3, 10, 12–13, 22–5, 31, 51. cf. C. Holmes, *Seventeenth Century Lincolnshire* (Lincoln, 1980), p. 245.

[75] *Vox Angliae* (1682), p. 19.   [76] *Vox Angliae* (1682), p. 21.

[77] *A Dialogue between the Pope and a Phanatick* (1680), p. 18.

[78] *Vox Angliae* (1682), p. 3.   [79] *Vox Angliae* (1682), p. 22.

[80] Jeffreys, who presented an address of thanks, 'was there with his sword and told his Ma[jes]tie that he used to appeare before him in his Gowne but now came w[i]th his weapon (and Laying his hand thereon) and said the Lives and Fortunes were at his Ma[jes]ties command' (UCNW, Mostyn MS 9090, f. 127, newsletter, 21 May 1681). Burnet saw in the addressers' attitude 'the old valour and swaggering of the Cavaliers' (Burnet, *History*, ii. 290).

[81] *True Protestant Mercury*, no. 28, 30 March–2 April 1681; Newdigate newsletter, Lc.1060, 2 April 1681; *CSPD 1680–1*, p. 229; Luttrell, *Brief Relation*, i. 72, 76.

[82] Congress newsletter 7/184, 28 April 1681.

King and a strict adherence to the established church was also made by the address of thanks from Leeds, which declared that the church was 'the most Pure for Principles of Faith and Worship and alone truly Loyal'.[83] It is clear that Danby's draft and the 'anonymous' draft shared arguments and emphasised views that many loyalists at the time found convincing and which were expressed in the presented addresses of thanks. Indeed some of the presented addresses actually went further than the draft declarations in their assertion of the King's powers. Several, for example, stated that the right of calling and dissolving Parliament lay wholly in the Crown,[84] and the one from Cambridge University was the quintessence of Toryism, asserting that

our kings derive not their Titles from the People, but from God; that to him only they are accountable; that it belongs not to Subjects either to create or censure, but to Honour and Obey their Sovereign, who comes to be so, by a Fundamental Hereditary Right of Succession, which no Religion, no Law, no Fault or Forfeiture can alter or diminish.[85]

Yet despite striking a chord with many loyalists, the draft declarations were not used probably because they were too immoderate in tone, and appealed to too narrow an audience. The published *Declaration* was more subtle, aiming to cover its partisanship with a layer of moderation. It used the argument that the experience of the civil wars prevented the King from agreeing to any measure (such as exclusion) which might return the country to chaos; but did not linger on this theme in the way that the drafts do, and made no mention of any association of loyalists. Even more significantly, the printed version omitted any specific castigation of the dissenters. A separate proclamation against conventicles was planned,[86] but was never issued because a number of Charles's advisers thought it 'very improper att this time, when all encouragement is to be given for the uniting of all protestants'.[87] The threat of repression was therefore veiled beneath the statement that 'the due and Impartial Execution of our Laws' had been found to be the best support of the Protestant interest. The printed version of the declaration was also careful to show the unreasonableness of the House of Commons in the last two Parliaments without antagonising the country with threats of retribution. Instead

---

83 *Vox Angliae* (1682), pp. 44–5.
84 *Vox Angliae* (1682), p. 6 (Wigan), p. 21 (Durham), p. 25 (Chesterfield), *Vox Angliae (Part Two)* (1682), p. 1 (Glamorgan), p. 13 (Lincoln), p. 16 (Stafford).
85 *Vox Angliae (Part Two)* (1682), p. 4. cf. *Vox Angliae* (1682), p. 4, Gloucester's address for the assertion that it was by God that Kings reigned.
86 *CSPD 1680–1*, p. 229; Newdigate newsletter Lc.1060, 2 April 1681. The plan seems to have been to raise money through prosecutions (Luttrell, *Brief Relation*, i. 72). Although he stopped short of this, Charles nevertheless told the privy council about his intention to prosecute nonconformists (*EHD*, viii. 394–5).
87 Nottingham University Library, DDSR/219/14, L. Champion to Halifax, 14 June 1681. The earl of Radnor and some others on privy council had opposed its publication (Bucks. RO, Verney mss, M11/35, John Verney to Sir Ralph Verney, 11 April 1681).

of exhorting the nation to elect worthy, anglican men, it did not even mention elections. Unlike the draft declarations, which speak in a divisive tone of the righteous against the 'ill affected' and 'ill minded', the printed *Declaration* preferred insinuation to explicit statement; whilst not excusing anything unjust, it tried not to be offensive or provocative. As Roger North remarked, the document was 'penned or adjusted with all the prudent cautions imaginable'.[88] Moreover, the printed *Declaration* promised that the King would rule by law, that he would summon Parliament frequently, and claimed that Parliament had acted arbitrarily, whilst the King had acted for the security of the nation. In other words Charles was claiming the high ground previously occupied by his critics. He was claiming moderation against fanaticism, and the defence of liberty and peace against those who used those cries to whip up discontent. He was arguing that there was no crisis of popery and arbitrary government, except that created by his opponents.

Some evidence suggests that right up to its date of publication the King was considering the various versions of the *Declaration* in an effort to choose between them. On 2 April 1681 John Braman was informed that the Court attempted 'to fit a declaration to the hewmer of the people but ... it is laid aside and some other measures taking'.[89] Three days before the declaration was officially released, Francis Gwyn, secretary to the council, informed the duke of Ormonde that although a declaration was expected, he could not 'tell what [was] resolved upon that matter as yet'.[90] The rejection of the two draft declarations in favour of the shorter published version, if that is what happened, may partly have been due to their length. The *Declaration* needed to be a succinct defence, brief enough to be read out loud to a congregation in order to emphasise the bond of church and state. On the other hand, Burnet thought that the archbishop of Canterbury's suggestion that the pulpit be used for disseminating the propaganda was only made in council when the King showed the *Declaration* to his advisers;[91] so that, unless Charles primed the archbishop beforehand to voice this idea, a decision in favour of the printed version had already been made. The decision not to choose either of the draft declarations was based on more than a preference for brevity. Charles was aware that he needed to win back the support of moderates who had been temporarily blinded by their fear of popery and arbitrary government, and that he would do so by a moderate, broad appeal rather than by the threats and divisive language that some of his advisers seemed to be advocating. Barrillon reported that Charles even contemplated not publishing

---

[88] North, *Lives of Norths*, i. 380.   [89] *CSPD 1680–1*, p. 228.
[90] *HMC Ormonde*, vi. 27.
[91] Burnet, *History*, ii. 288–9. Burnet may have been misinformed since one loyalist pamphleteer noted that Charles put the declaration before privy council 'without desiring their advice' (Bod., MS Jones 17, 'answer to a vindication', f. 213 verso).

the *Declaration* for fear of the opposition it would provoke.[92] A moderate statement was therefore required.[93] Moreover, Charles liked to be free from restrictions on his decisions, and he was concerned to remain above 'party', even a loyal one. He was not even initially in favour of a campaign of addresses of thanks for his *Declaration*, but thought himself 'compelled to it' once they had begun to be presented.[94]

THE RESPONSE TO THE *DECLARATION*

Despite its moderate nature, the *Declaration* was not universally well received. The contemporary historian White Kennett later wrote that 'however smooth and fair, [it] was by no means Popular. Some thought it nothing but a Torrent of Words: Others had a Worse Opinion of it, as a Stretch of Prerogative, and a Profess'd insult upon the late Members of both Houses. Many question'd the Validity of it.'[95] Barrillon believed that the *Declaration* had not calmed men's minds,[96] and Luttrell records that it 'was not very pleasing, but afforded matter of sport to some persons'.[97] Nevertheless, *direct* opposition to the *Declaration* seems to have been very limited.[98] The evidence suggests that few, if any, of the clergy refused to read it as ordered,[99] though

92 PRO, 31/3/148, f. 107, Barrillon dispatch, 7/17 April 1681. Charles may also have disliked having to explain his actions, especially since a loyalist propagandist had insisted that the petitioners of 1679–80 were incapable of understanding state affairs (*A Petition to the Petitioners* [1680], p. 3).

93 Sir William Coventry observed that the final version of the *Declaration* would 'put into the mouths of all whoe hate troubles & would be moderate, authentick arguments, & those whoe are not farre engaged will bee soe farr swayed, as that when the next Parl[iamen]t will bee chosen will encline to moderate men' (BL, Longleat mss, M/904, reel ix, Thynne papers, vol. xvi, f. 340, Coventry to Sir Thomas Thynne, 15 April 1681).

94 *CSPD 1680–1*, p. 267. Arran informed Ormonde that Charles had not encouraged the addresses (*HMC Ormonde*, vi. 61). Hyde and Halifax also had reservations about the campaign (John Rylands Library, Legh mss, Laurence Hyde to Richard Legh, 7 July 1681: 'I doe not give you any advice one way or other c[on]cerning an Addresse [of w[hi]ch I am as little fond as you can be] and I am sure, if there be any good in them, it can only consist in the unanimity of it'; Burnet, *History*, ii. 290: Halifax remarked that though the petitioners had spat in the King's face, the addressers spat in the King's mouth).

95 Kennett, *Complete History*, iii. 399.

96 PRO, 31/3/148, f. 111, Barrillon dispatch, 24 April 1681.

97 Luttrell, *Brief Relation*, i. 73, 77.

98 Nottingham University Library, DDSR 219/114, L. Champion to Halifax, 23 April 1681.

99 According to *The Impartial Protestant Mercury*, no. 6, 12 May 1681, a minister was to be called before the privy council for refusing or neglecting to read the declaration. Reresby was told that in parts of Yorkshire the declaration's distribution was sporadic (Leeds AO, Mexborough mss, Reresby 19/27, John Wentworth to Reresby, 25 April 1681). Muddiman, however, claimed that in London, where one would expect greatest opposition, that it was read and 'enterteined with a Reverence that became so great a condescension' (Longleat, Muddiman newsbook, 28 April 1681), and even the earl of Essex's chaplain read it at Osterley Park (Newdigate newsletter Lc.1079, 21 May 1681).

in some places it provoked outbursts from elements of the congregation. John Verney reported that 'when the Declaration was read on Sunday where Sir W[illia]m Rob[er]ts was he stood up & told the people that Parl[iamen]t did nothing but what he would maintain with his life & fortune'; and at Stepney there was another commotion after its reading, though an eye witness claimed this was due only to a boy running into the church crying for his mother.[100] One newsletter reported that at Chiswell 'sev[er]all Gentlemen made a disturbance & went out' of the church where the declaration was read.[101] The *Impartial Protestant Mercury* reported that a lord in Oxfordshire, possibly Lord Lovelace, would be questioned 'for opposing His Majesties late Declaration about the Parliament, when it was read out in his church, and saying it was false, or words to that effect, and caused his Man when they came out of the Church, to read the Protestation of the Lords in the Church Yard'.[102]

Such reactions were, however, rare and it was left to two tracts, *A Letter from a Person of Quality to his Friend concerning His Majesties Late Declaration* and *A Just and Modest Vindication of the Proceedings of the Last Two Parliaments*[103] to attack the wording and argument of the *Declaration*.[104] Both of these appear to have been written by a cabal, possibly the same cabal, of opposition writers.[105] *A Just and Modest Vindication*, which has been

---

[100] Bucks. RO, Verney mss, M11/35, John Verney to Sir Ralph Verney, 21 April 1681.

[101] Newdigate newsletter Lc.1079, 21 May 1681.

[102] *The Impartial Protestant Mercury*, no. 12, 3–7 June 1681. The 'Protestation' was presumably that made by twenty peers against the rejection of the impeachment of Edward Fitzharris (Haley, *Shaftesbury*, p. 636).

[103] It was not published until June (*CSPD 1680–1*, p. 312; *Observator*, no. 23, 15 June 1681), and according to Burnet's manuscript history 'was not so much considered over England' (BL, Add. 63,057B, f. 58).

[104] There appears to have been a third reply, intended particularly for foreign consumption. William Carr reported that 'a most treasonable paper called a letter to a friend in Amsterdam concerning the dissolution of the Parliament, which is full of treason and Impudent language,' replied to the *Declaration* (BL, Add. 37,981, f. 32, Carr to Conway, 19/29 April 1681), but no copy of a tract with that appears to have survived. *The Loyalty of the Last Long Parliament* (1681), pp. 14–16, indirectly attacked the *Declaration*.

[105] Burnet refers to an answer to the Kings's *Declaration*, having been originally penned by Algernon Sidney, but subsequently redrafted by Somers, and corrected by Sir William Jones (Burnet, *History*, ii. 289). In the original version of his history (BL, Add. 63,057B, f. 58) Burnet claimed that Wildman had written it, with help from Jones, Sidney and Col. Titus. It is not definite that Burnet was referring to *A Just and Modest Vindication* since he does not name the tract. Evidence in favour of Sidney's involvement lies in the fact that a paragraph of the tract appears in his *Discourses Concerning Government* [B. Worden, 'The Commonwealth Kidney of Algernon Sidney', *JBS*, xxiv (1985), p. 15], and Scott has also pointed to other similarities (*Restoration Crisis*, pp.184–95), though Sidney could of course have borrowed from the pamphlet. A rough draft of the tract also survives among the Somers papers (E. Ellis, 'The Whig Junto', Oxford D.Phil., 1961, p. 64). On the other hand, Robert Ferguson also admitted to having written it (Bod., MS Smith 31, f. 30), and his claim was backed at the time by L'Estrange, who 'took for granted' that the author of the tract was also

[*continued on next page*

described as bristling with republicanism,[106] put forward the argument that although the King had the power to call and dissolve Parliaments, dismissing a Parliament 'when nothing but the Legislative power ... could relieve us from our just fears or secure us from our certain dangers, is very unsuitable to the great trust reposed in the Prince'.[107] The tract asserted that the Court had prevented a peaceful resolution to the conflict, and, like Locke's *Second Treatise*, that the people must now decide how to act.[108] *A Letter from a Person of Quality* also argued in Lockean terms when it claimed that the King's prerogative of calling Parliament was 'but subservient ... to the great end and design of the Government and must be accommodated to it'.[109] By directly attacking the King's own moderate words, both tracts played into the loyalists' hands. Thus Sir William Coventry thought a written reply to a royal declaration to be 'a very strange thing, it not being usuall till absolute breakes; and I think the reply from a private hand would leave the answerer the gainer'.[110] The pamphlet response to the *Declaration* focused opposition fire on the King's own actions rather than on the fears of popery and arbitrary government in a future reign, but the naked attack on Charles was exploited by the replies they provoked. Halifax's *Observations upon a late libel* expertly exposed the nature of *The Letter*'s assault on the position of the King, who would only be left 'to eat and drink and perform some offices of nature'. He claimed it proved that the King's opponents sought a House of Commons 'that may do how they will, and as long as they will, that is for ever'; that the House undermined liberty; that the deliberate delay in the trial of Fitzharris,

the writer of *No Protestant Plot* (1681), a pamphlet which has been ascribed to Ferguson. L'Estrange does confirm Burnet's belief that the material for *A Just and Modest Vindication* (1681) was gathered by more than one hand (*CSPD 1680–1*, p. 532). *A Letter from a Person of Quality to His Friend* (1681) seems to have drawn most contemporary attention. *The Observator*, no. 17, 26 May 1681, described it as 'one of the most Daring Papers that has yet to come to light', and both Halifax and Dryden answered it, rather than *A Just and Modest Vindication* (1681). Dryden's *His Majesties Declaration Defended* (1681) p. 3, refers to five pens having been involved in the drafting of *A Letter from a Person of Quality to His Friend* (1681), and Halifax also referred to it (*Observations upon a late Libel* (1681), p. 1) as the product of consults. It seems possible that the cabal of writers was responsible for both. This would explain similarities of content, style, and the common use of the unusual example of the law regulating the use of bows and arrows (*A Letter from a Person of Quality to His Friend* (1681), p. 7; *Just and Modest Vindication* (1681), p. 25).

106 See Scott, *Restoration Crisis*, pp. 184–97, for a discussion of the tract.

107 *A Just and Modest Vindication* (1681), pp. 1–2.

108 Ibid, p. 48. cf. Ashcraft, *Revolutionary Politics*, pp. 317–18. *A Just and Modest Vindication* (1681), however, unlike Locke, argued for annual Parliaments (p. 1). cf. *A Dialogue at Oxford* (1681), p. 8, for similar arguments.

109 *A Letter from a Person of Quality to His Friend* (1681), p. 8.

110 BL, Longleat mss, M/904, reel ix, Thynne papers, vol. xvi, f. 340, Coventry to Thynne, 15 April 1681.

who had written a call to arms, looked like an attempt to allow men to commit treason with impunity; and that the opposition used the plot 'for a buttress to support arguments that are too weak to bear up themselves'. Pursuing his quarrel with Shaftesbury, Halifax sneered that the little earl would now be distraught 'for want of sufficient matter to trouble himself and the world with'.[111]

Dryden also attacked the *Letter*'s adoration of the Commons as the sovereign power and its attempt to reduce the King to a Venetian Doge. He attacked Shaftesbury for having broken with the Dutch when he was in power in 1672, and consequently allowing the growth of France. The House of Commons, he claimed, had been 'incroaching into sovereignty and arbitrary power while they seemed to fear it from the king', and the unrest was now being driven on by an 'anti-monarchical party', who artificially kept up imaginary fears of popery and arbitrary government. Dryden also attacked the resistance theory implicit in much of his opponent's argument, asserting that the law of nature and self preservation did not empower a man to rise in arms against the sovereign Prince, and he championed the King's right to dismiss MPs when he saw fit to do so, otherwise Parliaments would be perpetual. Dryden, the historiographer royal, thus highlighted the dangerousness of the ideology that underpinned the parliamentary opposition's actions, even though most of those members would have resented the imputation of republicanism in the sense of deposing the King. He and other loyalists had succeeded in smearing Restoration republicanism, which was the pursuit of a mixed monarchy and politics of virtue, with old-style King-killing republicanism. As a result, 'the nation beg[an] to awake', and the opposition was noticed to be 'mould'ring away, ... suspecting each other so very fast that every man is shifting for himself, by a separate Treaty'.[112]

---

[111] *Observations upon a late Libel*, pp. 2–7. For a discussion about the grounds for Halifax's authorship of the tract see *Works of George Savile*, ed. M. Brown (Oxford, 1989), i. 13–33. Assuming Halifax was the author, his snide remark about a 'Venetian shape' of monarchy (p. 2) raises questions about the sincerity of his commitment to limitations on a popish successor as a solution to the succession crisis, or at least about the extent to which he wished to see royal powers curtailed.

[112] *His Majesties Declaration Defended* (1681), pp. 5–20. The reference to members of the opposition making peace with the Court echoes Halifax's comment that 'if the confederates fall out amongst themselves they will bee so shaken, that a little care in the Gov[ernmen]t will dissolve the Corporation' (BL M/904, reel viii, Thynne papers, vol. xv, f. 27, Halifax to Thynne, 16 April 1681). Monmouth was restless, and took advantage of the fact that Sunderland was still on good terms with the duchess of Portsmouth to try to effect a reconciliation with his father (Congress newsletter 7/175, 7 April 1681; Clarke, *James II*, i. 681; *HMC Ormonde*, vi. 40; BL, Add. 28,042, f. 85. memorandum 27 May 1681). Although Monmouth eventually refused to leave his friends, others were successfully won over. The most notorious convert was the opportunistic Lord Howard of Escrick, who then quarrelled fiercely with Shaftesbury, but Lords Macclesfield and Manchester also made their peace, and others were believed to 'slacken in theyre way', so that it was 'observed in generall that that Party is very much broken since the last dissolution' (Luttrell, *Brief Relation*, i. 77; BL,

A lengthy reply to *A Just and Modest Vindication* was written, and though apparently never published, pursued many similar themes.[113] The author denied that the power of calling and dissolving Parliaments lay with the people, or else 'instead of a k[in]g we make him but the common cryer of the nation, who at every discontented person's pleasure is obliged to summon' MPs, and never dismiss them. Praising the *Declaration*, the author thought it was 'a great indication that a prince has not infringed the privileges of his people, when he does thus without necessity put himself (as it were) upon his countrye and makes his subjects judges of his actions'. The real design of the *Vindication*, he suggested, was 'to cast all odium upon the k[in]g imaginable'. The manuscript tract continued by attacking the three previous Parliaments, and in particular the Commons' refusal to agree to limitations on a popish successor, by which the House had 'dasht what might have proved its security'. Thus rather than being its preservers, MPs should be labelled 'the destroyers of the nation'. Security now lay in 'a good understanding and mutual trust and confidence between the K[in]g and his people'. In two telling phrases the author explained how he regarded 'civill warre as a more dreadfull thing than persecution' by a popish king, and that there were 'a great many who profess themselves protestants that do the Church as much harme as the Papists while they are more industrious to pull down episcopacy than popery'. This was now the dominant philosophy.

The *Declaration* had thus further encouraged loyalists to claim that the House of Commons, not the King, threatened liberty, security and religion. Having replaced the opposition's interpretation of key slogans with their own versions, the next step for the loyalists was to replace mass petitioning with loyalist addresses which thanked the King for publishing the reasons behind the dissolution of the last two Parliaments.

'THE HUMOUR OF ADDRESSING IS NOW OF OUR SIDE'[114]

It was within London, the heart of the petitioning campaign of 1679/80, that the *Declaration* and the addressers found most opposition. 'The City is now struggling within itself', remarked one observer of the rivalry between petitioners and addressers.[115] The City's common council was one of the

---

Althorp mss, B6, Countess Sunderland to Countess of Cork and Burlington, 12 May 1681; Bod., MS Carte 222, f. 290, newsletter 23 April 1681). It was reported soon after the dissolution that Sir William Jones, one of the most prominent MPs in the 1680–1 Parliament in support of exclusion, would be made Lord Chief Justice, and that Cavendish had also returned to Court (Newdigate newsletter, Lc.1069, 26 April 1681; Luttrell, *Brief Relation*, i. 89) The Whigs were slimming down to their ideological core.

113 Bod., MS Jones 17, ff. 212–32, 'An Answer to a Vindication'. It must have been written after July, since it refers to Shaftesbury's arrest.
114 *HMC Ormonde*, vi. 48.   115 Ibid.

arenas for this struggle. Immediately after the dissolution Jenkins had reported that 'the old Boulefeux' endeavoured to persuade the City to petition for a new Parliament,[116] and pressure was exerted by lords Bedford and Salisbury to have the common council summoned so that a petition might be presented.[117] With still no meeting called by the end of April, two rival petitions were prepared and presented to the court of aldermen: one signed by 'regular Protestants of the Church of England' thanked the King for his *Declaration*, but was otherwise very moderate in tone,[118] and the other called for a Parliament.[119] The address of thanks was presented, but Sir Thomas Player objected to it on technical procedural grounds, allowing alderman Hayes and Papillon to present the petition for a Parliament, and, although recorder Treby sent both parties away with 'a faire speech ... admonishing them to peace and union',[120] the matter did not end there. Rejecting advice from Jenkins, who argued that the rival petitions would 'unavoidably be brought in to the Common Councill and become a matter of great contrast between the subscribers and promoters of those petitions',[121] the lord mayor called a meeting, believing that the citizens could not be 'hindered from petitioning, considering the fears or rather the terrors and amazements that all good men [were] under'.[122] Although Charles had directed the court of

---

116 PRO, SP.104/67, f. 30, Jenkins to William of Orange, 1 April 1681. The other demands were a pardon for Fitzharris, and that none of the Lords in the Tower should be released on bail. Jenkins noted that although supported by 'the troublesome & factious spirits' the demands were less appealing to 'the sober & quiet men'.

117 *HMC Ormonde*, vi. 27; Newdigate newsletter Lc.1060, 2 April 1681. Several citizens 'went to Clayton, who told them to search for precedents [for calling a council without the lord mayor] but they could find none' (*Domestick Intelligence*, no.111, 5 Apr. 1681).

118 *The Protestants' Petition and Address*. Kent AO, U1015/07/7 is a copy of this petition, with twenty-two original signatures, with a note that it was presented by Mr Deputy Hawes and Mr Loades. Newdigate newsletter Lc.1070, 30 April 1681, put the number of subscribers at 'aboute sixty', but it is possible that a much larger list of names had also been collected, since other reports estimated 1,500–2,000 signatures (*CSPD 1680–1*, p.256; Nottingham University Library, DDSR/14, L. Champion to Halifax, 17 May 1681), and when it was printed claimed to have 'many thousands' of signatures, gathered in 'a day and a half'. For the text see below.

119 Kent AO, U1015/07/6, draft petition of 28 April 1681. The petition gave an account of the rise of popery and popish designs since the Great Fire, and the Court's failure to stem the growth of popery. It concluded that the petitioners 'humbly conceive That it is not a declaration to have frequent parliam[en]ts that can contribute any thing to the safety and preservation of his Ma[jes]ties Royall person ... But it must bee the sitting of a Parliam[en]t.' Muddiman thought that the petition was promoted by 'the busy dissenting party in London' (Longleat, Muddiman newsbook, 30 April 1681). It was printed as *The Petition of Divers Eminent Citizens*.

120 Bod., MS Carte 222, f.295, newsletter, 30 April 1681. A manuscript endorsement by Papillon noted that Treby's comment was 'well taken by everyone' (Kent AO, U1015/07/7b).

121 *CSPD 1680–1*, p.269.

122 Ibid. Jenkins ascribed the mayor's decision to a meeting with Clayton, Sir John Lawrence, and Treby at Pollexfen's chambers. For Treby's and Pollexfen's role in the petitioning in 1679 see *HMC Fitzherbert*, pp.21–2.

aldermen to take the petitions 'out of the way of the Common Councell',[123] a petition thanking the city's MPs for their service was accepted on 13 May after a close vote, and a new petition calling for a Parliament was introduced and passed 'with little opposition'.[124] Charles was determined to show his disapproval of these proceedings. He first refused to meet the petition's presenters, and then 'gratiously' received the address of thanks for his *Declaration* which had initially been offered to the court of aldermen and was now presented by Sir William Turner.[125] When the petitioners for a Parliament were eventually received, the lord chancellor was instructed to give them a sharp reprimand,[126] in contrast to the enthusiastic reception accorded to the rival Southwark addressers of thanks.[127] On 27 June the common council responded by passing another petition repeating the call for a Parliament, and emphasising that the earlier petition had been representative of the City's views.[128]

The struggle was not confined to the City's elected body. A Middlesex grand jury asked the judges to inform the King of their petition for an immediate sitting of Parliament. MPs were not to be dismissed until provisions had been made against a popish successor, a danger which the petition claimed 'may be easily and only cured by annual and effectual Parliaments'.[129] The jury gave thanks to the City's representatives,[130] and, as if to insult the loyalists further, also presented the Norwich address of thanks as a

---

123 Bod., MS Carte 222, f. 302, newsletter, 14 May 1681.

124 *True Protestant Mercury*, no. 37, 11–14 May 1681. The majority was only 14 (*CSPD 1680–1*, pp.275–6; Bod., MS Carte 222, f. 302, newsletter, 14 June 1681; *Observator*, no. 14, 18 May 1681). Verney blamed the Court's defeat on 'ill management' (Bucks. RO, Verney mss, M11/35, John Verney to Sir Ralph Verney, 16 May 1681), but a newsletter 'wondred that there were so many noes in a common councell that the Brethren had been so industrious, so prevalent too, in the choosing of' (Bod., MS Carte 222, f. 302, 14 May 1681). The petition is catalogued as being in the Alchin collection at the CLRO, but appears to have been lost or misplaced.

125 Nottingham University Library, DDSR 219/14, L. Champion to Halifax, 17 May 1681. According to Congress newsletter 7/191, 14 May 1681, the address was also to be presented by Sir John Moore, an important City figure sympathetic to dissent; if this report was true, his support may be an indication that some low-Churchmen disapproved of the immoderacy of the City 'faction'.

126 *The Answers Commanded by His Majesty* (1681). There is an annotated copy of this amongst Papillon's papers (Kent AO, U1015/07/11). All Souls, MS 239, f. 128 is a manuscript version of the lord chancellor's speech.

127 Bod., MS Carte 222, f. 303, newsletter, 21 May 1681.

128 Papillon recorded that 'at the word Parliam[en]t in the middle of the Petition ther was a great shout. At the end of the Petition ther was another great shout' (Kent AO, U1015/07/12). There had been reports that 'the Tory party' would attempt an address of thanks (*CSPD 1680–1*, p. 331–2), but this did not materialise.

129 *CSPD 1680–1*, p.283. It was promoted by Sir William Roberts and Sir William Cowper (Bod., MS Carte 222, f. 308, newsletter, 17 May 1681; *The Proceedings of the Grand Jury of Middlesex in Easter Term* [1681]).

130 *CSPD 1680–1*, p.285.

seditious libel.[131] In response, a different jury disowned the petition for containing expressions 'not at all becoming the duty of loyall subjects to their sovereign ... well knowing that the time for calling and sitting of Parliaments is the King's prerogative ... and that his Majesty is the only judge when to call them and how long they shall sit'.[132] The rivalry between the petitioners and abhorrers was also vigorous amongst the London apprentices.[133] In reply to the loyalist apprentices who addressed with thanks for the *Declaration*,[134] a number of apprentices expressed their veneration for Parliaments and sought action against those who aspersed them.[135]

The Inns of Court, too, were divided. At the Middle Temple there were two or three meetings in a tavern to discuss the acceptability of an address of thanks to the King. When the organisers of those meetings were accused of fostering a private address, the matter was put before the Inn's governing Hall. This formal meeting proved chaotic. After a contest over the choice of Speaker (the chairman of the meeting), the loyalists placed their nominee in the chair and voted for the address; but when many of the jubilant loyalists had left, their opponents called for a poll, had their own Speaker nominated

---

131 *The Loyal Protestant*, no. 21, 17 May 1681: 'and tis said they had His Majesties late Declaration in dispute, but there being a parity of votes, nothing was done against it'. *The Impartial Protestant Mercury*, no. 12, 31 May–3 June 1681, claimed that few in Norwich had supported the address of thanks, which was 'believed to have been Prepared by a Person, against whom there have been great complaints in Parliament, and whose guilt made him abscond till the Dissolution of the Parliament at Westminster' [probably Norwich's MP, Hon. William Paston, who had been denounced as an abhorrer, and subsequently defaulted on a call of the House: *History of Parliament*, iii. 213].

132 Greater London RO, calendar of sessions books, vol. vi/386; *Loyal Protestant*, no. 24, 28 May 1681.

133 See *A Letter of Advice to the Petitioning Apprentices* (1681), *A Friendly Dialogue* (1681), *A Vindication of the Protestant Petitioning Apprentices* (1681), *The Address of Above Twenty Thousand of the loyal Protestant Apprentices* (1681), *A Just and Modest Vindication of the Many Thousand and Loyal Apprentices* (1681), *Vox Juvinilis* (1681), and *A Vindication of the Loyal London Apprentices* (1681).

134 They dined at Sadler's Hall (Luttrell, *Brief Relation*, i. 114). According to some reports 12,000 signed the petition (*CSPD 1680–1*, p. 340; Bulstrode newsletter, 2 July 1681) but accounts of the numbers varied widely: *A Vindication of the Protestant Petitioning Apprentices* (1681), p. 4, claimed that Nathanial Thompson, who supported the loyalist address, had himself only estimated 2,000 signatures. The *True Protestant Mercury*, no. 44, 4–8 June 1681, and *A Friendly Dialogue* (1681), p. 2, observed that the address was left at taverns and other public houses for subscription at the beginning of June. An apprentice bookseller, John Dunton, estimated that 5,000 signed the 'Tory' apprentices' address (*The Life and Errors of John Dunton* [1705], p. 50).

135 *CSPD 1680–1*, p. 392. Newdigate newsletter Lc.1111, 11 August 1681, reported that the petitioning apprentices agreed to lay theirs aside 'being fully satisfied that all such proceedings are altogether displeasing to his Majesty'. John Dunton claimed that he helped organise this petition, and that at least 30,000 apprentices signed (*Life and Errors*, p. 50). Luttrell thought that 20,000 subscribed (*Brief Relation*, i. 123). *A Friendly Dialogue* (1681), p. 2 claimed it was signed by 10,000 within three days.

and voted the earlier proceedings of the day irregular.[136] Similar disputes ruffled the other Inns. At the Inner Temple 'a proposition was made for returning thankes to his majestie for his late declaration, which occasioned great heats', though the motion was eventually defeated by a mere three votes.[137] On 15 June a project to send an address of thanks from Gray's Inn was similarly rejected, 'but the other side seeing they could doe noe good this way, they gott about 40 togeather and went to the tavern, and there subscribed the said addresse in the name of the truly loyall gentlemen of Grays Inn'.[138] In London the struggle between petitioners and abhorrers had thus polarised the community.

Outside the capital, however, the addressers encountered far less opposition, despite the later claim by a Rye House Plotter that after the dissolution he 'could travill into no parts but found a great dissatisfaction in the people'.[139] Reports about petitions for a Parliament promoted at Lyme Regis and Hereford proved false,[140] and petitions rumoured to be imminent at Exeter[141] and York,[142] also failed to materialise, although petitions for a Parliament were presented from Tower Hamlets,[143] County Clare in Ireland[144] and Leicestershire, the latter 'subscribed by some thousands of hands'.[145]

Although few in number, the paucity of counter-petitions does not mean that addressing was universally accepted. The most common form of protest against the addresses of thanks was a simple refusal to sign. Thus at Wakefield the earl of Strafford refused to sign the address of thanks shown him, because 'he thought no part of the King's declaration deserved thanks but that part

---

[136] *A Vindication of Addresses in General* (1681), p. 4; *Loyal Protestant*, no. 30, 18 June 1681; Newdigate newsletter Lc.1089, 18 June 1681.

[137] Luttrell, *Brief Relation*, i. 94.

[138] Ibid., i. 99.

[139] BL, Add. 62,453, f. 3, account of the Rye House Plot, by James Holloway. Francis Barrowby of Ripon was reported to have said that the *Declaration* 'had given great dissatisfaction' (*CSPD 1680–1*, p. 257).

[140] *Loyal Protestant*, no. 24, 28 May 1681; Newdigate newsletter Lc.1078, 19 May 1681. The reports were retracted in *Loyal Protestant*, no. 25 and 26. Lyme presented a loyal address of thanks, though it encountered opposition from at least one man there who said all addressers were fools and knaves (*Currant Intelligence*, no. 26, 20 July 1681).

[141] *Impartial Protestant Mercury*, no. 15, 10–14 June 1681.

[142] *Impartial Protestant Mercury*, no. 28, 26–9 July 1681; Leeds AO, Mexborough mss, Reresby 18/117, Richard Grahme to Reresby, 20 July 1681.

[143] *Loyal Protestant*, no. 25, 31 May 1681; Congress newsletter 7/198, 31 May 1681; *CSPD 1680–1*, p. 305. Newdigate newsletter Lc.1083, 4 June 1681, reported that Charles was 'not so angry with [the presenters] as others', perhaps because they were 'sea officers'.

[144] Congress newsletter 7/187, 5 May 1681; *CSPD 1680–1*, p. 291 (Lord Clare had promoted it).

[145] Luttrell, *Brief Relation*, i. 110. It was presented on 15 July 1681.

wherein he said he would have frequent Parliaments'.[146] At Great Yarmouth a common council vote for an address of thanks failed, and when the matter was reconsidered, a ready-drafted address was produced and accepted, even though several councillors had left the meeting in disgust at the voting procedure, leaving the assembly inquorate.[147] In Kent Sir Vere Fane refused to subscribe an address 'because the Arbitrary powers therein mentioned (as hee sayd) reflected on the late Parliaments', and six other JPs also refused to sign.[148] At Durham Sir Gilbert Gerard and John Parkhurst refused to sign,[149] and Lord Bridgwater refused another in Buckinghamshire,[150] an action followed by others.[151] In Oxford the address was opposed by the mayor, Robert Pawling,[152] and Northumberland was said to be 'much Divided about Addressing'.[153] In Lincolnshire Sir Robert Carr successfully opposed an address promoted by the earl of Lindsey, even though the latter had organised a feast to encourage it, where Reresby thought there was so much food 'that if good meat and drinke will make men loyall ... my Lord spares noe cost to effect it'.[154] A large minority of the grand assize jury in Hampshire opposed

---

[146] Leeds AO, Mexborough mss, Reresby 17/45, Christopher Tancred to Reresby, 15 June 1681. Strafford was shown several different addresses of thanks, including one thanking Charles for 'every particular' of his Declaration (Mexborough mss, Reresby 17/46a, draft address). Three hundred gentlemen and 100 clergy were said to have attended. An address which Strafford was prepared to sign was eventually found, but it was not as 'home' as Lord Burlington had wanted (Mexborough mss, Reresby 17/44, Christopher Tancred to Reresby, 27 June 1681). Archdeacon Lake's name was added to the address, but he objected because the address was too moderate (Bod., MS Eng.Hist.e.47, f. 5, Lake to Francis Drake, vicar at Pontefract, 27 June 1681).

[147] *Impartial Protestant Mercury*, no. 13, 3–7 June 1681.

[148] BL, Eg.2985, f. 243b, notes on back of address. Five new names were suggested for promotion to the commission of the peace. Newdigate newsletter Lc.1080, 26 May 1681, reported a purge of Somerset JPs 'for not joyning at the Q[uarter] Sessions to thank his Ma[jes]tie for his Declara[tion]'. See Luttrell, *Brief Relation*, i. 83, for a purge of London's lieutenancy at this time.

[149] Congress newsletter 7/221, 2 August 1681; Newdigate newsletter Lc.1081, 28 May 1681.

[150] Huntington Library, Stowe mss STT 124, William Bowyer to Sir Richard Temple, 15 September 1681. Bridgwater said he would support an address if Temple could 'procure such an Address as may looke Unanimous & proper to be p[re]sented to his Ma[jes]tye' (Stowe mss, STT 2543, Thomas Weedon to Temple, 12 August 1681).

[151] Bucks. RO, Verney mss, M11/35, Temple to Verney, 17 July 1681. A newsletter records that two addresses were presented from Buckingham, 'one from the Court party & t'other from the opposite, both which the King received kindly' (Leeds AO, Mexborough mss, Reresby 18/5[3a], 26 July 1681).

[152] Wood, *Life and Times*, ii. 541.

[153] *Impartial Protestant Mercury*, no. 30, 2–5 August 1681; *CSPD 1682*, p. 321.

[154] Reresby, *Memoirs*, p. 228; BL, Althorp MS C2/27, John Millington to Halifax, 27 July 1681; Newdigate newsletter Lc.1108, 4 August 1681. For the opposition to the address see Holmes, *Seventeenth Century Lincolnshire*, pp. 245–6 and PRO, SP.29/416/107I, list of JPs and deputy lieutenants who did not sign.

the address promoted there, and at Exeter a number of aldermen refused to sign.[155] The address put before the Winchester grand jury split them into two equal parts, with ten supporters and ten who thought 'the said address tended to bring one part of the constitution into Contempt'.[156] Afraid of exacerbating such division the aldermen of Coventry, when besieged by rival camps for support, at first 'declined to meddle therein on either side'.[157]

Nevertheless a total of 210 addresses were presented,[158] many more than the petitioners of 1679–80 had been able to achieve; and, unlike the opposition petitions, the 1681 addresses came from all parts of the country.[159] Although most drew support from as wide a constituency as possible, forty-three were presented solely from borough corporations, fourteen solely from militia officers, ten from Grand Juries and two solely from JPs.[160] Others came from the Bristol Mariners, the Cornish Tinners and from as far away as Barbados. One of the most surprising features of the campaign is that despite the reliance of many addresses for sanction by elected or appointed officials, twenty-eight addresses came solely from the 'inhabitants', and a further seventy-one claimed to have their support.

The fact that the addresses attracted mass support has often been overlooked. Yet 1,000 were claimed to have signed the Exeter address, 6,000 the Northamptonshire address, 1,600 the Leicestershire address, 1,600 in Nottinghamshire, 2,000 in Cambridgeshire, 1,200 in Rutland, 2,000 of the Thames watermen, 2,500 in Derbyshire and over 2,000 of the Norwich

---

[155] Coleby, *Central Government and the Localities*, p. 213; *Impartial Protestant Mercury*, no. 15, 10–14 June 1681

[156] *CSPD 1680–1*, p. 370; *Loyal Protestant*, no. 43, 2 August 1681. Eight of the objectors were salt traders, suggesting that economic grievances may have played a part in their opposition to the addresses.

[157] *Impartial Protestant Mercury*, no. 12, 31 May–3 June 1681. The clothiers and eminent citizens were reported to have wanted a petition for Parliament to sit. The *Currant Intelligence*, no. 20, 28 June 1681, claimed that another address was therefore drawn up and carried up to London by Sir Robert Townsend and Alderman Farryman. The address (*Vox Angliae* [1682], pp. 22–3) came from the deputy lieutenants, gentry, inhabitants, freeholders and freemen.

[158] Several survive in manuscript form: PRO, SP.29/416/60, Bridgwater address, with signatures; BL, Eg.2985, f. 226, Gravesend and Milton address, ff. 236–7, draft Kent address, f. 241, Kent county address, f. 243, Maidstone address, with account of objectors; Lancs. RO, DDKe/2/20/1, draft Lancashire address; Essex RO, D/DKW08, address from grand jury of Essex, and address by deputy lieutenants and militia officers of Essex; Durham University Library, Old Library MS E.i.9, f. 146A, city of Durham address; Surrey RO, KB10/1, Kingston-upon-Thames address, with signatures; Berkshire RO, R/AC/1/1/15, f. 241, Reading corporation address, with signatures.

[159] *The True Englishman* (1681), p. 13, concluded that 'there are Addresses, very many Addresses, from all or most parts of the Kingdom'. Bulstrode newsletter, 30 May 1681, reported that the addresses 'came in very thicke'.

[160] Grand juries backed thirty-seven addresses, JPs forty-three, militia officers thirty-nine, inhabitants ninety-nine and corporations ninety-eight.

apprentices were said to have signed.[161] The total for the 207 addresses printed in *Vox Angliae*, a pamphlet which gathered them together, is almost 27,500,[162] to which the 'many thousands' of London apprentices,[163] the 'many thousands' of citizens of London,[164] 'some thousands' in Westminster,[165] and a reputed 10,000 Cornish 'tinners',[166] must be added. The overall total must have been 40,000 at the least.[167]

Ironically the loyalists had resorted to popular approval and claimed that 'seldom in any case of importance are they outdone by many score'.[168] This claim was answered by the argument that though the addresses were 'said to come from numerous Bodies of men ... the Temper of their Representation in Parliament doth better show the Temper of the People than those Addresses, which many Times are gained by sinister arts, and from a few that take upon them the Name of the Many'.[169] Another opposition pamphleteer complained that although the addresses claimed to represent the nation 'they contain[ed] and express[ed] only the sentiments of a few persons of little interest'.[170] The opposition therefore began to turn the loyalists' earlier arguments about the factious and unrepresentative nature of petitioning back on the addressers, and resorted to the defence that elections, not addresses, were the best litmus test of opinion. They therefore attacked the addresses as being signed by 'the scum and refuse of the places',[171] and even sought to use civil war memories against the loyalists to smear the campaign as subversive. Thus one opposition pamphleteer pointed out that 'the first contrivance of Addresses was from Oliver Cromwell ... and thus we most evidently see that those who most bitterly desire and seem to abominate the proceedings of

---

161   *Vox Angliae* (1682), pp. 8, 21, 45–6, 50–1, *Vox Angliae (Part Two)* (1682), p. 7; CSPD *1680–1*, p. 533. Oldmixon claimed that 16,000 signed an address from Devon which was presented by Sir Edward Seymour (*Oldmixon History of Addresses*, i. 48), but it is not mentioned in *Vox Angliae*. *Vox Angliae* also does not give the total number of subscribers of the Northamptonshire address, but Jenkins claimed a figure of 10,000 (NLW, MS 5389C, Jenkins to Bulstrode, 19 August 1681).

162   This is an underestimate of the true figure since many of the addresses which mention they had support from a number of the inhabitants fail to say how many. Because most of the addresses are now lost it is impossible to give an accurate total.

163   *Vox Angliae* (1682), p. 24.

164   *Vox Angliae* (1682), p. 1. See above for the estimate that 1,500–2,000 signed.

165   *Vox Angliae* (1682), p. 27.

166   Newdigate newsletter Lc.1125, 17 September 1681.

167   Oldmixon, *History of Addresses*, i. 53, estimated a total of no more than 40,000 signatures. The *Observator*, no. 15, 21 May 1681, claimed that the addressing had 'carried away at least Six out of Ten throughout the Kingdom'. An opposition tract claimed that the total was 'not so great a number as we have seen not long since to one Petition for a Parliament' (*An Impartial Account* (1681), p. 10).

168   *The True Englishman* (1681), p. 11; *Observator*, no. 8, 30 April 1681.

169   *The Loyalty of the Last Long Parliament* (1681), p. 20.

170   *An Impartial Account* (1681), p. 7.

171   *An Impartial Account* (1681), p. 12.

these times, still reject not to repeat the same method of addressing'.[172] Just as the loyalists had accused the petitioners of numbering their forces, so opposition tracts argued that the loyalists were doing exactly the same thing in 1681: 'by reading the Addresses one would be inclined to think that these men construe the King's Declaration, as the Erection of the Royal Standard; and that they intend these Papers for the Muster Rolls of those that are to fight under His Majesties Ensigns', complained one tract.[173] There seemed to be substance to this charge because 169 addresses promised to stand by the King with the lives and fortunes of their subscribers.

But, although the loyalists were in a sense appealing to the people in a way they had previously condemned, the opposition found it difficult to exploit this irony for three main reasons. The first was that Parliament had championed the right of the subject to petition. 'If they blame us for Addressing in general, they condemn their own Acts and the Parliament's votes', argued one pamphleteer supporter of the addresses.[174] Secondly, the loyalists argued that they had been forced to show that the opposition did not represent the sense of the nation: 'since the Petitioners began to number their Friends, it was time to examine what proportion for Number or Quality the dislikers of those Petitions bore to the other Party'.[175] Thirdly, the addressers had the support of a significant number of the gentry and clergy. It was thus quality as well as quantity that was important. Whereas it had been said that the petitions of January 1680 had only won support from the rabble, the 1681 addresses more properly represented the will of the nation because they came from the corporations' ruling bodies, from officers of the militia, from JPs and from Grand Juries.[176] And to show that they did so in emulation of earlier campaigns in defence of the established church, Sir Thomas Aston's 1642 *Collection* of addresses was reprinted.[177]

That the addresses received support from a large number of people, and from corporations which had returned MPs opposed to the Court in the last three elections, bewildered some contemporaries.[178] In fact, only twenty-one addresses promised to elect men of 'approved loyalty and good

---

172 *An Historical Account* (1681), p. 1. *A Vindication of the Protestant Petitioning Apprentices* (1681), p. 5, argued that the loyal apprentices' clamourings about 1641 and rebellion 'rake[d] up the Ashes of their Parents and disturb[ed] their own Fathers' Urns'.

173 *An Impartial Account* (1681), p. 38.

174 *Religion and Loyalty* (1681), p. 3.

175 Ibid. See also the Surrey and Wiltshire addresses (*Vox Angliae* [1682], pp. 40–2) which excused themselves on the grounds that the seditious practices of a few made their action necessary.

176 The 1661 Act against tumultuous petitioning allowed for addresses from these bodies.

177 *A Collection of Sundry Petitions* (1681).

178 Luttrell, *Brief Relation*, i. 85; Ailesbury, *Memoirs*, i. 58–9. Coleby notes that Newport, which had returned the exclusionist Sir Robert Dillington, was one of the first corporations to respond with an address (Coleby, *Central Government and the Localities*, p. 213).

moderation', and eight of those came from constituencies that had not returned a single opposition MP in the 1681 elections, and were thus merely a confirmation of the loyalty already shown.[179] Even so, fifty-five addresses were presented from boroughs or counties where two MPs hostile to the Court had been elected; and a further forty-one from boroughs or counties that had elected one 'opposition' MP. Ten of the Winchester corporation who supported the loyal address in May had voted for the two opposition candidates in the February election,[180] and at Reading four men who signed the corporation's address had voted for John Blagrave, an MP who had sat on the committee to draw up the exclusion bill.[181] Sir William Portman and Sir Nathanial Napier, both MPs who supported exclusion, also signed addresses.[182] These actions need some explanation because they seem to suggest that since the elections in February and March the country had turned Tory.[183] Were such paradoxical actions simply due to pragmatism, or was it possible to sign an address and remain consistent to principles that had earlier expressed themselves in hostility to the Court?

The most important reason why the addressing campaign of thanks for the King's *Declaration* was able to silence much of the unrest in the country was that it was, as we have seen, a masterpiece of careful wording. The moderation of the *Declaration* allowed it to be all things to all men. The address from the loyal inhabitants of London did not mention the succession, and thanked Charles for his promise to hold frequent Parliaments, to extirpate popery, to redress grievances and to govern according to the laws, principles to which even critics of the Court would have been able to put their name.[184] Grantham, which had returned two opposition MPs, thanked Charles

---

[179] *Vox Angliae* (1682), p.33. Only four (Lancashire, Worcester, Lyme Regis and Westbury) came from constituencies which had returned two opposition MPs, though Monmouth also disowned its 'Patriot' MP, John Arnold, who had become a national hero after an attempted assassination in 1680, supposedly committed by papists.

[180] Coleby, *Central Government and the Localities*, p. 212, note 30.

[181] Berkshire RO, R/AC/1/1/15, f. 241, address dated 27 May 1681. One of the men, John Bacon, even co-ordinated the presentation of the address.

[182] *A Letter from A Person of Quality to His Friend about Abhorrers and Addressers* (1682), p. 1. The earl of Ailesbury thought, however, that 'few or none' of the MPs signed the addresses (*Memoirs*, i. 59). One pamphleteer thought that 'some of our late senators refused signing the addresses, not because they had any objection to it (for they advised others to it) but because they were Parliament men!' (Bod., MS Jones 17, f. 232, 'Answer to a Vindication').

[183] North claimed that the addresses 'made the whole [opposition] party shoot the Pit and retire' (*Examen*, p. 327). Reresby was informed at the end of April that the coffee houses had become 'modeste in their discourses', and that in the country 'the people talk a much different dialect than what they were wonted to doe; as to Quaere one to another what the P[arliament] had done for them' (Leeds AO, Mexborough mss, Reresby 19/27, J. Wentworth to Reresby, 25 April 1681).

[184] It did, however, promise to defend the 'government both of Church and State as it is settled by law' (*Vox Angliae* [1682], pp. 1–2).

for his promise to defend and maintain the just rights and liberties of the subjects, to rule according to law, to 'pass any Bill, that shall be fairly offered you in a Parliamentary way, that truly tend[ed] to the Preservation of our sacred and civil Enjoyments'.[185] It concluded somewhat ominously by resolving to keep the oaths of allegiance and supremacy in the 'old Protestant sense'. Liverpool's address similarly reflected the City's sympathy for the opposition's aims.[186]

Careful wording, therefore, allowed some corporations which had returned opposition MPs to present addresses of thanks; and in some cases this allowed individuals or institutions to sign without altering their political opinions. Oxford, for example, was able to send an address of thanks, but at the same time to give a vote of thanks to its opposition MPs, Whorwood and Wright.[187] Retaining opposition views and subscribing a loyalist address were thus not totally incompatible. Arthur Onslow, MP, signed the Surrey address despite remaining a supporter of exclusion,[188] whilst Reresby was informed that an address from the Cutler's Corporation would 'not change theire opinions but they will be ready to rebell if an opportunity would offer itselfe', and that if they did subscribe it would be 'in hopes to keep the trade in their towne'.[189] One scathing loyalist thought the addresses were designed for 'such a sort of farme cattle that they think they are obliged to follow the bell weathers of the houre', and Henry Sidney cynically believed that the addresses signified nothing, and that they grew 'every day more ridiculous'.[190]

---

185 *Vox Angliae* (1682), p. 52.
186 *Vox Angliae* (*Part Two*) (1682), p. 2; M. Mullett, 'The Politics of Liverpool 1660–1688', *Transactions of the Historic Society of Lancashire and Cheshire*, cxxiv (1972), p. 49. For its drafters, one of whom only seems to have taken the oaths in 1679, see Sir James Picton, *Selections from the Municipal Archives [of Liverpool]* (1883), pp. 249, 251–2. Compare also the Evesham and Shropshire addresses (*Vox Angliae* [1682], pp. 39, 49).
187 *Impartial Protestant Mercury*, no. 14, 7–10 June 1681.
188 *CSPD 1680–1*, p. 357; *Impartial Protestant Mercury*, no. 12, 3–7 June 1681.
189 Leeds AO, Mexborough mss, Reresby 19/10, Blythman to Reresby, 18 September 1681. The duke of Newcastle congratulated Reresby on working 'a miricle' with the rebellious cutlers (Mexborough mss, Reresby 18/51, Newcastle to Reresby, 23 September 1681). John Heath tried to persuade one of the boroughs in Kent to send an address by appealing to their self-interest when he informed them that it would be for the 'advantage of your Corporation in the future' (BL, Eg.2985, f. 235, letter from Heath dated 11 June 1681).
190 Bod., MS Jones 17, ff. 232, 'an Answer to a Vindication'; *Diary of Henry Sidney*, ii. 217. The address from Chipping Wycombe (*Vox Angliae [Part Two]*, p. 4) is a good example of the hyperbole developed by the addressers. It promised to support the King 'to the utmost stress of our Sinews, to the latest gasp of our Lives, and the last Solitary Mite in our Coffers'. Henry Killigrew supposedly made a suit for Charles with one large pocket and one so tiny that the King could not get his hand in it; Killigrew told the King that the large pocket was 'for the loyal addresses of your subjects, whilst the other is full large enough to hold all the money they will give you' (quoted by Ronalds, *Attempted Revolution*, p. 79, from D. Senior, *The Gay King*, p. 308). It was reported that Norfolk, Suffolk and Bristol collected 'a considerable sum of Money' for the King (*Loyal Protestant*, no. 20, 14 May 1681; ibid., no. 22, 21 May

Although Burnet recognised that there were some moderate addresses, he claimed that 'the greater number, and the most acceptable, were those which declared they would adhere to the unalterable succession of the crown, in the lineal and legal descent, and that condemned the bill of exclusion'.[191] But, initially at least, the campaign did not concentrate on the succession issue. This can be shown by analysing *Vox Angliae*, the pamphlet which collected together all the addresses of thanks. Only eighty-three addresses, about half of those printed in the first part of the tract which covered roughly the period up to the end of July 1681, promised loyalty to the legal hereditary succession, or thanked Charles for the defence of his brother's rights. Many addresses simply ignored the matter, preferring instead to offer their lives in the defence of the present King, monarchy or protestantism. Others referred to the duke of York's rights only in a vague and guarded way. The otherwise loyal address from Ludlow resolved only to defend the King and his 'Royal Family', an ambiguous phrase that could even encompass Monmouth or William of Orange;[192] and Appleby prayed 'That there may never want one of your Royal Loyns to sway the scepter of these Kingdoms.'[193]

The reluctance to declare for the 'lawful' succession did, however, decline as the campaign gathered momentum. Only seven out of the fifty-five addresses printed in the second part of *Vox Angliae*, which collected the addresses presented between August and November 1681, failed to promise to stand by an uninterrupted succession. The duke of York must have taken heart from the Northumberland address which thanked Charles 'for opposing, with such incomparable Resolution, the Arbitrary and unnatural Proceedings against the undoubted Right of Your Succession in the person of your Royal Brother',[194] and from the increasing tendency of later addresses to affirm a willingness to defend the succession with the addressers' lives and fortunes. On the other hand, this development may have been part of the process whereby even addressers recognised that they competed to 'out-go each other in expressions of Loyalty'.[195]

Another feature which may partly explain the apparent success of the campaign was the way in which it was promoted. Traditional obligations between a local magnate and his neighbours were often exploited for political reasons, and the local initiative was in turn supported by central government. Thus Sir Leoline Jenkins seems to have organised and co-ordinated several

---

1681; ibid, no. 46, 13 August 1681; Luttrell, *Brief Relation*, i. 84; Newdigate newsletter Lc.1075, 12 May 1681; Nottingham University Library, DDSR 219/14, L. Champion to Halifax, 10 May 1681; Bod., MS Carte 222, f. 300, newsletter, 10 May 1681).

[191] Burnet, *History*, ii. 289.   [192] *Vox Angliae* (1682), p. 9.
[193] *Vox Angliae* (1682), p. 36.   [194] *Vox Angliae (Part Two)* (1682), p. 2.
[195] *Vox Angliae (Part Two)* (1682), p. 15, Lyme Regis address.

addresses, such as those of Middlesex, Southwark and the Hamlets of London.[196] The church also threw its weight behind the campaign, with a number of clergy fostering and signing the addresses,[197] and the addresses caught the tide turning against dissent. The one from Holland, in Lincolnshire, desired that the Act of 35 Elizabeth against recusants and dissenters be enforced,[198] and the Sussex address thanked the King for not repealing the law.[199] The Chesterfield and Bridgwater addresses asked for the enforcement of all laws against papists and dissenters,[200] and many others attacked 'fanatics' and 'dissenters' or advocated a strict adherence to the practices of the 'orthodox' Church of England as the best bulwark against its enemies.[201] Moreover, to increase their efficiency the loyal addressers even organised themselves into committees in London,[202] as their rival petitioners were supposed to have done, and adopted some of the petitioners' practices. In Hertford the addressers carried their text about 'in great Privacy, shewing it only to some and refusing it to others', and it was claimed that they had altered the wording to cover up the fact that honorary freemen had been created to increase the number of subscribers.[203] Moreover, since the addresses were printed, the campaign achieved a momentum of its own that

[196] *CSPD 1680–1*, pp. 267, 269. Sir Edward Phelips, who had been taken into custody for his abhorring activities, was handed the address from Bridgwater and promoted the Dorset address (*CSPD 1680–1*, p. 360; *History of Parliament*, iii. 237; Oldmixon, *History of Addresses*, i. 40). The earl of Peterborough also encouraged addresses (Halstead, *Succinct Genealogies* [1685], p. 439), as did Sir Edward Seymour (Oldmixon, *History of Addresses*, i. 48). Sir Richard Grahme consulted Reresby about whether he should procure an address of thanks (Leeds AO, Mexborough mss, Reresby 19/15, Grahme to Reresby, 6 May 1681).

[197] Burnet, in the 1683 version of his history, claimed the addresses were so full of flattery that they must have been written by parsons (BL, Add. 63,057B, f. 58). *The Second Part of the Growth of Popery* (1682), p. 297, said that clergymen were 'as diligent as bees to get such Addresses signed'. Oldmixon hints that the Dean of Ripon, Dr Cartwright, penned the city's address of thanks (*History of Addresses*, i. 29). 18 addresses claimed to have been signed by clergymen.

[198] *Vox Angliae* (1682), pp. 7, 43.

[199] *Vox Angliae* (1682), p. 10.

[200] *Vox Angliae* (1682), pp. 25, 37.

[201] *Vox Angliae* (1682), p. 11 (Oxon), p. 16 (Andover), p. 15 (Clifton), p. 19 (Nottingham), p. 20 (Brecknock or Brecon), pp. 25–6 (Canterbury, calling it the 'Orthodox Church of England'), p. 32 (Durham), pp. 33–4 (Dudden, Cumberland), p. 39 (Lancashire), p. 41 (Carmarthen), p. 44 (Southampton), p. 50 (Norfolk), p. 51 (Huntingdonshire), *Vox Angliae (Part Two)* (1682), p. 1 (Glamorgan), p. 7 (Exeter artillery company), pp. 15–16 (Worcester clothiers corporation).

[202] PRO, SP.29/415/159, the 'Honest Committee, 6 May 1681'. Those who met to promote the address in the eastern half of the City are given as Sir Jonathan Raymond, Sir William Russell, Mr Loades, Mr Hawes, Mr Daniel and Mr Vernon (for the activity of Loades and Hawes see above); and Sir William Dodson, Mr Charlton, Mr Gosnell, Mr Wyseman, William Browne and Mr Johnson in the west.

[203] *Impartial Protestant Mercury*, no. 20, 28 June–1 July 1681.

was difficult to resist. Several addresses recognised that they were 'provoked to Emulation'.[204]

These factors may go some way to explaining why the movement spread across the country; but the fifty-five boroughs and counties that returned two anti-Court MPs in the elections and yet presented addresses of thanks for the King's *Declaration* still seem puzzling. Was the electorate fickle? Were party loyalties skin deep?

One reason for the paradox is straightforward: the body which elected the members for Parliament was not always the same as that which subscribed the address of thanks. Thus at Windsor the inhabitants paying scot and lot taxes had elected Richard Winwood and Samuel Starkey, but the address came from the borough's corporation;[205] similarly at Reading the freemen elected the MPs, but the address came from the mayor, burgesses and aldermen.[206] The boroughs of Derby,[207] Nottingham,[208] Taunton,[209] Dover[210] and Bridgwater[211] all had exclusionist MPs elected by a different group to that which presented the borough's address of thanks. The same is also true in some of the counties. Surrey's addresses came from its militia, JPs and grand jury, so that although the campaign there reveals much about the importance of the purges of those institutions, these groups hardly represented the whole of the county's electorate. Similarly the Berkshire, Herefordshire and Cheshire addresses came only from their grand juries.[212]

In some cases, even when they came from the qualified voters, the addresses did not always have the backing of a majority of the electorate. Thus only 600 of Norfolk's 6,000 voters signed the county's address of thanks;[213] and only 200 of Bedfordshire's 2,000 voters signed.[214] In each case the views of about 10 per cent of the county electorate appeared to represent the views of the other 90 per cent as well. Although this much larger silent majority was prepared to acquiesce in an address, it must be highly questionable if this

---

[204] *Vox Angliae* (1682), p. 16 (Andover). See also *Vox Angliae (Part Two)* (1682), p. 5 (Merioneth). The Monmouth address thought it necessary to deny that its address had been motivated by 'the Example of Neighbouring Countries' (*Vox Angliae* (1682), p. 17) cf. Brecknock address (ibid. p. 20).

[205] *Vox Angliae* (1682), p. 2; *History of Parliament*, i. 130. The mayor and alderman who presented the address beseeched the King 'to have a candid opinion of them, and that if a part of the Borough had dissented from them … yet they hoped that would no ways reflect upon them' (*Benskin's Domestick Intelligence*, no. 1, 13 May 1681).

[206] *Vox Angliae* (1682), p. 10; *History of Parliament*, i. 132.

[207] *Vox Angliae* (1682), pp. 12–13; *History of Parliament*, i. 188.

[208] *Vox Angliae* (1682), p. 19; *History of Parliament*, i. 355.

[209] *Vox Angliae* (1682), p. 29; *History of Parliament*, i. 378.

[210] *CSPD 1680–1*, p. 261; *Currant Intelligence*, no. 2, 30 April 1681.

[211] *Vox Angliae* (1682), pp. 37–8; *History of Parliament*, i. 372.

[212] *Vox Angliae* (1682), pp. 30, 32–3; *Vox Angliae (Part Two)*, p. 6.

[213] *Vox Angliae* (1682), p. 50; *History of Parliament*, i. 319.

[214] *Vox Angliae* (1682), p. 20; *History of Parliament*, i. 125.

could be converted into electoral support.[215] Analysis of the boroughs also shows that unanimity of support behind the addresses was often elusive. Many simply remained silent about the number they represented, with few brave enough to emulate the Sandwich address's admission that it came only from 'the Major Part' of the militia, common councillors and inhabitants,[216] or Berwick's confession that only 'some' of its burgesses had signed.[217] It is no wonder that both corporations were remodelled in 1684.

In some areas, however, a real shift in opinion seems to have taken place. This partly reflected the success of the *Declaration* itself in winning moderate support. The Durham militia's address claimed that it had 'been so wonderfully successful, that there is quite another Spirit and Temper of Men than of late'.[218] Edward L'Estrange told the earl of Yarmouth that the *Declaration* had 'put new Life, and Soul, into all his Ma[jes]ties Loyall Subjects',[219] and Sir Richard Grahme said the *Declaration* had been read 'to the generall applause of all'.[220] But in some ways the addresses should be regarded as indicative of a change of opinion that preceded the recent elections.[221] Of the fifty-five constituencies that returned both opposition MPs and addresses, only thirteen had seen contested elections in 1681. Without a Court candidate to vote for, there had been no way of showing loyalty. Although it is difficult to prove, there are indications that a large loyalist vote had remained untapped in these areas. In Leicestershire at least half the county electorate signed the address;[222] at Great Marlow 222 inhabitants signed, almost double the electorate of scot and lot voters;[223] at Aylesbury 270 of the inhabitants signed an address, and the electorate of inhabitant householders not receiving arms was only 360;[224] in Nottinghamshire 1,600 freeholders signed, though the county electorate was only 2,000;[225] and in York as many as 13,000–14,000 had signed, vastly more than the 1,700 freemen qualified to vote.[226] In none of these cases had a Court candidate been presented for

[215] Lord Windsor reported that dissenters sent their journeymen to sign an address of thanks which promised the election of men acceptable to the King, yet knew they would oppose 'the honest party' at a new election (BL, Althorp MS C1, Windsor to Halifax, 22 October 1681).
[216] *Vox Angliae* (1682), p. 36.
[217] *Vox Angliae (Part Two)* (1682), p. 10. *History of Parliament*, i. 345 states that Berwick failed to produce a loyal address.
[218] *Vox Angliae* (1682), p. 32.
[219] BL, Add. 27,448, f. 16, L'Estrange to Yarmouth, 15 April 1681.
[220] Leeds AO, Mexborough mss, Reresby 19/15, Grahme to Reresby, 6 May 1681.
[221] R. Beddard, 'The Retreat on Toryism: Lionel Ducket MP for Calne and the Politics of Conservatism', *The Wiltshire Archaeological Magazine*, lxxii–iii (1977–8), p. 84.
[222] *Vox Angliae* (1682), p. 21; *History of Parliament*, i. 294.
[223] *Vox Angliae* (1682), p. 25; *History of Parliament*, i. 143.
[224] *Vox Angliae* (1682), p. 28; *History of Parliament*, i. 138.
[225] *Vox Angliae* (1682), p. 41; *History of Parliament*, i. 349.
[226] *Vox Angliae (Part Two)* (1682), p. 5; *History of Parliament*, i. 489.

election. Thus, even allowing for the impact the Oxford Parliament had on public opinion and for the fact that not all those who signed may have been eligible to vote, if there had been Court candidates standing in early 1681 it seems quite possible that they might have been returned, or at least been serious challengers. If the Court had been prepared to encourage its supporters more vigorously to contest elections, the results earlier in the year might have been significantly different.

At the same time as the Court was winning the propaganda war in terms of addresses, which complained about the penetration of seditious literature in the localities,[227] its supporters were also asserting themselves through the press. The spring and summer of 1681 witnessed a pamphlet war of great vigour,[228] but the loyalists gradually emerged as the victors.[229] Indeed, they were so successful that the opposition began to complain. *England's Appeal to the Parliament at Oxford*, a pro-exclusion sheet which was printed immediately prior to the Oxford Parliament, urged MPs to suppress the 'base pamphleteers, who would gladly set us together by the Ears',[230] and in August 1681 an opposition pamphlet complained that 'new and fresh trash' was for sale in the coffee houses.[231] Production of loyalist material now appears to have outstripped that of opposition material.[232] Ironically, the strength of the loyalist counter-attack forced the government's opponents into assuming support for censorship. In May 1681 the City of London sessions heard a charge against *An Apostrophe of the Loyal Party*;[233] the City's petition to the King complained about pamphlets that aspersed Parliament;[234] and in June 1681 Essex, Shaftesbury and Salisbury went to call on the King to ask him 'to

---

227 *Vox Angliae* (1682), p. 3 (Southampton), p. 9 (Cambridge), p. 21 (Durham), p. 31 (Essex), p. 40 (Surrey), *Vox Angliae (Part Two)* (1682), p. 16 (Stafford).

228 Luttrell, *Brief Relation*, i. 76; *HMC Ormonde*, vi. 31. Pamphlets printed at this time are marked in the bibliography.

229 Jones, *First Whigs*, p. 180; Burnet, *History*, ii. 290. For loyalist newspapers appearing at this time see *Heraclitus Ridens*, which began publication on 1 February, *The Weekly Discovery*, which started on 5 February, and *The Loyal Protestant*, which first went on sale on 9 March. On 13 April *The Observator* began publication with the declaration that its business was 'to encounter the Faction, and to Vindicate the Government'.

230 *England's Appeal to the Parliament at Oxford* (1682), verso.

231 *News from Colchester* (1681), p. 2.

232 In the Brindley pamphlet volume of Luttrell's collection of poetry in the Huntington Library, of the twenty-seven poems dated from the end of the Oxford Parliament to Shaftesbury's arrest in July, only four could be described as supporting the opposition (Huntington 135779–806).

233 *Impartial Protestant Mercury*, no. 12, 31 May–3 June 1681. In August the publishers of the principal loyalist newspapers were presented for prosecution for dividing 'his majesties true protestant subjects, and much reflecting on the magistracy of the citty of London' (Luttrell, *Brief Relation*, i. 119–20).

234 For the lord chancellor's reply see All Souls, MS 239, f. 128, 'Speech', 19 May 1681.

issue out an order to supresse pamphlets'.[235] These actions were tantamount to an admission of defeat.

CONCLUSION

The crisis of Parliament, which in 1679 and 1680 was characterised by controversy over its assembly, took a new turn in early 1681, when loyalists endeavoured to portray the House of Commons, rather than the King or his brother, as the greatest threat to liberty and the church. Loyalists argued that Parliament was unrepresentative, arbitrary and a grievance rather than a means of redress, charges which were refuted by appeals to the doctrine of popular sovereignty in the legislature; this defence in turn exposed a tension between opposition groups who had seen Parliament's actions as endeavouring to preserve the constitutional powers of the King and the strength of the church, and those who saw them as a means of curbing royal powers and/or reforming the church. The loyalists claimed that the real design of the discontented was the destruction of the monarchy and the church, and the promotion of rebellion. Accordingly, they asserted that dissent posed at least as great a threat to the church as popery, and that the real unity of protestants lay in uniformity and conformity. Moderates who had only ever sought peace and security therefore increasingly shyed away from the radical ideological reformers who seemed by 1681 to threaten rather than achieve those objectives. The loyalists had successfully appealed to the conservatism about tinkering with the status quo that had been one of the principal legacies of the civil war and interregnum years.

In order to further neutralise opposition, Charles issued a *Declaration*, which justified the King's reasons for ending the last two Parliaments, an implicit recognition that the crux of the crisis lay in the period between October 1680 and March 1681, rather than in the immediate aftermath of the Popish Plot. The *Declaration*'s wording is a good example of how the loyalists put forward their own version of the opposition slogans of 'rule by law', 'security' and 'frequent Parliaments', and challenged their opponents concept of popery and arbitrary government. Yet the King appears to have deliberately rejected aggressive drafts in favour of a text of moderate tone, that allowed the *Declaration* to appeal to as wide a section of opinion as possible. So successful was it, that a torrent of addresses of thanks were presented to the King, though these should not be taken at face value, for their

---

[235] Newdigate newsletter Lc.1085, 8 June 1681. Orders had already been given to the Stationer's Company to enforce a by-law passed 22 August 1679 (stating that names of printers must appear on printed works), to the lord mayor concerning the suppression of seditious papers and letters, and to Middlesex JPs to suppress pamphlets (*CSPD 1680–1*, pp. 208, 213; Newdigate newsletter Lc.1053, 12 March 1681).

form often belied complex motives behind their promotion. The country had not simply turned completely Tory by the summer of 1681, despite appearances. One observer, admittedly a fierce critic of the government, reckoned that the addresses represented no more than a tenth of the nation.[236] In London, especially, where rival petitions were presented, the divisions were bitter, and although elsewhere opposition to loyalist addresses mainly took the form of refusing to sign, some of the addresses picked out of the *Declaration* the King's commitment to frequent Parliaments and upholding the law.

On the other hand, a shift of attitudes, or at least in the representation of attitudes, does seem to have taken place. The loyalists attracted a hitherto unacknowledged, and startling, number of signatories to their addresses, allowing them to claim that by their opponents' own standard of mass subscriptions they expressed the sense of the nation, and forcing all but the most radical into acquiescence or neutrality. This process was largely the result of a desire for unity and the appearance of loyalty, at a time when civil war seemed the only alternative; overt opposition had become impossible without being labelled republican or disloyal. The flood of addresses of thanks shows how the overlap in tactics and slogans could lead to division, but also how common rhetoric and action could serve to hide some of the rifts. No doubt much of the unity portrayed by the addresses was more apparent than real, but in an age when propaganda was an integral part of politics the appearance of unity behind the Court was in itself a victory. It was not so much, as has recently been suggested,[237] that the 'Whigs' of 1678 had become the 'Tories' of 1681, as that those years saw a struggle between ideologically committed men to represent their opinion as the will of the nation. The rhetoric was the same not because the same people were expressing it – though clearly some, such as Warcup, do fit that pattern – but because the language was the means by which the rest of the nation could be led. Our concept of the structure of politics must therefore recognise the fixed and increasingly sophisticated polarities of the ideologues, whilst at the same time recognising that it was fluid enough for the majority of the nation to alter the *emphasis* of their beliefs even though they remained loyal to those positions and were consistent in holding them. The language of popery and arbitrary government had given legitimacy to discontent – Anthony Wood grumbled that 'under pretence of speaking against popery and arbitrary government people say what they please'[238] – but the licentiousness of that talk had allowed the loyalists to reinterpret the meaning of the slogans, so that they could be used against dissent and its sympathisers, and even against Parliament itself. Opposition was left without a legitimate voice, not only because

---

[236] *CSPD 1683–4*, p. 369.   [237] Scott, *Restoration Crisis*, p. 47.
[238] Wood, *Life and Times*, ii. 419.

Parliament was not called again in Charles's reign, but also because its slogans and tactics had been usurped by the loyalists. As the newswriter Henry Muddiman put it, the fanatics had been 'outdone at theire owne weapon'.[239] The Court had regained the initiative in most areas except London. Propaganda was once more the preserve of government, not of faction.

The unrest which had marked the country since the autumn of 1678 was not, of course, entirely over by mid 1681. It took some time longer for the suppression of discontent, or at least of its public expression, and, most importantly of all, the government still had to regain control of the capital.[240] But mid 1681 marked a turning point in loyalist fortunes. Thereafter, loyalists were pushing at a door that was at least ajar, if not half open. This is not to say that the period after 1681 is uninteresting in terms of political and religious ideology and organisation; but that it developed a number of trends that were already apparent, and whose origins have already been probed.

The second half of this book has charted shifts in public opinion. By taking propaganda to have been an integral part of the political and religious crisis, and viewing events themselves as propaganda, it has suggested a number of key points at which opinion can be gauged and changes in it determined. In essence, it has told the story of how the loyalist interpretation of popery and arbitrary government began to outweigh opposition versions of those rallying cries. Yet the preceding chapters have sought to emphasise that the path to dominance was not a smooth one. The movement of petitions, addresses and counter-addresses involved the country in a real struggle to represent the will of the people, a struggle in which first one side and then the other seemed to be winning. Thus rather than a series of pitched battles between two regimented sides, we should regard the contest as a tug of war, and the oscillations in that confrontation to be just as important as the conflict itself.

---

[239] Longleat, Muddiman newsbook, 2 June 1681. William Carr had the Declaration translated and distributed to Hamburgh, Denmark, Sweden, Brandenberg, Heidelberg and Italy (BL, Add. 37,981, f. 32, Carr to Conway, 19/29 April 1681).

[240] See Haley, *Shaftesbury*, chapter xxix; J.Levin, *The Charter Controversy in the City of London 1660–88 and its Consequences* (1969).

Conclusion

> There has not been any point, perhaps, in the whole of English story,
> either so dangerous to be mistaken or so difficult, and yet so necessary to
> be understood, as the mystery of this detestable plot now in agitation.
>
> R. L'Estrange, *A Further Discovery of the Plot* (1681), p. 5.

The interpretation of the period 1679–81 which has, until very recently,
found most widespread acceptance is that put forward by J.R. Jones in *The
First Whigs*. 'Exclusion', he argues, 'was the drastic response to an apparently
imminent and appalling danger which put liberties, religion and property in
peril and forced the Whigs to unite in self-preservation'. Concentrating on
that one single issue, the Whigs, 'who were essentially a parliamentary party',
achieved formidable 'discipline, ruthlessness, and mass effort' under the
leadership of the earl of Shaftesbury:

The first Whigs had necessarily to possess, or rather develop, the organisation,
cohesion, discipline and mass appeal that made them a party, because of the intensity
of the crisis through which they were living ... They followed Shaftesbury's somewhat
autocratic leadership and subordinated their particular grievances and interests to the
common cause.

Whig organisation was 'entirely geared to the immediate purpose of forcing
through Exclusion at all costs', and this did not aim at transforming the
structure of politics. Indeed, the 'immediate and polemical' nature of the
struggle meant that 'the Whigs had no developed, definite or coherent
political philosophy'. They were held together simply by their shared demand
for exclusion.[1]

Although Jones made it clear that the 'over-riding unity which the crisis
forced the Whigs to develop, with its organisation, cohesion and discipline,
could not have lasted',[2] his argument has been vigorously attacked by Jonathan Scott on the grounds that it is 'historically inappropriate' to treat
1679–81 in the context of the structure of early eighteenth-century party

---

[1] Jones, *First Whigs*, pp. 211–16.   [2] Ibid., p. 216.

politics. Scott places the crisis firmly in a seventeenth-century perspective, and asserts that the causes of conflict lay not in the attempts to pass the exclusion bill but in the failures of the Restoration settlement, in the force 'not of party organisation, but of public religious and political belief':

In the face of this hurricane, numerous individuals and groups made what political running they could ... the result was not parties but ideology. The Restoration crisis crystallised political belief. This crystallisation took place through the lens of the past, the lens of history ... when the words 'whig' and 'tory' appeared, they were coined to identify not 'parties' but polarities of belief.[3]

Each of these polarities was

primarily religious in its significance, and each referred to one of the past (and foreign) rebellions, by the destabilising influence of which the English church and state had previously been destroyed. 'Whig' pointed to the protestant 'fanaticism' of Scotland, behind the crucial military challenge of 1637–40 ... 'Tory', on the other sides, pointed to the darkest event in the protestant calendar: the Irish rebellion of 1641. The difference between 'whigs' and 'tories' in 1681–3 was not what it later became.[4]

Whiggery thus 'identified the counter-Reformation threat, allied with a popish and arbitrary crown', whilst Toryism saw a greater danger in the consequences of rebellion.[5]

Although he differs with Scott over the role of constitutional factors and over the idea of the birth of parties, Tim Harris has also stressed the primacy of a religious division. Religious factors, he suggests, were more important than constitutional ones in the determination of party identity, 'with the Whigs being the party sympathetic towards dissent and the Tories the champions of High Anglican intolerance. The language which contemporaries used to describe the partisan conflicts of their day reflected the priority of religious considerations.'[6] Yet he differs with Scott by claiming that parties did form after the Popish Plot, having had a twenty-year gestation period since the Restoration.

The debate about how to interpret the period therefore centres around three main ideas: the traditional model of an exclusion party; a refinement of that model which stresses that parties coalesced primarily around religious polarities (or, as Ashcraft has suggested, one where the secular ideological dimensions were far more coherently expressed than Jones admitted);[7] or an outright rejection of the party system in favour of a nonparty structure of ideological and religious dimensions reminiscent of the early seventeenth century.

---

[3] Scott, *Restoration Crisis*, pp. 11–14.
[4] Ibid., pp. 48–9. [5] Ibid., p. 49.
[6] Harris, *Politics under the later Stuarts*, p. 8.
[7] Ashcraft, *Revolutionary Politics*, pp. 181–3.

The questions currently being asked about the nature of politics and religion between 1679 and 1681 are fundamental to our understanding of the period. Is the concept of a crisis revolving around exclusion untenable? Is exclusion merely a red-herring distracting us from the real causes of the crisis? If so, does this mean that we have to abandon the idea of the party organisation which was said to have formed around the single issue? If there were parties, how does the traditional view of them need revision? If there were no parties, what political and/or religious framework are we to employ? Was the structure of politics essentially the same as that of the earlier seventeenth century?

The first part of this book examined 'high politics' at Parliament and Whitehall in an attempt to answer these basic questions from the angle of the succession crisis. In order to do so, it was necessary to re-examine the parliamentary crisis in some detail, and to focus on determining the true nature of the exclusion issue. Chapters 2–4 examined the role of the exclusion bill, and sought to challenge the 'single-issue' approach by placing the debate over the bill within the context of a larger succession crisis, arguing for the existence of a broad controversy which embraced a host of different projects to settle the succession problem. Exclusion was not the only project under consideration, and right up to the eve of the introduction of the first exclusion bill contemporaries remarked on the variety of opinion about to how to proceed. MPs moved slowly and cautiously towards adopting the bill, and even after the dissolution of the 1679 Parliament its promotion was still not a rule of faith carved in stone. Thus in the winter of 1679–80 Shaftesbury, with whom the policy of exclusion was most identified, was prepared to discuss the King's divorce as a means to safeguard the future. Plans to limit the powers of a popish king, or for the executive to be exercised by a regent, were actively discussed throughout the period, and other expedients were also hammered out in the frequent discussions and negotiations between the Court and the cabals. There was no ideological barrier between exclusion or limitations, for both were seen by their opponents as altering the form of monarchy, either by rendering it elective or by reducing the King to the role of a Venetian Doge. For this reason limitations were supported by commonwealthmen, and found few loyalist supporters, even though restrictions on the power of a catholic successor were for a long time advocated by the Court. Thus a broader succession crisis is often more apparent than a simple, single-issued exclusion crisis.

When talking about an 'exclusion crisis', therefore, it is worth remembering that it was only after Parliament resumed sitting in October 1680, and particularly after the rejection of the exclusion bill by the Lords the following month, that exclusion topped the Parliamentary agenda. Even during this later period a number of alternatives to the bill continued to be considered, particularly in the House of Lords, whilst in the Commons there was an increasingly loud demand that many of the proposed limitations on a catholic king should be applied in the present reign. Parliamentary control over officeholders of all types, from JPs to judges, together with an association of protestants and automatic assemblies of Parliament thus came to supplement, rather than replace, calls for exclusion. This development signified an important, and increasingly exposed, division amongst opposition groups, between those who saw exclusion as a means of preserving the status quo and those who saw an opportunity to remodel the constitution, or re-align it on what they believed were ancient or fundamental principles. Charles, and many others, took fright at the prospect of what he perceived as an assault on his prerogatives, believing that both monarchy and the established church, rather than the succession of James, appeared to be at stake. The government therefore changed its policy, from supporting and indeed advocating limitations on the Crown, to one of a regency administered by William of Orange. Yet this scheme foundered because William was not yet the protestant hero of 1688; even if fear of France was increasingly outweighing antagonisms with the Dutch, suspicions still remained about the Prince, who was perceived as a Stuart in his tastes for authority. The regency expedient proposed at the Oxford Parliament therefore failed to attract sufficient support, and exclusion seemed the only realistic alternative.

As the doubts about William suggest, the succession crisis was shaped, and its course influenced, by European considerations. William shared James's hostility to limitations even if he did not wish to see his francophile father-in-law James succeed to the throne. Moreover, the balance of Europe circumscribed Charles's freedom of manoeuvre at home. The peace of 1678 had ended hostilities, but it had not settled unease about French expansionism, nor resolved the inherent contradictions in Charles's policy of public alliance with the Dutch against France and private treating with Louis XIV. Louis had in any case tired of Charles's unreliability, and sought to foment, or at least take advantage of, unrest in England in order to give a sharp reminder about client relationships. Charles therefore faced diplomatic isolation unless he actively sided with the Dutch, a policy which would force him to rely on Parliament for supply, and hence to listen to, and to some extent accommodate, the grievances voiced by MPs. Since the succession had become one of those grievances, Charles was forced to keep his back-stairs open to those who proposed means by which King and Parliament might be reconciled. Charles may have had little or no intention of complying with what was suggested if he could possibly avoid doing so, but he had to be prepared to accept the hard fact that circumstances were forcing his hand. To a king who sometimes valued the possibility of different courses of action over action itself, this constraint was thoroughly unpleasant; yet Charles was, ironically, rescued by the apparent collapse of his own power and by the difficulties caused by the succession crisis, for France could see no value in allowing the emergence of an aggressive, and probably francophobic, republic across the channel, or clearing the way for William to accede to the throne. In early 1681 a secret Anglo-French agreement was once more possible, with James an enthusiastic supporter of such an alliance.

The problem of the succession must also be seen within the context of the collapse of Court power in the wake of Danby's fall from office. With no replacement ministry to hand, Danby's impeachment had far-reaching consequences. The first was that the long-simmering, and at times boiling, hostility to Danby's administration (and hence to the Court as a whole) vented itself in spectacular fashion. The antipathy erupted on to, and disrupted, the political scene, so that much of the proceedings of the 1679 Parliament revolved around the matter of Danby's fate. Whilst they did so, the Country party of the 1670s, which had largely been formed to oppose his ministry, remained largely united with the radical elements within the House who sought to use the crisis to effect far-reaching changes in church and state, including barring a catholic successor.

Secondly, Danby's legacy of widespread mistrust of the Court seriously undermined all attempts by the Court to settle the succession question. Distrust of Danby's political motivation and objectives effectively crushed support for the proposed limitations on a popish successor announced in November 1678. Moreover, Danby's administration had made Court organisation both more obvious and more obviously corrupt than previous administrations, provoking an aversion to management, officeholders and pensioners that lasted long after his demise. As one pamphleteer lamented, the term 'Courtier' had come to mean

an enemy to law and liberty and propriety and everything that is dear to the people ... the case is come to this, that no man what ever can attend the person of the King or serve him in any of the most honourable offices at Court, but he must be looked upon as a dangerous person to the people, and as the worst of men.[8]

Consequently, those members of the Country opposition taken into the privy council in April 1679 found that their new places actually damaged their credit and influence in the House, without giving them the means to create a Court party. Suspicion and mistrust of the Court continued to plague attempts to solve the succession crisis, and in December 1680 negotiations between Charles and the cabal of parliamentary leaders known as the Southamptons foundered on the rock of mutual distrust.

Thirdly, as those talks indicate, the loss of Danby's advice forced Charles to listen to opposition groups, even though this meant losing a clear Court stance or long-term policy. Essentially Charles reacted to events, albeit with

---

[8] *Advice to the Nobility, Gentry and Commonalty of this Nation* [1679], p. 2.

clever short-term tactics, and was intent on keeping as many avenues open as possible, both at home and abroad, in order to allow maximum freedom of manoeuvre and hence, so he believed, to ensure his survival. His opinions, opaque at the best of times, became impenetrable to even the closest observer of the Court, and his readiness to listen to conflicting sources of advice both frustrated and undermined his ministers, as well as confusing those who looked for a coherent and consistent line of action to follow. There was even uncertainty about the King's attitude to exclusion. For a long while it appeared that he may not have been averse to the bill, and when his opposition to the measure became more obvious, his resolution to adhere to his brother was still highly questionable. Even when he was thought to have decided to defend his brother's rights, there remained the distinct possibility that he could be forced to capitulate.

Fourthly, and most importantly, Danby's fall meant that Charles was to spend the next few years searching for a cohesive ministry. With power so openly available to the strongest, it was inevitable that factions jockeyed for position at Court, or tried to gain influence from outside the Court by harnessing popular pressure. The ramification of this struggle was that the succession became one of the keys to preferment. Thus, if Charles had yielded in December 1680 to the Southampton group which pressed for exclusion, they would all have expected office and influence. Similarly, in April 1679 both Shaftesbury and Halifax expected to dominate, but found themselves in competition with one another. The personal rivalry and factionalism between these two figures was to shape the struggle between limitationists, supported by Halifax, and exclusionists, supported by Shaftesbury, not only in the 1679 Parliament but also in 1680, when the debate in the Lords about the passage of the exclusion bill became a quality slanging-match between the two men. Yet Halifax never enjoyed, or fostered, the personal following enjoyed by his rival, and therefore had to rely on the personal nature of his relationship with the King. This meant that for much of the period he appeared to court power, only to shy away from it when it was within his grasp, and Charles was always rightly wary about relying on Halifax as a sole minister because the earl's uncertain credit and influence in the Commons limited his usefulness. Even when Halifax appeared to have bettered Shaftesbury, he pursued a factional struggle in 1680 with Sunderland, who had become Shaftesbury's ally and a threat to Halifax's influence over the King; and, when Sunderland was dismissed, he was still in rivalry with Hyde and Seymour. Always, and self consciously, a counter-balancing force in politics, rivalry with other ministers was Halifax's real trademark. He and Seymour agreed on the need for limitations or an expedient to settle the succession, but proved unable to work together. Charles listened to their advice in order to place something new before the 1681 Parliament, but it was Hyde who proved the eventual victor of the power struggle. Halifax was still a useful tool to employ against Shaftesbury, but the ministry was basically a Yorkist one, with the indefatigable Jenkins taking on the burden of day-to-day administration. Rifts remained within the group, most notably over foreign policy, but without the pressure of an imminent Parliament these no longer seriously undermined government effectiveness. In any case, the ministry was buttressed by an aggressive loyalism in the counties which needed relatively little government inducement or co-ordination.

Once the weakness of the Court during much of the period has been recognised, it is possible to turn to a proper assessment of opposition groups. Their strength was always to some extent illusory, because they often filled a power vacuum created by Court shortcomings and hence appeared a more effectively organised party than they actually were, and because for much of the period they dominated the means of representing public opinion, not just at elections but also through the press and the petitioning campaigns. But we need to go further than simply pointing to the appearance of power. The conclusions reached by the first part of the book that exclusion was part of a wider succession crisis, that this crisis was shaped by European factors, that mistrust of the Court sabotaged the possible success of alternatives to exclusion, and that the succession issue was bound up in personal and factional rivalry as well as ideology, all suggest the need to revise the interpretation of the crisis which depicts a tightly organised, thrusting opposition formed around the single issue of exclusion. Chapter 5 therefore sought to re-evaluate the structure of politics in Parliament.

Within Parliament contemporaries saw, and research confirms, a faction of leaders and an association of politicians held together more by informal ties, ambition and ideology than by party discipline and central organisation. The House was managed by a steering group of influential Members, relatively small in number, who were recognised as leaders of the House, even though a hostility to management had been militated against Danby and was resented by MPs of all opinions. The composition of this steering group was constantly shifting, and the motives of its members were diverse. A detailed study of its personnel points to the tensions amongst the leaders, especially when local or personal issues cut across collective loyalty. Suspicions and jealousies within the group were particularly apparent when it was suspected that the government was offering offices to some and not to others. Yet, although a degree of factionalism was ever-present amongst the top rank of parliamentary leaders, the crisis did force a co-operation between Members that was fostered by meetings at taverns, clubs or houses, gatherings that many contemporaries remarked on as though their scale was new, and which did lead to some idea of a programme of action to be followed. Moreover, amongst the second-rank of parliamentarians, those just below the level of possible ministerial quality for whom ambition was a much smaller motive, a degree of personal obligation and shared ideological commitment did create a powerful bond. In addition to, and on occasion overlapping with, the steering group of MPs, there were also pressure groups, such as Monmouth's supporters and an alliance of anti-Court critics encouraged by the French ambassador to oppose anti-French motions. Barrillon also made use of a republican group, but suggestions that its members were at odds with Shaftesbury and dominated the House gives them a coherence and command that they did not possess.

Shaftesbury's role as the grand puppet-master tugging at his disciples' strings also needs revision. It has been suggested that the 'Whigs owed almost everything to him', and that he directed activities from the party headquarters of the Green Ribbon Club,[9] but the earl's influence was nevertheless inflated by Tory propagandists, especially after his arrest in July 1681, to give credence to the concept of an evil, powerful and self-seeking politician leading honest men astray. This is not to deny that he played an important role in shaping and formulating overall strategy, that he was intimate with a significant number of MPs, or that he was closely associated with a coterie of London radicals; but it does need to be stressed that his associates were highly motivated individuals who needed little organisation, and whose network also embraced other co-ordinating figures such as the duke of Buckingham and the City's MPs. Similarly, Shaftesbury's was not the only influence on the Commons, and his lack of a widespread personal electoral interest made him reliant on Member's goodwill and agreement. In short, pivotal as he was, there is no need to see him as the director of all the unrest, and whilst it would be foolish to paint him out of the picture, his stature does need to be put in proper perspective. His status and credit fluctuated significantly during the period, so that by 1681 his mass appeal had largely evaporated. Moreover, the concentration on Shaftesbury has obscured the lead offered by others. Lord Holles, for example, was an influential figure in drawing up programmes of action, which covered a wide field of issues relating to popery and arbitrary government, but his death in February 1680 removed one of the mediating figures between the opposition cabals. Consequently the agenda set during the discussions amongst MPs became increasingly unwieldy and unfocused.

Some of the features outlined here and throughout the book could be found in the 1670s, and perhaps also before then, suggesting that 1679–81 was not so much of a watershed in the development of parliamentary parties as was once thought. Certainly the 1670s are important for an understanding of the process of local polarisation on to which the national crisis of 1678–81 was

---

[9] Simms, 'Organisation of the Whig Party', pp. 373, 378.

superimposed; but a stress on earlier political developments, and the playing down of exclusion as *the* dividing issue, does not mean that we must abandon the concept of the birth of party altogether, for although it is difficult to discern a radically new direction for political debate or tactics, an intensification and proliferation of division is more than apparent. When we examine the language used to describe the crisis we find that contemporaries did see parties in opposition to one another, though we must be sensitive about how we employ their labels. Throughout the period observers saw a 'loyal party' and an 'adverse party' or 'factious party'. I have therefore employed the terms loyalist and opposition to denote this division, with the understanding that I am referring to *an*, rather than to *the*, opposition, and that the loyalism was to the established state and church. The terms Whig and Tory were not in common usage until early 1681, and a Whig–Tory analysis is best used to describe the outcome of the crisis, to describe the extremes it produced, rather than to explain the cause of, or the course of, the unrest. This is because the period was a process of polarisation, not a static and uniform entity, and it possessed a strong dynamic of its own that is hidden by employing anachronistic terms. Nebulous and purposefully vague terms are needed to describe shades of opinion and interest groups that were allied together, for, as Shaftesbury's friend Robert Ferguson observed, 'so different were the principles, aims and interests of those, who had both the same apprehensions of what the Court was driving on and who were equally minded to save themselves and the nation that they could not agree in the means whereby to effect it, nor center in the same ends, in case it should have been compassed'.[10]

How then are we to view the structure of politics outside Parliament and what is meant by the emergence of Whig and Tory polarities? The answer, in short, is that the period witnessed a widening and deepening of ideological polarities that gives relevance to the language of party, though the term must be used very carefully to describe how the process of the crystallisation of belief, recognised by Scott as one of the main features of the crisis,[11] was accompanied by the sophistication of political groupings which shared those beliefs. The three elections, the sharply divided press, the promotion of petitions and addresses, and the religious crisis all drew the localities into national politics and forced men to ally with rival groups. It is that division at a local level which must be counted as one of the most far-reaching effects of the period. Many men had given public proof of where their loyalties, prejudices and fears lay, and these would not be quickly or easily forgotten.

The ideological divide relied on two main issues: religion and the constitution. In 1681 it became possible to characterise the Whigs in religious terms as calvinists who believed that the Church of England was imperfectly reformed and still contained popish elements. They sought to remodel the

---

[10] Ferguson, *Ferguson the Plotter*, p. 409.   [11] Scott, *Restoration Crisis*, p. 14.

national church by removing offensive dogmas in order to strengthen a broader protestant church either within which dissenters could be comprehended or from which they could be indulged. The Tories, on the other hand, regarded the established church, with all its ceremonies, as the true church, and believed that attempts to alter it were part of a popish conspiracy to destroy the principal defence against Rome. Both groups, by externalising the religious threat, either in the form of popery or dissent, papered over the existence of controversy within the church. Yet religion was also part of a broader shared ideology, since it was part of a subject's liberty and property and as such was inseparable from constitutional safeguards. Whigs wanted to defend liberty and property from the arbitrary government, and were prepared to alter the established church and state in order to do so, justifying their proposals on the grounds of natural right. The opposition radicals wished to ensure that Parliament met, most often on fixed terms, and should be allowed to continue sitting until MPs had redressed the nation's grievances. The Whigs argued that Parliament rightfully played a central role in government because civil authority was derived from the people, and that mutual compacts between the Prince and his people had determined the power of the executive. Magistrates who became tyrants therefore forfeited their right to govern, and could be resisted by an association of subjects employing the force of arms. These were the tenets explicitly condemned by Oxford University in 1683 on the grounds that they led to rebellion, regicide and atheism.[12]

As the burning of books at the university made clear, the Tories rejected such ideas. They emphasised that civil authority was derived from God, not from the people, and that monarchs ruled by divine right. Refuting the idea that government was instituted for the good of the people governed, Tories asserted that the King, although bound by good policy to avoid tyranny, could not be forced to respect the law. Believing that the concept of popular sovereignty ultimately led to anarchy and confusion, Tories rejected the idea that the people could resume a sovereignty that they never possessed, and asserted that they could therefore not make any pact with the King. Thus the power of Parliament derived from the King, who in turn received his authority solely from God. Tories believed that attempts to alter the established church and state undermined the security of the subject and the power of the King, and they denied the people's right to make such changes or even to meddle in state affairs. They refused to accept 'that tyranny in a king dissolves the Gordian knot of obedience ... admit this for law and down goes monarchy'.[13]

---

[12] *The Judgment and Decree of the University of Oxford* (1683), printed in *Somers Tracts*, viii. 420–4. cf. T. Sprat, *A True Account and Declaration of the Horrid Conspiracy* (1685), pp. 42, 53.

[13] *Heraclitus Ridens* no. 14, 3 May 1681.

Indeed, they believed that dissent, republicanism and a tyrannous Parliament posed the greatest threat of arbitrary government.

The succession issue helped to focus the polarity of these two sets of convictions. Altering the blood line, or even restricting royal prerogatives, was either lawful because Parliament had the right to direct the line of inheritance, or it was unlawful because Parliament did not possess such power. If the former, then the people, as represented by the legislature, were an integral part of government; if not, the King alone was sovereign, answerable only to God. Either the people could resist a popish successor to protect their fundamental liberties or properties, or they must bear whatever providence had in store and uphold a duty of obedience to a popish successor which nothing could break. As Secretary Jenkins told MPs, exclusion implied 'the orig[ina]ll of governm[en]t to derive from the people', with the result that 'we [would] have K[ings] by Auth[ori]ty of Parl[iamen]t':

Since after the Exclusion of the royall line it is in [MPs'] power whether they cho[o]se any king or no, they may introduce another form, and if they may thus depose of the supream and sovereigned authority, by the same reason they can dispose of their own that is but subordinate, and change the order of Parliament, excluding one House or abrogating both, and bringing in a new fasheon of government; there is no stopping when once we begin to make a change in fundamentalls.[14]

The succession and Parliament's role in government could thus be seen as two aspects of the same question about the nature and origins of government, and about the extent of the obligations of allegiance and obedience owed to Princes.

Most contemporaries, however, did not see the crisis in such terms, and the terms Whig and Tory are best reserved for those who espoused polarised ideological positions. When we study individuals rather than ideas it becomes less easy to pigeon-hole contemporaries, for a large number of factors shaped attitudes, and these factors varied in influence during different stages of the crisis. It is thus difficult to talk in terms of an exclusionist party, partly because the views of the majority on the matter are not known, but also because MPs were not elected solely, or even mainly, on their attitude to the bill. Whilst the succession issue did become more important as the crisis progressed, the elections show a more general Court–Country divide, although this dichotomy must also be handled carefully because support for the Country party of the 1670s did not, as Harris has recently emphasised, translate automatically into support for exclusion. Both Sir Francis Winnington and Sir William Jones had been employed by the Court under Danby, though both were dissatisfied with his administration; yet Winnington voted against the first exclusion bill, and Jones allegedly procured a drafting of the bill designed to ensure its rejection in the Lords, though by 1680 they were

---

[14] All Souls, MS 242, ff. 119, 256, notes for speeches, n.d.

two of the most influential Members pressing for exclusion. By contrast, Sir Thomas Meres had been one of the leaders of the Country party against Danby in the late 1670s, but by 1681 had become a spokesman for the Court's alternative to exclusion. Indeed during the period the leaders of the old Country party lost credit in the House, and were replaced by new men. The Country party, which had in any case never been an entirely united one, thus split: for some, such as Lord Cavendish and Lord William Russell, anti-popery, hostility to Court corruption and the need for security against arbitrary government led them, with different degrees of enthusiasm, to support exclusion; whilst for others, such as Sir Thomas Clarges and Sir William Coventry, fear that the monarchy and the church were threatened by forces that might lead to civil war drew them away from erstwhile colleagues. Both groups aimed at security and peace, but differed in their analysis of what constituted the greatest threat to peace, and on how that threat should be countered. Yet, although politically fractured, Country attitudes, particularly in respect to officeholding, public morality and corruption could still cut across the new polarities and reunite the different wings of loyalist and opposition groups. Indeed, a Court–Country polarity had more relevance after, rather than during the crisis itself, for whilst during much of 1678–81 'the anti-Court party was very great within even within the Court itself',[15] there was no confusion by 1681, once the Court was basically purged of all but loyalists.

The system of politics used to describe 1678–81 must therefore be fluid enough to take account of these factors, and to allow for personal, local and practical considerations which pulled forcefully at different times. Different motivation and changing circumstances thus make it difficult to talk of an 'exclusionist party'. A large number of the bill's supporters regarded barring James from the throne as a means for preserving the status quo of the constitution rather than as a means for reforming it or emphasising the role of the people in government; there were also moderates who supported the bill on practical grounds, because it offered the best prospect of peace and security; whilst others supported it because their anti-popery drove them into an extreme measure to prevent the destruction of the church. Each of these groups could be detached from the radical, ideological supporters of the bill, and the arguments used to do so were relatively simple because they were an extrapolation of the ideas used to justify exclusion. The claim that Parliament could determine the succession, the fusion of limitations on the King's powers with exclusion, the need for an armed association of protestants, the demands for religious reformation and the attack on Charles's own decisions to prorogue or dissolve Parliaments were all interpreted by loyalists as proof that the entire opposition aimed at overthrowing the present and established

---

[15] Dalrymple, *Memoirs*, ii. 322 (quoting lord chief justice North).

forms of religious and political government. Thus any criticism of the Court was regarded as parallel with civil war republicanism and fanaticism, and as those charges were driven home it became increasingly difficult for moderate opponents of popery and arbitrary government to support the radicals, particularly as the waning of anti-popery removed a veil that had given opposition its political legitimacy. It is this process of stripping moderates, trimmers and time-servers away from the core of radicals that was described in the second part of the book.

Chapters 6–10 addressed the question of public opinion, and charted shifts in moods, as well as pointing to events which caused such movements and studying the interplay between central and local politics. A major theme running through these sections was that opinion can and could only be understood in terms of propaganda, and that the means of representing the will of the nation therefore became inextricably combined with the political process.

The second part of the book sought to move away from an explanation of the conflict solely in terms of exclusion, to explore a wider religious and constitutional crisis outside Parliament and the Court. One major factor behind the turbulence of the period was the freedom of the press. Printed newspapers, pamphlets and manuscript newsletters achieved a wide and influential circulation, helping both to shape and reflect public opinion, though the impact of propaganda varied according to the strength of attempts by the government to re-establish control after the expiry of the Licensing Act, and according to the vigour of the debate between loyalist and opposition propagandists. The election campaigns in 1679 and the early months of 1681 also generated and maintained political excitement, and widened the extent of popular participation in the crisis, whilst the elections themselves were not fought over the single issue of exclusion, and were much more complex than has previously been admitted. A Court–Country conflict centering on the issues of popery and arbitrary government, a growing religious division between dissenters and low-churchmen, on the one hand, and strict conformists, on the other, together with local issues and interests, helped shape the character of the contests at the polls, and it is worth noting that, unlike the party system even of the early eighteenth century, the result of the elections did not determine control of the government or the composition of the ministry.

The campaigns of petitions and addresses, most relating in some way to the issue of Parliament's sitting, also provide an important thread linking the period. With Parliament increasingly seen by loyalists as unrepresentative, and by critics of the Court as sitting far too rarely, and for too short a time, to fully express grievances (Parliament sat for less than thirty-five weeks between October 1678 and July 1681), both groups needed an extra-parliamentary voice. The petitions and addresses that were promoted throughout 1680 and 1681 gave them such a means of expression, though they therefore ensured that the struggle became one to represent the will of the nation in propagandist terms. The loyalists were eventually prepared not only to copy the tactics of the opposition, in promoting rival addresses, but also in certain cases to formulate their own interpretation of key slogans. Thus by the spring of 1681 the loyalists were claiming that it was they, not their opponents, who stood for the rights of the subject against popery and arbitrary government, and for protestantism, liberty and property.

Analysis of the petitioning and addressing campaigns showed a changing and fluid situation, both in the capital and in the provinces, where particular caution is needed in explaining local divisions in terms of national ones. Each stage in the process of statement, response and counter-response had its own characteristic. After several abortive campaigns in 1679, the petitions in the winter of 1679/80 were successfully promoted in London, and a handful of other places; but although encouraged by Shaftesbury, and representing one of the high-points of opposition organisation during the period, they never fulfilled their anticipated strength or objective. Nevertheless they show how popular opinion could be galvanised not so much by the succession controversy as by the issue of Parliament's sitting in order to pass safeguards against the threats of popery and arbitrary government. The loyalist response to the petitioning was initially muted, and limited to a handful of 'abhorrences', but these in turn provoked new attempts to petition for a Parliament in the summer of 1680, and the loyalist 'abhorrences' were then taken up in Parliament on grounds of principle and faction. In the 1681 election addresses were made to MPs which were shaped by local factors, and did not blindly follow the lead offered by Shaftesbury and other peers, who had petitioned for Parliament to be held in London rather than Oxford. Although many of the addresses did call for exclusion, they were more than mandates on that single issue, and show the range of religious and political grievances that contemporaries wished to see addressed and redressed. The loyalist reaction to the so-called 'instructions', in terms of promoting rival addresses, was much stronger than has previously been thought, and reflected changing public attitudes. Loyalists concentrated on the need to defend the established church, and urged MPs to seek a reconciliation with the King by granting him supply, thereby directly refuting the previous Parliament's tactic of withholding money until its demands had been met. A number of factors combined after the dissolution of the Oxford Parliament to nurture a local-driven loyalist reaction against the perceived threat to church and state. The greater coherence of the Court, encouraged by Charles's own greater resolution, the willingness of loyalists in the localities to copy opposition tactics, and the assertiveness of propagandists against dissent and 'commonwealth principles' all contributed to the success of the nationwide campaign to publicly thank the King for his *Declaration* justifying the dissolution. The resulting addresses also drew much greater mass support than has previously been recognised, though they cannot be used as evidence that the country had simply turned 'Tory', for, whilst open opposition became submerged beneath a general desire to appear loyal and united in the face of civil war, divides still existed. The addresses and counter-addresses highlight the important response of the localities, where a loyalist faction was usually able to dominate the representation of the sense of the nation, and thereby add a dimension to the discussion of the period that is sometimes neglected. Indeed, further study of the political and religious groupings in the boroughs and counties seems one of the most productive approaches for new research if we are to enlarge our understanding of the structure of politics in the country as a whole, since the examination of public opinion at the local level can reveal regional variations as well as relate national shifts of opinion to events and concerns at the grass roots.

Political and religious attitudes after the Restoration were imbued for many with a strong strand of conservatism, a dislike of what Cambridge's address in 1681 called the 'restlessness of such as are addicted to innovation',[16] and a great part of the loyalist identity in 1681 concerned the fear of civil war. Virtually every loyalist pamphlet referred to the nation's sufferings before the Restoration and warned of the danger of relapsing into chaos. It was this appeal to the nation's collective memory of internecine warfare that gave the Tory doctrines of nonresistance, passive obedience and allegiance to the established church and state so much of their strength. Indeed, debates during the crisis often relied on the manipulation of people's fears, and principle was often tinged with, and even distorted by, considerations of emotion or practicality. Security from danger was the central thrust of both sides' arguments, even though interpretations differed as to what would contribute to security, and as to what constituted the greatest danger. It was this common concern over safeguards for the future that could lead to shifting opinions. In 1679 it was possible to believe that popery was the greatest threat, and exclusion the means of security; but by 1681 it was equally possible to see the power of dissent and the prospect of civil war as the greatest dangers, and to believe that an insistence on exclusion was the way to precipitate chaos. The cry of '41 is come again' therefore removed the legitimacy of political opposition that the Popish Plot had provided, and allowed the loyalists to reclaim the word loyal by challenging the interpretation of opposition rallying cries such as 'Liberty', 'Property' and 'Protestantism'. The 'Whig' camp held no monopoly of 'Country' ideology, and dread of a standing army, of chaos, of arbitrary government, and fears for the

---

[16] *Vox Angliae* (1682), p. 9.

future of protestantism were feelings harboured by many who in 1681 rallied to the established state and church. Thus as the crisis developed, 'Country' opinions increasingly expressed themselves in loyalist tones. Yet, whilst the rival exploitation of similar fears and anxieties from different perspectives helped divide the nation, the common rhetoric, arguments and tactics also helped to promote the appearance of unity once the parliamentary base of the opposition had been removed by the dissolution of the Oxford Parliament. Thus, although there was some shift in attitudes, discontent had not evaporated but been neutralised by the skilful wording of Charles's Declaration justifying his dissolution of the 1680–1 Parliaments, and by a fear of civil war that united all but the most radical. Even though the Tories were represented as persecuting, popishly affected, divine-righters, the loyalists had succeeded by 1681 in creating an image of all opposition as dissenting, republican and rebellious, an image that proved both too plausible and too powerfully drawn to resist.

The chronological study of opinion during the period emphasises the fact that there were fluctuations in the intensity of the crisis, that there was no smooth line of drift away from opposition, but periods of reversing fortunes. In the late summer of 1679 the first signs of a loyalist reaction are visible, yet the discovery of the Meal Tub Plot, the ill-conceived attempt by catholics to fabricate a 'presbyterian plot', re-animated anti-popery and encouraged demands for Parliament to meet. The decision to promote mass petitions to awe Charles into allowing MPs to assemble in January 1680 raised the crisis to a new level of intensity, involving the provinces and all social orders in the political conflict; the campaign was perceived as a direct attack on the King's prerogative, and raised the spectre of civil war, with the result that the petitions attracted far fewer numbers than had been hoped for. Moderates, alienated by these tactics, were further wooed by loyalist propaganda which refuted the ideas of popular sovereignty and the right of resistance, and a period of calm in the spring of 1680 rendered subsequent unrest more factious; but the Court still had to win over the moderates, and the loyalists still had to assert themselves. This process occurred when the proceedings in the 1680–1 Parliament were interpreted as arbitrary and extreme, and the winter of 1680–1 saw the expression of an increasingly aggressive loyalism, apparent to some extent during the elections of 1681, but more obviously in the aftermath of the dissolution of the Oxford Parliament.

These fluctuations in tension and the representation of opinion help explain why the three themes of succession, popery and arbitrary power were strongest at different times during 1678–81. The fear of popery, unleashed in such a dramatic way by the story told by Titus Oates, dominated public opinion until the summer of 1679. Just as its influence was waning, the discovery in the autumn of 1679 of the Meal Tub Plot induced a second wave of anti-popery. This, however, was not long-lasting, and by early 1680 belief in all the allegations of the plot was far from universal. Indeed the threat to the church from dissent, seen to be undermining the established religion on behalf of the papists, was increasingly regarded by many as more dangerous.

The succession issue, by contrast, grew in importance, though it was at first primarily a parliamentary one. Placed on the agenda by the 1679 session, it nevertheless did not greatly impact on the nation as a whole for some time, affecting London and its environs in the autumn of 1679, but thereafter subsiding as an issue until at least the following summer. When Parliament met in October 1680, although MPs did consider a range of issues, the provision of safeguards for the future centred on the impossibility of James's accession to the throne. The rejection of the exclusion bill by the Lords provoked a crisis for the exclusionists within Parliament about how to proceed, and the Parliament that met at Oxford in 1681 was again focused on the problem of the succession.

Like the term 'popery', the rallying cry of arbitrary government changed its appeal during the period. The fear of a corrupt, factional government was strongest between 1678 and 1679, when Danby's prosecution headed MPs' concerns. For those who focused on the King's own arbitrary actions, rather than the prospect of those of his brother, agitation was undoubtedly strongest when Charles prorogued or dissolved Parliament, decisions which seemed part of a conspiracy against the liberties of the subject and the safety of the nation. 'I cannot but think the Court's designe is to make parliaments useless or rid the crowne of them', wrote the puritan Ralph Josselin, and a leading MP, Thomas Papillon, suggested that Charles's frequent dissolutions aimed 'to bring parliam[en]ts into contempt and destroy the very constitution'.[17] The petitions of the winter of 1679–80, and the propaganda struggle a year later represent the high points when Parliament's assembly and its role within government were the subject of fierce controversy; but the radical ideological debate about the King's powers was always built on the back of moderate outrage at Charles's unwillingness to let MPs assemble in times of real crisis, and once the value in Parliament's sitting was perceived to decline, the opposition withered in terms of numbers, though not in terms of the conviction of a relatively small number of highly motivated men. Loyalists, on the other hand, had always been convinced that the cry of arbitrary government was a recipe for chaos and a republic. In September 1679 one MP 'idolised for being the Guardian of the People's Liberties', was warned that although men wanted to curb the powers of the monarchy and church because of the fears of arbitrary government, the steps of reform would inevitably lead to the destruction of both institutions; hence it was 'far better patiently to endure

[17] *Diary of Ralph Josselin*, p. 625; Kent AO, U1015/07/11, annotations, on a printed copy of *The Answers Commanded by His Majesty* (1681).

some tolerable inconveniencies under a lawful and long-settled government, than to ruin ourselves upon the hazard of an intestine war and the intolerable mischief of anarchy and confusion'.[18] But, although the author of this statement complained that anyone who tried to 'instil principles of Loyalty and Conformity' was 'decry'd as a promoter of arbitrary power and a friend to popery', loyalists became increasingly brave in their endeavour to denounce what they saw as 'wild and groundless clamours against the government'. By late 1680 loyalists argued that Parliament itself acted arbitrarily, that MPs aimed at perpetuating their power at the expense of the rights of the people and the King, and that they did so in alliance with the dissenters who wanted to destroy the church. 'If you hear any Person inveigh against the Government, or Discourse of the fear of Arbitrary Designes', wrote John Nalson in the spring of 1681, 'you may pawn your life on't, you may find him in a conventicle upon a Sunday.' The issue of arbitrary government had therefore also become 'a point of Religion', and had 'been set up as a mark and estimate of a true Protestant'.[19]

There has been a good deal of debate about what constituted the pivotal issue around which the unrest of the period really revolved. A stark choice between *either* exclusion *or* more fundamental problems about popery and arbitrary power is a false one, for, although the succession problem was not simply a by-product of a deeper malaise about popery and arbitrary government, it was an integral part of it. This inter-relationship is neatly captured by one of the pamphleteers of the period, who wrote that 'the same hour your religion is altered (which a Popish King ... will certainly effect), the same day the whole Law will be destroyed, and the English Nation will be reduced to absolute slavery'.[20] The succession, on the one hand, and popery and arbitrary government, on the other, are thus not mutually exclusive themes. Each of the three elements fed off each other, and concentration by historians on any one issue to the exclusion of the others therefore distorts the true picture.

The issues of religion, the succession and arbitrary government all helped to divide the nation during the period and held different sway at different times; they were all distorted by local and personal factors, and it is not very useful to try to prioritise them in sweeping generalisations. It is more helpful to ask what was new or unique to 1679–81. Religious tensions were crucial in stimulating, and to some extent characterising, the resulting divisions. But, whilst it is true that the Popish Plot gave the debate about the unity of protestants a new urgency, and that the struggle for a second reformation of

---

18 BL, Add.33,573, f. 132, John Savage to William Bourne, 6 September 1679; f. 130, Savage to Major William Hale, 5 September 1679.
19 *The Complaint of Liberty and Property* (1681), pp. 1–2.
20 *An Abstract of the Contents of Several Letters* (1679), p. 2.

the church reached new heights, the alarm about popery intensified polarities which had existed since the Restoration religious settlement, and which had flared up at intervals ever since. The arguments between the two sides were thus not particularly new, especially since clerics and divines had always been articulate in expressing their opinions. What was new was the intensity of the debate within the church, and this was in large part the legacy of Danby's self-conscious exploitation of the growing unease about the place of dissent, and the perceived growth of popery. The events of the period 1678–81 broke the accommodation and compromise reached in many areas since the Restoration, but they did so with such vigour because the peace had always been a very fragile one and had already become increasingly strained.

Moreover, an interpretation of the crisis which puts religion as the most important factor in the polarisation of the nation runs the risk of seeing attacks on dissenters and their allies as having been motivated solely by religious motives. Undoubtedly there were those who saw nonconformity as a theological threat, and nonconformists found the established church wanting in its dogma; but it should not be forgotten that, in ideological terms, dissent was so strongly attacked in part because it was seen as *politically* disruptive. Just as measures for the freedom or repression of conventiclers had often been determined by political considerations in the 1660s and 1670s, so the persecution of nonconformists after 1681 had political reasoning behind it. The government by 1681 wholeheartedly espoused L'Estrange's belief that dissent went hand in hand with an attack on the established government of both church and state, and it was the temporal factiousness and radicalism of conventiclers, their alleged republicanism and urge for civil war, that brought about the need for action. Loyalty to the established church was therefore taken as a touchstone for political loyalty. Since some dissenters rejected divine right ideas, attacked the church hierarchy and encouraged personal resistance based on conscience and fundamental rights, the toleration of noncomformists was therefore deemed incompatible with the maintenance of a stable society, or at least of the type of society accepted by the Restoration settlement. The political motivation behind the suppression of dissent after 1681 can be seen in the presentment made by the Westminster grand jury in January 1682, when it was publicly stated that the aim was to end meetings 'which, if not timely suppressed, will not only endanger the monarchy but keep up that division in this kingdom which in all probability will destroy both Church and state'.[21] The established church and state thus survived or fell together, a lesson which James unfortunately failed to learn. Persecution was, ironically, seen as 'an essay towards union' because it strove to build a

---

[21] G.L.R.O., Calendar of Sessions Books, vi/394.

single protestant national church.[22] Religion had an overtly political context, of a different character to that of the early seventeenth century. Part of the legacy of the civil war was a deeply held desire to maintain the established order after the Restoration. History could thus never exactly repeat itself, partly because the meaning of republicanism had shifted since the 1650s, and also because the past itself was constantly being used as a warning guide to show which steps would lead to rebellion. Popery and arbitrary government were such potent rallying cries because catholicism and tyranny threatened the religious and political status quo; so too did those who sought to remodel church or state. Moreover, from the dissenters' point of view, their religious demands had to be advanced by a political campaign, for they had been placed outside the law, and thus required a political solution to their predicament, a factor which made opinion in Parliament of crucial importance to their cause.

What was new about 1679–81 for the Restoration period, even if it was not so novel for the seventeenth century as a whole, was the depth of the constitutional crisis and fears of arbitrary government. Not since the civil wars had the role of Parliament, the origin of government, the obligations owed to a prince and the rights of the subject been debated so prominently and fervently. Although these issues had been raised in the 1660s and more forcefully in the 1670s, they had, unlike the religious question, remained largely the concern of MPs and perhaps also of persecuted dissenters. Only after the Popish Plot, and the lapse of the licensing laws to allow free debate, did they become truly national issues, attracting wider popular support or opposition when linked to the issue of Parliament's survival or meeting. Such widespread support temporarily faded in 1681, although the government's policy of remodelling the borough charters renewed national concern over the rights and privileges of the subject and the prerogatives of the Crown. Such local struggles over corporation rights helped buttress national constitutional concerns. Even if constitutional demands had been prompted or fuelled by religious ones, it was nevertheless the debate about the constitution that provided the crisis with much of its real depth and fire, and gave the period its radicalism. If party politics first emerged between 1679 and 1681 it was because the constitutional conflict added a new layer of polarity over, and to a large extent overlapping with, the religious one and because antipopery both drew men into political controversy and to some extent justified their expressions of discontent. Politics was so intense and so influenced by religious factors because of the conjunction of religious and constitutional controversies that seemed to threaten both church and state.

The suggestion that not one, but three, main issues were important in

[22] Ibid., vi/401, presentment of December 1682.

1679–81 urges a revision of the idea of the emergence of a party master-minded and directed by the earl of Shaftesbury, formed round support for exclusion alone. A more balanced interpretation would emphasise the personal, local and factional elements still displayed in the formation of allegiances, and stress what might be called partisan rather than party politics, but also point to the shared ideological commitment leading to co-operation and association amongst MPs and London or provincial cabals. A fluid structure of politics allowed groupings to coalesce into new polarities based on attitudes to dissent, to the succession, and to the idea of arbitrary government. Commitment to these fundamentals did not often change, but the expression of them in all but the most ideologically committed could vary according to the pull of personal, local and national considerations. More-over, party politics could only emerge when there was conflict along a sharply defined axis, requiring two sides, not just one pressure group, and the coherence of the Court and loyalists only really evolved in late 1680 and early 1681. It should also be said that neither side wished to remain a party, but aimed to represent the will of the whole nation, and that few contemporaries were yet prepared to sacrifice the pretence of unity. However we like to describe them, polarities were re-aligned, intensified and clarified during 1679–81. Whilst recognising that during those years opinion was not so tightly organised as we once believed, we can also conclude that it was a period of accelerated, and sophisticated, development for the structure of politics within a longer-term gradual process of change, marking a formative stage in the evolution of political and religious allegiances, and another nail in the coffin of consensual politics. We thus need to graft new layers of analysis onto often oversimplified interpretations, and recognise that the crisis and men's responses to it were more complex than was once thought.

BIBLIOGRAPHY

MANUSCRIPT SOURCES

(Manuscript tracts are listed under 'Printed sources')

All Souls College, Oxford

Papers of Sir Leoline Jenkins: MS 116, 169, 202, 206, 211, 229, 233, 239, 240, 241, 242, 243, 247, 251, 264, 275
Papers of Narcissus Luttrell: MS 117, 171

Bodleian Library, Oxford

Additional MS	D.23	Burnet papers
Aubrey MS	13	Letters to John Aubrey 1644–95
Ballard MS	70	Notes, chiefly relating to Oxford's history
Carte MS	39	Ormonde Correspondence
	72	Newsletters 1660–85
	80	Ormonde papers
	81	Wharton Correspondence
	103	Wharton and Huntingdon Papers
	104	Middleton Papers 1680–1
	146	Ormonde Correspondence 1677–80
	219	Ormonde Correspondence
	222	Newsletters 1662–84
	228	Miscellaneous Papers
	232	Ormonde Correspondence
	233	Miscellaneous Papers
	243	Ormonde Correspondence
Clarendon MS	87	Miscellaneous Papers
	92	Miscellaneous Papers
Don.	B.8	Miscellaneous Papers
	C.38	Fleming Newsletters
	C.169	Ashurst letterbook
	F.7	Notebook of Questions relating to Shaftesbury's Trial, 1681
Eng. Hist.	B.204	Papers of Sir Edmund Warcupp
	E.47	Letters of John Lake 1681–8
Eng. Letters	C.28–9	Letters of Henry Dodwell
	C.210	Letters to Rev. John Palmer

	D.60	Correspondence of Robert Bodmyn
	D.72	Letters from Owen Wynne 1680–4
Eng. Misc.	e.4:	Papers of George Hickes
Fairfax MS	33	Papers 1660–98
Firth MS	C.2	Miscellaneous Papers
	C.13	Miscellaneous Papers
Jones MS	17	Miscellaneous Tracts
Locke MS	B.4	Miscellaneous Papers
	C.25	Miscellaneous Papers
	C.3–23	Correspondence
	E.5	Diary of proceedings in Parliament 1660–1681
	F.4	Journal for 1680
North Papers		
Petty MSS		(Microfilm Deposit)
Poet	C.25	Miscellaneous Papers
Rawlinson MS	A.162	Copies of failed bills 1662–1685
	A.175	Pepys Papers
	A.135	Popish Plot Papers
	A.137	Proceedings in the House of Commons 1679
	C.727	Dispatches from Sir Gabriel Sylvius
	D.1064	Tracts
	letters 48	Letters of Sir Edmund Warcupp
	letters 93	Letters to Dr Francis Turner
Smith MS	31	Miscellaneous Papers
	50, 54	Letters to Dr Thomas Smith 1661–1709
	125	Miscellaneous Notes by Dr Thomas Smith
Tanner MS	37–9*	Letters 1678–81
	129	Bristol Diocese Correspondence
	148, 149	Chichester Diocese Letters
Topographical MS	Top. Oxon	Local History Collection relating to Oxfordshire
Wood MS	F.39–41	Correspondence
	F.43–4	Correspondence

Berkshire Record Office

Reading Corporation (uncatalogued) Papers

British Library, London

	10,118–19	Financial Papers relating to State Revenue
Additional	15,643	Register of the Committee of
MS		Intelligence 1679–82
	15,892	Hyde Papers
	17,107–8	Hyde Papers
	18,730	Diary of the Earl of Anglesey
	19,872	Letters to Tangier
	21,554	Fairfax Correspondence
	27,402	Tracts
	27,440	Allestree Papers
	27,447–8	Paston Correspondence

	28,042–3	Danby Papers
	28,046–7	Danby Papers
	28,049	Danby Papers
	28,053	Danby Papers
	28,054	Danby Papers
	28,087	Danby Papers
	28,091	Parliamentary Papers
	28,875	Ellis Papers
	28,930	Ellis Papers
	28,938	Ellis Papers
	29,556–8	Hatton-Finch Correspondence
	29,910	Swinfen Papers
	32,095	State Papers
	32,518–20	Papers of Lord Keeper North
	32,680–1	Papers of Henry Sidney
	33,573	Hale Family Papers
	35,099	Southwell Papers
	35,865	Hardwicke Papers
	36,988	Paston Correspondence
	37,985	Letters of Sir Philip Warwick
	37,981	Dispatches of William Carr
	38,847	Southwell Papers
	40,856	Hone Papers
	41,568	Newsletters to Sir Francis Parry
	41,656	Townshend Papers
	46,956A	Egmont Papers
	52,475A	Papers of Sir Richard Temple
	61,126	Blenheim Papers
	61,488	Blenheim Papers
	61,903	Diary of Peter Le Neve
	62,453	Papers relating to Monmouth's Rebellion
	62,585	Bulstrode Memoirs and Letterbook
	63,057A and B	Burnet's 'History of My Own Time' 1683
	63,755	Preston Papers
	63,773	Preston Papers
	70,013	Harley papers
	70,081–2	Harley Papers
	70,097–9	Harley Papers
	70,141	Harley Papers
	70,223	Harley Papers
Althorp MS	C.1–C.8	Correspondence of Halifax and Sunderland
Egmont MS	2540	Nicholas Papers
	2979	Heath and Verney Papers
	2985	Heath and Verney Papers
	3331	Leeds Papers
	3345	Leeds Papers
	3678	Bulstrode Papers
	3680	Bulstrode Papers
	3684B	Bulstrode Papers
Harleian MS	6495	Miscellaneous Tracts

Microfilm	M/863	Longleat Papers
	M/874	Longleat Papers
	M/904	Longleat Papers
Stowe MS	82	'The History of the Execrable Irish Rebellion'
	180	Miscellaneous Papers
	191	Historical Papers 1651–80
	354	Speeches and Collections relating to Parliament
	425	Miscellaneous Papers
	746	Miscellaneous Papers
Unclassified		Trumbull Papers

Buckinghamshire Record Office

Verney Correspondence (Microfilm) M11/32–5 – another microfilm of this is available at the BL.

Chatsworth

Devonshire Collection

Cheshire Record Office

Mainwaring Diaries
Cholmondeley MSS

Christ Church Library, Oxford

John Evelyn's Letter Book

Library of Congress, Washington

MF.18, 124 London Newsletter collection

Corporation of London Record Office

Common Council Papers 1679–83

Corpus Christi College, Oxford

Wood-Fullman Correspondence (transcript at Bod., MS Top. Oxen. C.102)

Cumbria Record Office

Lonsdale MSS

Dorset Record Office

Trenchard Papers

Dr Williams's Library

MS 31.P: Roger Morrice's Ent'ring Book

Durham University Library

Old University Library MS E.i.9

Folger Shakespeare Library

Newdigate Newsletters

Guildhall Library, London

Durham Election Polls
Hooke Papers

Hereford and Worcester Record Office (Hereford)

W15/1 'Sir Harry Connigsby's Expedient'

Hull Record Office

Letters to the Corporation

The Huntington Library, San Marino

| HM | 68 | London Petition 1680 |
| HM | 30314–15 | Newsletters of Francis Benson to Sir Leoline Jenkins, 1676–9 |

Stowe MSS
Hastings MSS
Bridgwater MSS
Ellesmere MSS

Kent Archives Office

Dering Papers
Papillon Papers

Lancashire Record Office

Kenyon MSS

Leeds Archive Office

Mexborough MSS (Reresby Papers)

Leicestershire Record Office

Finch MSS

Longleat House

Muddiman Papers

National Library of Ireland

MS 2395 Ormonde Papers

National Library of Scotland

Tweeddale Correspondence

374 *Bibliography*

National Library of Wales, Aberystwyth

Canon Trevor Owen MSS (William Williams Papers)
Chirk Castle MSS
Wynnstay MSS
Coedyman Papers

MS	5389C	Letters of Sir Leoline Jenkins to Sir Richard Bulstrode
MS	6272C	Henry Taylor Papers
MS	9346B	Henry Herbert Papers

Norfolk Record Office

Bradfer-Lawrence MSS
Hobart Papers

Nottingham University Library

DDSR/219/14, Halifax Papers

Pepys Library, Magdalene College, Cambridge

Pepys Papers

The John Rylands Library, Manchester

Legh MSS

Public Record Office, Chancery Lane

SP.8	King William's Chest
SP.9/165	Williamson's Memorandum Book
SP.9/193	Letters of Henry Savile
SP.29	State Papers
SP.77/52	Flanders Papers
SP.84/215	Holland Papers 1679–80
SP.101/61	Newsletters from Holland
SP.104/3	Letters to Denmark
SP.104/67	Foreign Entry Book
SP.104/189–90	Foreign Entry Book
PC.2	Privy Council Registers
30/24	Shaftesbury Papers
31/3	Baschet Transcripts of Barrillon's Dispatches to Louis XIV

Public Record Office, Kew

F.O.95	Transcripts of D'Avaux's Dispatches from the Hague

Queen's College, Oxford

MS.33	'Fragmenta Parliamentaria'

Surrey Record Office

Kingston-Upon-Thames Archives

Texas University (Harry Ransom Humanities Research Centre)

Newsletters to Sir Richard Bulstrode

Tollemache MSS (privately owned)

Lauderdale Papers

University College of North Wales, Bangor

Mostyn MSS

West Sussex Record Office

Petworth House Archives

Wiltshire Record Office

Shaftesbury Borough Polls

PRINTED SOURCES

Primary material

Pamphlets
* denotes that the tract deals at length with the succession issue. E denotes that the tract deals with elections. Because so many of the pamphlets are anonymous, they are listed by their titles rather than by their author. Where the author is known, or his initials are known, the information is supplied in square brackets. If the tracts are listed in D. Wing's *Short Title Catalogue 1641–1700* (second edition, 1972–8), their catalogue number is also given. If the date by which a tract was on sale is known it has been given at the end of each entry, prefixed by a number denoting information derived from: (1) Narcissus Luttrell's *Popish Plot Catalogues*, (2) Luttrell's collection of poems at Worcester College, Oxford, (3) Nichols Newspaper collection at Bodleian, with many endorsements apparently in Luttrell's hand, (4) annotations on the Verney collection of pamphlets in the Cambridge University Library, (5) the manuscripts and printed collections made by Anthony Wood at the Bodleian, (6) advertisements or references in newspapers, many of which appeared very shortly after publication [one useful source in this category is the *Weekly Advertisement of Books*, which began production on 1 October 1680], (7) state papers, (8) printed date on the pamphlet, (9) term catalogues of the Stationers' Company (10) Luttrell's endorsements on a volume of pamphlets held at Victoria Public Library, Melbourne, Australia, and catalogued by W.J. Cameron in the *Short-Title Catalogue of Books*

Printed in Britain ... 1641–1700 (1962). The earliest date is given for each pamphlet if a number of sources offer variants; interestingly this does not mean that Luttrell's always comes first, suggesting that in at least some instances he noted date of purchase rather than publication. For a fuller discussion of the Luttrell's methodology see J.M. Osborn, 'Reflections on Narcissus Luttrell', *Book Collector*, vi (1957), 15–27.

1678

An Account of the Bloody Massacre in Ireland, Wing A250
The Common Interest of King and People, Wing C5569
The Grand Designs of the Papists, Wing 3972A [William Prynne]
A Letter from Amsterdam, Wing L1439 .
A Short Answer to Several Questions, Wing M2463 [Sir John Monson]
Tyranny and Popery Lording it over the Consciences, Wing L1321 [Sir Roger L'Estrange]

1679

* *An Abstract of the Contents of Several Letters*, Wing A131
   An Accompt of Scotland's Grievances, Wing []
   An Account of the French Usurpation Upon the Trade of England, Wing B2062 [Slingsby Bethel]
   An Account of the Proceedings at the Guildhall, Wing A357
   An Account, Together With the Writing It Self [of Lawrence Hill's denial], Wing []
* *The Act of Parliament of the 27th of Queen Elizabeth To Preserve the Queen's Person*, Wing E1146
E *Advice to the Nobility, Gentry and Commonalty of this Nation*, Wing A660 – (3) 18 July
   Ananias and Saphira Discover'd, Wing A3048 – (9) Michaelmas
   The Answer of ... Sir William Scroggs, Wing O29 [Titus Oates]
E *The Answer of the Burgesses and Other Inhabitants of Buckingham*, Wing A3288
E *An Answer to a False and Scandalous Pamphlet, Entitled The Case of the Burrough of New Windsor*, Wing []
   An Answer to a Letter written by a Member of Parliament in the Country, Wing A3320
   An Answer to the Appeal from the Country to the City, Wing L1197 [Sir Roger L'Estrange] – (9) Michaelmas
   An Answer to the Excellent and Elegant Speech made by Sir Thomas Player, Wing B72 [H.B] – (4) 16 September
   An Antidote against the Present Fears, Wing A3496
* *An Appeal from the Country to the City*, Wing B3300 [Charles Blount]
   Articles of High Misdemeanor ... [against Scroggs], Wing O29 [Titus Oates; this tract is appended to *The answer of ... Sir William Scroggs*]
   Behemoth, Wing H2213 [T. Hobbes]
E *The Benefit of the Ballot*, Wing H806A [James Harrington]
E *The Bill for Regulating Abuses in Elections*, Wing E2532
   The Bishop of Carlisle's Speech, Wing []
* *The Case of Succession to the Crown*, Wing G67 [W.G]
E *The Case of the Borough of New Windsor*, Wing C1023
* *The Case Put Concerning the Succession*, Wing L1206 [Sir Roger L'Estrange] – (9) Michaelmas

Certain Considerations Tending to Promote Peace, Wing C1695

E *The Character of Popery and Arbitrary Government*, Wing C2023

E *The Cloak in its Colours; or the Presbyterian Unmask'd*, Wing C4719

Clod-pate's Ghost, Wing S4025 [Francis Smith]

* *A Coffee House Dialogue*, Wing Y10 [Andrew Yárranton?]

A Coffee House Dialogue Examined, Wing C4885

The Common's Address against the Duke of Lauderdale, Wing []

A Congratulatory Poem, Wing C5829A

E *The Countries Vindication*, Wing C6573 – (3) 17 August

Day Fatality, Wing G647 [John Gibbon]

Declaratory Considerations upon the Present State of Affairs, Wing []

A Discourse of the Peerage, Wing B829 [Bishop Barlow]

A Disputation proving that it is not convenient to grant unto Ministers Secular Jurisdiction, Wing D1677

The Divine Right of Kings Asserted, Wing P128 [W.P]

England Facing towards Rome, Wing []

England's Alarm, Wing E2939

E *England's Great Interest in the Choice of the New Parliament*, Wing P1278 [William Penn]

England's Grievances in Times of Popery, Wing E2975

England's Happiness Restored, Wing E2979

England's Overjoy at the Duke of Monmouth's Return, Wing E3008

* *England's Safety*, Wing E3045

Episcopal Government, Wing E3160

E *Essex's Excellency*, Wing E3343

An Exact Collection of all Orders, Votes, Debates, Wing E1531

An Explanation of the Lord Treasurer's Letter, Wing L923 [Earl of Danby]

E *A Faithful and Impartial Account of the Behaviour of a Party of the Essex Freeholders*, Wing F266 – (9) Michaelmas

* *Fiat Justicia*, Wing F845 – (5) 'latter end' of July

Flagellum Mercuris, Wing G649A [John Gibbon]

The Freeborn Subject, Wing L1248 [Sir Roger L'Estrange] – (9) Michaelmas

E *The Freeholders Choice*, Wing F2114

A Friendly Call or a Seasonable Perswasive to Unity, Wing A1064 [William Allen]

Great and Horrible News from the West of England, Wing G1657

* *Great and Weighty Considerations*, Wing G1660

The Grounds of Unity in Religion, Wing G 2144

His Majesties Most Gracious Speech, Wing C3184A

The History of the Civil Wars, Wing H2239 [Thomas Hobbes]

The Humble Address and Advice of Several of the Peeres, Wing H3371

An Impartial Account of Divers Remarkable Proceedings, Wing I63 – (3) 17 June

An Impartial Consideration of Those Speeches [of Five Jesuits lately executed], Wing W2709 [John Williams]

E *An Impartial Survey of...Candidates*, Wing P24 [G.P]

The Instrument or Writing of Association, Wing I256

The Jesuits Letter of Thanks To the Covenanters, Wing J720

The Judges Opinion, Wing J1169

A Just Vindication of Learning, Wing B3307 [Charles Blount]

The Late Proposal of Union amongst Protestants Review'd and Rectified, Wing W3345 [Laurence Womock] – (6) 28 November

E A *Letter from a Freeholder of Buckinghamshire*, Wing L1372A [Wing dates it as 1689]
E A *Letter from a Friend in Abingdon*, Wing B11 [A.B]
   A *Letter from a Gentleman in the Country to some of his Familiar Friends at London*, Wing N39 [N.N]
* A *Letter from a Gentleman of Quality in the Country to his Friend upon His being Chosen a Member*, Wing F14 [E.F]
   A *Letter from a Gentleman of the Isle of Ely*, Wing L1398 – (3) 28 November
   A *Letter from a Jesuit at Paris*, Wing N110 [John Nalson]
   A *Letter from a Minister to a Person of Quality*, Wing B14 [A.B] – (4) September
   A *Letter from an Impartial Hater of the Papists*, Wing L90 [W.L]
   A *Letter from Legorn*, Wing L1484A – (8) 1 December
   A *Letter from Nobody*, Wing L1491
   A *Letter from Somebody*, Wing l1510
* A *Letter on the Subject of the Succession*, Wing L1584 – (4) 18 September
* A *Letter to a Baron of England*, Wing L1631
   A *Letter to a Friend about the Late Proclamation on the 11th December*, Wing L1637
* A *Letter to a Friend in the Country: Being a Vindication*, Wing P55 [J.P]
   A *Letter to a Friend shewing from Scripture*, Wing L1655
   A *Letter to an Honourable Member of the House of Commons*, Wing L1699 – (8) 1 March
   A *Letter to both Houses of Parliament*, Wing P19 [E.P]
E A *List of One Unanimous Club of Voters*, Wing L2403
   The Litany of the D[uke] of B[uckingham], Wing []
E *London's Choice of Citizens*, Wing E9 [E.E]
   London's Defiance to Rome, Wing L2923
   London's Flames, Wing L2927
   London's Loyalty, Wing L2490
   Mr Francis Jenk's Speech Spoken in a Common Hall, the 24th of June 1679, Wing J627 – (4) 24 June
   Mr Thomas Dangerfield's Particular Narrative, Wing D192
E A *Mild but Searching Expostulatory Letter*, Wing M2039
E *The Moderate Parliament Considered*, Wing P24 [G.P]
   The Moderation of the Church of England Considered, Wing []
E* A *Most Serious Expostulation*, Wing M2919A – (4) October
   The Narrative and Reasons of the Honourable House of Commons, Wing E2625
   The Narrative of Mr John Smith, Wing S4127
E *The Nation's Aggrievance*, Wing N236
   New Advice to a Painter, Wing N533A
E *New News of a Strange Monster found in Stow Wood*, Wing N688
   Notes taken in Short Hand, Wing S2897A [The Earl of Shaftesbury]
   One Project for the Good of England, Wing P1334 [William Penn]
   Omnia Comesta a Bello, Wing O291 [first printed 1667]
   The Parallel, or an Account of the Growth of Knavery, Wing L1284 [L'Estrange]
* A *Plea to the Dukes Answers*, Wing P2526
   The Plowman's Complaint, Wing P2614 – (8), 1 March
* A *Poem upon the Right of Succession*, Wing P2716A
   A *Political Catechism*, Wing P417 (gives date as 1643, reprinted 1679], Wing P417 [Henry Parker])

A Political Discourse of the Ruine of States, Wing P2766
Popery and Tyranny, or the Present State of France, Wing P2922
The Pope's Downfall at Abergavenny, Wing P2931
The Popish Damnable Plot, Wing P2945
The Popish Massacre, Wing G1827
The Present Great Interest Both of King and People, Wing K8 [F.K] – (4) 16 September
A Proposal of Union amongst Protestants, Wing P3709A
The Proposals for Promoting the Woollen Manufactory, Promoted, Wing P3737
The Protestants Congratulation to the City, Wing P3848
Reasons and Narrative of Proceedings betwixt the two Houses, Wing E2693
The Reasons for Nonconformity Examined, Wing B26 [A.B]
A Relation of the Birth...[of Monmouth], Wing R816
A Satyr against the Pen-Men, Wing S4848
A Seasonable Advice to all True Protestants, Wing D63 [M.D]
E *A Seasonable Warning to the Commons of England*, Wing S2248
E *Sober and Seasonable Queries*, Wing S4402
Some reflections upon the Earl of Danby, Wing B127 [J.B]
Spectrum Anti-Monarchicum, Wing S4848
A Speech Made by a True Protestant English Gentleman, Wing S4854
E *The Speech of Ferdinando Huddleston*, Wing H3248
The Speech of Sir Robert Clayton, Wing C4615 [Sir Robert Clayton] – (4) 29 September
E *Tell Truth's Answer*, Wing T623B [Wing dates it as 1680]
To the Right Honourable the Lords and Commons, Wing T1698 [gives date as 1677 but MS note on Bodleian G.Pamph.1125 (14) dates it as 1679]
A Touch of the Times, Wing G653 [John Gibbon]
* *A True Account of the Invitation and Entertainment of the Duke of York*, Wing T2376
A True Account of the Rising of the Rebels, Wing T2399
E *A True Account of What Past at the Election of ... Bucks*, Wing T2409
E *A True and Impartial account ... [of the Essex Freeholders]*, Wing []
A True Relation of the Inhuman Cruelties lately acted by the Rebels, Wing T2971
Truth and Honesty in Plain English, Wing T3149
Venn and His Myrmidons, Wing V193 – (9) Michaelmas
The Vindication of Sir Thomas Player, Wing B81 [H.B] – (4) 20 September
The Vindicator Vindicated, Wing V538
Wife for a Husband, Wing W2094
A Word to the Approaching Parliament, Wing W3570 – (4) October
* *A Word without Doors*, Wing D48 [J.D]

1680

Absalom's Conspiracy, Wing A109 – (4) June
* *An Account of Queen Mary's Methods*, Wing S150 [T.S]
An Account of the Grounds and Reasons in Which Protestant Dissenters desire their Liberty, Wing A299
An Account of the Proceedings at the Sessions for the City of Westminster, Wing A360 – (1) 14 January

An Answer Returned to the Letter from Legorn, Wing F46 – (4) 15 January.

An Answer to the Appeal, Wing L1197 [L'Estrange]

An Answer to the Appeal Expounded, Wing A3385 – (1) 26 January

An Answer to the Merchant's Letter, Wing A3425 – (4) 19 January

An Answer to the Pretended Letter to a Friend in the Country, Wing A3433 – (4) 15 March

Behemoth Arraign'd, Wing W1865 [John Whitehall] – (9) Hilary

A Brief Answer to Mr L'Estrange's Appeal, Wing B4543

A Brief Remonstrance of the Grand Grievances, Wing []

A Brief Survey (Historical and Political) of the Life and Reign of Henry III, Wing B4649 – (1) 6 May

Britannia Languens, Wing – (1) 19 February

The Cabal, Wing C179 – (1) 18 February

* *Captain Thorogood His Opinion*, Wing T1062 [B. Thorogood] – (8), 3 January 1679/80

The Case of Protestant Dissenters, Wing R2178 [Thomas Rudyard] – (1) 4 November

* *The Case of Protestants In England Under a Popish Successor*, Wing C4569 – (1) 19 October

A Catalogue of the Names of all his Majesties Justices of the Peace, Wing N67 [S.N]

A Caution against Tumultuous Petitioning, Wing C1555 – (1) 7 January

Certain Material and Useful Considerations, Wing M1288 [John Mathew]

Certain Proposals Humbly Offered, Wing C1727

The Cities Just Vindication, Wing C4329 [1682 ?] – (1) 7 August

* *Citt and Bumpkin*, Wing L1216 [Sir Roger L'Estrange] – (1) 10 February

Citt and Bumpkin, the Second Part, Wing L1221 [Sir Roger L'Estrange] – (1) 31 March

A Compendious History of the Most Remarkable Passages, Wing L1228 [Sir Roger L'Estrange]

Compendium Politicum, Wing Y6 [John Yalden] – (9) Easter

Concerning Penal Laws, Wing C5695A – (8) 12 July

Considerations Upon the Reputation, Loyalty, Manners [of Hobbes], Wing H2218 [Thomas Hobbes] – (1) 1 April

The Conspiracy; or the Change of a Government, Wing W1716 [William Whitaker]

Curse ye Meroz, Wing H1803 [Edmund Hickeringill]

The Dialogue between Citt and Bumpkin Answered, Wing P17 [E.P] – (1) 14 June

* *A Dialogue between the Pope and a Phanatick*, Wing D1333 – (1) 19 March

A Dialogue between Tom and Dick, Wing D1337 – (1) 16 March

A Discourse Concerning Supreme Power, Wing M2462 [Sir John Monson] – (6) 15 March

Discourses Upon the Modern Affairs of Europe, Wing D1630

Discovery upon Discovery, Wing L1238 [Sir Roger L'Estrange] – (1) 23 April

The Disloyal Forty and Forty One, Wing D1670

The Duke Of Monmouth and Earl of Essex ... Vindicated, Wing N5 [C.N]

An Endeavour for Peace among Protestants, Wing H3341 [William Hughes]

England's Black Tribunal, Wing E2949 [3rd edition] – (9) Hilary

* *England's Concern*, Wing E2953

England's Delight in this Parliament, Wing S526 [William Sambach]

England's Improvements Justified, Wing Y14 [Andrew Yarranton]

The Englishman's Right, Wing H1185 [Sir John Hawles] – (1) 13 May

An Essay upon Satyr, Wing E3299 – (1) 9 February
The Essex Ballad, Wing E3341
An Exact and True Narrative of the late Popish Intrigue, Wing M514 [Roderick Mansell]
A Farewell to his Royal Highness James Duke of York, Wing F424
* *A Few Words among Many*, Wing F838AB – (1) 24 January
Friendly Advice to Protestants, Wing D60 [M.D]
Foxes and Firebrands, Wing N102 [John Nalson] – (9) Trinity
A Full and Final Proof of the Plot, Wing C23 [E.C]
A Full Relation of the Contents of the Black Box, Wing F2361
A Further Discovery of the Plot, Wing L1251 [Sir Roger L'Estrange] – (1 + 4) 23 January
The Genius of True Englishmen, Wing G518
* *God and the King*, Wing C5935 [Robert Constable] – (6) 22 April
Goodman Country, Wing L1255A [Sir Roger L'Estrange] – (1) 5 August
* *The Grand Inquest*, Wing G203 [John Garbrand] – (1) 14 September
* *Great and Weighty Considerations ... Considered*, Wing H3751 [Thomas Hunt]
His Grace the Duke of Monmouth Honoured, Wing C4456 [Henry Clark]
A Historical Narration Concerning Heresy, Wing H2238 – (6) 24 February
Honest Hodge and Ralph, Wing H2584 – (6) 16 April
An Humble Address to all the Truely Loyal Commons of England, Wing H3388
Humble and Modest Proposals, Wing S3294A [Richard Sherlock]
The Inconvenience of a long Continuance of the same Parliament, Wing I139 – (1) 28 January
The Information of Francisco de Faria, Wing F425
The Interest of Princes and States, Wing B2064 [Slingsby Bethel] – (9) Easter
The Interest of the Three Kingdoms, Wing I270 – (1) 25 June
An Intimation of the Deputies of the States General, Wing I275
Irenicum, or an Essay for Union, Wing M1282 [Samuel Mather]
The Judges Opinions concerning Petitions, Wing J1169
The Judgment or Resolution of all the Lords ... Touching Procuring Hands to Petitions, Wing J1184aA
* *Jura Coronae*, Wing B5260 [John Brydall] – (9) Hilary
* *A Just and Modest Vindication of His Royal Highness*, Wing J1222
* *The King's Prerogative*, Wing J592A [David Jenkins] – (1) 20 January
The Last Memorial of the Spanish Ambassador, Wing R1916 [Ronquillo] – (8) 19 December
The Last Sayings [of Hobbes], Wing H2245 [Thomas Hobbes]
The Last Speech and dying words of Thomas ... Pride, Wing L505aA
The Late Keepers of the English Liberties, Wing L549 – (1) 14 February
L'Estrange's Case, Wing L1204 [Sir Roger L'Estrange] – (1) 13 October
* *A Letter from a Gentleman in the City to one in the Country concerning the Bill*, Wing L1390 – (5) 19 November
A Letter from a Gentleman in the Country to a Person of Honour in London, Wing L1391
A Letter from Jack the Cobler to Any Body, Wing L1480
A Letter to a Friend in the Country Touching the Present Fears, Wing L1652 – (4) 29 February

* *A Letter to a Friend Reflecting upon the present Condition of this Nation*, Wing P1
     – (1) 10 February
* *A Letter to a Person of Honour, concerning the King's Disavowing the having been
     married to the Duke of Monmouth's Mother*, Wing F750 [Robert Ferguson] –
     (1) 17 June
* *A Letter to a Person of Honour ... concerning the Black Box*, Wing F749 [Robert
     Ferguson] – (1) 15 May
   A Letter to His Grace the Duke of Monmouth, Wing F3 [C.F] – (8) 15 July
   A Letter to the Earl of Shaftesbury, Wing L1734 – (8) 9 July
   A Letter wherein is shewed, first, what worship is due to Images, Wing B176 [J.B]
   A Letter written out of the Country to a Person of Quality in the City, Wing H3031
     [John Howe]
   Liberty of Conscience, Wing L1965 – (1) 20 October
   The Life of Thomas Hobbes, Wing H2251
   Love and Truth, Wing W673 [Isaac Walton] – (9) Trinity
   The Matter of Fact à la Mode de France, Wing M1303 – (1) 16 February
   A Memento for English Protestants, Wing A3030A [S. Amy] – (1) 18 February
   The Method of Turning the Militia of Scotland into a Standing Army, Wing M1948
     – (1) 19 August
   The Mischief of Separation, Wing S5605A [Edward Stillingfleet] – (1) 19 May
   Modesty Triumphing over Impudence, Wing M2379
   A Moral Prognostication, Wing B1311 [Richard Baxter]
   A Most Learned, Conscientious and devout Exercise, Wing M2906
   The Naked Truth. The Second Part, Wing H1821 [E. Hickeringill]
   News from Guildhall, Wing N961A
   The Northern Star, Wing T1879 [Ezerel Tonge] – (1) 10 May
   The Opinions of Divers Learned and Leading Dissenters, Wing O352 – (1) 17
     March
   A Panegyric to his Royal Highness, Wing P266 – (1) 23 October
   A Parallel between Episcopacy and Presbytery, Wing P334 – (1) 7 June
   A Pattern or President for Princes, Wing P875
   The Perfect Politician, Wing F1335 [Henry Fletcher, first printed 1660]
   A Perswasive to Reformation and Union, Wing B4844 [Francis Brokesby]
   A Petition to the Petitioners, Wing P1860 – (1) 5 February
   A Plea for the Bringing in of Irish Cattel [sic], Wing C5379 [J. Collins]
   The Plot Revived, Wing P2601 – (4) April
   Popery Display'd in its Proper Colours, Wing S83 [J.S] – (6) 28 December
   The Popish Courant, Wing []
   The Popish Damnable Plot ... fairly Laid Open, Wing T1879A [Ezerel Tonge]
* *The Power of Parliaments in Case of Succession*, Wing R1444 [Mathew Rider]
   The Power of the Lords and Commons in Parliament, Wing S927 [Henry Scobell] –
     (1) 8 January
* *A Praefatory Discourse*, Wing A3031 [S.Amy] – (1) 3 November, but printed date
     of 1681
   The Privileges and Practices of Parliaments, Wing P3535
   A Proposal humbly offered, Wing B119 [J.B] – (1) 8 November
   The Protestant Antidote, Wing P3822 – (4) 20 July
   A Protestant Prentice's Loyal Advice, Wing S176 [T.S] – (8) 27 Mar.
* *Reasons for the Indictment of the Duke of York*, Wing H3776 [The Earl of
     Huntingdon]

Reasons offered by a Well-Wisher, Wing R577 – (1) 4 February

E *A Safe and Easy Way to obtain Free and Peaceable Elections*, Wing S282A – (3) 25 November

A Seasonable Address to the Right Honourable the Lord Mayor, Wing S2205 – (4) 19 July

A Seasonable Corrective to the One Project, Wing S2226

* *A Seasonable Memento*, Wing S2232 – (1) 4 February

A Seasonable Memorial in some Historical Notes, Wing L1301 [Sir Roger L'Estrange] – (1) 19 January

The Second Part of the Nonconformists Plea for Peace, Wing B1402 [Richard Baxter]

A Short Answer to a whole Litter of Libels, Wing L1307A [Sir Roger L'Estrange] – (1) 17 June

* *A Short Historical Collection Touching the Succession*, Wing H3595, giving 1689 as first edition [Thomas Hunt] – (4) 15 November

A Sober Discourse of the Honest Cavalier, Wing O350 – (8) 26 April

Some Considerations about Union, Wing S4409B – (6) 9 December

The Soveraign, Wing S4777 – (1) 6 March

A Speech Made By a True Protestant Gentleman, Wing S4854 – (1) 13 January

The Spirit of Popery, Wing H1874 [G. Hickes]

* *The State and Interest of the Nation*, Wing L1309 [Sir Roger L'Estrange] – (1) 28 February

Study to be Quiet, Wing S6092

A Survey of the Lord High Steward, Wing []

* *Three Great Questions Concerning The Succession*, Wing R49 [M.R]

A Time-serving Speech, Wing T1279

To the King's Most Excellent Majesty, Wing T1520

To the Right Honourable Sir Robert Clayton, Wing T1613A

* *Treason, Popery etc. Brought to a Publique Test*, Wing T2079 – (9) Trinity

Treason's Masterpiece, Wing C19 [C.C] – (6) 16 March

The Trial, Conviction and Condemnation of Popery, Wing T2177

A True Account of the Proceedings at the Common Hall, Wing T2392A

A True and Exact Copy of a Treasonable and Bloody Paper, Wing T2431

The True and Only Way of Concord, Wing B1432 [Richard Baxter] – (6) 3 November

A True and Perfect Collection of all Messages, Addresses, Wing E2746

The True Englishman, Wing T2697 – (8) 23 September

A True List of the Names of the Persons Appointed by the Rump Parliament to sit as Council of State, Wing T2733A

A True Narrative of the Duke of Monmouth's late Journey, Wing T2786

A True Narrative of the Popish Plot against Charles I, Wing T2805 – (3) 29 March

The True Protestant Subject, Wing T2865 – (9) Hilary

Twenty Four Sober Queries, Wing T3411

* *Unio Dissidentium*, Wing G653A [John Gibbon] – (1) 27 February

Will with a Whisp, Wing W2259 – (4) August

The Wiltshire Ballad, Wing W2958

* *The White Rose*, Wing B5268 [John Brydall] – (1) 9 March

A Word in Season, Wing W3546 –(1) 3 January

* *A Word within Doors*, Wing W3576

Pamphlets marked + were, judging from internal evidence, published immediately prior to the Oxford Parliament.

Absalom and Achitophel, Wing 2215 [J. Dryden]

The Absurdity of that new devised State Principle, Wing B5251 [John Brydall]

An Account of the State of His Majesties Revenue, Wing H2990 [Sir R. Howard]

* *An Act Acknowledging and Asserting the Right of Succession*, Wing S1023 – (10) 19 August

The Address of Above Twenty Thousand of the Loyal Protestant Apprentices, Wing A543

An Address of the Freeholders of the County of Middlesex, Wing A548

E+ *An Address to the Honourable City of London*, Wing B40 [C.B]

E+ *Advice to the Freemen of England*, Wing A656

Advice to the Men of Monmouth, Wing A658 – (4) June

Advice to the Men of Shaftesbury, Wing A659 – (4) 20 April

Animadversions on the late Vindication of Slingsby Bethel, Wing W138 [W.W] – (10) 3 May

The Answer of a Citizen of London, Wing P86 [N.P]

* *An Answer to a late Pamphlet entitled A Character of A Popish Successor*, Wing A3307

An Answer to a Scoffing and Lying Lybell, Wing A3347

* *An Answer to Pereat Papa*, Wing A3372

An Answer to the Noble Speech and Petition, Wing []

The Answers commanded by his Majesty, Wing C2890 – (10) 24 May

Antidotum Britannicum, Wing W140 [W.W]

An Apostrophe From The Loyal Party, Wing A3562 – (10) 30 May

An Argument For Toleration, Wing W1700 [Edward Whitaker]

The Birth and Burning of the Image called St. Michael, Wing S3382 [Edward Sherman] – (10) 26 May

The Bishops Courts Dissolved, Wing W1701 which gives it the date of 1689 [Edward Whitaker] – (10) 9 June

A Brief Account of What pass'd at the Common Council, Wing L2882 – (10) 16 May

A Brief Answer to Mr L'Estrange's Appeal, Wing B4543

A Brief History of the Life of Mary Queen of Scots, Wing D57 [M.D]

* *A Brief History of the Succession*, Wing S4638 [John Somers]

The Caracter [sic] of a Leading Petitioner, Wing C1978

A Caution to all true Englishmen, Wing C1558 – (4) October

Certain Proposals Humbly Offered by the Bailiff, Wing C1727

E+ *The Certain Way to Save England*, Wing C1764 – (3) 7 February

The Character of a Fanatick, Wing C1973 – (10) 10 August

The Character of a Church Papist, Wing C1965 – (10) 22 August

The Character of a Good Man, neither Whig nor Tory, Wing C1974 – (10) 17 August

The Character of a Modern Sham Plotter, Wing C1980 – (10) 20 August

The Character of a Modern Whig, Wing C1981 – (4) July

The Character of a Rebellion, Wing N91 [John Nalson] – (9) Easter

The Character of a Papist in Masquerade, Wing L1215 [Sir Roger L'Estrange] – (9) Easter

*+ *The Character of a Popish Successor*, Wing S2670 [Elkanah Settle] – (6) 11 February

* *The Character of a Popish Successor Compleat*, Wing P2081 [John Phillips] – (7) 6 May

* *The Character of a Popish Successor Part Two*, Wing P2080 [John Phillips]

The Character of a Tory, Wing B5335 – (10) 4 August

A Collection of Sundry Petitions, Wing A4076 [Sir Thomas Aston, first printed 1642] – (10) 9 June

*+ *A Collection of the Substance of Several Speeches and Debates*, Wing E2538 – (6) 7 March

The Complaint of Liberty and Property, Wing N94 [John Nalson] – (10) 31 March

E+ *Considerations Offered to all the Corporations of England*, Wing C5912

Cromwell's Complaint, Wing C7192 – (10) 30 June

The Death, Burial and Resurrection of the Act of the 35th of Elizabeth, Wing W1701A [Edward Whitaker] – (10) 22 April

The Debates in the House of Commons, Wing E2546 – (3 and 10) 28 April

The Devonshire Ballad, Wing D1235

* *A Dialogue at Oxford*, Wing D1290

E+ *A Dialogue between two Burgesses*, Wing D1339 – (1) 3 February

A Dialogue between two Jesuits, Wing D1340 – (4) February

A Dialogue betwixt Sam the Ferriman, Wing D1353

* *A Discourse between a Romanist*, Wing D1573

+ *A Discourse concerning Popish Perjurers*, Wing B1561 [Richard Beane]

* *The Earl of Shaftesbury's Expedient*, Wing S2891A

The Emperour and Empire Betray'd, Wing C1672A [J.P. Comte de Cerdan]

E+ *England Bought and Sold*, Wing N101 [John Nalson] – (9) Easter

* *England Enslaved under a Popish Successor*, Wing E2932 – (6) 14 April

+ *England's Appeal to the Parliament at Oxford*, Wing E2945

+ *England's Triumph and Joy*, Wing E3061

E *English Liberties*, Wing C515 [Henry Care]

The Englishman's Happiness under a Protestant Prince, Wing E3100 – (4) February

Europe a Slave, Unless England Break Her Chains, Wing C1673 [J.P. Comte de Cerdan]

An Exact Collection of the Most Considerable Debates, Wing E2575 – (6) 14 June

An Excellent New Ballad between Tom the Tory and Toney the Whig, Wing E3803. The imprint is 1678 but it was published in 1681 [see chapter 3]

E *A Faithful Account of the Manner of the Election*, Wing S108 [L.S]

The Field of Blood, Wing F870 – (9) Easter

Five Important Queries, Wing F1107

The French Intreagues Discovered, Wing F2185 – (10) 2 June

A Friendly Dialogue, Wing F2220 – (10) 23 August

+ *From Aboard the Van-Herring. Being a full Relation of the Present State*, Wing F2239 – (4) February

The Glory of the English Nation, Wing 9877

The Grand Question Resolved, Wing G1509

* *The Great Case put Home*, Wing G1674

* *The Great Point of Succession Discussed*, Wing B4191 [Robert Brady] – (6) 25 April

* *Grimalkin*, Wing G2026 – (10) 4 May
* *A Help to Discourse*, Wing H1405
* *His Majesties Declaration*, Wing C3000
* *His Majesties Declaration Defended*, Wing D2286 [John Dryden] – (10) 15 June
  An Historical Account of the Rise and Progress of Addressing, Wing H2098 – (10) 12 July
  Historical Collections, Wing H2099
  An Humble Essay toward the Settlement of Peace, Wing H777
  The Humble Petition and Address, Wing H3429
* *An Impartial Account of the Nature*, Wing I73
* *The Impostor Expos'd*, Wing I104 – (9) Easter
+ *Iter Oxoniense*, Wing I1093 – (2) 9 March
  Jesuita Vapulans, Wing N54 [C.N] – (3) 1 February
  Jesuite in Masquerade: or The Sheriff's Case Uncas'd, Wing J704 – (10) 4 July
  Jus Anglorum, Wing A4175 [William Atwood] – (6) 1 June
  Jus Caesaris, Wing D1066 [William Denton]
* *A Just and Modest Vindication*, Wing F741 [Robert Ferguson??]
  A Just and Modest Vindication of the Many Thousand and Loyal Apprentices, Wing J1223 – (6) 15 June
  A Justification of the Paper, Entituled A Short History, Wing W1703 [Edward Whitaker] – (10) 28 April
  A Landmark for all True Englishmen, Wing L323 – (10) 10 August
  The Lawyers Demurrer, Wing L740 – (10) 22 June
  L'Estrange His Appeal, Wing L2102 [Sir Roger L'Estrange]
+ *A Letter from a Person Of Honour in the Country to the Earl of Castlehaven*, Wing A3170 [The Earl of Anglesey]
* *A Letter from a Person of Quality in Scotland*, Wing L1424
  A Letter from a Person of Quality to His Friend, Wing L1428
*+ *A Letter from a Student At Oxford*, Wing K301 [White Kennett] – (5) 15 March
  A Letter from Mr Edward Whitaker, Wing W1704
  A Letter from Scotland, Wing L1931B [Earl of Roscommon] – (4) January
  A Letter in Answer to a Friend, Wing L1555
  A Letter of Advice to the Petitioning Apprentices, Wing L1569
E+ *A Letter to a Friend Concerning the next Parliament's sitting at Oxford*, Wing L1644
  A Letter to a Friend in the Country concerning the Prorogation, Wing L1649 – (8) 11 January
+ *A Letter to a Noble Lord*, Wing M13 [D.M]
+ *A Letter to a Noble Peer of the Realm about His Late Speech and Petition*, Wing S109A [L.S]
* *A Letter to his Royal Highness*, Wing L1707 – (6) 27 July
  A List of Abhorrers, Wing L2376
  The Loyal Address [of Lynn Regis], Wing L3335
  The Loyal London Prentice, Wing L3350
  The Loyalty of the Last Long Parliament, Wing B187 [T.B]
E *The Manner of the Election of the Honourable Approved Patriots*, Wing M468
+ *Materials For Union*, Wing H3685 [John Humfrey]
  Memoirs of the Most Remarkable Enterprises, Wing M1672
E *The Memorable Case of Denzil Onslow*, Wing M1676 – (10) 15 August
  Miscellania, Wing T647 [Sir William Temple]

The Mischiefs and Unreasonableness, Wing M2238 – (8) 24 May
* *A Moderate Decision on the Point of Succession*, Wing M2323B
A Modest Answer to a Printed Pamphlet, Wing M2355
More Shams Still, Wing D191 [Thomas Dangerfield]
Mr John Milton's Character of the Long Parliament, Wing M2098 [John Milton]
   – (6) 4 April
Multum in Parvo, Wing M3061 – (10) 13 July
The Narrative of a Strange and Sudden Apparition, Wing S746B [J. Saunders]
The Narrow Way, Wing N232
A New Answer to a Speech, Wing J8 [E.J]
A New Letter from Windsor, Wing F2133 [John Freeman] – (10) 8 July
A New Narrative of a Fiery Apparition, Wing S746C [J. Saunders] – (10) 2 April
News From Colchester, Wing B24 [A.B] – (10) 19 August
No Protestant Plot, Wing F756 [Robert Ferguson]
Notes Upon Stephen College, Wing L1281 [Roger L'Estrange]
Obsequium et Veritas, Wing H1308 [Robert Hearne] – (10) 18 April
* *Observations upon a late Libel*, Wing H316 [The Earl of Halifax] – (10) 16 June
Of the Unity of the Church, Wing []
+ *Oliver Cromwell's Ghost*, Wing W2143 [Robert Wild]
The Oxford Health, Wing O855
Oxford In Mourning, Wing O856
A Panegyric Upon the Ensuing Spring, Wing P271
The Parliament Dissolved at Oxford, Wing P501
Patriarcha Non Monarcha, Wing T3591 [James Tyrrell] – (6) 18 May
* *Pereat Papa*, Wing P1465
Persecutio Undecima, Wing C3786 [Chestlin, first printed 1648] – (10) 13
   June
The Petition of Divers Eminent Citizens of London, Wing P1762 – (8) 28 April
The Petitioning Comet, Wing P1864
The Phanatick in his Colours, Wing F394 – (10) 24 August
E *Plain Dealing*, Wing P2353 – (4) 1 February
+ *The Plain Truth*, Wing P2369 – (8) 4 March
Plato Redivivus, Wing N513 [listed as 1680/1 in Wing; Henry Nevile] – (6) 22
   February
A Plea for Moderation, Wing P2514
A Pleasant Battle between two lap dogs, Wing P2537
A Pleasant Discourse between Two Sea Men, Wing P2545 – (10) 29 April
The Plotting Cards Revived, Wing P2605B
The Politician Discovered, Wing P2767
The Portraiture of Roger L'Estrange, Wing M2995 [Laurence Mowbray]
* *The Power of Parliaments Asserted*, Wing H34 [G.H]
A Praefatory Discourse – see 1680
The Present State of England, Wing P3263 – (9) Hilary
The Presentment and Humble Petition, Wing P3280 – (10) 23 May
The Proceedings at the Session House in the Old Baily ... on Thursday 24th of
   November 1681, Wing P3563
 ˙ *The Proceedings of the Grand Jury of Middlesex in Easter Term*, Wing P3586
The Progress Of Honesty, Wing D2764 [Thomas D'Urfey]
A Proper New Brummingham Ballad, Wing P3672
* *A Prospect of a Popish Successor*, Wing P3804

*   *The Protestant Admirer*, Wing P3819
    Protestant Loyalty Fairly drawn, Wing P3837 – (6) 3 August
    The Protestants' Petition and Address, Wing P3839 – (8 and 10) 30 April
    The Protestants' Remonstrance, Wing P1345
E+ *Reasons for Chusing Sir Robert Atkyns and Sir John Knight*, Wing R487
*+ *Reasons for His Majesties Passing the Bill*, Wing D1233 [Lord Cavendish]
    The Reformation Reformed, Wing L1287 [Sir Roger L'Estrange] – (8) 2 September
*   *Religion and Loyalty*, Wing C5486 [Thomas Comber] – (9) Michaelmas
*   *A Reply to the Second Part of the Character of a Popish Successor*, Wing L1298 [Sir Roger L'Estrange]
*   *The Right of Primogeniture*, Wing L691 [William Lawrence]
    Salus populi, Wing S514
*+ *A Scheme of Popish Cruelties*, Wing S864A – (6) 8 February
*+ *A Seasonable Address to Both Houses*, Wing H320 [attributed to the earl of Halifax, but authorship disputed]
    Seasonable Advice to all Protestant People, Wing 2692A [W. Lloyd] – (9) Easter
    A Seasonable Answer to ... the Vindication of Slingsby Bethel, Wing S2217 – (10) 11 July
E+ *A Seasonable Momento for all that Have Voyces*, Wing S2233
    Sejanus or the Popular Favourite, Wing S2419 – (4) November
+   *Serious Advice*, Wing W1687 [James Whiston]
    A Serious Enquiry into the Means of an Happy Union, Wing S805
    The Sham Indictment Quashed, Wing S747 [J. Saunders]
    A Short Defence of the Church, Wing G2160 [Robert Grove]
    A Short History of the Life and Death of the Act made the 35th of Elizabeth, Wing W1707 [Edward Whitaker] – (10) 16 April
+   *A Sober and Seasonable Commemoration*, Wing S440A
    A Sober and Seasonable Discourse, Wing S4401 – (6) 16 August
*   *Some Observations upon the Tickling Query*, Wing S4542 –(9) Easter
+   *Some Reflections upon a late Pamphlet*, Wing A3974 [Thomas Ashenden] – (4) February
    The Southwark Address, Wing S4773
    The Speech and Carriage of Stephen Colledge, Wing C5228
*   *A Speech lately made by a Noble Peer*, Wing S2901 [The Earl of Shaftesbury?]
+   *The Speech of the Honourable Henry Booth*, Wing D881 – (3) 24 March
    A Speech Without Doors, Wing S4874
    Strange and Wonderful News from Norwich, Wing W132 [T.W]
    The Tears of the Press, Wing T609 – (9) Trinity
    The Time Servers, Wing T1278
    To The King's Most Excellent Majesty, Wing T1551
    Treason in Graine, Wing T2076A – (6) 24 May
    The Trial Of Henry Care, Wing T2190
E   *A True Account of the Election at Cambridge*, Wing T2366
    A True Account of the Last Parliament, Wing T2380
    A True and Brief Relation of the Proceedings of the Common Council, Wing T2419A – (10) 24 May
*   *A True and Exact History of the Succession*, Wing B4195 [Robert Brady] – (6) 27 July
*   *The True Englishman*, Wing T2696 – (6) 15 October

The True Notion of Government, Wing L82 [T.L] – (9) Trinity

+ *The True Protestant's Appeal to the City and Country*, Wing N119 [John Nalson] – (4) 12 February

The Tryal of Slingsby Bethel, Wing T2223

The Two Associations, Wing T3428

* *Two Great Questions Determined by the Principles*, Wing L97 – (6) 21 April

* *The Two Great Questions whereon in this Present Conjucture*, Wing L692A [William Lawrence]

The Unreasonableness of Separation, Wing S5675 [Stillingfleet]

Vestigia Veritatis, Wing V289 – (10) 29 April

A Vindication of Addresses in General, Wing V469 – (10) 19 August

A Vindication of His Grace, James Duke of Monmouth, Wing V478A

A Vindication of Slingsby Bethel, Wing B2078 – (10) 28 April

* *A Vindication of the Character of a Popish Successor*, Wing S2728A [Elkanah Settle]

A Vindication of the Loyal London Apprentices, Wing M52 [J.M] – (10) 17 June

A Vindication of the Protestant Petitioning Apprentices, Wing V528 – (10) 29 August

Votes of the Honourable the Commons, Wing E2762 – (10) 1 Sept.

Vox Juvenilis, Wing V720 – (10) 14 July

Vox Patriae, Wing V725 – (10) 13 April

Vox Populi, Wing V729 – (6) 4 April

Vox Populi, Fax Populi, Wing N121 [John Nalson] (9) Easter

Vox Regis, Wing J148 [James I]

The Waking Vision, Wing W282

The Wars in England, Scotland and Ireland, Wing C7357 [Nathanial Crouch]

The Wicked Petition, Wing []

The Worcestershire Ballad, Wing W3538

A Word Concerning Libels and Libelers, Wing L1327 [Sir Roger L'Estrange]

* *The Zealous and Impartial Protestant*, Wing G837 [Joseph Glanvill]

1682

Absalom Senior, Wing S2652 [Elkanah Settle]

An Address to the Freemen and Freeholders of the Nation [In three parts], Wing B3445 [Edmund Bohun]

* *The Apostate Protestant*, Wing P1075 [Edward Pelling]

A Brief Discourse between a Sober Tory and a Moderate Whig, Wing B4577

The Case of Present Distresses on Nonconformists Examined, Wing C967

The Character of a True Protestant, Wing C1999

The Character of the True Blue Protestant Poet, Wing C2028

The Country Man's Petition for a Parliament, Wing C6557

A Discourse Touching the Addresses, Wing D1622

The Form of an Address, expressing the True Sense of the Dissenting Protestants, Wing F1563

A Gentle Reflection on the Modest Account, Wing A3121 [John Andrewes]

The History of the Association, Wing H2144

The History of Whiggism, Wing H1809 [E. Hickeringill]

A Letter from a Person of Quality to his Friend about Abhorrers and Addressers, Wing L1427

A Letter from his Grace James Duke of Ormonde, Wing O448
A Letter from the Right Honourable Earl of Anglesey, Wing A3172
Mr Hunt's Postscript, Wing H3758
A New Ballad with the Definition of the Word Tory, Wing N579B
* *A Plea for the Succession*, Wing P2516
Remarks on the Growth and Progress of Nonconformity, Wing L1296 [Roger L'Estrange]
The Rights of the Kingdom, Wing S279 [Richard Sadler, first printed 1649]
The Second Part of No Protestant Plot, Wing F759 [Robert Ferguson]
The Second Part of the Growth of Popery (1682) [Printed in Cologne, written under pseudonym of Philo-Veritas, probably by Robert Ferguson, not listed in Wing]
A Sermon prepared to be preached ... by the Reverend Toryrory, Wing S2643A
* *A Tory Plot*, Wing T1946
A True Account of the Whole Proceedings, Wing T2408
Vox Angliae (Parts One and Two), Wing V711

Undated and miscellaneous

An Abstract of the Contents of Several Letters (1679?), Wing A131
An Account of the Presentment of the Grand Jury ... of Northampton (1683), Wing []
* *An Answer to Pereat Papa* (1681?), Wing A3372
The Carman's Poem (1680?), Wing C595
A Commentary upon the Present Condition of the Kingdom (1677), Wing []
Comprehension Promoted (1673 or 1679–80), Wing H3675 [John Humfrey]
The Deliquium (1679–80), Wing D908
The Design of Enslaving England Discovered (1689), Wing F734 [Algernon Sidney *et al.*]
A Discourse of Trade (1675), Wing D1610
The Earl of Anglesey's State of the Government (1694), Wing T1000 [Sir John Thompson]
Essexian Triumviri (1684), Wing D4 [B.D.]
An Exact Collection of the Debates of the House Commons, (1689), Wing E2574
E *The Fanatick Rampant* (1679–80), Wing F400
The Good Old Cause Revived (1680?), Wing G1079
The History of the Whiggish Plot (1684), Wing H2190B
A Hue and Cry after R.L. (1680?), Wing H3283
The Intrigues of the Popish Plot Laid Open (1685)
A Journal for the Proceedings of the House of Commons (1674), Wing P2167A
The Judgment and Decree of the University of Oxford (1683), Wing O891
The Judgement or resolution of all the Lords (1679?), Wing J1184aA
The Lawyer Outlaw'd (1683), Wing L1266 [Roger L'Estrange]
The Legacy of John Wilmer (1692), Wing W2884.
A Letter from a Parliament Man (1675), Wing S2896 [Earl of Shaftesbury]
A Letter of Remarks upon Jovian (1683), Wing A3174 [The Earl of Anglesey]
* *A Letter to the King when Duke of York* (1685), Wing J614 [Sir Leoline Jenkins]
Memoires of the Life of Anthony late Earl of Shaftesbury (1683), Wing M1671
The Mischief of Cabals (1685), Wing M2233
A Moderate Expedient for Preventing of Popery (1680?), Wing M2324

E   *Observations on the Single Query* [1679 or 1681??], Wing O106
    A Pacquet of Advices and Animdaversions ... to the Men of Shaftesbury (1676),
       Wing N400 [M. Nedham]
    The Parallel or an Account of the Growth of Knavery
    The Present State of Christendom (1677), Wing P3257
    Reflections on a Pamphlet stiled A Just and Modest Vindication (1683), Wing
       B3459 [Edmund Bohun]
    *The Report of the Committee of the Commons Appointed to Examine the
       Proceedings of the Judges*, Wing []
    A Seasonable Speech made by Alderman Atkins (first printed 1660, reprinted
       1680), Wing S2244.
    A Short Discourse upon the Designs, Practices and Counsels of France (1677),
       Wing S3589
*   *A Short Historical Collection Touching the Succession*, Wing S3596 [gives date as
       post-1700 but 1679 in BL catalogue]
    A Speech made by the Earl of Buckingham (1677)
    A True Account and Declaration of the Horrid Conspiracy (1685)
    The Tryals of Henry Cornish Esq. (1685), Wing T2250
    Two Seasonable Discourses (1675), Wing S2906 [Earl of Shaftesbury]
    A Vindication of His Royal Highness (1683), Wing []
    Vox Regni (1680?), Wing V738

Newspapers and periodicals

(The year given is that when the paper started publication)

1678

The Weekly Pacquet of Advice from Rome

1679

The Domestick Intelligence (became the *Protestant Domestick Intelligence* after issue
   no. 56, but original name retained in citations)
The English Intelligencer
The English Courant
The Faithfull Mercury
The Friendly Intelligence
Mercurius Anglicus (becomes the *True News or Mercurius Anglicus* after no. 10, but
   original title retained in citations)
Mercurius Domesticus
Poor Robbins Intelligence Revived
The Snotty Noze Gazette
The True Domestic Intelligence
The Weekly Character
The Weekly Pacquet of Advice from Germany

1680

The Catholic Intelligence
The City Mercury
The Currant Intelligence [became *Smith's Currant Intelligence* after no. 10]
The Haarlem Courant
The London Gazette
The Loyal Intelligence
Mercurius Civicus
Mercurius Infernus
Mercurius Publicus
The New Anti-Roman Pacquet
The Rotterdam Courant
The True Protestant (Domestick) Intelligence
The True Protestant Mercury
The Weekly Advertisement

1681

Advice from Parnassus
Benskin's Domestick Intelligence
Democritus Ridens
Heraclitus Ridens
The Impartial London Intelligence
The Impartial Protestant Mercury
The Loyal Protestant and True Domestick Intelligence
The Merchants Remembrance
Mercurius Bifrons
Mercurius Veridicus
The Mock Press
The Monthly Recorder
News from Parnassus
The Observator
The Observator Observed
The Protestant Oxford Intelligence
Smith's Protestant Intelligence
The Universal Intelligence
The Weekly Discovery
The Weekly Discovery Stripp'd Naked
The Weekly Pacquet of Advice from Geneva

Manuscript tracts

'Animadversions upon a Pamphlet Entitled A Brief History of the Succession' [BL, Add. 22,589, f. 98–105]
'An Answer to A Vindication of the last Two Parliaments' [Bod., MS Jones 17, ff. 212–232]

'Concerning the power of the Parl[iamen]t to exclude' [BL, Add. 32,518, ff. 75–81]
'A Letter from a true zealous Protestant to his worthy friend and patriot', by 'J.P' [1679] [All Souls, MS 167].
'The Scheme of a Paper to be offered to publique Consideration. The Title. An Address to all the free born subjects of England' [All Souls, MS 240, f. 363]
'Some Modest Reflections upon a bill lately designed against his Royall highnes succession' [Bod., MS Rawl.D.1064, ff. 74–9]
'That Parliaments can not alter or invert the graduall succession of the Royal Family' [Bod., MS Rawl.D.1064, ff. 19–72]
Untitled tract dated June 1679 [All Souls, MS 240, ff. 314–51]

Other printed primary sources

(The place of print is London unless otherwise stated)

Archives ou Correspondance inédite de la Maison d'Orange-Nassau, ed. G. Groen Van Prinsterer (Utrecht 1861), vol. v, 1650–88
Aubrey, J. *Brief Lives*, ed. Clark, A. (Oxford 1898)
d'Avaux, *Négociations de Monsieur le Comte d'Avaux en Hollande Depuis 1679 Jusqu'en 1684* (1752, translated 1754), vol.i
Baxter, R. *Reliquiae Baxterianae* (1696)
Bohun, E. *The Diary and Autobiography of Edmund Bohun*, ed. Rix, S.W. (1853)
Bramston, J. *The Autobiography of Sir John Bramston of Skreens in Chelmsford*, ed. Braybrooke, P. (Camden Series, Old Series, xxxii, 1845)
Browning, A. *English Historical Documents 1660–1714* (1953)
Browning, A. and Milne, D.J. 'An Exclusion Bill Division List', *BIHR*, xxiii (1950), 205–25
Bruce, T. *The Memoirs of Thomas Bruce, Earl of Ailesbury*, ed. Buckley, W.E. (The Roxburghe Club, 1890)
Bulstrode, R. *Memoirs and Recollections Upon the Reign and Government of King Charles I and King Charles II* (1721)
Burnet, G. *History of My Own Time*, ed. Airy, O. (1897)
    Supplement to Burnet's History of My Own Time, ed. Foxcroft, H.C. (1897)
    Some Unpublished Letters of Gilbert Burnet, ed. Foxcroft, H.C. (Camden Miscellany, third series, xi, 1807)
Calamy, E. *An Historical Account of My Own Life* (1829)
Calendar of State Papers Domestic
Calendar of Treasury Books
Cavelli, Campana de. *Les Derniers Stuarts à St Germain* (Paris 1871)
Clarke, J.S. *The Life of James II* (1816)
A Collection of Scarce and Valuable Tracts, ed. Scott, Sir Walter (1809–15)
Collins, A. *Letters and Memorials of State* (1746)
A Complete Collection of the Protests of the Lords, ed. Thorold-Rogers, E.J. (1895)
Crino, A.M. *Il Popish Plot* (Rome 1954)
Crouch, N. *The Secret History of the Four Last Monarchs* (1691)
Dalrymple, J. *Memoirs of Great Britain and Ireland* (Edinburgh 1771)
Diaries of the Popish Plot, ed. Greene, D. (New York, 1977)
Dering, E. *The Diaries and Papers of Sir Edward Dering, Second Bart 1664–84*, ed. Bond, M.F. (House of Lords Record Office Occasional Publications, 1976)
Dryden, J. *The Works of John Dryden*, ed. Swedenberg, H.T. (1972)

Dunton, J. *The Life and Errors of John Dunton* (1705), ed. Parks, S. facsimile reprint New York 1974

Essex Papers, ed. Airy, O. (Camden Society, New Series, xlvii, 1890)

Evelyn, J. *Diary of John Evelyn*, ed. de Beer, E.S. (Oxford 1955), vol. iv, 1673–89

Filmer, R. *Patriarcha*, ed. Laslett, P. (Oxford 1949)

The Flemings in Oxford, ed. Magrath, J.R. (Oxford History Society, xliv, 1904)

Gardiner, T. *A General Survey of the Post Office 1677–82*, ed. Bond, M.F. (Postal History Society, Series No. 5, 1958)

Grey, A. *Debates of the House of Commons 1667–1694* (1769)

Grey, Lord Ford. *The Secret History of the Rye House Plot* (1754)

Halstead, R. *Succinct Genealogies* (1685; written by the Earl of Peterborough under pseudonym)

Harleian Miscellany, ed. Oldys, W. and Park, T. (1809)

Henry, P. *The Diaries and Letters of Philip Henry*, ed. Lee, M.H. (1882)

Historical Manuscript Commission

   Legh (3rd Report)

   Verney (7th Report, Part 1, Appendix)

   Drummond–Moray (10th Report, Appendix i)

   Lords 1678–1688 (11th Report, Appendix ii)

   Dartmouth i (11th Report, Appendix v)

   Rutland ii (12th Report, Appendix v)

   Le Fleming (12th Report, Appendix vii)

   Beaufort (12th Report, Appendix ix)

   Fitzherbert (13th Report, Appendix iv)

   Kenyon (14th Report, Appendix iv)

   Portland iii (14th Report, Appendix ii)

   Ormonde iv–vii (14th Report, Appendix vii)

   Buckingham (14th Report, Appendix ix)

   Onslow (14th Report, Appendix ix)

   Lindsey (14th Report, Appendix ix and Series 79)

   Hodgkin (15th Report, Appendix ii)

   Foljambe (15th Report, Appendix v)

   Frankland (Series 52)

   Bath (Series 58)

   Egmont (Series 63)

   Finch ii (Series 71)

   R.R. Hastings (Series 78)

Hobbes, T. *Behemoth*, ed. Tonnies, F. *(1969)*

Hooke, R. *The Diary of Robert Hooke 1672–1680*, ed. Robinson, H.W. and Adams, W. (1968)

Howell, T.B. *A Complete Collection of State Trials* (1816), vol. ix (1682–4)

Hyde, H. and L. *The Correspondence of Henry Hyde, Earl of Clarendon and his Brother Lawrence Hyde, Earl of Rochester*, ed. Singer, S.W. (1828)

Jeaffreson, J.C. (ed.) *Middlesex County Records* (Middlesex County Record Society 1892)

Jeake, S. *An Astrological Diary of the Seventeenth Century: Samuel Jeake of Rye 1652–99*, ed. Hunter, M. and Gregory, A. (Oxford, 1988)

Josselin, R. *The Diary of Ralph Josselin*, ed. Macfarlane, A. (Oxford, 1976)

Kennett, W. *A Complete History of England* (1706)

   Memoir of the Family of Cavendish (1708)

Klopp, O. *Der Fall des Hauses Stuart* (Vienna 1875)

The Lauderdale Papers, vol. iii (1673–9), ed. Airy, O. (Camden Society, New Series, xxxviii, 1885)

Lawrence, W. *The Diary of William Lawrence 1662–81*, ed. Aylmer, G.E. (1961)
    Records of the Borough of Leicester 1603–1688, ed. Stocks, H. (Cambridge, 1923)

Leicester, P. *Charges to the Grand Jury at Quarter Sessions 1660–1677*, ed. Halcrow, E.M. (Cheatham Society, 1953)

L'Estrange, R. *Selections from the Observator*, ed. Jordain, V. (Augustan Reprint Society Publication, no. 141, 1970)

Locke, J. *Two Tracts on Government*, ed. Abrams, P. (Cambridge, 1967a)
    Two Treaties of Government, ed. Laslett, P. (Cambridge, 1967, second edition)
    The Correspondence of John Locke, ed. de Beer, E.S. (Oxford, 1976)

The London Sessions Records 1695–85, ed. Bowler, H. (Catholic Record Society, xxxiv, 1937)

Ludlow, E. *A Voyce from the Watch Tower. Part v*, ed. Worden, B. (Camden Society, Fourth Series, xxi, 1978)

Luttrell, N. *A Brief Historical Relation of State Affairs* (Oxford 1857)
    Narcissus Luttrell's Popish Plot Catalogues, ed. Francis, F.C. (1956)

Lyme Letters 1660–1760, ed. Lady Newton (1925)

Marvell, A. *The Letters of Andrew Marvell*, ed. Margoliouth, A. (Oxford 1971)
    An Account of the Growth of Popery and Arbitrary Government in *The Complete Works of Andrew Marvell*, ed. Grossart, A.B. (1875), iv. 258–414

McCulloch, J. R. *Early English tracts on Commerce* (Cambridge, 1952)
    Memoirs of the Verney Family, ed. Verney, Lady F. and M. (1925 third edition), vol. ii, 1660–1696

North, R. *Examen* (1740)
    The Lives of the Norths (1826 edition)

Oldmixon, J. *The History of Addresses* (1709)
    The History of England (1730)

Original Letters of John Locke, Algernon Sidney and Anthony Lord Shaftesbury, ed. Foster, T. (1830)

Original Papers; containing the Secret History of Great Britain, ed. MacPherson, J. (1776) vol. i. 'The Life of James II as written by himself'

'The Osborn Collection', *Yale University Library Gazette*, xliv, no. 3 (1970), ed. Parks, S.

Papillon, T. *The Memoirs of Thomas Papillon of London 1623–1702*, ed. Papillon, A.F.W. (Reading 1887)

Penn, W. *The Papers of William Penn*, vol. i, ed. Dunn, M.M. and R.S. (1981); vol. v, ed. Bronner, E.B. and Fraser, D.

Pepys, S. *The Letters and Second Diary of Samuel Pepys*, ed. Howarth, R.G. (1932)

Plott, T. *The Dispatches of Thomas Plott*, ed. Middlebush, F.A. (1926)

Poems on Affairs of State, ed. Mengel, E.F. (New Haven, 1965–6), vol. ii.

Political Ballads of the Seventeenth and Eighteenth Centuries, ed. Wilkins, W.W. (1860)

Potenger, J. *Private Memoirs (Never Before Published) of John Potenger Esq.*, ed. Bingham, C.W. (1841)

Prideaux, H. *The Letters of Humphrey Prideaux to John Ellis*, ed. Thompson, E.M. (Camden Society, New Series, xv, 1875)

The Pythouse Papers, ed. Day, W.A. (1879)

Ralph, J. *The History of England* (1744)

Reresby, J. *The Memoirs of Sir John Reresby*, ed. Browning, A. (Glasgow 1936)

Robbins, C. *Two English Republican Tracts* (Cambridge, 1969)

Russell, R. *The Letters of Rachel Lady Russell*, ed. Russell, R. (1853)

Savile, G. 'Some Unpublished Letters of George Savile, Lord Halifax', ed. Poole, D.L., *EHR*, xxvi (1911), 535–42

    The Works of George Savile, Marquis of Halifax, ed. Brown, M.N. (Oxford, 1989)

Savile, H. *The Savile Correspondence: Letters to and from Henry Savile*, ed. Cooper, W.D. (Camden Society, lxix, 1858)

Scott, W. *A Collection of Scarce and Valuable Tracts [80 belonging to Lord Somers]* (1809–15)

Sidney, A. *Discourses Concerning Government* (1968 republication of the edition of 1751)

    Discourses Concerning Government by Algernon Sidney with his letters, trial, apology and some memoirs of his life, ed. Hollis, T. (1763)

Sidney, H. *Diary of the Times of Charles II by Henry Sidney*, ed. Blencowe, R.W. (1843)

Sprat, T. *A True Account and Declaration of the Horrid Conspiracy* (1685)

Stanhope, P. *The Letters of Philip Second Earl of Chesterfield* (1837)

Stephens, F.G. *A Catalogue of Prints and Drawings in the British Museum Division I: Political and Personal Satires* (1870), vol. i (1320–1689)

Temple, W. *Memoirs, The Third Part, from the Peace Concluded 1679 to the Time of the Author's Retirement from Publick Business*, ed. Swift, J. (1720)

The Term Catalogues, vol. i. 1668–1682, ed. Arber, E. (1903)

Thibaudeau, A.W. (ed.) *A Catalogue of the Collection of Autograph Letters and Historical Documents ... Collected by Alfred Morrison*, (1883–92, printed privately)

Tillotson, J. *The Works of John Tillotson*, ed. Birch, T. (1752)

Van Prinsterer, G. *Archives ou correspondance inédite de la Maison d'Orange – Nassau*, ed. Van Prinsterer, G. Groen (Utrecht, 1861), vol. v (1650–88)

Walwyn, W. *The Writings of William Walwyn*, ed. Taft, J. and B. (1989)

Warcup, E. 'The Journal of Edmund Warcup', ed. Feiling, K. and Needham, F., *EHR*, xl (April 1925), 235–60

Warner, J. *The History of the English Persecution of Catholics*, ed. Birrell, T.A., translated by Bligh, Rev. J. (Catholic Record Society, vols. xlvii–viii, 1953–5).

Williamson, J. *Letters ... to Sir Joseph Williamson* (Camden Society, New Series, viii and ix, 1874)

Wood, A. *The Life and Times of Anthony Wood*, ed. Clark, A. (Oxford 1892), vol. ii 1664–81.

SECONDARY SOURCES

Printed

Abbott, W.C. 'The Origins of Titus Oates's Story', *EHR*, xxv, no. 97 (January 1910), 126–9

    'What was a Whig?', in *The Quest for Political Unity in World History*, ed. Pargellis, S. (Washington 1944)

Allen, D.F. 'The Role of the London Trained Bands during the Exclusion Crisis 1678–81', *EHR*, lxxxvii (1972), 287–303

'Political Clubs in Restoration London', *HJ, xix, no. 3 (1976), 561–580.*

'The Political Function of Charles II' Chiffinch', *HLQ,* xxxix, no. 3 (May 1976), 277–90

Ashcraft, R. 'Revolutionary Politics and Locke's Two Treatises of Government: Radicalism and Lockean Political Theory', *Political Theory,* viii, no. 4 (November 1980), 429–88

'The Two Treatises and the Exclusion Crisis: The Problem of Lockean Political Theory as Bourgeois Ideology', *Papers Read at the Clark Library Seminar, 10 December 1977* (published 1980).

Revolutionary Politics and Locke's Two Treatises of Government (Princeton, 1986)

Ashley, M. *John Wildman, Plotter and Postmaster* (1947)

Charles II (1971)

James II (1977)

Astbury, R. 'The Renewal of the Licensing Act in 1693 and its lapse in 1695', *The Library,* xxxiii (1978), 296–322

Aylmer, G. 'Place Bills and the Separation of Powers', *TRHS,* xv (1965), 45–69.

Barbour, V. *Henry Bennet, Earl of Arlington* (1914)

Barry, J. 'The Press and the Politics of Culture of Bristol 1660–1775', in *Culture, Politics and Society in Britain 1660–1800,* ed. Black, J. and Gregory, J. (Manchester, 1991), 49–81

Beaver, D. 'Conscience and Context: The Popish Plot and the Politics of Ritual 1678–1682', *HJ,* xxxiv, no. 2 (1991), 297–327

Beddard, R. 'The Commission for Ecclesiastical Promotions 1681–4: An Instrument of Tory Reaction', *HJ,* x (1967), 11–40

'Vincent Alsop and the Emancipation of Restoration Dissent', *Journal of Ecclesiastical History,* xxiv (1973), 161–84

'The Retreat on Toryism: Lionel Ducket MP for Calne and the Politics of Conservatism', *Wiltshire Archaeological Magazine,* vol. lxxii–iii (1977–8, published 1980), 75–106

'The Revolution of 1688', in *The Unexpected Whig Revolution,* ed. Beddard, R. (Oxford, 1991)

de Beer, E.S. 'The House of Lords in the Parliament of 1680', *BIHR,* xx (1943–5), 22–37

Behrens, B. 'The Whig Theory of the Constitution in the Reign of Charles II', *CHJ,* vii (1941), 42–71

Beier, A.L and Finlay, R. *London 1500–1700: The Making of the Metropolis* (1986)

Benham, W.G. 'The Essex Petition of 1679–80', *The Essex Review,* xxxiii, no. 172 (October 1934), 193–9.

Benson, D.R. 'Halifax and the Trimmers', *HLQ,* xxvii (1963–4), 115–34

Brown, L.F. *The First Earl of Shaftesbury* (New York, 1933)

Browning, A. *Thomas Osborne, Earl of Danby* (Glasgow, 1944–51)

'Parties and Party Organisation in the Reign of Charles II', *TRHS,* xxx (1948), 21–36

Bruce, C.S.C. *The Life and Loyalties of Thomas Bruce* (1951)

Burghclere, Lady W. (née Gardner) *George Villiers, Second Duke of Buckingham* (1903)

Bushman, R.L. 'English Franchise Reform in the Seventeenth Century', *JBS,* iii, no. 1 (1963), 36–56

Campbell, J. *Lives of the Lord Chancellors* (1846)

Cannon, J. *Parliamentary Reform 1640–1832* (Cambridge, 1973)

Capp, B. *Astrology and the Popular Press* (1979)

Carte, T. *The Life of James Duke of Ormonde* (Oxford, 1851)

Challinor, P.J. 'Restoration and Exclusion in the County of Cheshire', *Bulletin of the John Rylands University Library of Manchester*, vol. lxiv (1981–2), 360–85

Chandaman, C.D. *The English Public Revenue 1660–88* (Oxford, 1975)

Childs, J. 'The Army and the Oxford Parliament of 1681', *EHR*, xciv (1979), 580–7
'1688', *History*, lxxiii (1988), 398–424

Christie, W.D. *The Life of Anthony Ashley Cooper, First Earl W.D of Shaftesbury* (1871)

Clarke, E.S and Foxcroft, H. *A Life of Gilbert Burnet, Bishop of Salisbury* (Cambridge, 1907)

Clifton, R. *The Last Popular Rebellion* (1984)

Cockburn, J.S. *A History of English Assizes 1558–1714* (Cambridge, 1972)

Coleby, A.M. *Central Government and the Localities: Hampshire 1649–89* (Cambridge, 1987)

Cragg, G.R. *Puritanism in the Period of the Great Persecution* (Cambridge, 1957)

Cranston, M. *John Locke, a Biography* (1957)

Crawford, P. *Denzil Holles, a study of his political career* (1979)

Cressy, D. *Literacy and the Social Order* (Cambridge, 1980)

Crist, T. 'Government Control of the Press after the Expiration of the Licensing Act in 1679', *Publishing History*, v (1979), 49–77

Croft, P. 'Annual Parliaments and the Long Parliament', *BIHR*, lix, no. 140 (1986), 155–71

Cruickshanks, E. 'Religion and Royal Succession: The Rage of Party', in *Britain in the First Age of Party*, ed. Jones, C. (1987)

Cust, R. 'News and Politics in the early Seventeenth Century', *P&P*, no. 112 (1986), 60–90

Daly, J. *Sir Robert Filmer and English Political Thought* (Toronto 1979)

Davies, G. 'Council and Cabinet 1679–88', *EHR*, xxxvii, no. 145 (1922), 47–66
'The By-Election at Grantham', *HLQ*, vii, no. 2 (1943–4), 179–182
'The Political Career of Sir Richard Temple 1634–97 and Buckingham Politics', *HLQ*, iv, no. 1 (October 1940), 47–83

Davies, J.D. 'Pepys and the Admiralty Commission of 1679–84', *BIHR*, lxii, no. 147 (1989), 34–53
'The Navy, Parliament and Political Crisis in the Reign of Charles II', *HJ*, xxxvi (1993), 271–288

Davis, R. 'English Foreign Trade 1660–1700', *Economic History Review*, 2nd series, vii (1954) 150–66
'The Presbyterian Opposition and the Emergence of Party in the House of Lords in the Reign of Charles II', in *Party and Management in Parliament 1660–1784*, ed. Jones, C. (Leicester, 1987)

De Krey, G. *A Fractured Society: The Politics of London in the First Age of Party 1688–1715* (Oxford, 1985)
'The London Whigs and the Exclusion Crisis Reconsidered' in *The First Modern Society*, ed. Beier, L., Cannadine, D. and Rosenheim, J. (Cambridge, 1989), 457–82

Dickinson, H.T. 'The Precursors of Political Radicalism in Augustan Britain', in *Britain in the First Age of Party 1680–1750*, ed. Jones, C. (1987)

D'Oyly, G. *The Life of William Sancroft* (1821)

Dunn, J. *The Political Thought of John Locke* (Cambridge, 1969)

Dunn, M.M. *William Penn: Politics and Conscience* (Princeton, 1967)

Edie, C. 'Succession and Monarchy: The Controversy of 1679–81', *American Historical Review*, lxx, no. 2 (January 1965), 350–70

'The Irish Cattle Bills: A Study in Restoration Politics', *Transactions of the American Philosophical Society*, vi, no. 2 (1970), 5–62

Elrington, C.R. (ed.) *Victorian County History of Cheshire* vol.ii (1979)

Evans, J.T. *Seventeenth Century Norwich: Politics, Religion and Government 1620–1690* (Oxford, 1979)

Ewald, A.C. *The Life and Times of Algernon Sidney* (1873)

Feiling, K. *A History of the Tory Party 1640–1714* (Oxford, 1924)

Ferguson, J. *Robert Ferguson 'The Plotter'* (Edinburgh, 1887)

Figgis, J.N. *The Theory of the Divine Right of Kings* (Cambridge, 1896)

Fink, Z. *The Classical Republicans* (Northwestern University Studies, no. 9, 1945)

Finlayson, M. *Historians, Puritanism and the English Revolution* (1983)

Fletcher, A. 'The Religious Motivation of Cromwell's Major Generals', *Studies in Church History*, xv (1978), 259–266

The Outbreak of the English Civil War (1981)

'The Enforcement of the Conventicle Acts 1664–79', *Studies in Church History: Persecution and Toleration*, ed. Sheils, W.J, xxi (1984)

Reform in the Provinces (1986)

Forster, G. 'Government in Provincial England under the Later Stuarts', *TRHS*, xxxiii (1983), 29–48

Foss, M. *The Age of Patronage* (1971)

Foxcroft, H. *Life and Works of Sir George Savile ... Earl of Halifax* (1898)

A Character of a Trimmer (Cambridge, 1946)

Fraser, P. *The Intelligence of the Secretaries of State* (Cambridge, 1956)

Furley, O.W. 'Pamphlet Literature in the Exclusion Crisis 1679–81', *CHJ*, xiii (1957), 19–36

'Pope Burning Processions of the late Seventeenth Century', *History*, xliv (1959), 16–23

Gardiner, T. *A General Survey of the Post Office 1677–82*, ed. Bond, F.W. (Postal History Society Special Series, no. 3, 1958)

Geiter, M. and Speck, W. 'The Reliability of Sir John Reresby's Memoirs and his account of the Oxford Parliament of 1681', *BIHR*, lxii, no. 147 (1989), 104–113

Genest, J. *Some Account of the English Stage 1660–1830* (1832)

George, M.D. 'Elections and Electioneering 1679–81', *EHR*, xlv, no. 180 (1930), 552–578

Glassey, L.K. *Politics and the Appointment of Justices of the Peace 1675–1720* (Oxford, 1979)

Goldie, M. 'The Revolution of 1689 and the Structure of Political Argument', *Bulletin of Research in the Humanities*, vol. 83, no. 4 (1980), 573–664

'The Roots of True Whiggism 1688–94', *History of Political Thought*, i, no. 2 (June 1980), 195–236

'John Locke and Anglican Royalism', *Political Studies*, xxxi (1983), 61–85

'Sir Peter Pett, Sceptical Toryism and the Science of Toleration in the 1680s', *Studies in Church History*, xxi (1984)

'The Huguenot Experience and the problem of toleration in Restoration England', in *The Huguenots and Ireland: Anatomy of an Emigration*, ed. Caldicott, C. and Pittion, J- P. (Dublin, 1987)

'Priestcraft and the Birth of Whiggism', in *Political Discourse in Early Modern Britain*, ed. Phillipson, N. and Skinner, G. (Cambridge, 1993)

Gooder, A. (ed.) 'The Parliamentary Representation of York 1258–1832', *Yorkshire Archaeological Society Record Series*, xcvi (1937)

Greaves, R.L. *Deliver Us From Evil – The Radical Underground in Britain 1660–3* (Oxford, 1986)
  Enemies Under His Feet: Radicals and Nonconformists in Britain 1664–1677 (Stanford, California, 1990)
  Secrets of the Kingdom: British Radicals from the Popish Plot to the Revolution of 1688–9 (Stanford, California, 1992)

Grose, C.L. 'French Ambassador's Reports on Financial Relations with Members of Parliament 1677–81', *EHR*, xliv (1929a), 625–8
  'Louis XIV's Financial Relations with Charles II and the English Parliament', *Journal of Modern History*, i (1929b), 177–204

Gunn, J.A. *Politics and the Public Interest in the Seventeenth Century* (1969)

Haley, K.H.D. *The First Earl of Shaftesbury* (Oxford 1968)
  'No Popery in the Reign of Charles II', in *Britain and the Netherlands*, v (The Hague 1975), 102–119

Hall, D. 'Anglo-French Trade Relations Under Charles II', *History*, new series, vii (1923), 17–30

Halle, M. *Mary of Modena* (1905)

Harris, M. 'The Structure, Ownership and Control of the Press 1620–1780', in *Newspaper History*, ed. Bryce, G. (1978)

Harris, T. *London Crowds in the Reign of Charles II: Propaganda and Politics from the Restoration to the Exclusion Crisis* (Cambridge, 1987)
  Politics Under the Later Stuarts: Party Conflict in a Divided Society 1660–1715 (1993)
  'Was the Tory Reaction Popular? Attitudes of Londoners towards the Persecution of Dissent 1681–6', *London Journal*, xiii (1987–8), 106–20

ed. Harris, T, Seaward, P. and Goldie, M. *The Politics of Religion in Restoration England* (Oxford, 1990)

Harrison, F.M. 'Nathanial Ponder. The Publisher of the Pilgrim's Progress', *The Library*, xv, no. 3 (1934), 257–294

Harrison, J. and Laslett, P. *The Library of John Locke* (Oxford Bibliographical Society, New Series, xiii, Oxford, 1965)

Hart, W.H. *Index Expurgatorius Anglicanus* (1872–88)

Havighurst, A.F. 'The Judiciary and Politics in the Reign of Charles II', *Law Quarterly Review*, lxvi (1950), 62–78, 229–252

Hawkes, A.J. *Sir Roger Bradshaigh of Haigh 1628–84* (Chetham Society, cix, 1945)

Henning, B.D. (ed.) *The History of Parliament: The House of Commons 1660–1690* (1983)

Hinton, R.W. 'A Note on the Dating of Locke's Second Treatise', *Political Studies*, xxii, no. 4 (1974), 471–8

Hirst, D. *The Representative of the People?* (Cambridge, 1975)
  'The Conciliatoriness of the Cavalier House of Commons Reconsidered', *Parliamentary History* vi, pt. 2 (1987), 221–35

Hirst, D. and Bowler, S. 'Voting in Hertford 1679–1721', *History and Computing* i, no. 1 (1989), 14–18

Holmes, C. *Seventeenth Century Lincolnshire* (History of Lincolnshire Series, vol. vii, Lincoln 1980)

Holmes, G. *Politics, Religion and Society in England 1679–1742* (1986)
  British Politics in the Age of Anne (1987, revised edition)
Hopkins, P. 'The Verney Collection of Popish Plot Pamphlets', *Bulletin of the Friends of Cambridge University Library*, ix (1988), 5–11
Horwitz, H. 'Protestant Reconciliation in the Exclusion Crisis', *Journal of Ecclesiastical History*, xv (1964), 201–17
  Revolution Politics: The Career of Daniel Finch, Second Earl of Nottingham 1647–1730 (Cambridge, 1968)
Hurwich, J. 'Dissent and Catholicism in English Society: A Study of Warwickshire 1660–1720', *JBS*, xvi, no. 1 (1976), 24–59
  '"A Fanatick Town"; The Political Influence of Dissenters in Coventry 1660–1720', *Midland History*, iv, no. 1 (1977), 15–48
Hutchinson, F. *Henry Vaughan* (1947)
Hutton, R. *The Restoration* (Oxford, 1985)
  'The Making of the Secret Treaty of Dover 1668–1670', *HJ*, xxix, no. 2 (1986), 297–318
  Charles II (Oxford, 1989)
Jacob, J.R. *Henry Stubbe, Radical Protestantism and the early Enlightenment* (Cambridge, 1983)
Jenkins, P. *The Making of a Ruling Class: The Glamorgan Gentry 1640–1790* (Cambridge, 1983)
Jones, C. (ed.) *Britain in the First Age of Party 1680–1750: Essays Presented to Geoffrey Holmes* (1987)
  Party and Management in Parliament 1660–1784 (Leicester, 1987)
Jones, J.R. 'The First Whig Party in Norfolk', *Durham University Journal*, xlvi (December 1953), 13–21
  'The Green Ribbon Club', *Durham University Journal*, xlix, no. 1 (December 1956), 17–20
  'Shaftesbury's "Worthy Men"', *BIHR*, vol.xxx (1957), 232–41
  The First Whigs (Oxford, 1961)
  'Restoration Election Petitions', *Durham University Journal*, vol.liii, no. 2 (March 1961), 49–57
  The Revolution of 1688 in England (1972)
  Country and Court (1978)
  'Parties and Parliament', in *The Restored Monarchy*, ed. Jones, J.R. (1979)
  'William Penn: A Representative of the Alternative Society of Restoration England?', in *The World of William Penn*, ed. Dunn, R.S. and M.M. (1986)
  Charles II: Royal Politician (1987)
Karraker, C. *The Seventeenth Century Sheriff* (1930)
Kelly, P. 'Constituents Instructions to MPs in the Eighteenth Century', in *Britain in the First Age of Party 1680–1750*, ed. Jones, C. (1987)
Kemp, B. *King and Commons 1660–1832* (1957)
Kent, C.B.R. *The Early History of the Tories 1660–1702* (1908)
Kenyon, J.P. 'Charles II and William of Orange in 1680', *BIHR*, xxx (1957), 95–101
  Robert Spencer, Earl of Sunderland 1641–1702 (1958)
  The Popish Plot (1974)
  Revolution Principles: The Politics of Party 1689–1720 (Cambridge, 1977)
Kirby, J.W. 'Restoration Leeds and the Aldermen of the Corporation', *Northern History*, xxii (1986), 123–75

Kishlansky, M. *Parliamentary Selection. Social and Political Choice in Early Modern England* (Cambridge, 1986)
'The Emergence of Adversarial Politics in the Long Parliament', *JMH*, xlix (1977), 617–40

Kitchin, G. *Sir Roger L'Estrange: A Contribution to the History of the Press in the Seventeenth Century* (1913)

Knights, M. 'Petitioning and the Political Theorists: John Locke, Algernon Sidney and London's "Monster" Petition of 1680', *P&P*, no. 138 (1993), 94–111
'London's "Monster" Petition of 1680', *HJ*, xxxvi, no. 1 (1993), 39–67
'London Petitions and Parliamentary Politics in 1679', *Parliamentary History*, xii (1993), 29–46

Knott, D. 'The Booksellers and the Plot', *The Book Collector*, xxiii (1974), 194–206

Lacey, D.R. *Dissent and Parliamentary Politics 1661–89* (New Jersey, 1969)

Lambert, S. *Printing for Parliament 1641–1700* (List and Index Society, xx, 1984)

Landau, N. *The Justices of the Peace 1679–1760* (California, 1984)

Landon, M. *The Triumph of the Lawyers. Their Role in English Politics 1678–1689* (Alabama, 1970)

Laslett, P. 'The English Revolution and Locke's Two Treatises of Government', *CHJ*, xii, no. 1 (1956), 40–55

Latimer, J. *The Annals of Bristol in the Seventeenth Century* (Bristol, 1900)

Lee, C. '"Fanatic Magistrates": Religious and Political Conflict in Three Kent Boroughs 1680–4', *HJ* xxxv, no. 1 (1991), 43–61

Levin, J. *The Charter Controversy in the City of London 1660–88 and its Consequences* (1969)

Lillywhite, B. *London Coffee Houses* (1963)

Lipson, E. 'The Elections to the Exclusion Parliaments 1679–81', *EHR*, xviii, (1913), 59–85

Locke, A.A. *The Seymour Family* (1911)

Lord, G.De F. 'Satire and Sedition: The Life and Work of John Ayloffe', *HLQ*, xxxix, no. 1 (1965–6), 255–73

M, J. *An Enquiry into the Authority for Echard's Statement in his History of England* (1852)

MacGillivray, R. *Restoration Historians and the English Civil War* (The Hague, 1974)

Marsh, J.B. *The Story of Hare Court* (1871)

Marshall, A. 'Colonel Thomas Blood and the Restoration Political Scene', *HJ*, xxxii, no. 3 (1989), 561–82

Mason, W.G. 'The Annual Output of Wing-Listed Titles 1649–1684', *The Library*, xxxix (1974), 219–20

McKenzie, D.F. 'The London Book Trade in 1668', *Words*, iv (January 1974), 75–92

McKeon, M. *Politics and Poetry in Restoration England* (Harvard 1975)

Merewether, H.A *The History of the Boroughs and Municipal Corporations* (1835)

Miller, J. *Popery and Politics in England 1660–1688* (Cambridge, 1973)
'The Correspondence of Edward Coleman 1674–8', *Recusant History*, xiv, no. 4 (1978), 261–75
'The Later Stuart Monarchy', in *The Restored Monarchy*, ed. Jones, J.R. (1979), 30–47
'Charles II and his Parliaments', *TRHS*, xxxii (1982), 1–24
'The Potential for Absolutism in Later Stuart England', *History*, vol. 69, no. 226 (1984), 187–207

'The Crown and the Borough Charters in the Reign of Charles II', *EHR*, c (1985) 53–84

Charles II (1991)

Milne, D.J. 'The Results of the Rye House Plot and their Influence on the 1688 Revolution', *TRHS*, i (1951), 91–108

Mood, F. 'William Penn and English Politics 1680–1', *Journal of the Friends Historical Society*, xxxii (1935), 3–21

Moore, T.K. and Horwitz, H. 'Who Runs the House? Aspects of Parliamentary Organisation in the later Seventeenth Century', *JMH*, xliii, no. 2 (1971), 205–27

Morgan, W.T. 'What was a Tory?', in *The Quest for Political Unity in World History*, ed. Pargellis, S. (Washington, 1944)

Morrah, P. *Restoration England* (1979)

Morrison, P.G. *Index to Wing's Short Title Catalogue* (Virginia, 1955)

Muddiman, J.G. *The King's Journalist 1659–89* (1923)

Mullett, C.F. 'Toleration and Persecution in England 1660–89', *Church History*, (1949), 18–43

Mullett, M. 'The Politics of Liverpool 1660–688', *Transactions of the Historic Society of Lancashire and Cheshire*, vol. cxxiv (1972), 31–56

'"Deprived of our former place" – The Internal Politics of Bedford 1660–1688', *Bedfordshire Historical Record Society*, lix (1980), 1–42

'Conflict, Politics and Elections in Lancaster 1660–1688', *Northern History*, xix (1983), 61–87

Munby, L.M. 'Politics and Religion in Hertfordshire 1660–1740', *East Anglian Studies*, ed. Munby (1968)

Neal, D. *The History of the Puritans* (1837)

Nenner, H. *By Colour of Law. Legal and Constitutional Politics in England 1660–89* (Chicago, 1977)

Newton, T.F.M. 'The Mask of Heraclitus: A Problem in Restoration Journalism', *Harvard Studies and Notes in Philology and Literature*, vol. xvi (1934), 145–60

Nicholls, F.J. and Taylor, J. *Bristol Past and Present* (1881)

Norrey, P.J. 'The Restoration Regime in Action: the Relationship between Central and Local Government in Dorset, Somerset and Wiltshire', *HJ*, xxxi, no. 4 (1988), 789–813.

Nuttall, G.F. and Chadwick, O. *From Uniformity to Unity 1662–1962* (1962)

Ogg, D. *England in the Reign of Charles II* (Oxford, 1984 edition)

Oliver, H.J. *Sir Robert Howard 1626–1698* (Duke University, 1963)

Ollard, R.L. *The Escape of Charles II after the Battle of Worcester* (1966)

O'Malley, L.C. 'The Whig Prince: Prince Rupert and the Court against Country Factions', *Albion* (1976), 333–50

O'Malley, T. 'Religion and the Newspaper Press 1660–1685' in *The Press in English Society from the Seventeenth Century to the Nineteenth Century*, ed. Harris, M. and Lee, A. (1986), 25–46

Osborn, J.M. 'Reflections on Narcissus Luttrell', *The Book Collector*, vi (1957), 15–27

Pearl, V. 'Change and Stability in Seventeenth Century London', *London Journal*, v (1979), 3–34

Phelps, W.H. 'The Will of Randall Taylor, a Restoration Bookseller', *Papers of the Bibliographical Society of America*, vol. 72 (1978), 335–8

Pincus, S. 'From Butterboxes to Wooden Shoes: the Shift in English Popular Sentiment from hatred of Holland to hatred of France in the 1670s', *HJ*, forthcoming 1994

Plumb, J.H. 'The Growth of the Electorate in England 1660–1715', *P&P*, vol. 45 (1969), 90–116

The Growth of Political Stability 1675–1725 (1967)

Pocock, J.G. 'Robert Brady 1627–1700', *CHJ*, x (1951), 186–204

The Ancient Constitution and the Feudal Law (Cambridge, 1957)

Politics, Language and Time (1960)

The Machiavellian Moment (Princeton, 1975)

Virtue, Commerce and History (Cambridge, 1985)

Pollock, J. *The Popish Plot* (1903)

Powell, A. *John Aubrey and his Friends* (1963)

Price, C. *Cold Caleb: Ford Grey, first Earl of Tankerville 1655–1701* (1956)

Priestley, M. 'London Merchants and Opposition Politics in Charles II's Reign', *HR*, xxix (1956), 205–19

'Anglo-French Trade and the "Unfavourable Balance" Controversy 1660–1685', *Economic History Review*, 2nd series, iv (1951–2), 37–52

Rahn, B.J. 'A Ra-ree Show – A Rare Cartoon: Revolutionary Propaganda in the Treason Trial of Stephen College', in *Studies in Change and Revolution*, ed. Korshin, P.J (1972)

Reay, B. (ed.) *Popular Culture in Seventeenth Century England* (1985)

Robbins, C. *The Eighteenth Century Commonwealthmen* (Harvard, 1959)

'Algernon Sidney's Discourses Concerning Government, Textbook of Revolution', *William and Mary Quarterly*, (July 1947), 267–96

Roberts, C. *The Growth of Responsible Government in Stuart England* (Cambridge, 1966)

'Party and Patronage in Later Stuart England', in *England's Rise to Greatness*, ed. Baxter, S. (California, 1983), 185–212

Schemes and Undertakings. A Study of English Politics in the Seventeenth Century (Ohio, 1985)

Roberts, G. *The Life, Progesses and Rebellion of James Duke of Monmouth* (1844)

Ronalds, F.S. *The Attempted Whig Revolution of 1678–1681* (Urbana, 1974)

Roper, A. 'Dryden, Sunderland and the Metamorphosis of a Trimmer', *HLQ*, liv (1991), 43–72

Rosenheim, J.M. 'Party Organisation at the Local Level: the Norfolk Sheriff Subscriptions of 1676', *HJ*, xxix, no. 3 (1986), 713–22

Rostenberg, L. 'Richard and Anne Baldwin, Whig Patriot Publishers', *Papers of the Bibliographical Society of America*, vol. 47 (1953), 1–42

Literary, Political, Scientific, Religious and Legal Publishing, Printing and Bookselling in England 1551–1700 (New York, 1965)

Sacret, J.H. 'The Restoration Government and the Municipal Corporations', *EHR*, xlv (1930), 232–59

Schlatter, R. *The Social Ideas of Religious Leaders 1660–1688* (1940)

Schochet, G. 'Patriarchalism, Politics and Mass Attitudes in Stuart England', *HJ*, xii, no. 3 (1969), 413–41

Restoration, Ideology and Revolution (Washington, 1990)

Patriarchalism in Political Thought (Oxford, 1975)

Schwoerer, L. 'William Lord Russell', *JBS*, xxiv (1985), 41–71

No Standing Armies! (Johns Hopkins University, 1974)

'Press and Parliament in the Revolution of 1689', *HJ*, xx, no.3 (1977), 545–67

The Declaration of Rights (1981)

Scott, J. *Algernon Sidney and the English Republic 1623–77* (Cambridge, 1988)

'Radicalism and Restoration: the Shape of the Stuart Experience', *HJ*, xxxi, no.2 (1988), 453–67

Algernon Sidney and the Restoration Crisis 1677–1683 (Cambridge 1991)

Scott, W.R. *The Constitution and Finance of English, Scottish and Irish Joint-Stock Companies to 1720* (Cambridge, 1912)

Seaward, P. *The Cavalier Parliament and the Reconstruction of the Old Regime 1661–7* (Cambridge, 1989)

Sensabaugh, G.F. *That Grand Whig Milton* (Stanford, California, 1952)

Sharpe, R. *London and the Kingdom* (1894)

Siebert, F.S. *Freedom of the Press in England 1476–1776* (University of Illinois, 1952)

Simon, W.G. 'Comprehension in the Age of Charles II', *Church History*, xxxi (1962), 440–8

Sissons, C. 'Marks as Signatures', *The Library*, ix, no. 1 (June 1928), 1–38

Sitwell, G. *The First Whig* (Scarborough, 1894)

Skinner, Q. 'History and Ideology in the English Revolution', *HJ*, viii, no. 2 (1965), 151–78

Somerville, T. *The History of Political Transactions and of Parties from the Restoration of King Charles II to the Death of King William* (1792)

Sommerville, C.J. *Popular Religion in Restoration England* (1977)

Speck, W.A. 'The Electorate in the First Age of Party', in *Britain in the First Age of Party*, ed. Jones, C. (1987)

'Political Propaganda in Augustan England', *TRHS*, xxii (1972), 17–32

Spurr, J. 'Latitudinarianism and the Restoration Church', *HJ*, xxxi, no. 1 (1988), 61–82

'The Church of England, Comprehension and the Toleration Act of 1689', *EHR*, civ, no. 413 (1989), 927–46

'Schism and the Restoration Church', *Journal of Ecclesiastical History*, xli, no. 3 (1990), 408–24

The Restoration Church of England 1646–1689 (1991)

Stone, L. 'Literacy and Education in England 1640–1900', *P&P*, Vol. xlii (1969), 69–139

Sutherland, J. *The Restoration Newspaper and its Development* (Cambridge, 1986)

Swedenberg, H.T (ed.) *Essential Articles for the Study of John Dryden* (1966)

Sykes, N. *From Sheldon to Secker: Aspects of Church History 1660–1768* (Cambridge, 1958)

Tarlton, C.T. 'The Exclusion Controversy, Pamphleteering and Locke's Two Treatises', *HJ*, xxiv (1981), 49–68

'A Rope of Sand: Interpreting Locke's First Treatise of Government', *HJ*, xxi, no. 1 (1978), 43–73

Thomas, P.D. 'The Montgomery Borough Constituency 1660–1728', *Bulletin of the Board of Celtic Studies*, xx, pt 3 (November 1963)

Thompson, M.P.. 'Significant Silences in Locke's Two Treatises of Government: Constitutional History, Contract and Law', *HJ*, xxxi, no. 2 (1988), 275–94.

Todd, T. *William Dockwra and the Rest of the Undertakers: The Story of the London Penny Post 1680–2* (1952)

Toulmin, J. *The History of Taunton* (1827)

Treadwell, M. 'London Trade Publishers 1675–1750', *The Library*, 6th Series, iv (1982), 99–135

Turbeville, A.S. 'The House of Lords under Charles II', *EHR*, lv, no. 177 (1930), 58–79

Turner, E.R. 'The Privy Council of 1679', *EHR*, xxx (1915), 251–70

Underdown, D. 'Party Management in the Recruiter Elections', *EHR*, lxxxiii (1968), 235–64

Van Lennep, W. *The London Stage 1660–1800. Part I 1660–1700* (Southern Illinois University, 1965)

Von Maltzahn, N. *Milton's History of Britain* (Oxford, 1991)

Von Ranke, L. *A History of England* (1875), vol. iv

Walcott, R. *English Politics in the early Eighteenth Century* (Oxford, 1956)

Walker, J. 'The Secret Services under Charles II and James II', *TRHS*, xv (1932), 211–42

'The English Exiles in Holland during the Reigns of Charles II and James II', *TRHS*, xxx (1948), 111–25

'Censorship of the Press under Charles II', *History*, xxxv (1950), 219–38

Walker, J.W. 'Records Relating to a Seventeenth Century Election', *Yorkshire Archeaological Journal*, xxxiv (1939), 25–34

Wallerstein, R. 'To Madness Near Allied', *HLQ*, vi (1943), 445–71

Webb, S.S. *The Governors General. The English Army and the Defintion of Empire 1569–1681* (University of N. Carolina, 1979)

Weston, C.C. 'Co-ordination: A Radicalising Principle in Stuart Politics', in *The Origins of Anglo-American Radicalism*, ed. Jacob, M. and J. (1984)

Weston, C.C. and Greenberg, J. *Subjects and Sovereigns* (Cambridge, 1981)

Whiteman, A. (ed.) *The Compton Census of 1676* (1986)

Whiting, C.E. 'Sir Patience Ward of Tanshelf', *Yorkshire Archaeological Journal*, xxxiv (1939), 245–72

Whiting, G.W. 'The Condition of the London Theatres 1679–83: A Reflection of the Political Situation', *Modern Philology*, xxv, no. 2 (1927), 195–206

'Political Satire in London Stage Plays 1680–3', *Modern Philology*, xxviii (1930), 29–43

Williams, J.A. 'English Catholicism under Charles II: The Legal Position', *Recusant History*, vii (1963), 123–43

Williams, J.B. 'The Newsbooks and Letters of News of the Restoration', *EHR*, xxiii (1908), 252–76

Williams, S. 'The Pope Burning Processions of 1679, 1680 and 1681', *Journal of the Warburg and Courtauld Institute*, xxi, no. 1 (1958), 104–18

Willman, R. 'The Origins of Whig and Tory in English Political Language', *HJ*, xvii (1974), 247–64

Wing, D. *Short Title Catalogue 1641–1700* (Second edition 1972–88)

Witcombe, D.T. *Charles II and the Cavalier House of Commons 1663–1674* (Manchester University, 1966)

Wood, A. C. *A History of the Levant Company* (Oxford, 1935)

Woodhead, J.R. *The Rulers of London* (1965)

Worden, B. 'Toleration and the Cromwellian Protectorate', *Studies in Church History*, xxi (1984), 199–233.

'The Commonwealth Kidney of Algernon Sidney', *JBS*, xxiv (1985), 1–40

'English Republicanism', in *Cambridge History of Political Thought 1450–1700*, ed. J. Burns and M. Goldie (Cambridge, 1991), pp. 443–75.

Wrigley, E.A. 'A Simple Model of London's Importance in Changing English Society and Economy 1650–1750', *P&P*, vol. 37 (1967), 44–71

Wyndham, H.A. *A Family History 1410–1688* (1939)

Wynne, W. *The Life of Sir Leoline Jenkins* (1724)

Zwicker, S. 'Lines of Authority: Politics and Literary Culture in the Restoration', in *The Politics of Discourse*, ed. Zwicker, S. and Sharpe, K. (California, 1987)

Zwicker, S. and Hirst, D. 'Rhetoric and Disguise: Political Language and Political Argument in *Absalom and Achitophel*', *JBS*, xxi, no. 1 (1981), 39–55

Theses

Allen, D.F. 'The Crown and the Corporation of London in the Exclusion Crisis 1678–1681' (Cambridge Ph.D., 1976)

de Beer, E.S. 'The Development of Parties during the Ministry of Danby' (London MA, 1923)

Carter, D.P. 'The Lancashire Lieutenancy 1660–88' (Oxford M.Litt., 1981)

Child, M.S. 'Prelude to Revolution: The Structure of Politics in County Durham 1678–1688' (University of Maryland Ph.D., 1972)

Clark, R. 'Anglicanism, Recusancy and Dissent in Derbyshire 1603–1730' (Oxford D.Phil., 1979)

Clayton, R.W. 'The Political Career of Sir Edward Seymour Bart. 1633–1708' (York Ph.D., 1975)

Crist, T. 'Francis Smith and the Opposition Press in England 1660–1688' (Cambridge D.Phil., 1977)

Davies, C.E. 'The Enforcement of Religious Uniformity in England 1668–1700, with special reference to the dioceses of Cheshire and Worcester' (Oxford D.Phil., 1982)

Ellis, E. 'The Whig Junto' (Oxford D.Phil., 1961)

Furley, O.W. 'The Origins and Early Development of the Whig Party, with special reference to Shaftesbury and Locke 1675–92' (Oxford B.Litt., 1952)

Gauci, P. 'The Corporation and the Country: Great Yarmouth 1660–1722' (Oxford D.Phil., 1991), being revised for publication by OUP

Glines, T. 'Politics and Government in the Borough of Colchester 1660–1693' (Wisconsin Ph.D., 1974)

Goodman, P.H. 'The Political Career of William, Third Lord Howard of Escrick 1626?–1694' (Oxford B.Litt., 1948)

Hetet, J. 'A Literary Underground in Restoration England 1660–1689' (Cambridge Ph.D., 1987)

Houlbrooke, M. 'Paul Barrillon's Embassy in England 1677–1688' (Oxford B.Litt., 1971)

Jones, G.F.T. 'The Political Career of Philip Lord Wharton' (Oxford D.Phil., 1957)

Marshall, J.A. 'Sir Joseph Williamson and the Development of the Government Intelligence System in Restoration England 1660–1680' (Lancaster Ph.D., 1991), being revised for publication by CUP

Milne, D.J. 'The Rye House Plot, with special reference to its place in the Exclusion contest, and its consequences until 1685' (London Ph.D., 1949)

Montano, J. 'Courting the Moderates: Ideology, Propaganda and Parties in the 1670s' (Harvard Ph.D., 1987)

Mullin, A.M. 'Lancashire and the Exclusion Crisis' (Lancaster Polytechnic M.Phil., 1984)

Murrell, P.E. 'Suffolk: The Political Behaviour of the County and its Parliamentary Boroughs from the Exclusion Crisis to the Accesssion of the House of Hanover' (Newcastle Ph.D., 1982)

Pickavance, R.G. 'The English Borough and the King's Government: A Study of the Tory Reaction 1681–5' (Oxford D.Phil., 1976)

Rutter, M. 'Politics and Religion in Sussex 1678–84' (Durham BA thesis, 1991)

Scott, D. 'Politics, Dissent and Quakers in York 1640–1700' (York Ph.D., 1990)

Simms, V.H. 'The Organisation of the Whig Party during the Exclusion Crisis' (London MA, 1934)

Smith, A.G. 'London and the Crown 1681–5' (University of Wisconsin Ph.D., 1967)

Swatland, A. 'The House of Lords in the Reign of Charles II 1660–1681' (Birmingham Ph.D., 1985), being revised for publication by CUP

Taylor, D.F. 'Sir Leoline Jenkins 1625–85' (London M.Phil., 1973)

Yardley, B. 'The Political Career of George Villiers, 2nd Duke of Buckingham' (Oxford D.Phil., 1989)

Walker, J. 'The Republican Party in England from the Restoration to the Revolution 1660–1688' (Manchester Ph.D., 1930)

Witcombe, D.T. 'The Parliamentary Careers of Sir William and Mr Henry Coventry' (Oxford B.Litt., 1954)

INDEX

Cambridge Studies in Early Modern British History